JOHN MAYNARD
KEYNES

VOLUME THREE

FIGHTING FOR FREEDOM

1937-1946

Books by Robert Skidelsky:

POLITICIANS AND THE SLUMP

ENGLISH PROGRESSIVE SCHOOLS

OSWALD MOSLEY

JOHN MAYNARD KEYNES VOL. 1 – HOPES BETRAYED

JOHN MAYNARD KEYNES VOL. 2 – THE ECONOMIST AS SAVIOUR

INTERESTS AND OBSESSIONS

THE ROAD FROM SERFDOM

John Maynard Keynes in his study at Gordon Square, May 1944

JOHN MAYNARD

KEYNES

VOLUME THREE

FIGHTING FOR FREEDOM

1937–1946

Robert Skidelsky

VIKING

TO WILLIAM

VIKING
Published by the Penguin Group
Penguin Putnam Inc., 375 Hudson Street,
New York, New York 10014, U.S.A.
Penguin Books Ltd, 80 Strand,
London WC2R ORL, England
Penguin Books Australia Ltd, Ringwood,
Victoria, Australia
Penguin Books Canada Ltd, 10 Alcorn Avenue,
Toronto, Ontario, Canada M4V 3B2
Penguin Books (N.Z.) Ltd, 182–190 Wairau Road,
Auckland 10, New Zealand

Penguin Books Ltd, Registered Offices:
Harmondsworth, Middlesex, England

First American edition
Published in 2001 by Viking Penguin,
a member of Penguin Putnam Inc.

1   3   5   7   9   10   8   6   4   2

Acknowledgments for permission to reprint copyrighted
texts appear on page xi-xii.

ISBN 0-670-03022-8

CIP data available.

This book is printed on acid–free paper. ∞

Printed in the United States of America
Set in New Baskervillie

Contents

PART TWO: BETTER THAN LAST TIME

PART THREE: THE LAST BATTLE

UK Retail Price Index and US Consumer Price Index

Year	United Kingdom (£)		United States ($)	
	Index	Factor	Index	Factor
1913	100	47.6	100	17.3
1915	124	38.5	102	16.9
1920	249	19.1	202	8.5
1925	176	27.0	177	9.8
1930	159	30.0	168	10.3
1935	143	33.3	138	12.5
1940	184	25.9	141	12.2
1945	204	23.4	181	9.5
1950	232	20.5	243	7.1
1955	304	15.7	270	6.4
1960	346	13.8	299	5.8
1965	412	11.6	318	5.4
1970	515	9.2	392	4.4
1975	967	4.9	543	3.2
1980	1892	2.5	831	2.1
1985	2676	1.8	1085	1.6
1990	3569	1.3	1318	1.3
1995	4218	1.1	1537	1.1
2000	4760	1.0	1727	1.0

List of Illustrations

Acknowledgements

My thanks above all go to my wife and our three children for sustaining me with their love, understanding and support, through twenty years of Keynesian labour.

I would like to thank David Calleo, Peter Clarke, Paul Davidson, Meghnad Desai, Jean Floud, Geoffrey Harcourt, José Harris, Vijay Joshi, Alastair Kilmarnock, Deepak Lal, Ian Little, Nicholas Mosley, George Peden, Larry Siedentop, and Timothy Renton who read the whole or substantial parts of this book in manuscript and contributed valuable comments.

The following have, in smaller or greater degree, and occasionally unbeknown to themselves, helped me in various ways: the late Paul Bareau, James Beechey, Terence Benton, the late Edward Bernstein, Daniele Besomi, John Morton Blum, James Boughton, Terence Burns, Damon Clark, Bruce Craig, Jo Elwyn-Jones, Iraci Fedelli, Francis Gladstone, Angus Graham Campbell, Joe Grice, Chris Guest, Liam Halligan, Frances Anne Hardin, Daphne Harmer, the late Frederic Harmer, Mavis Hicks, Bryan Hopkin, Alan Hopkins, Michael Howard, Jeremy Hutchinson, Michael Ignatieff, G. John Ikenberry, Charles Jones, Evan Jones, Anne Keynes, Milo Keynes, Richard Keynes, Simon Keynes, Harvey Klehr, Robyn Lee, Clive Lennox, Fiona MacCarthy, Don McCarthy, Donald MacDougall, James Marcouyeux, Kalin Nikolov, Rod O'Donnell, Peter Oppenheimer, F. T. Ostrander, Peter Plesch, David Rees, Tom Rivers, Kenneth Rose, Roger Sandilands, Arthur Schlesinger Jr, Edward Skidelsky, William Skidelsky, Iain Smith, Sam Tannenhaus, Douglass Wass, Andrei Weller and Jean Whiter. I would like to thank them all.

My thanks also go to the staff of the Bank of England; Christopher Webb, Archivist of the Borthwick Institute of Historical Research, York University; Helen Langley, Modern Political Papers, Bodleian Library; Sue Donnelly, Archivist of the British Library of Political and Economic Science; Fred Bauman and David Wigdor of the Manuscript Division of the Library of Congress; Mrs P. Hatfield, College Archivist, Eton College Library; Tanya Thompson of Thompson Henry Ltd; Peter Jones, Fellow and Librarian, and Jacqueline Cox and Rosalind Moad, past and present Archivists, King's College, Cambridge; the staff of the House of Lords Library; Raymond Teichman, Supervisory Archivist of the Franklin D. Roosevelt Library.

I am grateful to Macmillan, for their patience over the life of this enterprise, to my agent Michael Sissons whose irrefutable economic arguments kept me moving forward, if not up to speed, to Georgina Morley, my publisher, and to my editor Peter James, whose exact eye has been as invaluable in this as in the previous volume.

Successive Vice-Chancellors of Warwick University, first Jack Butterworth, then Clark Brundin, and latterly Brian Follett, as well as my colleagues in the Department of Economics, have treated me with the greatest kindness and consideration. Without that understanding, I doubt whether I could have completed this work.

Extracts from the Lydia Lopokova Keynes Papers reproduced by permission of King's College Cambridge. Unpublished writings of Lydia Lopokova copyright © The Provost and Scholars of King's College, Cambridge, 2000.

Extracts from the Keynes Papers reproduced by permission of King's College, Cambridge. Unpublished writings of J. M. Keynes copyright © The Provost and Scholars of King's College, Cambridge, 2000.

Every effort has been made to contact all copyright holders of material reproduced in this book. If any have been inadvertently overlooked, the publishers will be pleased to make the necessary arrangement at the first opportunity.

Preface to the American Edition

'Fighting for Freedom' is a better subtitle for the American edition of this book than its British subtitle, 'Fighting for Britain'. It identifies the supreme value for which both Britain and the United States fought. The victory of freedom—requiring the defeat of Hitler's Germany and, a little later, Imperial Japan—was the overriding war aim of the Anglo-American alliance forged in the Second World War. Keynes fully accepted this, and all his actions have to be seen in this context.

The British subtitle was designed to remind readers of something else: that national interests do not disappear just because the cause is noble. Britain and America spent much of the war jockeying for post-war position. The battleground of this war was finance. I have called it 'Keynes's War' to distinguish it from 'Churchill's War'—because without Lend-Lease Britain could not have fought Churchill's War, and financial negotiations with the United States took up most of Keynes's time from 1941 till his death in 1946. The plot of this war was simple: America tried to get the highest price, Britain to pay the lowest price, for Lend-Lease. Keynes summed up this British 'war aim' in a nutshell: 'the retention by us of enough assets to leave us capable of independent action'.

The novelty of my treatment is to place this financial 'war' in the foreground of my narrative, the military war in the background. This seems to be only right, inasmuch as this is a biography of Keynes, not of Churchill. It does not mean that I regard Keynes's War as important as Churchill's War. To say that Britain paid a much higher price than did the United States for victory over Hitler does does not mean that it would not have paid an even higher price had it lost.

American readers might be shocked by the revelation in these pages of the bitterness of Anglo-American rivalry. They should not be. Commercial and financial conflict had embittered relations between the two countries in the 1930s, with each one blaming the other for breakdown of the world economy. It was as natural for the United States to use its wartime financial leverage to weaken Britain as a financial and commercial rival as it was for the British to try to minimise or evade the strings attached to American help. But it is not easy to get this message across, first because it shatters

the myth of the united front against evil, secondly, because Americans tend
to believe that their nation is uniquely idealistic, and therefore exempt
from calculation of self- interest.

In a bold pre-emptive strike, the American economist Bradford DeLong
has posted a rejoinder to my theme on his home Web page
(www.j-bradford-delong.net). Essentially he denies or minimises the existence of wartime economic conflict between Britain and the United States.
That I argue the contrary must be due to the fact I am not an economist,
or that I have fallen 'under the influence of a strange and sinister set of
British imperial conservatives . . .'

DeLong's technique of refutation leaves much to be desired. He seems
to think that I accuse America of having provided Britain with such 'niggardly' Lend-Lease help that it destroyed Britain as a great power. He
refutes this by saying that even had the United States paid for the whole of
Britain's wartime import surplus, Britain would have been too weak to have
become the post-war leader of the western alliance. The proposition he
attributes to me is nowhere to be found in this book, and the counter-
argument is therefore irrelevant.

What I do say is that the United States demanded that in return for
Lend-Lease Britain pledge itself to abandon its imperial preference and
sterling area systems, and that the way Washington managed the flow of
Lend-Lease supplies had the effect, and possibly the intention, of leaving
Britain dependent on US help after the war on whatever terms America
chose to impose. Rather than deal with this argument, DeLong simply sets
up an Aunt Sally to knock down.

DeLong claims that I widen the differences between the Keynes and
White Plans for post-war monetary reconstruction 'to an immense gulf' in
order to dramatise the conflict between the two sides, whereas he is struck
by the 'extraordinary similarities between the two plans'. He quotes me as
writing on p. 245: 'The White and Keynes Plans were based on different
concepts . . . loans out of subscribed capital . . . [or] overdrafts [created]
out of nothing . . .' But this was Keynes's own view of the essential difference between the two schemes (pp. 250–1).

Keynes's Clearing Union was based on his theory of liquidity preference.
In a global trading economy mass unemployment, he thought, resulted
from the propensity of some countries—particularly the United States—to
hoard their surpluses, which forced deflation on the deficit countries,
leading to a contractionary global spiral. The Keynes Plan was designed to
prevent such an outcome by forcing adjustment on surplus countries.
Countries which accumulated surplus balances would be forced to accept
'bancor' cheques in payment for their unrequited exports, ie, to accept
money created by the global monetary authority as payment for exports
which they did not match by corresponding imports. By contrast, the
White Plan upheld the orthodox doctrine of debtor adjustment, and

aimed to provide only modest help to deficit countries whilst they put their houses in order. In due course they would be required to contract their demand for imports or to sell more exports in competition with those from surplus countries. Keynes believed that this would not check any pressure towards global recession.

Keynes's Clearing Bank was, in effect, to be the central manager of global aggregate demand, varying the supply of 'bancor' according to the demand for it; White's IMF was conceived as a modest monetary add-on to a revamped gold standard.

This was not a trivial technical disagreement. Keynes and the British Treasury thought that adoption of something like the British Plan was an essential condition of Britain's acceptance of a post-war liberal economic order. That is why they fought so hard for it. The triumph of the White Plan led Keynes back to the view that responsibility for full employment would inevitably remain national, not global. He insisted on inserting into the Bretton Woods Agreement clauses which exempted member countries from IMF rules for a prolonged, and potentially indefinite, 'transition' period. This might well have led back to the 'bloc economics' and trade and currency wars of the 1930s had not the United States, starting with Marshall Aid, pumped large quantities of extra spending power into the 'free' world economy for geopolitical reasons.

To be reminded of the realities of alliance politics, even in the case of such close partners as Britain and the United States, is timely in the aftermath of the tragic events of 11 September, when the United States is working to construct a global coalition against terrorism. In 1940, it was British vulnerability which threw it into the arms of the United States. America did not fail its fellow-democracy; but also used the occasion to settle old scores, and secure pole position in the post-war international order. Today, the United States, faced with an unexpected vulnerability, calls in the Old World to redress the balance of the New. It, too, will have to pay a price for victory, though it will not be as high a price as Britain paid.

Keynes was an economist, thinker, and writer of genius who developed the theories he thought the times demanded. During the Second World War, propelled by events onto the field of action, he fought for the British position within the Anglo-American Alliance as a patriot, and, with eloquence and imagination of the highest quality, conjured up a post-war economic order which could combine full employment with liberty. These are the culminating themes of this biography.

6 October, 2001

Introduction

When I started this concluding volume of my Keynes trilogy I intended to call it 'The Economist as Prince'. My idea was to juxtapose the theorist who wrote the *General Theory of Employment, Interest and Money* with the economic statesman of the war years. However, as the writing went on, I decided that such a sub-title would miss what this book was really about, which was Keynes's part in Britain's struggle for survival. This is a story, above all else, about Keynes's patriotism. When he died, Lionel Robbins wrote to his widow: 'Maynard had given his life for his country, as surely as if he had fallen on the field of battle.'

Keynes's war was different from Churchill's war. Nazi Germany, to be sure, had to be defeated; this was the *ultima ratio* of both their efforts. But, whereas the military struggle occupies the foreground of Churchill's war, it was the backcloth only to Keynes's war, which was financial and economic. In this war, the United States occupies the foreground – as ally but also as rival. Churchill fought to preserve Britain and its Empire against Nazi Germany. Keynes fought to preserve Britain as a Great Power against the United States. The war against Germany was won; but, in helping to win it, Britain lost both Empire and greatness. Hence, the title of the concluding volume of Churchill's war history, *Triumph and Tragedy*, also fits this volume.

In his narrower, and subordinate, sphere, Keynes rivalled Churchill. He was, in fact, the Churchill of war finance and post-war financial planning. His achievement was the more remarkable in that he held no official position. He was merely an unpaid adviser to the Chancellor of the Exchequer, with a room in the Treasury. His peerage in 1942 gave him rank, but no responsibilities. In a Presidential (or dictatorial) system he would probably have been Minister of Finance. In the British system he was, for many purposes, *de facto* Chancellor of the Exchequer. Certainly he was regarded as such by the Americans, and sometimes as President of the Board of Trade as well. But his authority was largely personal.

In the years covered by this volume, he was also a sick man. Following his 'heart attack' in May 1937, he had been diagnosed as suffering from subacute bacterial endocarditis, for which there was then no cure. In 1939 he was brought back to relatively good health by a remarkable Hungarian doctor, Janos Plesch, who gave him injections of Prontosil, an anti-bacterial drug recently discovered in Germany. Unfortunately, it was only partly effective, and, as the war progressed, so did Keynes's heart disease, so that towards the end his attacks became more frequent, and he had to spend an increasing part of each day in bed. From the time of the Bretton Woods negotiations in July 1944 it was obvious to those around him that Keynes was living on borrowed time. His illness did not diminish his prodigious energy, though it may have affected his judgement.

In his years of failing health, Keynes was sustained by the devotion of his wife, the Russian ballerina Lydia Lopokova. An improbable marriage, much disparaged by Keynes's Bloomsbury friends, blossomed into a magical union. She was his fairy princess who acquired the solid qualities of a nurse. He was her fairy prince, her mentor and protector in the world of affairs. Lydia was not clever, but she was intelligent. Her unexpected-ness, wit and inspired misuse of the English language never failed to delight Keynes, an accomplished wordsmith himself. They never bored each other, while her sparkling performances captivated Keynes's staider friends from business, politics and administration on both sides of the Atlantic, and added to the attraction of his own presence.

Like Churchill, Keynes made mistakes. His most important was the strategy he masterminded for the Anglo-American loan negotiation of 1945. He persuaded himself, against all the evidence, that he could obtain a large gift from the United States to cover Britain's temporary post-war balance of payments deficit, without any unacceptable strings. When this hope was disappointed, he proved too slow-moving and indecisive in the actual negotiation, though he was not helped by the government in London. As a negotiator on this occasion, and in other Anglo-American negotiations, Keynes was fallible. It was as an advocate that he was supreme.

Taking his life as a whole, Keynes was a successful, not a tragic, hero – an Odysseus rather than an Achilles. In his private life as in his public activities he generally managed to get the best of both worlds. He was a rebel who entered the Establishment, not by succumbing to it, but by shifting it towards his own ground. He owed this achievement, above all, to his ability to think orthogonally – at right angles from existing ideas. Time and again, in great things and in small, Keynes was able to carry the discussion on to a new plane, where the old antitheses became irrelevant. In a world in which *laissez-faire* and central planning, free trade and protectionism, conservatism and socialism were opposite poles of political and intellectual attraction, the *General Theo of Unemployment, Interest and Money* represented a break-out into a new dimension – in which one could have continuous full employment without suppressing political and econ-omic freedom. He showed the same quality on two occasions in the

Second World War – in his pamphlet *How to Pay for the War* and in his plan for an International Clearing Union, both of which were applications of his fundamental theoretical insights into the nature of economic life.

It is tempting to think of him as the philosopher of the Middle Way, and he was wont so to describe himself. But it is misleading, nevertheless. Like the projection of a ray of light his mind pointed not to a Middle Way between two established points but to a New Way. Such originality can never 'win' in an absolute sense – at least not in human life. The biases of temperament, position and feeling which inclined people to one or other side of the old debates were too deep, had too long a history, to be eradicated by an intellectual *tour de force*. Keynes's ideas entered as new ingredients into established habits of thought, where they have lodged.

His genius was lonely, as all genius is. In time Keynesianism became the new orthodoxy, against which a reaction was inevitable. The economics profession came to be divided into Keynesians and anti-Keynesians, because his followers, who numbered many outstanding men and one outstanding woman, lacked his deep originality. When in the 1970s and 1980s the cry was often heard for a 'new Keynes', people were calling for the reappearance of a phenomenon that has occurred very rarely in human history.

II

The plan of the book is as follows. Part I, called 'Paying for the War', opens in 1937 and closes with a general survey of Keynes's wartime activities and an assessment of the qualities he brought to them. It deals largely with his role in shaping the financing of the war, on both its domestic and external sides.

Part II, 'Better than Last Time', is mainly concerned with planning for the post-war world. Horrible though the war was, it gave an opportunity, missed after the previous war, to rebuild the world on more solid and hopeful foundations. Here Keynes took the decisive lead with his proposal for an International Clearing Union to overcome the economic conflicts of the 1930s. A parallel initiative from Harry Dexter White, of the US Treasury, led to the signing of the Bretton Woods Agreement of July 1944. A large part of this section is taken up with the gestation of the two plans, and the difficult technical negotiations between the British and American experts which led to the Agreement. But Keynes also modified the Beveridge Plan for Social Security and influenced British (as well as American) thinking on post-war fiscal, monetary and employment policy. His chairmanship of the Council for the Encouragement of Music and the Arts (CEMA), subsequently the Arts Council of Great Britain, undertaken on top of all his other duties, was personal testimony to his commitment to the 'good life'.

In Part III, Germany is crushed, but Britain is bankrupt. 'The Last Battle' traces Keynes's desperate attempt to claw back some of the costs of the war from the United States and the sterling area, so as to leave Britain room for independent action. The nighmarish negotiations in Washington in the autumn of 1945, in which a rapidly fading Keynes fights unavailingly on two fronts – against the US administration and his own government – to get a settlement which makes economic sense, is the climax of this book. Four months later he was dead. A post-war epilogue, ending with the death of Lydia Lopokova and the eclipse of the Keynesian Revolution, rounds off the story.

What does this account add to our knowledge of Keynes and the momentous events in which he was involved? The first thing to say is that my biography is conceived on a larger scale than those of Roy Harrod (1951) and Donald Moggridge (1992) and there is, therefore, in this volume as well as the previous two, more room for both private and public detail. Two examples from this book are the attention I give to Keynes's attitudes to pre-war foreign policy in the first chapter, and the space given to his service as a fellow of Eton College in Chapter 5. Some may see this second topic as a distraction from the main theme. However, it serves to remind the reader that Keynes had considerable diplomatic gifts when he chose to exert them, as well as offering, I hope, a comic respite from the grimness of the war.

From the biographical point of view, perhaps the main element added to previous accounts is the revelation of Keynes's ability to work as an effective and loyal member of a team. It is true that Roy Harrod repeatedly asserts this, but I try to show it, notably in Chapter 5. The other theme I try to convey is the relentless strain of the war for those in charge of the 'home front'. Few of middle age in government service during the war survived to a ripe old age. Keynes himself was fighting a losing battle against heart disease. There is probably more to be said about his medical problems – a neglected subject in biography – and their effect on his time-horizon and performance under stress than I have been able to manage.

Keynes was a masterly user of English. This was the key to his persuasiveness. His language, logical and robust, could suddenly take wing as his mind soared beyond the strict requirements of his argument. A study of Keynes's use of rhetoric remains to be done. I simply alert the reader to its importance. I also offer more practical help. Keynes is the most quotable of men, though his contributions to the English language have scarcely been recognised by compilers of anthologies, who seem to believe that only 'writers' say things memorably. Under Keynes's name in the Index I have supplied page references to the 'quotable quotes' from this period of his life.

This is a book about practical applications, not theory. However, the theoretical substratum shines through all of Keynes's wartime plans. I have emphasised the influence of five theoretical or intellectual predispositions which emerged from the debates of the 1920s and 1930s. First, there was Keynes's liquidity preference theory, which led him to advocate cheap money, capital controls, and creditor adjustment in his International Clearing Union plan. Secondly, the aggregate supply and demand analysis of the *General Theory* framed his fiscal plans to counter both inflation and depression. Thirdly, his conviction that private industry was 'socialising' itself, dating from the 1920s, underpins his technique of fiscal stabilisation, discussed in chapter 8. Fourthly, his 'elasticity pessimism' explains his preference for fixed, over floating, exchange rates. Finally, all his plans exemplify the philosophy of the Middle Way which he developed in the 1920s.

The early chapters on 'Paying for the War' bring out three points which have been insufficiently stressed. The first is Keynes's role, between 1937 and 1939, as the impresario of his own Revolution. The fact that he was around for ten years after the *General Theory* was published, six of them in the Treasury, was a vital factor in the success of the Keynesian Revolution. The key was his ability to show how his theory could be used accurately and successfully for anti-inflationary policy. That the *General Theory* could be turned to this purpose is now obvious. But it was Keynes who pointed it out, in a series of anti-inflationary articles in *The Times*, starting in 1939. These brought about a reconciliation between Keynesians and non-Keynesians, especially in the Treasury and Bank of England, which only broke down in the 1960s. Amusingly, some of his followers thought that he had become anti-Keynesian.

Secondly, I show that his influential anti-inflationary tract *How to Pay for the War*, published at the end of 1939 and expanded in 1940, sprang directly from his anti-inflationary writings of the previous two years. What he did, in essence, was to turn the fiscal policies for 'boom control' which he had been advocating since 1937 into financial policy for a fully employed war economy. Specifically, the idea that policy in 1937 should aim for a 'rightly distributed demand' rather than for an expansion of total demand could readily be adapted to the need to transfer resources to the war effort without inflation once the war had started. Acknowledgement of his achievement came from Friedrich Hayek, his most intransigent critic. Hayek wrote to him on 3 March 1940: 'It is reassuring to know that we agree so completely on the economics of scarcity, even if we differ on when it applies.'

Thirdly, I bring out the underlying liberalism of his approach to wartime problems. His 'fiscal theory' of war finance was put forward explicitly as an alternative to physical planning of resources, buttressed by price controls and rationing, which he dubbed the economics of a 'slave' state. Provided total purchasing power could be controlled, the price mechanism should be allowed to allocate resources – in war as well as in peace. This was his Big Idea, his alternative to economic 'totalitarianism'. He called the price mechanism the 'element of freedom' in the economic system. Here we have a prime example of his intellectual fearlessness. In practice, Keynes lost the battle for economic freedom in war, and the price mechanism was suppressed along with consumer demand. This was inevitable once the war became 'total'. The episode is important, nonetheless, in showing that, by instinct, he was not a controller but a lover of freedom. Bringing out the liberal strand in *How to Pay for the War* makes it much easier to understand why Keynes wrote to Hayek in 1944, of the latter's *Road to Serfdom*, 'Morally and philosophically I find myself in agreement with virtually the whole of it; and not only in agreement, but in a deeply moved agreement.'

I have emphasised more than other writers have the intensity and often bitterness of the struggle between Britain and America for post-war position which went on under the façade of the Grand Alliance. When the European war started, Britain, not Germany, was seen by most American leaders as America's chief rival. America's main war aim, after the defeat of Germany and Japan, was the liquidation of the British Empire. Both sides understood – perhaps wrongly – that the terms on which American help was rendered to Britain during the war would decide whether or not Britain remained a Great Power. To condense a complicated story, the Americans tried to use Lend–Lease as a lever to destroy Britain's pre-war financial and trading system, based on the sterling area and imperial preference. Early in 1941 Keynes tautly summarised what was to become Britain's chief aim in all its financial negotiations with the United States: 'the retention by us of enough assets to leave us capable of independent action'. The story of Anglo-American rivalry is given a further twist by the fact that the man with whom Keynes mainly negotiated in Washington, Harry Dexter White of the US Treasury, wanted to cripple Britain in order to clear the ground for a post-war American–Soviet alliance. That he and other senior administration officials were passing classified information to the Soviets cannot now be reasonably doubted.

The battle over Britain's post-war future was fought not just with the Americans but within the British government. Should Britain try to base its post-war economic future on its Empire? Or should it agree to dismantle its imperial system in return for American aid? Keynes was neither anti-liberal nor anti-American. He dismissed the idea that Britain should form a bloc with all the countries to which it owed money. He never considered the possibility of Britain joining forces with the liberated and post-Nazi countries of Western Europe to balance American power – though one or two of his colleagues in the Treasury were starting to. But he mistrusted the United States as discretionary manager of a new world system and he rebelled against Britain being forced by its weakness to beg America for favours. He wanted partnership with the Americans during and after the war on equal terms. But he had no bargaining power. Few things are more poignant than the letter he wrote to his mother on 21 November 1945 at the lowest point of the Washington loan negotiation: 'May it never fall to my lot to have to *persuade* anyone to do what I want, with so few cards in my hand.'

Could Britain have taken another road? I do not accept the argument implied in the work of some revisionist historians like John Charmley (in his *Churchill: the End of Glory*, 1993) that it should have made peace with Hitler's Germany. It takes two to parley, and Hitler, as well as being a moral barbarian, lacked every genuine attribute of statesmanship. He left others with no choice but to conquer him or be conquered by him. It was a tragedy for Continental Europe, as well as for Britain, that such a man was in charge of a great nation. It threw Britain into the arms of America as a suppliant, and therefore subordinate: a subordination masked by the illusion of a 'special relationship', which continues to this day.

These, and other, differences in emphases and interpretations from previous books on Keynes stem from differences of curiosity and competence. I currently 'profess' political economy at Warwick University. Though I trust that I have learnt some economics, I instinctively approached the subject matter of this book as a historian, not as an economist. That is to say, my trained instinct is always to set economic debates in their historical and political contexts. This book is, therefore, a history of the Second World War, from a particular point of view, as well as a history of Keynes's intellectual and financial projects. I would claim that this is the right approach for two reasons. First, Keynes himself was always acutely aware of the importance of relevance, practicability and political presentation. Every proposition or proposal had to be intellectually robust; but it was not worth putting forward unless it had a chance of being acted on in a reasonable time-scale. What was true of his approach at all times, was even more urgently the case in wartime. Thus, to understand the import of what Keynes was saying, it is always necessary to be aware of why he was saying it at that particular time. It is not enough just to refer to the *General Theory*, because the *General Theory* is a book which allows almost infinite elasticity of applications.

Secondly, although the technicians argued the pros and cons of different economic plans in technical terms, politics decided which ones were adopted. Thus some parts of Keynes's original *How to Pay for the War* were more politically acceptable than others; the Bretton Woods Agreement reflected Harry Dexter White's ideas rather than Keynes's not because it was technically superior, but because the Americans had the power; Keynes failed to achieve his objects in the loan negotiation of 1945, not because he had poor arguments, but because he had poor political weapons. This book is, therefore, much more about the relationship between politics and economics than previous biographies of Keynes have been.

Did Keynes make a difference? This is the hardest test for any individual to pass. Monsters in power do. Hitler certainly did, in the sense that had he never existed, or had he died in 1937, the world would have been very different. The same is true of Stalin. Of good men, even great men, it is more difficult to give a clear answer. Roosevelt probably did; also Churchill (at least in 1940). Of those who wield the power of the pen rather than the sword it is even harder to answer. Keynes's *General Theory* was one of the most influential books of the twentieth century. Yet it is impossible to demonstrate conclusively that economic conditions would have been very different had it never been written. In the years covered by this volume, the achievements with which his name is chiefly associated – Kingsley Wood's budget of 1941, the Full Employment White Paper of May 1944, the International Monetary Fund – were largely the work of others. His effect is rather to be found in the authority his ideas and presence gave to propositions and policies which would have been held or pursued more feebly or in a more muddled way without it. He was the fifth wheel on the coach. If this biography has rescued Keynes from the economists, and placed him in the world of history where he properly belongs, it will have achieved its aim.

III

Recalling his final deliverance from *The Decline and Fall of the Roman Empire*, Gibbon wrote: 'I will not dissemble the first emotions of joy at the recovery of my freedom, and, perhaps, the establishment of my fame. But my pride was soon humbled, and a sober melancholy was spread over my mind, by the idea that I had taken an everlasting leave of an old and agreeable companion. . . .' No author, at the point of finishing a large project which has taken many years, can fail to share Gibbon's mingled joy and melancholy. I started researching on Keynes at the end of the 1970s. Over twenty years or more, my work on him stopped me doing many things I wanted to do; it also became my 'old and agreeable companion'.

Agreeable? Certainly. No one would (or perhaps should) write books unless he or she got pleasure from doing so. But is a highly demanding and disciplined kind of pleasure, and I was often afflicted with doubts as to whether I would or could finish the project, and even more about whether I could do justice to my subject. At such times, I would start re-reading Keynes – anything, anywhere – and my resolve to press on would revive.

He was not just a brilliant person; there are many of these. We are even told that a sizeable fraction of any population consists of 'geniuses'. What makes Keynes stand out from the throng of the highly gifted is what

Lytton Strachey might have called 'the fearlessness of his cerebration'. He was incapable of banality; on any subject he turned his mind to, even momentarily, he would come up with a thought unexpected, arresting, original. This could make him exhausting to live with at close quarters. As the art historian Kenneth Clark once said, 'He never dipped his headlights.' This quality, I now realise, sustained my joy in his company for over twenty years – a pleasure enhanced by the fact that, when I felt like arguing with him, I always had the last word.

Nevertheless, I now look forward to my own personal 'Post-Keynesian' era. Keynes is one of my skins and I will never be able to slough him off. But there are others, not entirely harmonious with it, and I will have to work out a peace treaty between them.

Robert Skidelsky 3 June 2000

PART ONE

PAYING FOR
THE WAR

Well here am I, like a recurring decimal, doing very similar work in the same place for a similar emergency. JMK

CHAPTER ONE

Curing Invalidism

I

Dominating the upper part of the vale of the Clwyd, in north-eastern Wales, is the ruin of Ruthin Castle. It stands on a rock 270 feet above sea level. Nestling under its walls on their northern slope is the ancient town of Ruthin. Rhudd-ddin means Red Fortress in Welsh, and it was so called because it was built from the red sandstone on which it stood. The original castle was founded by Edward I in 1281 as a royal base, part of a chain of forts built to garrison the country he had just conquered in a brutal war. The outer walls, fortified by seven great towers, enclosed an area of about a hundred acres, including the castle proper, a chapel and a well a hundred feet deep. It was at Ruthin that the Welsh patriot Owen Glendower raised the standard of revolt against Henry IV in 1400, 'plundering the English who had come [to the fair] with their goods, slaying many of them, sacking the town and concluding his day's work by firing it'.[1] In the Civil War the Castle was held for the King by Colonel Marcus Trevor, who surrendered it to Parliament after a two months' siege on 12 April 1646. General Thomas Mytton wrote to Parliament: 'The reducing of the Castle of Ruthin has cost me more time and ammunition than I expected . . .'. It was then demolished. From the Myddletons who owned it, the property came, by marriage, into the hands of the West family, which, in the mid-nineteenth century, built a strange three-storeyed, red-sandstone, castellated edifice on the edge of the old ruins. Colonel William Cornwallis West entertained the Prince of Wales there in 1899; a year later his son George (aged twenty-six) married another of his house guests on that occasion, the widowed Lady Randolph Churchill, Winston Churchill's mother (aged forty-six). The Colonel started selling off the Ruthin Castle estate in 1919. Today it is a luxury hotel.

When Keynes was conveyed there by car on 18 June 1937, it had been for fourteen years a private sanatorium, a kind of convalescent home for the sickly rich. He had been preceded by Calouste Gulbenkian and Lady Ottoline Morrell, and would be followed by John Buchan. Keynes had been moved from Cambridge as soon as he safely could be following his coronary attack a month earlier. F. C. Scott, a fellow director of the

Provincial Insurance Company, had recommended it as 'supreme in diagnosis' if rather primitive in its methods of treatment. Started at Duff House, Banff, in Scotland, it had moved to more accessible premises in 1923, and now advertised itself as a 'clinic or private hospital for the scientific investigation and treatment of illness, and for the maintenance of health . . . the first institution of its kind in the United Kingdom'. It comprised three groups of buildings set in 475 acres, including the old castle ruins, with sixty-four patient rooms, as well as a grand reception room, library, dining room, consulting rooms, laboratories, kitchens, larders, staff rooms, offices, diet rooms, an X-ray department and medical baths. The Vale of Clwyd enjoyed what the brochure called 'a mild and equable but not relaxing climate', being buffeted by mountain and moorland air, supplemented by breezes from the Irish Sea. But 'the friends and relations of patients', it promised, 'will find abundant interest in the neighbourhood. The town has a nine hole golf course . . .'. The weekly charge, inclusive of meals, nursing and 'ordinary X-ray examinations', was 15 guineas upwards. Keynes stayed in the superior Castle Wing, in a huge, red-carpeted room with views on to the Clwydian hills and with a private bathroom. He would have paid 30 guineas a week. He spent over three months at Ruthin altogether, from 18 June to 25 September. He then went back to his country house, Tilton, in East Sussex, where he was based for a further eighteen months in a twilight between sickness and health.

When Keynes came to Ruthin he was the most famous economist, and even then one of the most famous men, in England. But his reputation was precariously poised. His *General Theory of Employment, Interest and Money*, published the previous year, had claimed to prove that full employment might be beyond the reach of an unmanaged market economy. This being so, it ought to be the goal of government policy. Critical reaction to his great book was inconclusive. To young economists it was a 'Manifesto of Reason and Cheerfulness'.[2] To most of their elders it was little more than an inflationist tract, 'the dying voice of the bourgeois crying in the wilderness for the profits it dare not fight for', as Joseph Schumpeter put it.[3] Most of Keynes's Cambridge colleagues sat on the fence, shaken but sceptical.

The fate of the Keynesian Revolution thus depended on economic and political events. Had Keynes diagnosed the condition of contemporary capitalism aright? It was a subtle reading. His capitalist system was no longer in a state of rude health, as in the nineteenth century; but neither was it mortally wounded as Marxists claimed. Its 'natural' twentieth-century state was one of *invalidism*. Bereft of its old vigour, it might still get on perfectly well with the aid of stimulating tonics. In the late 1930s these propositions started to be put to the test. By the spring of 1937 Britain's national government had presided over four years of strong private-sector-led economic recovery from depression. Balanced budgets and huge Conservative majorities had restored business confidence; cheap money had fuelled a building boom; lower taxes and rising incomes had led to a consumption boom. This is as the orthodox economists would have expected. Nor was there as yet any undue apprehension of war. Despite the disturbing presence of Hitler and Mussolini, the times, it seemed, were slowly returning to 'normal'; and even Hitler and Mussolini might be bought off with African colonies. In the immediate aftermath of the *General Theory*, Keynes seemed more isolated than he had been at any time in the inter-war years – not altogether unlike Winston Churchill, whose warnings of a coming war went unheeded.

Yet by 1939 Keynes had recaptured a central, if not yet commanding, position in British public life. After four years of recovery, the American economy went into a steep decline in the summer of 1937, and the British economy followed suit. The patient was not yet cured. The decisive push, though, came from two men. It was Hitler who forced Keynesian economics on to Neville Chamberlain's anti-Keynesian government; and it was Keynes himself who made sure that the rearmament programme would be understood as an experimental test of his employment theory. The author of the Keynesian Revolution became its impresario. For two years the cure for an invalid economy was propounded by the invalid at Tilton.

II

THE INVALID

What exactly was wrong with Keynes? The enquiry was conducted by the magnficent Sir Edmund Spriggs, KCVO, who had been consulting physician to King Edward VII, and was now consulting senior physician at Ruthin; he was assisted by the resident physician, Sydney Wentworth Patterson, a bacteriologist. Sir Edmund was resident, too. He lived in one of the smaller neo-Gothic castles on the estate and was driven around in a splendid Rolls-Royce of buff colour. In the former library, now the hotel bar, are seventy-five bound copies of volume one of the *Duff House Papers*, which Spriggs edited, dealing with disorders of the stomach. These, together with the antique Rolls-Royce, still garaged on the estate, appear to be the only relics of Sir Edmund Spriggs's regime at Ruthin Castle.

The official diagnosis was 'coronary disease, large heart and aorta; septic tonsils. . . . The condition is due to coronary and myocardial trouble probably associated with the tonsils.' The doctors discovered, Maynard told his brother Geoffrey, that his tonsils were in a 'shocking condition, covered with pus to the naked eye and creeping apparently with animals called fusillaria. . . . I gather he [Patterson] took the view that there was enough poison distilling in the system here to account for all the other symptoms. They have been tackling this by painting the tonsils . . . with a preparation of organic arsenic.' The Ruthin doctors, that is, had diagnosed subacute bacterial endocarditis, caused by streptococcus viridans, green bacteria which lodge in and attack the valves of the heart, or, in Lydia's phrase, 'dripped poison into the systeme'. This diagnosis was almost certainly right. It suggests that Keynes had been in trouble since the bouts of the intercostal rheumatism he had been experiencing since 1931. Unfortunately, no known treatment of it was effective. Antibiotics had not yet been invented. Neither treating the throat with arsenic (more familiar in treating syphilis), nor applying Mandl's paint, a compound of iodine, which succeeded Keynes's arsenic preparation, would have cleared up the bacterial infection. So the Ruthin diagnosticians fell back on the two most ancient of remedies: rest and hope.

Keynes spent his first six weeks at Ruthin in bed. He started in a 'luxurious' private room, with a four-foot-wide bed which Edward VII, he gossiped, had shared 'in happier days' with Mrs Cornwallis West – a slightly inaccurate reference to Lady Randolph Churchill, known later in life as Lady Randy, who had stayed with the Prince of Wales at Ruthin in 1899. 'I am in outrageously good general health and very cheerful,' he wrote to his mother on 25 June, though he was somewhat disturbed by the snores of his fellow patients, who included Lord Derby and 'the American Ambassador (who drinks, I should suspect!)'. The ambassador, R. W. Bingham, died a few months later. On 19 July Keynes was moved into a less palatial room and put into a Bergonie's chair, a traction machine for restoring movement. On the 27th he was freed from his 'horrible chair' and allowed up for the first time. He hoped he would soon be able to walk again 'like a human being instead of a poodle on its hind legs'.

Lydia stayed in the town of Ruthin in a 'mousy room' in the Castle Hotel, with a 'hen party of Castle widows'. Except for a couple of short visits, Florence Keynes tactfully left Lydia in charge. Lydia sent her reports on Maynard's condition, in her own inimitable style. On 19 July she told Florence that 'the throat does not smell any more for the last three days, it shows the grubs are cornered and destroyed'. When the unrelaxing weather allowed, she and Maynard went for drives, interspersed by walks. When it rained, she translated articles from the Russian émigré press. One of them stated that 'out of 2,000,000 Communists belonging strictly to the party 1,000,000 ha[ve] been wiped out'. Maynard had a 'flop' in mid-August, 'yet I can't help seeing that he is improving, the wounded bird's look in his eyes is disappearing'. He now realised that 'mental effort upsets the heart, which he refused to believe before'. On 22 August 'cardiag is definitely better'. He was walking a little more every day. By 13 September Maynard was sleeping 'without a dope', but fretting to leave. 'The change will be welcome for both of us, because my nerves are getting very ragged, and sometimes I simply break up in torrents of tears.'

Maynard was allowed a modest amount of work in the mornings. 'I get my papers alright,' he wrote to Richard Kahn two days after arriving. 'Markets seem stoner dead than ever. . . . Don't hang on to the maize. . . . 24/6 is now looking good.' A letter to the Chancellor of the Exchequer followed a few days later. 'Lying in bed, I think a good deal about foreign policy,' he wrote to Kingsley Martin on 1 July. An article in the *New Statesman* duly followed on 10 July. Duncan Grant, who read it, wrote to his old friend: 'Do you write under your bed clothes without the knowledge of your Doctor?' His secretary, Mrs Stephens, visited fortnightly. He bombarded Norman Higgins, manager of the Cambridge Arts Theatre, with programming instructions and Richard Kahn, now assistant bursar at King's, with investment instructions. 'I wish I knew how far linseed oil and cotton oil are substitutes,' worried the imperious patient at Ruthin. 'I am sending Weller some short notes on gilt-edged for the Bursars' meeting.' He apologised to Kahn for causing him so much trouble over commodities. 'But it's a pure game,' he added lightly, 'and should not use time available for serious tasks.' Kahn, too, made the pilgrimage to Ruthin – with an inflamed Achilles tendon.

Keynes did not give up the 'management' of his Revolution. Illness made him no less combative. 'It seems to me the work of a sick man,' the far from sprightly Keynes commented after reading an attempted refutation of his theory by Arthur Pigou, his Cambridge colleague. Pigou, too, had heart trouble. 'Why is there such obstinacy and wilfulness in error?' he asked about Gottfried Haberler's *Prosperity and Depression*, which he got Kahn to savage in the *Economic Journal*, which he edited. As for Miss Myra Curtis (subsequently Principal of Newnham), who had written something on money, 'the poor girl seems to have taken complete leave of her senses. I am writing to Lerner to suggest that he might deal with it . . . in a couple of pages.'

In her final report from Ruthin on 22 September Lydia wrote that 'The dilated muscle is diminishing, but the complete recovery is still to come for a long time, and Maynard is to go on with the same regime. . . . he still has pains in the chest (not what they were). . . .' Dr Patterson left written instructions for his convalescence. Apart from a diet which looks surprisingly ample, Keynes was to take breakfast in bed, have a good rest after lunch, retire to bed before dinner, stay in bed one day a week. As he explained to Virginia Woolf, 'I have got to continue my present semi-bed regime for a considerable time to come. But a point has now been reached when it is admitted that I can do it quite as well at home.' Keynes returned to Tilton on 30 September, after a stopover in London. In retrospect, he and Lydia agreed that the Ruthin regime had been a 'strange mixture of first-class medicine and first-class humbug'.

He left Ruthin in an upbeat mood, with the doctors promising him recovery within six months.[4] He would take the autumn off from

Cambridge, but would spend most of it in London, gradually picking up the threads of 'real life'.[5] In fact, he stayed at Tilton till February. There was a three-week visit to London and Cambridge in February–March and another of the same length to Cambridge in May–June, with mixed results. After that he did not leave Tilton again till October 1938. The reason is that his recovery turned out to be much slower than he expected. Till Janos Plesch took over his treatment in March 1939, he remained an invalid, subject to almost daily fluctuations in health, and serious setbacks whenever he came under any strain.

Lydia now became his heroic, devoted nurse. Love certainly, but also basic peasant instinct dictated that she tend her sick mate. Keynes's debility redressed the internal balance of their marriage. Lydia had been his responsibility; for the rest of his life he became hers. She had been necessary for the completion of his egoism; now he depended on her for his survival. Without being asked, she took control. To her care she brought the discipline she had shown as a *prima ballerina*. For three years, she recorded every fluctuation in his health, mood, appearance; enforced his regime; kept at bay unnecessary business or visitors. For the first time, she found herself useful, in fact indispensable, to Maynard. Besides, Maynard was now her whole life. Her acting career was petering out, though she still did occasional broadcasts for the BBC; she had no children; her family was far away in Russia. Maynard understood and accepted the rearrangement. He never went far without Lydia again. He increasingly invoked her authority to protect him against irksome or tiring demands. He hated being an invalid; at the same time, as Dadie Rylands shrewdly noticed, he 'enjoys the atmosphere of the nursery'. This was the first of Keynes's illnesses when he had not been nursed by his mother. It says a great deal for her understanding of the situation that Florence Keynes willingly surrendered the care of her adored, famous son to a Russian ballerina, dismissed by Bloomsbury as canary-brained.

Lydia set out to enforce the programme of rest prescribed by the Ruthin doctors. Since Keynes could barely crawl up the stairs, his bedroom at Tilton was moved to the ground-floor 'boot room' to the right of the front door as one entered, a Cézanne hung on the wall, and Lydia installed next door in the wing Keynes had built for guests. He spent half the day in bed. He was allowed to work for two or three hours in the mornings, propped up in bed or on a couch with his writing board. In the afternoons, taking advantage of the exceptional sunshine that October, he and Lydia were driven to nearby places like Glynde, Firle, Lewes or Eastbourne, so that he might be 'aired', as Lydia put it in a letter to her friend Samuel Courtauld, 'in harmonious foliage'. Tea would be followed by rest. After an early supper, Keynes would be back in bed again, relaxing with a book, a play or the wireless. He often took what Lydia called 'dope' to fall asleep. Mrs Stephens (known as 'Missie') came once a week for his correspondence, but if these sessions continued too long they were liable to leave him 'aggressive' and 'chippy'. Visitors were discouraged, as talk made him too excited, leaving him flat and depressed. If she thought they had stayed too long, Lydia would suddenly throw them out, as the doctor had told her to: 'Now you must go.' She saw at once when Maynard was tired, and told him to lie down and stop talking – 'the only cure for the heart pain'.

His long convalescence and growing involvement in the affairs of his small estate made Tilton increasingly important to Keynes in the last years of his life. As his mother described it, it was 'essentially a house with views – north, south, east and west'. The front door, almost invariably wide open, framed 'an enchanting view of meadows fading into the distance at the foot of the South Downs'. The long drawing room, early brightened by the morning sun, opened on to a stretch of lawn, backed by an ancient orchard 'more remarkable for the fantastic forms of the aged trees than for the fruit they bore'. To the south, connected to the house by a covered way, was the loggia built by George Kennedy in the 1920s, now glassed in, giving a wide view of the South Downs to Firle Beacon. Here Keynes would spend part of the day reading. Finally, to the west was the guest wing, which Lydia now occupied.

Tilton had an ample if fluctuating staff. Penny Weller, otherwise 'Auntie', Lydia's old dresser, together with her nephew Edgar Weller and his wife Ruby, formed the core. Edgar Weller was now confined to the garden, his erratic place at the wheel of Keynes's Rolls having been taken by Fred Woollard, Auntie's nephew-in-law and apparently a great mechanical genius, whom Lydia adored and who combined the improbable duties of 'librarian–chauffeur–masseur'. Beatty, an attractive twenty-six-year-old, cooked 'delicious' meals. Her mind, though, was 'beyond belief'. There were two housemaids, Roma, who was Swiss, and a Norwegian girl (unnamed). The household was completed by Patsy, the survivor of the Keyneses' three dogs, a 'squat, yapping brown-and-white mongrel'[6] with evil breath. 'It is rumoured that Patsy has caught a rat with his breath,' Maynard scribbled on one of Lydia's letters to Richard Kahn.

With staff came staff problems. The servants' health fluctuated alarmingly. 'Oh! This staff business. We never have a complete quorum, one is always in bed,' Lydia wrote in despair. In January 1938, Auntie developed pneumonia, and Maynard ordered a trained nurse for her – 'most charming, not a dragon like me', Lydia noted. With Fred also down with a heavy cold, 'the master and the mistress are by far the healthiest'. Auntie recovered, and by the summer was 'running round like a gazelle, turning socks in and out', but Beatty developed dreadful eczema and shingles. 'I hope she will get married, it is the only salvation for her.' On 25 January 1939, she and her Dick were wedded in Lewes by a 'sympathetic Reverend', Lydia and Maynard signing the register. 'Beatty was beautiful, aristocratic and Dick charming, distinguished. They look so much better than the upper classes.' They spent their honeymoon at the Keynes's London house, 46 Gordon Square, where Mrs Turtle still cleaned. Roma was now promoted to the Tilton kitchen. The saga of ill-health continued when Mrs Stephens developed chest pains and a high temperature in the spring of 1938. She returned after two months, 'looking fragile, poor girl'.

Keynes could not give up work. He was yoked to activity by his passions and commitments. Some of the latter were suspended rather than renounced. He gave up attending the London meetings of his company boards and the Committee on Economic Information, though he maintained his connections from Tilton, upbraiding the Committee's chairman, Sir Josiah Stamp, on the 'appalling verbosity' of its latest quarterly report.[7] Richard Kahn managed his bursarial business in Cambridge. But he could not escape his broker, and he would not give up the Arts Theatre, though for tax reasons he transferred control of it to a charitable trust.*

Lydia kept a tight control on visitors. The Woolfs came to tea early in October. Virginia found Maynard looking much better, 'not so white and heavy', and transformed into a medical expert. 'All London specialists were wrong about him. The only cure for all diseases is at Ruthin's.'[8] Their first non-local visitors were Auden and Isherwood, who came down from London on 11 November with Rupert Doone (director of the Group Theatre) to discuss their new 'morality play' *On the Frontier*, which Keynes wanted to put on at the Arts Theatre. He and Lydia walked 'with the boys' down from Firle Beacon, and found them 'very stimulating and interesting'. Keynes was disturbed to discover that the Group Theatre had no funds, but agreed to put up the money for a production at Cambridge and act as agent for the play. As the two authors were about to go to China, the Cambridge performances had to be postponed for a year. The McKennas and Walter Layton came down in the spring. Lydia tried to avoid lunch parties: 'it is two hours of continuous talk, but we couldn't put Layton off, he seemed to me a case for a breakdown, very stammery and yellow . . .'.

With his fifty-year lease on Tilton Farm and Tilton Wood, signed in 1936, Keynes was also a farmer; and he now had the leisure to play the rural squire on an estate of about 200 acres. Tilton Farm was run by his farm manager Logan Thomson, a Yorkshireman with a taste for novels, while the gamekeeper, Mr Churchill, reared pheasants and partridges in Tilton Wood. Thomson's heart, Lydia said, was broken by the Norwegian maid who came in 1938; 'she and Logan used to drive round the farm together and seemed . . . all through the summer of 1938, to be insepar-

---

* In January 1938, to avoid entertainment tax and to get income tax relief on his own contributions. His own control as chairman of the Trustees was little affected.

able'. Quentin Bell, Vanessa and Clive Bell's younger son, who tells this story, thinks it was old Mrs Thomson, who with Thomson's father lived with Logan in the pink bailiff's house, who ended the affair.[9]* The convalescent Keynes loved to potter round his farm, watching the corn being threshed, the sheep being sheared, checking the quality of the milk and the condition of the pigs. He gave a big bonfire party on Guy Fawkes Day: Quentin Bell made the mask for the guy, there was beer and sausages for the farm labourers, a little speech from Maynard. Lydia attended dressed as a pig. The Saturday shoots, in which Clive Bell and members of the Keynes family sometimes took part – Keynes himself never shot – had decidedly unbucolic accompaniments. The farmers would gather in Keynes's spacious hall, reconstructed by George Kennedy, whose walls were hung with Post-Impressionist paintings, and be directed by Lydia to a lavatory leading off, where a Matisse hung, with the words, 'Now you boys will want to do your little water in here.' On Christmas Day Lydia made her own contribution to the feudal system by distributing presents to the 'forty-five people in the little community'. The locals thought it was all a bit of a pretence, one of the farm workers remarking, 'Lord Gage [Maynard's landlord] is a lord and knows how the thing should be done.'

Keynes continued to scribble away on his writing board. Among his autumn productions was a memoir of Julian Bell, who had been killed that summer in the Spanish Civil War. Virginia Woolf's appreciative letter was touched with envy. 'I wish you'd go on to do a whole portrait gallery, reluctant as I am to recognise your gift in that line when it seems obvious that nature gave me none for mathematics. Is portrait writing hard work compared with economics?'[10] Keynes would have said no: it was 'writing arguments' which was really difficult. Not that there was as much falling-off in that department as his doctors would have liked. The controversy with Bertil Ohlin and Dennis Robertson on interest-rate theory rumbled on through the autumn, and Keynes had to draft his reply to the 'Prof.' – Pigou – on flexible wages. This involved extensive correspondence with Richard Kahn, Nicholas Kaldor (who was preparing an independent reply to Pigou's article), Dennis Robertson and Pigou himself. The result was two articles by Keynes in the December issue of the *Economic Journal*, 'The "Ex-Ante" Theory of the Rate of Interest', and 'Professor Pigou on Money Wages in Relation to Unemployment'. A review of James Meade's book *Consumer Credits and Unemployment* followed in the March 1938 issue of the *Journal*. Meade was advocating varying payments to, and contributions from, pensioners and insured workers to even out fluctuations in demand. 'Indeed the policy is obviously an extension and working out of the idea

---

* In his book *Keynes: A Critical Life* (1999), 208, David Felix misinterprets Quentin Bell to be saying that it was Logan Thomson and *Lydia* who used to drive round the farm together and be inseparable, and develops some fanciful speculation based on this non-event.

of budgeting for a deficit in depressions and a surplus in recoveries,' Keynes wrote. But he was not wholly convinced.[11]

Lighter tasks included browsing through his antiquarian book catalogues, adding to his collection of Newton manuscripts with purchases from Bertram Rota, and doing 'a little Newton research'. In December he wrote a review of W. R. Scott's biography of Adam Smith. 'Very good material but written in a most confused and boring way,' he told his mother. What the review shows is his delight in the small details of the lives of great economists. He noted Smith's habit, in writing, of lifting his pen in the middle of words 'so that no rapid cursive could be achieved'. Keynes had no such problem.[12]

Dating from this leisurely period is the introduction he wrote to the reprint of an anonymous *Abstract* of David Hume's *A Treatise on Human Nature*, the original of which he owned, which was published by the Cambridge University Press in March 1938. Although his Cambridge friend Piero Sraffa appears as joint author of the introduction, Keynes must have written at least the first draft, as Sraffa had a horror of writing for publication. In their introduction, Keynes and Sraffa argue ingeniously that the *Abstract* was in fact written by Hume and not by the juvenile Adam Smith, as hitherto thought, in order to stimulate the flagging sales of his *Treatise* by publishing an anonymous 'puff' for his own work.

Keynes kept in touch with public events. On 14 November 1937 he summarised his views on the world situation to Walter Stewart, who had taken over from Walter Case at the US merchant bank Case, Pomeroy & Co.* 'I do not expect a war, and I do not expect a major recession. On the other hand, international politics will interfere with the development of full business confidence, and some sort of recession seems obviously to be in progress on your side.'[13] That Britain, too, was in recession was apparent by December 1937. On this occasion, there was no Keynes Plan. The deepening recession in the United States did, though, prompt him to write another of his letters to the American President, Franklin Roosevelt, on 1 February 1938, this time private.

The slump in Maynard's health was accompanied, and aggravated, by the slump in his wealth. Wall Street's decline started about the time of Keynes's heart attack, with London following more gently. Most of Keynes's investments were in equities in the two markets; he was also highly leveraged. True to his philosophy of 'faithfulness' he hung on, but with growing anxiety. 'I don't want to have a big loan, even though the cover position is perfectly good,' he wrote to Richard Kahn from Ruthin on 2 September. 'I've not got to the point of being a bear, but I am *much*

---

* Walter Case had died in October, soon after visiting Keynes at Ruthin, apparently cured of his cancer. Keynes was a consultant for his firm.

more disinclined to be bull on borrowed money. And to bring loans down sufficiently is a necessarily tedious and difficult process.'

Nevertheless, it was the course he now embarked on. His brokers, Buckmaster and Moore, demanded an increase in cover. The only way Keynes could reduce his liability was by selling on a falling market. The increasingly steep decline in share prices slowed down his own recovery, while the alternation of brief recoveries with deeper collapses produced fluctuations in his heart. 'Specs are awful,' he wrote to his mother on 10 October. 'But . . . my hunch is that prices must now be somewhere near bottom.' In fact, Wall Street took another plunge nine days later. Keynes wrote to Florence on 21 October: 'Big losses, many decisions to make and many telephones. But although one's nerves itch badly on such days, there was nothing *really* to worry about.' A month later Lydia noted in her medical diary, 'Slump fatal for health.' On 16 November 1937, Maynard wrote to G. H. Recknell of the National Mutual, 'Of course the right time to sell was in the spring but that was *very* difficult to detect.'[14] On 7 December he wrote to Spriggs at Ruthin that 'a week of what seems almost excellent health has been followed by two or three days when I am not myself'. Two days later came a collapse in health which lasted for nine days. Spriggs urged rest, not realising that the cause of Maynard's 'flutters' was not work, but worry.

Keynes recovered enough to have dinner with Clive, Duncan and Vanessa at Charleston and lunch with the Woolfs at Rodmell over Christmas, his first evening engagements for nine months. 'We put Maynard to bed on 2 chairs,' wrote Virginia to her niece Angelica, 'and talked and talked until he worked himself into such a fury about politics, that Lydia called the car and off they drove.'[15] Almost certainly Keynes was lashing out at the imbecility of the Labour Party and the *New Statesman* about Spain and foreign policy, with Leonard Woolf trying to defend them (see pp. 32–4 below). The Provost of King's, Sir John Sheppard, came for the last weekend in January 1938. On 30 January Lydia told Richard Kahn that Maynard was taking things easier, 'reads the light books at the same time with BBC butting in'. With Keynes on the mend, Lydia felt able to take on some engagements herself, appearing on television on 23 December reading the Hans Christian Andersen story 'Little Red Shoes'. In the spring she broadcast a series of programmes, 'Studies of Childhood and Adolescence from the Russian Masters'. Their producer was Guy Burgess.

On 2 February there was another slump in Maynard's health. 'Is it spring?' asked Lydia. 'Or is it the nature of his disease? I cannot explain it. And yet on the whole he looks much better even with a sleepless night.' Keynes quickly rallied. The 5th of February saw him and Lydia sleeping in the garden 'wrapped up like eskimos'. The following day 'he had a glass of red wine with Mrs Stephens and me' for dinner.

Keynes returned to Ruthin on 11 February 1938 for a check-up. He was worried by a new localised heart pain, which usually appeared after a day of exertion just as he was about to go to sleep. The report from Ruthin was encouraging. His heart was still enlarged, but the quality of its pumping had improved. The yellow streptococci had been replaced by green ones, but the fight was easier. The throat swabs, Lydia explained, 'refused to grow vegetables, whilst the last time we were here, they grew at once into an orchard'. His blood pressure was still too low. The doctors would allow a 'mild return to public appearances in the near future, provided it is followed by a long summer's rest'. Lydia thought Wales was 'lovely for a week. . . . we went to the Old Chester Road, and walked with the winds behind, and the sun streaming, and the dead bracon [sic] to caress the eyes. . . . We are disturbed over the political news. To make friends with Italy! What a world.'[16] (Chamberlain had announced official talks with Italy the previous day.) A little later Lydia wrote to Florence: 'Have you seen atrocious photo of Mussolini looking like a starved gorilla? What a sight.'

On their return they spent three weeks in London. They now occupied two houses, Keynes having acquired the lease of 47 Gordon Square shortly before his illness. The drawing room at Number 47, connected by a door to the one in Number 46, now housed his library. While they walked in the parks, took drives in the countryside, saw old friends, political tension mounted. Hitler was piling pressure on Austria; Chamberlain was trying to get Mussolini to stand up for Austrian independence; on 21 February Eden resigned as Foreign Secretary. Lydia noted: 'Weather bad, political news bad, therefore it reflects on health.' Maynard wrote to Virginia Woolf: '[The] state of foreign politics is nearly giving me a heart attack. I always knew that Neville [Chamberlain] was the lowest (I can't spell it) flatest-footed [sic] creature that creeps. But will the country follow him [in his appeasement policy]?' Leonard and Virginia came to tea at 46 Gordon Square and found 'M. recumbent, but with a stock of ideas. Bentham the origin of evil. Lydia like a peasant woman, wringing her hands, on a stool.'[17] On 23 February 1938, Keynes made his annual chairman's speech to the National Mutual, his first public appearance since his illness; the following day he chaired a meeting of the Royal Economic Society. He carried both off with aplomb, but the controversy in the press following his speech left him exhausted. They went to tea with Maynard's brother Geoffrey. 'What a duck Stephen [Geoffrey's son] is!' wrote Lydia, in what she took to be colloquial English. 'He tells me he will never be a Communist.'

Maynard and Lydia spent the weekend of 10–14 March in Cambridge for the Fellowship Elections, his first visit since being taken to Ruthin. While they were there, German troops crossed the Austrian frontier, and Hitler declared the Anschluss. Keynes thought the government was 'almost wholly out of touch with the swiftly growing anti-dictator emotions of the public'.[18] They got back to Tilton on 18 March.

More bad news, this time from Wall Street in late March, brought another slump in health for Maynard, who still had 'a huge American position'. Lydia took it philosophically: 'it is quite natural after so much work, change of weather, the world situation, Wall Street and life in general'. In the last fortnight in March he sold £40,000 to £50,000 worth of securities, steadily reducing his debt to Buckmaster and Moore, while preserving most of his liquid resources. In the year of 'terrific decline' which had started in the spring of 1937 he lost nearly two-thirds of his money. His net assets fell from £506,222 at the end of 1936 to £181,244 by the end of 1938, with his gross income cut by two-thirds, from £18,801 in 1937–8 to £6,192 in 1938–9. The institutions whose investment policy he largely dictated – his College, the Provincial Insurance Company, the National Mutual – had also suffered heavy losses, and Keynes was driven to justifying his philosophy of 'hanging on for a rise' in lengthy letters and memoranda. To Francis Curzon, who chaired the weekly meetings of the board of the National Mutual in his absence, he wrote on 18 March: 'I feel no shame at being found still owning a share when the bottom of the market comes. . . . I would go much further than that. I should say that it is from time to time the duty of a serious investor to accept the depreciation of his holdings with equanimity and without reproaching himself. Any other policy is anti-social, destructive of confidence, and incompatible with the working of the economic system. An investor . . . should be aiming primarily at long-period results, and should be solely judged by these.'[19] Curzon and the board were not convinced, and Keynes resigned his chairmanship in October 1938, explaining to Falk, 'One naturally chooses [to give up] that part of one's activities in which one finds the least satisfaction.'[20]

With spring turning into summer, and Wall Street at last recovering, Keynes's health slowly improved. On 29 April Lydia wrote to Kahn: 'Yesterday Maynard walked very well for a whole hour, we saw butterflies out of their cocoons tangled to their husbands, resting on the branches from time to time.' In the middle of May he risked three weeks in Cambridge, living with Lydia in their new flat at 17a St Edward's Passage. Lydia's medical diary tells the story of energetic occasions ('carried the Congregation brilliantly') interspersed with fatigue, pain, bad nights ('entered the room like a corpse . . . took dope, very tired'). Still, he got by without severe damage. Sam Courtauld found him looking 'much better' at Tilton on 26 June, 'but he has to be very careful not to strain his heart, and must not talk too long. We went on a slow walk about an hour in the afternoon. Lydia seemed happier. . . .'[21] On 28 June Keynes felt well enough to tell Spriggs that he was not coming back to Ruthin.

The pains in his heart were getting less, for the first time in life he had completed a year without a cold, he was putting on weight.

Maynard and Lydia remained at Tilton for four months. 'What a relief to settle with one's bags & pillows in one place . . .' Lydia wrote to Florence. They found Fred Woollard 'intoxicated with his television [so] he has no time to drive us'. For much of this time Maynard was, as Lydia records, 'flat', sometimes sleeping or resting the whole day, taking pills for his heart and 'dope' at night. The lanky, stooped economist in his serge jacket and straw hat and his tiny, birdlike wife with her Russian accent and exotic headscarfs must have made a strange impression on the rustics as they puffed their way slowly round their little estate. Maynard loved to think of himself as a benevolent landlord, dispensing protection, festivals and fun in the traditional way – a thought not unconnected, Quentin Bell suggests, with 'a mistrust of communists and cryto-communists'. But the performance was unconvincing. Lord Gage was an aristocrat with intellectual interests, Keynes was an intellectual with squirearchical pretensions. It was the idea of the role, not the role itself, which appealed to him. He was no countryman. He talked about his labourers as fantastical, two-dimensional creatures, comic but not sympathetic. They in turn were disconcerted by his calculations, his inquisitiveness, his ferocious intelligence. Quentin Bell writes: 'They did not know what to do with so much brilliance. In a way they admired him and and were proud of him but . . . they did not love him. In matters of business he came amongst them like a man armed with a rapier who meets rustics armed only with clubs.' Such was a neighbouring tenant whom Maynard persuaded to erect and maintain an expensive fence between their properties at his expense – pointing out with scintillating logic why it would be enormously to his neighbour's benefit to shoulder the cost of the erection. On one of their potters round the farm, when Lydia had been trying to get Maynard not to overtax his strength, he turned to his shepherd and said: 'What would you do if an old sheep looked at you as Lydia is looking at me now?' – a question, Bell remarks, 'which anyone might have found it difficult to answer'.[22]

Water was a continuing problem, especially in the summer, owing to the smallness of their private well. In July 1938, Lydia recorded that neither she nor any one else at Tilton had had a bath for a month. Maynard got the farm workers to start digging a new well. There was still no water 'after six weeks boring'. Finally, at 222 feet they struck water and 'now there is so much beautiful water that it cannot start on its own and gets oppressed by the sand, so we'll have to drink mud and take mud baths'.

Keynes's economising instincts, never far from the surface, were strengthened by the decline in his own income. In March 1938 some hay at Tilton caught fire. Keynes summoned the fire brigade, which billed him for £21 9s 6d. Keynes calculated that he owed only £11 9s. A six-month correspondence now ensued with the Lewes Borough Council, the points at issue being how many firemen had answered the call, and whether Keynes was liable to pay for the extra people who had had to man the station in Lewes while the Lewes Fire Brigade was at Tilton. Keynes justified his reluctance to pay in terms of high moral principle: 'If only on public grounds, it seems to me inadvisable that costs should be unnecessarily inflated with the result of making the public reluctant to call the fire brigade. . . .' Eventually, Keynes agreed to pay £15 8s 6d. 'Rarely has so much correspondence passed over an account of this nature,' wrote Henry Cottrill, the borough treasurer, 'and I trust that . . . you will let me have settlement without delay.'

A happier connection with Lewes arose from Keynes's sponsorship of a project to build a theatre there. In 1936 he had met Kenneth Rawlings, rector of St. Michael's Church, and director of an amateur theatre company called Lewes Players. Rawlings, a practical visionary much like Keynes, wanted to build a theatre for the many amateur dramatic societies which then flourished in the area, as well as for professional productions.* In December 1937, Keynes lent him £125 to buy a disused garage, but, with his investments collapsing, would do no more. He became trustee of an appeal to raise £5000 to convert it into a small, modern theatre. The appeal raised £76. Despite this setback, a rudimentary 'Little Theatre' was constructed which still exists.

Lydia was now allowing more visitors. Her husband needed 'stimulus', even though it left him tired. His mother and father came down, as did his brother Geoffrey and his wife Margaret together with their children. Richard Kahn was almost family, though Lydia had to put Maynard to bed to avoid the excitement of conversation with Richard about bursarial matters. Other visitors who flit through the pages of Lydia's medical diary are his old undergraduate friend Robin Furness, Samuel Courtauld, Kingsley Martin, Rupert Trouton and the American economists Walter Stewart and William Riefler. Most of these just came for lunch or tea. Maynard and Lydia did not seek out county society. They occasionally had tea with their landlord, Lord Gage; relations with Glyndebourne, where John Christie had started a small opera house in 1933, were frosty, Keynes and Christie having disliked each other ever since they had been contemporaries at Eton. Duncan Grant and Vanessa and Clive Bell at Charleston and Virginia and Leonard Woolf at Rodmell were the Keyneses only local friends. Lydia notes a visit from Clive Bell to discuss partridge shooting – 'a suitable man for all occasions'. It was about as near to an acid comment

* The connection was through Dorothy Rawlings, Kenneth's wife, and friend of Margaret Masterman who was married to the philosopher Richard Braithwaite, a colleague of Keynes at King's College, Cambridge.

as Lydia got. But she and Maynard saw little of their Bloomsbury friends either. To Bloomsbury's continuing astonishment, their enjoyment of each other's company seemed complete.

Keynes's one major production over the summer of 1938 was a paper on buffer stocks, which he discussed with Walter Layton and Arthur Salter at Tilton, and which was read for him by his King's College colleague Gerald Shove at a meeting of Section F of the British Association in Cambridge on 19 August (see p. 25 below). Isherwood, back from China, paid a return visit to Tilton with Rupert Doone and Benjamin Britten, to finalise plans for staging *On the Frontier* in Cambridge. They agreed it should be done in November, with Lydia in the female starring role. A 'crummy piano' was bought to enable Benjamin Britten to rehearse the score. On 23 August Keynes gave an upbeat report on his health to Richard Kahn. He had made more progress in the previous month than at any other time since his illness: 'my off days and bad moments are nothing like so bad as they used to be either in duration or intensity . . . serious pain has almost entirely disappeared and I recover rapidly from fatigue'. Alas, his calm and health were to be shattered by the Czech crisis in September which led to Munich. 'I get on awfully slowly,' he gloomily wrote to his old Cambridge friend Bob Trevy (Trevelyan) on 27 September. 'We had a meeting of the Memoir Club last month and I read a paper on the effect of Principia Ethica on me when I was an undergraduate; and writing about Moore brought back to me vivid memories of you in those days.'[23] In fact the meeting took place at Tilton on 11 September. Virginia Woolf recorded that Keynes read 'a very packed profound & impressive paper' to a collection of Bloomsberries, old and young, then had to be 'slowly conveyed' to his ground-floor bedroom for a rest, while Lydia chirpily fed them ham sandwiches and hot cakes.[24] This was his paper 'My Early Beliefs', published posthumously, in which he partly confirmed and partly repudiated them.[25] He and Lydia were driven up to Cambridge from London on 16 October 1938 – 'dinner with Kahn, a bit tired, looks pale, went to bed early, no pain, but might be lurking around the heart'.

III

IMPRESARIO OF THE KEYNESIAN REVOLUTION

It was in the twilight years between peace and war that the Keynesian Revolution started to take hold. The reconciliation between Keynes and the anti-Keynesians began in 1937. Its setting was the worsening international situation, which brought about massive British rearmament. But the architect of the reconciliation was Keynes himself. Bypassing contentious theoretical issues, he showed how the aggregative approach of the *General Theory* could be applied not just to the unemployment problem but to the problem of inflationary pressure at full employment, and the management of a war economy. The *General Theory*, cunningly so called, had the potential so to be applied. But Keynes's exploitation of this potential was an astonishing performance, a captivating mixture of assurance, style, intellectual flexibility and administrative fertility. Admittedly, the circle of the captivated was quite small. The Conservative MP for Lewes, Admiral Tufton Beamish, who had joined Keynes as a trustee of the Little Theatre appeal, denounced his 'hoary proposal for vast schemes of public works'. John Buchan painted an unflattering portrait of Keynes as the 'half-adventurer, half-squire' and wholly amoral financier Barralty in his novel *The Island of Sheep* (1936). This reflected the standard right-wing Tory opinion of Keynes as a man of first-class brains but second-class character. The left still preferred socialism to managed capitalism, although it was starting to see how capitalism might be managed to further socialism's cause. It was the clever centre, always susceptible to Keynes's intellectual charm, which was reconciled. But that was enough.

On the surface there remained a wide gap between the startling and paradoxical propositions of the *General Theory* and what even the clever orthodox believed. Like Nietzsche or Copernicus, Keynes had turned their world upside down – mainly, his critics asserted, for a perverse pleasure in doing so. He had denied that a market system has any automatic tendency to full employment. He had propounded his 'paradox of thrift': that in a depression the attempt to save more will make a community poorer, but that a community which invests enough will never be short of saving. He had said that the rate of interest is the price of money, not of capital – a return, it seemed, to the doctrines of the medieval schoolmen. He had likened the stock market to a casino. He had pooh-poohed the doctrine of the balanced budget. He had even endorsed the heresy of protection. But the beauty of the *General Theory* was that one did not have to accept Keynes's 'wisecracks', as Hubert Henderson disobligingly called them, to appreciate the usefulness of his analytical framework, especially when it could be used to support or justify what the government wanted to do for other reasons. Keynes himself was well aware of how 'general' his *General Theory* was.

> I would emphasise again [he wrote to the American economist Gardner Means on 10 August 1939] the distinction between my *General Theory*, regarded as a more or less all-embracing theory, and the applications of it which can be made in different circumstances according to the different sets of realistic assumptions. . . . I regard the theory as equally applicable to flexible economies, inflexible economies, and intermediate conditions. But, of course, the results

to which the Theory would lead in the different cases would be widely different.[26]

From 1937 onwards, Keynes started applying the *General Theory* framework to the problems which would occur as Britain neared full employment and started preparing for the war. Of particular concern to the Treasury was the need to create room for rearmament without running into inflationary or balance of payments pressures. It was above all Keynes's anti-inflationary perspective which reconciled Keynesian economics to Treasury orthodoxy. Keynes's *How to Pay for the War*, and the wartime budgetary policy it inspired, were crystallisations of these pre-war discussions.

In February 1937 the Chancellor of the Exchequer, Neville Chamberlain, announced an addition to the rearmament programme, in the form of a £400m. defence loan, to be spent over five years. Those schooled in the old views asked the old questions. Where would the extra resources come from? Would they not be diverted from other uses, like the export trade, which the Treasury regarded as the 'fourth arm of defence'? Would not the borrowing raise interest rates? Would it be inflationary? But times had changed. The Treasury was now committed to borrowing increasing sums for rearmament. The only theory on offer which promised both guns *and* butter and the low interest rates the Treasury wanted for its borrowing was Keynes's. At the same time, the approach of full employment gave Keynes the chance to establish his anti-inflationary credentials. From 1937 to 1939 he repeatedly used *The Times* and other platforms to hammer home the message that there was enough spare capacity ('elasticity of supply' as he called it) in the economy to absorb extra public spending without inflation, provided the extra spending was targeted on areas with high unemployment; that fiscal, not monetary, policy should be the instrument for controlling booms; that central planning of demand was needed as the limit of capacity approached; and that national income and output statistics were needed to estimate the size of the gap between aggregate supply and demand, as well as to pinpoint relative imbalances across regions and industries. What Keynes did was to show how the *ad hoc* measures to which the government was being driven might become the basis for the permanent management of a peacetime economy.

Five strands in these polemics are worth following. The first is Keynes's sketch of stabilisation technique, in three articles he wrote for *The Times* on 12–14 January 1937 – a topic absent from the *General Theory*. In a section headed 'Boom Control' Keynes suggested what would now be called a 'cyclically balanced budget' policy – governments should incur debt in the downswing and repay debt in the upswing of the business cycle. 'The boom, not the slump,' he declared, 'is the right time for austerity at the Treasury.' The policy was to work by discretionary variations in public spending, managed by a public investment board. He also advocated countercyclical variations in trade policy: just as in a slump tariffs should be raised to check imports, so in a boom they should be lowered to divert a 'temporarily inflated demand in the home market' to imports. In the longer run, 'as the profit to be gained from adding to our capital goods [falls]', tax policy should be directed towards increasing consumption. This fiscal theory of demand management had a powerful influence on orthodox Keynesianism after the war.[27]

Secondly, Keynes repeatedly emphasised that there was no overall shortage of resources in the British economy, but that the 'unfortunate rigidity' of Britain's industrial structure meant that heavy surpluses of labour in the 'distressed areas' coexisted with shortages in some industries and localities, so that 'we are in more need today of a rightly distributed demand than of a greater aggregate demand'.[28] This implied cutting back public spending in the booming south and increasing it in the depressed north and Celtic fringe. This had special relevance to the rearmament programme. In *The Times* of 11 March 1937 Keynes argued that defence orders should be placed, as far as possible, in the special areas of heavy unemployment.

> It is a mistake [he wrote] to suppose that this is merely a form of charity to a distressed part of the country. On the contrary, it is in the general interest. Whether demand is or is not inflationary depends on whether it is directed towards trades and localities which have no surplus capacity. To organise output in the Special Areas is a means of obtaining rearmament without inflation.[29]

For purposes of policy, Keynes was dividing Britain into two halves. Overall unemployment then stood at 12 per cent, but it was much higher in the North and in the Celtic fringe than in the South and Midlands. Keynes thought that the explanation for the high unemployment in the distressed areas might lie in the fact that the old staple industries – engineering, textiles, coal – had, through productivity gains, been shedding labour faster than the 'distributing trades' had been capable of absorbing them.[30] Targeting rearmament spending on these areas while postponing civilian spending – particularly on council house building – in the prosperous ones would allow a closer approach to full employment without inflation.

Thirdly, Keynes stressed the need for a board of public investment to plan investment demand, so that a stock of new investment projects was ready to be activated as the profits from other types started to fall.[31] This became even more imperative in the twilight zone between peace and war through which Britain started to move in 1938 and 1939. He wrote to Oswald Falk on 5 September 1938: 'The trouble is that we are governed by utter boobies. Instead of devoting themselves to the none too easy task of ensuring the preparedness of this country, senior civil servants seem to devote themselves in almost every sphere of activity to providing their ministers with more or less plausible excuses for doing nothing.'[32]

Fourthly, national income statistics were needed to manage demand. At what levels of unemployment would serious inflationary pressures arise? Would it be 10 per cent, 5 per cent? No one knew. In his *Times* article of 11 March 1937 Keynes used some back-of-envelope arithmetic to calculate the size of the 'output gap'. This led him to conclude that 'the Chancellor's loan expenditure *need* not be inflationary'. But he complained that lack of adequate statistics had reduced his calculations to 'bold guesses'.[33] In *The Times* of 13 September 1938 he exploded in exasperation: 'How can economists be expected to produce a clear and unanimous diagnosis when the facts they have to go upon are so obscure and imperfectly known?'[34] Keynes's demand for national income statistics would soon be supplied. There is a point here of more than passing interest. Planning requires centralised knowledge and power of prediction which a *laissez-faire* system can do without. Yet Keynes himself was famously sceptical of econometric forecasting models. It was a contradiction, or subtlety, of which his practically minded disciples could make no sense.

The final strand of Keynes's argument was his advocacy of permanently cheap money. Short-term interest rates should be kept continuously low, in order to avoid uncertainty about the future of long-term rates. 'We must avoid [dear money] . . . as we would hell-fire,' he wrote in *The Times* of 12 January 1937. This doctrine would determine monetary policy till 1951.

Cheap money was not specifically Keynesian. It was the classical response to – and it was presumed the natural result of – depression. Bank rate was set at 2 per cent in 1932. The Treasury's massive conversion operation of 1932, whereby £2bn of the 5 per cent War Loan of 1917, about a quarter of the National Debt, was converted to 3.5 per cent, was designed both to relieve the budget and to support lower short-term interest rates. The Treasury, though, did not doubt that interest rates would have to rise in boom conditions.

In the traditional view, a rise in interest rates signalled a 'shortage of saving' – a sign that demand was pressing against the limit of resources. Thus any increased government borrowing, four years into recovery, was bound to push up interest rates. This prospect alarmed the Treasury, which wanted to borrow the money to finance rearmament as cheaply as possible. It was in these circumstances that Keynes's 'monetary' theory of the rate of interest started bells ringing in the Treasury and Bank of England. According to this theory, a rise in interest rates signalled a shortage not of saving but of liquidity.

Here was the nub of the theoretical debate which followed the publication of Keynes's *General Theory*. The older school's theory of the self-regulating economy rested heavily on its view of the rate of interest as the price which balanced saving and investment. Keynes denied this. Saving rose and fell with income; the rate of interest was the price of giving up liquidity. A loan-financed rearmament programme which raised the level of national income would generate the savings to pay for it, *without requiring interest rates to rise*. But this did not explain the rise in short-term rates in early 1937 – which is exactly what the classical school would have predicted as the economy started booming. This happening in the 'real world' stimulated Keynes's last burst of theory-building. In an article published in the *Economic Journal* of July 1937, written from his sickbed in Cambridge, he argued that an investment decision may involve 'a temporary demand for money . . . before the corresponding saving has taken place'. Normally this 'finance' is supplied by the banking system from a 'revolving fund' as the loans for projected investments are paid out of repayments to the banks for completed ones. But if investment demand rises unexpectedly the 'pressure to secure more finance than usual may easily affect the rate of interest through its influence on the demand for money'. Thus, although extra investment (private or public) could not be limited by a 'shortage of saving', it could exceed the supply of financial facilities 'if the banking system is unwilling to increase the supply of money and the supply from existing holders [of inactive balances] is inelastic'. But, Keynes went on, 'if the banking system chooses to make the finance available and the investment projected by the new issues actually takes place, the appropriate level of incomes will be generated out of which there will necessarily remain over an amount of saving exactly sufficient to take care of the new investment'. In other words, the monetary authority could always create the 'finance' for additional investment by printing more money, 'a potent, though sometimes dangerous, method'.[35] This is the origin of the famous 'finance' demand for money, which Keynes had not mentioned in the *General Theory* and which he now offered as a 'bridge' between his liquidity preference theory of interest and Dennis Robertson's savings-derived loanable fund theory. It is a classic example of what Professor Clarke called 'making up theory on the hoof' to meet objections to his proposals. In his chairman's speech to the National Mutual on 23 February 1938 Keynes invented an ingenious argument based on his new theory. The rise in interest rates in 1937 had resulted not from the raising of the rearmament loan, but from the fact that it had been raised before it was spent. 'Borrowing in advance of expenditure amounts to a sort of hoarding which may cause a grave credit stringency.' The rise in interest rates could have been prevented had the government, instead of issuing defence bonds well in advance of requirements, started its investment programme 'a little before the borrowing, or at any rate . . . *pari passu*'.[36] Keynes was enraged by the comments in the financial press which greeted his speech. 'Practically all City Editors (like Civil Servants and others who are in touch with money making and not themselves money-makers and so dislike the nasty thing) are congenital deflationists,' he wrote to Richard Kahn on 5 March 1938.

Keynes's other technique for avoiding high interest rates was for the Treasury to satisfy the public's desire for liquidity by borrowing more at the short end of the market, avoiding premature funding. The use of this technique by the US Treasury allowed it to borrow 'at a materially lower average rate' than the British Treasury was able to do, since the rate of interest rose with the length of maturity.[37]

The reception of Keynes's doctrine in the Treasury was cordial. The Treasury's countercyclical approach to interest rate policy was coming to be overshadowed by its concern to keep down the cost of borrowing. Keynes's liquidity preference theory of the rate of interest suggested the technique by which this might be done. It implied that monetary policy could fix interest rates at whatever level the government wished, provided the money supply was deliberately expanded to 'feed the hoarder', and the terms of maturity arranged to suit the tastes of the investor.

Keynes continued to plug this theme over the coming year, notably in articles in *The Times* of 17 and 18 April ('Crisis Finance') and 24 and 25 July 1939 ('Borrowing by the State'), the latter based on a memorandum he had prepared for the Chancellor of the Exchequer and the governor of the Bank of England in May 1939.[38] In the fiscal year 1939–40, the government proposed to borrow an extra £220m. for defence. This implied that national saving would have to increase by this amount. Keynes rejected the argument that interest rates would have to rise to evoke the additional saving. The required saving would be necessarily forthcoming, 'irrespective of whether the rate of interest rises or falls', as a result of the physical increase in output and income. Thus, 'so long as the Government's programme can be physically carried out . . . the savings to finance it must necessarily be available' at existing interest rates and price levels. The problem was a different one: how to ensure what he called a 'national service for savings' – that the added savings were invested in government securities rather than hoarded or exported or spent on private domestic investment. Once again Keynes rejected pressing them into government service by means of higher interest rates. Inflation was to be avoided, not by arranging for government debt to be held by the public rather than by the banking system, but by higher taxes. The Chancellor of the Exchequer should announce that in no circumstances would he borrow at more than 2.5 per cent. (This was raised to 3 per cent in the second set of articles.) Lenders should be left in no doubt that these were the best terms obtainable for bonds with the longest maturities. In order to enforce this rate, the market should be given 'an increased amount of liquidity' to prevent the 'congestion of credit' of which Keynes had warned in 1938. (As he put it in *The Times* of 18 April 1939, 'Loans must be raised after the expenditure has been incurred and not before'); and the Treasury should 'wait until the market is ready' before funding its loans. These principles amounted to a policy of arranging the forms of loans to suit the liquidity preferences of the public. 'If the public prefer short-dated debt, nothing can be gained and much will be lost in terms of interest and in the disturbance to the financial fabric by attempting to force long-dated loans on them.' Thus 'In the first instance a large addition to the volume of Treasury bills will be right and probably inevitable. Thereafter loans of varying maturities might be offered with rates of interest rising according to maturity from ½ to 2½ per cent.' These were not just to be expedients of 'emergency finance'. Keynes was anxious that the 'emergency', or war if it came, should end with low rates of interest in place to check the post-emergency slump which would follow the withdrawal of the 'abnormal' government expenditure. But, to be effective, these techniques would need to be buttressed by control of domestic capital issues, prioritising the use of physical resources, and an embargo on foreign lending.

Keynes admitted that 'the proportion of the increased income which is spent on imported goods raises a dangerous complication. For both directly and indirectly the Government's loan expenditure will worsen the foreign balance.' Allowing sterling to depreciate might have seemed the natural answer, but this was resisted by Keynes and the Treasury alike because of the need to maintain Britain's creditworthiness. Instead, Keynes urged, in addition to the embargo on capital exports, a new machinery for bilateral clearing 'so as to make sure that those from whom we buy spend a reasonable proportion of the proceeds in corresponding purchases from us',[39] and building up stocks of foodstuffs and raw materials. This last proposal, stimulated by the government's announcement, in May 1938, that it intended to accumulate reserves of essential war commodities, brought out the full range of Keynes's ingenuity, as he argued that accumulating a commodity reserve at relatively low prices in advance of war would not only be an essential security measure, but could be used in peacetime to moderate price fluctuations and stabilise the business-cycle as well as exchange rates, thus assuring a steady income for Empire producers and a steady demand for Britain's exports. Although the policy would cost Britain gold, it would also obviate the need to hold such a large gold reserve.[40] His old King's colleague Nathaniel Wedd enthused that 'it gives hope not just for a war crisis, but for the future permanently'.[41]

These sketches of Keynesian policy reveal not just his capacity for theoretical invention, but his flair in applying theory, new and old, to the problems of administration. They were devised in the shadow of war, which gave them a *dirigiste* flavour that was by no means an ineluctable conclusion of his 'general theory'.

Keynes's promotion of his theory was starting to shift the Treasury out of its Chamberlainite orthodoxy. Susan Howson and Donald Winch show that 'by 1937 the macroeconomic position which we associate with Keynes's *General Theory* had altered the thinking of the most important policy-making civil servants in the Treasury'.[42] They cite, in particular, the argument for countercyclical public works put forward in the Twenty-Second Report (19 February 1937) of the Economic Advisory Council's Committee on Economic Information, chaired by Sir Josiah Stamp, on which Keynes and two senior Treasury officials, Sir Frederick Phillips and Sir Frederick Leith-Ross, served.[43] This was virtually identical to the case Keynes put forward in his *Times* articles in January 1937. More important was Keynes's influence on monetary thinking. The last report of the Committee on Economic Information in July 1939, and the Treasury Committee on the Control of Savings and Investment, set up on 30 June 1939, under Sir Frederick Phillips, echoed the arguments and proposals of Keynes's *Times* articles of that year. When a 3 per cent maximum borrowing rate was decided on in October 1939 'the methods subsequently used to maintain this level were the same as those favoured by Keynes . . .'.[44] Keynes's ideas became central to the policy discussion in the 1937–9 period, not because most of those concerned 'bought' his *General Theory*, but because they fitted the preoccupations of the policy-making elite. There was still widespread mistrust of his over-cleverness. As Schumpeter – a jaundiced witness – wrote, 'Most people who admire Keynes accept the stimulus, take from him what is congenial to them and leave the rest.'[45]

IV

PRUDENCE VERSUS APPEASEMENT

In his *Economic Consequences of the Peace*, Keynes had written: 'If we aim at the impoverishment of Central Europe, vengeance, I dare predict, will not limp.' His impassioned outburst against the Treaty of Versailles has been subject to much brutal criticism, most of it misplaced. Much less has been written about his reaction to the coming of the vengeance, in the shape of Adolf Hitler. Keynes's first biographer Roy Harrod has almost nothing to say on Keynes's extensive commentary on foreign policy in the 1930s, surmising that 'the convalescent had resort to a little wishful thinking in this horrible period'[46] – Harrod's usual technique for dealing with distressing aspects of his hero. D. E. Moggridge gives a factual summary, but makes no attempt to relate Keynes's commentary to the contemporary, or subsequent, foreign policy debate.[47] In an unpublished chapter of autobiography, Kingsley Martin, editor of the *New Statesman*, of whose board Keynes was chairman, wrote: '[Keynes] usually, with some lapses, supported Baldwin and even Chamberlain, and even put up a half-hearted support, though an angry one, for Munich. He found it almost impossible, as I did, to "start a war" in defence of Eastern Europe when some sort of peace was offered to us and we were not necessarily engaged.' C. H. Rolph, Martin's biographer, comments: 'If Kingsley had followed Keynes's line throughout the late 1930s the *New Statesman* would have been on the whole an appeasement paper.'[48] Professor Carr, while emphasising Keynes's criticisms of the conduct of British foreign policy, wrote that his 'strong aversion to war brought him, in practice, very close to Chamberlain's position at the time of the Munich Conference'.[49] That most perceptive of contemporary Keynes-watchers, Oswald Falk, wrote about 'the conflicts in his mind between his undoubted pacifism and his wish, at times at any rate, to fight evil and aggression'.[50] Most recently, Donald Markwell, in an unpublished doctoral dissertation, argues that the view of Keynes as an appeaser was, 'at best, simplistic'.[51]

The truth is that Keynes was *not* an appeaser in the technical sense, to be defined below, but the point of distinction sometimes seemed recondite. Nor were his writings on foreign policy of the same quality as his economic pronouncements. Keynes's genius as an economist owed a great deal to his intimate knowledge of the workings of Whitehall and the City of London. In foreign policy he had no such comparative advantage. He had no particular expertise to offer and no contacts at the heart of the policymaking machine; his knowledge of the United States and the Soviet Union was sketchy. So his approach was often amateurish. He ruminated from a distance; his writing was untypically vague; his influence on policy was virtually nil.

Why then bother with his views? The main answer is that they are of great biographical interest, showing the way his mind worked and how his sympathies were distributed in areas where they could not be concealed by technical language. There are two additional reasons. First, through his contributions to the influential *New Statesman* he took part in the debate on the left of politics, which is historically important as revealing the climate of opinion in which foreign policy was conducted. Secondly, Keynes himself had helped form that climate with his attack on the Treaty of Versailles. He has been called the 'spiritual father' of appeasement. A. J. P. Taylor succinctly, and not unfairly, summarised the message of *The Economic Consequences of the Peace* as: 'Precautions should be taken against German grievances, not against German aggression.'[52]

Let us try to recreate Keynes's state of mind as he contemplated the gathering war clouds. We can readily agree that 'the effects of *The Economic Consequences of the Peace* were irrelevant to Keynes's own views of how to deal with Hitler'.[53] Unlike Philip Kerr (now Marquess of Lothian), who, as Lloyd George's private secretary, had drafted the infamous 'war guilt' clause, Keynes had no personal reason to feel guilty about the 'harsh' peace at Versailles, since he had opposed it. Furthermore, since he had never supported the Wilsonian principle of 'national self-determination' – that multiplication of frontiers and sovereignties which he thought had disrupted the pre-war economic unity of Europe – he never felt the need to urge territorial concessions to Germany on ethnic or linguistic grounds. Finally, the Germany whose cause he had supported in 1919 was not the Germany of the 1930s. He loathed the Nazi regime, never visited Germany after 1933, and never drew attention to the successes of Hitler's economic policies – a commendable feat of self-denial in the circumstances.

Secondly, Keynes, was 90 per cent pacifist. Like most liberals, he regarded peace as an almost overriding good – one which should be sacrificed only in extremity, for the defence of vital interests. In this he reflected the pacificism of the democracies. His overwhelming bias in favour of peace comes out in his disinclination to underwrite the European or global status quo; his excessive faith in economic sanctions as an alternative to war; and his genuine puzzlement about how to deal with people like Hitler and Mussolini who were willing to risk war to secure their aims. The appeal of war or warlikeness lay beyond his imaginative understanding – a defect or virtue he shared with most British liberals. Of course, he understood that there were rational reasons for conflict. In fact, the *General Theory* pointed to a peace policy: 'If nations can learn to provide themselves with full employment by their domestic policy there need be no important economic forces calculated to set the interest of one country against that of its neighbours.'[54] Here was the intellectual basis of an updated pacifism, to which Keynes added at various times support for disarmament, the League of Nations and supranational financial institutions. But the conditions of peace in general had little to do with the conditions of peace in 1938. Nor did Keynes – unlike Oswald Mosley – ever think of turning this kind of argument into advocacy of a political agreement with Nazi Germany.

Thirdly, it was an extension of Keynes's pacifism to believe that governments had no right to risk war for a principle without popular support. On 24 July 1937, he wrote to Richard Kahn on Julian Bell's death in Spain: 'He had a personal right to make his protest with his life. I feel that, though I feel ever more strongly that the NS and N [*New Statesman and Nation*] and the Labour Party are *not* entitled to urge the Govt. to make protest with the lives of the community at large when it would be entirely against feelings of the great majority of them.'

Fourthly, Keynes's foreign policy convictions in the 1930s were highly influenced by his conception of prudence. This was a set philosophical attitude, which goes back to his undergraduate essay on Burke and his distinctive theory of probability. One passage from his 1904 paper on Burke is worth recalling: 'Burke ever held, and held rightly, that it can seldom be right . . . to sacrifice a present benefit for a doubtful advantage in the future. . . . [Moreover] it is not sufficient that the state of affairs which we seek to promote should be better than the state of affairs which preceded it; it must be sufficiently better to make up for the evils of the transition.'[55] Applied to the 1930s, the logic is very simple. At any moment in time peace is better than war. Therefore we should not risk war unless we know that it will make peace more secure; and we should not fight a war unless we know that it will make a future peace sufficiently better than the existing peace to offset the costs of war. But this kind of knowledge is rarely available. Therefore we should 'prolong peace, hour by hour, day by day, for as long as we can'. This is not an ineluctable deduction from the existence of uncertainty. One could say: if one cannot calculate the probability of an outcome, one should simply do what history and honour teaches is right. This was Churchill's view.

Fifthly, Keynes attached an enormous significance to the use of language as an element of power, especially since armaments were in short supply. As a masterly user of language himself, he understood the power of words, and particularly admired Churchill for his quality of utterance. It was not the language of moral indignation he demanded, but the language of moral eloquence. In the years leading up to the war he repeatedly accused the government of neglecting 'the power of courageous bearing', 'the capacity to appear formidable'. Such neglect would not lessen the risk of war, only ensure that we would fight it 'with no friends and no common cause'.[56] Keynes believed that a prouder bearing by Britain would have brought the United States much sooner into the moral – and eventually military – balance against the dictators.

Finally, we must distinguish Keynes's policy from Neville Chamberlain's. Personal antipathy played a part. Keynes genuinely liked Baldwin; he hardly knew his successor, and had no reason to love him, or hope much from him. Chamberlain had one of those unmalleable personalities, peculiarly resistant to Keynes's charms and spells. Keynes's only published personal comment on him, dating from 1939, sees him as the main obstacle to all his hopes: 'In the Prime Minister's case this blindness [to the most obvious aspects of the contemporary world] is an essential element in his strength. If he could see even a little, if he became even faintly cognisant of the turmoil of ideas and projects and schemes to save the country which are tormenting the rest of us, his superbly brazen self-confidence would be fatally impaired.'[57]

As Chancellor, Chamberlain rigidly pursued the policy of balanced budgets and believed they had brought prosperity. He was appalled by the drift and lethargy of Baldwin's foreign policy, and when he became Prime Minister in May 1937 he determined to apply equally clear-cut principles to his dealings with the dictators. His policy has been aptly called 'armed appeasement'. His hope was, as he put it in a letter to his sister Hilda on 1 August 1937, that 'a double policy of rearmament and better relations with Germany and Italy would carry us safely through the danger period'. 'Better relations' meant, in that context, recognising Italy's conquest of Abyssinia and securing 'reasonable agreements with Germany reasonably reached'.[58] Chamberlain was driven by a horror of war and the conviction that *if only* Germany's political grievances could be met on reasonable terms a new age of prosperity would dawn, with trade liberalised and defence spending cut. This assumed, however, that German grievances and Hitler's aims were the same. It ignored the fact that Hitler's aims were, in principle, unlimited. By seeking agreements in advance of crisis Chamberlain simply handed Hitler an expansionist agenda he would have been hard put to conjure up himself.

The difference between Chamberlain and Keynes was that Keynes rejected the policy of actively seeking an agreement with what he called the 'brigand powers'. Intuitively he knew one could not do business with the Nazis on any terms acceptable to British public opinion. But that did not commit him to the defence of the European, or extra-European, status quo. The line he most consistently favoured was strong armaments, no clear-cut commitments, building up a defensive alliance of peaceful powers including the USA and the Soviet Union, and adopting a vaguely menacing posture. It was closest to the view of Anthony Eden, Baldwin's Minister for League of Nations Affairs and subsequently Chamberlain's first Foreign Secretary. Eden's policy was to keep the dictators 'guessing' while getting on to 'better terms' with the USA and Soviet Russia – the exact opposite of Chamberlain's aim of getting on 'better relations' with the dictators. The trouble was that two could play the game of bluff, so that brinkmanship offered alarmingly easy victories to the player with the stronger nerve; while, given US isolationism and Stalin's bestiality, the putative alliance for peace with the Soviet Union and the United States was never plausible. The real logic of Keynes's peace policy was British isolationism behind the defensive shield of the Channel and the Royal Navy – a logic he never accepted.

Keynes's commentary on foreign affairs started with Italy's preparations to invade Abyssinia. On 28 September 1935 he urged a combination of financial assistance to Abyssinia and 'mild' sanctions against Italy to deter Mussolini's attack.[59] The sanctions he proposed were roughly the same as those the League imposed when Mussolini invaded: they did not prevent Italy from completing its conquest of Abyssinia in May 1936. Despite this outcome, Keynes attacked the government's policy as 'cowardly and misguided', and claimed that 'firm action [could] have simply put a stop to the whole thing'.[60] It is not clear what 'firm action' he would have taken, since he ruled out blockade; and, without blockade, the oil sanction, which Eden tentatively suggested at Geneva, would have been ineffective. The truth is that if Eden 'entertained illusions that Mussolini might be persuaded to back down ... in the face of pressures short of military sanctions',[61] so did Keynes. On 10 June, Chamberlain called the continuation of sanctions 'the very midsummer of madness'; they were abandoned by the Cabinet a week later. On 15 July Keynes tried to assure his by now distraught father that peace was secure for the time being. 'Our immediate interests', he wrote, 'are *not* threatened by any early ambitions either of Germany or Italy.' The real dilemma was 'how far we are prepared to go to the assistance, if at all, of other victims'. He was apparently not unduly worried about the military balance, and thought that 'at sea we are much too powerful for [Germany] to want to try conclusions [against us]'.

At this stage Keynes's foreign policy polemics, conducted mainly in the *New Statesman*, were directed much more against the left than against the government. The Labour Party believed, with good reason following the Abyssinian fiasco,* that the government was not serious about collective security through the League of Nations. But it drew from this the illogical conclusion that it must, therefore, be pro-fascist. This conviction was confirmed when the British government announced its policy of 'non-intervention' in the Spanish Civil War, started on 17 July 1936 by General Franco with Italian support. So Labour opposed Baldwin's modest measures of rearmament. Its left wing, heavily represented in the *New Statesman*, went further, demanding civil resistance to rearmament, military sanctions against Italy and 'Arms for Spain'.

This attitude infuriated Keynes, and he castigated the left's folly in angry letters to Kingsley Martin and in the correspondence columns of the *New Statesman*. The nub of his position was that 'it is better to have strong forces and no clear-cut foreign policy than to advocate no armaments one week and warlike alliances the next'.[62] The policy of the government reflected the people's aversion to war, not pro-fascist sympathies. His alternative to Martin's policy of 'war resistance' to British rearmament was for Britain to head a bloc of peaceful nations, including France, Russia and the USA, and 'make it collectively so formidable that only a madman will affront it' – a proposal which, Kingsley Martin cogently pointed out, rested on the 'delusion' that the British government would form a military alliance with the Soviet Union to uphold collective security.[63] Martin's delusion was to suppose that Stalin would co-operate with Baldwin for the same purpose. Keynes tried to counter the attacks on

---

* On 8 December 1935, Sir Samuel Hoare, Britain's Foreign Secretary, and Pierre Laval, the French Foreign Minister, agreed a plan to end the Abyssinian War by giving Mussolini about one-third of Abyssinia. Laval's main aim was to bribe Mussolini to support the European status quo against Germany. When the plan was leaked, a public outcry forced Baldwin to repudiate it. Hoare resigned and was replaced by Eden. Since the national government had fought (and won) the general election of October 1935 on support for 'collective security, the League and sanctions against aggression', what the Hoare–Laval Plan did 'was to harden the belief on the Left that Baldwin and Chamberlain were utterly untrustworthy in meeting the Fascist menace' (Michael Foot, *Aneurin Bevan*, 212–13).

his support for non-intervention in the Spanish Civil War. 'The fatal dilemma', he recognised in a letter of 29 August 1936, 'arises precisely because the Fascist Powers are readier to go to war for their objects than we are for ours. This . . . provides those powers with unsurpassable opportunities to bluff. I see no possible reply except to build up a navy enormously superior to those of the potential adversaries, without committing ourselves to use or not to use it. . . .'[64] Thus Keynes came down on the side of the Baldwin–Eden policy of 'unheroic cunctation', wishing only that it could be coupled with 'some clear declaration of where this country's sympathies stand, or ought to stand'. The left claimed that Keynes's foreign policy was as utopian as his economic policy: it failed to recognise the worldwide character of the struggle between socialism and monopoly capitalism in its Baldwinite or fascist form. Replying to one such stricture on 12 September Keynes wrote:

Mr Lerner and Mr Sweezy see everything in terms of Capitalism and Communism. This leads them to misinterpret the slant of British opinion to-day. Capitalists and Communists in this country are, I suppose, about equally numerous, each 1 per cent, perhaps, of the population. The great majority of people are neither one nor the other, and are just private individuals. But in that capacity, they have one overwhelming preoccupation – the avoidance of war. . . . Those . . . who interpret everything in terms of Capitalist and Communist are blind to their surroundings.[65]

Keynes's next intervention, in July 1937, was prompted by the *New Statesman*'s call on the government to abandon non-intervention in Spain. On 12 July he wrote to Richard Kahn – who favoured the *New Statesman* line – from Ruthin Castle:

I wish I knew what you wanted about Spain. Would you follow the same policy as the brigands, but on the other side? Or would you send ultimatums to the brigands [threatening war] unless they desisted from their present policy? If so, would you do this anyhow as a matter of principle, or only because you estimate the risk of a general conflagration negligible? Furthermore, would you so act because you believe that the mass of public opinion would support you, or would you, if you had the power, go ahead as a matter of principle irrespective of public opinion? I have never been able to discover from the New Statesman what, in practice, they would really want to do.

The published article from his sickbed at Ruthin contains the most philosophical lines he ever wrote on foreign policy:

... I maintain that the claims of peace are paramount; though this seems to be an out-of-date view in what used to be pacifist circles. It is our duty to prolong peace, hour by hour, day by day, for as long as we can. We do not know what the future will bring, except that it will be quite different from anything we could predict. I have said in another context that ... in the long run we are all dead. But I could have said equally well that ... in the short run we are still alive. Life and history are made up of short runs. If we are at peace in the short run, that is something. The best we can do is put off disaster, if only in the hope, which is not necessarily a remote one, that something will turn up. While there is peace, there is peace. ... By postponement we gain peace – to-day. Have we anything to lose by it? Our capacity for cunctation is one of our powerful and characteristic national weapons. It has been our age-long instrument against dictators. Since Fabius Maximus there has scarcely been a stronger case for cunctation than there is to-day. It is maddening and humiliating to have to take so much lip. We may, conceivably, have to submit to greater humiliations and worse betrayals than any yet. Those who applaud war and believe they have something to gain from it have an inevitable advantage ... in a game of bluff and in the preliminary manoeuvres; though all the time they may be running unperceived risks, which one day will catch them out. But we have to look further ahead; believing that time and chance are with us, and taking precautions that, if we are forced to act, we can make quite sure.

Britain should build up its naval strength and wait for the dictators *to make mistakes.*[66]

Even Keynes's optimism was dented by the scale of Stalin's purges, of which Lydia apprised him. 'In truth,' he wrote to Kingsley Martin on 25 July, 'there are only two [ideologies]: the totalitarian states ... and the liberal states. The latter put peace and personal liberty first, the others put them nowhere.' He correctly predicted an eventual Nazi–Soviet pact.[67] But he still hoped to wean the United States from its isolation. In October 1937 he wrote a letter to *The Times* which urged the British Empire to join the USA in warning Japan that they would sever 'all trade relations' with it unless it called off its war on China. 'If America will not play, then, of course, we cannot proceed,' he privately admitted. 'But it would be a splendid thing at least to put the proposition to her.'[68] In fact, 'Eden tried unceasingly (though unavailingly) to interest the Americans in common action.'[69] Once anti-Japanese sanctions failed to materialise, Keynes attacked Kingsley Martin for his 'imbecile' policy of urging China to fight on to the end without any hope of effective assistance from outside. He suggested that China should sue for peace 'even if it involves ... ceding a large area of territory', and that Spain, too, should be divided between the Francoists and Republicans.[70] As he explained to Kingsley Martin on 10 November:

> our sole and overriding purpose should be to make quite sure of countering the Fascist powers at long last. It is precisely because I believe the position to be critical and dangerous that I believe strategic retreats to be necessary and the gradual consolidation of forces absolutely essential. There is no chance except by achieving an almost worldwide consolidation of opinion on very broad issues.... You, on the other hand, are perpetually engaged in conducting an indignation meeting.... It is no good to spit and fume against the powers that be and all the real forces in the world, keeping in reserve, as the final expedient of escapism, throwing in your hand and lying flat on your face before the advancing forces.... Another feeling ... plays a not unimportant part in my own mind. I cannot accept the policy of non-resistance, but I have a very strong objection to sending the average man to fight on an occasion, or at a time, or in circumstances ... for reasons which only appeal to a minority. There are no issues on which the rights of the majority are so paramount as in the case of war and peace.
>
> Thus if the issue is to be joined, it must be for reasons which unite the vast majority of right-thinking men.... What I am objecting to is ... the old non-conformist urge to save *one's own soul.* But we are at a juncture of the world's affairs when these virtues are vices.[71]

To his sister-in-law Margaret Keynes he wrote on 16 October: 'I, being an optimist, believe the brigands are exceptionally liable to make mistakes. Meanwhile nothing can be better for us than to increase our armaments, be far more reasonable than is reasonable, allow world opinion, especially in America, to veer the right way, get complete solidity of sentiment at home, and then trust that the villains will either think better of it or make bloomers.'[72]

Keynes never appreciated the extent of Anglophobia in the United States. This was the real force behind isolationism. Throughout the 1930s, dislike of the fascist 'villains' was balanced by dislike of British imperialism. Bruce Bliven, who had taken Keynes's articles for the *New Republic*, was not untypical of American 'liberals' in seeing a moral equivalence between British and Japanese methods in China – much to Keynes's disgust. Americans particularly resented Britain's repudiation of its war debt in 1933. This led directly to the Johnson Act, which banned private loans to countries which had defaulted on their loans. H. C. Engelbrecht's and F. C. Hanighen's bestselling book *Merchants of Death* (1934) argued that arms manufacturers and international bankers had combined with British interests to inveigle America into the First World War. It led to the setting up of the Nye Senatorial Committee, whose findings 'included a veritable laundry list of British sins during the war' and led to the passage of the two Neutrality Acts of 1935 and 1936. Where Keynes was right was in thinking that appeasement as practised by Baldwin and Chamberlain reduced Britain's prestige in America. Americans don't like to back losers. But it is highly unlikely that a 'prouder bearing' by Britain would have helped forge an anti-fascist alliance ahead of war.[73]

Nineteen-thirty-eight was Hitler's *annus mirabilis.* In two bloodless coups, he annexed Austria and the German-speaking areas of Czecho-slovakia. Following German occupation of Austria on 12 March, Keynes put forward his own 'Positive Peace Programme' in the *New Statesman* of 25 March 1938. It was not one of his happiest productions. The core of his idea was sound enough: Czechoslovakia should 'at least attempt to negotiate with Germany a reasonable solution to the problem of the Sudeten Germans, even if this means a rectification of the Bohemian frontier'; and Britain and France should form a military alliance with Russia. But this *Realpolitik* project was muddied by being decked out in the fantastic garments of a new European 'League of Nations' (minus Germany and Italy), equipped with sanctions against aggression to be activated by majority vote, and forming a single market, with free movement of goods, capital and labour.[74] It was opportunistic without being practical: the idea of inviting Stalin's Russia to join a league of freedom violated his own emphasis on the need to unite all *right-thinking* people; the idea that Stalin might accept the invitation was bizarre.

The Czech crisis hotted up in August 1938. The three million Sudeten Germans started clamouring for 'national self-determination'; Hitler screwed up the tension, hoping the Czech state would disintegrate of its own accord; Chamberlain sent Lord Runciman to Prague to 'mediate'. Keynes thought Hitler was bluffing. Czechoslovakia was guaranteed by both France and Russia. 'In a world war', Keynes wrote to Kingsley Martin on 26 August, 'Hitler will be beaten and he knows it.' But he added: 'I agree with you that we should bluff to the hilt; and if the bluff is called, back out. I prefer, meanwhile, meiosis and bogus optimism in public.' Keynes, that is, was no more willing to fight for Czechoslovakia than was Chamberlain, but was against telling Hitler so. That is why he was furious with Martin for raising the issue of frontier changes in the *New Statesman* of 27 August. He wrote to Martin on 11 September: 'Please don't imagine I have weakened on the wisdom of frontier revisions. Indeed the latest concessions [the Czech President Beneš had accepted the principle of a Czechoslovakia of co-equal national groups] are such as to make one feel even more than before that in the long run frontier revision is a cleaner and *safer* remedy. [But] . . . it is plain as a pikestaff that at this juncture we must back up the Czechs, and particularly *not* suggest to Hitler that he can get what to him seems more.'[75] Keynes's main proposal was to call Hitler's bluff by asking him to state his intentions. Chamberlain did not believe Hitler was bluffing; he knew the French would not fight, and had good reason to believe the Russians would not either. On 15 September he flew to meet Hitler at Berchtesgaden and conceded the principle of separating the Sudeten Germans from Czechoslovakia before Hitler had even suggested it. Delighted that Chamberlain was doing his work for him, Hitler raised his demands: German troops must occupy the ceded territory at once, he told Chamberlain at Godesberg on 22 September. Chamberlain rejected this 'ultimatum'. The French called up reservists; the British mobilised the Fleet. Chamberlain broadcast to the British nation: 'If I were convinced that a nation had made up its mind to dominate the world by fear of its force, I should feel that it must be resisted.' For a few days it seemed that war was inevitable. Hitler then backed down. He agreed to a new conference, with Mussolini as 'mediator'. On the afternoon of 28 September, Chamberlain announced that he was flying to Munich the next day in a last effort to save world peace. The House of Commons broke into hysterical cheering.

Glued to his wireless at Tilton, Keynes had followed these twists and turns with mounting anxiety. Lydia had reported him 'worried over the world war' on 23 September, 'very worried, upset' on the 26th. On the 27th he was 'much more cheerful, thinks there won't be a war, in spite of everything . . .'. On the 29th his 'health improved with news and weather'. As Chamberlain winged his way to Germany, Keynes wrote to his mother:

> it was a tremendous relief to get last night's news – though my reasoning self has never wavered from the conclusion that H[itler] was totally against war. Hitler has never had much to gain from calling off his bluff until the very last possible moment; and he needed the Fleet Mobilization and ARP precautions in London to convince him that we should really act. Given the latter, I have always believed that the former must follow. The Prime Minister has shown extraordinary character and courage and good motives. But his sympathies are distasteful. If he gets us out of the hole, it was he (and *The Times*) who got us into it by leading the Nazis into the belief that at bottom the sympathies of the English ruling class were with them. . . . We are not out of the trouble yet – but we *shall* be, if only the PM can bring himself to be just a little harsh to the Fuhrer.[76]

At Munich Mussolini suggested that the German-speaking areas should be occupied by German troops in ten days rather than one. Hitler agreed at once, not surprisingly, since the German Foreign Ministry had drafted Mussolini's proposal. The settlement was announced on 30 September, with Chamberlain returning to London, to an outburst of rejoicing, waving a bit of paper and proclaiming 'peace with honour . . . peace in our time'. That night Keynes slept well: '*no war*, feels basically tired after the war-strain, but health is not bad at all, directed himself at a sale of sheep, bought 140, slept in the afternoon'. But on 1 October Lydia reported him 'angry at PM's cheating the nation'. His immediate reaction, conveyed in a letter to Kingsley Martin written that day, was 'painful in the way in which only a *mixed* state can be. Intense relief and satisfied cowardice join with rage and indignation, *plus* that special emotion appropriate to the state of having been *swindled* . . . the whole nation *swindled* as never before in its history'. The intense relief was from his own heart pains; the shame he shared with many others. His tirade to Kingsley Martin continued:

> Honourable international policy has suffered a terrific reverse by the unscrupulous intrigues, quite unsupported by public opinion, of our own pro-Nazis. . . . (The attitude of *The Times* must have been revolting to almost everyone.)
>
> Russia (and of course France . . .) has been greatly to blame. . . . There has never been any convincing evidence of Russia's reliability, and she has played straight into Chamberlain's hands. . . .
>
> It is *not certain* that the present settlement may not be a good thing in the long run. Viewed quite drily, there is a great deal to be said for it. . . . The settlement itself cannot be rightly denounced as indefensible and monstrous. What is certain is . . . that the sympathies and methods which have brought it about cannot be safely allowed to continue in charge. This time they may, by historic luck, have carried through a necessary thing which decent men could not have accomplished. . . .
>
> I suppose that popular emotion will shortly be capitalised in the shape of a General Election. The most important immediate political objective should be a union of forces against Chamberlain. This is much wider than a Popular Front. . . .[77]

Despite these fulminations, the rational difference between Keynes and Chamberlain was wafer thin. It boiled down to thinking that Chamberlain could have got a better deal for the Czechs (what sort of deal?) had he gone on bluffing a bit longer; and disgust at the way he had clothed his surrender in fraudulent phrases. Keynes's view that Hitler was bluffing is shared by Alan Taylor, but not by all historians. Like many others Keynes was convinced that both sides had been play-acting, the purpose of the play being to clear Hitler's path to the East. Virginia Woolf reported a tea-time conversation with Keynes at Rodmell on 2 October:

> His view is that the whole thing was staged by Chamb.; that there was never any fear of war; that he never even consulted Russia; that

it was a put up job between him and Hitler; that he would now call a general election; that our business is to fight Chamberlain; that we are sure of peace during our lifetime; that Hitler wants the Ukraine; that he'll get it; that Italy will be wiped out; that we shall do a deal with the colonies; that Chamberlain is a mere Birmingham politician; and so on. We all analysed our complexities of shame, and fear. . . .[78]

More presciently Keynes suggested that 'who knows that in the end Herr Hitler will be the second dictator to retreat from Moscow'.[79] He chose to ignore the fact that by guaranteeing the rump of the Czech state, the British had implictly guaranteed the existing territorial order in Eastern Europe.[80]

V

RECOVERY

Maynard and Lydia spent most of the autumn of 1938 in Cambridge. Keynes's resignation from the chairmanship of the National Mutual Life Assurance Company spared him his old mid-week trips to London. He did no teaching, concentrating on the Arts Theatre, College business, and writing. The big event in the autumn term was the long-delayed production of the Auden–Isherwood play *On the Frontier*, which opened at the Arts Theatre on 14 November for six performances. Rehearsals soon revealed it as an amazingly feeble Marxist pastiche on anti-war themes, structured as an operatic melodrama, with a nonsensical fascist 'Leader' manipulated by a sinister arms manufacturer, Valerian, and two young lovers (one of whom, Anna Vrodny, was played by Lydia) divided by the 'frontier' of the warring states, Westland and Eastland. Keynes himself realised it was out of touch with the post-Munich mood. 'Do you think you can go ahead with it in precisely its present form without feeling at all silly?' he asked Christopher Isherwood. Interestingly, a number of passages, considered offensive to Hitler and Nazism, were censored by the Lord Chamberlain's office. Despite a glittering production – Rupert Doone directed, Robin Medley did the scenery and sets, Benjamin Britten wrote the music and played the piano – and a warm send-off from Keynes, who, allowing himself a rare evening out, hosted a post-performance dinner party – the play flopped with the critics and never got a West End run. T. S. Eliot wrote to Keynes grimly: 'I'm afraid that Hitler is not the simpleton the authors make him out to be.'[81]

Keynes's continuing presence so close at hand unnerved the theatre manager, Norman Higgins. Keynes treated him, as he did all his subordinates, with a mixture of kindness and wilfulness. Even in sickness, he drove himself harder than anyone, but in return he expected Higgins to be at his beck and call, and could be unsparing in his criticisms. Higgins, for his part, adored Keynes, tried to please him in every way, but became terrified of making mistakes. Keynes now also had plenty of time for the fusses which he so enjoyed. He convinced himself that the restaurant's pricing policy was all wrong. The existence of a high elasticity of demand for wine would justify reducing the price to Cambridge's champagne drinkers of 1929 Cliquot and 1928 Krug to fifteen shillings a bottle. Dadie Rylands insisted that Cambridge was far too 'priggish and Left Book Club' to drink good wine, even at reduced prices. But Keynes persisted with his reductions, and then tried to prove his hypothesis by examining the restaurant's wine accounts. These showed that the sales of wine were 14 per cent higher after the reductions than before. After a few months of this Higgins had a nervous breakdown and had to be sent off on a convalescent cruise, which Keynes, characteristically, paid for out of his own pocket.

Keynes's own health bore up remarkably well. On 24 October Lydia noted with pleasure that his blood pressure was higher ('120') which made him 'much better, but care is necessary as the heart is not right yet, puffs when walking'. On 29 November he made 'twenty speeches [at the Annual Congregation] carried it out very well, came [back] after 6 o'clock, had massage, restored'. He lived a compressed version of his old existence, talking chiefly to Piero Sraffa and Richard Kahn, seeing his parents on Sunday at Harvey Road, even venturing to London occasionally for meetings of the Committee on Economic Information and other business.

On 18 January 1939 Keynes had dinner in London with Kingsley Martin. They ate woodcock and talked about 'Democracy and Efficiency'. This 'conversation' was published in the *New Statesman* ten days later. It is the starkest statement of Keynes's view that the 'war economy' which was slowly taking shape might serve as some sort of model for the peacetime regulation of economic life. On the one hand, there was the need for planning and organisation. At the same time, he urged the 'profound connection between personal and political liberty and the rights of private property and private enterprise'. He argued that the threat to liberty from the measures of planning he proposed was 'so remote from the first and the next and the next things that want doing, that it is not now, and is a long way from being, a practical issue'. There is a clear lineage from the 'middle way' views Keynes had developed in the mid-1920s in such essays as 'The End of Laissez-Faire' and 'Am I a Liberal?' But its pith, as always with Keynes, had a precise reference to immediate circumstances. On 9 January, Sir Stafford Cripps had launched his appeal for a popular front of anti-appeasers 'ranging from Amery and Churchill on the right to Pollitt and Maxton on the left' as the only way to topple Chamberlain at the next general election. Keynes, as we have seen, had advocated this course immediately after Munich, and his 'conversation' was designed to puff the idea, by suggesting that there was a potential 'liberal' consensus on practically everything, excluding only some 'old jossers' like Chamberlain, a few right-wingers and a reactionary civil service. This is the context for his call for an 'amalgam of private capitalism and state socialism'.[82]

On 28 February Keynes went from Cambridge to London and caught influenza. Lydia's entry on 1 March is terse: 'Bad. Called Plesch. Bad.' That was the end of the Cambridge term for him. He did not leave 46 Gordon Square till the end of March, returning with Lydia to Tilton on 6 April. How Keynes got to hear of Plesch is unrecorded. But Plesch's entry into his life was a decisive turning point in his illness. For 'undoubtedly it was he, and he alone, who brought me back into active life'.[83]

Keynes came to regard Janos Plesch as 'something between a genius and a quack', an impression confirmed by Plesch's memoirs, in which he sounds off about every subject under the sun. It says much for Keynes's intuition that he was willing to entrust himself to this very unEnglish medical practitioner – also for his desperation at the slow pace of his recovery. Janos Plesch, then aged sixty, was a self-made Hungarian Jew, who had established a fashionable medical practice in Berlin in 1910. He had married Melanie Paula, the daughter of a wealthy Frankfurt dyestuffs manufacturer, Adolf Gans, who had gone to him to relieve the spinal pain from which she suffered. She met 'a dark-haired gypsy-like young man, a cigarette in his mouth,' who told her, 'You will have to learn to live with that pain. There is nothing that anyone can do to cure you.' It was the first honest, straightforward diagnosis she had heard. Having served as a doctor with the Austro-Hungarian army in the war, Plesch re-established his practice in Berlin. The family lived in a grand house in the Budapesterstrasse and had also an estate in Gatow outside Berlin, entertained in great style, and drove a Rolls-Royce, one of only two in Berlin. Plesch was a versatile linguist, connoisseur of the arts and a more than competent painter. He was consulted by Pope Pius X and the Kaiser's wife; in fact he seems to have known and/or treated every important person in Central Europe, including Albert Einstein, to whom he dedicated his book *The Physiology and Pathology of the Heart and Blood Vessels.* One patient he treated early in his career married the Hungarian diplomat Tibor Scitovsky, father of the economist, who became a lifelong friend. In 1933 he left Germany (on a Hungarian passport), settled in England and, having passed the necessary examinations, started a private practice at Hereford House, off Park Lane. As his son Peter Plesch tells it, he did not try to join Harley Street, heart of the English medical establishment, as such a move would have been blocked by its leaders, Lord Horder and Lord Dawson of Penn (of whom it was said he 'killed many men'), but he did join the much more congenial Peckham Health Centre. There a patient would be seen by a group of like-minded doctors from different disciplines, all in one place.

The requirements of a 'great doctor', as listed by Plesch, were evidently tailored to fit his own qualities: 'He must be of good and agreeable appearance, he must be well educated, he must be cultured, he must be clever, he must have good manners, and, of course, he must know a thing or two about his job. But if a doctor has real personality he can do without almost all the rest.' Plesch brought some decided opinions to his treatment of his patients, which were not unlike Keynes's ministrations for sick economies. Good diagnosis was a mixture of science and imagination. The doctor must study the patient, not the symptom, letting his 'imaginative intuition' play on the evidence. Secondly, Plesch had a strong belief in assisted self-healing, declaring that 'a satisfactorily compensated sickness is very similar to health'. Thirdly, he was utterly opposed to invalidism. The instinct for life was more powerful than any other. It was fatal to tell old people to 'take it easy'; it was best 'to die in harness, and in that event death will probably be postponed to the very last minute'. Finally, Plesch rejected 'the medieval tradition of secrecy and mystification' in medical matters. Medical knowledge should be communicated in ordinary language.[84] Keynes was quick to recognise a kindred spirit. He noticed that Plesch said something with great assurance one week and exactly the opposite the next week. 'His treatments', he said, either revived his patients or 'failed completely'. Keynes collected stories of his 'peculiar and amusing cures'. Margot Asquith, another Plesch devotee, advised him that if Plesch told him to eat an apricot at two o'clock in the morning, 'tell him to go to hell'. More appealing was his advice to Jack Hutchinson, who also suffered from heart trouble, that some good sex did no harm at all. Einstein, having read some chapters from Plesch's memoirs, summed up the good doctor thus in 1944: 'Talented to your fingertips, keen of hearing and sensitive, but slovenly and lacking a sense of responsibility. A true angel, but already "fallen" at birth. . . .'

It was on this fallen angel that Keynes's hopes for better health now rested. Plesch certainly had a Keynesian approach to healing. On 28 May 1939, Keynes wrote to Bob Brand, who had just become a Plesch patient:

> With English doctors one goes on for two or three years incapacitated from active work and exercise, and is given no definite treatment whatsoever, merely being advised to 'rest'. This is never Plesch's method. Successfully or unsuccessfully, too drastically perhaps sometimes, he begins at once with every kind of active treatment, very fertile and ingenious in ideas, trying on every sort of thing imaginable until he finds something useful. For the first 35 days after I went to him, he gave up half an hour a day to me, and is unquestionably extraordinarily thorough in his care. He now has a

very prosperous Park Lane practice, and is greatly disapproved of by all the English doctors.[85]

Plesch set out not just to treat Keynes for his influenza, but to get him off his couch. He started him off on a saltless diet to reduce body fluids, ordered an icebag to be placed on his heart for three hours a day, prescribed opium pills, and even jumped on him as he lay in bed. A bacteriological examination showed Keynes's throat swarming with strep-tococci. Plesch told his patient that, until the streptococcus had been defeated, recovery was a 'Sisyphus task'. He decided on drastic measures. He gave him an elaborate and stringent treatment of a new drug, Prontosil, a brilliant red dye product, discovered in 1935 by Gerhard Domagk, director of research at the Bayer company, one of the firms from which the I. G. Farben combine had been formed, which was found to have powerful anti-bacterial properties. Plesch would have known about this work from his father-in-law Adolf Gans. Domagk found that when this red dye extract was injected into mice which had been given lethal injections of haemolytic streptococci, they recovered. A year later, a French husband-and-wife team, the Trefouels, working at the Pasteur Institute, showed that chemicals in the body broke down the Prontosil compound into two different components, and it was one of these, sulphanilamide, which attacked the bacteria. In 1936 Laurence Colebrook was leading research into puerperal fever caused by streptococci at Queen Charlotte's Maternity Hospital in West London. His assistant Robert Hare pricked his finger on a sliver of glass infected with streptococci. Within a couple of days it looked as if he was going to die. But Colebrook administered Prontosil. Hare turned bright pink as the dyestuff went into his system, and felt 'so much worse that I began to wonder whether I was dying because of the drug or the microbes'. But he recovered in ten days. Patterson's failure to try Prontosil on Keynes at Ruthin in mid-1937 suggests either ignorance of Germany's anti-bacterial therapy or a closed mind.

The sulpha drugs, as they came to be called, were the precursors of penicillin. Whether Keynes turned bright pink is not recorded. His Prontosil injections made him feel iller than he had ever been before, and he could scarcely stand. But Plesch assured him that once the streptococci were eliminated, he would make a full recovery, as his heart muscle was not fundamentally injured. He and Lydia returned to Tilton on 6 April; the following night he 'slept well, feels drowsy, foggy with all the poisons inside of him, but the heart has no sensations'.

By 13 April he was telling Plesch that he was completely free from all heart symptoms, 'so very many thanks indeed'. He had even run after a train, for which indulgence his doctor sternly rebuked him from Monte Carlo. By this time he had taken to addressing Plesch as 'My dear Rabbi'.

Lydia called him 'The Ogre'. On 28 May, back in Cambridge, Keynes invited Plesch to a chapel service at King's College: 'You would hear English Church music in its most exquisite form and in the grandest possible environment. To my thinking, though exquisite, it is lifeless and even moribund. . . . But if you have never been to one of these highly respectable, quasi-aesthetic Victorian performances, where deathly moderation and pseudo-good taste have drowned all genuine emotions, you might find it an interesting experience.'

There is no reason to doubt Keynes's own view that it was Prontosil which had brought about his dramatic improvement. Unfortunately, it was subsequently discovered that Prontosil was effective against the green streptococci lodged in the throat but not against those already firmly established in the valves of the heart.[86] So Keynes would almost certainly not live into old age. Whether, or how soon, this ever became clear to Plesch or Keynes cannot now be discovered.

Plesch treated Keynes for the rest of his (Keynes's) life. They had a lively correspondence, which ranged over matters not purely medical. Keynes enjoyed Plesch's vast fund of Jewish jokes about the famously effete Austro-Hungarian aristocracy. His favourite was one about young Count Bobby visiting his tailor in the company of his friend Count Aristide. After Bobby had ordered a suit, Aristide turned to him and said, 'Why on earth did you bargain so long with that old man, getting him to agree to a ridiculously low price when you know that you will never pay him?' To which Bobby replied, 'I just did not want to cheat the poor fellow out of such a lot of money.'

Keynes now started to work at more like his old pace. At Cambridge he examined for the Tripos. With war finance on his mind he wrote two articles for *The Times* on 17 and 18 April 1939, arguing for low interest rates, control of capital exports and a Department of Co-ordination with an economic general staff. Tactfully, he suggested this should be attached to the Treasury. He broadcast on the effect of rearmament on employment conditions, helped draft the Twenty-Seventh (and last) Report of the Committee on Economic Information, and wrote two more articles in *The Times* on 24 and 25 July developing his arguments for a low interest policy. In his broadcast, he asserted that rearmament expenditure was about to bring to an end the years of 'abnormal' unemployment, and that 'we shall never go back all the way to the old state of affairs'.[87] In his last pre-war articles he wrote: 'The key to sound public finance in the present emergency is a rigid refusal to fund short-term debt at high interest rates and a stern stiffening of taxation when we have reached the full employment of our productive resources.'[88]

By 12 July he was back at Tilton. He and Lydia went to Verdi's *Macbeth* at Glyndebourne; on 13 August he walked to the top of Firle Beacon for the first time since his illness, without ill effects. He was clearly in a buoyant, active mood. He had installed an electric fence to keep out marauders from his estate; he had ordered covered cattleyards for the winter; he had bought his manager Logan Thomson a 'very smart new car, which makes Fred [his chauffeur], to whom I have just refused a new one, very jealous'. He told his mother that he considered himself 'two thirds back to normal'. On 15 August he and Lydia flew off to Paris for a holiday in France, to take the refreshing baths at Royat, near Vichy, and get away from the latest war scare over Poland. When Clive Bell told him that another 'hullabaloo' (their name for the Munich Agreement) was unlikely, Keynes rebuked him for being a pessimist. 'I shall be most surprised if it ends in war,' he wrote to Kahn the day before they left. 'It seems to me that Hitler's argument is unanswerable that he must get Danzig, because it matters so little either to him or to anyone else. They will fix up some formula. . . .' He wrote in much the same terms to Kingsley Martin.

He described his 'cure' in a chatty letter to his mother from the Royal Palace Hotel:

> At 7.30 I drink tea water (L. drinks it at 11 and at 6). After breakfast I do an hour or two's work at correspondence and serious reading. Then the visit to the baths . . . inhalation for 8–10 minutes of a strong current of the water vaporised into steam to clear the tonsils; then alternate days massage sans l'eau and the bath proper; after the bath an hour's rest and meditation in one's 'cabine de luxe'; then an automobile takes one back to the Hotel for an other hour's rest in bed; then dejeuner; then sleep for ½ to 1 hour in bed . . . by 3 o'clock ready for an excursion – which are varied and agreeable . . . and sit in the evenings listening to the hotel orchestra which plays the sort of music father would like. . . . I reckon I spend 18 hours of the 24 in bed or its equivalent.

There was a trip to Clermont, and a visit from the Ogre, who was staying at Vichy. No doubt they talked about the world's health as well as Keynes's own. By 22 August Keynes was getting worried that 'Hitler does not seem to be keeping open much of an emergency exit. He seems to show in high degree what Scotland Yard says is particularly characteristic of nearly all criminals, namely an inability to vary his methods.' However, he took comfort from one point, 'that if he has made up his mind to take Danzig, or other Polish territory by force, it would have paid him to do it before rather than wait'.

On 25 August he wrote to Kahn that 'it still looks to me much more like politics than war'. He assumed, that is, that Hitler was waiting for the British to make him an offer, which would lead to another Munich. But no offer came. The British had had enough, and anyway they could not control the Poles as they could the Czechs. On 27 August Maynard decided to come home, not because he expected 'serious developments just yet', but because the hotel was closing down as the result of French mobilisation. 'First our waiter went, then the violinist, then the cellist, then both the pastry cooks, and the culmination was the departure of Monsieur Jacques, the nice and clever . . . concierge, round whom all the goings on in the hotel revolved.'

They got back to Tilton on 29 August. Maynard still hoped war might be averted, but he was much less nervous than at the time of Munich. On 1 September German troops invaded Poland. Britain declared war on Germany two days later. Maynard and Lydia took the news calmly. Some sort of die had been cast. It was not one he would have cast. Britain had gone to war for an object he did not think worth fighting for – and without the United States. But he accepted the conflict as inevitable. The British people had forced the hand of their rulers. Keynes's most important test for going to war had been met.

CHAPTER TWO

The Middle Way in War

I

OLD DOGS

The politicians and generals occupied themselves with how to fight the war – or whether, at first, to fight it at all. For the first two years of it, Maynard Keynes was chiefly concerned with how to pay for it. The finance of war has two aspects, domestic and foreign. A government may draw resources from its own people, or from abroad – from its allies, dependants and trading partners. At first Keynes was mainly concerned with the first – how to mobilise available domestic resources for the war effort most efficiently and fairly and, on a long view, with least damage to the practices of peace. Once the war hotted up in the summer of 1940, he became increasingly involved in the second – how to pay for the imports which Britain needed to keep its war effort going full blast.

He started his efforts without any official position, nor indeed expecting one. With the outbreak of war, the government began to assemble an administrative machine to run a war economy. Although certain contingency plans had been made, the first steps were tiny. Sir Josiah, now Lord, Stamp, chairman of the London, Midland and Scottish Railway, was made a part-time adviser on economic co-ordination. Stamp's job was to prepare a 'survey' of departmental war plans, reporting to a Cabinet committee chaired by the Chancellor of the Exchequer, Sir John Simon. He was given a room in the offices of the War Cabinet at Gwydr House, a secretary, Francis Hemming, and two economists, Hubert Henderson and Henry Clay, the latter seconded from the Bank of England. Henderson was given a room at the Treasury and told to divide his time between the Stamp survey and ill-defined advisory duties. Dennis Robertson was made 'temporary administrative officer' at the Treasury to Sir Frederick Phillips, head of the Finance Division. In December 1939 a start was made to setting up a Central Economic Information Service under the direction of Henderson and Clay. The economists recruited to it were Austin Robinson, Fellow of Sidney Sussex College, Cambridge and assistant editor of the *Economic Journal,* and John Jewkes and Henry Campion from Manchester University. This lackadaisical transition to wartime administration was much attacked in Parliament.

Keynes drew comfort from the fact that the Committee which Stamp was to advise 'brings in the Treasury. . . . But an adviser without executive functions and with no staff, and himself part time, is only too easily frozen out. . . .'[1]

Keynes was not one of the chosen. He was fifty-six and sickly. Apart from the question of his health, there was no obvious slot for him. He was too eminent to be made an ordinary civil servant, and too stimulating to be let loose in Whitehall. He did not expect a government job. His first thought was to get Richard Kahn into the Treasury to do 'the sort of thing I used to do last time', while he would take over Kahn's bursarial and teaching duties at King's, and draft memoranda quietly in his room, with only occasional visits to London. This, he implied, was all he was fit for.[2] The Treasury quickly scotched the idea of letting Keynes in through the back door: Kahn was eventually appointed assistant secretary at the Board of Trade, on condition that he steered clear of currency questions. However, the thought that Keynes would be confined to King's was never quite plausible. His health, he told his friends, was 80 per cent of what it had been; and the Ogre had promised him full health eighteen months after his treatment started – that is, by September 1940. His usefulness was bound to suck him into Whitehall in the end, if the war became serious. This was by no means certain. Chamberlain was still Prime Minister, though he brought Churchill back into the government as First Lord of the Admiralty. Appeasement had not turned out as he had expected, since Hitler had taken to seizing countries without waiting for Chamberlain to offer them to him. But as Britain and France were in no position to stop Germany conquering Poland, and had no offensive plans of their own, it was not clear where the war would go. There was a long lull after the fall of Poland. Had Hitler made a seductive peace offer – for example, by suggesting an international conference – it might well have ended there and then.

The war opened with a flurry of controls over imports, transport, prices and assembly – and a stream of letters and memoranda from Keynes protesting against them. 'It might be sounder in every way to make motoring expensive than to make it the subject of wangling [to get additional petrol coupons]; – it might even save more petrol,' he observed acidly in his first note to the Treasury, written on 14 September, as the German armies crashed through Poland. He looked to free prices to stimulate domestic production of essentials, not unmindful that the prices of Tilton's breeding sows had collapsed disastrously because the farmers could not afford to sell bacon at the tariff fixed by the Ministry of Agriculture.[3] In a note on exchange regulations, which he supplied on 24 September at the Treasury's request, he argued against 'complete exchange control on the German model' and in favour of allowing a modest 'black exchange'.[4] Rationing money was Keynes's alternative to rationing supplies, and he held fast to the distinction even when the claims of war became more clamant.

Keynes's quietist inclinations were soon overcome by the pull of events. He started coming to London regularly in mid-week, plugging himself back into his old circuits of influence and persuasion. On Wednesday 20 September he hosted the first of a number of weekly meetings at 46 Gordon Square for William Beveridge, Walter Layton, Arthur Salter and Hubert Henderson: the Conservative MP Robert Boothby formed a link between this group and an all-party parliamentary committee headed by the Liberal MP Clement Davies, who was to be useful a little later in arranging meetings with MPs. The 'Old Dogs', as the Keynes group called themselves, had served government in the last war; except for Henderson, they were reluctantly unemployed in this one. They growled away, as Old Dogs tend to, at the chaotic state of administration – 'fifty times worse than anything we had in the last war,' Keynes told Henderson.[5] Keynes was particularly scathing about the Air Raid Precautions regulations, which he called 'a pure piece of muddle and imbecility'.[6] Of Sir Horace Wilson (Head of the Treasury), who had thought up a scheme for dispersing departments in the event of bombing, he remarked that 'it is rather terrifying that a brain that could think of such a mad plan should be in charge of so many of our affairs'.[7] Keynes had a horror of what he called the 'empty minded busybodyness' which war always caused to luxuriate. The Old Dogs put bright ideas to the departments, from where they received polite, non-committal responses. Early in October Keynes sent Sir Frederick Leith-Ross, the newly appointed director-general of the Ministry of Economic Warfare, a plan to put the Rumanian oil refineries out of action.[8] Keynes was never afraid to chance his arm on the basis of a hunch and a snippet of information.

For the first time since his illness Keynes started going to his two dining clubs – the Other Club and the Tuesday Club.* The first brought him into regular contact with its founder, Winston Churchill. The second kept him in touch with Whitehall. He wrote to Oswald Falk: 'The departments are at sixes and sevens, the home front is a real mess. There is more need even than there was last time of a method such as the Tuesday Club presents of conveying constructive criticism.'[9] He used these intimate gatherings of the great, the good and the almost good to put forward his own ideas and pick up gossip. At the Other Club dinner on 12 October he urged on Churchill his idea – concocted with Salter – of removing

---

* The Other Club was founded by Winston Churchill and F. E. Smith in 1911 for politicians and wits; Keynes had been elected in 1927. Rule 12 stated: 'Nothing in the rules of the Club shall interfere with the rancour or asperity of party politics.' The Tuesday Club, a financial and economic dining club, was started by Oswald Falk in 1917. Keynes was a founder member.

wheat from the contraband list to tempt Germany to squander precious foreign exchange on non-essential imports. But, as he told Beveridge, he 'met with great discouragement. [Winston] does not like the suggestion that the war will not be carried out by totalitarian methods on our side.'[10]

Keynes summed up his view on the failings of early war administration in a letter to Sir George Schuster, a National Liberal MP who had sought a briefing for a parliamentary debate. 'The main point', he wrote on 16 October, 'seems to me that price policy, rationing policy, wage policy, budget policy, export policy, manpower policy, cost of ARP in actual cash and reduced efficiency cannot be properly dealt with in isolation and without any sort of economic policy co-ordinating the whole thing into an intelligible and consistent whole.' The only remedy was to have a powerful minister in charge of the home front.[11] Keynes realised that his memoranda were not having much effect: 'you must either be right in or right out', he told Brand.

On 27 September German troops entered Warsaw; the next day Germany and Russia settled their zones of occupation. Bernard Shaw wrote to Nancy Astor: 'Everyone who can see three moves in front of his or her nose knows that the war is over.'[12] Some members of the Cabinet agreed. There was much defeatist talk at dinner parties and beyond: in the House of Commons on 3 October, the seventy-six-year-old Lloyd George urged a negotiated settlement. Keynes was worried about Kingsley Martin. 'His mind', he wrote to Edward Whitley, a fellow *New Statesman* board member, on 3 October, 'is . . . subject from time to time to moods of extreme defeatism. I cannot feel perfectly sure that he might not suddenly come out in the paper with a leader demanding immediate peace on almost any terms.'[13]

Martin came to see him in London on the evening of 4 October with the proof of an article by Bernard Shaw called 'Uncommon Sense about the War'. Uncommon sense, according to Shaw, demanded that '[we] make peace with [Hitler] and with all the world instead of making more mischief and ruining our people in the process'. Martin's decision to publish Shaw's article gave Keynes a sleepless night. The next morning Martin found a note from him on his desk, denouncing Shaw's views as 'mischievous' and advising Martin to reject his contribution, but in any case to submit it to the Censor. Keynes and Shaw then had a row on the telephone, marred by Shaw's inability to hear almost anything Keynes said to him: as Shaw later explained, he was 'too old and deaf for normal treatment on that instrument: only an oratorical performance reaches me effectively'. Keynes agreed: 'Even the one phrase you caught was wrong. To your question, whether I was crazy, I replied merely that I thought the article was a very bad one. On which there came from you a cheerful laugh, which seemed the appropriate response. . . .' Keynes was so upset by this episode – he had a 'heart attack' according to Virginia Woolf –

that he applied to Plesch for a sedative. To his surprise, the Foreign Office recommended publication. Shaw was not in the least surprised. He wrote irrepressibly to Keynes after their telephone conversation: 'I was sure they would rise up and call me blessed for saying what they all wanted to say, but dared not,' attributing to his Irish extraction his insight into the true nature of the war. He added more gently, 'you must bear with me. I am sometimes useful.'[14]

Keynes did not regard Shaw's article, published on 7 October, as at all useful, though he thought that, with the deletions Shaw accepted, it was now 'harmless'. His own reply to Shaw, published on 14 October, harked back to his polemics of the mid-1930s: 'The intelligentsia of the Left were the loudest in demanding that the Nazi aggression be resisted at all costs. When it comes to a showdown, scarce four weeks have passed before they remember that they are pacifists, and write defeatist letters to your columns, leaving the defence of freedom and of civilisation to Colonel Blimp and the Old School Tie, for whom Three Cheers.'[15] He was congratulated on his letter by Samuel Courtauld, Bob Brand and others. 'I think old Shaw really ought to dry up,' Courtauld wrote to Christabel Aberconway. 'I suppose only a discredited rag like the NS welcomes him today.'[16] A further letter published on 21 October makes it clear Keynes was not anticipating a short war. He refused to rule out a compromise peace, but 'for myself, I am not ready yet to rule out the ideal peace'[17] – one which would not just remove Hitler and the Nazis from the scene, but also abolish the economic and political causes of war. Keynes was always convinced that Hitler would create the winning anti-fascist coalition by making mistakes, and it was Britain's duty to hang on till that happened.*

Like Churchill, and unlike Chamberlain, Keynes attached the greatest importance to drawing America into the Allied net. He was much encouraged by a visit from Leonard and Dorothy Elmhirst of Dartington Hall. Leonard Elmhirst had sounded out opinion in Washington and New York, and returned convinced that Britain could get 'a complete economic front with America, whilst not asking them to send troops'.[18] Keynes's own reading of American opinion was filtered through the articles Walter Lippmann and Dorothy Thompson were writing for the *New York Herald Tribune*, which he thought were the 'best anti-Nazi propaganda' appearing anywhere. When Lord Macmillan at the Ministry of Information refused

---

* I cannot accept Professor Wilson's view of this letter as evidence that Keynes thought the war would be short (T. Wilson, 'Policy in War and Peace: The Recommendations of J. M. Keynes,' in A. P. Thirlwall (ed.), *Keynes as a Policy Adviser*, 45 and 66, n. 6). Keynes wanted Hitler and Nazism removed, and never thought this could be done quickly by force of arms. The phrase in his letter 'For a compromise peace must depend on circumstances which we cannot anticipate' was most likely a veiled reference either to a possible German coup against the Nazis or to a possible Allied defeat.

to distribute them in neutral and Empire countries on grounds of expense, Keynes wrote to him: 'Alas, your letter confirms the prevailing opinion that money is only available for what is useless.'[19] Sir George Schuster approached him with a plan to set up unofficial Anglo-American contact groups. Keynes drafted some 'Notes on the War for the President' on 7 November, which he correctly decided inadvisable to send. Perhaps word had got through to him that Roosevelt had not welcomed his previous attempts to advise him on how to run his administration. 'Obviously American opinion ought to be allowed to stew and develop for a long time yet,' he explained to Walter Lippmann.[20]

Keynes was testing out his capacity for the active life. He stood the strain well, often getting tired, but rapidly recovering. He was convinced that a special course of injections, devised by the Ogre, kept him free of colds all winter. Lydia reported exhausting meetings (including one with an 'Australian magnet'), visits to the Cambridge Arts Theatre, late nights. Keynes's care for the Arts Theatre and the well-being of artists did not cease with the war. He persuaded Norman Higgins not to volunteer for the RAF. He interceded with R. A. Butler at the Foreign Office to get ballet dancers exempted from military service; both Germany and Russia had let off ballet dancers in the last war, 'and we ought not to be less civilised than they were then'. Although Butler tried, Ernest Brown, the Minister of Labour, refused. 'I am afraid he is a savage,' Keynes reported to Raymond Mortimer.[21] A notable event was the appearance of the Ballet Jooss in Cambridge, the proceeds of the gala on 12 December going to Jewish refugees. After telling the assembled audience that there were now a thousand Germans in Cambridge, Keynes continued memorably, in phrases suggested by Dorothy Thompson:

> The truth is that there are now two Germanies. The presence here of Germany in exile is one more symptom of what has been called the queerness of this war. It is a sign that this is a war not between nationalities and imperialism, but between two opposed ways of life and over what we are to mean by civilisation. Our object in this mad, unavoidable struggle is not to conquer Germany, but to convert her, to bring her back within the historic fold of Western civilisation of which the institutional foundations are ... the Christian Ethic, the Scientific Spirit and the Rule of Law. It is only on these foundations that the personal life can be lived.[22]

One commitment he did manage to evade was an invitation from A. B. Ramsay, Master of Magdalene College, and chairman of the University Conservative Committee, to stand for Parliament for Cambridge University as an unopposed Independent. Rather to his surprise, Plesch declared him fit for the job; but after some hesitation Keynes declined, expaining that 'the active political life is not my right and true activity'.[23] His

brother-in-law A. V. Hill took his place and was Independent MP for
Cambridge from 1940 to 1945. Hubert Henderson, one of many whom
Keynes consulted, hoped his refusal would not preclude him 'doing
something Ministerial later on, if your health is completely restored'.[24]

II

COMPULSORY SAVINGS

When not fussing about petrol coupons, Bernard Shaw and such like,
Keynes was germinating his grand plan on 'how to pay for the war' – a
project which kept him occupied until the partial triumph of his ideas in
April 1941. The 'Keynes Plan', as it was soon known, was triggered by Sir
John Simon's first war budget of 27 September 1939, but it was the
crystallisation of much of what Keynes had been writing and saying in the
previous two years. In the proto-war period from 1937 to 1939 the
Treasury had relied heavily on borrowing for rearmament, fearing the
depressing effect of increased taxes on employment and the tax yield.
Simon's emergency budget of September 1939 continued this policy. He
imposed additional taxes of £107m. for the financial year 1939–40, but
defence spending was set to rise by £600m. over the year. Since he had
already projected a deficit of £500m. in his March 1939 budget, this left a
new projected deficit of £1000m. – or 25 per cent of GDP – to be met by
borrowing. This was deficit finance with a vengeance. The Treasury had
evidently absorbed the lesson that no great danger of inflation threatened
while the percentage of insured workers unemployed still stood at over 9
per cent. But if it thereby congratulated itself on its up-to-date 'Keynesian'
approach, it was quickly disabused. Keynes had hopped over the unemployment problem to new ground. As he explained in *The Times* on 28
September, the problem was, or would soon be, one not of inadequate,
but of excess, demand. The need was to limit civilian consumption of the
products of a fully employed war economy, and to this the budget made
hardly any contribution: the new taxes, 'appalling as [they] may seem to
individuals, [are] chicken-feed to the dragons of war'.[25] In a letter to *The
Times* of 4 October he elaborated the point: 'If working-class incomes are
to rise by 10 to 20 per cent [as a result of fuller employment and longer
hours worked] and the taxes they pay by only 5 per cent, either their real
consumption must rise appreciably above their pre-war standard or they
must save a large proportion of the increase in their incomes, or prices
must rise.'[26] One was back in the world of physical scarcity.

From the start he was clear about one point. The government must
find some way of stopping the public consuming the extra resources
which government spending would create, otherwise they would be lost to
the war effort. The main technique used in the last war – stumbled into

rather than deliberate – was inflation. The government printed the money to pay for its domestic war spending; increased government spending caused prices to rise; workers whose wages lagged behind the rise in prices were forced to consume less; the 'windfall' profits of entrepreneurs were commandeered by the government in the form of loans and taxes. As a result of this, the price level doubled in the four years of war. Technically, the First World War was financed by an 'inflation tax' levied on the workers, which accrued to the government in the form of taxes on, or loans from, businessmen.[27]

Keynes's ideas about how to improve on this system did not crystallise at once. At first he seemed to accept inflation as an acceptable alternative to higher taxes.[28] He never deviated from the view that the cost of wartime borrowing could and should be kept low, despite a prescient letter from the economist John Hicks, to the effect that the immediate post-war problem would be boom, not slump, and that the policy of 'piling up liquid funds in the hands of the public . . . is likely to make the problem of controlling the post-war boom even more intractable'. Keynes predicted cavalierly that the boom 'would only be an event of a few months and that our real post-war problem would be inadequate effective demand'. He was more receptive to Hicks's contention that the inflation tax on working-class purchasing power would no longer work. Hicks wrote on 4 October: 'I simply cannot see how we can expect that organised labour . . . will possibly be persuaded to content itself with a fall in the standard of living induced in that way. Surely they will say . . . wages must go up with the cost of living.'[29] Hubert Henderson agreed: 'where strongly placed', labour 'doesn't wait for the cost of living to rise, before demanding higher wage-rates'.[30] In short, the government could no longer rely on a 'lag' between price rises and wage rises – estimated at six months to a year in the first two years of the First World War – to get it the extra resources it needed. But the alternative of imposing income tax – for the first time – on low earners was political dynamite. Keynes conceded that the problem called 'for special measures of an unorthodox kind', which he was working on.[31]

His 'big' idea was first revealed in what Lydia called a 'brilliant lecture' on 'War Potential and War Finance' to Cambridge's Marshall Society on 20 October, which left him 'healthily tired' but with no chest pains. He worked up this lecture into an article for *The Times*, 'Paying for the War', which he submitted to its editor Geoffrey Dawson on 26 October, calling it 'the most important proposal I have ever sent you'. At the same time he circulated copies for comment.[32] Cut in two, it appeared in *The Times* on 14 and 15 November. It had been scooped by the *Investors Review*, which published an extensive summary on 4 November, based on the Cambridge lecture of 20 October, and a proof had been leaked to the *Frankfurter Zeitung*, which published the articles on 7 November. When an uncorrected version of his articles also appeared in the Johannesburg *Star* on 17 November, Keynes wrote ponderously to Dawson: 'I have regarded contributions to *The Times* itself as a sort of public service, analogous to making a public address, where questions of remuneration were entirely secondary, and the object of reaching the right public primary. But the supply of the article throughout the world is quite another matter.'[33]

This is the gist of what he wrote:

The problem we face is that the aggregate of purchasing power is increasing faster than the available supply of goods. Increased defence spending is bringing about much fuller employment, and with it a rising national income. An increase in the purchasing power of wage earners of at least £500m. a year is to be expected, and far more when we have reached our maximum production. Failing special measures much of this sum will be spent in the shops. But wage earners cannot be allowed to buy any more goods than before if the increased resources brought into being are to be used for war purposes; and any further increase towards our maximum war effort must be at the expense of pre-war consumption. The solution of the problem requires the coordination of price policy, budget policy, and wages policy.

Before coming to the real solutions let us dispose of two pseudo-remedies. The first is rationing. Rationing may be needed when an essential consumption good is in such short supply that a modest rise in price will not restore market equilibrium. But it is useless against a general increase in purchasing power. Partial rationing merely diverts demand to unrationed goods; universal rationing is a bad method of control because it assumes that all tastes are identical and imposes an intolerable bureaucratic burden. A tax on excess profits tries to deal with the least important cause of rising prices – which is the increase in working-class purchasing power.

Two genuine remedies are inflation and higher taxation. Some price rises are inevitable due to higher shipping costs and higher world prices. But since workers have become much more index conscious, an excessive rise in prices will merely spark off the vicious spiral of wage-price inflation, as well as being a cause of great social injustice. To solve the present problem taxation must be extended to the working class, since ⅗ths of net expenditure on consumption is by those who earn less than £250 a year and it is this class whose incomes are likely to rise by upwards of 15 per cent. A turnover, or sales, tax on non-essentials should be considered, yet a general turnover tax would be highly regressive. Both inflation and taxation aim to deprive the working class of any benefit from their increased earnings. Yet a large part of these earnings represent increased effort. We must find a way of preventing individuals from spending more than before, but in a way which avoids penal taxation of the wealthy and which rewards the working class for increased effort by giving them claims on future resources. They can only enjoy an increase in real earnings if they are prepared to accept deferred pay.

My proposal is as follows. A graduated percentage of all incomes above a stipulated minimum should be paid over to the government, partly as direct taxes, partly as compulsory savings. This will subsume the existing system of direct taxation. Part of the levy will be used to discharge income tax and surtax obligations, if any. The rest will be credited to interest-bearing individual accounts in the Post Office Savings Bank, will be collected (for most wage earners) through the National Insurance machinery, and will be repayable after the war in instalments to help us through the first post-war slump. The higher the incomes the lower will be the repayable percentage. For a married man with two children earning less than £300 a year, the whole of the levy will be repayable. At an income level of £20,000, the levy will come to £16,000 of which £13,000 will be tax, and only £3000 repayable. The yield of the levy might amount to £400m. more than existing direct taxation. Compulsory savings will not obviate normal borrowing out of voluntary savings of various kinds.

Critics must compare it with the alternatives. At present the income group between £3 and £10 a week pays almost no direct taxes. Imposing compulsory savings on this group will be incomparably better than to deprive them of their reward by higher prices or direct taxation, while for the higher incomes the practicable limit of direct taxation is already reached. Moreover, there will be great social advantages in spreading the inevitable increase in the National Debt as widely as possible. If the Chancellor does not choose a positive method, he will inevitably slip into inflation merely by hesitating.[34]

The central point in 'Paying for the War' was the rejection of inflation-cum-rationing as a way of reducing working-class consumption. This automatically excluded reliance on traditional debt finance, which depended in large part on borrowing from the inflated incomes of the business class. Compulsory saving was put forward as a novel form of debt finance. It killed several birds with one stone: it restricted working-class consumption without robbing workers of the rewards of greater effort; it drastically restricted the consumption of the wealthy without imposing penal, disincentive tax rates; surcharging post-tax or non-taxable incomes rather than increasing taxes would ensure that peace started with a more modest burden of taxation; and it avoided the need for comprehensive rationing and price controls.

Keynes explained this last advantage in a talk he gave on 'Price Policy' to the Tuesday Club on 6 December. Inflation, he said, could not be prevented 'by forbidding prices to rise', only by stopping purchasing power from rising faster than available supplies. Keynes went on: 'You will see that my object is to maintain a system of natural prices to the utmost possible extent.' This would make it possible to 'revoke many of the minor and perhaps some of the major controls'. Fortunately, the traditions and atmosphere of Britain made impossible 'a totalitarian system which will work well'. But if the situation got out of hand through a failure to implement his policy, then there might be no alternative to forbidding by law any further rise in wage rates, accompanying this by a standard food ration at prices fixed in relation to wages.

The Keynes Plan received enormous press coverage, confirming Dawson's belief that 'an important article in *The Times* gets publicity everywhere else'.[35] Keynes hoped that his scheme might form the basis for the next budget, and over the ensuing months he canvassed it tirelessly in Whitehall, Parliament and press, his persuasive efforts climaxing with the publication of his booklet *How to Pay for the War* on 27 February 1940. Keynes was a heroic controversialist. As well as taking on his critics in public, and explaining his Plan to private gatherings of politicians, businessmen and trade unionists, he replied mainly courteously, and often at length, to most letters he received. He made it plain that he was more committed to the logic of his approach than to the details of his proposals, which he modified in response to criticism and suggestions.

What was the character of the response? We must distinguish between inside and outside opinion, and the partly overlapping reactions to the logical structure and detailed provisions of Keynes's proposals. From the start, the economics profession was unanimously in favour of Keynes's logic. This is not particularly surprising, since Keynes had moved the discussion on to a terrain where non-Keynesian and Keynesian economics agreed. A particularly significant endorsement came from his self-styled 'scientific antipode' Friedrich Hayek, who publicly praised the Keynes Plan in the *Spectator* of 24 November. As Hayek put it to Keynes: 'It is reassuring to know that we agree so completely on the economics of scarcity, even if we differ on when it applies.'[36] The eager embrace by all economists of the 'economics of scarcity' suggests that the 'economics of plenty' which was the real subject of the *General Theory* still had only a very limited appeal. Of the inner core of Keynesians, only Richard Kahn had doubts about Keynes's anti-inflationary emphasis (see p. 80 below). Interestingly, the feature of the Keynes Plan which got least support from the economics profession was the proposal to release the blocked credits to counteract the post-war slump. Hayek did not believe in increased spending as a cure for slumps; in any case, the immediate post-war prospect was not for a slump but for an inflationary boom. Like Hicks, he favoured a capital levy to reduce effective demand after the war.

The economist–administrators in Whitehall, men like Stamp, Henderson and Clay, were also firmly behind Keynes's logic, though critical of the details of his Plan. It was a mistake to guarantee the post-war value of the blocked credits; Keynes's levy, being graduated by size, rather than increment, of income, would catch people whose real incomes had gone down since the start of the war as a result of the inflation already taking place; he should include minimum rations at fixed prices and/or family allowances as a protection for the poorest.[37] Keynes deleted the section of his pre-publication draft guaranteeing the purchasing power of the blocked deposits. But he rejected Henderson's amendment to tax only overtime pay. 'Under your plan,' he wrote to Henderson, 'everyone would have as large an income as before, and even the overtimer would have a considerably larger one,' leaving aggregate consumption 'appreciably higher than pre-war'.[38]

Another old friend, Bob Brand of Lazard Brothers, thought Keynes dismissed the possibility of raising revenue from orthodox taxes too readily. He also feared the effect of compulsory savings on voluntary savings – a view influenced by his close association with Sir Robert Kindersley, chairman of Lazards and chairman of the National Savings Committee. Keynes replied that it would be politically easier to raise the extra money from compulsory saving than from taxation.[39] Brand told Hubert Henderson that Keynes's Plan 'looks nice & simple & just', with 'obvious merits over crude inflation',[40] but thought that rationing of essentials at fixed prices was an essential *quid pro quo* for trade union wage restraint. Keynes was unconvinced. When Brand supplied him with details of the German rationing scheme, he wrote back scathingly: 'The policy of fixed prices plus having nothing in the shops to buy – an expedient pursued for many years by the Russian authorities – is undoubtedly one of the very best ways of preventing inflation!'[41] When Arthur Salter, Brand, and John and Ursula Hicks publicly suggested a Treasury subsidy for an 'iron ration' of necessaries, Keynes initially resisted on cost grounds – 'As an old Treasury man I am scared of it' – but was eventually persuaded that it was politically necessary. It must, however, be conditional on acceptance of compulsory saving.[42]

Keynes thought that Kindersley's optimism concerning voluntary savings was 'obviously clouded by emotional disturbance'. Brand disagreed. 'He holds the strongest conviction that as his movement gets more intense he can raise very large additional sums from the public, much larger than people think. . . . He complains, too, that you have never answered his argument that if you compel the population to save they will to a considerable extent balance their position by withdrawing existing savings

from the Post Office and the friendly societies. . . .' Keynes agreed that
'there will be some leakages through the withdrawals of existing savings.
But this seems to me to apply to any drastic remedy whatever. . . . It is true
of high surtax.' Part of Kindersley's own successes was due to withdrawals
from other sources. Keynes still believed that the amount of saving
Kindersley could achieve 'above the normal' was 'terribly small'. The
figures bear him out. The National Savings Movement campaigned vigorously to mobilise small savings throughout the war, but it seems that 'the
switching of assets was the main source of the "savings" totals achieved'.[43]

Keynes was astounded by the hostile reaction to his proposals outside
the magic circle of economists, experts and insiders. The horror of
'compulsion' united Kindersley, the Beaverbrook press and the Labour
Party in defence of voluntary saving and free trade unionism. The *Daily
Express* of 16 November 1939 rubbished his Plan in terms which would not
discredit the *Sun* today:

> Another enemy attacks the liberty of the people! Mr Keynes, the
> economist. He takes out his textbooks, he flourishes his fountain
> pen, and he rushes out of his study to demand that compulsory
> saving should be imposed. The Government, he says, should take
> away part of the workers' wages, force the public to lend them
> money. What an insult to the patriotism of our people! What a
> slander on their eagerness for voluntary sacrifice to suggest that they
> will not freely lend every pound and penny they are asked for!

What made Keynes's 'propaganda' so attractive to officials was that it
drove home the point that, as Stamp put it, 'the war can only be paid for
by annexing a large part of the increased purchasing power of the wage
earning class and also encroaching on the pre-war standard of living'.[44]
But it was precisely this feature that made it so hard to sell to the leaders
of the Labour Party (including the trade union movement), whose
support was absolutely essential. Keynes made great efforts with the
Labour Party – indeed most of his persuasive efforts were directed at
them. He had carefully sent the manuscript of his *Times* articles to
Clement Attlee on 24 October, with a personal letter which said that his
plan offered 'the only way of handling the financial end of the war that is
at the same time just and advantageous to the working class'. Attlee's
reply devastated him: the leader of the Labour Party wrote back that
Keynes's proposals would impose a 'crushing' burden on Attlee himself!
Keynes sent him a testy four-page letter: 'The question is, do you prefer
to be mulcted in alternative ways? . . . There is not the slightest good your
saying that you cannot afford any of them. You have got to suffer the
reduction one way or another.' The great advantage of compulsory saving
over orthodox taxation or inflation was that workers would not lose the
benefit of their higher wages, only be obliged to defer their spending.[45]

Even worse was Labour's public response. Arthur Greenwood, Labour's deputy leader, wrote in the *Daily Express* that the Keynes Plan smacked of Hitlerism.[46] Frederick Pethick-Lawrence in the *Forward* of 25 November argued that no attempt should be made to depress the living standards of the working class, that the rich should be subjected to a capital levy to prevent them living off capital, and that individuals' circumstances differed so much that it would be better to rely on voluntary savings in the first instance. Douglas Jay argued in the *Daily Herald* of 16 November – on Keynesian grounds! – that inflation would not be a problem till full employment was reached. Ernest Bevin, leader of the Transport and General Workers Union and the dominant figure in the trade union movement, said it was the government's duty to control prices, and, if it failed to do so, he would use collective bargaining to prevent any erosion of workers' real wages.[47] Keynes was particularly upset by Bevin's attitude – 'almost the worst thing I have read since the beginning of the war'[48] – as he had formed a high opinion of him when they had served together on the Macmillan Committee in 1930–1. He made repeated efforts to see Bevin, using the Liberal MP Clement Davies as his intermediary, but without success. Trade union opposition to increased burdens on their members was a key factor in stopping the government imposing heavier taxes on the working class, even in the Keynesian form of deferred pay, the Treasury's expectation being that it would stimulate equivalent claims for wage increases.[49]

Keynes found Labour's response 'frivolous and unthinking'.[50] He wrote to Greenwood on 19 November, 'I had devised [the scheme for compulsory savings] *solely* in the interests of the working class, particularly the poorer members'.[51] In a reply to his critics in *The Times* of 28 November he pointed out that the workers did not face a choice between increased consumption and voluntary saving, it was 'compulsory savings or compulsory inflation'.[52] As for the argument that his scheme was premature, he was 'entirely in agreement with you [Pethick-Lawrence] . . . that the problem I am tackling does not really arise until we are approaching full employment. But I have assumed that . . . that position cannot be far off . . . [and that] we want to be prepared beforehand for the problem it will then set us'.[53] In a discussion with Douglas Jay in the *Daily Herald*, Keynes attacked as mythical the idea that the war could be financed by those with over £10,000 a year, but conceded that there might be a case for 'establishing a standard subsistence ration of primary necessities . . . at a fixed price'. Keynes soon recognised he had made a tactical mistake in talking about compulsory savings and substituted the more diplomatic 'deferred pay' in subsequent expositions.[54]

It was the Labour intellectual Harold Laski who pointed out the problem. Laski, who liked Keynes's Plan, wrote to him on 5 December that 'your propagandist support, and, to some extent, your own method of statement, have done it the maximum possible harm with Labour people'. Hurt, Keynes replied on 11 December, 'Honestly, I did my best to approach the Labour leaders in the right way before publishing my articles in *The Times*.' Since then he had been trying to arrange a meeting without success. 'So you see, I really have been trying. . . . But the official leaders seem almost past praying for. Is there anything positive which they are known to be in favour of?' It turned out that Greenwood had been paid £100 for his article, which had been written for him, Greenwood having no idea what it was all about. Evidently 'Beaverbrook understands the right technique [of persuasion] better than I do.'[55]

Had Keynes bothered to read Labour's own booklet, also called *How to Pay for the War*, published that autumn, he would have been less surprised at the Party's frosty response. Drawn up by the economists Evan Durbin, Hugh Gaitskell and Douglas Jay of Labour's War Finance Group, it argued that, with a limited tax base and lack of direct controls on industry, large-scale borrowing was inevitable. This would be inflationary, but a 'moderate and controlled' inflation, accompanied by rationing and other restrictions on consumption, was desirable, as it would increase the profits and hence output of the war industries, increase saving when consumption was restricted, and reduce the real burden of debt. The burden of post-war debt could be further reduced by a capital levy after the end of the war.[56] Both the Keynes and the Labour Plans aimed to restrict working-class consumption. But, whereas Keynes aimed to achieve this by compulsory saving, the Labour economists preferred a mixture of controlled inflation, comprehensive rationing and voluntary saving. Keynes greatly weakened his persuasive effort by not engaging directly with Labour's argument. Also, as in the First World War,[57] he grossly underestimated the appeal of rationing. Oliver Lyttelton, controller of non-ferrous metals, who had heard Keynes at the Tuesday Club on 6 December, made a brutal political point: 'Nobody cares a damn about justice: equality is what matters.'[58]

It was a relief to Lydia when they finally got back to Tilton on 14 December. At least he could work away quietly, without being sucked into endless meetings and dinners. Richard Kahn was their only house-guest. They took Christmas Day off, drank Sam Courtauld's champagne and retired to bed early. On Boxing Day, Keynes was back at work, going over to Charleston for tea with Duncan Grant, Clive and Vanessa Bell, and the Bells' son Quentin, whom Maynard was employing as a farm labourer. There had been a sortie to Rodmell for tea with the Woolfs on 23 December, and they returned the visit on 27 December. Such reunions, with their opportunities for reminiscence, gossip and exploration of personal standards, were now rare for Keynes – not just on account of the war, his busyness and Lydia's inaptness for the Bloomsbury style of cerebration, but because his attitude of omniscience on all topics had become too overwhelming for intimacy. Virginia Woolf described the scene at Rodmell, with Maynard 'lying extended on the sofa . . . with the two fog lamps burning, & Lydia a sort of fairy elf in her fur cap. . . . He is now supreme, mounted on his sick throne, a successful man – farmer, bursar, a man of business, he called himself, applying for petrol. A heavy man with a thick moustache. A moralist. As interested in Patsy the[ir] black dog with the bald patch as in Europe. He was saying – odd how hard it is to remember – he was telling us about salt; water; heat and cold & their effect on the urine.'

Their conversation turned to Roger Fry, whose biography Viriginia Woolf was writing. 'Can I mention erection?' Virginia asked, in Blooms-bury shorthand for Fry's affair with her sister Vanessa Bell. Maynard made his usual decisive pronouncement. 'No you can't,' he said. 'I should mind your discussing it. Such revelations have to be in key with their time. The time has not yet come.' So 'sodomy and the WC' would have to be 'disinfected', Virginia reflected. She did not mention the affair in her published book.[59]

III

EFFORTS AT PERSUASION

With so many comments coming in, Keynes had suggested to Harold Macmillan on 27 November that the material of his articles be turned into a short book, initially to be called 'The Economic Consequences of the War'. On Macmillan's agreement, he set to work on revisions. These were specifically aimed at winning over Labour support. He incorporated several new suggestions. 'I am sure', he wrote to one correspondent, 'that there is an overwhelming case for dealing with a rising cost of living by means of family allowances, rather than by an all-round rise in wages, irrespective of family.'[60] The previous summer Keynes had discussed the idea of children's allowances with his niece Polly Hill, and suggested paying for them out of the surplus of the Unemployment Insurance Fund.[61] Now the details of a more comprehensive scheme, financed by taxes, were worked out after a meeting on 17 January 1940 with, as Lydia put it, 'ladies of economics Miss Rathbone and Mrs Hubback'. Families would get cash payments of 5s a week for each child up to fifteen, at a cost to the Exchequer of £100m. Family allowances were offered as a *quid pro quo* for wage moderation. Keynes preferred this method of reducing wage pressure to that of subsidising the sale of necessaries at fixed prices.

Keynes's concession of a capital levy after the war was a less happy compromise with his critics, for it enabled anti-Keynesians to claim, much later, that he was hostile to private enterprise.[62] He had considered the question of the 'ultimate repayment of the compulsory savings' as the 'least of the difficulties'. He assumed that a post-war slump would follow fairly soon on the heels of an inflationary boom (as happened in 1920), as military spending fell off and men were demobilised from the armed forces. The release of the deferred pay would add to demand and substitute old debt for the new debt the Treasury would otherwise need to incur for public works; this automatic repayment mechanism, he thought, was 'the strongest feature of the scheme, worth having for its own sake'.[63] However, critics of both right and left wanted a capital levy: Hayek and Hicks because they saw the blocked balances as merely postponing inflationary pressure; the Labour economists because they wanted the rich to pay for the war after all – later if it could not be sooner. Keynes unwisely conceded the case for a capital levy if the National Debt created by deferred pay exceeded the sums which needed to be released to offset serious post-war unemployment, but argued that levy and release should not be synchronised, the tax being levied in the inflationary period, the release timed for the onset of the depression.[64]

The public and private discussion about 'what to do' with the deferred pay offers a fascinating counterfactual perspective on the history of the welfare state. The most interesting suggestion, which came from several of Keynes's correspondents, was that compulsory savings be turned into life assurance policies. This would not just guard against the danger of premature release but give all earners a security against post-war hazards. This foreshadows the later fashionable Singapore model of social insurance. Keynes was interested, but pointed out that for such security to be achieved compulsory saving would need to be made permanent, not just temporary.[65] Hayek's suggestion of repayment in the form of shares rather than cash[66] was another idea whose time came in the 1980s. Continuing compulsory savings into peacetime to endow wage-earners with personal assets was a neglected alternative to the 'social insurance' route to social protection mapped out in the Beveridge Report of 1942. Keynes was diverted from this line of thought by his conviction that the post-war world would need more consumption, not more saving.

Through the efforts of Pethick-Lawrence and Walter Citrine, meetings with the Labour Party front bench and the Economic Committee of the General Council of the TUC were arranged on the morning and afternoon respectively of 24 January. The revised proposals Keynes now presented included administration of deferred pay by trade union and friendly societies, family allowances, and a capital levy after the war. He estimated that his new protections would maintain the pre-war consumption standard of all earning less than £250 a year, while reducing by a third the consumption of those earning over £250 a year. As he explained to Stamp on 29 January, his plan was 'not now merely a piece of technique, but aims at actually using the opportunity of war finance for constructive social reforms, and a bigger move towards equality than any we have made for a long time'.[67] He was much less satisfied with the morning than with the afternoon session. The Party leader, Clement Attlee, 'obviously extremely hostile', escaped after fifteen minutes. 'Daddy' Dalton, who had never liked Keynes, was hostile, but shaken. Gulping down bad food while arguing with Pethick-Lawrence, 'a good old Liberal' who reminded him of Snowden, Keynes felt ill in the taxi taking him from Parliament to Congress House, but the TUC session went a lot better, with the discussion 'serious and intelligent' and George Woodcock, secretary of the TUC's research department, summing up very well. But Bevin was absent.[68] For all his verbal eloquence, Keynes was finding the job of persuasion incredibly frustrating. 'The trouble is not with public opinion,' he exploded to his First World War Treasury chief Reginald McKenna, 'but [with] the bloody politicians whose bloody minds have not been sufficiently prepared for anything unfamiliar to their ancestors. If the things were to be sponsored and put across with reponsible leadership, there would be practically no opposition at all.'[69]

Keynes went on trying, addressing a group of MPs on 20 February and the Fabian Society the next day. He told the Fabians that from the start of the war he had been 'obsessed with the task of finding the right solution' to the problem of reducing consumption in a way which satisfied popular psychology and social justice. He disliked the 'old-fashioned laissez-faire' solution of inflation, the 'new fashioned totalitarian' method of comprehensive rationing which would reduce Britain to a slave state, and the compromise between them of 'a totalitarian solution for a narrow range of necessaries and inflation over the remaining field of consumption'. The right solution was to fix purchasing power and allow freedom to spend the balance; to make sure that the National Debt was owned by everyone who had earned it; and to arrange the details so as to make the fiscal system an engine of social reform. He had been overwhelmed by the 'violence of the criticism' his Plan had incurred. He admitted that he 'had been too much preoccupied' in his first version 'with . . . financial technique, and had not made sure of the full gain in social justice for which this technique opened the way', but he was a 'highly teachable person' and his proposals were now much improved.

> Before this audience [Keynes said after explaining the revised details of his plan] I claim justly that this is the right Socialist solution. . . . But I would also claim that it is the solution which best preserves the rights and interests of the individual. It is for the state to say how much a man is entitled to spend out of his earnings. It is for him to say how he will spend it. Liberty and the right to personal choice is thus harmonised with the overriding demands of the community as a whole.[70]

Keynes's dislike of rationing and price controls ran deep. He objected to them because they eliminated consumer choice. 'This is the overwhelming argument for tackling the problem at the income end rather than at the expenditure end.'[71] But, as Brand told him, much more psychologically important than consumer choice in war was 'that the wage-earners should feel that as regards *consumption* we are all on the same level'.[72] Keynes only gradually accepted the force of this argument, which ran counter to all his liberal instincts. He did not mention a 'cheap ration for necessaries' in his speeches or writings prior to the publication of his pamphlet. After its publication, Keynes explained to the nutritionist V. H. Mottram, who had supplied him with a list of healthy foodstuffs, that 'the iron ration is a little bit of a concession to others. I would much rather diminish spending power . . . and deal with the wages question by family allowances'.[73]

Lydia's medical diary records a life lived at high pressure, full of meetings, concerts, ballets and plays, dinner parties and late nights. All the while Keynes scribbled away at the final version of his Plan in Cambridge, with 'rings under the eyes'. He finished writing the pamphlet on the morning of Sunday 11 February, having lunch with his parents at Harvey Road, and walking back to College, just as he had always done before his illness. At the last minute there was a publishing hitch. Harold Macmillan had agreed to print a first run of 10,000 at a shilling a copy. Now Roland Heath, deputising for him, told Keynes they would print only 5000. Keynes's explosion differed only from the usual writer's pique in being backed by precise statistics. 'I have never written any book on economics . . . which has sold less than 5000 copies; nor any pamphlet which has sold less than 12,000, though these have had vastly less advance publicity than this one.' If necessary he would publish at his own expense, with Macmillan getting a commission for distribution, as in his previous arrangements with the firm. Heath capitulated: there would be a first print run of 11,500 and £154 would be spent on advertising.[74]

How to Pay for the War was published by Macmillan on 27 February. Keynes had done his best to make his Plan more widely acceptable: to the working class by incorporating extra protections for the lowest paid in the form of family allowances and 'iron rations' at subsidised prices,[75] and to the financially orthodox by adding a capital levy to discharge the liability created by deferred pay.[76] He now conceded that subsidy might be a useful *quid pro quo* for the promise of wage moderation.[77] The extra protections required offsetting reductions in children's allowances under the income tax system and increased progression in repayable tax;[78] the capital levy might be the prelude to an annual wealth tax.[79]

Keynes's private publicity machine had gone into action with 380 presentation copies, and he puffed his pamphlet tirelessly in the precincts of Whitehall. On 28 February he spoke to 250 MPs from all parties in the Commons without fatigue; on 6 March he addressed the Trade Union Club, with the octogenarian Ben Tillett in the chair; the same day Lord

Balfour of Burleigh initiated a debate in the House of Lords, Keynes briefing Lord Hankey, who replied for the government. Difficult meetings at the Treasury and with the Chancellor of the Exchequer followed the next day, with Keynes having dinner in bed to recover from the strain. On 8 March he came back to Cambridge, after seeing the governor of the Bank of England Montagu Norman, 'fresh as a button [and] in the evening went to the theatre'. On Saturday there were 'sausages and Troilus' at the Cambridge Arts Theatre, with noisy undergraduates making sleep in St Edward's Passage impossible. On 11 March he did a broadcast interview with Donald Tyerman for the BBC, for which he was paid thirty guineas. There was a meeting with the Parliamentary Monetary Committee on 19 March, at which he concentrated mainly on foreign exchange matters, but also answered questions on his deferred pay proposals. He was still dissatisfied with his publisher. Nearly two weeks after publication, no copy was to be seen at the St Pancras, Liverpool Street or Cambridge railway bookstalls. A month later he was 'shocked bibliographically' that no indication had been given of the second printing (of 10,000 copies), though he had revised the text. A week later, 'Words fail me to express my feelings that your firm thought fit to send only 75 copies to Australia.' Thirty-eight thousand copies were eventually sold.[80]

Keynes gave detailed accounts of the reactions to his pamphlet, largely based on public comment and private correspondence, to Geoffrey Dawson, editor of *The Times*. The trade union leaders were sympathetic, though Bevin was unapproachable. The economic advisers of the Labour Party – Cole, Laski, Crossman and Barbara Wootton – were 'strongly in favour'. Among academic economists there was 'almost universal agreement on principle, though some differences on points of detail'. (Robertson told Keynes it was his 'best work since E[conomic] C[onsequences of the] P[eace]' – a backhanded compliment.)[81] Montagu Norman had asked to see Keynes on 8 March. Keynes reported that, 'after long estrangement, this scheme has brought about a personal reconciliation,' he thinks 'it is the only solution,' and the other leading bankers were in favour. The only outspoken opposition, 'apart from the dark questionings by the Labour Front Bench', came from Kindersley, Beaverbrook, 'who says frankly that he prefers inflation', and the *Daily Worker*. (The Communist Party, opposed to what it regarded as an 'imperialist war', savaged Keynes's Plan as an attack on the working class in a pamphlet, *Mr Keynes Answered*, written by Emile Burns.)

As always, Keynes overestimated his support. J. L. Garvin of the *Observer*, while praising his 'power of stirring thought', did not feel that 'your psychologicals are right for the hour'.[82] The large postbag which Keynes received after his broadcast was discouraging. Although many of the letters clearly came from the 'lunatic, the violently irritable and unstable and anti-war', many 'reasonable and sensible souls' clearly felt that he was trying to rob 'ordinary people' of their hard-won earnings.[83] One pleasing, if unexpected, letter, must have stirred memories of long-buried emotions. It came from Arthur Hobhouse, now chairman of the Somerset County Council. Praising Keynes's pamphlet for its 'clearness, precision and its humanity', Hobhouse wrote that Keynes owed the first two qualities to the fact that 'you were once a mathematician . . . For the third, you are probably indebted to your chromosomes.'[84]

Lydia and Maynard were back at Tilton on 22 March for Easter. His health had stood the strain of war work pretty well. 'I have certainly been taking in the last few weeks a burden of intellectual and nervous activities which I had scarcely expected to be able to support,' he reported to Sir Edmund Spriggs at Ruthin Castle on 13 March.[85] On 18 March he had gone to Plesch complaining of a 'feeling of distress in the aorta' from time to time. Plesch prescribed a porous plaster to be worn constantly under his left armpit. At Tilton, he had his first setback for some months, Lydia reporting him looking 'old and worn out' after a potter round the farm with Logan Thomson on 31 March. Next day, Sunday, he was discussing details of the forthcoming Cambridge Arts Theatre productions with the actor–manager Donald Wolfit. Ford's play *'Tis Pity She's a Whore* must be done, he told Wolfit in the authoritative tone he now brought to all topics, 'with gusto and in the Italian manner'. (Dadie Rylands thought no one would come 'unless the title stimulates the curiosity of the RAF'.) On Sunday 7 April, they entertained the Woolfs, Maynard telling Virginia that the war was practically won.[86] Two days later, the Germans invaded Norway – 'the first main clinch of the war', as Churchill put it. At Charleston, Lydia had a fierce argument with Clive Bell, who had made the mistake of saying he thought the Germans were winning.[87]

Keynes knew that Britain was still far from being fully prepared for war. As one account puts it:

In whatever direction one looked, the war effort was endangered by growing shortages while civilian consumption had hardly been touched. Unemployment was still relatively high – it was nearly one million . . . in the autumn [of 1940] – but this left a relatively small margin in relation to the rapidly growing manpower requirements of the armed forces. There was also a major balance of payments constraint and very little foreign exchange. The import programme would have to be cut for lack of shipping, stocks were being run down, manpower was moving too slowly into the metal and engineering trades. . . . In the background, too, was the ever-present danger of inflation if the claims over resources continued to be excessive or if efforts were made to speed up labour transfers by the offer of higher wages.[88]

No appraisal of Keynes's political legacy can leave out *How to Pay for the War*. (For its economic legacy, see pp. 87–90 below.) After the war ended, Lionel Robbins wrote that there were two views about how to run a war economy – the fiscal theory and the planning theory. According to the fiscal theory the government should withdraw as much purchasing power as was necessary to avoid inflation, and allow the price system to allocate resources. By contrast, the planning theory fixes wages and prices, with the government commandeering resources and allocating them between the armed forces, productive instruments and final goods according to the strategic plan.[89] Both theories agree that in war civilian consumption should be a residual; the crucial disagreement is over the role that the price system might play in allocating resources. Robbins, a Hayekian in peacetime, argued that 'for the conduct of small wars' the fiscal recipe might be adequate, but for modern 'total' war, where rapidity of response to war demands was of the essence, there was no alternative to 'totalitarianism'.[90]

Since Keynes is so often unthinkingly placed in the *dirigiste* camp, it is important to insist that he favoured the fiscal theory of war control. More importantly, he *invented* the fiscal theory, precisely in order to avoid 'totalitarian' planning. He did not see demand management as a useful adjunct to planning, price fixing, rationing, bureaucratic controls and so on, but as an alternative to them, in war as in peace. In the First World War he had quipped: 'If we put prices low enough and wages high enough, we could achieve the most magnificent queues even in peacetime; there never has been anything like enough caviar to go round.' This position proved increasingly difficult to maintain after the fall of France in June 1940. 'As the war developed the need for central allocation of resources increased progressively.'[91] Nor did Keynes's approach necessarily fit the popular mood. The issue here is not whether he was right or wrong, but the spirit in which he approached wartime problems. Harrod and Moggridge fail to bring out the liberal presuppositions underlying his Plan, especially his belief that prices were the essential element of freedom in the economic system, however restricted their scope might have to be.[92] After a long search, Keynes had found his own point of equilibrium between individualism and collectivism and he held fast to it.

Keynes's fiscal theory was an alternative to inflation as well as to physical planning. Indeed, he believed that the first would inevitably lead to the second. What he called 'totalitarianism' was an inevitable outcome of failing to control inflation in a modern economy – a conclusion strikingly similar to that of Hayek in his *Road to Serfdom*, published in 1944.

A case can be made out for *How to Pay for the War* as the quintessence of Keynes's achievement. It engaged all the qualities of his complex nature. The union of theory and practice, the linking of economic doctrine to political philosophy here achieved its most compelling artistic expression. At the core of his vision was his understanding that modern society would no longer stand 'Nature's cures' of inflation and unemployment for the malfunctioning of the market system. His answer was a permanent scheme of regulating spending to avoid booms and slumps, of which his war Plan was a first instalment, politically easier to start off as an anti-inflationary policy. This logic was still resisted by politicians and economists of the right, wedded to *laissez-faire*. But there was a sting in the tail for the left as well. For most socialists, the war offered a chance to introduce physical planning not just for war but as a permanent system. Against these temptations Keynes steadfastly defended the price system and consumer choice. 'The abolition of consumers' choice in favour of universal rationing is a typical product . . . of Bolshevism,' he wrote.[93] Similarly, the release of deferred pay after the war, 'by allowing individuals to choose for themselves what they want, will save us from having to devise large-scale government plans of expenditure which may not correspond so closely to personal need'. He wrote: 'I am seizing the opportunity to introduce a principle of policy which may be thought of as marking the line of division between the totalitarian and the free economy. For if the community's aggregate rate of spending can be regulated, the way in which personal incomes are spent can be safely left free and individual.'[94] This was his philosophy for both war and peace. Keynes resisted the stampede to state socialism, because he felt he had worked out a way of making individualism safe for the community. He summed up his philosophy of the Middle Way in an article for an American audience, published in the *New Republic* on 29 July 1940:

> The reformers must believe that it is worth while to concede a great deal to preserve that decentralisation of decisions and of power which is the prime virtue of the old individualism. In a world of destroyers, they must zealously protect the variously woven fabric of society, even when this means that some abuses must be spared. Civilisation is a tradition from the past, a miraculous construction made by our fathers . . . hard to come by and easily lost. We have to escape from the *invalidism* of the Left which has eaten up the wisdom and inner strength of many good causes.
>
> The old guard of the Right, on their side, must surely recognise, if any reason or prudence is theirs, that the existing system is palpably disabled, that the idea of its continuing to function unmodified with half the world in dissolution is just sclerotic. Let them learn from the experience of Great Britain and of Europe that there has been a rottenness at the heart of our society, and do not let them suppose that America is healthy.[95]

IV

The fate of the Keynes Plan depended on the Treasury. Keynes was heartened by the interest of the the Chancellor of the Exchequer, who did not raise any insuperable objections. The government had no real alternative to his Plan, he told Dawson, but 'they are extremely reluctant to adopt any drastic remedy until the necessity of it is obvious, and more than obvious, to the densest member of the public'. But with such a weight of 'authoritative support' they need not feel so scared of public opinion, if only they would 'grasp the nettle'.[96]

This was greatly to oversimplify the Treasury's problem. The general Treasury attitude to Keynes's policy proposals, going back to the 1920s, was that they were invariably stimulating but that, as one Treasury official commented on his 'Means to Prosperity' in 1933, 'he has never allowed questions of time-lag or of practical feasibility to interfere with the even flow of his argument...'.[97] On one point there was no disagreement: Keynes's resistance to the use of high interest rates to check a boom coincided with the Treasury's desire to borrow large sums for war as cheaply as possible, as well as 'an appreciation that the social and political climate would not permit a repeat of the *rentier*-friendly policy of the First World War'.[98] This put the burden of anti-inflationary policy on the budget. Here there was as yet no meeting of minds. The pre-Keynesian orthodoxy was that the use of borrowed money to supplement taxes was not inflationary if matched by the flow of voluntary saving. 'Chancellors imposed tax increases as sharp as they thought that the public would stomach and then hoped that the amounts they would have to squeeze out of the capital markets would not exceed the supply of voluntary saving.'[99] That is why they were so keen to encourage the National Savings Movement. Officials were only dimly aware that borrowing could be inflationary if the savings being borrowed were themselves being created by increased government spending. Keynes was the first to put clearly into circulation two propositions: (a) that 'paying for the war' meant reducing civilian consumption to the extent required by the war effort and (b) that the required reduction would not be brought about without inflation simply by the government meeting its expenditure by taxes and loans.

There was also an overwhelming administrative objection. Any *deliberate* withdrawal of spending power from the public required information about how much the 'aggregate of purchasing power' exceeded the 'available supply of goods'. This knowledge was not available to the Treasury early in 1940. The Inland Revenue knew the total amount of incomes it was taxing, but in 1939 income tax was far from being a mass tax, since about three-fifths of wage-earners paid no income tax at all. Squeezing more money out of existing taxpayers would do nothing to stop the majority of wage-earners spending their increased earnings in the shops. An anti-inflationary budgetary policy required national or 'social' accounts. The government needed to know the value, at pre-war prices, of the national output becoming available for all uses during the year, and the total money demand on that output from all sources, and how it was distributed. Only then could it work out how much purchasing power it had to remove from the consumer goods market to stop prices rising, and how to distribute the burden of sacrifice.

Keynes had been calling in vain for official national income statistics since 1937. 'Every government since the last war', he complained, 'has been unscientific and obscurantist, and has regarded the collection of essential facts as a waste of money.'[100] What he omitted to point out was that such facts were essential only for the purposes of 'demand management' which the pre-war Treasury regarded as neither feasible nor desirable.[101] Though an Inland Revenue effort in 1929 to calculate the national income languished, unknown, in its pigeonholes, Keynes, in making his calculations in 1939, had to rely on pioneering work by Colin Clark in 1938, updated by a young émigré economist, Erwin Rothbarth, working as an assistant in statistical research at the Cambridge Economics and Politics Faculty.

On 12 October 1939 Keynes had asked Rothbarth to prepare estimates of the national income, national savings, incomes below £500 a year and so on for the year 1938–9 for his Marshall Society lecture of 20 October, which became the text for his *Times* articles. He used these estimates in a note to Sir Richard Hopkins, second secretary at the Treasury, on 16 November, a revised version of which appeared in the *Economic Journal* of December 1939; and his 'budget of national resources' was published as an appendix to his pamphlet *How to Pay for the War*. It was based on his *General Theory* concepts of aggregate demand and aggregate supply, measured in prices, and subdivided into components, to which he applied, for the first time in a macroeconomic context, the golden rule of double-entry book-keeping, that the sums on both sides of the ledger must balance. Both conceptual and statistical problems had to be finessed on the way. There was no agreement about definitions of national income and national output – a matter which Keynes debated with both Rothbarth and Nicholas Kaldor.[102] Working-class saving behaviour had only recently started to be studied by the Cambridge graduate Charles Madge, co-founder with Tom Harrisson of 'Mass Observation', for whose work Keynes obtained a grant. Rothbarth marvelled at 'what one can do with such imperfect information'. Keynes was characteristically forthright: 'When statistics do not make sense I find it generally wiser to prefer sense to statistics.'[103]

In what were little more than back-of-envelope calculations, Keynes estimated that government spending in 1939–40 was set to rise by £1.8bn out of a national income of £4.85bn, measured in 1939 prices. About half, he thought, would come to the government through the 'realisation and diversion of existing capital assets'; the remainder would serve to increase output by increasing the amount and intensity of employment. The problem then was to stop the public from spending their increased incomes on consumption. The full-year yield of Simon's taxes and other fiscal devices was expected to bring in about £500m., leaving a 'gap' of between £400m. and £500m. to be filled by extra taxes or compulsory saving if inflation was to be avoided.[104]

The logic of all this was serviceable, if crude; but the bold and fluctuating 'guesstimates' about magnitudes seemed to the Treasury too flimsy a basis for fiscal policy. The Treasury was influenced not just by public opposition to Keynes's proposals, but also by workload and administrative objections to his specific Plan raised by the Inland Revenue. It agreed that Britain could not expect both more guns and more butter. But its feeling was that temporary inflation was the least bad option, especially as the war might not last or explode into full action. In the meantime, Keynes's agitation would help prepare public opinion for higher taxes if and when they became necessary.[105] There was no need for his 'ingenious devices'.[106] The one concrete result of Keynes's agitation was that the Stamp Committee authorised the start of work on compiling national income statistics.

In these circumstances the Chancellor's interest was deceptive. Keynes hoped that the budget statement would at least announce the setting up of the machinery to implement his Plan. In fact, his suggestions were searchingly examined, but the Treasury still shrank from imposing extra burdens on the working class. So, in his budget of 23 April, Sir John Simon proclaimed that 'voluntarism is on trial', imposed minor indirect tax increases, raised Excess Profits Tax to 100 per cent, projected a deficit of almost £1500m. and produced 'absurdly optimistic estimates' of voluntary lending. Specifically, he rejected compulsory savings, saying that they would 'kill' voluntary savings. He minuted, 'video meliora proboque, deteriora sequor' – 'I see the right and approve it too / Condemn the wrong, and yet the wrong pursue.'[107] Keynes told Victor Gollancz on 25 April: 'For the time being the Chancellor has committed himself to inflation, very slightly mitigated by a tax falling mainly on boots and clothing. We shall have to see how this works. I am inclined to think that shop shortages will be the first consequence.'[108] In a letter to *The Times* the same day he remarked tartly that it was only the government's failure to increase war output which was protecting it from the financial problem. 'Sir John Simon may claim that this is his fortune and not his fault. For the rest of us it is our misfortune and far from our intention . . . how little the country understands what sacrifices victory will require.'[109]

The military and political calculations underpinning this relaxed financial strategy were soon to be shattered, and with it Keynes's own semi-detached role. On 10 May the Third Reich sprang its military might on Belgium, Holland and France; the same day the Chamberlain government fell. Winston Churchill became Prime Minister and formed a coalition with the Labour and Liberal parties. On Monday evening, 13 May, Keynes saw 'Tis Pity She's a Whore at Cambridge, gave a party for Wolfit, and early the next morning had a 'heart attack' in St Edward's Passage. He 'seems very weak, bad under the eyes, blue lips, lies in pyjamas and rests with the lovely sun from the windows,' Lydia wrote in her diary. 'It is sad after 4 years of illness.' There was a further attack on Friday. Lydia wrote: 'I cried. I cannot stand the strain of illness and war.'

CHAPTER THREE

The Dragons of War

I

MAD DOGS AND ENGLISHMEN

Maynard Keynes's setback in May was a warning that his health might never fully recover. Throughout May and June he continued lecturing in Cambridge, icebags on his heart whenever he lay down. The increasingly dreadful war news so affected him that he had to have the wireless turned off. On 24 May he saw the Ogre, who prescribed the theological cure of fasting. For five days he lived on coffee, tea, raw cabbage and sour oranges. A regime of cold baths followed. Not till France capitulated on 17 June, with the British army safely evacuated from Dunkirk, did Keynes recover. It was not just the succession of blows, but the constant sense of foreboding that had been so hard to bear. He told Bruce Bliven, editor of the *New Republic*, that he had been a 'complete pessimist from the first moment of the break through at Sedan [13 May]'. However, he was not one of those who thought that the time had come to make peace with Hitler. It was a relief that Britain was now on its own, 'where, speaking for myself, I do not feel the least anxiety as to the eventual outcome'.[1]

Keynes's confidence in victory was shared by the British people. In Keynes's case, it seems to have rested on little more than the conviction that Britain was invulnerable to invasion, that Hitler would start making blunders, and that sooner or later the United States was bound to come in. He was not alone in thinking that the Nazi–Soviet Pact was a loveless union which would soon collapse. At a lunch he had with Maisky, the Soviet ambassador, on 12 June, he predicted that 'Hitler would meet his Waterloo a long way East of Berlin and that we should be there'.[2] The Grand Alliance had thus formed in Keynes's mind, long before it came about in fact. It was a flimsy enough basis on which to continue the struggle.

Hitler thought the British were mad, and in the Reichstag on 16 July appealed to their 'common sense' to make peace. The appeal fell on deaf ears. Britain's moment of total isolation from the Continent was to be its 'finest hour'. The British had never trusted the French, and the Germans were now beyond the pale. At that moment, in June 1940, history lived up to the British people's conception of themselves – and their relationship with the Continent of Europe. It was to be an enduring image.

These traumatic events stimulated Keynes to wider reflection on the character of his age. Two days after the fall of France, he wrote to Sterling P. Lamprecht of Amherst College, who had sent him a lecture on Hobbes:

> I have found it far from an irrelevant matter to have my mind brought back by you to Hobbes in these days. The events of the modern world are surely a dreadful confirmation of Hobbes's diagnosis of human nature and of what is required to preserve civilisation. From one point of view, we can regard what is now happening as the final destruction of the optimistic liberalism which Locke inaugurated. Our age forces us to return to the pessimistic view which the horrors of the seventeenth century impressed on Hobbes. I find your explanation of Hobbes as a passionate lover of his fellow men and far removed from the monster of Hobbism altogether convincing. For the first time for more than two centuries Hobbes has more message for us than Locke.[3]

II

BACK TO THE TREASURY

Parallel with his public campaign on the budget Keynes had been conducting a guerilla campaign with the Treasury on exchange control. Any 'budget of national resources' had to include not just domestic resources but those which could be attracted from abroad – through export of goods or gold, the sale of foreign securities owned by British nationals, and foreign loans. Early in 1940 Keynes had become convinced that foreign exchange vital to importing war supplies was leaking out through gaps in the exchange control system the Treasury had set up on the outbreak of war. This had aimed to channel the flow of all foreign exchange transactions involving 'hard currencies' – mainly dollars – through the Treasury's Exchange Equalisation Account. It had required all British exporters to sell their 'hard currency' receipts to designated clearing banks for sterling at a fixed exchange rate ($4.03 to the pound), the banks making available the foreign exchange needed to buy approved imports from the designated-currency countries; and it had forbidden British residents to sell securities marketable outside the United Kingdom. Free payment in sterling was allowed within all the countries of the British Empire except Canada, on the understanding that their governments imposed similar exchange restrictions to those in Britain, and sold their excess hard-currency receipts to the Bank of England in return for sterling. This was the start of the 'fortified' sterling area. 'The ring fence obstructing payments was thus to run not round the United Kingdom alone, but around the entire Sterling Area,' writes Richard Sayers. However, the Treasury continued to allow non-residents to sell their sterling securities for dollars in an unsupported currency market, believing that this freedom was essential to attract and retain foreign balances (or loans) in London.[4] This was one source of the 'dollar' drain. Another was the chaotic licensing system, which allowed precious dollars to be squandered on non-essential imports.

Keynes's intererest in the problem was triggered in February 1940 when the Treasury, having requisitioned £30m. worth of British-owned American securities – which left Keynes himself with £1m. to invest in replacement shares for himself, King's College and the Provincial Insurance Company – tried to sell large blocks of British Imperial Tobacco shares in the United States. American holders of sterling bought shares in Imperial Tobacco by selling their sterling securities for dollars, thus nullifying the intention of the policy: the dollars earned by the Treasury from the sale of American securities were those it was losing through the free exchange in London. This episode disposed Keynes to 'go on the warpath'; he would 'follow in Dr. Schacht's footsteps and block foreign balances as a whole'.[5] (For Schacht and his system, see pp. 189–90.) On 20 March Keynes told the Parliamentary Monetary Committee: 'It is a major scandal that what easily may be tens of millions of resources which would be available otherwise to finance our adverse balance of trade should be allowed to escape in this way'; the drain could be stopped with 'a stroke of the pen'.[6] Keynes primed two Conservative members of the Monetary Committee, Robert Boothby and P. C. Loftus, to ask the Chancellor in Parliament whether he proposed to stop foreign nationals taking money out of the country. Simon replied dourly that freedom to sell sterling for foreign currencies was the only way of keeping non-Empire balances in London.[7]

Keynes was not ready to put pen to paper till 10 April. It proved almost impossible to get useful statistics: the Treasury, he scornfully informed Boothby, had not the 'foggiest' idea of how much they had lost in the last six months.[8] In his fact-gathering he was helped by Thomas Balogh, a young Hungarian economist at the National Institute for Economic and Social Research, Richard Kahn, Austin Robinson and his stockbroker, Ian McPherson. He was soon able to estimate losses of £100m. since the war started through the various leakages. He sent a first draft of a memorandum to Henry Clay at the Bank of England on 29 April and discussed it with him and Henry Siepmann on 8 May. The Bank was the Treasury's agent in operating the system of exchange control, and Keynes found it much more eager than the Treasury to make exchange control effective. It was a most heartening experience, he told Clay, to 'discover for once people in executive positions who were in a drastic state of mind, seemed completely competent and equal to their job and were *not* enjoying living in a perpetual twilight, dim and incomplete'. On Keynes's letter, Montagu Norman scribbled the 'once . . . unimaginable' words: 'He must come again: his support of Exch. policy will be most important under new Cabinet. Treasy have neither time nor knowledge to help. . . .'[9] Keynes's rapprochement with the Bank was now well advanced. It was nevertheless based on a misconception. The Bank came to see itself as manager of an imperial currency bloc, fortified by permanent exchange controls; Keynes viewed these controls as a necessary wartime measure, to be discontinued once the emergency was over. The Bank would lead the opposition to his Clearing Union Plan and, even more emphatically, to the Bretton Woods Agreement and the American loan.

With the German attack on France and the Low Countries, events took control of Keynes's drafting. The Treasury blocked all sales of sterling securities owned by non-residents; Keynes refashioned his suggestions to take into account the worsening military situation and lay the basis for financial co-operation with the United States. His revised Plan, which went to the Chancellor on 24 May, and was supplemented by several further notes, consisted of an immediately enforceable policy to block further leakages of sterling; the negotiation of bilateral payments agreements between the sterling area and neutral countries; the setting up of new foreign exchange and import control authorities; and a 'spectacular' policy of pooling the foreign financial resources of the four Allied empires (Britain, France, Belgium and Holland), and exploiting their combined bargaining strength to negotiate credits with the United States.[10] The Treasury at last acted along the lines Keynes proposed: 'great minds', Sir Frederick Phillips brightly told him, 'think alike'. In the summer of 1940, it negotiated a series of payments agreements with neutral countries, whereby the proceeds of their exports to Britain could be spent only on buying British and sterling area goods, the countries concerned undertaking to keep any unused sterling on account in London. However, the 'pooling' suggestion was not proceeded with. The collapsing empires managed to get their gold reserves abroad (in France's case to Canada), but Britain never regarded them as part of its own reserve, treating them as obligations to be repaid. This was a costly mistake. 'I am now absolutely clear', Keynes wrote to Kahn on 2 June, 'that the first step to anything worth mentioning is the complete deposition of the Treasury. The more I come to understand what has been happening, the more ghastly their record seems to be.'[11]

On 11 June, after seeing Emmanuel Monick, the French financial attaché in London, he drafted a proclamation, for use by Churchill or the Chancellor, promising that all aid to France should 'freely be given for the common cause'. He took this round to the new Chancellor, Kingsley Wood, that afternoon, explaining that its two objects were to encourage the French and to create a good precedent for the terms of impending United States aid to Britain. Even at this desperate moment of the war, Keynes was determined that it should not end with a debt problem. On 13 June, Wood issued a statement proposing that France and Britain should 'shar[e] together the burden of repairing the ravages of war', which nevertheless fell short of the pledge Keynes wanted. 'Were it not for this desperate battle in France, I should get my Master to pump some oxygen into Kingsley Wood,' explained Brendan Bracken, Churchill's Parliamentary Private Secretary. Churchill was thinking in even more grandiose terms. On 16 June, he authorised the offer of an indissoluble Franco-British Union. But it was too late. France surrendered the next day. After the armistice, Monick, with whom Keynes had established a warm relationship, told him that he was returning to France. 'It is no use running away from one's country. One must do the best one can on the spot.'[12] After the liberation he became governor of the Bank of France.

Foreign exchange control was not the only matter in which Keynes found the Treasury at fault. He blamed it for failing to authorise expenditure at home.[13] Richard Kahn, at the Board of Trade, pointed out that the real problem was manpower shortages, particularly in engineering. Far too many skilled people were still being employed in producing for private consumption, so the spending departments could not spend up to their authorised limits. In a letter to *The Times* of 5 June, Keynes urged employers to get rid of 'unessential' jobs. He acted on his own principles by instructing Norman Higgins to run the Cambridge Arts Theatre with women only, releasing able-bodied men for war work.[14]

Underemployed himself, Keynes was still spending his weekends in Cambridge, keeping up a semblance of normal term-time activity. From the Prof. – Arthur Pigou, also one of Plesch's patients – he received a reminder of more parochial concerns:

The chief bad thing [about the Tripos results] we [Sraffa and Pigou were examiners] found was that a very large number of people had been stuffed like sausages with bits of your stuff in such a way that (1) they were quite incapable of applying their own intelligence to it, and (2) they perpetually dragged it in regardless of its relevance to the question. . . . My own guess . . . is that the parrot-like treatment of your stuff is due to the lectures and supervision of the beautiful Mrs [Joan] Robinson – a magpie breeding innumerable parrots. I gather that she puts in the Truth, with an enormous T, with such Prussian efficiency, that the wretched men become identical sausages without minds of their own.

Keynes replied that 'if there can be a few of reasonable merit at the top, I do not so much mind what happens at the bottom'.[15]

The universities, hitherto a sanctuary for refugees from fascism, were now required to offer up sacrificial victims to the dragons of war. In June Piero Sraffa was interned as an 'enemy alien', together with Erwin Rothbarth – who had helped Keynes on *How to Pay for the War* – and two other economists, Hans Singer and Edward Rosenbaum at Manchester University. Keynes petitioned tirelessly for their release, to the Home Secretary downwards. His own work on bringing his national income statistics up to date had been held up because of Rothbarth's internment. He called their treatment – and that of other refugees – 'the most disgraceful and humiliating thing which has happened for a long time. . . . If there are any Nazi sympathisers at large in this country look for them in the War Office and our secret service. . . .'[16] He obtained an order for Rothbarth's release in August, and the others were freed soon afterwards. But a year later he was still trying to get Kurt Jooss, who had brought his ballet to Cambridge in December 1939, out of internment in the Isle of Wight.

On 28 June Kingsley Wood offered Keynes membership of a Consultative Council to advise on special problems facing the Treasury. Explaining his appointment to a 'new super-dud Committee'[17] to his parents, Keynes wrote:

> [it] seems well suited to try out my present capacities without involving any strain. It will require no regular attendance. I should say that most of the other members [S. K. Beales, Colin F. Campbell, Sir Walter Citrine, Hubert Henderson, Sir Bertram Hornsby, George Riddle, Lord Riverdale] are people who will do no work at all and that I can make my own work just what I choose. I have, as you know, a strong prejudice against advisory as compared with executive jobs. But I think it is wise to start with something minor like this, and it will have the great advantage of giving me direct access to the Chancellor . . . with any bright ideas I may have. . . . I am guessing that it may prove compatible with our spending Friday to Tuesday each week at Tilton.[18]

A week later he wrote to his mother: 'I am pretty sure that the work of the Council itself will be exiguous. But I am hopeful that I may perhaps be able to use the position to establish helpful relations with the paramount Treasury people and persuade them to make use of me.'[19] The bright ideas soon started to flow. Three memoranda followed a brief to the Consultative Committee to investigate the issue of compensation for war damage. There was a series of notes to the Chancellor before the supplementary budget introduced on 23 July, a memorandum arguing against the closing down of the Stock Exchange, and a further note on exchange controls and payments agreements – eight meaty documents, totalling fifty-two printed pages, in one month.[20] 'Whether it is possible to produce any effect in this way remains to be seen,' he wrote to his mother. The note on the Stock Exchange emphasised a point Keynes was never tired of making: with foreign exchange controls and a closed market for new security issues, all savings were bound to reach the Treasury in one way or another, making cheap borrowing relatively easy.[21] In his first series of 'Notes to the Chancellor' Keynes conceded that the time-lag in increasing spending, external disinvestment, voluntary saving and modest inflation had succeeded in 'paying for the war' to an extent he had not anticipated, but that these expedients were now exhausted, and heavy new taxes needed to be imposed to meet mounting expenditure. After Kingsley Wood's supplementary budget of 23 July, which put a shilling on the standard rate and imposed a miscellany of indirect taxes, had been widely criticised for being inadequate, Keynes comforted him by pointing out that accruing revenues from the current taxes had been greatly underestimated by the press.[22]

For almost a year Keynes had been knocking at the Treasury's door. At last he was let in. On 12 August, without being assigned official duties, he was given 'a sort of roving commission'; put on several 'high up committees' with access to secret information – including the Exchange Control Conference – and, at the behest of Sir Richard Hopkins, given an office and a part-time secretary in Treasury Chambers in Great George Street. His office was next to that of Lord Catto, who resigned as director of the Bank of England to take up, like Keynes, an unpaid Treasury job. They soon became friends, and, as 'Catto and Doggo', worked in the greatest harmony for three years before Catto became governor of the Bank of England. Fortified by a 'drastically improved' report on his heart, Keynes immediately started putting in five hours a day. But, as he told his mother on 24 August, 'like Polly [Hill – his niece and a temporary civil servant at the Board of Trade] I am only just able to occupy my time, and have not *really* enough work to do. You know how Keyneses hate that.'

The Battle of Britain started on 10 July, with the German air force concentrating its attacks on the Channel ports, before switching to London on 18 August. 'We hear all day bombs and anti-aircraft guns, feel while it lasts a bit restless, but English air men are wonderful and protect us,' Lydia wrote to Florence Keynes from Tilton on 16 August. 'It is a strange war, we walk in the fields, and yet the war rages right in the midst of it.' They had 'Bunny' and Angelica Garnett for the weekend, with a 'skeleton' meeting of the Memoir Club at Charleston, where Virginia Woolf found Maynard 'severe, snubbing, truculent'.[23] At 46 Gordon Square, Maynard and Polly Hill slept in bunks in the basement during the weeks of nightly air-raids, 'rather like life on board ship'. Keynes was amazed at how little damage the Germans were doing in London, 'nothing that the building industry could not put right in a couple of days'. The problem was not the damage but lack of transport. 'I have not walked so much for years,' he told his mother, 'and what with perpetually running up and down the stairs to the deep Treasury basement – much more than meets with Lydia's approval – I am thoroughly exercised. . . .' Even when much heavier air-raids on London and industrial centres started in the autumn, he thought the estimates of the damage much exaggerated, especially to machine tools which were immune to blast.

> Last night [he wrote to Florence Keynes on 6 September] I went to my Other Club and was put next to Winston, so I had some two or three hours conversation with him and listening to him. I found him in absolutely perfect condition, extremely well, serene, full of normal human feelings and completely un-inflated. Perhaps this moment is the height of his power and glory, but I have never seen anyone less infected with dictatorial airs or hubris. There was not the faintest trace of the insolence which LL.G, for example, so quickly acquired. As perhaps you saw, he placed my new war damage scheme in his speech in the afternoon, so that I am now hopeful that that will really get through.

On Friday 13 September he went up to London to record a BBC broadcast to the United States and the Empire on Britain's financial position, and found 700 to 800 people sleeping in the corridors all over Broadcasting House. He delivered a dose of soothing syrup, emphasising the small scale of war damage, the success in avoiding 'the social evil of inflation', the austerity of Sir Kingsley Wood's supplementary budget, and his belief that America would pay up when the chips were down.[24] Richard Kahn disliked Keynes's concentration on preventing inflation. The sole object of policy should be to speed up manpower mobilisation, and this had been done to only a 'negligible' extent.[25] Kahn was right. Keynes's liberal prejudices made him slow to face up to the need for the direction of labour.

On 18 September he, Polly, Fred Woollard (their chauffeur), Mrs Stephens and Mary (their maid) were eating a duck from Fortnum and Mason for supper when a landmine burst opposite their house. The shutters saved them from injury, but all the windows were broken and the front door unhinged. Maynard was 'wonderfully calm'. Bloomsbury, he said, was evidently getting the Luftwaffe's near misses on nearby Euston Station and the Ministry of Information tower. Repairs on Number 46 could not start till another bomb was defused, so for three weeks Keynes commuted between Tilton and London every weekday, this time by car as trains in the south-east were disrupted, the dusky evening journey made more mysterious because all roadsigns had been removed as a precaution against the expected German invasion. He now got up at 7 a.m., left Tilton at 8 a.m., and got back by 8.30 p.m. 'I never thought I should again be able to put in such a long day. I get tired, but am extremely well,' he wrote to his mother on 27 September. The only drawback was that Lydia still subjected him to nightly icebags. But it was worth even the icebags to sleep at Tilton:

> I get a really good night, the beauty of the early country morning, great content for Lydia, who stays in the country continuously, and I have managed so far, by cutting meetings, to take a long week-end. . . . And, fortunately, this is really in the interests of my work, since I can compose the more important memoranda quietly in the country, for which I have never had the peace in the Treasury building itself. . . . I am now occupied in trying to put across the big guns a comprehensive budget of financial policy.

III

KINGSLEY WOOD'S BUDGET

Between 21 September and 6 October 1940 Keynes produced four 'Notes on the Budget' designed to change the Treasury's approach to war finance. Their main purpose was not to argue for his own specific of deferred pay but to win Treasury acceptance for his theoretical approach to making the 'budget judgement'.

At the beginning of 1940 Keynes had estimated a 'financing gap' of about £400m.–£500m., which he had proposed to plug by compulsory saving. In practice, it had been largely met by increased voluntary saving from increased output, with negligible 'budgetary inflation'. However, by the autumn of 1940 full employment had been achieved, and government spending was expected to rise further, leaving a 'prospective Budget problem . . . of the order of £400 million'. The reduction in the standard of life through inflation, Keynes repeated, would necessarily be *just as great* as through taxation. 'So it would be a mug's game *not* to solve the Budget problem.' Working-class assent for higher taxes should be sought by guaranteeing to stabilise the cost of living.

Keynes recommended that an extra £450m. of revenue should be raised by a graduated war *surcharge*, superimposed on the existing income tax and surtax. For presentational reasons he attached 'great importance' to expressing the new impost as a percentage of net – that is, post-tax – rather than gross income, since simply to slap on extra taxes (by raising the rate of income tax and reducing personal allowances) would seem to leave the poor worse off and the rich better off than would really be the case: the reverse of the psychological effect being aimed at. But only the first £50 or £100 of this surcharge on individual incomes should take the form of deferred pay, the rest being outright tax. This would deprive the rich of the incentive to sell capital assets against their prospective deferred income, while retaining the attraction of deferred pay for the poor.[26]

Keynes's 'Notes' caused a considerable stir in the higher reaches of the Treasury. On 21 October he joined Catto, Sir Horace Wilson, Sir Richard Hopkins and Sir Frederick Phillips with Kingsley Wood to discuss budget strategy. After explaining his thinking, he was put on the Treasury's Budget Committee. At this point there were a number of competing proposals for increasing revenue: Keynes's for a graduated surcharge on net incomes, coupled with deferred pay; Catto's for a flat-rate surcharge on all incomes; Stamp's proposal – first made by Hubert Henderson – for an excess earnings tax, analogous to the Excess Profits Tax; and straight-forward increases in direct taxes, championed by the Inland Revenue, which objected to the other three proposals on conceptual and adminis-trative grounds. Kingsley Wood ordered all four to be thoroughly exam-ined. Over the next three months Keynes fought vigorously for the logic, psychology and arithmetic of his approach. He felt strongly that the administrative obstructiveness of Sir Gerald Canny, head of Inland Rev-enue, would maximise discontent with the increased taxes. At one point he minuted testily: 'A tinkering with the existing income tax, however drastic, will have no popular or political appeal.'[27] According to Sayers, Keynes's 'frequent impatience with the Inland Revenue Department's memoranda perhaps reduced the effectiveness of his presentation'.[28] He produced evidence from the Madge Surveys which showed that, although most people preferred rationing to deferred pay, a large majority favoured deferred pay to higher taxes and prices.[29] He wrote to his mother, 'I spend my time trying to make them face up to the possible alternatives and choose wisely between them.' The first week in December also found Keynes hard at work preparing a War Damage Bill which provided full compensation by the state, while levying a contribution on property-owners.

Early in January 1941 the Treasury moved out of its bomb-damaged quarters in Great George Street into 'hideous' new government offices at the top of Whitehall, where, Keynes told his mother, he was 'deep into all the big questions and sit in the huddle (as we call it) with the Chancellor and the permanent secretaries'. In his summing up for the Chancellor on 10 January, Sir Horace Wilson threw out the Catto and Stamp proposals. This left Keynes's surcharge and increases in income tax as the only runners.[30] Kingsley Wood was in the mood for a bold stroke. He was 'most attracted by the War Surcharge suggested by Mr Keynes' and called for its further study 'as a matter of urgency'. He also asked for the 'considered views of the Treasury on the suggestion that as part and parcel of a severe Budget I should agree to stabilise the Cost of Living Index'.[31] Canny at the Inland Revenue once more unrolled his objections to a surcharge in a nine-page memorandum; he did, however, concede (on 15 January) that a 'withholding tax' would be feasible provided the repayable portion was 'confined to an increase in the reduced rate or to a reduction of the earned income and personal allowances'. The way was clear for a compromise. Keynes would drop the surcharge, accepting that additional revenue had to be raised through income tax; Canny would accept that part of the increased income tax would be repayable.[32] Responding to a request from Hopkins, Keynes worked out an income tax formula which would give the same yield as his surcharge. He also worked out a repayable tax formula which met the Inland Revenue's stipulation that any scheme of deferred pay must take the form of a credit against the higher taxes to be levied on lower incomes.[33]

Kingsley Wood came to his decision on 1 February. Keynes's surcharge was 'impracticable' because 'its presentation to the House of Commons and the country seems bound to sound like a rehash of the Income Tax and Surtax'; it let off the surtax payer too lightly; it made life too difficult for the Inland Revenue; and it brought in only 750,000 new taxpayers. The novelty in Keynes's proposal was the 'deferred pay' part and this could be preserved by treating as deferred income 'some (indeed the greater part) of the possible increase based on income tax arrangements'. Kingsley Wood was attracted by the thought of being able to present deferred pay as part of 'saving' rather than taxes. He also accepted Keynes's plan for subsidising the cost of living.[34]

There still remained the question of how much purchasing power needed to be withdrawn. In July 1940, Hopkins had doubted whether Keynes's 'guesstimates' of the 'inflationary gap' were 'as useful as might appear'.[35] Confidence was not increased by the fact that the numbers fluctuated from month to month. In July it was £200m. In September it was £400m. By December it was £500m., the problem of excess purchasing power having been 'significantly' increased by a growing shortage of goods.[36]

By the time the notion of an 'inflationary gap' started to appear in Treasury memoranda in the winter of 1940, much more authoritative national income estimates, commissioned by the Stamp survey earlier in the year, were becoming available. On his appointment to the Central Economic Information Service in June 1940, James Meade had evolved a 'complicated system of balancing tables', based on Colin Clark's 1937 estimates and independently of the Keynes–Rothbarth effort. At the end of August he was joined by Richard Stone, a twenty-seven-year-old Cambridge economist–statistician. There was some initial Treasury resistance to Meade's enterprise, based on jealousy and what Robbins called 'prescriptive right'.[37] By 6 January 1941 they had prepared the first draft of their paper 'National Income, Saving and Consumption', which Keynes circulated to the Chancellor and Treasury Budget Committee. On 1 February, the *Economist* alarmed the Treasury by suggesting that the national income had almost doubled since before the war, which implied that inflation was spinning out of control. 'I really think', Hopkins wrote to Keynes, 'that something must be done both about the national income and about the gap. Perhaps we should talk.' Richard Stone, on whom this account is based, believes that the furore aroused by the *Economist* article was crucial in persuading the Chancellor to base the budget judgement explicitly on the new national arithmetic, and to publish the Meade–Stone document, redrafted by Keynes, as a White Paper accompanying the budget.[38]

This is not very plausible. The figure of £250m.–£300m. as the amount which needed to be raised in new taxation had been around for some time, based on Keynes's educated guesses and estimated yields of the politically acceptable levels of taxation. The truth seems to be that the Treasury accepted the Keynes–Meade–Stone method of analysing the budgetary problem because it gave roughly the same results as its own traditional method, but seemed to provide a more accurate basis for making policy. Keynes defined the inflationary gap as 'the amount of purchasing power [which] has to be withdrawn either by taxation or primary saving . . . in order that the remaining purchasing power should be equal to the available supplies on the market at the existing level of prices'.[39] In fact there were two kinds of gap: the excess of the government's domestic spending over its revenue and the excess of aggregate demand over aggregate supply.[40] As it happened, the two methods produced roughly the same result – early in 1941 a 'gap' of £500m. The problem with what Keynes called the 'budget method' was that it did not give enough information on how to close the 'inflationary gap'. For example, how much new saving would the extra spending produce? This depended on information about the saving propensities of different classes. The national income–expenditure approach was therefore more useful for both anti-inflationary and social policy. It told policymakers how much to take in taxes and how much to leave to saving, and how to distribute the burden of sacrifice. 'What was new in 1941', Sayers concludes, 'was the universal acceptance of the Keynesian formulation and the existence of Keynesian arithmetic as one weighty element – but only one element – in the emergence of the "decisive" hunches'.[41]

In the weeks leading up to the budget Keynes was working up to thirteen hours a day, but was in such good health that the Ogre released him from his icebags. Suddenly it was all over, 'with no more work to do than occupies the mornings'. Kingsley Wood's budget of 7 April 1941 was the first budget which Keynes had helped shape and (astonishingly) the first he had heard delivered in person. Characteristically he thought the MPs sitting below him on the floor of the chamber 'a truly sub-human collection'.

In his budget speech Kingsley Wood estimated a total central government expenditure of £4,207m. for 1941–2, with £500m. being met by overseas loans and realisation of foreign assets. Of the remaining £3700m., £1636m. was expected to be covered by existing taxes, and £1600m. from existing savings of individuals and institutions and sums set aside for depreciation, leaving an 'inflationary gap' of around £500m. Wood decided to assume that personal savings would increase by £200m. to £300m. – mainly because there were fewer things to buy – and therefore that he should aim for £250m. only in new taxation. He decided to raise the standard rate of income tax to 50 per cent, with a top marginal rate of 97.5 per cent, raise the reduced rate which applied to the first £165 of taxable income, and lower earned income and personal allowances, bringing 3.25 million new taxpayers into the income tax net. The extra tax paid by an individual resulting from the reduction in personal and earned income allowances would be 'offset after the war by a credit which will be given in his favour in the Post Office Savings Bank' which would provide 'an additional fund of post-war savings for himself and his dependents'. The credits would amount to £125m. or half the increased tax yield. An analogous concession was made in respect of the 100 per cent Excess Profits Tax. The Chancellor also undertook to stabilise the price index at its existing level, about 25 to 30 per cent above pre-war, by subsidising the cost of necessaries, particularly food, warning that, if wage rates rose, the government would have to increase taxes further.

The framework set up in the 1941 budget continued through the war. Although Keynes remained on the Budget Committee, his own contributions to subsequent fiscal policy tailed off. In his 'Budget Notes' of 3 November 1941, he advocated increased taxes on non-rationed luxuries and employment taxes on non-essential work – a precursor of Nicholas Kaldor's Selective Employment Tax introduced in 1967 – as well as universal family allowances.[42] There was some increase in indirect taxes, but the introduction of universal family allowances was postponed till after the war. Keynes advised on the Pay-As-You-Earn Scheme – compulsory deductions at source assessed on current earnings – introduced in 1943 for all incomes under £600 a year.[43]* In 1944 and 1945 he devoted his efforts to trying to get rebates on the Excess Profits Tax made unconditional, and taxes on small businesses reduced. 'If we . . . want to remain a private enterprise country we must not kill the goose (which is what our tax system is doing), even though it is such a goose as not to be able to explain its sufferings in an intelligible human voice.'[44] On the borrowing side, he inspired the Tax Reserve Certificate scheme, announced in December 1941. This was a two-year Treasury bond, carrying 1 per cent interest and tax-free, designed to tap bank deposits set aside for paying tax liabilities accrued but not yet collected.[45]† More

* PAYE was considered indispensable to widening the tax base. (See R. S. Sayers, *Financial Policy 1939–1945*, 99–100.)
† Keynes got the idea from the Americans in his mission to Washington in the summer of 1941. It attracted the enthusiastic support of Sir Robert Kindersley. As Sayers writes (212), 'A

generally, he continued to argue, with limited success, that with cheap borrowing assured the government should 'cater to the needs of the market' in its maturities policy, issuing much more short-dated stock.[46]

But his main work was done. Among the many congratulations he received was one from his old Treasury boss, Reginald McKenna. Keynes wrote to him on 10 April 1941:

> The deferred pay proposals were those most associated with me in the public eye, but there are in fact two other features of the Budget where I played a part, of which the importance seems to me almost greater. First of all, the stabilisation of prices which, in combination with the limitation of the rate of interest on government loans, will give us a firm basis to work on. (Between 1916 and 1918 there was hardly any increase in real expenditure. All our hideous troubles were due to the race upwards of prices and the fact that we were always collecting revenue a year late.) The second was the method of analysing the genuine requirements of the Budget – You may imagine what an effort it was to get so unorthodox a document [as the National Income White Paper] into day light.[47]

On 14 April Keynes wrote to his mother:

> The chief officials, Sir Richard Hopkins and Sir Horace Wilson, as well as the Chancellor, have been extraordinarily good to me and open-minded ready to be persuaded; and Lord Catto has been a great help all through. Indeed we were a wonderfully united team. The opposition which has given me most trouble and worn out my nerves was mainly from Hubert Henderson.

Keynes's budget triumph coincided with a dreadful personal blow. At the Keyneses' traditional Christmas tea with the Woolfs, Virginia had found Maynard pugnacious, puritanical and disapproving, melting a little only when she kissed him.[48] It was the last time they saw each other. On 28 March 1941, Virginia Woolf drowned herself in the River Ouse. Maynard, who had never felt despair, and could not understand it, reported the news to his mother in his usual factual style:

> We have been much upset this week-end by the sad fate of our dear friend Virginia Woolf. Her old troubles came back on her, and she drowned herself last Friday. She had seemed so very well and normal last time we saw her. We rang up on Saturday to ask her over to tea and got this answer. It is nearly 30 years now since she poisoned herself in Brunswick Square and Geoffrey raced to Barts for a

---

combined Keynes–Kindersley front on a matter of Government borrowing was as formidable as it was unusual.'

stomach pump and brought her round. I thought she had safely
steered through all that as the result of the devoted care of . . .
Leonard. The two of them were our dearest friends.

IV

KEYNES'S INFLUENCE

Kingsley Wood's budget was far from being a copy of *How to Pay for the
War*. In his pamphlet, Keynes had recommended that about 15 per cent
of domestic government spending be financed by compulsory saving; in
the upshot it was under 3 per cent. This reflects both the delay in
implementing his scheme – with the 'gap' being filled by higher 'straight'
taxes, shortages, rationing and inflation, all of which *How to Pay for the
War* was designed to obviate – and the agitation to minimise the amount
of repayable taxes, whether from fear of post-war inflation or from fear
that the rich would be enabled to 'live off capital'.

The social contract struck in Kingsley Wood's budget was different
from the one Keynes had sought. In the original *Times* articles the reward
for increased effort was simply to be postponed. There was no explicit
attention to the wages problem. In the revised and expanded pamphlet,
How to Pay for the War, wage moderation was to be secured by family
allowances and an 'iron ration' of subsidised necessities. With deferred
pay marginalised, and family allowances postponed, the 1941 budget
sought to win consent for taxing working-class earnings by punitive
taxation of the wealthy (including a 100 per cent Excess Profits Tax),
price fixing and universal rationing. The Chancellor bought Keynes's
technique, but the philosophy of the budget was socialist rather than
Keynesian.

Total domestic government spending from 1940 to 1945 came to
£19.4bn. Had 15 rather than 3 per cent of this spending been covered by
deferred pay, the total of 'blocked balances' by the end of the war would
have been nearer £3bn. than £600m. What would the consequences have
been? Social policy might have taken a different turn: Beveridge, for
example, could scarcely have avoided the possibilities opened up by such
a huge increase and wide distribution of personal savings for the post-war
financing of social insurance. On the other hand, premature adoption of
the Keynes Plan might well have made government policy too deflationary
in the first period of war. What would have happened had £400m.–£500m.
of private demand, almost 10 per cent of GNP, been withdrawn from the
economy early in 1940, with unemployment still at 9 per cent? Would it
have hastened the absorption of civilian manpower into the war industries? Or would it simply have led to higher unemployment, given the
inescapable time-lags in converting to war production? Perhaps it was

good for Keynes's reputation that the experiment was not made when he proposed it.

It is now generally agreed that the Treasury's acceptance of Keynes's logic to deal with inflation did not imply acceptance of that logic to deal with unemployment. The idea of using the budget to 'balance the accounts' of the nation did not extend to *augmenting* purchasing power when an 'output gap' developed. For the inflation problem, the orthodox and Keynesian logics coincided: for the unemployment problem, they diverged. Professor Peden rightly says that 'The 1941 "revolution in public finance" and the "Keynesian revolution" in employment policy . . . deserve to be treated as separate issues.'[49]

Keynes's influence on the domestic war finance was fivefold. First, his theoretically based advocacy emboldened the Treasury and the Bank to go for cheap money. The government's maximum borrowing rate was 3 per cent, and most of its war debt was borrowed at cheaper cost than this. Even though inflation was controlled, it got most of its money at negative real interest rates.

Secondly, Keynes turned the budget into an effective weapon against inflation, by clarifying what was meant by inflationary finance. He never tired of pointing out that government spending would automatically be financed 'to the nearest ½d'. The only question was about the means by which excess private purchasing power was liquidated. One could still have what Keynes called 'budgetary inflation', even when the government was 'balancing its books', if the extra taxes and loans were being pulled in by rising money incomes. However, the 'revolution in public finance' of which Keynes talked was only partial. As we have seen it was the *coincidence* between the 'budget method' and the 'purchasing power' method for calculating the inflationary gap which produced Kingsley Wood's 'budget judgement' of 1941. This double approach governed all the subsequent war budgets. As a result, the goverment covered 54 per cent of its spending by taxation in the six years 1940–5, as opposed to 32 per cent only in the four years 1915–18, and the price level in 1945 was only 30 per cent higher than in 1939, as compared to a doubling of prices in the 1914–18 war, virtually the whole of the rise having occurred before the 1941 budget.*

Thirdly, the new budgetary arithmetic brought out clearly the fact that that part of total government expenditure being financed from abroad was irrelevant to the domestic fiscal balance. From 1941 wartime demand

---

* As Professor Peden points out, the policy of price stabilisation was founded on a cost-of-living index based on Edwardian working-class patterns of spending. The more complete consumer price index rose by 17 per cent between 1941 and 1945, giving a total inflation over the war of about 50 per cent. This was still half of what it had been in the First World War.

management was pursued without reference to the balance of payments. But to the extent that the external deficit was being financed by *ad hoc* methods, the budgetary problem was not being solved, only postponed till after the war.

Fourthly, Keynes's particular contribution to the 1941 budget was to drive home the connection between taxes and subsidies. R. S. Sayers credits him with having established in Kingsley Wood's mind the 'vital link' between the two. 'Failure to stabilise the cost of living would render the taxation proposals inadequate, and failure to absorb extra purchasing power would make it difficult to hold the cost of living down.'[50] The problem of cost-push inflation at full employment was identified clearly for the first time. With Keynes's proposal for 'confiscating' pay ruled out, and wage controls impracticable, the government was inevitably driven back to subsidies, price controls and rationing. The subsequent Achilles' heel of full employment policy in a free society had thus emerged by 1940, though it was finessed in the special circumstances of war.

Finally, Keynes put the social function of the budget centre stage. The purpose of the wartime budget was not to divert resources to the government – that would happen anyway – but to do so with justice and efficiency. 'The importance of a war Budget', Keynes wrote, 'is . . . *social*: to prevent the social evils of inflation now and later; to do this in a way which satisfies the popular sense of social justice; whilst maintaining adequate incentives to work and economy.'[51] That a major function of the budget was to achieve social objectives was accepted till the advent of Thatcherism in the 1980s, but fiscal policy was only intermittently inspired by Keynes's own social philosophy.

It is the fate of all philosophies of the Middle Way to be attacked by both left and right, and so it was with the Keynes Plan. Some of these attacks were revived in the 1990s. It is alleged that Keynes was too protective of the interests of capital, a criticism which echoes that of Emile Burns in 1939.[52] It is true that he greatly underestimated the buoyancy of the existing tax base. Far from the limits of taxation having been reached in late 1939, as he alleged, the budgets of April and July 1940 and April 1941 imposed large tax increases on the better-off. However, it is not evident that top marginal tax rates of 97.5 per cent and an Excess Profits Tax of 100 per cent – both of which he opposed – were the best way to preserve incentives and promote efficiency even in war. Keynes may also have got his working-class 'psychologicals' wrong. High taxes on the rich and universal rationing were more popular than deferred pay and family allowances. Those who believe there is a place for liberty even in war will praise, not blame, Keynes for resisting the common sentiment.

Left-wing Keynesianism was represented by the Kalecki Plan, published in the *Oxford Bulletin of Statistics* on 26 April 1941. Michal Kalecki, a Polish émigré, attacked the view that the inflationary gap could or should be closed by financial measures. He concluded that 'the only fair and efficient way to stop the inflationary tendencies is some type of comprehensive rationing'.[53] This showed that the Keynesian logic could be used for regimentation by those who did not share Keynes's political values. The Kalecki Plan was supported by Thomas Balogh at Balliol College. The American banker Russell Leffingwell called it 'a communist system to put everyone on the bread line, not merely for bread but for clothes and most everything'. On the other hand, Leffingwell was just as dismissive of the Keynes Plan for compulsory saving: 'It is wrong for a necessitous Treasury burdened with financing the war to use the tax power to sell bonds instead of tax receipts. It would aggravate the danger of post-war inflation.'[54] Keynes himself remained wholly opposed to comprehensive rationing, for Leffingwell's reasons.[55]

An opposite criticism of the Keynesian approach was that it jeopardised the long-run future of British capitalism. This case has been made by two American economists, Thomas Cooley and Lee Ohanian. Essentially they allege two things: that high British wartime taxes, continued into peace, lowered investment after the war, reducing Britain's growth rate relative to that of the United States, whose wartime taxes were much lower; and that Keynes was the author and inspirer of this punitive tax philosophy.[56] The first charge may or may not be true, though the two economists overlook the extent to which Britain was more heavily mobilised for war than the United States was; the second is patently false. It ignores the fact that the Keynes Plan called for a *temporary* war surcharge on top of tax rates only modestly raised from their pre-war levels. It was not his doing that the tax burden was more than doubled, with punitive top marginal rates persisting into the 1980s. Compulsory savings can also be seen as a type of debt finance. In effect government would borrow the savings of the people for war purposes and return them at staggered intervals after the war. In both respects, the Keynes Plan was much more like the scheme Cooley and Ohanian think should have been adopted than like the Kingsley Wood budget of 1941.

The general proposition that Britain was seriously weakened by the war is incontestable. This was the price of survival. Britain's leaders, from Churchill downwards, mortgaged their country's economic future with open eyes, Keynes playing his part. Any critique of his wartime legacy needs to start here. And the critics have to face honestly the question: was there a better choice? Should Britain have tried to negotiate a peace with Nazi Germany? Should it have fought a different, less expensive, kind of war? Could it have survived if it had? They set themselves too easy a task if they point out the bad consequences of the policies actually pursued and ignore the opportunity costs of the alternatives. These considerations come dramatically to the fore when the subject switches to external finance, and Keynes's part in Anglo-American relations.

CHAPTER FOUR

Envoy Extraordinary

I

ENGAGING THE UNITED STATES

The British and French governments went to war with Germany in the belief that the Roosevelt administration would not risk the defeat of its fellow democracies. Not that they thought that the risk was great. The Western Front was regarded as invulnerable to German attack; even more important to the financial mind, the Germans lacked the 'credits' for a long fight. This being so, Britain and France had only to sit still, tighten their blockade, drop subversive leaflets and wait for the Germans themselves to overthrow Hitler. Alternatively, the war itself might peter out. In any case the United States was not central to their early calculations.

This was not Keynes's view. In the 1930s he had regarded the United States as Britain's natural, and necessary, ally in the defence of freedom against the 'brigand' powers. In his 'Notes on the War for the President', written in November 1939, but never sent (see p. 51 above), he urged the United States to join Britain in a religious crusade against fascism, initially by advancing credits to the Allied governments, to be repayable to a fund to reconstruct Europe after the war and save it from communism – 'the indemnity . . . paid by the victor to the vanquished'. But even Keynes did not think a British defeat was possible: he was thinking about the post-war world.

Like most liberal Englishmen, Keynes overestimated support for Britain in the United States. British expectations of assistance concentrated on the President, ignored Congress and assumed that the (largely Republican) east-coast WASP elite represented US public opinion.

The British tendency to discount Congress as an independent actor in American politics persisted throughout the war. This was because both Houses had Democratic majorities, though severely shrunken by the mid-term elections of 1938. Drawing an analogy with their own system, British policymakers believed that a government with a majority in Parliament could do more or less what it wanted. Keynes never stopped believing that with proper 'leadership' the President could extend to Britain all the help it needed. The British, that is, did not take the separation of powers seriously.

The British were not good at reading the motives and intentions of the President. This is not surprising, since few Americans were any more successful at penetrating his apparently fathomless ambiguities. Keynes's comments on Roosevelt were generally laudatory, and, when not laudatory, at least optimistic. He was right not to doubt Roosevelt's democratic sympathies, his loathing of fascism. But he seriously overestimated the extent to which Roosevelt – and the New Dealers as a whole – saw Britain as a satisfactory defender of these values. To the American left, Britain was the arch-imperialist power. The United States had won its independence fighting Britain's armies. Thomas Gage, an ancestor of Viscount Gage, Keynes's landlord at Tilton, had commanded British troops, with poor generalship, in the first major engagement of the American War of Independence – the Battle of Bunker Hill on 17 June 1775. When the European war broke out, Britain still held India and much of the Middle East and Africa by force. It was also the centre of the bankers' capitalism against which the New Deal was directed. Roosevelt himself hated the British Empire, mistrusted England's aristocracy, and suspected the Foreign Office of pro-fascist tendencies. He also thought the British were very foxy, and was determined to prevent the United States becoming a 'tail to the British kite' – that is, being trapped into defending purely British interests. His famed relationship with Churchill was also less cordial than it later became. FDR's first question about Churchill to Wendell Wilkie, when the latter returned from a visit to England in February 1941, was: 'Is he a drunk?'[1] There was much talk in New Deal circles of 'a fundamental moral equivalency between Germany's war of conquest and England's efforts to protect her empire'.[2] Keynes was enraged by the anti-imperialist diatribes of his *New Republic* editor, Bruce Bliven, and stopped writing for the journal. Anti-British sentiment was supported by the large numbers of Irish and Italian immigrants who dominated the big-city Democratic machines.

Republicans were not so much anti-British as anti-Roosevelt. They wanted America to keep out of the war, because war spelt government interventionism and extension of the hated New Deal. One Republican Congressman was to tell the British ambassador that Roosevelt was more dangerous than Hitler, Mussolini or Stalin.[3] But Anglophobia was also rife in an important segment of the Republican electorate made up of the German-descended communities of the Mid-West.

Economic rivalry in the 1920s and 1930s had soured relations between the two countries. By the mid-1930s the Americans had started to look to the expansion of trade to solve the unemployment problem left over from the Great Depression. Standing in the way was Britain's imperial preference system, erected in 1932, which discriminated against American goods. No real mitigation of this economic rivalry had been achieved by the time war broke out.

After the fall of France, isolationists had a new argument: Anglopessi-mism. Joseph Kennedy, Roosevelt's ambassador in London, returned to America in the summer of 1940 saying that Britain was finished. America should not bind itself to a 'loser'. Anne Morrow, wife of the aviator Charles Lindbergh, published a bestselling book called *The Wave of the Future*. Britain was not part of it. This was the setting for the isolationist, largely conservative 'America First' movement formed in September 1940.

Throughout 1940, and well into 1941, American public opinion was strongly against American intervention in the European war. However, sympathy for 'plucky' Britain in its stand against the Nazi bully never extended to generalised support for Britain's world position. This is the clue to Anglo-American relations, economic as well as political, both in the pre-war period and once the Grand Alliance had been forged.

American isolationism was entrenched in legislation. Britain's default on its American war debt in 1933 led to the passage of the Debt Default Act of 1934, sponsored by the arch-isolationist Hiram Johnson, forbidding private loans to any country 'delinquent in its war obligations'. The investigations of the Nye Committee led to a series of Neutrality Acts between 1935 and 1937 forbidding sales of arms, war materials and loans to belligerents.

The Allied cause received an early and, as it turned out, crucial boost. The 'cash and carry' legislation of November 1939, devised by Bernard Baruch, amended the Neutrality Acts by allowing belligerents to buy arms which they could pay for and carry in their own ships. This favoured Britain, which had both reserves and ships. At the same time, though, Cordell Hull, the American Secretary of State, protested against British restrictions on imports of American tobacco and motor cars, designed to conserve foreign exchange.[4] This, together with the British export drive in Latin America, set the two countries on a commercial collision course. Walter Lippmann hoped 'cash and carry' would promote a negotiated peace, by preventing the Allies from fighting an unlimited war. To Keynes it seemed as if the United States were placing the democracies and dictatorships on the same footing. He wrote to Lippmann on 6 January 1940, 'There is a lot to be said for neutrality but moral beauty, no.'[5] 'Cash and carry' furnished the sole legal basis for British war imports from the United States in the first year and a half of the war. As Britain's exporting capacity declined, it was forced to cover its imports of food, raw materials and war materials from the United States by shipping gold and selling American securities. This could continue only as long as there remained gold to ship, securities to sell – and, of course, ships to carry the gold and goods. At the end of February 1940, Sir Frederick Phillips of the British Treasury estimated that Britain's gold and dollar reserves, which stood at £545m. in December 1939, were running down at a rate of £200m. a year.

The assumptions underlying US 'benevolent neutrality' were shattered by Hitler's rapid conquest of Continental Western Europe in the spring of 1940. For the first time a British defeat, and consequent German control of the Atlantic, seemed possible. Britain's supply problem was compounded by the loss of its army's equipment at Dunkirk. Moreover, as war mobilisation accelerated, Britain's exporting capacity declined even further. In June 1940, the British government dropped its decision, taken at the outbreak of the war, to husband its gold and dollar reserves for a three-year war: its Purchasing Mission, headed by a brilliant Scottish-Canadian businessman, Arthur Purvis, started ordering in the United States and Canada as much war material as the Chiefs of Staff needed, leaving future financial problems, as Churchill put it, 'on the lap of the Eternal Gods'. Keynes himself never seems to have doubted that America would continue supplying Britain, even if Britain could no longer pay. Writing to his friend Felix Frankfurter on 4 June 1940, he hoped that the time would soon be ripe for 'something decisively encouraging and hopeful on your part'.[6]

This hope was only partly fulfilled. Sir Frederick Phillips was summoned to Washington in July to discuss Britain's financial needs. He projected a net balance of payments deficit of $1.6bn (£400m.) for the year ending June 1941, against which Britain held reserves of $1.5bn (£375m.). The drain would have been even larger but for the overdraft Britain was running up with Canada for Canadian purchases in the United States on Britain's behalf. But these were draining Canada of its reserves as well. 'How about selling some of those securities you have in Argentina?' Roosevelt asked Phillips.[7] Secretary of the Treasury Henry Morgenthau also advised him to arrange for the sale of large British-owned American companies. Fixed assets were to be included in the balance sheet. The Americans expected the British to pay to the utmost out of their – and the Empire's – capacity. Nor was there any promise of help after that. Warren Kimball's view is that in pressuring Britain to sell its foreign assets Washington was not deliberately trying to take advantage of Britain's woes, but that it needed to convince domestic opinion that Britain was not trying to drag the USA into the war by means of American loans. Also, Phillips failed to convey any sense of urgency.[8]

The drain on British reserves was compounded by the lack of an American defence industry. Keynes later claimed that before Lend–Lease Britain spent about $2bn on capital construction in the United States. A particularly heavy burden was the $880m. Britain paid for constructing aircraft factories in July 1940. These orders, of course, required payments well in advance of delivery of the goods. British-owned factories were later 'sold' to the Americans without payment. Keynes certainly regarded these capital expenditures in the United States as moral debts to Britain. They were the basis of his request for a 'grant' not a loan in 1945. As American arms production grew, so did the debate about whether the USA should concentrate on hemispheric defence or ship arms to Britain. In the month following Dunkirk, 95 per cent of Americans expected the British to lose the war. This made it seem foolhardy to sell the British scarce weapons: a position most clearly articulated by Charles Lindbergh, whose still boyishly handsome presence now adorned the platforms of the 'America First' movement. A further complication was that it was Presidential election year. Both Roosevelt and his Republican opponent Wendell Wilkie vied in their promises to keep 'our boys' out of the fighting. At Buffalo, on 2 November 1940, Roosevelt gave this pledge: 'Your President says this country is not going to war.'

Alerted by the British ambassador, Philip Lothian, to the danger of a British defeat and surrender of the Royal Navy, Roosevelt decided to act. In June 1940, he authorised the sale of a large stock of old rifles to Britain at knock-down prices. (He got round the neutrality legislation forbidding government-to-government weapons sales by selling the rifles to the US Steel Corporation, which resold them the same day to the Anglo-French Purchasing Commission.) In September, he agreed the transfer to Britain of fifty ancient destroyers, in return for leasing naval bases to the United States in Newfoundland and the Caribbean, and British promises to transfer the Royal Navy to the United States in the event of a successful German invasion. By these means Roosevelt moved his country from neutrality to non-belligerence. These measures were defensive, and were presented as such. The British hoped they would lead to America's entry into the war on their side – the sooner the better.

Britain was well served by its ambassador, Philip Kerr, Marquess of Lothian. As a leading supporter of appeasement in the 1930s – confusing German grievances with Hitler's motives – he was not obviously destined for success in his new post. But Lothian had a chameleon-like ability to adapt himself to changed circumstances. He also had a deep underlying belief in Anglo-American partnership as the basis of future world order. As a long-serving secretary of the Rhodes Trust he was very much at home in the United States. From the moment he arrived in 1939, he argued from every platform available to him that American and British security were indivisible. The British Navy had underwritten the Monroe Doctrine in the nineteenth century, and still stood guard over the Atlantic. To this national security perspective he added the idealistic patina of an Anglo-American partnership in the cause of freedom – a reading of history which befitted a product of Alfred Milner's 'kindergarten', but neatly sidestepped the problem of Britain's dependent Empire.* Lothian's lofty

---

* Milner's kindergarten is the name given to a formidably clever group of young Oxford graduates assembled by Lord Milner, high commissioner of the Cape Colony, which conjured up the Union of South Africa in 1909 from the ruins of the Boer War. In 1910 they started

sentiments, which he combined with an ascetic presence, informal manners which dispelled fear of the aristocratic embrace, and a hard-headed
appeal to America's self-interest, played well to American audiences and
the press. As military disasters rained down in 1940, he expounded one
simple idea: the best way to keep America out of the war was to keep
Britain in it. The message sank in. As Henry Morgenthau put it on 23 July
1940, 'the longer we keep them going, that much longer we stay out of
this war'.[9] This was a decision for prioritising arms shipments to Britain; it
represented no softening of the view that the British must pay for them.
Morgenthau was the key link between the US administration and the
British Purchasing Mission. If the British mobilised their foreign assets, he
would do his best to ensure a continuing flow of war supplies.

By November 1940 the British cause in America had been strengthened
by the defeat of the Luftwaffe in the Battle of Britain, so removing the
immmediate threat of invasion, and by Roosevelt's re-election as President
(on 4 November) for an unprecedented third term. However, Britain's
financial position had deteriorated. It had taken over French orders, but
not French gold reserves shipped to Ottawa, fearing to inflame Quebec
separatism already outraged by the Royal Navy's sinking of the French
fleet at Mers-el-Kebir in July. It needed to order more supplies than ever
before, as well as more ships to carry them in, because Germany's
submarines were sinking so many. And American exporters were insisting
on larger advance payments, which reflected 'doubts about [Britain's]
ability to pay all the bills she was running up'.[10] Britain lost $668m.
(£167m.) in the third quarter of 1940. At this rate it would be virtually
out of gold and dollars by the end of the year.

On 13 October, Lothian warned Morgenthau that Britain's reserves
were nearing exhaustion. This produced another summons to Phillips to
come to Washington as soon as the Presidential election was over. On 23
November, alighting from his plane at La Guardia after a trip to London,
Lothian told the waiting reporters: 'Well, boys, Britain's broke; it's your
money we want.' The Treasury in London was furious. Lothian explained
that it was necessary once and for all to disabuse Washington of the view
that Britain had 'vast resources available which we have not yet disclosed'.
He was hopeful that 'substantial financial assistance' would be forthcoming, but warned that it might take up to six months to legislate, that
Americans expected Britain to show that it had exhausted its available
resources, including its direct investments in the United States and its

the magazine *The Round Table*, edited by Kerr, which aimed to promote the 'organic' unity
of the British Empire by setting up an imperial government for purposes of defence and
foreign policy, on which the self-governing Dominions would be represented. This idea came
to be transmuted, through organisations such as the Rhodes Trust, into the looser concept
of a union of English-speaking peoples. Keynes's friend Robert Brand was one of the leading
members of the kindergarten.

investments in Latin America, and that the administration would raise the question of acquiring a share in Britain's tin and rubber investments in Malaya – propositions which, not surprisingly, the British government found disquieting.[11]

Lothian's bombshell 'forced the Roosevelt Administration publicly to face up to the question of the British dollar shortage'.[12] The drain had slowed down in the fourth quarter, largely owing to delays in delivery, but in December the reserves stood at just over £100m. or $400m. against payments owed of $1bn. If the haemorrhage continued, Britain would have to default. The US authorities were alive to Britain's problem, but did not know how to address it, technically or politically, and anyway believed it was not as urgent as the British claimed. They were still mesmerised by the 'opulence' of the British Empire. Above all, they had not made up their mind on what Lothian called 'the fundamental question . . . whether [US] policy is to . . . help Britain within the limits of the Neutrality Act but acquiesce in [its] defeat if these half measures do not suffice, or to adopt the policy in America's own interests that it is going to see Great Britain is not defeated whatever it may cost . . .'.[13]

Although Phillips and David Waley controlled Overseas Finance at the Treasury, Keynes from the first interpreted his Treasury role as a licence to encamp in his First World War bailiwick. So he helped draw up the Treasury brief for Phillips's forthcoming American trip. His memorandum, dated 27 October, proposed that the US Treasury should take over the financing of all approved British military purchases in the United States from 1 January 1941. (If legislative sanction had not been secured by that date, any gold spent after 1 January should be refunded.) That way, the American government and people would know 'exactly what they were paying for'. Britain, and more generally the sterling area, could pay its way with the rest of the world, with the help of a gradual mobilisation of Britain's overseas assets. Keynes's strategy of partial self-reliance depended crucially on Britain getting help from the USA *before* its 'cupboard was stripped bare'. He pointed out that not only would Britain run out of ready cash before its assets could be sold, but that the 'stripping' policy would have 'exceedingly inconvenient' consequence for the United States of saddling it with Britain's overseas liabilities. He argued against selling off Britain's direct investments in the United States. These were part of Britain's exporting capacity. If they were lost to Britain, Britain would be forced to restrict imports from the United States after the war. Another crucial point in his memorandum was that American assistance should be by way of grant, not loan. There must be no repetition of the debt problem which so soured relations between the two countries between the wars. The British would not for a second time 'accept the dishonour and the reproaches of default whilst allowing to the US all the consequent conveniences to their trade. This time if we are asked to pay, we shall pay' – by means of 'revolutionary changes in the commercial relations' between the two countries. What Keynes was implying was that the British would, if forced to do so, close all the markets they controlled to American goods after the war.[14]

Keynes's memorandum made the questionable assumption that Britain and America were already allies, despite the inconvenient fact that America was not actually at war. His aim was to ensure that the terms under which aid was given should not reduce Britain to satellite status during the war, or destroy its independence after it. In a typical flash of anger he minuted: 'America must not be allowed to pick out the eyes of the British Empire.'

There was no disagreement in the Treasury with these propositions, though no one expressed them as vehemently as did Keynes. On Sir Frederick Phillips fell the daunting task of persuading the Americans of their validity. Phillips went to Washington hoping to obtain a grant (not loan) from the US government to cover all payments due on Purchasing Commission contracts, both outstanding and future, from 1 January 1941. This would allow Britain to restore its minimum required reserve of $600m. from the Empire's gold and dollar surpluses, while taking care of the rest of its deficits, including the adverse balance with Canada. The question of the disposal of Britain's North American assets was left open.[15]

Phillips's most urgent task was to convince Roosevelt's Treasury Secretary, Henry Morgenthau. London had not got Morgenthau properly into focus. He was known as a loyal executant of Roosevelt's policies, and was suspected of being rather anti-British. Keynes had never met him. In fact, he was passionately anti-Nazi. But he mistrusted Britain's motives, and harboured long-term plans for American financial hegemony.

He came from a German Jewish background. His dominating father had prospered in real estate and politics, being rewarded by Woodrow Wilson with an ambassadorship to Turkey. New and old money met in 1913 when Henry Morgenthau Jr bought a thousand-acre estate in Dutchess County, in New York, close to Hyde Park, the Hudson Valley family property of Franklin Roosevelt. He owed his position in Washington to his personal friendship with Roosevelt, who appointed him his Treasury Secretary in 1934. Herbert Feis, a State Department official and close Morgenthau-watcher, writes of him: 'He was a person of basic good will and kindly intentions, but his mind was slow, his self-knowledge little, and his sense of humour adolescent. He was at once shrewd, gullible and suspicious. Two purposes were to dominate his thought and actions: a wish to serve and please his neighbour, friend and boss, Roosevelt; and a determination to down the Nazis.'[16] Morgenthau served Roosevelt, not just by being impeccably loyal, but by being an excellent administrator, fiercely loyal to his staff. His frail constitution led him to impose a strict routine at the Treasury, of which the group meetings with top staffers almost every working morning were a notable feature.[17] The second aim gives an important clue to his dealings with the British: he was not so much pro-British as Germanophobic. With America neutral, Britain was the reed that had to be supported, *faute de mieux*, despite the inaptness of imperial Britain as a champion of freedom. Morgenthau also shared the New Deal suspicion of international finance. His aim was to shift financial power from New York and London to Washington. The dollar would become the instrument of a global 'New Deal'. At the same time, his lack of financial expertise made him dependent on a small group of trusted technicians. Gradually, Feis writes, Morgenthau became 'more and more influenced by the viciously assertive staff assembed around him, led by Harry White. They used him, and he used them. . . .'[18] He would support Britain in the war against Germany, but not to preserve Britain's world position. The United States, not Britain, would be the leader of the post-war free world, the dollar would replace the pound as the world's leading currency. He would do all he could to help Britain, but as a satellite, not as an ally.

In 1940 he started putting pressure on the British to sell off their big American companies – Shell Oil, Lever Brothers and Brown & Williamson Tobacco. The Secretary, writes his biographer John Morton Blum, 'recognised that the loss of [Britain's overseas] investments would cripple the British economy after the war, but he maintained that England could not afford to worry about this in 1940'.[19] For the first time in its history, Britain found itself a suppliant for means-tested benefits, with Morgenthau running the benefit office. Little wonder he was cast as the villain in Keynes's, and London's, eyes.

II

LEND–LEASE

'Suave, balding Sir Frederick Phillips,' as *Time* magazine called him, finally reached Washington early in December. He found his talks with Morgenthau 'heavy going'. The Secretary of the Treasury insisted that the British should turn their pockets 'inside out' and give him full details of their assets in the United States and Latin America, and what they were willing to take for them. But rescue was to hand. On 8 December, prompted by Lothian, Churchill had dispatched a desperate but dignified letter to Roosevelt which the President received while recuperating from the election on board the cruiser *Tuscaloosa* in the Caribbean. Churchill told Roosevelt that Britain was running out of the money to pay for the supplies of ships, aircraft, munitions and machine tools it needed from the United States to win the Battle of the Atlantic, carry the air war to the

Continent, and maintain a military presence in the Far East. Cleverly phrased to suggest that Britain was America's forward line of defence against the Axis offensive in both the Atlantic and Pacific, Churchill's letter, 'one of the most important I ever wrote', was read and re-read by 'our great friend' as he sat alone in his deck chair.[20] After two days' brooding, Roosevelt came to his decision. Britain was to be kept in the war at any price. Lawyers found the means.

At a press conference in Washington on 17 December the President announced a programme of 'lend–lease', in the homely image of lending a neighbour a hose to put out a fire. The best security for the United States, Roosevelt said, was the defence of Britain; British orders were galvanising the American defence industry. The United States would be willing to lend or lease Britain equipment for 'fire-fighting' which would be returned after the war. This method would get rid of 'the foolish, silly old dollar sign'. In a fireside radio chat on 29 December, the night German bombers destroyed much of the City of London, Roosevelt called America 'the arsenal of democracy'.

Roosevelt followed up his words with deeds. He sent a Bill, symbolically entitled HR [House of Representatives] 1776, to Congress on 11 January 1941, authorising the President to make available to belligerents any materials necessary, in the President's judgement, 'for the defence of the United States', subject to an undisclosed non-cash 'benefit'. Britain could go on buying what it could pay for in cash and carry in its ships, and nothing more. But the American War Departments would ask for extra appropriations for supplies to 'lend' or 'lease' to the British. They would remain American property; their return after the fire was put out was, of course, purely fictional. So strong was anti-British sentiment, in the opinion of Sir Frederick Phillips, that only the President's 'brilliant handling' of the situation had made aid practical politics.[21]

Lend–Lease was the most adventurous political coup of Roosevelt's presidency. It was the one occasion in the war when he led decisively from the front on Britain's behalf. Lend–Lease not only bypassed the Neutrality and Johnson Acts, isolating the isolationists; it broke with the whole American tradition of making loans on business terms. It set the precedent for post-war Marshall Aid. Devastated by the stickiness of the American loan negotiations in Washington in 1945 after Roosevelt's death, Keynes pined for the 'gay, generous and brilliant spirit' which had conjured up this solution to Britain's problems in the hour of its need. That this British view of Roosevelt survived unscathed through all the subsequent torment of Anglo-American financial dealings testifies to the supreme psychological importance of that moment.

Why did Roosevelt throw Britain this lifeline? Was it to keep America out of the war, as he said? Or to get America into it, as the isolationists claimed? Roosevelt remains an enigma. Warren Kimball calls him 'The

Juggler'. A leading New Deal official, Rexford Tugwell, wrote a book called *In Search of Roosevelt*. He never found him. Roosevelt's own Secretary of War, Henry Stimson, recalled that a conversation with Roosevelt was 'very much like chasing a vagrant beam of sunshine around a vacant room'.[22] The likeliest explanation is that Roosevelt had come to believe that at some point the dictators had to be faced and defeated, and that Britain had to be kept going till American military preparations and public opinion were ready to undertake the job. He must also have known that Lend–Lease would make war with Germany more likely, if only because America was bound to protect its 'property', being conveyed across the Atlantic in American merchant ships, from being sunk by German U-boats. Roosevelt was thus playing it both ways: Lend–Lease would keep Britain in the war and provoke Nazi Germany into attacking American ships in the Atlantic – just like in 1917, when Roosevelt had been Assistant Secretary of the Navy.* That Lend–Lease might also be used to secure the United States post-war commercial advantages was certainly not absent from the mind of the President and his advisers. Getting away from the 'dollar sign' did not imply the absence of a *quid pro quo*. And the fact that Britain would be given a discretionary grant of supplies rather than being loaned a definite sum of money with which to buy them placed the control of the flow firmly in the hands of the administration and Congress.

Getting Churchill to write as he did to Roosevelt was Lothian's last public service. Nancy Astor had converted him to Christian Science, which proscribed the use of doctors; and he died on 12 December from a liver complaint which orthodox medicine could have treated. In his last speech, read for him on the day before his death, he said, 'If you back us, you won't be backing a quitter.' On 7 January 1941 Roosevelt sent Harry Hopkins to London as his envoy, to find out Britain's needs first-hand. Though still nominally a Cabinet officer, Hopkins was Roosevelt's *familiar*, the main channel through which his intimations were conveyed to other members of the administration. A large part of his stomach had been removed at the Mayo Clinic in 1937; from 1940 to 1943 he conducted most of his business from his bedroom in the White House, 'a combination of Chief of Staff and National Security Adviser'.[23] To impress him, Churchill took him up to Scapa Flow in the Orkneys to see off Lothian's successor, Lord Halifax, to Washington in Britain's newest battleship, *King George V*. His account of his acrobatic leaps from minesweeper to destroyer to battleship in the heavy winter seas at Scapa, with Churchill surveying the performance from the deck of *King George V*, cigar in hand,

---

* Given the First World War precedent, I find it hard to accept Kimball's view that Roosevelt hoped that Lend–Lease would eliminate 'any need for large-scale American intervention' (for example in Kimball, *The Juggler*, 12).

delighted Washington on his return. Churchill's seduction had the required effect. 'This island needs our help now, Mr President, with everything we can give them,' he cabled on 14 January.[24] On the 31st Hopkins saw Keynes, who told him that the Lend–Lease Bill would meet Britain's requirements if the President interpreted it as covering both direct and indirect war purchases in USA, *and* reimbursed Britain in cash for advance payment on orders in the pipeline, so that it could rebuild its working balances.[25]

The announcement of Lend–Lease guaranteed Britain that it would eventually get the supplies it needed. However, it did not solve the immediate problem of assuring supplies before lend–leased goods came on stream. The enabling legislation would take some months to enact; the British claimed they could not pay for the orders already placed, much less order new goods. Churchill weighed in with a further message to the President on 2 January: 'What would be the effect upon the world situation if we had to default on payments to your contractors? . . . Substantial advance payments on these . . . orders have already denuded our resources.'[26] American officials simply did not believe him. Sir Frederick Phillips was giving little away. Asked by Cordell Hull why Britain could not put up collateral as security for orders, 'Sir Frederick was reticent as to most of the figures I desired.' Further enquiries produced 'similar scant results'.[27] The British believed that the USA was trying to 'strip them bare,' the Americans that the British were distinctly understating their opulence.

Much of the dispute hinged on what counted as disposable assets. There was considerable haziness about the size of Britain's 'war chest'. Did it, for example, include the stocks of refugee gold deposited in London for safekeeping by Britain's defeated allies? The Americans thought it did. The British said it did not. These stocks were debts to foreign governments – even though these governments now had only a shadowy existence in a few terraced London houses. Then there was South African gold. South Africa was in the British Empire; Washington seemed to believe that Britain could simply seize the production of the South African mines. Even while the Lend–Lease weapon was being forged, Roosevelt 'helpfully' insisted, over Churchill's objection, on sending a cruiser to South Africa to ship to Washington £42m. of gold held there. Keynes was driven to remark that the Americans believed the British owned their empire 'lock, stock, and barrel'. Finally, there were Britain's overseas investments. Surely they could and should be mobilised before Britain got help from the United States? Morgenthau used to tell Roosevelt, 'Never worry, the British will always find means of paying if they cannot get out of it.' Most of these misunderstandings were cleared up by an improved flow of information. But the disputed definitions of wealth also hid different priorities and clashing interests. The British overstated their poverty because they wanted to lock the Americans into the war *and* maintain some independence of action; the Americans demanded payment 'up front' because they doubted the British could win it, and because they wanted to control British policy.

On 18 December Morgenthau told Phillips that Britain should go ahead and place as many contracts as it wanted. When Phillips asked who would pay, Morgenthau said, 'the President had said it was all right to place the orders now'.[28] The British Treasury interpreted this as a moral commitment to pay for all new orders. However, Morgenthau interpreted his remark as giving Phillips permission to place orders 'for anything they wanted if they said they had the money to pay for it'[29] – in other words, simply as reasserting that priority would be given to British orders for American defence goods. As Kimball puts it, 'Roosevelt gave the green light to Great Britain to make commitments they could not meet.'[30]

Put by Roosevelt in charge of selling the Lend–Lease Bill to Congress, Morgenthau decided to argue the case on the ground that the British would soon run out of means of payment, not that they had already done so. He told the Senate Foreign Relations Committee on 28 January: 'If Lord and Lady Astor own real estate in New York their assets will be on the auction block with the rest.'[31] Roosevelt now instructed Morgenthau to get the US Army to take over as many British contracts as they could from their ordinary budgets.[32] On 1 February Morgenthau authorised payment for $35m. of new orders a week; but he was infuriated when spectacular sales of British securities failed to materialise. By 6 March he was 'boiling over. . . . Here I stake my reputation . . . and they don't make a god damn move on this thing. . . . They have just got to do it, and I'm still not convinced that they want to do it. . . .'[33]

Morgenthau's political problems got little sympathy in London. Keynes's explosion of 11 March 1941 is typical: '[Morgenthau] has been aiming, partly perhaps . . . to placate opposition in Congress, and partly . . . connected with his future power to impose his will on us, at stripping us of our liquid assets to the greatest extent possible *before* the Lend Lease Bill comes into operation, so as to leave us with the minimum in hand to meet during the rest of the war the numerous obligations which will not be covered by the Lend Lease Bill.' He was aiming to reduce Britain's gold reserves to nil, 'treat[ing] us worse than we have ever ourselves thought it proper to treat the humblest and least responsible Balkan country'. The main British objective must be '*the retention by us of enough assets to leave us capable of independent action*' (italics added).[34] While exempting the President from ill-intent, Keynes never forgave the US Treasury – and later the State Department – for taking advantage of Britain's weakness, incurred in a joint cause. He had convinced himself that the defeat of the Axis had precisely the same significance for the US as it had for Britain. America's failure to live up to his ideal of equality of sacrifice gave an edge to all his subsequent financial negotiations with the US administration.

The Lend–Lease Act became law on 11 March, but Congress still had to approve the Appropriation Bill of $7bn. Any hope that it would allow some of it to be used to take over either Britain's 'old commitments' or the 'interim' (post-January 1941) orders were dashed when, on 16 March, Harold Smith, director of the Bureau of the Budget, assured the House Appropriations Committee that none of the $7bn would be used for materials ordered before 11 March. This was the logical sequel to Morgenthau's earlier assurance that Britain could pay for them. Another explosion from Keynes in London: 'Morgenthau', he wrote 'has burnt our boats, as usual, without telling us beforehand.'[35] Keynes did not understand that the Budget Bureau Director worked at the White House, not the US Treasury. Roosevelt too was insuring himself against Congressional rebuff. To smooth the Bill's passage the President also demanded the quick sale of a major British asset. On 15 March, Lord Halifax, the new ambassador, and Sir Edward Peacock of the Bank of England agreed to sell Courtauld's Viscose Corporation to an American banking group for $54m., about half its real value. As Kimball writes, 'the dispute over th[e] ... "old commitments" acted as a strong warning to the British that America would continue to insist on the artificial separation between political alliance and profit-motivated economic policy'.[36]

In an effort to prevent further sales of British assets, Keynes took up Purvis's suggestion that the Reconstruction Finance Corporation, one of Roosevelt's New Deal agencies headed by the Texan businessman Jesse Jones, the Secretary of Commerce, might lend Britain $900m. against the collateral of all Britain's direct US investments. He put this to Benjamin Cohen, adviser to John Winant, US ambassador in London, on 19 March. This plan, which had the advantage that it would 'not interfere with the future export organisation of Great Britain', would, Keynes thought, 'carry the discussion onto a new terrain'.[37] Cohen was attracted by the technique of what came to be known as the 'Jesse Jones Loan', but warned Keynes about the politics: Morgenthau would interpret any approach to Jesse Jones as going behind his back. Keynes was taken by surprise: he had sought the approach to Jones because he had assumed that, following Harold Smith's statement, Morgenthau 'no longer has legal powers to assist us in any way'. Now it seemed that 'in his career of double-crossing everyone and providing false assurance on both sides', Morgenthau might still be able to raise some money to meet the 'old commitments'.[38] Morgenthau told Phillips on 19 March that the President, Hopkins and himself 'had agreed that the Army and Reconstruction Finance Corporation should take over $300–$400 million' of outstanding British orders.[39] Thereafter the British always included this 'Morgenthau pledge' in their calculations of promised relief. When Phillips, too, warned against the

Jesse Jones Loan, Keynes demanded to know his alternative. Was it 'to sell by hook or by crook every direct investment which can conceivably find even a bad market in the course of the next six months or so? If so, this is capitulation. . . . Surely, we cannot contemplate that without a struggle.'[40]

The new American ambassador to London, John Gilbert Winant, was much more helpful than his anti-British predecessor, Joseph Kennedy. A patrician New Englander and former Governor of New Hampshire, Winant was an ardent Anglophile and though a Republican was a supporter of the New Deal and a friend of Roosevelt. When he took his own life, by a pistol shot to the head, in 1947, the *Times* obituary was headed simply 'Friend of Britain'. Described by Breckenridge Long as 'an intense, melodramatic theorist . . . with a philosophy embedded in humanitarianism', he had been sent to London 'with the possibility that the Labour Party might succeed to power . . .'.[41] Winant was tall and swarthy, and was said to have Red Indian blood. Dalton found him 'incredibly tongue-tied' and 'almost inaudible' when he did speak. 'He must be brighter than his outward form or how did he get anywhere? But he is, I think, a good friend of ours and herein a sharp contrast to his crook predecessor. . . .'[42] He and Keynes met soon after his arrival in London in March, and from the start got on famously. He was captivated by Keynes's intellectual fizz and by Lydia's vivacity. As the war went on the Winants and Keyneses often dined with each other round the kitchen table at 46 Gordon Square. Keynes also established a rapport with the ambassador's more intellectually formidable economic adviser, E. F. Penrose. Keynes's personal line to Winant reinforced his authority in the Treasury.

Winant agreed with Keynes that they should try and get away from 'the business side of things'. He even welcomed Keynes's suggestion that Americans should go without cheese one day a week to secure a better psychological bonding between the two peoples.[43] Keynes poured out his frustration at the lack of official bonding. Why not go to Washington to put the British Treasury position in person, Winant suggested? It was soon arranged that Keynes should go over as the Chancellor's personal representative to try to clear up the financing of Britain's pre-Lend–Lease orders. 'It might be useful and would certainly be exciting,' Keynes wrote to his mother of his prospective trip on 14 April, 'but the task would be difficult and unrepaying, the climate awful and the fatigue severe.' He had taken a series of vows: (a) not to talk too much, (b) never once to speak his mind or tell the truth, (c) not to drink cocktails, (d) to obey Lydia in all things. Keynes went without specific instructions, but with a general mandate to replenish Britain's reserves up to the golden minimum of $600m.

This was to be the first of Keynes's six Treasury missions to the United States, four of them during the war. By sending Lothian, then Halifax, then Keynes to Washington, Churchill's government hoped to overcome the weakness of Britain's bargaining position by the distinction of its representatives. It was given out to the press that Keynes was going to Washington 'to establish a clearer definition of what is to be included in Lend Lease' and that his visit had 'no direct connection with deals relating to direct investments'. The *Financial Times* wrote: 'It is agreed on all sides that Mr Keynes is a man of constantly fresh ideas whose freedom from any hidebound economic tradition fits him peculiarly well for the job of placing new suggestions before the American mind. . . .'[44] It was a gamble both for the government and for Keynes, for without official position he was expected to succeed, by sheer personal authority, where Phillips had failed. The irony that 'Mr Governor [Montagu Norman] now regards [me] as the sole salvation' did not escape him.

Keynes was in reasonable health when he set out on this arduous trip, despite the fact that he had been working up to twelve hours a day, to such disagreeable accompaniments as continuous air-raids, the Ogre's 'lenten fast' and nightly icebags on his heart. Air trips across the Atlantic were scarcely faster than by boat, though at that time considerably safer. He and Lydia spent the night of Thursday 1 May in Bournemouth in the Branksome Towers, a 'hotel like a tomb', before stepping into a flying boat at Poole Harbour, which flew them, his secretary Mrs Stephens and Lucius Thompson-McCausland, a Bank of England official and former scholar of King's College, Cambridge, off to the Costa do Sol, Portugal, where they arrived at 7 p.m. on Friday. They were welcomed by 'dark Portuguese sailors in white British Airways uniforms' and taken to the Estoril Hotel. After a day of sightseeing, some financial discussions for Keynes and a surfeit of food, Lydia decided that the people were pro-British, but business pro-German, that Lisbon had become very prosperous 'since they put an economist Dr Zalazar [sic] in charge of the state' and that Thompson was a 'nice boy', with plans for a huge family.

On Sunday morning they took off in an American Clipper with a 'delicious cool drawing room', reaching the Azores in the evening. They set off the same night, but had to turn back with engine trouble, as apparently the Clipper was too heavily loaded, so they spent a night in the American Club, leaving on Monday minus Mrs Stephens, who flew out on the next plane. It took them nearly two days to get to Bermuda, and they finally reached New York at 7 a.m. on Thursay 8 May, where the press was waiting.

Keynes was soon deep in discussions with Sir Edward Peacock and Thomas Gifford of the Bank of England and their American adviser Clarence Dillon of J. P. Morgan: that evening he dined with Peacock and Gifford at the Knickerbocker Club. He said that it was no part of his instructions or intentions to get involved in the Viscose sale, but he wanted to be kept informed. They discussed the political difficulty of selling Viscose too cheaply, and agreed a strategy for assigning the revenues of other British companies in the United States to the Reconstruction Finance Corporation as collateral for a loan. Keynes learnt at first hand about the lack of co-ordination between British officials (neither Peacock or Gifford, who were charged with selling Britain's American assets, had been told by Phillips about the urgency of the cash position) and was briefed about the personalities in the US administration: about Morgenthau's bad moods, his fear of hostile senators and his jealousy of Jesse Jones, about the Secretary of Commerce's determination to have his finger in every pie. Peacock said there had been a marked improvement in Morgenthau's attitude in the previous few weeks, due in part to the seriousness of the war news, also to Britain's willingness to 'sell, indeed sacrifice' Viscose.

Maynard and Lydia travelled to Washington by train next day, booked into the Mayflower Hotel, familiar from their stay in 1934, and dined that evening with Sir Frederick Phillips and Edward Playfair, who was attached to the British Supply Council (successor to the Purchasing Commission). Gerald Pinsent, Treasury adviser to the British Embassy, joined them on Saturday morning. Phillips, who was 'extremely genial and easy', was eager to hear London and purvey Washington gossip. He confirmed the great improvement in atmosphere brought about by the Viscose sale, for which Britain was receiving value well above its sale price. Keynes outlined his strategy for negotiations with Morgenthau. Because Britain's reserves had unexpectedly stabilised (albeit at a low level) there was no longer any need to try to squeeze every last dollar out of Lend–Lease. Phillips and Playfair expressed relief at not having to face a 're-casting' of the Lend–Lease negotiations, but this was, in fact, exactly what Keynes was proposing. The question of the 'consideration' for Lend–Lease cropped up. The US Treasury had previously urged that bits of the British Empire be surrendered in return, but the State Department had quashed them. They all favoured postponing the issue for six months. By then, Keynes said, they would know whether America would be in the war. Playfair and Pinsent independently confirmed that Harry Dexter White, the US Treasury's statistician, was 'deeply suspicious of us'. It was clear, though, that 'the rooted general suspicions of the Americans are encouraged by the fact that we have told then we shall be bankrupt by such and such a date ... and then that date has come and we continue perfectly solvent'.[45] 'Maynard sees people continually,' Lydia wrote to Florence on 12 May, 'talks a lot, but in good health. Often we go out together to dine ... tomorrow with Morgenthaus.'

III

ENCOUNTERS WITH MORGENTHAU

This was Keynes's first visit to the United States since 1934, and he had to discover the feel of Washington all over again. He understood no better than most Englishmen how the American political system worked, Roosevelt's predilection, like Hitler's, for governing through competing agencies, or the relative indifference in Washington to Britain's financial problems. British and American soulmates were few, suspicion and misunderstanding rife, liaison between the two sides – in economics, strategy, intelligence – virtually non-existent.

Churchill had taken 'a monumental risk with Anglo-American relations' by appointing as Lothian's successor 'a Conservative fox-hunting aristocrat with an ill-disguised contempt for the media, a reputation for being aloof, who was furthermore the Foreign Secretary during Munich'.[46] Packing off Halifax to Washington (and Hoare to Madrid) was part of Churchill's sweep-out of Chamberlainites from his government. It strengthened his position in London, but it made little sense in 1940 to send a prominent 'appeaser' to Washington. Known in the Foreign Office as Holy Fox, Halifax spent the first few months of his ambassadorship wandering round America like a visitor from another planet, noting its strange social and political customs. He found the Americans 'very crude and semi-educated', marvelled at their capacity for turning private entertainments into public meetings, and found their leaders dangerously afraid of uninstructed public opinion. 'When they confess dislike of what they call our aristocratic system, I am tempted to reply (but hold my tongue), that at least it gives us a certain tradition of leadership. . . .'[47] His patrician aloofness and proconsular gravity were unfavourably contrasted with Lothian's informality and oratorical uplift; by the time Keynes arrived, his popularity had barely 'risen from zero to freezing point'.[48] It was not till August 1941, when he faced down an egg-throwing crowd in Detroit with the unflappable remark that Americans were lucky to have eggs to spare, that his relations with the press started to thaw. Although he was a public relations disaster, Halifax, helped by his sparkling wife Dorothy, got on well with the President and leading administration officials. From time to time Churchill toyed with replacing him with one of his favourites – Beaverbrook or Brendan Bracken – but the thought of having him back home was enough to secure his job for the rest of the war.

Britain's other representatives scarcely fared better. Morgenthau thought Peacock 'dilatory' in arranging sales of British investments. Keynes's old friend Bob Brand, the merchant banker, joined the Supply Council, but he seemed old and tired and depressed, as well he might be.

His adored wife Phyllis, Nancy Astor's sister, had died in 1937; his lifelong friend Philip Lothian in December 1940; now he faced the dismal prospect of the forced sale of British-owned insurance companies. Arthur Purvis, head of the British Supply Council, was popular with all, but the taciturn Sir Frederick Phillips was an acquired taste. His unexpectedly warm relationship with Morgenthau was based on an unusual affinity. 'I like that man,' Morgenthau was to tell Lionel Robbins. 'I suspect he's a little slow of speech as I am myself.'[49] Phillips's weakness as an envoy was professional: he had a civil servant's refusal to go beyond his brief. He seemed to embody the British reluctance to disclose information and 'explain themselves' which both Harrod and Sayers have identified as a major weakness in Britain's negotiating technique.[50] He could do business with Morgenthau, not explain why the business was necessary or suggest how it might be better done.

Keynes himself came with a mixed reputation, dating from the First World War, and reinforced by his controversial economic theories and his intellectual arrogance. He had made a 'terrible impression for rudeness' on his first visit to Washington in 1917, and his attack on Woodrow Wilson in *Economic Consequences of the Peace* had not been forgotten or forgiven. To conservative bankers like Thomas Lamont and Russell Leffingwell he was the evil genius behind the destruction of the gold standard and the unsound experiments of the New Deal. Nor was he especially popular with the senior New Dealers. Morgenthau regarded Keynesian economics as a dangerous heresy and was instinctively suspicious of their author. On the other hand, there was now a fervent band of 'Young Keynesians' among economists working in Roosevelt's New Deal agencies. Lauchlin Currie was administrative assistant to the President: his influential Memorandum on Full Employment, dated 18 March 1940, was explicitly based on 'the analysis . . . of J. M. Keynes'. Anti-British as he was, Harry Dexter White at the Treasury 'revered Keynes as the greatest living economist'[51] Alvin Hansen of Harvard University, the most notable Keynesian convert of the 1930s, was installed in the Federal Reserve Board. Keynesians were sprinkled round the Departments of Commerce and Agriculture, and the Office of Price Administration. Admiration for Keynes as an economist did not, of course, extend to personal liking, nor support for all the demands he made on Britain's behalf. But it gave some of the officials he would have to work with an initial respect for him, and lent him a greater authority than that of an ordinary British official. On his return, Keynes told Oliver Harvey, a Foreign Office official, that ' "New Dealers" were like the Jesuits or German General Staff and had their representatives in [every] Government department who were more loyal to each other than to their departments.'[52]

Keynes's personality was a source of friction. He had a natural affinity with practically minded Anglophile intellectuals like Walter Case, Felix

Frankfurter, Walter Lippmann and Dean Acheson; but he was too esoteric for most politicians, and he held them in contempt. It would have been beyond him to conceal his dissatisfaction at the inefficient processes of American administration; and he suffered from an incurable tendency to tell Americans how they ought to be running their country. The Treasury official Sir Frederick Leith-Ross, by no means an unqualified admirer, was not the only one to notice that Keynes's professorial manner and tendency to score points off his opponents hampered him as a negotiator.[53] Keynes was not a patient man, and was prone to exasperated outbursts. He sometimes picked unnecessary, and wearing, fights on small matters. His great intelligence often led him to over-complicate an argument, when a simple, down-to-earth approach would have served better. This was to prove a handicap in dealing with Morgenthau, whose understanding of technicalities was zero. Even so, Keynes's mixture of gifts made him a powerful plenipotentiary. He had a unique capacity to translate visions into plans; his language was eloquent, yet precise; and he was good at figures. Lionel Robbins, who accompanied him on three of his North American missions, wrote after his death: 'He was not always a good *negotiator*. . . . But as an *envoy* he was supreme. Not even Mr Churchill could state more magnificently the case for this country than Keynes at his eloquent best.'[54]

Beyond the personal, Keynes's relations with Americans reflected tensions between Britain and the United States generally in an era when power, but not reputation, had shifted across the Atlantic. The gap between the two was a fundamental factor in the wartime relationships between the two Allies. Although the United States held most of the trumps, American officials felt culturally unconfident and inexperienced in dealing with the British. They felt the British would 'pull a fast one' over them unless they were always on guard. There was a strong feeling that British wiles had inveigled them into the First World War; to add insult to injury, the British had got out of paying their debts. To many Americans Keynes, with his subtle intelligence, epitomised the traps which a declining civilisation could set for a rising one. And, of course, there were traps. The British were trying to maximise American support at least long-term cost to themselves. The Americans were not enthusiastic about pulling Britain's chestnuts out of the fire for a second time in a generation. A substantial minority did not want to do so at all. Those who were convinced it was necessary were determined that this time the operation should be on American terms. They were determined not to be 'bamboozled' again, as Lloyd George, on Keynes's own testimony, had bamboozled President Wilson. Once America entered the war, Soviet Russia seemed to some American officials the more convincing, and certainly the more powerful, partner in war and peace. Thus the plot was set for Anglo-American relations till Keynes's death.

Keynes's first encounter with Morgenthau, on Tuesday 13 May, crystallised these personal as well as political tensions. It was a disaster – typically veiled in Harrod's cloying account.[55] Keynes started well by thanking the administration for the concept of Lend–Lease and the US Treasury for helping Britain continue its purchases in the interval before it was legislated. Morgenthau probed by suggesting that the British ambassador had been unhappy about the forced sale of Viscose. Keynes avoided the trap by saying that 'there was no change whatever in the policy which Sir Frederick had followed of disposing of British gold, listed dollar securities, and direct investments in the United States'. So far so good. But at this point Keynes started to bewilder Morgenthau and his officials. Speaking at 'some length', he told them the British Treasury was concerned that they were using Lend–Lease facilities too freely. Keynes thought that Lend–Lease should be restricted to armaments and agricultural products, leaving Britain to buy other items with dollars. Morgenthau responded that Britain had been best aided by a generous interpretation of Lend–Lease. Keynes responded that he wanted to build up British reserves 'to meet unforeseen situations'. When Morgenthau asked him whether this was for financial or military reasons, Keynes fudged. When Morgenthau asked him if what he had said represented an 'amendment' to the Phillips programme, he fudged again by saying that 'he was working closely with Sir Frederick'. This gave Morgenthau his chance of suggesting that Phillips attend their next meeting. When Keynes called in at the office of Merle Cochran, Morgenthau's special adviser, to collect his hat afterwards, Cochran warned him – ominously – of US concern that Britain should build up excessive 'cash balances' under cover of Lend–Lease. He advised Keynes to keep his remarks in future short and snappy 'since we were accustomed to dealing that way'.[56]

The evident failure of his first meeting with the Treasury Secretary left Keynes baffled and depressed. 'I have seldom struck anything stickier than my first interview,' he reported to London. 'One seemed to be able to get no human reaction whatever, which is, I suppose, his method of protection until he is quite sure what you are after. It is also most difficult to get him to see one's real point, and misunderstandings peep out at every corner. Everybody agrees that he is jealous and suspicious and subject to moods of depression and irritation.'[57] Lydia cheered him up. The evening of the disastrous encounter, she sat next to Morgenthau at dinner. With a quick flash of perception, she told Maynard that the Secretary was 'a good man and will do you no harm *on purpose*', a phrase he was so pleased with that he cabled it back to London. Keynes's mistake is obvious. He had used a courtesy visit to plunge into unfamiliar substance, at considerable length, in the course of it seeming to pour cold water over the efforts of both Morgenthau and Phillips, and implying that he, Keynes, had come to Washington to sort the whole matter out. Eddie

Playfair put the misunderstanding down to another cause. Morgenthau, he wrote in one of his racy letters to Sigismund Waley in London, was bound to be suspicious of someone as clever as Keynes. 'When Maynard arrived he went to see Henry & expounded for an hour. Henry received him coldly and did not understand one word (he said so himself). Next day F[rederick]P[hillips] wrote it all down in words of one syllable and read it out to Henry, who understood perfectly.'[58] The marked difference between Keynes's and Morgenthau's ways of doing business was to hamper all their subsequent dealings. Morgenthau was prickly and insecure; Keynes lacked the common touch. It is impossible to imagine the two men ruminating together, and striking deals over brandy and cigars.

But even Phillips's translation made Keynes's intervention no more palatable. Keynes wanted to reduce Britain's dependence on Lend–Lease, and thus American control over its balance of payments. Morgenthau was aiming to maximise Britain's dependence on Lend–Lease, partly to maximise Britain's mobilisation, partly to minimise Britain's ability to rebuild its reserves. Both sides were jockeying for post-war position.

On 16 May, Keynes sent Morgenthau a memorandum offering a 'clean-cut arrangement'. Britain would undertake not to press for certain politically, administratively or legally 'difficult' purchases to be lend-leased, saving an estimated $650m. from the projected Lend–Lease budget over two years, if in return the US Treasury would apply these – hypothetical – savings to 'taking over existing British commitments'. Basically, Keynes was asking the US Treasury to refund $700m. of advances already paid on contracts worth $2bn outstanding on 1 May. Britain would pay off the rest with the help of Morgenthau's promised $300m. to $400m. and by the elimination, through Lend–Lease, of its balance of payments deficit with the US. The refund would immediately replenish Britain's dollar reserves. 'If the British Treasury had a reasonable reserve against contingencies,' Keynes wrote, 'they could face with far greater assurance the various unforeseen risks and contingencies which may face them in any part of the world. . . .'[59] His memorandum did not mention the loan the British were negotiating with Jesse Jones. In other words, Keynes thought it better for Britain to buy more from the United States and have dollars to do it than to receive more and be entirely dependent on America's goodwill.

Keynes's plan, which had seemed so clear-cut and rational in London, was not practical politics in Washington. Its subtlety alone – with its suggestion of a trap – would have ruled it out. In practical terms, it fell foul of the administration's undertaking to Congress not to pay for pre-Lend–Lease orders – as Harry Hopkins pointed out when Keynes visited the ailing Lend–Lease czar on 19 May. It also fell foul of Morgenthau's conception of himself as a sugar-daddy, keeping Britain dangling on the string of his generosity. It was worth a try, but its rejection was inevitable.

Keynes's attempt to get on to human terms with the Secretary was equally unsuccessful. His 'brilliant' covering letter to Morgenthau dwelling on the 'anxieties and preoccupations' faced by the British 'moved me [Playfair] to tears & I thought would move Henry to tears, but Henry read passages out to F[rederick]P[hillips] in derisive tones (Maynard does not *know* this). Henry also believes that the sole purpose [of his visit] is to sabotage the Viscose deal.' The only redeeming feature of the situation, noted Playfair, was that Morgenthau's spat with Keynes had 'restored [Sir Frederick Phillips] to his original position of being Henry's second girl, after Purvis'.[60]

As Playfair perceptively noted, Morgenthau would have responded better to a begging letter. But this was never Keynes's style. 'Maynard thinks we are a great & independent nation, which on the financial side is patently not true. . . . I think he is inclined to ask as of right what they are only prepared to give as a favour.'[61] Britain's greatness and independence were under jeopardy from military events as well. The war was going disastrously: the British had been driven out of Greece and Crete, Rommel was on the offensive in North Africa, German air raids were were continuing; worst of all, one-third of the supplies coming from the United States were not getting through because of the U-boat campaign. Britain's one military success while Keynes was in Washington was the sinking of the *Bismarck* on 27 May. Not till Hitler invaded Russia on 21 June 1941 was some of the pressure taken off Britain. Keynes had a dreadful hand to play; and he was too proud to beg.

Keynes spent a week wandering round rooms filled with cigar smoke, meeting officials, arguing for his 'solution', without yet realising that it was not practical politics. It was impossible to find out who was responsible for what, or even engage the interest of those who mattered. 'My particular problem', he wrote back home in some despair on 20 May, 'cannot be solved unless I can simultaneously square Morgenthau about the old commitments, Harry Hopkins about the new commitments and the Director of the Budget about the relation of these to the appropriations.'[62]

Morgenthau was not altogether wrong to suspect Keynes's interference in the Viscose deal. Maynard's old friend Samuel Courtauld certainly thought that his presence in New York would increase the chances of saving his company,[63] and, in his discussions with Peacock and Gifford, Keynes had raised the political problem which would arise if the Treasury was forced to pay a much higher compensation price to Courtauld in sterling than it received in dollars. He was also actively promoting the strategy of getting a loan on the security of British companies as an alternative to distress sales. He had proposed that 'the rate of selling might be slowed down' as the Treasury's need for dollars was less than expected.[64] All this was anathema to Morgenthau, who had heard about the New York discussions.

Keynes's arrival in Washington threatened Morgenthau's own position as the manager of Britain's support system. He rang up Halifax from the White House, expressing his dismay at Keynes's memorandum, and demanding to know who represented the British Treasury in Washington–Keynes or Phillips? When Halifax replied, 'Phillips,' Morgenthau asked Phillips why he had not signed Keynes's proposal, and demanded that he do so. Morgenthau had received no word from the Chancellor of the Exchequer or the British Embassy about Keynes's visit. This suggested to him that it had an ulterior purpose. He detected Keynes's influence behind Phillips's attempt to delay the Viscose sale, and was much perturbed to learn that Jesse Jones had offered to lend $65m. against the Viscose stock, more than the sale price. He cabled Winant in London to ask exactly why Keynes had come to America. Winant cabled back: 'It was my belief that both you and President Roosevelt knew Keynes and liked him.'[65] Keynes's care to get his visit sponsored by the American ambassador had spectacularly misfired, as Morgenthau suspected Winant of being in cahoots with Jesse Jones. 'It is rather harassing to have to live in an atmosphere of such morbidity,' Keynes wrote to Horace Wilson.[66] It took several days and a cascade of telegrams, letters, telephone calls and meetings to calm Morgenthau down. Keynes was in Washington solely on Lend–Lease business, Phillips assured him. He came with 'the Chancellor's full authority', Halifax explained.

Keynes himself saw the suspicious Treasury Secretary on 24 May, to find him beaming, shaking his hand and saying all was forgiven and forgotten, 'though exactly what it was that was forgiven and forgotten I shall never know for certain'.[67] Keynes now told Halifax that he thought that the root of Morgenthau's hostility had been not the Viscose issue itself, but the suspicion that Winant and Ben Cohen had been using him (Keynes) to undermine Morgenthau's authority with the President. Now Morgenthau was insisting that the Viscose sale go through to undermine Jesse Jones. 'One can never remember, I find, in this place,' Keynes wrote to the ambassador, 'to make allowance for the extreme jealousy of colleagues.' Nevertheless, Morgenthau 'is one of Great Britain's best and truest friends in the Administration'. Halifax replied sourly: 'it is a pity that his desire to help us should be diluted with a desire to make things hot for Jesse Jones'. Both agreed that Washington was a 'very odd place'.[68]

IV

A WASHINGTON SUMMER

After he got back from America Keynes wrote to a friend: 'I always regard a visit [to the USA] as in the nature of a serious illness to be followed by convalescence.'[69] He was in Washington for eleven weeks. Most of his waking hours were devoted to government business. He had decided not to stay at the Embassy, so as to keep his independence, and probably to reduce the amount of travelling he had to do. He moved mainly between the Mayflower Hotel on Connecticut Avenue, the Willard Hotel, whose entire ninth floor had been leased by the British Purchasing Commission in 1940, and the Treasury, State and Executive Offices of the President. These buildings formed a fairly compact governmental cluster in downtown Washington. But they were all grand, Washington was more widely spaced out than London, and, though Keynes went everywhere by car, his stamina was taxed by his peregrinations through long halls and corridors. The British Embassy, where he went to consult and dine with Halifax, was an outlier, a Lutyens mansion way up Massachusetts Avenue in north Washington. He and Lydia were able to take the occasional weekends out of Washington, and Keynes also fitted in a few meetings with American economists, mainly Keynesians and mainly working for the government, at which they discussed American macroeconomic policy.

He kept up a flow of letters and telegrams to the Treasury in London which record not only the progress of his negotiations, but his reflections on the institutions and personalities of American government. Certain themes, which splay his subsequent letters, were starting to appear: the lack of orderly business procedures, the incoherence of government organs, the infestation of lawyers, the power and calumnies of the press, the timidity of the administration, and the consequences of the division of power between the executive and legislature.

Doing business in Washington was a very different matter from working in London's centralised machine. Keynes was slow to grasp the fundamental truth that – as he put it on his return – 'the Administration, not being in control of Congress, is not in a position to enter into commitments on anything'.[70] Keynes never visited Congress, and knew few legislators; he dealt exclusively with government officials and his comments focused on the incoherence of the administration itself. This was a product of design, not inattention. Roosevelt, in Richard Hofstadter's phrase, was 'the patrician as opportunist'. His technique for preserving his own freedom of action was, as J. A. Schlesinger wrote, to 'keep grants of authority incomplete, jurisdictions uncertain, charters overlapping'.[71] Keynes only gradually realised that it was incomplete authority, not animosity, which lay behind Morgenthau's failure to deliver on his promises.

The American 'organs of government' struck Keynes as so 'incredibly inefficient' that 'one wonders how decisions are ever reached at all'.

There is no clear hierarchy of authority [he wrote to the Chancellor on 2 June]. The different departments of the Government criticise one another in public and produce rival programmes. There is perpetual internecine warfare between prominent personalities. Individuals rise and fall in general esteem with bewildering rapidity. New groupings of administrative power and influence spring up every day. Members of the so-called Cabinet make public speeches containing urgent proposals which are not agreed as part of the Government policy. In the higher ranges of government no work ever seems to be done on paper; no decisions are recorded on paper; no-one seems to read a document and no-one ever answers a communication in writing. Nothing is ever settled in principle. There is just endless debate and sitting around. . . . Suddenly some drastic clear-cut decision is reached, by what process one cannot understand, and all the talk seems to have gone for nothing, being the fifth wheel to the coach. . . .[72]

Keynes came to believe that an important cause of the defectiveness of the executive organs was that everyone in the higher reaches of government was either old or ill. Hopkins was an invalid, Morgenthau was tired, Cordell Hull was both old and ill, Stimson, Secretary of War, was very old. This meant that they either failed to grasp the point or were unavailable. 'Their professional advisers work, therefore, under a severe handicap . . . as they are only too anxious to explain to one. On the other hand the younger Civil Servants and advisers strike me as exceptionally capable and vigorous (with the very gritty Jewish type perhaps a little too prominent). . . .'[73]

Keynes was taken by Halifax for two meetings with Roosevelt. The first was on 28 May, the day after Roosevelt's broadcast proclaiming an unlimited state of national emergency. They had gone to discuss Eden's draft on post-war economic aims (prepared for him by Keynes, see p. 196 below). If Roosevelt had resented Keynes's letters of advice in the 1930s, he showed no sign of it. The conversation ranged widely as Roosevelt, sitting at his desk 'without ever moving or getting up', handed his visitors, sitting on either side of him without much room for their long legs (both were over six foot), morsels of food to convey from their napkins to their mouths. Keynes believed the President's strategy was to get into the war step by step. Roosevelt said that after the war Continental Europe should be disarmed, with Germany and perhaps Europe as a whole federalised, but Britain and the USA alone retaining offensive weapons. 'What about Russia?' Keynes asked pertinently. 'Now you are making things difficult,' Roosevelt smiled. Keynes particularly noted Roosevelt's suggestion of an Anglo-American 'police force'. He found the President 'in grand form', quite recovered from his recent prolonged attack of acute diarrhoea, 'calm and gay and in full possession of his own personality and his will and purpose and clarity of mind . . . head and shoulders above everyone else'.[74] Halifax concurred: 'he was in good form, looking much better than when I saw him last, sheaves of telegrams were coming in [approving of his speech the day before]'.[75]

The second time Keynes was not so sure: 'He is not a sick man, but he is not exactly a fit one. I thought he was fundamentally weak and tired and using his courage and willpower to keep going. . . . Whilst I have been in Washington he has had three attacks of low [high?] fever with other minor symptoms. I am told by those round him that he is still suffering from more or less chronic [and most painful] sinus trouble.' The President complained bitterly about the heat, and was plainly suffering from the humidity and discomfort, but refused to turn on the noisy, antique air-conditioning system in the Oval Office, which was all Congress allowed him. Keynes was convinced he was suffering from the streptococcal infection which he had himself experienced, and that he would slowly conk out unless he got proper medical attention.[76] Halifax disagreed. 'The President was in good form, though Keynes thought he was tired. I don't think I had that impression. The truth I think was that he was not greatly interested in the detail of Keynes's subject. I stopped and had a bit of talk to him after Keynes left. He said that he thought that Hitler's attack on Russia was based on a political miscalculation as to the psychological effect it would have on the world.'[77]

Keynes's comments on Roosevelt – he saw him once more in 1944 – while admiring, were by no means wholly uncritical. In particular he was sceptical of what he ironically called his 'famous political instinct', which to him simply meant appeasing rather than leading Congress and American public opinion. This analysis was simplistic. Roosevelt may have been over-sensitive to political dangers. But brandishing Congress before the British was also a political tactic – an excuse for not doing what the British wanted or a lever to get the British to do what he wanted. Keynes could never understand that American and British interests were not identical, attributing differences to deficiencies in the American political system, and thus over-relying on logic and eloquence to overcome them.

Keynes found a country ruled by newspapers and lawyers. Nothing was secret: everyone and every department leaked like mad. He suggested to Roosevelt that the American method of deceiving the Germans was to publish so much vital information that they would not have the time to read it. The President laughed heartily. 'Almost before you are out of the door of [Morgenthau's office or the Oval Office] you are assaulted by the reporters for a full account of what has passed inside,' he wrote home. Keynes never completely learnt to repress his talent for the witty or caustic phrase which, speeding round Washington, sometimes undermined the relationships he was trying to build up.

From the start Keynes was exposed to American legalism. The first time he saw Morgenthau, Morgenthau's officials asked Thompson-McCausland, who accompanied him, 'Where is your lawyer?' When Thompson-

McCausland explained there was none, they said, 'Who does your thinking for you?' It became one of Keynes's *mots* that when the *Mayflower* sailed from Plymouth, it must have been filled with lawyers. Americans refused to write down any oral agreement until it had been turned into a legal contract, whereas Keynes regarded legal precision as inappropriate to international agreements. What he wanted from lawyers – he was to explain at Bretton Woods – was to devise means 'by which it will be lawful for me to go on being sensible in unforeseen conditions. . . .' On his return to Washington in 1943 he continued in the same vein: 'Surely the plague of lawyers . . . is a worse plague of Egypt than the Pharaoh ever knew. It is only by a rare and lucky coincidence that what is administratively sensible is also lawful. The late Lord Hewart [British Lord Chief Justice, whose book *The New Despotism* (1929) attacked the growth of delegated legislation] should have visited Washington to discover what the substitution of administrative law for administrative decision means in practice.'[78] Too often lawyers busied themselves to make commonsense illegal.[79] His favourite expression for legalese was 'Cherokee'.

Also from the 1943 visit comes this diatribe against telephones (he would have hated mobiles):

> Indeed in Washington the Ancient Mariner would have found it necessary to use a telephone to detain the wedding guest. For it is only on the telephone that one can obtain undivided attention. If you seek an interview, your American friend will spend half the time talking on the telephone to all quarters of the compass, until in despair you return to your office and yourself ring him up, when you can expect to secure his concentrated mind for as long as you like, while someone else wastes his time . . . in the chair you have so wisely vacated.[80]

Keynes built up good working relations with other members of the British mission, after a rocky start. 'Maynard's visit', wrote Playfair on 22 May 'has been & is a great joy. He is a fine gadfly to us & to the Americans. . . . I am certain his visit will do nothing but good.' He first got to see Halifax on 19 May in the middle of his spat with Morgenthau. Lydia Keynes turned up for the luncheon which followed – 'an odder little person I never saw,' the ambassador wrote in his diary. 'I believe she used to be in the Russian Ballet – very fresh and sprightly, and after an initial shock, I rather liked her.' Thereafter he and Keynes saw each other fairly frequently. Halifax and Keynes had overlapped at Eton, but this did not make for perfect sympathy, Halifax having the traditional Oppidan's mistrust for the over-clever Colleger. He had had some dealing with Keynes in 1925 when he was Minister of Agriculture, Keynes coming in to discuss tithes. Halifax did not claim to understand the intricacies of this, or any other financial, question. He had no understanding of the 'Treas-

ury' mind; his mollifying touch ran up against Keynes's edgy realism; he
sometimes felt that Keynes attached more importance to getting the
figures right than to getting on with the war. He summed up his
impression in his diary on 14 July: 'He [Keynes] has got a very acute but
obstinate mind. He is a good fellow to do business with, and in spite of
one or two tiresome qualities, I like him.'

It is a tribute both to Keynes and to the permanent British officials in
the United States that his arrival in Washington, with his clear plans which
cut across theirs, caused so little friction. In particular, Sir Frederick
Phillips showed very little resentment at the incursion of this strong-willed,
opinionated plenipotentiary from London. In his dispatches home Keynes
was generous in his praise of Peacock, Purvis and Phillips. They sank their
differences, and worked as a team for Britain's survival.

Keynes's position as plenipotentiary at large was powerfully reinforced
by the slowness and erratic nature of communications between Washington and London, which had almost reverted to their sailing-ship days.
Diplomatic bags weighing half a ton went once a week by ship to Lisbon
and took three weeks to reach London. With cipher facilities at the
Embassy heavily overburdened, even telegrams of instructions took days
to reach Keynes, often responding to his own telegrams of a week or so
before. All this gave Keynes, himself a punctilious correspondent, considerable latitude in framing his own proposals. This was especially true
of the negotiations over the 'consideration' (see p. 128 below). There
were occasional signs of alarm in London; but London had little choice
but to trust him and hope that the thunderbolts he was forging would not
turn into boomerangs.

'I shouldn't have survived without Lydia who provides constant rest,
discipline and comfort. So when I do get away from the insistent world,
all is very good and re-creating.' So Keynes wrote to his mother on 28
June. Lydia's own letters to Florence, amusing though rather uninformative, give tiny glimpses of their joint life.

When they arrived in Washington, it was already hot and humid and
grew progressively more so. The Mayflower, opened in 1925, billed itself
as the 'Renaissance Hotel', and boasted a long, cool marble-floored
'Promenade', running its length, with frescoed ceilings. But the Keyneses'
suite was not air-conditioned, and Maynard had to buy a tropical suit.
Lydia reported to the doting Florence that it made him look 'as slim as a
dragon fly . . . most elegant, distinguished and really nice looking'. He
and Mrs Stephens had been reduced by the heat to taking constant cold
baths, unlike Lydia, who only sprinkled water on her 'sweaty parts & that
lasts a week'. After a month Lydia took to cold baths as well. It was not till
early July that they managed to get air-conditioned rooms.

Keynes began his visit working flat out – often starting his dictating to
Mrs Stephens at eight in the morning, and only getting back to the

Mayflower twelve hours later. On 17 June Lydia reported that he often worked seventeen hours a day. However, a month later he told his mother he was now 'very far from overworked' and was only hanging on because 'the job that is really keeping me here [negotiations about the consideration] advanced by a stage about once a week'. Lydia's attempts to control his diet were undermined by the quantity of working and social meals. After five weeks, Maynard reported to his mother with statistical precision that he had lunched and dined out forty-seven times, 'which really is service at the front and certainly much more dangerous than the blitz'. The main social event of his fourth week was a big birthday party given in his honour by T. V. Soong, China's Finance Minister, consisting of sixteen courses, and a birthday song sung by Soong's daughter. In his last month the 'entertainments' became 'much more reasonable', and he and Lydia were often able to eat out on their own, in a little French restaurant across from the Mayflower. Despite the work and the meals, his health stood up well. The hot weather, he told his brother Geoffrey, was very good for his heart and his digestion was perfect.

There was time for a few trips out of Washington. On their first weekend, he and Lydia took their nephew Quentin Keynes – 'sweet, a little pale' and working at the British Embassy – on a picnic in Shenandoah Park, driving out on the 'wonderful road ... built by the unemployed'. On 17 June they gave him a birthday party, the guests including John Sparrow (with whom Quentin was rooming) and Michael Straight, Dorothy Elmhirst's son, whom Maynard had taught economics at Cambridge.[81]

Two weekends later they were in Princeton, Keynes talking to 'the economists', while Lydia stayed with Mary Case, Walter's widow, in the country. At Princeton, Keynes renewed his acquaintance with Einstein. They found him, Lydia wrote, 'in bed with the curly hair and the big toe out'. (Keynes reported him telling them that 'if we bomb Germany continuously ... they most certainly will not stand for it',[82] a common, though fallacious, view at the time.) At the end of June, they managed to escape Washington's tropical weather for a weekend in Virginia, at the foot of the Appalachians, Quentin driving them in a 'smart Buick'.

Keynes came to America not just as the envoy of the Chancellor of the Exchequer, but as the most famous, and controversial, economist in the world. Naturally enough his views on what US domestic policy should be were eagerly sought by the younger Keynesians working in the administration. The most important discussions – confrontations might be a better word – were held at Lauchlin Currie's house on 22 May and at a dinner meeting of officials of the Office of Price Administration at the National Press Club on 10 June. The American Keynesians had all read his *How to Pay for the War*, but were more worried about stagnation than inflation. Higher taxes and price controls were to be postponed until full employment was reached. Currie reported to Roosevelt in December 1940 that 'reasonably full utilization of our labor forces in 1943 would yield us a national income, with no advance in prices, of between $105b and $110b, or from $35b to $40b higher than our income from 1940'. They expected Keynes to support their expansionary policies. Instead, he shocked them by warning of the need to combat inflation by heavy taxation and a high-pressure savings campaign. He wondered if his American disciples had forgotten that 'when the supply of consumable goods is increased, the incomes of those producing them are likewise increased and the [inflationary] gap would be reduced only insofar as saving and taxes increase'.[83] Taylor Ostrander, a US Treasury official, remembers that at one of these dinners Keynes said to Walker Salant, 'Well, I have to tell you that you are more Keynesian than I am.' Although the arguments involved theoretical and empirical issues, at root they reflected the economic and psychological distance between the two countries. The American Keynesians wanted to continue the New Deal in war, whereas Keynes wanted to convert the economy from peacetime to wartime production.[84] Of some theoretical interest is Keynes's insistence that investment is responsive to changes in interest rates as well as to changes in demand – something his radical followers tended to forget.[85]

V

THE OLD COMMITMENTS

Keynes's opening gambit having failed, he had to change tack. If Britain's reserves were to be replenished, there was now no alternative to offloading as many current imports from the United States as possible on to Lend–Lease, while averting the distress sale of Britain's remaining American assets by means of the Jesse Jones Loan. The second part of the operation, unsurprisingly, proved the easier. The Reconstruction Finance Corporation became an enthusiastic convert to lending the British government money at high interest rates, with the juiciest British investments put up as collateral. 'There is . . . very strong reason to hope and believe', Keynes wrote home on 8 June, 'that, if we can get a substantial Jesse Jones loan with the earnings of the more obvious direct and market investments earmarked to its repayment, we shall hear no more of the disposal of the equities of any of them. . . . So the horrible Viscose business may after all bear fruit.'[86] Legal authorisation for a loan of $425m. against collateral of $700m. was given by a Congressional amendment to the Neutrality legislation, passed on 10 June, and a provisional agreement signed a few days later.

On 17 June Keynes fired off to Harry Hopkins a new scheme for extending Lend–Lease to cover additional items. This recognised that the amount available 'for relieving us of existing commitments . . . will not go far to satisfying the needs which I outlined in my memorandum [of 16 May]'.[87] Hopkins did not appreciate Keynes's letter; nor did Morgenthau, to whom he sent a copy. Had Keynes heard their telephone conversation, he might have thought he had wandered into a bad B movie. Harry Hopkins plays the heavy, with Morgenthau as his more or less incoherent stooge:

> HH: Because I've got a long letter from Keynes – a long-winded letter from Keynes. . . . I don't like his style and approach. My own opinion is that except from the point of view of the British Treasury, he'd just be well off at home.
> HM: You and me, both.
> HH: You see, he says he's been sent here on a mission, and his mission has got to be complete.
> HM: Yeah.
> HH: Well, God Almighty, seems to me you might well say, 'Well, what the hell has Phillips been doing here all the time?'
> HM: That's right.
> . . . .
> HH: Here's the point about Keynes. If he hangs around here until we get mixed up in a new Lend–Lease bill, he's apt to pull something and he'll be telling us how to write a Lend–Lease bill and people will get madder than hell here about it.

The two statesmen then discuss whether they can send a 'bee' to Winant to get Keynes recalled. Morgenthau recounts that Keynes had made remarks 'quite critical of how the President is running the country'. This is a reference to a dinner party given by Felix Frankfurter in which Frankfurter and Dean Acheson had discussed 'how and when' America would enter the war. It was only later that Morgenthau heard from Frankfurter that Keynes had been 'enthusiastic' about him at dinner, an observation which greatly surprised the Secretary.[88]

> HH: Yeah, you see how what's he doing, too. He now moves in on me – writes me a letter and sends you a copy, see?
> HM: Yeah.
> HH: Well, now God damn it, if he's here for the Treasury . . . his business is to be writing you letters and sending me copies. You see what he's going to do, he's going to move on any front he thinks he can move on . . . if I'd got a two line note or copy of a note from Phillips, which . . . would have said, well, now, we're in quite a jam and wish you would help us out – personally, I undoubtedly would stir my stumps far more than getting a six

page letter from Keynes, you see? . . . He's one of those fellows
that just knows all the answers, you see?[89]

Whatever Morgenthau thought, Keynes's logic of trading old for new
commitments was appreciated by US Treasury officials Harry White,
Daniel Bell and Jacob Viner.[90] They persuaded Morgenthau to set up a
Treasury committee, which would meet to decide which British orders
should be lend-leased against daily reports of the Bank of England's
reserve position. Starting 19 June, Keynes, Phillips (followed by his
temporary replacement Kenneth Bewley) and Purvis met a shifting collection of American officials most weekdays for the next month to approve
British purchases. At meetings of the 'Committee' Keynes found Morgenthau 'all smiles and helpfulness' in his efforts to 'replenish our dollars'. It
was Keynes's first continuous contact with Harry Dexter White, the
'suspicious' director of monetary research at the US Treasury.

The threads were coming together. The extension of Lend–Lease to
cover additional products and orders for the Dominions might save
$250m. of reserves a year. Morgenthau had renewed his pledge to Phillips
to find $400m. for the old commitments. The Jesse Jones Loan would
bring in $425m. The US Treasury now accepted the principle of allowing
Britain to build up a 'free reserve' of about $600m. Lunching with the
Secretary on 25 June, Keynes said he felt his original mission had been
successfully accomplished. Suspicious to the last Morgenthau asked him
to put it in writing, which Keynes graciously did, using a phrase he had
picked up from Morgenthau. 'Everything depends, of course, on what you
call the McCoy . . . going through – that is certain tanks and aeroplane
engines contracted by us being taken over by your War Department and
certain shipping contracts being replaced by deferred contracts for a later
date.'[91] At a press conference at the British Embassy on 14 July he denied
Congressional and newspaper charges that Britain was using lend-leased
goods to undercut American exporters in Latin America. This problem
would cause bitter mutual recrimination in the months and years ahead.[92]

How successful had Keynes been? In terms of his original logic he, and
the British Treasury, had been defeated. The settlement left Britain more,
not less, dependent on Lend–Lease, and therefore on the United States.
Phillips had argued against allowing the USA to exercise control over the
British balance of payments.[93] Yet this, in effect, is what Morgenthau's
Committee had been set up to do. Given the impossibility of getting the
administration officially to accept responsibility for Britain's pre-Lend–
Lease orders, this was an inevitable conclusion. It was the insistent logic
of Keynes's demands which brought the matter to a head. Yet it set a
precedent for the Office of Lend–Lease Administration to police Britain's
export policy – and thus level of reserves – throughout the war. The one
clear success for the original strategy was the Jesse Jones Loan, which

ended the danger of further asset stripping. After a dour start, Keynes had got on to reasonable terms with most Washington officials. He had spotted White as 'one of the few constructive brains in the Treasury'.[94] He had even started to appreciate Morgenthau, 'despite that dreadful, leery smirk of his'.[95]

In terms of figures, the result was highly successful. Keynes claimed to have exceeded his hopes and the Treasury's expectations. He had secured a sufficient enlargement of the scope of Lend–Lease to leave Britain with a net annual surplus of $500m. on its trade balance with the United States. In addition, 'we have . . . good reason to hope' that $450m. of old commitments will be taken over by Morgenthau, and a further $425m. made available by the Jesse Jones Loan. As the payments outstanding on the old commitments came to $1.17bn on 1 July, Britain was left with no more than $300m. to meet on outstanding orders. 'Since our estimated surplus income in gold and dollars available to meet this is at the rate of $500m. a year, we can hope to add $450m. to reserves in the course of the next eighteen months. . . . As we start out on 1 July of this year with a balance of about $180m. [£45m.] this raises the aggregate reserves to $630m. without making allowance for further windfalls. . . .'[96] Keynes's confidence was not misplaced. Britain's 'war chest' was back to $564m. by December 1941, and reached $900m. by December 1942. It was not getting supplies out of the United States which proved difficult; it was getting supplies *and* preserving independence.

The mystery is how the British went on paying for the pre-Lend–Lease orders through till April 1941, after which Lend–Lease started taking some of the strain. Official figures show that British reserves had sunk to £12m. in April before picking up slightly. (For changes in the reserve position during the war see Appendix at the end of this chapter.) The answer almost certainly is that deliveries (and therefore payments) were held up by supply and shipping shortages. Playfair was suitably cynical: 'I am rather impressed by the unreality of it all: all our figures are false, & we always have just enough money, to our own surprise.'[97] In fact, what with delays and the onset of Lend–Lease, the extreme crisis had already passed by the time Keynes got to the United States.

It is hard to be sure whether Keynes's visit improved Anglo-American relations. He himself thought that six months before 'we felt that they were trying to strip us of everything. . . . Today . . . they are still sensitive to real or imagined political difficulties and want to expose the least possible surface to Congress. But, subject to this, they are going out of their way to find means of relieving us of dollar obligations and of allowing us to build up a free reserve of $600 million. . . .'[98] But the 'improvement' in the American attitude had already been registered by the British before Keynes arrived. It is doubtful whether he helped it mature. Morgenthau certainly felt that Lend–Lease was under control before Keynes burst on the scene, and that his presence only delayed and complicated matters. Phillips and Playfair also believed that 'But for Maynard we should have started back already.'[99] Not only did the first 'Keynes Plan' prove to be a red herring, but Keynes imparted an edge to the Lend–Lease negotiations which might be thought inappropriate to the situation at the time. On the other hand, he explained Britain's financial needs with a frankness and boldness which the taciturn Phillips could not match. Keynes's mission is notable not for what he achieved, but as a revelation of his attitude, and for the contacts he made in Washington, which were to serve him in good stead for his subsequent missions.

It is worth stepping back for a moment to consider the effects of the way Britain 'paid' the external cost of the war. Of total wartime British imports of £17bn ($68bn), only £7bn ($28bn) or 40 per cent were paid for by exports and reserves. Of Britain's external deficit of £10bn (or $40bn) over the six years of war, $22bn were covered by Mutual Aid, $14bn by accumulating sterling balances in London, and $4bn by disinvestment in overseas securities.* As Alec Cairncross has written, 'the extreme to which it [Lend–Lease] allowed Britain to push her military effort enhanced the risk of economic collapse when peace returned'.[100] Had Britain fought the war entirely from its own resources it would have had $36bn less to spend on the war. It might have survived. A massive proportion of its war effort went into defending the Empire against Germany and Italy in the Middle East and against Japan in the Far East. It could have surrendered these positions and concentrated on the defence of the Atlantic sea routes, but only at the cost of greatly strengthening Germany's strategic position. The Empire's contribution to Britain's war effort was vital. But it was very different from America's contribution, and this, too, was to cause great problems. Both Lend–Lease and the accumulation of sterling balances were at the expense of British exports. But whereas the former was a gift, the latter was a debt. So Britain would start the peace not just with an export trade 30 per cent of pre-war, but with approximately £3.5bn ($14bn) of external debt – the largest in its history. The build-up of debt and the growing size of Britain's prospective balance of payments deficit were constant worries to Keynes, and indeed to the Treasury, right through the war; but there seemed no remedy, given the policy of victory at any price.

---

* Lend–Lease came to be known formally as Mutual Aid after Britain agreed to supply the United States with war materials on a somewhat different basis. These terms were used interchangeably.

VI

THE CONSIDERATION

Keynes remained in Washington through July to deal with the 'consideration'. Although Britain was to get its goods free of the 'dollar sign', they were not to come without strings. Section 3(b) of the Lend–Lease Act had authorised aid to Britain on 'terms and conditions' designed to 'benefit' the United States, the benefit being 'payment or repayment in kind or property or any other direct or indirect benefit which the President deems satisfactory'. The first two conditions made possible not just the return of 'leased' material, but also the transfer of assets in the Empire; the third was inserted with future benefits to US commerce in mind. Roosevelt, who had only the vaguest idea of what he wanted, might have been content with general promises. But in America an agreement is a contract, and a contract requires terms.

The US Treasury and State Department had different ideas about what should go in the contract, and fought for the right to draw it up. The Treasury's aim was to keep Britain in the war, but to render it financially dependent on the United States. Morgenthau had insisted that Britain sell its overseas assets as the price for aid. With Lend–Lease on tap, the Treasury's main aim became to use it as a lever to control Britain's gold and dollar reserves. By contrast, the State Department was keen to dismantle Britain's imperial preference system. The two aims were contradictory: a post-war Britain left with exiguous reserves would be more, not less, inclined to maintain imperial preference as the only basis of commercial survival. In a key move, Roosevelt, on 16 May, handed responsibility for negotiating the consideration to the State Department. This gave Secretary of State Cordell Hull, backed by his Assistant Secretary, Harry Hawkins, the chance to commit the British to a free-trade agenda. For the British, the only consideration which seemed just was that 'we should go on fighting'.[101] But, beyond this, there were two rather different kinds of British objections to the State Department's plans. The Treasury wanted to retain the right to use exchange and import controls to deal with Britain's post-war balance of payments problem; the imperialist wing of the Conservative Party wanted to retain imperial preference as a means to Empire unity.

Although the consideration was now a State Department (and therefore, on the British side, a Foreign Office) matter, Keynes soon got involved, partly because he was Keynes, partly because the consideration was bound to have economic implications, partly because Halifax, whose understanding of economics was limited, chose to involve him.

From the first Keynes got on splendidly with Assistant Secretary of State Dean Acheson, the man charged by Hull with drafting the consideration.

With his imposing height, clipped moustache and tweeds, Acheson looked the picture of an English gentleman. A product of Groton, Yale and the Harvard Law School, and a protégé of Felix Frankfurter, Acheson shared many of Keynes's friends, values and cultural interests. From the moment the Germans invaded Poland, Acheson and his wife Alice were fully committed to the Allied cause: it was Acheson who supplied the legal opinion which produced the destroyer-for-leases swap in 1940. Acheson was a legal pragmatist. Although he supported the State Department line, he was, like Keynes, a pragmatic, rather than ideological, free trader. The two men matched each other in both intellect and arrogance. Acheson's biographer James Chase writes: 'He relished clever argument and outrageous humour and hated cant, hypocrisy, the pompous, the obvious, the pedantic.'[102] Acheson wrote of Keynes that he 'was not only one of the most delightful and engaging men I have ever known, but also, in a true sense of the word, one of the most brilliant. His many-faceted and highly polished mind sparkled and danced with light.'[103] Acheson, unlike Morgenthau, was a genuine Anglophile. He accused the US Treasury of 'envisaging a victory where both enemies and allies were prostrate – enemies by military action, allies by bankruptcy.' He wanted Britain to be left financially strong enough after the war to accept the liberal agenda.

At first, Keynes sensed little danger. Acheson led him to believe that the main point of the State Department draft was that Britain should be prepared to trade the Ottawa Agreement for a reduction in the US Hawley-Smoot tariff (see pp. 187–8 below). Keynes wrote that this 'seems to all of us here extraordinarily satisfactory'.[104] Keynes was clearly expecting a general declaration of intent, no more, to lower obstacles to trade. The two men also had no problems when they discussed post-war relief matters, rapidly agreeing that an Anglo-American committee should be set up to study how European requirements might be met out of food and commodity surpluses held by the two Allies, and broaching the subject of permanent buffer stocks to secure an 'ever normal granary'.[105]

However, Morgenthau told Acheson that 'Congress would require something more substantial' than vague promises in return for Lend-Lease.[106] On 8 June Keynes informed the permanent secretary at the Treasury, Sir Horace Wilson, in London that the amendments suggested by the Treasury to the State Department draft were 'far from improvements, and there is reason to think that tin, rubber and also jute raise their heads again'.[107] In a discussion with Acheson next day, he suggested an Anglo-American commission, with no precise terms of reference, to consider how best to restore 'the free and healthy flow of normal economic intercourse between nations'. He hoped this was not 'indiscreet'.[108] London authorised Keynes to continue his exploratory talks.

On 18 June Keynes was still confident that 'the background [to the consideration] is extraordinarily favourable and friendly, and I see no reason to expect that any terms to which we much object will be forced on us'. He felt sure that he and Acheson could easily draft something worth while 'with a few general directives' from the President.[109] On 21 June Keynes sent Kingsley Wood a 'skeleton draft' of an agreement he had prepared 'for my own purposes'. The President would be entitled to ask as part of the 'benefit' that Britain furnish the United States with bases and secret information; allow British-owned stocks to be used for post-war relief and reconstruction; and join the USA in promoting the 'free and healthy' flow of trade by granting free access to all purchasers of raw materials under their joint control, by participating in commodity and price regulation schemes, by reducing trade barriers and trade discrimination, and by maintaining, through 'an appropriate exchange and currency organisation', balance of payments equilibrium between national systems.[110] Keynes was warned to 'avoid making far-reaching suggestions'.[111] In a graciously phrased rebuke, the Chancellor cabled from London that the heads of agreement which Keynes had sketched out 'raise fundamental issues. . . . In these circumstances we felt it unwise for you, as my representative, to cast a fly, however lightly.'[112]

At this point Keynes stumbled into a set of parallel trade negotiations. John Stirling of the British Board of Trade had arrived in Washington in December 1940 to push British exports, offering as a *quid pro quo* for a reduction of US duties a wartime abatement of imperial preferences. Harry Hawkins, head of the State Department's Division of Commercial Policy, and, like Hull, a fervent free trader, suggested that Britain abolish imperial preference entirely in return for a 50 per cent reduction in the US tariff. When the British rejected this, Hawkins suggested that, in return for immediate trade concessions by the United States, Britain commit itself to reducing imperial preference and exchange controls and quantitative restrictions *after the war*.[113] This produced an outburst from the imperialists in Churchill's Cabinet, led by Leo Amery, the Secretary of State for India. But the Treasury in London also resisted any limitation on Britain's ability to continue its system of import licences and payments agreements. Meeting Hawkins and Stirling on 25 June Keynes upheld the Treasury view, but he 'stated the probability of postwar [trade] discrimination so forcefully that he effectively deadlocked the negotiations'.[114] Keynes sent London a spirited defence of his stand in a telegram (suppressed by Phillips and Stirling) in which he condemned as a 'lunatic proposition' any agreement 'which presumes the abolition of all controls whatever immediately after the war' when no one knew what the trading and monetary system in Europe or Latin America would be.[115] Keynes's outburst, in sharp contrast to the usual British style of gentle remonstrance, infuriated the State Department. Hawkins minuted that Keynes 'wholly fails to see that after the sacrifices the American people are called upon to make to help Great Britain in the present emergency (even though we are thereby helping ourselves), our public opinion simply would not tolerate discrimination against our products in Great Britain and, at Great Britain's insistence, in other countries'.[116] After Keynes left Washington, Hawkins tried to ensure against his return to complete the Lend–Lease negotiations, as his 'well-known obstinacy' would wreck the chance of an agreement.[117] However, the Chancellor, Foreign Secretary and President of the Board of Trade cabled the British Embassy backing Keynes's demand for 'full liberty of action at least during the transitional period'.[118] In leaky Washington, news soon got round that Keynes favoured bilateralism. Keynes was so upset by this characterisation of his stand, when it got back to him, that he wrote to Redvers Opie at the British Embassy, for transmission to Leo Pasvolsky at the State Department, that he was not advocating bilateralism, but emphasising 'the inadvisability of our signing away certain principles *before* the conditions necessary for multilateralism had been devised and agreed'.[119] If Keynes's outburst did have an effect, it was to convince Hawkins that the supplementary trade talks would get nowhere without 'specific provisions for postwar economic policy in the Consideration Agreement'.[120]

Following his meeting with Roosevelt on 7 July, Keynes called on Acheson 'at the President's request' to tell him to get on with drafting the *quid pro quo.* He 'did not appear to think it unusual that I should receive instructions from the President via the British Embassy'.[121] Keynes's discussions with Acheson crawled forward at a snail's pace. On 15 July Keynes handed Acheson a draft agreement drawn up in London, and approved by Churchill and Kingsley Wood. He was plainly exasperated by his instructions. He considered the British draft so 'jejune' that he delivered it as an 'aide memoire'. Acheson commented that it excused the British from any liability to deliver goods or assets, or make any post-war commitments at all – which, Keynes noted, 'is undoubtedly true'.[122] He was equally frustrated by the lack of progress with Acheson. Whenever they made ground, 'there is Mr Hull . . . whose attention is not easily gained. . . . And, finally, there is the President . . . whom one cannot expect to attend to one except at his own leisure. I am praying that, in spite of this, not too much time will elapse, since we are all dreadfully homesick.'[123]

A State Department draft of seven substantive articles was finally handed to Keynes on 28 July. Acheson recalled that it was 'simple and amazingly liberal'. Basically, it affirmed the principle of a reciprocal exchange of gifts between Britain and the United States. The crucial Article VII may have been liberal, but its simplicity was deceptive. Gone was the notion of trading British reductions in imperial preference for American tariff cuts. Instead:

The terms and conditions upon which the United Kingdom receives defense aid from the United States of America and the benefits to be received by the United States in return therefor, shall be such as not to burden commerce between the two countries but to promote mutually advantageous economic relations between them and the betterment of world-wide economic relations; they shall provide against discrimination in either the United States of America or the United Kingdom against the importation of any produce originating in the other country; and they shall provide for the formulation of measures for the achievement of these ends.[124]

Reading this brought on Keynes's second explosion. It was impossible, he raged, for the British to make such a commitment in good faith. It fastened upon the future an ironclad formula from the nineteenth century. It contemplated the impossible and hopeless task of returning to a gold standard where international trade was controlled by mechanical monetary devices. It banned exchange controls, which were the only way to maintain economies in balance. It allowed all kinds of cunningly devised tariffs which were in fact discriminatory, while prohibiting sound monetary controls. After the war, Britain would have a large surplus of imports over exports and the Article VII formula provided no remedy for this. One must imagine the torrent of words pouring out very fast, as they did when Keynes got excited. Redvers Opie confirmed to Harrod that Keynes had referred to this draft of Article VII as 'the lunatic proposals of Mr Hull'.[125]

As coldly as he could – 'which I have been told is fairly cold' – Acheson told Keynes that all the Americans were asking from the British was that, in return for receiving vast quantities of aid, they would not regard themselves free to take any measures they chose against US trade but work out with America steps which would make them unnecessary. This was Acheson's gloss, and it may have been what he believed. But it was a strained interpretation of what Article VII actually said.

Keynes was not an imperialist *per se*. But he was not prepared to dismantle imperial economics without something better put in its place; and he was very much alive to the gravity of Britain's prospective post-war economic position. Having heard Acheson out, he 'cooled off and spoke wisely about a postwar problem that he foresaw far more clearly than I did – our great capacity to export, the world's need for our goods, and the problems of payment'. He mentioned the divisions in Britain between the free traders, believers in a managed economy (among whom he numbered himself) and the imperialists. 'At the end of our talk,' Acheson wrote, 'he seemed more reconciled to the Article, but by no means wholly so.'[126]

Keynes felt guilty about his outburst, and before heading back for England the next day he wrote Acheson an explanation and apology. His reaction, he said, was the result of my feeling so passionately that our hands must be free to make something new and better of the post-war world; not that I want to discriminate in the old bad sense of that word – on the contrary, quite the opposite.

But the word [discrimination] calls up . . . all the old lumber, most-favoured-nation clause and the rest which . . . made such a hash of the old world. We know also that won't work. It is the clutch of the dead . . . hand. If it was accepted it would be the cover behind which all the unconstructive and truly reactionary people of both our countries would shelter. . . . Meanwhile forgive my vehemence which has deep causes in my hopes for the future.[127]

What exactly was the dead hand? It was *both* the nineteenth-century *laissez-faire* system which sacrificed domestic employment to free trade and the gold standard *and* the nineteenth-century reactions against it in the form of protectionism and imperialism. Keynes rejected both. What at this point had he to replace them with? His 'realistic' answer, exchange controls and import licensing, made no appeal to American idealism, and left out an important strand of his own. He accurately concluded his letter to Acheson: 'I know, *or partly know*, what I want. I know, and clearly know, what I fear' (italics added). Keynes flew back to London on 30 July. 'You and your wife gave both of us a great deal of joy and it was exhilarating to go on from where we had left off in England,' Felix Frankfurter wrote. 'And in wider fields your visit was productive in all sorts of ways, and not least – as old teachers like you and I know – in the stimulation that you afforded literally scores of able youngsters down here who are carrying heavy burdens now and will be carrying them increasingly.'

VII

MISUNDERSTANDINGS

As soon as Keynes got back to London the understandings he thought he had achieved in Washington started to unravel – a débâcle made worse by the death, on 14 August, of Arthur Purvis in an aeroplane accident. There had been a foretaste of what was to come in the unexpected hitches to the Jesse Jones Loan. Peacock returned to London on 21 June, with its broad principles seemingly settled. The Reconstruction Finance Corporation would lend the British Treasury $425m. for fifteen years at 3 per cent a year (Keynes had tried hard to get 2.5 per cent), received as pledged income from American branches of British insurance companies. However, the 'unusually favourable atmosphere' which marked agreement on the broad principles was succeeded by an attitude of 'ungenerous bargaining' by the Commerce Department's lawyers. The administration insisted on inserting a 'War Disaster Clause' allowing the RFC to take over the pledged assets in the event of a British default – a euphemism for a British defeat. 'The Chancellor of the Exchequer reluctantly swallowed the [modified] disaster clause ... and the agreement was signed in Washington on 21 July.'[128]

After Keynes left, Congress cut down the ordinary budget of the War Department, making it doubtful whether Morgenthau could meet his promise to take care of the 'old commitments'. On his return to Washington in August, Phillips doggedly went on reminding Morgenthau of his pledge. It was not till May 1942 that the War Department agreed to pay a total of $295m., partly in cash, partly in relief from contracts falling due.[129]

Much more important in the long run were the steps Congress took to prevent Britain exporting goods which contained lend-leased components. Keynes had tried to forestall this line of attack at his press conference in Washington on 10 July, but without success. General Burns, the executive officer of the Lend–Lease Administration, proposed that Britain's exports be limited to 'traditional' specialties like whisky and Harris tweed, to which Keynes ironically added haggis. A bitter three months' row followed between the two governments. American manufacturers saw an opportunity to capture Britain's export markets in Latin America; the British pointed out that their exports to Argentina were their only means of paying for the meat they were importing from that country. They also tried to secure the right to export goods, particularly cotton and steel, in which the source of the raw materials could not be identified – the so-called 'principle of substitution'. All to no avail: the British government's Export White Paper of September 1941 pledged that Britain would not export goods which incorporated Lend–Lease materials, contained materials 'similar' to those being lend–leased, or contained materials in 'short supply' in the United States. Although this was a unilateral undertaking, Lend–Lease could be be 'policed' from the supply end so as to prevent Britain's gold and dollar reserves rising above a certain maximum.

Britain failed to secure a revision of these arrangements when the United States entered the war. America had agreed to finance most of Britain's purchases of war materials in the United States, but had left Britain to pay for the local expenditure of its armies in the Middle and Far East out of its own resources. This led directly to the growth of the 'sterling balances' – the huge debts Britain started to pile up to Egypt and India. Despite much pressure from the British side, the Americans steadfastly resisted the principle of 'pooling' the financial resources of both countries.

Gabriel Kolko has seen in the steps America took to manage Lend–Lease a deliberate attempt to capture Britain's export markets in Latin America and to bend Britain to the State Department's post-war liberal trade agenda.[130] This is too simple: the Treasury and State Department had different agendas, which pointed in opposite directions. It was the fact that they were both pursued simultaneously which was so damaging to Britain's long-term position. To marginalise Britain's wartime export trade in order to control the level of its reserves was not consistent with the demand that it give up imperial preference after the war. Both in its management and in its *quid pro quo*, Lend–Lease became the main instrument of American foreign economic policy, and the main source of grievance to its wartime ally.

The wrangle over the exact wording of Article VII also continued for several months. The Mutual Aid Agreement was not finally signed till 23 February 1942, after Roosevelt had given Churchill a written assurance that 'it is the furthest thing from my mind that we are attempting in any way to ask you to trade the principle of imperial preference as a consideration for lend–lease'.

These developments left Keynes deeply depressed. On 4 November he wrote to Walter Lippmann:

Immediately after I left Washington, we went, during August and September, through a very bad spell in which every tiresome thing conceivable happened both on the financial and supply sides of Lend–Lease. The Administration did not seem prepared to risk the faintest criticism, however misconceived. . . . Now it is evident that things are much better and that the Administration was, as usual, unnecessarily timid. But we are very remote from Washington here, and the danger is of . . . our allowing awkwardness dating from the bad spell to crystallise. . . .'

On 28 April 1942 he concluded that the various Lend–Lease imbroglios had all resulted from 'the failure to revise Anglo-American relations . . . in any field outside the military and supply fields'.[131] This failure was never to be remedied.

APPENDIX

Britain's Gold and Dollar Reserves 1939–1945
(£ = US\$4.03)

On last day of	Exchange Equalisation Account holdings of gold, US and Canadian \$	Change
	£ million	£ million
September 1939–December 1940		− 395
August 1939	503	
September 1939	519	+ 16
December 1939	545	+ 26
March 1940	491	− 54
June 1940	390	− 101
September 1940	223	− 167
December 1940	108	− 115
1941		+ 33
March	70	− 38
June	65	− 5
September	69	+ 4
December	141	+ 72
1942		− 113
March	163	+ 22
June	205	+ 42
September	238	+ 33
December	254	+ 16
1943		+ 203
March	296	+ 42
June	352	+ 56
September	401	+ 49
December	457	+ 56
1944		+ 144
March	504	+ 47
June	571	+ 67
September	589	+ 18
December	601	+ 12
1945		+ 9
March	603	+ 2
June	624	+ 21
September	603	− 21
December	610	+ 7

Source: R. S. Sayers, *Financial Policy 1939–1945*, 496.

CHAPTER FIVE

Keynes in Wartime

I

MORE THE MASTER THAN THE SERVANT

'Well here am I, like a recurring decimal, doing very similar work in the same place for a similar emergency,' Keynes wrote to Russell Leffingwell on 1 July 1942. What sort of work was it, what position did he occupy? In one of his letters from Washington in 1941 Keynes described the director of the Bureau of the Budget, Harold Smith, as a 'peculiar animal, a real chimaera, half way between an official and a minister'.[1] Probably he was not thinking of himself, but the description fits his wartime role like a glove. Keynes retained his anomalous position at the Treasury from August 1940 till he died in 1946. He was enormously influential. This influence was based on personal authority rather than official position. Officially he remained an unpaid, part-time adviser to the Chancellor of the Exchequer. He was 'in the Treasury, but not of it'.[2] Despite this, he '*was* the Treasury', according to one of his colleagues, who cited in support of this contention 'the masterly war-time Budgets, the conception of Bretton Woods, and the gradual domination of overseas financial policy'.[3]

Much of the evidence for his activities can be found in 'Lord Keynes's Papers' at the Public Record Office – 130 Treasury files. They cover budgetary policy, financial and commercial negotiations with the United States and the Dominions, policies for the transition to peace. We can also follow in them the evolution of Keynes's Clearing Union Plan as it progressed through Whitehall and to negotiation with the Americans, the Dominions and the European Allies. These are the main threads, but Keynes's eye ranged over the whole field of economic policy, lighting on whatever interested him.

Since he had no formal executive or administrative responsibility for policy – except when he was representing the Chancellor in Washington – his influence was bound to be indirect. It is often hard to disentangle his own impact from that of many others, or his exact place within and in relation to the different centres of wartime power and influence. As often as not it was a memorandum from Keynes which clarified the intellectual and technical issues involved in some proposal, and thus nerved the

Treasury's 'administrators' to back it. What can be said is that, if Keynes chose to get fully engaged in something, his influence tended to be decisive, in the sense that policy was made within the framework of his analysis of the problem. This was as true in big matters as in small. Keynes left no less a mark on the legislation providing compensation for war damage than on the design of wartime budgetary policy or the post-war payments system. Once the main structure of wartime finance, domestic and external, had been decided in 1941–2, he turned his attention to securing the external basis of Britain's post-war existence, which included the many problems involved in the transition from war to peace.

A rough and ready measure of Keynes's importance is given by the index of Richard Sayers's authoritative *Financial Policy 1939–1945*. Keynes gets 84 page references followed by Churchill (39), Kingsley Wood (38), Morgenthau (35), Roosevelt (34), Simon (27) and Anderson (25). *How to Pay for the War*, with its associated technique of national income and expenditure forecasts, set the intellectual framework for wartime budgetary policy. The 'cheap money' policy was partly inspired by Keynes's theories; his influence was directly felt in the Treasury's wartime borrowing technique and in the Tax Reserve Certificate scheme. In external finance, Keynes influenced the technique of exchange control, and the policy of gold sales to India and the Middle East. He led for Britain in the two major Lend–Lease negotiations of 1941 and 1944. He devised the basic strategy for meeting the problems of 'Stage III', the transition to peace in 1945–6. And this leaves out the Clearing Union, the Bretton Woods compromise, and his many other contributions to planning for peace.

Most of Keynes's wartime activities and efforts eluded Churchill's grand geopolitical sweep. Keynes rates a single mention in his five-volume history of the Second World War. Not suprisingly, for as Keynes told Churchill's former private secretary Eddie Marsh, 'no-one on the economic or financial side ever, so far as I can make out, runs across him in Whitehall or Downing Street'.[4] As Keynes wrote of Winston's visit to Roosevelt early in 1942: 'It has been a question of buddies sitting around writing large numbers of tanks and planes on paper and talking about high strategy [with] no financial matter . . . given a minute's consideration.'[5]

Churchill's interest in finance was limited to its not being an impediment to deploying British power on a global scale. The terms on which the finance was obtained were of little interest to the War Leader, except when it led to rows in Cabinet. Churchill would grumble occasionally about taxes being too high. His tirades against Indian 'money lenders' grew longer as the war went on and Britain's sterling debts to India piled up. Nor was Churchill interested in post-war social and economic problems: sufficient unto the day was his motto. So the main spheres of Keynes's activity largely escaped his notice. Churchill did attach supreme importance to Anglo-American relations, and prized and cultivated his relationship with the President. His main concern here, which did impinge on Keynes's work, was to agree to nothing which would threaten the post-war position of the British Empire. Non-agreement took the form of refusing to discuss the matter with Roosevelt; and, when forced to do so, agreeing to pious declarations like the Atlantic Charter. Churchill preferred not to think about the implications of Article VII of the Lend–Lease Agreement. As for Keynes's Clearing Union Plan, the Bretton Woods Agreement, these were at the far periphery of his vision.

Churchill's indifference to the economic and financial aspects – and consequences – of the war was shared by most of his Party's high command, as well as by his Labour colleagues. Their economic attitudes were primitive. The gold standard was bad because it was associated with mass unemployment, the sterling area was good for Britain's prestige, imperial preference symbolised the fact that Britain still had an empire. Economic imperialism was, in fact, the one distinctive Conservative economic tradition, bequeathed by the disturbing Joseph Chamberlain and implemented by his son in the Ottawa Agreement of 1932. It was represented in Churchill's government by Max Beaverbrook (a Canadian), by Leopold Amery (half-German) and, intermittently, by Lord Cranborne. They, together with Robert Hudson, the Minister of Agriculture, became the chief Cabinet opponents of Keynes's internationalist post-war plans. The debate between 'imperialism' and 'internationalism' sputtered on for most of the war without ever coming to life. Unlike their American counterparts, Britain's political leaders fought the war not to gain advantages, but to hold on to what Britain already had. Both Secretary of State Cordell Hull and Secretary of the Treasury Morgenthau had economic war aims. Their British equivalents had none.

This indifference gave great latitude to the economic technicians to develop their own initiatives at the sub-political or 'expert' level. Keynes took full advantage of this opportunity, crossing the boundary between administration and policymaking. So in a very different way did Beveridge. But, unlike in the United States, the experts' post-war plans never became the policies of the government. No decisions were taken to endorse Beveridge's social security scheme, the Bretton Woods Agreement or the International Trade Organisation while the war lasted. The failure of Churchill's coalition government to define its attitude to the post-war world is one reason the coalition broke up, and the Conservative section of it was so heavily defeated in the general election of 1945. As for Keynes, he found himself, for much of the war, in the anomalous position of negotiating post-war arrangements with the American, the Dominion and the European Allied governments on behalf of the British government, but without the authority of the British government.

II

Keynes's wartime position needs to be set in the context of the Treasury's own partial eclipse. When Keynes re-entered his old department in 1940 its reputation was low. Churchill had a fixed antipathy to the 'Treasury view', which he believed had misled him as Chancellor in the 1920s and postponed rearmament in the 1930s; like Lloyd George in the First World War, he was determined to fight the war regardless of cost, and this initially kept his first Chancellor of the Exchequer, Kingsley Wood, outside the War Cabinet. Churchill set up a system of government which subordinated the traditional departments (including the Treasury) to a number of super-committees, whose work was co-ordinated by the Lord President's Committee. This soon came to dominate 'the whole field of home and economic policy'.[6] On the other hand, Churchill had considerable respect for Keynes, whom he judged to have been right over the gold standard, and with whom he dined regularly at the Other Club. The Treasury's incorporation of Keynes can be seen as a shrewd move in its longer-term effort to regain control over economic policy. Keynes's presence undoubtedly enhanced the prestige and influence of the Treasury, even though he disrupted its internal routines.

The Treasury's eclipse was due more to the pressure of war than to Churchill's antipathy. Its traditional job was to manage the government's finances. Keynes wanted it to manage the national economy through the budget. His *How to Pay for the War* was based on this philosophy. It was taken up by the Treasury partly because it was presented as an explicit alternative to physical planning. Once total war was forced on Britain by Germany, financial planning, being too slow and uncertain in its effect, necessarily gave way to the allocation of resources, especially manpower, by physical planning. The Lord President's Committee became the hub of the planning effort, co-ordinating the departmental plans through its powerful sectoral committees. The Treasury was left with three main tasks: to borrow the money the government needed as cheaply as possible; to keep the domestic price level stable, by means of a taxation scheme regarded as socially fair; and to arrange for the financing of Britain's overseas expenditure on the best possible terms.

The new machinery got off to a creaking start. The Lord President of the Council, Neville Chamberlain, was dying; his deputy, Arthur Greenwood, was incompetent. On 1 August 1940 Keynes wrote to Brand: 'The trouble is that the new Ministers in charge of economic policy – Chamberlain, Attlee and Greenwood – have provided us with a system quite a lot worse than what existed before; although before the change it seemed inconceivable that any alteration could not be for the better. . . . There is an almost complete divorce between thought and action.'[7] Only when John Anderson became Lord President on 2 November 1940 did the machinery start to work at full power.

The demands of the planning system led to an influx of economists into Whitehall. Most of these went not into the Treasury but into the Offices of the War Cabinet (where they serviced the Lord President's Committee) and into the Ministries chiefly concerned with supply. They were mostly young, and seconded from university posts.

Separate from this structure was the Prime Minister's Statistical – 'S' – Branch under the monumentally self-assured Lord Cherwell, formerly Professor Lindemann, Churchill's pre-war scientific adviser. 'S' Branch provided Churchill with an independent critique of policy implementation, and an up-to-date statistical digest, particularly as it bore on the military situation. Cherwell specialised in simplifying and shortening minutes for the Prime Minister to a double-spaced quarto page, and tracking statistics on multi-coloured charts. Interestingly, Roy Harrod, a university and wartime colleague of 'The Prof.', regarded him as more original than Keynes, because he took less for granted.[8]

The emergence of an economic secretariat at the heart of government happened by necessity rather than design. The planning system needed technicians, not administrators. Following the change of government in May 1940, the Central Economic Information Service, originally attached to the Stamp Survey (see p. 46 above) was greatly enlarged to serve the new super committees; in January 1941 it was split into an Economic Section and a Central Statistical Office, both based in the War Cabinet Offices, the former under the direct control of the Lord President of the Council. Known as 'Anderson's Circus', the Economic Section had between nine and twelve economists, the Central Statistical Office another seven or eight. Together they formed the economic and statistical 'brain' of the centrally planned war economy. The Economic Section's historians describe it as 'the first group of professional economists to operate full-time as government economic advisers in this country – perhaps in any country'.[9] Keynes called it 'the nucleus of that economic general staff which we have so long talked about'.[10] But, in English administrative style, they serviced rather than commanded the departments, briefing the Lord President on the items appearing on his Committee's agenda, ensuring economic consistency between departmental plans, servicing the sectoral committees, and studying subjects not covered by any department. Once the planning system was set up and running, members of the Economic Section like James Meade were left free to think about post-war problems.

Keynes served as the main bridge between the Treasury and the economists recruited into the Economic Section, the Central Statistical Office and the Ministries. They were his professional colleagues, many of them former students for whom he was a natural leader and ally. Keynes himself was suggested as first head of the CSO, in December 1940,[11] but refused, preferring to remain footloose in the Treasury. The Economic Section was immediately seen as a dangerous rival by the Treasury, which tried to curtail its scope and functions.[12] Keynes played an important part in arranging a *modus vivendi,* and he and Lionel Robbins, director of the Economic Section from September 1941 to November 1945, 'worked together in great harmony', despite their pre-war quarrels.[13] Keynes was happy with these fluid arrangements. He believed in preserving a balance of power between the technicians and the administrators, with himself as an avuncular go-between. He could use the economists to bolster his position in the Treasury, while using the Treasury to discipline their theoretical enthusiasms. He 'thought it a mistake to link the Economic Section to the Treasury, where they would either be too powerful or not powerful enough'.[14] When Anderson became Chancellor in 1943, the Economic Section, with its responsibility for manpower planning, continued to be separated from the Treasury. With the return of peacetime methods, the logic of this division evaporated, and the Economic Section was incorporated into the Treasury in 1953.

Keynes became more Treasury-minded as the war progressed. His more radical followers attributed his growing conservatism to the malign influence of his Treasury associates. Naturally enough everyone is influenced by his immediate associations; and there is some substance to the charge that Keynes 'went native'. It is a large simplification, nevertheless. By the time Keynes re-entered the Treasury in 1940 he was no longer the *enfant terrible* of his own legend. Events and his own powers of persuasion had jointly done their work in edging Whitehall's views closer to his own. He had always believed in being a few years ahead of the game. War brought a rapid catch-up. It was a catch-up helped by capture. The economists brought into the government by war were not all Keynesians, but their outlook had been permanently shifted by the Keynesian Revolution. Nevertheless, it is probably true that by the time he died what Keynes still wanted to achieve was no longer much in advance of what it was politically and administratively feasible to achieve.

Close linkage between the networks of economists and career civil servants was facilitated by Whitehall's structure and geography. Unlike Washington's sprawling, leaky and incoherent bureaucracy, Whitehall, in Keynes's day, was a lean, self-enclosed world, reflecting the British tradition of centralised government and administration. In his six years at the Treasury Keynes would have been in regular contact with no more than fifty people; and in close and continuous contact with no more than a dozen. All the great offices of state were bunched together. Treasury Chambers in Great George Street was embedded in a complex of government buildings, with St James's Park on the one side and the Palace of Westminster on the other, its dingy interior symbolisng the Treasury's traditional role as the guardian of the public purse. Treasury officials were reasonably, but by no means lavishly, paid. The permanent secretary (who was also head of the civil service) got £3,500; the second secretaries £3000; principals between £700 and £1000. These salaries were all frozen for the six years of war, though the price level by the war's end was about 50 per cent higher than at the start. Keynes was independently wealthy. His gross annual income between 1939–40 and 1945–6 averaged £12,623, most of it investment income. Even though punitive wartime taxation reduced his relative advantage, it was still substantial. Keynes was strategically located. His second-floor office, overlooking Parliament Square, with a painting by Duncan Grant as the sole concession to higher values, was immediately on the left of the Chancellor's; on the right was Thomas Catto, the Treasury's other economic adviser; across the corridor from Keynes was the permanent secretary (after 1942 Sir Richard Hopkins). The War Cabinet Offices, including the Economic Section, were in the same building. During air-raids, the government, headed by the Prime Minister, transferred to the basement, where a duplicate complex of offices had been constructed. Over the whole war, the Treasury had to be evacuated only once, in the winter of 1940, as a result of a direct hit. For Keynes, all this meant that he rarely had to leave the Treasury to conduct his business, the vast majority of meetings, including meetings of inter-departmental committees, taking place in his or adjoining rooms.

Geographical propinquity did not, however, produce an oral culture. There was no Whitehall equivalent of Morgenthau's daily 'brainstorming' sessions with his senior officials. The British system of administration was formal and hierarchical. Like other major departments, the Treasury had its structure of permanent, second, third, under, principal assistant, assistant, principal, assistant principal secretaries, to mention only the grades in the administrative class. Officials from the principal and assistant principal secretaries downwards were organised in divisions. Civil servants were responsible to ministers; ministers were responsible to Parliament. Decision-making proceeded by an upward shuffle of paper, not by means of deals in smoke-filled rooms. Keynes's major initiatives started as memoranda injected into the policymaking machine. They were then subjected to a searching process of scrutiny and criticism by the relevant officials within the Treasury and departments on which they impacted. In monetary and external financial policy, this involved the Bank of England. Before the days of photocopiers and personal computers, this scrutiny was a laborious and time-consuming business, involving the production and circulation of carbon-copied or stencilled documents, with comments from all the relevant officials received, discussed, incorporated or rejected at each stage in a hierarchical ascent to a final product for the Chancellor's consideration. The process was predominantly literary. There were numbers, of course, but no equations. The aim was to present a consensual Treasury (and if possible Whitehall) opinion, which it would be hard for the Chancellor to ignore. Keynes was able to use the critical machine to his advantage. Not only was he able to force his critics to accept the logic of his proposals; he was indefatigable in adapting them to objections and changing realities. Quite apart from the power of his conceptions, he knew how to work the Whitehall machine.

Once the domestic fiscal framework had been settled, it was inevitable that an increasing amount of Keynes's attention would be taken up by overseas finance. There were many reasons for this, including his own Treasury background as first head of 'A' Division in the First World War. Here it is only important to notice that the arena of Keynes's dominance was also the arena of his greatest single failure – which was to get Britain's rulers to understand the relationship between the economics of war and the economics of post-war survival. Once victory over Germany became certain, Keynes started to attack the 'Lady Bountiful' approach to waging war: the unfortunate Sir Frederick Leith-Ross at the Office of Economic Warfare was the frequent recipient of acerbic comment for his over-eagerness to commit Britain to expensive relief schemes which it could not afford. Keynes advocated cutting down on foreign military spending in order to halt the build-up of sterling debt, restarting the export trade and reaching agreement with Britain's creditors to 'fund' the 'abnormal' sterling balances. From the start of 1944, he urged a policy of retrench-ment for the remainder of the war in order to start the peace without having to borrow large sums from the United States. It was the defeat of this policy which forced Keynes – and Britain – to accept the humiliating terms of the American loan in 1945.

Keynes's failure to reactivate the limited war option goes back to the Cabinet's decision in the summer of 1940 to throw financial prudence to the winds. After the fall of France it was not possible to revive the debate about what kind of war Britain should fight. The German threat was too immediate and the number of Britain's allies too small for Britain to contemplate a limited war which would protect its reserves and trade connections. The export trade was sacrificed to the production of war goods; imports – from the Americas, the Empire and neutrals – were determined by war needs, not by what Britain could afford to pay. Total war was forced on Britain by Germany. There was no point in maintaining a trading economy if the Germans were determined to sink the ships transporting goods to and from Britain. It never apparently occurred to Germany's rulers that a less fully mobilised Britain would be a lesser threat to Germany than a fully mobilised one.

No account of Keynes's time in Whitehall should overlook the terrific strain under which he and everyone else worked – and not just from the continuous air-raids. The great advantage of private enterprise, Keynes used to say, was that it decentralised economic responsibility to the maximum possible degree. In the war it was centralised to an unprecedented extent. This meant much more work for government, with only a grudging increase in manpower to do it: quality was supposed to make up for lack of quantity. This was most vividly true in the negotiations with the Americans, but it was also true over the whole range of governmental activity. As the war went on, everyone became more and more exhausted. Churchill often appeared *non compos mentis* at Cabinet. In his case supreme responsibility was superimposed on a highly erratic lifestyle: prodigious alcohol consumption and inability to get to bed at night. At least he could sleep late: but the staff who attended his wakes had no such respite. Churchill was exceptional, but it was generally the case that few of those who worked in Whitehall had much idea about how to look after themselves. They did not live like athletes in training. Most smoked heavily; they took no exercise; they ate disgusting food. Of Keynes's own circle, Frederick Phillips died of cancer, Richard Hopkins and Hubert Henderson suffered coronary thromboses, Dennis Robertson had gall bladder trouble, James Meade suffered from stomach ulcers. For much of the war the sickly Keynes – who drank very sparingly and, at Lydia's insistence, went early to bed – stood forth as a paragon of good health.

III

KEYNES'S NETWORKS

Keynes served under three Chancellors – Kingsley Wood, John Anderson and Hugh Dalton. Kingsley Wood had replaced the indecisive and increasingly detached Sir John Simon in May 1940, Simon becoming Lord Chancellor. Wood was a solicitor by training. Despite a thin, reedy voice, he was an effective, hard-working politician, who had been in government throughout the 1930s. His reward for switching allegiance, at the last moment, from Chamberlain to Churchill was the Exchequer. He was never in Churchill's inner circle, failing to get a permanent position in the War Cabinet. This weakened the Treasury's standing in government. His strength as Chancellor was his 'capacity for hard work, for seeking and acting upon the best advice he could command, and for getting things done'.[15] Although his 1941 budget was not as revolutionary as legend made it out to be, it was at least consistent with Keynes's conception of the budget as an instrument of economic policy. The real innovation was the accompanying National Income and Expenditure White Paper – the forecast of the 'national accounts' for the following year – which came to supersede traditional Treasury arithmetic as the basis for the 'budget judgement' until the advent of Margaret Thatcher. Keynes's attitude to Kingsley Wood was affectionate and appreciative, without being overly admiring. He found drafting Wood's budget

speeches 'a heart-breaking job . . . for I know well by experience that the
better I make it the less likely it is to be used!' Sir Richard Hopkins put it
more politely: 'The Chancellor proceeds *from* the pedestrian.'[16] When
news of Wood's unexpected death reached Washington in September
1943, Keynes, who was there on a mission, rather shocked the Americans
by getting up at lunch and saying: 'No matter how . . . apparently
incomprehensible an economic proposition seemed to him to be, he . . .
had the gift of converting it . . . into a platitude intelligible to the merest
child. This is a great political gift, not to be despised. . . .'[17]

Sir John Anderson, his successor, was a civil servant, and former
chairman of the Board of Inland Revenue. Succeeding the dying Neville
Chamberlain as Lord President of the Council in October 1940, he was
judged by Robbins to have been 'the greatest public administrator of the
age'.[18] He had an exceptional capacity for hard work, an excellent
memory, efficient work habits, great persistence and a dispassionate
approach to problems which inspired confidence in his integrity: Sir
Richard Hopkins would say that he had never known a Chancellor so little
influenced by political considerations. He was also tremendously pompous
– people called him 'Pompous John' – though not without a pawky,
Presbyterian humour. When he became Chancellor in 1943, he relinquished his powerful Lord President's Committee to Clement Attlee, the
Deputy Prime Minister. Keynes did not, in truth, have much to do with
him. By the time Anderson became Chancellor, the war economy was
working on automatic pilot; all the major financial decisions had been
taken, at home and abroad. There was no intimacy between the creative
imp and the stiff, gloomy public servant, but there was no friction either,
and, as we shall see, Anderson backed Keynes in Cabinet to get the
Bretton Woods negotiations under way.

After the end of the German war, Keynes was chief economic adviser,
for eight months, to Hugh Dalton, Labour's first Chancellor. Their pre-
1914 Cambridge background (Dalton had attended Keynes's lectures)
linked the two together; mutual antipathy kept them apart: Keynes used
to call Dalton 'The Dirty Doctor'. Dalton had imbibed the earliest of
Keynes's doctrines, cheap money, and stopped there. Keynes's relations
with Dalton foundered during the American loan negotiations of 1945,
and when he died he was on the point of quitting Dalton's Treasury.

Keynes's first Treasury permanent secretary was Sir Horace Wilson, an
unusual appointment from outside the department or Inland Revenue,
made at the behest of Prime Minister Neville Chamberlain, whose close
friend and confidant he was. But he was too publicly identified with the
policy of appeasement to thrive in the new regime. He was allowed to stay
on till he reached sixty in 1942, the earliest retiring age. He was succeeded
by Sir Richard Hopkins, the second secretary, who was in turn followed by
Sir Edward Bridges in 1945.

At that time, the Treasury was organised into three main divisions – Finance, Supply and Establishments. Finance was split up into Home Finance and Overseas Finance. Home Finance dealt with government borrowing and debt management; Overseas Finance with the balance of payments. The controller of finance was Sir Frederick Phillips, who started the war as third secretary and in 1942 became joint second secretary with Sir Alan Barlow, in charge of Supply. Between 1940 and 1943 Phillips spent most of his time as British Treasury representative in Washington. Sir Wilfrid Eady took Phillips's place as head of Finance in London in 1942, David ('Sigi') Waley, promoted to under-secretary in 1943, taking charge of Overseas Finance. In 1944, the banker Robert Brand assumed Phillips's role as Treasury representative in Washington.

Keynes used to say that the Treasury was at its peak when Hopkins was in charge, with Sir Frederick Phillips as his lieutenant.[19] He thought of them as fine examples of the Treasury mind at its best – cautious but rigorous, and ultimately receptive. They did not accept, perhaps even understand, his characteristic doctrines. Sir Richard Hopkins read the *General Theory* only in 1945, after he had retired as permanent secretary. He aimed to use Keynes's brains, not his theories. But, of course, his theories, or rather his way of analysing problems, rubbed off on both men. In turn, their support for him, as well as his respect for them, was the bedrock of his institutional strength. He must have struck them at times like a spanner in the works. But they refused to allow themselves to be put off by his restless interference, and knew how to use his ideas to enhance the Treasury's prestige.

'Diminutive in stature, with a general appearance rather like that of an extremely intelligent monkey, on the subject of government finance [Hopkins] was an intellectual match for anyone of his generation.'[20] He had overlapped with Keynes at Cambridge, though there is no evidence that they knew each other then. Like many top civil servants, Hopkins's training was in classics: he took a first in Part I of the Classics Tripos, and a first in Part II of the History Tripos. He was also a rugby and fives blue. His special expertise was taxation: he had come to the Treasury via Inland Revenue. From the time he succeeded Otto Niemeyer as controller of finance in 1927, 'his was normally the last word, and accepted as the last word, of expert financial advice to the Chancellor of the Exchequer'.[21] His support for Keynes was thus absolutely crucial. He and Keynes had clashed famously on the Macmillan Committee on Finance and Industry in 1930 over the question of whether public works could cure unemployment.[22] On the Committee on Economic Information in the 1930s, Keynes had inched Phillips towards accepting the idea of countercyclical public spending, and this had rubbed off on Hopkins, to whom Phillips reported.[23] Hopkins was quiet, shy, reserved, with a powerful mind and a dry sense of humour. He had a small circle of intimate friends. One of them was 'Monty' Norman, governor of the Bank. His son, Alan Hopkins, remembers an evening when Norman came to supper. The two men dined in almost complete silence. On leaving, Montagu Norman thanked Hopkins for a 'most interesting evening'. Alan protested: 'But you never said anything.' 'Ah, but our minds were moving along parallel lines,' his father replied. Keynes treated him with affectionate, sometimes exasperated, respect, which Hopkins reciprocated. 'Dear Hoppy . . . how fearfully and dangerously rash you cautious people are,' he wrote to him on one occasion.[24] Like many cautious men, Hopkins could be fired by others' visions. He generated the Treasury consensus behind Keynes's approach to budgetary arithmetic and his Clearing Union Plan, and helped Meade's memorandum on post-war employment policy on its way to White Paper status.

Keynes got on equally well with Phillips, another reserved official susceptible to his intellectual charm. As we have seen, their ability to work together in Washington in 1941, under very trying circumstances, was key to the success of Keynes's mission. After Keynes's return, they kept up a fairly continuous correspondence, Phillips dry and factual, Keynes expansive, lively, gossipy. In 1943 Brand wrote from Washington: 'Phillips, I am sure, has valuable ideas on both schemes [Clearing Union, Stabilisation Fund] and I have had more than one monosyllabic conversation with him. But, as you know, a free discussion with him, either on this or on any other subject, is practically impossible – certainly not through any ill-will on his part, but because I think the habit has now become second nature to him.'[25] When Phillips died later that year, Keynes wrote of him in *The Times*: 'His laconic manner, or, more exactly, his grunts of assent or dispute, were as well known and as well understood in Washington or Ottawa as in Whitehall; at Geneva he could be silent in several languages.'[26]

Keynes's Treasury ramified beyond Whitehall. Keynes himself spent approximately one year of the war – or 20 per cent of his time – in Washington, where a parallel British administration, which came to number several hundreds, worked out of the Willard Hotel and the Embassy's Chancellery, with Halifax presiding as a constitutional, but not entirely powerless, monarch. Dennis Robertson and 'Sigi' Waley were there representing the Treasury for a large part of 1943–4. Apart from Phillips, Keynes was most continuously in touch with Redvers Opie, an Oxford economist who was counsellor and economic adviser to the British Embassy, and, after Phillips's death, with Bob Brand. Until Brand took over the function, Opie provided Keynes with much of his information about trends in American opinion, and Keynes supplied him with similarly atmospheric reports from London. But Opie was not penetrating enough to be an ideal intellectual companion for someone like Keynes, and tended to get lost in the technicalities of financial negotiations. The same could not be said about Bob Brand, who became chief Treasury representative in Washington in 1944. His friendship with Keynes dates from the Paris Peace Conference in 1919, though they started calling each other 'Bob' and 'Maynard' only in 1944. A Fellow of All Souls and a merchant banker, Brand was known, at least by his friends, as the 'wisest man in the Empire' before the First World War. An extremely intelligent, shrewd and accomplished financial diplomat, bald, bespectacled and diffident in manner, he was another official dazzled by Keynes's intelligence and lightning celerity. He said that with Keynes he always felt like the bottom boy in the class. But he was not afraid to argue with him, and Keynes greatly respected both his mind and his judgement. As we shall see, Brand was one of the few who faulted Keynes's judgement in the run-up to the American loan negotiations of 1945, but he lacked the confidence to make his views prevail.

The banker Thomas Catto – who had been ennobled in 1936 – was another important ally in Keynes's first four years at the Treasury. A short, self-made Scotsman, partner in Morgan Grenfell, and since 1940 a director of the Bank of England, he had been made unpaid adviser to the Chancellor shortly before Keynes. He had the office next to Keynes's at the Treasury. 'From the first time I walked into his room with some papers in my hand to discuss with him, we seemed to take to each other,' Catto recalled. 'I came to have considerable influence with him, partly because he liked me, and partly, I think, because he found that the quickness of his mind and his sometimes startling theories did not frighten me; for I applied to them in the friendliest spirit the test of long practical experience.' Catto and Keynes worked closely together on the 1941 budget as well as on the intractable problem of the sterling balances. Catto protected the Bank's interests in the Treasury; and protected Keynes's Clearing Union Plan from the full force of Bank hostility.

With the death of Phillips in 1943 and the decline of Hopkins's health at the end of the same year, the Treasury lost its cohesion. Keynes never established the same rapport with Sir Wilfrid Eady, the new controller of finance. Eady, who had been appointed to the Treasury from outside, was a pugnacious and effective negotiator. He was dazzled and awed by Keynes, and felt a 'deep affection' for him,[27] but he lacked Hopkins's intellectual grasp of complex problems. Keynes once said to him, after some argument, 'If I had taken you very young and had limitless patience, I might have taught you the elements of economics. As it is, I must assume that you understand your own art of administration.' One could not imagine Keynes teasing Hopkins like that; it is to Eady's credit that he took no offence and tells the story against himself.[28] Robert Armstrong, a later permanent secretary, delicately wrote on Eady's death that 'it was not an easy collaboration'.[29] Also, Eady, unlike Hopkins, had a nationalist, imperialist agenda which cut across Keynes's internationalist one. Because, however, he lacked authority, he could annoy Keynes, but not thwart him.

At the end, only Richard ('Otto') Clarke, another outsider, could stand up to Keynes in the Treasury. But he was a much younger man and, like everyone else, in awe of him. Keynes was left as a solitary mountain towering over the foothills.

Keynes dominated the Treasury physically as well as intellectually. By coincidence, the men with whom he worked closest – Wood, Hopkins, Catto, Eady – were all short, whereas Keynes was over six foot.

> The majesty of his appearance was notable. For three years he had been gravely ill, and he had to guard and save his strength. Tall and big-framed, he walked through the Treasury in slow processional dignity. Above his dark clothes, the ivory pallor of his face and the fine dark-blue eyes, steady and reflective, or filling with amusement, had often the effect of a light moving. Others, in Washington, noted this luminous aspect. His hands, also, were distinctive. He used them rarely in gesture, except to gather an argument together, or, ominously, to remove his glasses, which he placed before him, deliberately folded, with his hands cupped over them. This was the hoisting of a storm-cone. The slight stammer would reappear for a moment, the even, restful voice would darken, and all those who had been fishing in troubled waters would make for harbour. But the sky would clear with equal suddenness.[30]

His stature, as well as his isolation, became more obvious with the departure of Dennis Robertson and Hubert Henderson in 1944, to take up chairs in economics at Cambridge and Oxford respectively. The two men were economists of Keynes's generation, easily able to stand up to him – and each other – in debate. Robertson's 'first class brains' – temporarily transferred to Washington in 1943–4 – proved invaluable in the negotiations leading up to the Bretton Woods Agreement. But Robertson's subtle and penetrating criticisms were not to hand when Keynes drew up his strategy for handling 'Stage III' in 1945. Keynes's relationship with Henderson was far more stormy. Henderson's duties were as vague as Keynes's, and he made it his special concern to pour cold water over what he considered post-war projects for utopias, most of them inspired by his former mentor. He spent much of his time at the Treasury working on his history of the international economy between the wars, which he finished in December 1943. This was designed to underpin his case for continuing the planned economy into peacetime.

Hopkins's Treasury was wont to balance Keynes's optimism with Henderson's pessimism and split the difference. This was most obvious in the famous Employment White Paper of 1944, with its strong, though subsequently neglected, emphasis on getting the supply side of the economy right. Although their personal relations remained cordial enough, Henderson was the biggest thorn in Keynes's side throughout the war, disputing his positions on fiscal policy, the Clearing Union, buffer stocks, trade liberalisation, employment policy and a host of smaller matters. His coronary thrombosis in August 1942 barely interrupted the flow of his barbed memoranda. Despite this, Keynes treated Henderson with marked respect, and found much to approve in his consistently pessimistic analyses. Although Henderson's influence is said to have been diminished by his refusal to recognise 'the formidable organising power of economic analysis,'[31] it would be truer to say that in his arguments with Keynes he proceeded from an opposite postulate, that demand deficiency had not been the main cause of Britain's chronic inter-war unemployment problem, and consequently demand expansion, whether domestic or international, would inevitably promise more than it could deliver. Henderson was more of a planner than Keynes because he was less of a Keynesian.

The collapse of Keynes's Treasury networks drew him closer to two economists in the Economic Section, James Meade and Lionel Robbins. Meade, a future Nobel Prize Winner, was the most powerful economic thinker in the Section, as well as its main visionary. Early in the war, he was chiefly involved, with Richard Stone at the Central Statistical Office, in setting up the system of national accounts. Later he concentrated on post-war employment and commercial policy. Meade was a liberal socialist, who grafted the Keynesian analysis of unemployment on to the classical free-trade and redistribution framework. His deceptive mildness of manner hid a steely persistence in theoretical controversy and the pursuit of his plans. 'His interest lay in issues of principle; and, if ministerial decisions seemed to him mistaken in principle, he thought it his duty to contest them. . . .'[32] This is a polite way of saying that Meade rarely took political realities into account. The Treasury official 'Otto' Clarke called him 'ridiculously academic and perfectionist'. Meade worshipped Keynes, without being overawed by him. Keynes greatly respected Meade's analytical powers – at meetings of officials he would sometimes call on Meade to expound 'Keynesian' theory – but was sceptical of his utopianism, and, as we shall see, gave only limited support to his plan for stabilising demand by varying national insurance contributions (he thought the main emphasis should be on managing investment), and was much less of a free trader than Meade was.

Robbins was less of a Keynesian and more of a politician than was Meade. He had a powerful mind and personality, with 'a measured, eighteenth-century style that matched his Johnsonian figure and, if at times a little ponderous, he also achieved elegance and wit'. Robbins was Pompous John's favourite official, and their relationship, together with Anderson's own standing in the War Cabinet, was the key to the Economic Section's influence.[33] One of Robbins's main achievements was to secure points rationing for foodstuffs, against the strong opposition of the Ministry of Food. Robbins had been chastened by the theoretical defeats he had suffered at Keynes's hands in the 1930s. While he continued to find much of the *General Theory* 'confused and even wrong-headed', he had 'long realized that my earlier diagnosis of the Great Depression had missed the mark in not realizing sufficiently the paramount role played by the catastrophic contraction of incomes brought about by deflation . . .'.[34] The Keynes–Robbins axis became crucial in the years 1943–5, with Robbins strong in support of the Bretton Woods compromise and Keynes's positions on the loan negotiations.

By contrast, those most closely implicated in the Keynesian Revolution of the 1930s were not part of Keynes's Whitehall circuit. Joan Robinson stayed at Cambridge. Harrod desperately wanted a Treasury job. Keynes recommended him for one, but without success. Instead Harrod found a precarious perch in Cherwell's 'S' Section, from where he resigned to return to Oxford in 1942. In 'S' Section, he felt undervalued and underused. He was a man of ideas, not of multi-coloured diagrams. After quitting Cherwell's mini-empire, he tried hard to get suitable war work, but no one would have him. Despite his powerful intellect, he was said to 'lack judgement'. The truth seems to be that he was too donnish and self-regarding to be fitted happily into a team. He was a brilliant economist; his subsequent life was to be embittered by his wartime career failure.

Keynes also tried, without success, to get Richard Kahn into the Treasury. Hopkins probably thought that it was enough to have Christ, without having St Peter there as well. Instead Kahn went to the Board of Trade. In October 1941 he was sent to Egypt as economic adviser to Oliver Lyttelton, Minister of State. His work involved trying to save shipping space by encouraging local food production. He became Keynes's main source of information on the Middle East. In 1942, Keynes sponsored an ingenious initiative, transmitted by Kahn, to sell Egypt and Persia gold. Gold would provide an alternative to foodstuffs as a store of value, thus reducing their rate of inflation and slowing down their accumulation of sterling balances.[35] Kahn loved Keynes, and could only function properly in his shadow. Deprived of Keynes's constant stimulus – and peremptory demands – he languished. He languished in Egypt, complaining to Keynes on 16 August 1942 that he had 'ceased to be allowed any responsibility'. Keynes supported his desperate request to return, but it was delayed because Treasury Establishment couldn't discover who paid him. In January 1943 he came back to a job in the Ministry of Supply. From there he moved on to the Ministry of Production, and then back to the Board of Trade when the two departments merged after the war. Master and disciple continued to correspond, but, being out of the loop, Kahn played no real part in Keynes's two great wartime achievements – the Kingsley Wood budget of 1941 and the Clearing Union Plan. After the war, Keynes supported his department's request that he be allowed a further leave of absence from King's to work on British tariff policy in preparation for the International Trade Conference. As he explained to Sheppard on 20 February 1946, 'he is for the first time in the war [sic] thoroughly happy and contented in his work . . .'. But he advised Sheppard to 'order' Kahn to leave the Board of Trade on Friday night and not return till Monday morning, and spend three nights quietly at King's so he could help Dadie Rylands out with bursarial matters.

To conclude: Keynes was much less happy in Whitehall in his last sixteen months there. He talked increasingly of resigning. It was the passing of the inter-war generation he minded most, and its replacement by men of inferior or as yet untested calibre. In January 1945, Meade records him denouncing his department as 'utterly incapable and incompetent to deal with technical economic matters'.[36] In 1945, he was unchallengeable, but isolated. As Donald Moggridge says, 'he could be in a minority, not be believed . . . and still get most of his way'.[37] Only after the trauma of the American loan negotiations at the end of 1945 did his authority start to wane.

IV

THE KEYNESIAN TEMPERAMENT

Opportunity, temperament and qualities of mind and heart brought Keynes to a dominating position in the Treasury. Some of the opportunities were self-created, others more circumstantial, but it was Keynes's exploitation of the opportunities which the war opened up which makes his performance outstanding. He earned his entry ticket into the Treasury by writing *How to Pay for the War*, but lost no time in producing a series of powerful memoranda which got him put on the Budget Committee. His informal access to Churchill through the Other Club, his friendship with the American ambassador John Winant, his directorship of the Bank of England, finally his peerage: this dowry of external influence greatly increased his prestige within the Treasury; but it was his creative energy which caused it to multiply. Two other opportunities for leadership were created for him: the absence of Sir Frederick Phillips in Washington between 1940 and 1943 and the relative weakness of Eady gave him the chance to seize control of overseas finance in London; while the inability of the Chancellor to leave Britain for any extended period left Keynes as the obvious British official to 'represent the Chancellor' abroad in top-level negotiations – which he did on six missions to the United States between 1941 and 1946. Indeed, to the Americans, Keynes *was* Britain's Chancellor of the Exchequer. The Clearing Union Plan is, as we shall see, the classic example of Keynes taking the initiative. Article VII of the Lend–Lease Agreement gave him his opportunity. He was not asked to produce a plan. He could have contented himself with commentary. Instead, he turned the whole discussion by producing his own 'big idea'.

Keynes's temperamental activism, the counterpart of his confidence in his own competence, also determined the part he played. Even as a schoolboy he was writing to his father: 'I am finding . . . that whenever I am appointed to a committee I am invariably made to do all the work.' The undergraduate who told C. R. Fay soon after he arrived at King's College, Cambridge that 'I've had a good look round the place and come to the conclusion that it's pretty inefficient' was still recognisable in Keynes at the Treasury. As one Treasury official, Dennis Proctor, recalls, 'His instinctive attitude to any problem was, first, to assume that nobody was doing anything about it and, secondly, that, if they were, they were doing the wrong thing.' From his office, he would let fly a swarm of minutes, dictated to Mrs Stephens, which 'would turn up in somebody's in-tray the next morning – or probably several people's in-trays, since he liked to loose these missiles in a spray of carbon copies directed at several targets at once'. He preferred his own writing paper, which allowed him to feel the 'run and balance of his sentences', to what he called the toilet-paper provided by the Treasury. His distinctive, double-spaced missives would be received with a 'mixture of slight terror, some delight and immediate hostility' – the terror, no doubt, induced by the fear of having made some slip of commission or omission, the delight being in their prose style, and the hostility aroused by one or other of the two assumptions which inspired them. More often than not 'Maynard had got it all wrong, but this was going to cause a lot of trouble before it was finished with.'[38]

Within the Treasury, as within Whitehall as a whole, Keynes was a continuous stimulator of action, a great stirrer up. 'He accepted a description of his functions as those of the pike put into the Roman carp-ponds, to chase the carp around and keep them from getting lousy.'[39] He had a seemingly insatiable curiosity about anything touching war finance, however remote from the centre of his concerns; and for most of the war he had enough energy and speed of mind to sustain a huge scatter of interventions. By 10.30 in the morning he had already done an amount of dictating which would occupy another most of his day. His eye was a roving searchlight, illuminating examples of defective reasoning or action in dark quarters. He had no respect for administrative hierarchies or demarcations, would go to junior officials for facts or opinions, and would not scruple to use their testimony against obstructive superiors. This made him an unsettling colleague.

Keynes's hunches usually ran well ahead of his knowledge of the facts. This was almost inevitable: he was not a specialist, and he was not part of the administrative machine. But ignorance was no barrier to his forming decided opinions on what should be done, which he would propound and defend passionately, and with every device of argument, rhetoric and repartee at hastily assembled meetings of officials. His initial assumption of omniscience was, however, tempered by a marked respect for specialist knowledge, and once a plan or pet scheme had been declared unworkable or unsound, he would rapidly modify it or start on another tack. He could be devastatingly rude to those who, in his view, were lazy, incompetent or obtuse. Stories of his put-downs are legion. He once told a Colonial Office official, Gerald Clauson, who had submitted a critical memorandum on buffer stocks: 'I agree with everything in this if *not* is put in front of every statement.'[40] But, as Catto recalled after his death, 'among those whom he liked, he could differ with a curious and delightful gentleness'. There is ample testimony to the kick which people got out of working with him, even though it was they who sometimes got kicked.

Most important Treasury papers came to him for comment. He felt it his duty to enquire into any matter where he suspected action was lacking or inadequate. At times a passion for detail seized him, and he would burrow into 'low level' committees to find out how the matter was really being handled. Sometimes the Chancellor of the Exchequer wanted a word with him, and he would be discovered in the Board of Trade attending a committee no one had heard of. Keynes had more contacts than other high-ranking officials, with those both above and below him.

His interventions would often be triggered by a fragment of information which had come his way from outside. A typical example arose out of a correspondence with Rupert Trouton in the winter of 1940–1. A former 'A' Division colleague from the First World War, subsequently a director of the Hector Whaling Company, in which Keynes had invested, Trouton doubted that the real problem of getting supplies through from abroad was shortage of shipping. There was in fact a shipping surplus. The problem was congestion in discharge, due partly to labour shortages. 'On re-reading your letter,' Trouton wrote to Keynes, who had upheld the orthodox position, 'I am made to wonder – only ever so slightly of course – are you becoming "official-minded"?' Any such suggestion was like a red rag to Keynes. 'Thank you very much for a useful letter, – just what I wanted to get. You will realise that I only enter into this shipping question by a side-wind. . . .' Trouton's observations, accompanied by the familiar double-spaced letter, soon arrived on the appropriate departmental desks.[41] Soon after Keynes's arrival at the Treasury he got interested in Bolivian tin. The 'attached correspondence', he informed Waley ominously on 3 October 1940, showed that the Bolivians had 'ratted' on their tin agreement with Britain and it was 'merely a question of time before all the Bolivian tin goes to the USA to be smelted'. In Washington, Playfair wrote to Waley on 3 April 1941: 'Are we right in thinking that [Maynard] has recently become interested in Bolivian tin? Recent instructions to deliver a rather cock-eyed ultimatum on the subject to most of the

American Cabinet, nine months late & based on false premises, we assume
to be one of his wilder moments. Even Hermes nods.'[42]

In the autumn of 1941, Keynes took advantage of Richard Kahn's
presence in Cairo to send him a five-page plan for reorganising the
Middle East's transport system.[43] Early in 1942 we find him eloquent in
resisting a British loan to China – the so-called Niemeyer loan – demanded
by the army to help repel the Japanese advance in South-East Asia. In a
caustic note he told the story of Huxley looking up the word 'intelligence'
in the *Encyclopaedia Britannica* and finding 'Intelligence, human. Intelligence, animal. Intelligence, military'.[44] There is a file in his Treasury
papers marked 'Italy: Ancient Monuments and Art Treasures (Protection)'. In 1945, 'the question of the finance of reconstruction in Burma
... is a completely new subject to me. Perhaps it is lack of background
that makes me find this paper almost unintelligible. Any possibility of rewriting it so that one can see what it really amounts to?'[45] Even Keynes
had his limits. He resisted attemps to involve him in currency reform in
Ethiopia and the tangled affairs of the British Institute in Madrid. 'After
all, one must be allowed some moderate specialisation of functions,' he
wrote, in a rare tone of plaintiveness.[46]

In the last analysis, what made Keynes an extraordinary civil servant was
the same mixture of qualities which made him an extraordinary economist. There was, to start with, his life-enhancing vitality and optimism, like
Churchill's; his conviction that to every problem there was a solution. As
Austin Robinson notes, 'around Keynes something was always happening'.[47] To be with Keynes, on paper or in person, was the greatest possible
fun – even if his rudeness could sometimes reduce grown men to tears.
'The extraordinary thing about him', wrote one of his Treasury colleagues,
'was his intellectual sex appeal and zing, always fresh and interesting and
original and provocative. . . .'[48] The Canadian official Douglas LePan
pictured his Treasury office as a 'miraculous smithy', constantly sparking
off fresh ideas.[49] His brain, thought Robert Brand, was different from that
of even his brainiest colleagues: 'it was like something constantly throwing
off sparks. "Flashing" is the only epithet I can think of.'[50] Over a lifetime
of friendship, Virginia Woolf singled out the same qualities: 'that queer
imaginative ardour about history, humanity', his mind 'working always',
but equally amused by small incidents, his ideas overflowing 'vigorously
into byepaths'.[51] Keynes's intellectual vitality was accompanied by a
marked changeability. The questing mind was so ardent in its questing,
that no one could ever be sure where it would settle next. Partly this was
the effect of mere playfulness, the love of argument for its own sake, the
enjoyment of shocking the conventional. Partly it was due to quick
reactions to changes in facts. As Kingsley Martin said, when facts changed
he rearranged his views – 'a reasonable procedure which only seemed
inconsistent because he phrased both his objurgations and repentances

in such stirring and memorable language'.[52] He was often much too optimistic, so great was his belief in the power of thought and persuasion, especially his own. But this was a fault on the right side in the darkest days of the war, and there was no lack of counterbalancing scepticism.

But he was not all fizz. As Austin Robinson writes, doing something about a problem presented itself to Keynes in three stages: analysis, administrative technique, persuasion. His mind moved without break from theory to plan, the whole movement expressed in prose of compelling power. The war gave Keynes the chance to live up to his ideal of the 'master economist', who must touch 'abstract and concrete in the same flight of thought'. If this diluted the pure quality of his cerebration, it made him an outstanding policy adviser.

All Keynes's projects had a powerful analytical core. Specifically, the logic of the *General Theory* shone through *How to Pay for the War* and the Clearing Union Plan. Not all the Whitehall economists shared the same analytic system. But non-Keynesians like Robertson, Robbins and Henderson suffered from the disadvantage that their own systems were in considerable disarray after the *General Theory*'s assault on them. Except for Henderson, the non-Keynesian economists in any case supported Keynes's plans on more traditional grounds – for anti-inflationary reasons in the budget discussions, for internationalist reasons in the case of the Clearing Union. Politicians and officials might argue against Keynes's projects that they were politically or administratively impracticable, but they lacked the training or flair to challenge their underlying logic.

Keynes was not just a powerful theoretician. He always had a strong sense of what events required of theory. He aimed to supply serviceable theory, constantly adapting his theoretical approach to the preoccupations of government. The *General Theory* was a theory of employment, built for the situation of the early 1930s. We have already seen the way he manoeuvred it to meet the inflationary concerns of the Treasury (and economic orthodoxy) in the proto-war years and in *How to Pay for the War*. We shall see the same process at work in this Clearing Union Plan, where he used his liquidity preference theory as the intellectual pivot for a scheme of workable internationalism.

Keynes had a genius for translating theory into administrative technique. He was that rare bird who could think both strategically and administratively. Most intellectuals are baffled and frustrated by Whitehall. They come in with bold ideas which evaporate as they move towards implementation. Keynes surmounted this disillusioning progression. He had an instinctive sense of what might be made to work, and how it might be made to work; and an instinctive ability to distinguish real from spurious objections. A crucial element in his practical success was his feel for figures, or as he liked to put it, for 'magnitudes'. Although he was not a trained statistician, he was way ahead of most of his colleagues in his willingness to use figures or estimates to underpin his proposals. When officials told him that figures were not available, he resorted to his 'compression' technique. He demanded maximum and minimum estimates and split the difference. Strong numerical scaffolding gave his plans a solidity which could be misleading, but which was better than no scaffolding at all. Like many people with a strong feeling for figures, he had a poor memory for dates, and little historical sense. He lived overwhelmingly in the present. This was both his strength and weakness as an economist.

A less noted aspect of Keynes's administrative style was his willingness to compromise. Students of Keynes have been misled by the confrontational technique which, consciously or unconsciously, he used to probe the weaknesses of his own position as much as opposing ones. He was, of course, extremely clever, as well as quick-thinking. Bertrand Russell felt that in arguing with Keynes he 'took his life into his hands'. Keynes's first reaction to others' suggestions was frequently one of scorn. The words 'barmy', 'lunatic', 'nuts', tripped easily, much too easily, off his tongue. Kingsley Martin noticed that he was prone to dismiss people at first meeting as fools, 'often because he did not realise the paralysing effect of his own personality upon them'.[53] He could seldom resist a witty put-down: one observer thought that 'he must have been responsible for more inferiority complexes among those with whom he came into contact than anyone else in his generation'.[54] But his first reactions were not necessarily his second or his third. He could demolish any argument, including good ones, and pulverise people into accepting bad ones of his own. However, he had the saving grace of self-correction. Many noticed his habit of expounding opposite ideas with equal confidence.

The charge of inconsistency can be overdone. Keynes customarily distinguished logic from tactics. He understood the difference, expressed many years earlier in his essay on Burke, between the central fortifications which had to be defended, and the outposts which could be conceded. Certainty of general principles, and great flexibility and guile in applying them, was Keynes's recipe for political success. In some respects he had the mentality of a civil servant: unlike Meade, he was quick to understand political constraints, and adept at manoeuvring his forces within them.

Some said that he compromised too much, that under cover of tactical retreats he abandoned central positions, or even that there were no principles for which he would fight in the last ditch. He prized intelligence, ingenuity, flexibility over soundness, and gave the impression that one could usually have the best of all worlds – if one was Keynes or like Keynes; that is, sufficiently intelligent. We have already seen this rationalising tendency in his conduct of the Lend–Lease negotiations in 1941; we will see it again in the Bretton Woods compromise and in his acceptance of an American loan agreement which failed to meet any of his initial requirements. Keynes was not a politician, but it sometimes looks as though he carried the principled pursuit of pragmatism to excessive lengths.

Keynes's persuasive power was enormously heightened by his use of language. This must be given pride of place in any serious examination of the 'rhetoric' of economics. Keynes had a striking ability to move between logic and fancy, prose and poetry, advocacy and irony in the same argument, even in the same paragraph. Douglas LePan, a poet himself, likens his presentations to the 'song of birds'. His Treasury colleague David Waley remembered 'every paragraph . . . full of abounding vitality and a constant sense of drama'. Henry Phelps Brown wrote:

> His prose runs naturally, is sometimes slack in texture, yet even then, like an engine ticking over, conveys a sense of power in reserve. The reasonableness, the candour, the easy command of a sufficient vocabulary, sets us at our ease. But then as the argument quickens and nears its goal, an imagery and iridescence of phrase appear that enchant us. There is still no ornament, no manner, but the easy periods shine with a sudden light. Keynes indeed had the lyric gift of making simple words suddenly quicken our senses like the spurt of dust from a bullet; of writing a phrase, which once read . . . is 'unforgettable, unforgotten'.[55]

His memoranda to the Chancellor were famous for their eloquence and irony. And he had the readiest of wits. 'This is not an anthology, but an encyclopaedia, of truisms,' he once minuted, after reading a particularly laborious presentation. He was addicted to punning, describing Meade's proposal for a capital levy as 'capital levity', or remarking of the actor Sir Donald Wolfit, 'He will always be a lone Wolfit.' Keynes's phrase-making burnt incandescently in the humdrum world of affairs in which he moved. And it powerfully affected the prosaic practitioners of that world, who felt themselves in the presence of a divine visitor, who could speak their language, yet had another up his sleeve. It was his poetry as much as his logic which paralysed criticism. It was a sometimes unproductive gift. Those who did not adore Keynes were baffled and often enraged by his ability to slaughter them on both planes. Morgenthau was initially unreceptive to Keynes's linguistic charm, though he thawed to it over long exposure. And Keynes used his gifts to win arguments he should not have.

A final, and again underemphasised, element in Keynes's wartime influence was his loyalty. However many kites he flew internally, he won the respect of his Treasury colleagues by showing himself to be a team player. Once he was on the 'inside' Keynes played by insider rules. Unlike the publicity-seeking William Beveridge, he made no attempt to use insider knowledge to influence policy from the outside, confining his public pronouncements to agreed texts. A defining moment was when, having been made a peer, he decided not to make his maiden speech in the Lords on the Beveridge Report, whose proposals the Treasury judged to be unaffordable. He explained to his mother: 'I value too highly my present relations with everyone in the Treasury to want to run the risk of disobliging them.'[56]

Intellectual sparkle, analytic power, mental and physical vitality, a capacity to shape theory to events, administrative flair, an instinct for compromise, mastery of persuasive language, loyalty to his department: these were the pillars on which Keynes's wartime influence rested. 'The truth about Maynard', Lydia once told Bob Brand, 'is that he has abnormal will-power. There is nothing to be done about it. I suppose one is born like that.' Only towards the end are there signs of a decline. Brilliant phrases still abounded in his memoranda and conversation but they were embedded in increasingly wordy productions. At the end of his life Keynes started to lose his gift of concise expression; or, to put it another way, the habit of dictation, combined with great tiredness, finally took its toll.

Keynes was in reasonably good physical shape for his first three years in Whitehall. He told Mary Hutchinson on 28 August 1942 that he was now 'quite emancipated [from the Ogre], though I do look in on the old bird now and again. I felt I was under treatment the other night when I listened on the wireless to Valk doing Othello. In the early days, when he used to jump on me in bed I always used to feel like Desdemona!' From the autumn of 1943, his health started to fail at an increasing rate. Remarkably, in the light of modern conceptions, he still continued to smoke – mild Turkish cigarettes – though only moderately. But the major breakdown of his health was caused by his five difficult missions to the United States between 1943 and 1946. It was not work that was bad for Keynes's heart, but worry and anxiety. He was never happier than when drafting. Face-to-face meetings with the Americans, the constant moving around Washington, the crippling workload imposed by over-ambitious schedules, the small size of the British delegations, the fact that he doubled the roles of expert and plenipotentiary, his constant need to refer back to London – all tended to leave him exhausted, baffled, angry and frustrated. Almost till the end, he had remarkable powers of recuperation. On his returns, he would retreat to his beloved Tilton for ten days or so of rest and relaxation. The Treasury was worried by his absences, but even more worried by his returns, full of new, disturbing ideas to unleash on his wary colleagues.

V

EXTRA-CURRICULAR ACTIVITIES

Keynes added the Treasury job to the rest of his life, rather than cutting down on the latter. Telling Keynes to slow down would have had as much effect as telling a clock to lose time. His doctor, Plesch, understood this, and adopted the opposite strategy: when Keynes boasted of working ten hours a day, he told him to work twelve. From September 1940, Keynes took the view that he was completely recovered, in fact better than for a long time past. 'I am in the best of health and L[ydia] says the war agrees with me!' he wrote to his mother on 11 January 1941. 'It may be, I think, that I am benefiting from lying fallow for three years. Also, I had probably been suffering to some extent from chronic poisoning for a great number of years.'

Keynes could easily have got leave of absence from Cambridge – as he did in the First World War. Instead he continued to spend most weekends in term time 'in residence', usually with Lydia, with whom he shared a flat at 17a St Edward's Passage. His weekends followed a set pattern. On Friday evening a car would take him from the Treasury to King's Cross for the train to Cambridge, picking up Lydia from Gordon Square on the way. On Saturday morning there would be a meeting of the College Council, followed by lunch in Hall, and possibly the Estates Committee in the afternoon. On Saturday (occasionally Friday) evening he and Lydia would go to a play, opera or ballet at the Arts Theatre, entertaining guests to dinner at the restaurant before the performance. Sundays would be reserved for lunch with his parents and possibly a concert in Chapel. They would return to London on Monday morning.

He remained first bursar of King's till he died, though the detailed work of preparing the annual accounts fell to Dadie Rylands and the clerks. In 1943, Richard Kahn, who wanted to quit government service, suggested that he return to King's and take on Keynes's bursarial duties, freeing him to concentrate on his war work. Keynes indignantly rejected the idea. 'There is much of the College business which I actually enjoy and would miss, if I were without it. It does not put on me any burden which is unduly heavy. . . .'[57] On the other hand, he refused all thought of becoming the next Cambridge professor of economics on Pigou's retirement in 1943. He explained to Joan Robinson, who urged him to apply, that he couldn't go back to the grind of lecturing after the war. Richard Kahn declined to apply either; Dennis Robertson got the chair, with Keynes's blessing.[58]

He was keen to channel young economists into Cambridge jobs. Eustace Tillyard, Master of Jesus College, wondered about the suitability of Richard Stone as an economics fellow. Keynes advised him to elect

Stone straight away, without any commitment from him to come back to Cambridge after the war. The best alternative would be Nicholas Kaldor, then at Peterhouse as part of the evacuated LSE. ('Only his alien origin has prevented him from having a Government job.') He was not only one of the best young economists in the country, but would be 'an exceptionally delightful and acceptable member of High Table, a brilliant talker and one of the most attractive people about the place. He has a particularly nice English wife and family. The very best type of cultivated, civilised, learned Central European.'[59] Stone and Kaldor both became fellows of King's College, Cambridge after the war.

Keynes was far from a sleeping member of his own Governing Body. An outburst to Provost Sheppard at the end of his life showed he had lost little of his elitism in the war, though its occasion – a report of College Council which glossed over the reasons for the dismissal of a steward – hardly merited his letter's bad temper. Keynes railed to Sheppard against soppy humanitarianism, demanded a return of 'the honest plain speaking of our predecessors', insisted that the denial of differences in ability was 'sapping this country in every direction', and concluded that 'if we go down to perdition, it will . . . be in a foam of slop and soap'.[60]

The main pleasures of his Cambridge life were his parents and the Cambridge Arts Theatre. Sunday lunches with the 'starychki' at 6 Harvey Road remained fixed points in his Cambridge weekends, occasions enhanced by his parents' wholehearted acceptance of Lydia and joy in her company. Despite the inevitable alarms, Neville and Florence remained in tolerable health. Extreme old age had finally brought John Neville Keynes complete relief from the anxieties connected with his work and the state of the world which had clouded his more active years. His retirement routine of stamp collecting, listening to opera, playing bridge and drinking his best wines was hardly disturbed by the fluctuating course of the military struggle.

Keynes's short speech, on the occasion of a luncheon at King's on 30 August 1942 to mark his father's ninetieth birthday, summed up, with typical grace and tact, the promise, disappointments and consolations of Neville Keynes's long life:

> I should like to imagine him as he was *before* I knew him . . . elegant, mid-Victorian high-brow, reading Swinburne, Meredith, Ibsen, buying William Morris wall-paper, whiskered, modest and industrious, but rather rich, rather pleasure-loving, rather extravagant within carefully set limits, most generous, very sociable; loving entertaining, wine, games, novels, theatre, travel; but the shadow of work gradually growing, as migraine headaches set a readiness to look on the more gloomy or depressing side of any prospect. And then his withdrawal, gradual, very gradual, to his dear wife and the bosom of his fam-

ily. . . . He became a perfect, lovable, dependable parent, generous, reserved and shy, leaving you always to your own will and judgement but not concealing his own counsel.

For thirty-three years he was one of the best administrators there ever was, and during those years the University was a better place in my judgement than it has ever been before or since. Perfect order and accuracy without a shadow of pedantry or red tape, the machine existing for the sake of the University, and not the other way round. . . . He helped to create a framework within which learning and science and education could live and flourish without feeling restraint or a hampering hand.

So let us drink in gratitude and thankfulness for his well-fulfilled years, drink to his health, joining in our thoughts my dearest Mother without whom he could not have lived or wished to live.

Neville's withdrawn serenity contrasted sharply with the still active, restless intelligence of his wife Florence, nine years his younger. After she gave up most of her public activities in the mid-1930s, she took up research into Cambridge and family history, having two books on these topics published after Maynard's death. As her contribution to war work, she took in unmarried mothers at 6 Harvey Road.

She was especially delighted when Maynard succeeded Lord Eltisley as High Steward of the Borough of Cambridge, noting proudly that he united in his parentage 'University and Borough, his father having been Registrary of the University and his mother Mayor of the Borough'. His installation, on 6 March 1943, was almost a family affair, with both parents and many relatives in attendance. His acceptance speech, fortified by a few words of historical reminiscence provided by Florence, emphasised his local roots: Alderman Peck's father had pulled out his first teeth, rewarding him with an acid drop from a magic vase; his father had kept 213 consecutive terms of residence. Although he described the post as having 'no rights and no duties', he was soon helping to draft the University's and Borough Council's protest at the Air Ministry's attempt to requisition college and town property for defence purposes.[61]

Maynard's attitude towards his parents remained – as one feels it had always been – affectionate and attentive, without being overtly emotional. They were proud of him, and interested in his doings, without being inquisitive. So he plied them with what they, and especially his mother, wanted to hear: the facts about his life, news of his appointments, his opinions on matters great and small. His wartime letters to them, written from Tilton and on his foreign trips, are informative and chatty. He lists his public efforts, achievements, honours with an ironic detachment, a kind of amused wonder appropriate to a true son of Cambridge University, one whose real vocation lies in contemplation rather than in action.

They contain hardly a clue to the 'inner' Keynes – a Keynes capable of torment or self-doubt. Or had such a Keynes ceased to exist?

Nor were other family members neglected. He corresponded with his brother Geoffrey, now an air commodore, about family matters and their purchases of antiquarian books – Berkeley, Spinoza, Locke. He discussed military matters with his brother-in-law A. V. Hill, who had become Independent MP for Cambridge – the job which Keynes refused. Hill's service in the 1930s on the Tizard Committee, which developed the radar and early air warning systems, had left him with a profound contempt of politicians who meddled in scientific matters. He complained to Maynard that military strategy and tactics were being decided by people who knew nothing about weapons and equipment. Cherwell was a 'liability', Winston an 'amateur'. He said that the 'idea of bombing a well-defended enemy into submission, or even doing serious damage to him, is a complete illusion – and a very wasteful one'. It was Keynes who was being lectured, by an expert, and for once his famous ability to sound off was silenced.[62]

Aunt Jessie Lloyd, one of Florence's sisters, wanted his advice on her will. She planned to leave money to Newnham College, in memory of her daughter Muriel Lloyd. Myra Curtis, the Principal, wanted it to go to the Library, but Keynes urged, in his usual decided way, the merits of a new building with 'a very good flat for the Principal with a study, fairly large drawing room, decent-sized dining room and three bedrooms, with sets for the Fellows of three rooms each, the whole to be serviced by a staff of three domestics, not necessarily live in'. Eventually, Jessie Lloyd left £21,000 for a new Lodge for the Principal only, which was built after the war.

Maynard's benevolence and interest extended to the rest of his family, especially to his nephews and nieces, though the benevolence often seemed more apparent than the interest, as he showered covenants and annuities on them. 'I don't like just to get presents from you but *never* see you,' wrote Stephen, Geoffrey's youngest son.[63] To Milo Keynes, his uncle seemed like a 'very nice, benevolent patron whom no one really seems to know'.[64] Keynes's generosity extended to his friends. He gave them practical advice, often paid for the education of their children, and delighted to give them presents of rare old books. Accused by Bloomsbury of being mean in his entertainments, he did not hesitate to use his wealth in the service of friendship.

Keynes was too intimidating to get on easily with the children of his relations or friends. Jeremy Hutchinson, later an outstanding criminal lawyer, recalls being 'very frightened of him' when he came to dinner with his parents in the 1930s, 'with his curling lip and massive intellect – unlike Virginia Woolf & Leonard who were both great fun and unalarming, and of course Clive [Bell] even more so'.[65] Nevertheless, Keynes tried to be a good uncle. He arranged for Richard Keynes and his new bride

Anne Adrian to spend their honeymoon at Tilton early in 1945; he invited the nephews down to Tilton for the Christmas shoots. He dealt seriously with their questions. When Quentin Keynes wrote to him from Washington in 1943, disapproving of the capital controls' provisions of the Clearing Union Plan, because 'bringing it down to the simplest terms, this would mean that no one would be allowed to take out £10 for a week-end in Paris without applying to the Exchange Control for permission', Keynes took trouble with his reply. 'It is quite impossible to allow foreign investment ... by individuals irrespective of our collective capacity to finance it,' he wrote to Quentin. 'Unfortunately, that does have the consequence that, in order to enforce it, tourists and travellers will have to get permission to take money out of the country. I only hope that this will be interpreted with proper liberality.'[66]

Milo Keynes, then an undergraduate at Trinity College, Cambridge, wondered whether he ought to continue his medical studies or join up. His 'affectionate and ancestral uncle' advised him to 'stay where you are, – and with a good conscience', in a letter full of tact and good sense:

> The supply of doctors is going to be very short. It seems unlikely to me that the war will last long enough, at any rate in a fashion which requires great numbers of foot-soldiers, to make an interruption of your work really useful to the country.
>
> In time of war, fortune is not evenly distributed to the children of men. Some are lucky, some are unlucky. You, compared with many, are lucky, – both in the date of your birth, which settled a good deal, and in the accident of your chosen profession. So enjoy your luck and do not repine. Perhaps some version of abstract justice requires equal suffering. That, perhaps fortunately, is not what happens.
>
> I am not sorry that you have worried a bit about it. But, if the thing is once settled, do not tease yourself about it any more.[67]

Keynes took the time to impart the wisdom of a life spent in investment and speculation to his nephew David Hill. Should David sell his railway shares, which his broker had told him would be bound to slump after war? On the contrary, wrote Maynard, 'I cannot think of better or safer investments today than Railway shares.' This led him on to some typical reflections on the inadequacy of brokers:

> After all, one would expect brokers to be wrong. If, in addition to their other inside advantages, they were capable of good advice, clearly they would have retired long ago with a large fortune. Also there is a tendency for all brokers to advise the same thing, so that the shares of any company whose sale they are recommending are nearly always too cheap and those whose shares they recommend for purchase too dear. If only one could find out for certain what

brokers are recommending to their clients and do the opposite, the way to a fortune would be safe and secure.[68]

Keynes could rarely resist such didactic opportunities. His communications were saved from earnestness and pomposity by their sly humour and persistent undermining of conventional views.

Keynes attended the centenary of the birth of his old teacher Alfred Marshall in Cambridge on 7 November 1942.

> Everyone was there [he wrote to Richard Kahn on 13 November] and it was one of the pleasantest tea parties given for some time. The Prof [Pigou] appeared in an apparently new suit, which he was accused of having hired, but declared that he had it laid by in tissue paper since the last war. . . . Mrs Marshall spoke without a note for fully ten minutes. Piero [Sraffa] was hiding his abashed head for fear of any reference to his Ricardo fiasco, when he failed at the last moment to give the lecture. . . . Meanwhile [he] has been asked to join the Political Warfare Department to promote a revolution in Italy. But even that he seems to shilly-shally about and may be going to back out.

'Piero is still failing to finish Ricardo,' Keynes informed Kahn on 12 January 1942. Sraffa had started working on the Royal Economic Society's edition of Ricardo's works in 1930, the job Keynes had got him to keep him in Cambridge. Sraffa was detemined to track down every correspondence in which Ricardo had been engaged. On 5 July 1943 he wrote to Keynes in his beautiful handwriting: 'This is the most sensational news there has ever been about Ricardo. *His letters to [James] Mill have been found!*' It was Hayek who had alerted Sraffa to their discovery, in the house of C. K. Mill, a descendant of Mill living in Dublin. Keynes now exerted himself to get Sraffa (who had recently been interned as an enemy alien) the necessary papers to go to Dublin to examine the precious hoard. The director of the Passport Office was told in typically authoritative Keynes prose that it was a matter of the utmost urgency for Mr Sraffa to proceed in quest of documents 'mysteriously missing since the death of John Stuart Mill'. On 19 August Sraffa was on an aeroplane to Dublin.[69] The Ricardo editing continued to proceed at its stately pace, the first four volumes of the eleven-volume edition being published in 1951.

Keynes found time to write a substantial obituary of Mary Paley Marshall, who passed away on 7 March 1944. The death of Dilwyn Knox on 27 February 1943 was a painful reminder of the first love of his life. 'It is a sad thought to his old intimates of Eton and King's that we shall never see our beloved Dilly again,' Keynes wrote in *The Times* on 10 March.

In June 1943 Keynes read an essay on 'Newton the Man' at Trinity

College, Cambridge – a fragment of a much longer projected study for Newton's 300th birthday which he lacked the leisure to complete.* Studying Newton's life prompted him into a statement of a biographical credo. 'We suffer from the habit', he wrote to Eustace Tillyard, 'of interpreting the great men of the past by reference to what came after . . . instead of . . . what came before and what they were imbibing in their youth. Tradition treats [Newton] as a pure eighteenth century figure of almost Voltairean rationalism. In fact, the whole of his thought and temperament were rooted in what preceded him. He was, as I put it, the last of the magicians, and not the first of the rationalists'.[70] Close attention to context, that is, is crucial for understanding a thinker's ideas. This approach to writing intellectual history has now become commonplace, but Keynes's essay was then very much a pioneering effort. Did he also have in mind how he wished to be understood by later generations?

In December 1940 Keynes finally relinquished personal control over the bookings at the Arts Theatre. In future, he said, he would confine himself to general principles. But of course he did not. In 1942 he was active in getting Norman Marshall to form a resident company at the Arts Theatre, which in the spring of 1943 put on twelve weeks of Ibsen and Chekhov – 'just the sort of thing', Keynes told the manager Norman Higgins, 'we have dreamt of having for a long time past'. He advised Marshall, though, to do something 'to raise the average cheerfulness of the plays! In these times one can put up with only a moderate ration of gloom and perplexity.' Marshall proved something of a disappointment – 'idle and . . . unimaginative, rather a coward and incompetent over detail'; Higgins, by contrast, was 'energetic, loyal, intelligent . . . everything one could wish and a great deal more'.[71] The war years were a halcyon time, the theatre being full from the influx into Cambridge of evacuees and government and military personnel, including the American air force. Keynes himself paid for 3000 schoolchildren to see Toy Princess, a poetry and music entertainment devised by Dadie Rylands. He continued to enunciate the general principles he so loved:

> It is important to emphasise [he wrote in a memorandum of 24 March 1942] the significance of having enough financial resources . . . to be able to afford a long-sighted policy, which does not have to pay undue attention to day-to-day commercial considerations. One might also add [that] a spirit of generosity to all local people . . . is of great value. . . . Everyone who deals with the place must get the feeling that we are not hard or grasping or aiming all the time at saving or making a little money. . . . I should also emphasise that an

---

* Neither Harrod nor Moggridge mentions this reading in 1943. The essay was re-read to the Newton Society in Trinity College by Geoffrey Keynes on 17 July 1946. Keynes also may have read it to a gathering of Bloomsberries at Tilton on Boxing Day 1942.

institution must aim at financial independence in the long run. People always get tired of supporting what seems a sink for resources. You will never get the right spirit in the management of a concern which runs habitually at a loss.[72]

Here was the rub: how was the disdain for 'day-to-day' commercial considerations to be squared with long-run financial independence? Keynes's faith that good quality would pay was not tested in the war when cinema entertainment was heavily curtailed and when the profits of his theatre soared. It was to be otherwise in the long peace which followed.

Keynes managed to devote an extraordinary amount of attention to farming operations at Tilton which now, heavily subsidised, were part of the wartime drive for agricultural self-sufficiency. They were also much expanded, for in 1941 Keynes and his farm manager, Logan Thomson, jointly took over Charleston farm as well as Tilton – 'to stop its buildings falling into decay', writes Frances Spalding – Keynes lending Thomson the money to set up as an independent farmer, and giving him the profits of Charleston from which to pay it back. They now had 600 acres, and Keynes was in a position to sow 100 acres of wheat annually, Fred Woollard, his chauffeur, taking charge of a magnificent new tractor costing £600. The detailed correspondence between Keynes and Logan Thomson in the war occupies a fat folder in Keynes's papers at King's College. As was his wont, he wanted to know and understand everything. He gave detailed instructions to Thomson on what to plant in the kitchen garden; he wanted to know exactly why the wheat crop at Charleston had been so bad in 1944. In October 1941 there were twelve labourers altogether, including Quentin Bell, who was paid £2 1s 0d a week to look after the pigs. Quentin was not noted for his rural skills. When organising a pheasant shoot in December 1943, Logan Thomson wrote to Keynes: 'You can probably leave out Quentin . . . from the point of view of killing anything.'

Keynes was a canny employer. On one occasion, he announced a wage increase, but eliminated the free milk allowance, which was costing him more. In 1942 he applied to the Wages Board to reduce the wages of old labourers: 'The main reason . . . is not so much a lack of skill as the slow pace at which they perform.' On hearing that 'Old Horace' had finally been carried off to the workhouse, Keynes commented: 'Sorry to hear that Old Horace has . . . been taken to his last home but one.'

In February 1941 he had to ward off a request from a Captain Wills to requisition Tilton as a small headquarters. Keynes – justifiably – went through the roof. 'Quite out of the question,' he thundered back. He, his wife, his 'aged housekeeper', cook and cook's daughter were in continuous residence. Although he had a resident bailiff, he was in active control of Tilton farm and had to be there frequently to take part in the

Janos Plesch, the doctor who brought JMK 'back to life', and whom he called 'the Ogre'.

Above. JMK and Lydia in Gordon Square, march 1940

Below. JMK dictating letters on his day bed in Gordon Square, March 1940

Right. Kingsley Wood (and his wife) on Budget Day 7 April 1941

Below. Sir John Anderson (known as 'Pompous John')

JMK and Lydia arriving in New York on the 'Clipper', at 7 a.m., 8 May 1941. He had not had a chance to shave.

Right and below.
JMK in persuasive mode,
Washington DC,
12 May 1941

Sir Richard Hopkins. He reminded Lionel Robbins of an 'extremely
intelligent monkey'.

Above, left. Sir Frederick Phillips. JMK wrote that 'he could stay silent in several languages'.

Above, right. Sir Wilfrid Eady. JMK thought that, caught young, he might have understood the 'elements of economics'.

Right. Lionel Robbins: increasingly Johnsonian in manner and appearance

James Meade (*left*) with Lucius Thompson-MacLausland. James Meade, a later Nobel Prize winner, struck 'Otto' Clarke as 'ridiculously academic and perfectionist'.

Harry Dexter White, as Keynes would have seen him in 1944

management. After being seriously ill for three years, he had returned to full duty at the Treasury, but still needed to care for his health, with the country as his place for recuperation. 'I am afraid it would seriously interfere with my physical capacity to undertake my duties at the Treasury, which are of an important character, if I was deprived of my house and home,' he wrote back. No more was heard of requisition.

The Tilton household consisted of 'Auntie' (Penny Weller, Lydia's former dresser, the 'aged housekeeper'), Ruby Weller, who lived at Tilton Cottage and cleaned, the cook (known as 'Jewish Mary'), the cook's daughter, and the squat mongrel dog Patsy. Ruby's husband Edgar, Penny's nephew, now a hospital orderly, sent Keynes gardening verses. At the end of the war, a new 'cooking couple', Mr and Mrs Carter, arrived.

Keynes kept in touch with his old Bloomsbury friends as much as his duties would allow, and did his best to help them in dealing with wartime difficulties: meetings of the Memoir Club, convened by Molly McCarthy, continued to be the focal point of old and new Bloomsbury, Maynard attending as many as he could. Duncan Grant and Vanessa Bell sat out the war at Charleston, living a 'relatively quiet life, composed of painting, gardening, keeping chickens and seeing few people'.[73] During his recuperative holidays at Tilton, Maynard saw more of Duncan than he had done in the 1930s, and the Charlestonians would come to Tilton over the Christmas holidays, with Lydia and Duncan leading the 'entertainments'. Keynes helped finance the religious murals Duncan, Vanessa and Quentin painted in Berwick Church in 1942–3, and gave money, as well as lent pictures, to a remarkable art gallery opened in Lewes by 'the ladies of Miller', two eccentric sisters, Mrs Frances Byng Stamper and Miss Caroline Byng Lucas. With its 'Miller's House' and Little Theatre, Lewes, according to Duncan, was becoming the 'Athens of the South'. Keynes's own picture buying was in abeyance, though he added the occasional Ivor Hitchens to his collection. He joined with Duncan and Vanessa in disapproving of Bunny Garnett's marriage to their daughter Angelica in 1942. The thought of Duncan's former lover marrying Duncan's daughter was too bizarre even for his relaxed morals.

Though he was the most loyal and helpful of friends, even Keynes rebelled against some of the demands made on him. Asked by Frances Cornford, the sister of his brother Geoffrey's wife Margaret, to meet a young Bulgarian painter who wanted to establish a Bauhaus in Cambridge, he wrote back: 'I have reached saturation point. . . . So all I could do, if he talked about the School of Design, would be to try politely to keep him at bay and forget with what prejudice the name of Gropius fills me. . . .'[74] The same impulse led him to reject many invitations to serve on committees. 'I have a bad habit', he wrote of one such invitation, 'of not treating membership of committees . . . as sinecures. I should not feel happy to lend no assistance and cannot spare the time to take real trouble'.[75]

Keynes did not give up the editorship of the *Economic Journal* till February 1945. His main motive was to keep abreast of economic theory. *EJ* material went with him on all his wartime American journeys. He exerted himself to get decent obituaries for J. A. Hobson (d.1940) and for his old friend Beatrice Webb (d.1943) whom he considered 'the greatest woman of the generation which is now passing'.[76] It was at the end of a speech at the dinner marking his retirement from the editorship that he offered a toast 'to economists, who are the trustees, not of civilisation, but of the possibility of civilisation'. Harrod is quite right to emphasise Keynes's careful choice of words: 'He said what he wanted to say.'[77] Keynes remained chairman of the board of the *New Statesman* till his death, though he found its journalism increasingly distasteful. In 1945 he objected to an article by Aylmer Vallance 'full of the slants, snides, sneers, and smears which Communists and Fellow Travellers habitually employ as a means for building a perfect society'.[78]

In January 1943, he resigned as vice-president of the Malthusian League in protest against the decision of its Council to urge the government to take steps to restrict the fecundity of the poor – a policy of which he had approved as a young man, but which now struck him as grossly insensitive in the light of Hitler's eugenic experiments. By contrast, the Trusteeship of the National Gallery, which Keynes accepted in October 1941, was a 'very pleasant and honourable mild job'. His appointment led Simon Courtauld to remark that 'all our most respectable institutions are being revolutionised'.

Throughout the war, Keynes kept up his reading, and commented, often extensively, on books which interested him. His letter to Friedrich Hayek on the latter's *Road to Serfdom* was a key statement of his political and economic philosophy. (See p. 284 below.) He was 'so fascinated' by Ivor Brown's book on slang, *A Word in your Ear*, that he felt moved 'to send you one or two footnotes on it'.[79] A profile of Keynes by Brown appeared in the *Observer* in 1943. He managed a reader's report on a manuscript by the statistician Udny Yule, entitled 'Statistics of Literary Vocabulary', in which Yule had counted up authors' choice of nouns. 'This is far too narrow a front on which to advance with such large forces,' Keynes declared, but, as always, he found Yule's work 'queer, suggestive and original'.[80] The summer of 1942 found him reading the galleys of volume one of J. H. Clapham's history of the Bank of England, supplying eight pages of comment on a 'fascinating' work, and wondering how the Bank protected its reserve in its first hundred years.[81] He promoted the efforts of a Czech refugee, Werner Stark, to rediscover and rehabilitate Bentham, got him a job lecturing at Cambridge, and paid various grants to him out of his own pocket.[82]

In May 1943 Maisky, the Soviet ambassador, sent him an article by Academician M. Mitin on 'Twenty-Five Years of Philosophy in the USSR' which he hoped Keynes would be able to get published in a respectable English journal to 'strengthen the cultural ties between our two peoples'. Keynes passed on 'this interesting but rather pathetic document' which had 'nothing whatever to do with philosophy but is a sociological document of genuine interest' to Leonard Woolf, who was editing *Political Quarterly*. 'I wish I knew what dialectical materialism is. But I know from long experience and many efforts that this is doomed to be a sealed book to me. I shall never know.' Woolf rejected the article as total rubbish. Keynes persevered with Sydney Hooper, editor of *Philosophy*, who also rejected it. Keynes urged him to reconsider, if only to show 'how barmy the human race is'.[83] Keynes's 'blind spot' about Marxism remained. A few days' holiday gave him time to read Joan Robinson's short book *An Essay on Marxian Economics*. 'I found it most fascinating,' he wrote to her. 'This is in spite of the fact that there is something intrinsically boring in an attempt to make sense of what is in fact not sense. . . . I am left with the feeling . . . that he [Marx] had a penetrating and original flair but was a very poor thinker indeed. . . .'[84]

In the last years of his life, Keynes's book buying turned increasingly towards early editions of Elizabethan and Stuart drama and poetry, partly because he thought they were good bargains, partly because he enjoyed reading them. He bought fine editions at auction and through the catalogues of Maggs, Quaritch and other specialist booksellers. He would browse through them in the loggia on sunny afternoons at Tilton, particularly when bouts of ill-health gave him enforced leisure, and would correspond about their contents and market value with experts, in letters full of excitement and amateurish but learned assertion. A. N. L. Munby, librarian of King's College, wondered how he found time for those 'four-page letters about the frontispieces of Hobbes's *De Cive* or the translations, one by Bentham, of Voltaire's *Le Tareau Blanc*'.[85] Dadie Rylands was the frequent recipient of these literary outpourings. Keynes liked old books because they connected him with the culture of the past, because they enlarged his knowledge of Cambridge, and because they set him bibliographical puzzles which stimulated fanciful hypotheses. On 22 February 1945 he described his reading habits to Cyril Connolly:

> in my private reading I hardly ever take up contemporary stuff, which seems to me to be phoney for the time being, but not unpromising for the future; but have been dipping very widely and frequently into the minor Elizabethans and Jacobeans, who, unlike contemporaries, seem to me to be silly and neurotic in just the way I fancy. When I go for a voyage, I take up something more robust and read slowly and thoroughly such masterpieces as [Charles Reade's] The Cloister and the Hearth and [Walter Scott's] The Heart of Midlothian.[86]

VI

BACK AT SCHOOL

In addition to his Treasury job Keynes took on two substantial extra
responsibilities in the war. On 17 December 1941, Samuel Courtauld's
son-in-law R. A. Butler, President of the Board of Education, asked him to
become chairman of the Council for the Encouragement of Music and
the Arts (CEMA). His work for this body can be more conveniently
considered later (see pp. 286–99 below). But it scarcely exceeded in
volume his labours for his old school. In July 1940, accepting an invitation
from R. C. Martineau, he was elected to represent the eighty masters on
the Governing Body (called Fellows) of Eton. He was admitted as a fellow
on 5 October and at the same meeting was made a member of the
General Purposes Committee. Being Keynes, he interpreted his brief in
the broadest terms. At his very first meeting of the GPC 'he drew attention
to various points as regards the claims [for war damage to houses owned
by Eton in London]' and was soon advising on Eton's investment policies
and tax affairs, the management of trust funds and properties, and future
relations with the state system. This was in addition to sorting out staff
grievances. Keynes loved being back at school. Meetings of the General
Purposes Committee took place once every two months, meetings of the
Governing Body three times a year. He would generally arrive on Friday
evening, stay overnight with the headmaster, Claude Elliott, and continue
on Saturday to Cambridge by train. Between the meetings there were
often heavy bouts of correspondence; when other duties kept him from
attending, he would communicate his views in writing, often at considerable length. His four folders of Eton business contain over one thousand
items.

Keynes took on this extra chore not just because he enjoyed the work,
but because he was passionately committed to Eton's survival. This was an
aspect of his traditionalism, reinforced by his conspicuously happy memories of his schooldays. Once engaged, there was no controlling his restless
probing. Even before his formal election as fellow he had spied out
inefficiencies in the system – lack of adequate pension rights for the
Dames, 'barmy' retirement ages for the beaks.[87] Having denounced the
school's investment and pension policies as supremely tax inefficient, he
started an Investment Committee, and sketched out a new pension
scheme in a letter of several pages.[88] He took his duties as masters'
representative seriously, adjudicating in many disputes, often involving a
mountain of correspondence. To these contentious battles, Keynes
brought a remarkable tact and good sense. After a famous running battle
between two housemasters, Tait and Assheton, about who should get the
larger House (boys' boarding houses then being run by the housemasters

for profit), he came down firmly in favour of paying housemasters salaries, a reform introduced in 1945. Sometimes even his patience ran out. On 23 January 1943 he wrote to the bursar: 'Here is a copy of the letter which I have written to Colquhoun about his blasted gas-cooker. . . . I cannot see that this is the kind of case where there is justifiable ground for carrying the appeal to the House of Lords.'

Much of his time in 1943 was taken up by the business of Chalcots Estate, a collection of about a hundred mainly residential properties owned by the College in Hampstead, north London. This was most of what remained of the property of the Hospital of St James, founded before 1100 for '14 maidens that were leprous', and given to Eton by Henry VI in 1449. The estate brought in £6000 a year in ground rents. Keynes's first instinct was to sell the freehold outright as the leases expired, though not till some time after the war. It was very unsafe, he argued, to have so much money tied up in a single risk. 'Nothing is safe, least of all ground rents, in view of possible future legislation. . . .' Having gone round the estate on 23 June 1943, he was not so sure: 'If we could discover how to manage Chalcots with complete efficiency, I should expect we could increase our income by a cumulative amount of £1,000 a year . . . for ever. And it is easy to see how wonderfully this would ease the general situation.'[89] Although there were individual post-war sales, about half of the property was still in College ownership until the mid-1990s.

Many of Keynes's interventions belong to a history of Eton, but some of them are revealing of his attitudes. Students of Keynesian economics will be amused by the following note to him from the headmaster: 'I am going into your suggestions for balancing the budget.'[90] His closest ally on the Governing Body was the banker Jasper Ridley, but when Ridley refused to support his proposal to buy Australian dollar bonds, Keynes was provoked into a frustrated statement of his investment philosophy: 'My central principle . . . is to go contrary to general opinion, on the ground that, if everyone agreed about its merits, the investment is inevitably too dear and therefore unattractive. Now obviously I can't have it both ways – the whole point of the investment is that most people disagree with it. So, if others concerned don't feel enough confidence to give me a run, then it is in the nature of the case that I must retire from unequal combat.'[91]

Keynes's attitude to the future of the public schools is also of some interest. It was far from certain whether Eton would survive in the post-war world of punitive tax rates. R. A. Butler at the Board of Education was preparing his famous Act; the Fleming Committee was set up in 1942 with a brief to open up the public schools to non-fee-payers. Defensive action was called for. The Provost, Lord Quickswood, was clear that any state assistance to public schools should take the form of relief from income tax for educational expenses, rather than state scholarships, since the latter would inevitably bring 'some measure of State control or representation'. Keynes agreed. 'Next time we are discussing this sort of thing in the Treasury,' he wrote to the Provost on 10 October 1941, 'I will take the opportunity to bring your proposal to the notice of those concerned.' Nor was there any hint of a radical approach in his explanation to Archbishop Temple a couple of months later: 'The right line in my judgment is not to injure the Secondary Schools by stealing from them a limited number of their most promising pupils, but rather by gradually developing them so that there is no substantial difference between them and the public schools, either educationally or in the development of character and personality.'[92]

By 1944, influenced by New Jerusalem thinking, he had become cautiously receptive to limited integration of the two systems. The Fleming Report of 1944 recommended that local authorities be allowed to pay for up to 25 per cent of public school places froom the rates; Sir Will Spens, Master of Corpus Christi College, Cambridge and chairman of the Governors of Rugby School, was promoting a counter-proposal that public schools admit children from state primary schools on a co-payment basis, the schools themselves contributing to the state bursaries. After a reassuring talk with Butler, who said there was no intention to seek Board of Education control over public schools, Keynes pressed the Governing Body, on 3 February 1945, to accept one or other of these two possibilities on a seven years' trial: he had worked out that Spens's proposal would cost the Eton fee-payer only £10 per annum more. (Fees were then £245 a year.) However, no decision was made. These early versions of the Assisted Places Scheme of the 1980s foundered on the public schools' refusal to put up money for scholarships, most local authorities' refusal to pay boarding-school fees, and the schools' fear of loss of independence. A few 'Fleming' boys came to Eton in the first post-war years; then they came no more.[93]

Not least of Keynes's delights, though also irritations, was Eton's magnificently eccentric resident Provost, 'Linky' Quickswood, formerly Lord Hugh Cecil, a forensically ferocious High Church Tory of traditional habits – he went on wearing knee-breeches to dinner – and even more traditional views. He regarded the war as a vulgar interruption of time-hallowed routine, and resisted the provision of air-raid shelters, on the ground that the statutes did not provide for them. 'The relentless habits of a medieval schoolman to which he subjected human problems was not always appreciated,' writes Kenneth Rose.[94] Keynes arrived in the middle of a terrific row between Quickswood and the headmaster, who was trying to get control over the election of scholars, traditionally the prerogative of the Provost and Fellows. 'Linky' accused Claude Elliott, a man of 'brilliant administrative ability', but 'ambitious for power', of trying to reduce the Provost to even greater 'Merovingian' status. The scent of battle in his nostrils, the Provost combed ancient statutes in support of his position. 'A prize example of misdirected intellectual powers' was Keynes's verdict on a six-page letter he received from Quickswood on the subject of who was to chair the examiners' meeting. Exhaustion eventually brought a compromise. 'You will see on what statesmanlike lines [the dispute] has been conducted,' an amused Keynes told the scholars' examiner, Francis Cruso. 'His training in theology and mine in metaphysics enabled the Provost and me to reach a concordat, which I hope you will think satisfactory. The examiners are not to draw up an order of merit, but there will be no objection to their communicating to the electors the sort of list which they would have been inclined to draw up were they permitted to do so.'[95]

More serious was the dispute over the bursarship. As the bursar of King's, Keynes had decided views on bursarial efficiency, and concluded that the bursar, P. A. Macindoe, was incapable of learning new tricks. 'I doubt if Eton's finances have been what one could call *well managed* for at least half a century,' he told Quickswood. So he moved and carried, at the Governors' meeting of 3 December 1941, a motion to appoint a committee to consider bursarial arrangements. The Provost declared himself 'irreconcilably opposed to the reconstruction of the Bursary during the war'. He discovered a novel delaying tactic, announcing to Keynes that 'as he [Quickswood] was non compos. and expected to remain so as long as the war lasted, he thought no decision . . . ought to be reached until after the armistice had restored his sanity'. Keynes pressed on: 'The last meeting of the [Provost and Fellows],' he informed his old school friend Dundas on 5 June 1942, 'was . . . rather an abnormal occasion, in which, in order to obtain the absolutely necessary results, assault and battery had to be continued uninterruptedly for a considerable number of hours. . . . The trouble . . . is that not only the Provost and Vice-Provost are nuts, but they have gone a long way to driving everyone nuts too.' The upshot was that the Governing Body adopted a plan by which the bursar became emeritus and the junior bursar, R. E. Marsden (known as the Horse), became acting bursar, a new bursar not to be appointed till after the war.

This was not quite the end of the matter, though. The Horse, a prickly character, refused to accept the position of acting bursar. He wrote Keynes long letters on backs of old algebra exams, presumably to economise on paper, demanding detailed and impossible conditions if he were to take on the bursarship, which included the stipulation that the Vice-Provost should never enter his office. Quickswood, declaring that it would be quite intolerable for a person of 'Marsden's cranky temper' to become bursar on special terms, told Keynes that he would resign if Marsden's terms were accepted. 'Forgive me if I add that I do most earnestly hope that you and Ridley will not continue to interfere with the details of College management.' That the Provost should be 'constantly overruled by the Governing Body is inevitably painful to his feelings'. So, like Hitler, Keynes found himself having to fight a war on two fronts. First, he neutralised the Horse by getting him to accept the position of temporary bursar with modified conditions; then he addressed himself robustly to the Provost: 'You must remember that I represent by statute a considerable body of residents, and I do my best to inform myself about their views. The only apology which I feel I owe you and the rest of the Governing Body is that preoccupation in other directions has prevented me from doing my full duty. . . .' He wrote to the headmaster on 24 June 1942: 'My correspondence on this subject is now mountains high. But it is a scream, and I must confess that the amusement does a little outweigh the burden of the trouble.' By 30 June he was able to report a satisfactory outcome to Jasper Ridley: 'By dint of several letters, urging each of them to be extremely nice to the other, the Provost and the Horse have now become thick as thieves. . . . Indeed, the whole thing has settled down in the happiest possible manner, on the basis . . . that you and I are the villains of the piece. . . .' In August, the headmaster reported that 'The Horse is prancing.'

Soon after this, Keynes was having to use all his diplomatic skills to settle a dispute between the bursar and a College tenant, wife of an absent master, whose pear tree the bursar was trying to cut down. 'It looks like the old aporia – when an irrevocable ass meets an immovable horse,' Keynes commented. 'My dear Bursar, you must be patient with us . . .' Keynes was writing to the Horse on 5 February 1945, when the Governing Body refused to make him a fellow. Keynes proved to be the only person capable of riding the angry Horse, who repaid him with unstinted admiration and slavish devotion.

By 1944, Linky Quickswood was ready to go. Before the war, he had attacked bishops for refusing to retire before the onset of senility. On 14 October, having reached the age of seventy-five, he suddenly announced his own retirement. 'And so I go to Bournemouth in lieu of Paradise,' he told the assembled school. He was succeeded by the Vice-Provost, Henry Marten, who had taught Keynes history, and was now teaching Princess Elizabeth the same subject at neighbouring Windsor Castle.

Keynes himself sometimes thought of retiring from government service, particularly after 1943 – a course often urged on him in the interests of public enlightenment. His official position led him to refuse some tempting offers, including an invitation to deliver the Romanes Lectures for 1942, and, less demandingly, the Stamp Memorial Lecture at the London School of Economics. The key question was: should Keynes continue his Treasury work or try to prepare public opinion for post-war realities? In reply to one of these retiring suggestions, from Sir George Schuster, Keynes wrote on 7 February 1943: 'I think the time may well come when one can be more useful trying to affect public opinion. . . . But it does not seem to me that the time for that has yet come. . . . Whitehall . . . is in a very constructive and enterprising mood, – at least the Treasury is. So far we are all acting rather successfully as a team. So long as this is the case, I believe that team work can do more towards getting things actually done, than the baying of a lone dog.'[96] The constructive enterprise on which he and the Treasury were jointly engaged was the plan for an international clearing union.

PART TWO

BETTER THAN
LAST TIME

The day is not far off when the Economic Problem will take the back seat where it belongs, and the arena of the heart and head will be occupied where it belongs, or reoccupied by our real problems – the problems of life and human relations, of creation and behaviour and religion. JMK

CHAPTER SIX

Keynes's 'New Order'

I

SETTING THE SCENE

All those who thought about the future, even in the darkest days of the Second World War, shared one overriding aim: to do better than last time. To be sure, the First World War also hatched improving plans. But the Wilsonian programme – national self-determination, open covenants openly arrived at, the League of Nations – was primarily constitutional and political. In economics, though less so in social life, the cry was 'back to 1913'. In the Second World War, no one wanted to 'get back' to the 1930s. The problem of Germany, of peace-keeping, remained. But what distinguished the reformist efforts of the Second from those of the First World War was the much greater attention paid to economic and social policy. Most of those who pondered on such matters believed that it was defective economic arrangements which had made such a 'hash', as Keynes put it, of the inter-war years. Hitler himself could be seen as an extreme reaction to the extreme effect of the great depression on Germany. Full employment, social security, international partnership were to be the conscious goals of peace, not just the aberrant achievements of war.

The great unknown was the United States. Among policymakers in Britain and America, there was a widespread, though not universal, feeling that the isolation of the United States had been a major factor in the breakdown of both the economic and security systems of the inter-war years. Britain, as Keynes put it, had conducted the nineteenth-century international orchestra. After the First World War, it was palpably disabled from doing so. As a result, the orchestra had broken up into discordant sections. Was the United States willing to pick up the baton? This was far from clear. In 1941 it was not even in the war. But it had a post-war agenda – non-discrimination in trade – and in Lend–Lease a powerful lever to force Britain to sign up to it. To Keynes these were the 'lunatic proposals of Mr Hull'. They were lunatic, because apparently unqualified and religiously inspired. But Keynes was a pragmatist. So it might be possible to accept the American agenda, if the US administration could be got to see that it had to be underpinned by other policies and institutions, involving American money and leadership.

Qualifying all Keynes's battles with the Americans was the underlying belief that the New World had to be yoked, and kept yoked, to the Old World, if the latter were to enjoy durable peace and prosperity. It was in Britain's long-term interest to arrange for this, even if it meant having to swallow humble pie on the way. This was far from being the consensus view of Britain's elites, but it was probably the majority view. It goes far to explain what otherwise might seem inexplicable, namely the deference Britain paid to American wishes, both during and after the war, and its failure to exploit crucial elements in its bargaining position – like fighting a more limited war, or even making a separate peace with Germany – which might have appealed to the *Realpolitik* school of statesmanship.

Keynes had been handed the State Department draft of Article VII of the Lend–Lease Agreement before he left Washington in July 1941. As a 'consideration' for Lend–Lease, Britain would pledge itself not to 'discriminate' against American goods after the war. Between August 1941 and February 1942, British strategy for dealing with the draft Article VII followed two parallel courses. The first was to secure such amendments as to free Britain from any specific obligations in return for receiving American supplies. The second was to develop proposals for meeting, or seeming to meet, American requirements. Keynes wrote to Acheson on 17 October: 'When I got back here I found that Whitehall was very much more prepared to take a serious interest in post-war problems than before I left with various high up committees being established to think about this.'[1]

Keynes was involved in both endeavours. There was endless toing and froing between London and Washington about the wording of Article VII. The Treasury's aim was to avoid making any commitments which would limit Britain's freedom of action to protect its post-war balance of payments; the Foreign Office and Washington Embassy favoured Britain signing up to anything the Americans wanted, in the expectation of not having to honour its pledges when the time came. Keynes denounced the second course with his usual asperity. 'If there was *no one* left to appease, the FO would feel out of a job altogether,' he minuted. The worst thing would be 'our agreeing to unreasonable demands against our better judgment and then *inevitably* having to find some way of slipping out of our ill-advised words'.[2] On 7 December 1941, the whole context of the Lend–Lease negotiations seemed altered by the Japanese attack on Pearl Harbor, and US entry into the European war. The British now hoped that talk of a consideration owing for Lend–Lease would be drowned out by the rhetoric of mutual sacrifice for a common cause. They were alarmed by the pile-up of sterling balances which would ensue from the Pacific war. Montagu Norman wanted the British to urge on the Americans 'the policy of pooling resources without any talk of consideration now or hereafter'.[3] Halifax hoped to postpone final discussion of the consideration till after the war. There was neither pooling nor postponement. The United States insisted that a 'debt' had already been incurred; and made it clear that all future supplies to Britain would be lend–leased on the same conditions as before. Churchill, conscious of disunity in his Cabinet,[4] crossed out the words 'without discrimination' from the Atlantic Charter when he met Roosevelt at Placentia Bay, New Foundland in August 1941, and managed to avoid discussion of Article VII altogether when he visited Washington in December that year to cement the Grand Alliance.

Keynes's more serious preoccupation was to find some way by which it might be safe for Britain to accept the obligations of Article VII of the Lend–Lease Agreement. He was clear from the start that a return to the gold standard and free trade was out of the question. But might it not be possible, by a major reform of the currency system, to restore the system of multilateral payments which had underpinned trade expansion in the nineteenth century? Provided all countries were guaranteed sufficient quantities of reserves – something the old gold standard had been unable to do – it might be possible to dismantle most of the trade barriers which had grown up in the 1930s and during the war and restore that single world which had vanished in 1914. It was in this mood that Keynes started thinking about 'future currency arrangements' at Tilton in August 1941.[5] These thoughts were to occupy him for most of the rest of the war. Back in Washington, Harry Dexter White of the US Treasury was also thinking about 'future currency arrangements'. The compromise between the plans which the two men produced would be known as the Bretton Woods System.

It might seem odd that planning for economic disarmament started on the monetary rather than on the trade side, and made faster progress. After all, Article VII was about trade, not money. But it made sense logically and politically. World trade had broken down in the 1930s because the gold standard had disintegrated. So the way to start unblocking the channels of trade was to unblock the flow of money by which traded goods were paid for. This required an improvement on the old gold standard. It also seemed a lot easier for Britain and America to reach agreement about money. Money was too esoteric and boring to engage the attention of most politicians, whereas trade issues instantly aroused interests, passions, and prejudices. So technicians had a chance to make much more progress on money before their plans attracted political attention.

It must not be supposed that the technicians, as they were somewhat contemptuously called, operated in a historical or political vacuum. They brought to their work different understandings of what had gone wrong with the old gold standard; and different national experiences and interests. Above all the British and American plans came from two countries which expected to be very differently situated in the post-war world. The British expected to emerge from the war stripped of trade and assets and burdened with debts; the Americans in the opposite position. Keynes's, therefore, was a debtor's, White's a creditor's, perspective. The British wanted a scheme which would enable them to borrow without strings; the Americans one which would lend with strings. This difference was reinforced by another. The British plan came from a banking tradition, the American one from a legal tradition. The British wanted a scheme based on prudential maxims; the Americans one based on legal rules.

The technical debates were not merely a cover for national self-interest. Keynes and White were both interested in theory, and in finding technical solutions to technical problems. Economics often enables political conflicts which seem intractable if carried on in the language of politics to be bypassed by assuming (or the cynic would say pretending) that they can be reduced to the technical, and imposing a language of debate consistent with that assumption. As the technicians from both sides got to know each other better, a genuine camaraderie developed *contra mundis* – against the politicians, bankers, vested interests on both sides waiting in the wings to sabotage both the Keynes and White Plans. The fact that 'technicians' handled all the stages leading to the Bretton Woods Agreement ensured that there was an Agreement; it did not ensure that the politicians on either side signed up to it in good faith.

The challenge with which Article VII faced Keynes was to devise a plan to lock the USA into a system which would maintain balance of payments equilibrium between all countries without trade discrimination but also without forcing deflation, unemployment or debt-bondage on the deficit countries. He met it with the experience of the inter-war years and his economic theories, which were largely commentaries on the experience.

II

THE BACKGROUND

By tradition, Britain was internationalist, the United States protectionist and isolationist. Britain had virtually created the nineteenth-century 'world economy'; it was its lynchpin as well as its main beneficiary. The United States, by contrast, was a largely self-sufficient periphery, with a founding myth of freedom from foreign entanglements. In the 1930s Britain became protectionist and isolationist, the United States internationalist. This shift reflected the changing facts of power. Indeed, in one famous account, the financial and economic breakdown of the 1930s resulted from the incompleteness of the transfer. 'The British couldn't and the Americans wouldn't' take responsibility for stabilising the international economy.[6]

This would have seemed a strange idea to the central bankers who resuscitated the international gold standard in the mid-1920s after the disruptions of the war. The picture of the world economy in their minds was that of a self-equilibrating system in which international payments were automatically kept in balance by the condition that domestic currencies were freely convertible into gold at a fixed price. The whole textbook theory of international payments pivoted on this view; it had been endorsed in 1919 by the influential Cunliffe Report. The question of 'management' was therefore irrelevant: the virtue of the gold standard lay precisely in the fact that it was 'unmanaged'. Few glimpsed the truth, proclaimed by Keynes in his *Tract on Monetary Reform* (1923), that the gold standard was not a self-managing system, that its operation depended on policy, and that national interests might diverge. When the system broke down in 1931, everyone had come to understand this; but no one was quite sure who was to blame.

It is now generally agreed that under the restored gold standard of the 1920s the main currencies were seriously misaligned. Sterling, put back on gold in 1925, was overvalued at $4.86 to the pound – its pre-war parity – and the franc, fixed *de facto* in 1926, *de jure* in 1928, at a small fraction of its pre-war parity, was undervalued. The result was that Britain slumped in the second half of the 1920s, while America and France boomed – or so it seemed. The question of whose duty it was to adjust to whom was explicitly raised for the first time in the late 1920s in financial discussions between the Bank of England and the Bank of France. British officials accused the French of draining gold from London, the French replied that it was Britain's duty to readjust its domestic position so as to avoid gold loss. Looking back on the experience, after the gold standard had collapsed, the consensus British view was that France and the United States had not followed the 'rules of the game'. France had deliberately undervalued the franc. By maintaining a high tariff, America had made it extremely difficult for Europe to export to it and repay its own debts. As the world slithered into depression after 1929 the US had put up an even higher tariff (the Hawley–Smoot tariff) and repatriated its loans from Europe and Latin America, forcing their recipients into default. Thus was the doctrine of creditor adjustment born. Too late Britain's financial managers discovered that what had suited Britain as the world's leading creditor country in the nineteenth century did not suit others. The removal of sterling's 'golden fetters' in 1931, leading to an immediate depreciation of sterling against the dollar and franc, was welcomed as a liberation by Britain's business community, as enabling them to sell more of their exports and inaugurating a policy of cheap money at home.

In British self-perception, Britain was 'forced off' gold in September

1931 by selfish American (and French) policy. The Americans did not agree. The duty of adjustment lay with the country losing gold. When the Europeans complained about having to pay back their war debts, President Calvin Coolidge memorably responded: 'We hired them the money, didn't we?' In American eyes Britain should have re-established its economy by consuming less, saving more, working harder and exporting more. Thomas Lamont, a J. P. Morgan partner, denied that England had made a mistake in restoring the pound to its pre-war gold value in 1925. Any other action would have been a default. 'The mistake was in permitting the trade unions . . . to impose a rigid wage scale on British industries and subsidising the resulting unemployment by the dole.' In 1931, Britain should have cut wages and continued borrowing. The New York bankers also blamed British influence for the collapse of American prosperity in 1929. By allowing London to borrow dollars cheaply instead of putting up domestic interest rates, the US monetary authorities had, according to Lamont, allowed the New York Stock Exchange boom to get out of hand.[7] After 1931 American authorities blamed Britain's abandonment of the gold standard for the deepening banking crisis in the United States. 'The hurricane that swept our shores was of European origin,' declared President Hoover. This view was inherited by Roosevelt, though he blamed the New York bankers for their greedy and unsound loans to Central Europe.[8] It is a wild over-simplification. America's collapse in the early 1930s was domestically generated, for reasons which are still debated.[9] The upshot, nevertheless, was that the Americans did not accept Britain's abandonment of the gold standard as involuntary: it was a voluntary default.

These polemics at least exploded the myth of 'automatic adjustment'. Monetary conditions depended on policy; an international monetary system had to have agreed exchange rate rules, adjustment mechanisms, and escape clauses. The real charge against the gold standard was its inflexibility. This was because the exchange rates of currencies were determined by their relative gold content. In this kind of world, for a country to devalue its currency (that is, reduce its gold content) was seen, not as an act of adjustment, but as an act of default. The concepts, though not the practice, of the time did not allow for the middle way of currency management. You either fixed your currency irrevocably to gold, or you floated it. And floating – permitted under extreme circumstances – was seen as a prelude to refixing at the old rate, at least for a first-class monetary power.

The breakdown of the gold standard in 1931 was thus expected to be temporary; in fact it proved permanent. Attempts to restore it, even in modified form, at the World Economic Conference in London in July 1933 broke down after newly elected President Roosevelt denounced stabilisation efforts as 'the old fetishes of so-called central bankers'. The rivalry and mutual incomprehension between Britain and the United

States now exploded into full-blown economic warfare. Because the United States refused to accept sterling's depreciation as involuntary, and suspected Britain was using its Exchange Equalisation fund to keep it 'undervalued',[10] it too suspended dollar convertibility into gold in April 1933, despite ample reserves.[11] By the summer of 1933 the dollar had depreciated by 30 per cent and most of Britain's temporary competitive advantage had been wiped out.

But Roosevelt was determined to force down the value of the dollar even further. 'He told [the banker James] Warburg that now he wanted the dollar to fall until the pound became worth $5.00.'[12] He hit on a novel method. In their tree-planting activities in Dutchess County, Roosevelt and Morgenthau (not yet Secretary of the Treasury) had met two arboreal experts, George Warren and Frank Pearson, of nearby Cornell University, who were also agricultural economists. Professor Warren told them that the way to raise farm prices was by reducing the value of the dollar in terms of gold, and the way to do that was for the government to buy newly minted (or indeed any) gold for dollars at an ever rising price. The dollars could be obtained from the Reconstruction Finance Corporation, which had been set up in 1932 to refinance the banking system. So in the autumn of 1933 Roosevelt and his two cronies, Morgenthau (made acting Secretary of the Treasury) and Jesse Jones of the RFC, went on a gold-buying spree, meeting every morning round the President's bedside to raise the RFC's buying price for gold by a few percentage points. One morning it was increased by 21 cents since three times seven seemed a lucky number. By these methods the price of gold was pushed up to $35.00 an ounce compared to its par rate of $20.67. Keynes memorably described the policy as 'the gold standard on the booze'. It had little effect on domestic prices, but gold purchases in the world market drove down the international price of the dollar, so that by January 1934 Roosevelt had achieved his five-dollar pound. Thereafter, although Congress fixed the gold content of the dollar at $35 an ounce, sales of gold were at the discretion of the Treasury, and Roosevelt retained the right of currency retaliation to prevent sterling from depreciating again.[13] The British, who might have accepted a four-dollar pound, resolved instead 'to manage sterling so as to suit our own economy'.[14] Each country accused the other of pursuing 'beggar my neighbour' policies. But the real moral of the 1931–4 events was that changing an exchange rate is a two-way transaction. The US refused to accept the British devaluation, and there was nothing Britain could do about it.

When Harry Dexter White of the US Treasury came to London on a fact-finding mission in April–May 1935, he reported Keynes as telling him that a 'de facto stabilization was desirable' but the sterling rate would need to be lower before the British government would agree, an opinion echoed by Sir Richard Hopkins, Sir Frederick Phillips and Sir Frederick

Leith-Ross of the British Treasury.[15] In October 1935 Keynes was confident that he was expounding 'the British point of view' when he wrote of the three requirements of a 'permanent' system that (a) 'the *de facto* rates of exchange, from which we start out, should be in reasonable equilibrium', (b) central bank reserves should be pooled to prevent short-term exchange rate fluctuations and (c) exchange rates should be fixed, but adjustable enough to cope with 'deep-seated' disequilibria.[16] Keynes was expressing the by then consensus British belief that 'balanced trade' must be a precondition for restoring fixed exchange rates.

Why did Roosevelt refuse to accept sterling's depreciation? The answer lies in a combination of desperation, ignorance, interest and paranoia. The desperation was real enough: the American economy was crumbling and he was trying out every device he could think of to revive it. The ignorance relates to the method: this was the age of the monetary cranks. Roosevelt was also appealing to one very influential class of debtors – the food and raw-material producers, whose incomes had been catastrophically hit by the collapse of primary product prices. Farmers and miners welcomed the reduction of the gold content of the dollar as the way to higher prices at home and increased exports abroad. Politically, Roosevelt's tirade against the 'fetishes of central bankers' played well to a rural paranoia dating back to William Jennings Bryan and even earlier. A related paranoia gripped the administration. US economic policy was dominated by a grotesque overestimation of Britain's financial strength and a corresponding suspicion of Britain's motives. Vigilance against British Machiavellianism rather than the production of constructive ideas was the watchword of Morgenthau's Treasury, a tendency reinforced by British secretiveness. Americans' image of themselves as innocents abroad – 'The trouble is that when you sit around the table with a Britisher he usually gets 80 per cent of the deal and you get what is left,' Roosevelt told Morgenthau – promoted, in the early 1930s, an aggressive, self-righteous isolationism.

Roosevelt's monetary experiments were regarded as bizarre by many Americans at the time, and a longer perspective has not altered this verdict. It did nothing for US recovery, and strengthened the trend to currency and trading blocs by failing to address the problem of America's unbalanced creditor position. Carried to its logical conclusion it would have prevented three out of four continents from trading with the United States, leaving its huge gold stock largely redundant.

With the world economy breaking up, Britain regrouped its financial and trading relations on its Empire. When sterling went off gold in 1931, twenty-five countries joined it in a downward float against the dollar, linking their currencies to sterling for trading convenience, to protect their position in the British market and prevent a rise in the cost of their debt to Britain. This was the start of what was later called the sterling area.

At the heart of this grouping were about a dozen countries and dependencies of the British Empire which pegged their currencies to sterling, used sterling, not gold, to settle their accounts with each other, and held their reserves ('sterling balances') in London. Till 1939 sterling was freely convertible into other currencies on current account. The sterling area was a mutual benefit society in a disordered world. It offered its members interest on their balances, direct means of buying British goods, unrivalled means of converting sterling into dollars and other currencies, free access to loans, and protection, through the financial facilities offered by the London market, against fluctuations in prices, particularly valuable for primary producers. It protected most of Britain's external trade against exchange risk, and, with freedom to export capital within the area, preserved the role of the City of London as banker and lender, though on a much reduced scale. Britain was also able to use sterling area countries' dollar surpluses to balance its dollar deficits on trade with the United States. The accumulation of sterling balances had reached £780m. early in 1938.

In American eyes, the emergence of the sterling area compounded the offence of the British devaluation, by checking American exports to Latin America and elsewhere and retarding the rise of the dollar as the premier world currency. For Morgenthau, dollar–sterling rivalry had a geopolitical dimension. The fact that China, for trade purposes, pegged the yuan to sterling rather than to the dollar undermined his attempts to organise loans to stiffen Chinese resistance to Japanese aggression, which the British were in no position to supply. As his assistant Harry White put it with brutal candour, 'the US is a coming nation and England is a going one'.[17]

The trade war between the two countries proceeded parallel with the currency war. Britain's response to the US Hawley–Smoot tariff of 1930 was to set up the imperial preference system in 1932 – the abandonment of almost a hundred years of free trade. The inspiration behind imperial preference, going back to Joseph Chamberlain's tariff reform campaign of 1903, was to convert an empire of sentiment into a commercial and political union, on the basis of reciprocal tariff concessions for each other's products. Neville Chamberlain, the British Chancellor of the Exchequer, to whom it fell to implement his father's grand design, found little warmth in the imperial bargaining at Ottawa in July–August 1932. The theory was that Britain would use its quasi-monopsonist buying power in foodstuffs and raw materials to secure preferential entry for its manufactured exports in Empire countries in return for concessions to their products in the British market. The basic flaw in this strategy lay in the notion of a 'natural' division between British manufactures and Dominion primary products. In practice, Canada, Australia, South Africa and India were all interested in developing their 'infant industries', while Britain wanted to protect its farmers and also preserve its trade relations with third countries, some of which were members of the sterling area. The Ottawa preference system turned out to be a device for tariff increases all round. The Dominions gave British manufactures preference by increasing their tariffs on foreign goods rather than reducing them on British goods. Free or privileged entry for Empire primary products into the British market was coupled with a complicated duty and quota system to protect British farmers and preserve third-party entry. Judging by results, the British were comprehensively out-negotiated at Ottawa: a classic case of the weak exploiting the strong. Britain achieved only a small increase of exports to the Dominions; its exports to third countries were restricted, as it was deprived of bargaining flexibility and suffered increased competition in non-Empire markets; and Empire and foreign countries benefited largely from Britain's home-market-based recovery. As a result Britain's trade deficit soared, while income from 'invisibles' shrank. In the years immediately preceding the war Britain became, for the first time, a net importer of capital.

Although the sterling area had formed spontaneously while the Ottawa preference system had been negotiated, they soon came to be regarded in Britain as interlocking parts of the same defensive system. The large British market for Empire products caused Empire countries to hold sterling balances in London, which maintained London as a financial centre and sterling as a reserve currency, and enabled Britain to balance its trade with the United States. Once it had been set up, there was extreme reluctance in Britain to abandon a system which combined imperial sentiment with seemingly solid economic advantages.

Secretary of State Cordell Hull condemned imperial preference as 'a grevous injury' to US commerce.[18] But he appreciated that it was Britain's retaliation against the Hawley–Smoot tariff of 1930. Hull, a preacher by temperament, was a passionate advocate of non-discrimination, which is what he really meant by free trade. He believed that attempts to 'close off' markets were the most potent cause of war. Reading his memoirs one gets the curious impression that Hitler's worst offence was his trade policy, but that this was exceeded in iniquity by Britain's. His evangelical fervour coincided with a swing in American business sentiment towards freer trade. Historically, the United States had protected its manufactures behind high tariff walls and exported its agricultural surpluses. Now that the infants had grown into competitive giants, it was interested in general trade expansion. The 'Open Door' was also a way of extending America's economic reach, while preserving political isolationism. Hull would have allowed an adjustment of the dollar–sterling exchange in Britain's favour in order to facilitate mutual tariff reductions, but was overruled by Roosevelt and Morgenthau.[19] However, the view that a monetary agreement was the key to unblocking the channels of trade was growing in Washington.

Monetary rapprochement was triggered off by France's decision to devalue the franc in 1936, threatening another round of competitive currency depreciation. A Tripartite Monetary Agreement was signed on 25 September 1936, by which the USA and Britain accepted a 30 per cent franc devaluation, and the three countries agreed to use their exchange equalisation accounts to promote stable exchange rates between themselves. In an important policy shift the US Treasury agreed to sell gold to the British and French Treasuries at a daily quoted price: the gold standard on a twenty-four hours' basis, as one wag put it. These monetary arrangements soon embraced the core Western democracies. Separately, the Bank for International Settlements in Geneva offered its member central banks facilities for granting each other reciprocal credits for commercial transactions. In July 1937, Harry White negotiated a series of stabilisation arrangements with Latin American countries on behalf of the US Treasury. The Tripartite Agreement and its supporting institutions were to be very much in White's mind when he drew up his own scheme for an International Stabilisation Fund to support a fixed exchange rate system in 1941. The events of 1936 marked the end of the era of competitive exchange depreciation, though it fell far short of a full-blooded return to the gold standard.[20] After 1937 the United States acquiesced in a gradual decline in the value of sterling against the dollar.

The modest moves towards monetary rapprochement enabled some equally modest steps towards unblocking trade. Cordell Hull had secured the passage of a Trade Agreements Act in 1934, empowering the President to negotiate reciprocal tariff reductions. Hull plainly hinted that progress towards peace depended on Britain moving away from economic nationalism.[21] The British, accepting the need for closer relations with the United States in face of the challenge of the brigand powers, were in a mood to respond to an American initiative. The result was the Anglo-American Trade Agreement of 1938, which brought 'a marked benefit to American agriculture'.[22]

While the democracies were edging back towards a more liberal economic system, Germany had developed an illiberal variant of its own. This came to be known as the Schachtian system, after the name of Hitler's banker and Economics Minister, Hjalmar Schacht. Schacht made an unpleasing impression on the State Department's Herbert Feis when he came to Washington for financial talks in 1933: 'He spoke with voluble assurance akin to that of a schoolmaster lecturing to his pupils. His gray, mean face was pinched above his high, stiff collar, and his pale eyes gleamed sharply behind unrimmed spectacles as his glance darted about from person to person.'[23] But Schacht was a technical wizard, who pioneered an ingenious system for freeing his country from the external constraint on recovery and rearmament. Its rested on two pillars: an import-licensing scheme together with subsidiary controls on exports, and bilateral payments agreements with Germany's main trading partners, notably in South-East Europe and Latin America. As opposed to multilateral clearing, in which the only relevant account is a country's balance with the rest of the world, bilateral agreements were designed to balance the trade of each pair of countries, thus obviating the need for gold movements, or indeed any foreign exchange transactions. In its simplest form, the two trading partners open accounts for each other in their central banks, into which each pays for its imports from the other in its local currency. The balances in both accounts can only be cleared (that is, eliminated) by the exchange of goods. It was a modern form of barter trade: goods exchanged against goods, not money. By 1938 Germany had made clearing agreements with twenty-seven countries, covering half of its foreign trade. Technically, it remained on the gold standard, but it was a gold standard maintained by exchange controls. Paul Einzig dubbed it the 'Gold Insolvency Standard' since 'any currency can be maintained stable by preventing transfers which tend to cause its depreciation'.[24] In fact, Germany was able to accumulate mark balances (representing import surpluses) in the bilateral clearings much as Britain was able to run up sterling balances.

Although the Schachtian system was widely regarded in Britain as enabling Germany to obtain forced loans from its Danubian neighbours by blocking their balances, it undoubtedly 'solved' Germany's balance of payments problem in a way the sterling area/imperial preference system did not do for Britain, by allowing German economic recovery to proceed to full employment. (For a fuller discussion of the Schachtian system, see Appendix 1 to this chapter.)

The inter-war experience thus presented itself very differently to the British and the American technicians negotiating a post-war monetary system. The key to it was their different perceptions of the gold standard. In the 1920s both Britain and America were on the international gold standard, but Britain slumped, while America boomed. In the 1930s, the gold standard disintegrated, but Britain recovered while America slumped. Thus the British attributed their misfortunes to the gold standard, and their recovery to being liberated from it, while the Americans at least associated their prosperity with the gold standard, and the collapse of their economy with the monetary chaos which followed its breakdown. As a result, the British approached post-war monetary planning with a marked aversion to the gold standard, and the Americans with a marked preference for it.[25] Morgenthau's Treasury, recovered from its gold-buying binge, now regarded fixed exchange rates as a *sine qua non* of trade expansion. The British Treasury believed equally firmly that 'balanced trade' was the condition for stable exchange rates and that the main responsibility for securing this lay with the Americans. It was the middle ground of currency management and managed trade policy that seemed to offer the best hope of reconciling the two views.

Keynes provided a mordant commentary on the whole catastrophic sequence which illuminates the approach he would take to post-war reconstruction. The key to his attitude is his rejection of Lord Cunliffe's doctrine that the gold standard was automatically self-adjusting. It had only *seemed* that way in the nineteenth century because of the special role of London in financing world trade and capital exports. In the *Tract on Monetary Reform* (1923) he had argued that Britain could not rely on the United States replicating by policy what, before the First World War, had happened spontaneously. He thought it improbable that the post-war US creditor position would be voluntarily liquidated, at least quickly. Pegging sterling to the dollar (especially at the pre-war parity) would therefore force deflation on the British economy. So Britain must preserve its monetary independence. The world should be divided into dollar and sterling currency blocs which floated against each other. If both countries pursued policies of domestic price stability, the two currencies would be stable against each other for long periods, but their exchange rates should not be rigidly fixed.[26] Had his advice been taken, a lot of the subsequent trouble might have been avoided.

In his polemics of the 1920s, Keynes blamed British rather than American or French policymakers. He claimed that sterling had been overvalued against the dollar. This had forced deflation on the British economy. But 'Deflation does not reduce wages "automatically". It reduces them by causing unemployment.'[27] In 1924 he started advocating capital controls as a way of reducing deflationary pressure.[28] In the *Treatise on Money* (1930) he argued that the central object of national monetary policy should be to maintain a rate of interest consistent with domestic full employment. This was incompatible with a passive attitude to international gold flows.[29] All this was a logical following through of the idea that societies are sticky not fluid, and that therefore fixing the monetary thermometer does not automatically cool overheated economies or warm chilled ones. Almost single-handedly Keynes killed the allure of the gold standard for the British by calling it a 'barbarous relic'.[30] This characterisation conceals a crucial lack of clarity on the question of whether the gold standard was inherently deflationary, or whether its deflationary consequences on Britain were the result of the policy mistake of overvaluing the pound.

In the *Treatise on Money* Keynes first put forward his earliest plan for an 'ideal' system, managed by 'the plenary wisdom of a supernational body' which would secure currency stability while overcoming the defects of the gold standard. The essential condition was to ensure that countries never had to deflate because of a shortage of gold. A world bank should be set up with the power to create a fiduciary asset (supernational bank money or SBM). SBM would count equally with gold as legal reserves of the member central banks. The Bank would be able to lend SBM to the central banks of countries in temporary balance of payments difficulties in proportion to their deposits of gold and securities, and would vary the total quantity of SBM – partly by means of open-market operations – so as to stabilise its value in terms of a basket of commodities.[31] Essentially it was a plan to enlarge the world's monetary base, while retaining gold as the ultimate reserve asset. Two features of this scheme – technical management free from national politics and the power to create deposits – were to be repeated in Keynes's monetary plan of 1941.

In line with this ideal system, Keynes and Hubert Henderson produced a reflationary plan for the World Economic Conference of 1933 based on the creation of additional international reserves to raise the world price level, Keynes emphasising that the distribution of the additional reserves his plan would create 'should not be of an eleemosynary [that is, discretionary] character' but 'available ... to all participating countries in accordance with a general formula'.[32] He then produced another plan of his own, involving an all-round devaluation in terms of gold of the world's leading currencies. Despite the fact that Roosevelt's 'bombshell' had scuppered his own scheme, Keynes proclaimed that 'President Roosevelt is Magnificently Right' in choosing the path of domestic currency management. He hoped that Britain would now throw in its lot with the United States in a 'sterling–dollar bloc committed to economic progress and the restoration of economic health'.[33] He broadened his case for national monetary sovereignty to include the possibility of making social experiments: 'We each have our own fancy. Not believing we are saved already, we would each like to have a try at working out our own salvation ... and be free as we can make ourselves from the interferences of the outside world.'[34]

On 13 October 1936 he summed up his views to a German correspondent, W. Lück. This came just after the Tripartite Monetary Agreement and conveys Keynes's (and the Treasury's) sense of the limits of what was possible at that moment:

1. In general I remain in favour of independent national systems with fluctuating exchange rates.

2. Unless, however, a long period is considered, there need be no reason why the exchange rate should in practice be constantly fluctuating.

3. Since there are certain advantages in stability ... I am entirely in favour of practical measures towards de facto stability so long as there are no fundamental grounds for a different policy.

4. I would even go so far ... as to give some additional assurance

as to the magnitude of the fluctuations which would be normally allowed. . . . Provided there was no actual pledge, I think that in most ordinary circumstances a margin of 10 per cent should prove sufficient.

5. I would emphasise that the practicability of stability would depend (i) upon measures to control capital movements, and (ii) the existence of a tendency for broad wage movements to be similar in the different countries concerned.[35]

Keynes's wavering line in the inter-war years closely mirrored the opportunities opened up and foreclosed by policies and events. As Schumpeter shrewdly wrote: 'Keynes's advice was in the first instance always English advice, born of English problems. . . .'[36] At a formal level, there was a basic consistency in his views. A multilateral payments system, which preserved the advantages, while avoiding the defects, of the gold standard, was best; but, if it could not be achieved, Britain would have to be free to manage its exchange rate and trading policies in its own national interest. The key feature of an 'ideal' system was that deficit countries would never be forced to deflate. Surpluses would be liquidated by formula, not by discretion.

Despite the formal consistency, there was a tension, even a fissure, between Keynes's nationalism and internationalism, which required a fabulous formula to overcome. The nationalist tendency in his theory is clear from his insistence that the national authority must retain control over the domestic rate of interest in order to be free to pursue full employment and progressive social policies. It might be wondered what kind of international monetary system, except one which impelled the regular redistribution of reserves from creditor to debtor countries, could satisfy these requirements. A modern answer might be a system of floating exchange rates. But this was beyond the practical or theoretical imagination of the times, including Keynes's. For one thing it was associated with the currency wars of the 1930s. More deeply, most economists at the time doubted that currency depreciation could bring an economy closer to equilibrium: it could well have the opposite effect if it led to a country selling its exports too cheaply. The notion that serious misalignments could develop under a floating exchange rate system was to be rediscovered in the 1980s. In the earlier period, it ensured that floating was not considered a remedy for balance of payments disequilibrium. There was also an emotional fissure between Keynes's liberal internationalism and his patriotism. This had not been a problem in the nineteenth century when Britain, as he put it, had 'conducted the international orchestra'. It became a problem for him when the baton passed to the United States.

Old dogs do not learn new tricks, and Keynes was no exception. The two alternative approaches of his inter-war commentary run through his

Clearing Union proposals and the Anglo-American negotiations over the shape of the post-war international economic order. Keynes was able to take the principal role in these negotiations because events in peace and war had made his views orthodox in Whitehall; and he was their most persuasive and elegant advocate.

III

SCHACHTIAN TRICKS

In the 1930s, Keynes took no interest in Hjalmar Schacht's system of bilateral clearing agreements. But the Schachtian system was much on his mind in the summer of 1941. The reason is twofold: Britain had itself adopted 'Schachtian' methods to fight the war, and in the autumn of 1940 Keynes had got personally involved in a propaganda exercise designed to counter Germany's post-war plans.

As has been told, the sterling–dollar rate was fixed at $4.03 to the pound at the outbreak of the war and imports were made subject to licence. By the summer of 1940, all 'hard currency' transactions were subject to exchange control. Sterling area residents were free to spend the pounds they earned from their exports anywhere within the sterling area. As Britain's export trade shrank, sterling area countries started to run large export surpluses with Britain, so that sterling balances (British debts) accumulated in London. Sterling area countries also deposited their exporters' dollar earnings in London, drawing on the 'dollar pool' as required for their imports from the United States, which they undertook to keep to a minimum. American resentment at the existence of this 'pool', which in their view was a device to discriminate against American goods, rankled throughout the war. Bilateral payments agreements had been negotiated with non-sterling neutrals in Europe and Latin America. Under these agreements, the countries concerned were paid 'area pounds sterling' for their exports to Britain which they were free to spend anywhere in the sterling area, but not outside – that is, they could not convert their pounds into dollars. In effect, all exits of foreign exchange from the sterling area were sealed off except for British-approved military purchases from the United States, for which Britain paid from its gold reserves and dollar pool. The success of the British 'Control' in mobilising the nation for war convinced many in 'official circles' that Schachtian methods should be made a permanent part of Britain's peacetime system. At the same time the 'Control', which operated mainly through import licensing, clearly discriminated against US goods, since it diverted trade to within the sterling area to save precious dollars. Article VII of the Lend–Lease Agreement was thus aimed at two sources of discrimination against American goods, which got somewhat confused in the American mind: the pre-war system of imperial preference and the wartime system of exchange control.

In the summer of 1940 Hitler was master of Western and Central Europe. Here was a considerable paradox. What he wanted was a slave empire in the East. What he got was Western Europe. He had no policy for what to do with his conquests. The vacuum was partly filled by technocrats in the German Economics Ministry and the Reichsbank, who put forward a blueprint for European economic union. Because of the unexpected German victory – soon to be revealed as ephemeral – the Germans were the first post-war planners. Their plans had nothing to do with Germany's future relations with Russia, which, still governed by the Nazi–Soviet Pact of August 1939, was supplying Germany with war materials. They were concerned with Germany's future relationships with its conquered territories – and with the United States. In the latter respect, they arose from the same preoccupations and covered much the same ground as British ruminations on the same subject.

At a press conference in Berlin on 25 July 1940, Walther Funk (Schacht's successor as Economics Minister) announced a plan for a 'New Order'. It had two elements. Germany and Italy would use their combined productive power to reconstruct Europe after the war; and payments within Europe would be cleared multilaterally, instead of bilaterally as in Germany's pre-war system. Germany would set up a payments union managed by a central clearing office in Berlin. Within the Union there would be fixed exchange rates and a 'rational' division of labour. Trade with outside countries would be regulated by bilateral agreements made by the Union: European imports from the United States would exactly balance European exports to the United States. In any case, gold would no longer function as a means of payment.[37] The Funk Plan offered all the Continental countries of non-Soviet Europe the benefits of multilateral clearing. It was Germany's answer to Britain's 'fortified' sterling area. It was also the first blueprint for the economic union of Europe.* Its basic technical weakness (as compared with Keynes's 1941 plan) was the absence of a central bank. The Funk Plan envisaged completely planned

---

* The existence of this important fascist root of European Union has been ignored, largely for political reasons, but partly because it was regarded as fraudulent. Certainly Hitler had no interest in it. His mind was already set on extending the war to Russia. This does not mean that the technocrats who devised the Funk Plan thought it fraudulent. They were probably expecting the post-war era to start very soon, and were making economic preparations for it. The Funk scheme is an interesting example of the way the belligerents' economic plans influenced each other. Britain applied the Schachtian system to non-sterling area countries in 1940; and Germany sought in the Funk Plan a Continental version of the sterling area 'Control'. (John Laughland, *The Tainted Source: The Undemocratic Origins of the European Idea*, discusses, ch 2, wartime fascist pronouncements on European unity.)

trade, so that surpluses and deficits would never arise in the clearing accounts.

The 'New Order' dossier arrived on Keynes's desk at the Treasury on 19 November 1940, with a note from Harold Nicolson at the Ministry of Information suggesting that he do a broadcast for American and Dominion audiences to discredit it. The dossier did not in fact contain a coherent account of the Funk Plan, but consisted only of snippets from German newspapers and broadcasts, stitched together by the Ministry of Economic Warfare. However, Keynes had got a better idea of the German scheme from Claude Guillebaud's favourable economic assessment of 'Hitler's New Economic Order for Europe', submitted to the *Economic Journal* (which Keynes still edited) and published in December 1940; and this influenced his response. He wrote back to Nicolson that a broadcast on the lines implied by the Ministry of Economic Warfare's comments was hopeless: it was no use trying to outflank Funk by offering Europe the blessings of universal free trade and the gold standard. In fact the Funk Plan was 'excellent and just what we ourselves ought to be thinking of doing. If it is to be attacked, the way to do it would be to cast doubt and suspicion on its *bona fides*.'[38]

Keynes did not broadcast on the Funk Plan but he produced some propagandist points for use by the Foreign Office: Britain and the countries of the sterling area could offer neutrals – and an eventually liberated Europe – far more of what they needed for reconstruction and trade than could Germany and its allies; Germany would exploit its position, as it had before the war, to get 'something for nothing', whereas Britain's debts would be repaid; Funk's talk of a rational division of labour was merely a cloak for concentrating industry in Germany and pastoralising the rest of Europe; because of the lack of food and raw materials in its 'space', Germany would be bound to start new wars to carry its imperialist exploitation further. Keynes borrowed Roosevelt's phrase 'social security' to describe the main theme of British post-war policy, at home and abroad.[39] Anthony Eden used Keynes's remarks as the text for a speech at the Mansion House on 29 May 1941, 'well wrapped in Foreign Office wool'.[40]

More interesting is a letter Keynes wrote to his Treasury colleague 'Sigi' Waley on 11 November:

> If Hitler gets his new Europe going properly, with barter replacing gold . . . and with all the nations playing the cultural and ethnographical roles allotted to them, while the Vatican provides the slave states with a philosophy of life, then England can be made to look like an intolerably disruptive pirate nuisance in the eyes of Europe. We would become the real aliens, the Protestant dissenters, the Berbers of the North. In Hitler's favour is the fact that he has the

will and ambition to govern Europe, and that Rome, Berlin and Munich are the natural places to do it from. But as long as the blockade is effective he is compelled to loot, and while he has to loot the conquered territories, his propaganda must fail.[41]

Did Keynes really mean that the *only* reason the New Order would fail was the British blockade?

Much more important than his propagandist exercises was Keynes's acceptance of the fundamental postulates of Funk's permanent system:

> I have assumed [he wrote in a covering note] that we shall continue our existing exchange controls after the war, and that we do not propose to return to *laissez-faire* currency arrangements on pre-war lines by which goods were freely bought and sold internationally in terms of gold or its equivalent. Since we ourselves have very little gold left and will owe great quantities of sterling to overseas creditors, this seems only commonsense.... The virtue of free trade depends on international trade being carried on by means of what is, in effect, *barter*. After the last war *laissez-faire* in foreign exchange led to chaos. Tariffs offer no escape from this. But in Germany Schacht and Funk were led by force of necessity to evolve something better. In practice they have used their new system to the detriment of their neighbours. But the underlying idea is sound and good. In the last six months the Treasury and the Bank of England have been building up for this country an exchange system which has borrowed from the German experience all that was good in it. If we are to meet our obligations and avoid chaos in international trade after the war, we shall have to retain this system. But this same system will serve to protect the impoverished European countries and is an essential safeguard against a repetition of what happened last time.[42]

In a letter he wrote to Frank Ashton-Gwatkin of the Foreign Office on 25 April 1941, Keynes expanded on these initial observations as follows.

(a) Capital exports would be restricted to the case where the capital-exporting country had a favourable trade balance with the capital-importing country. 'Whatever one might wish, something of the sort seems to be inevitable, since we shall no longer have a cushion of gold or other liquid assets, by means of which the immediate effects of unbalanced capital movements can be handled.'

(b) Large elements of multilateral clearing would exist within the sterling area, but payments agreements would be required to handle relations between the area and the outside world. 'Unquestionably [this] would involve a discrimination against the United States if she persisted in maintaining an unbalanced creditor position. Again, whether we like it or not, this will be forced on us. We shall have no means after the war out of which we can pay for purchases in the United States except the equivalent of what they buy from us.'

(c) The exchange rate between sterling and the dollar should be fixed by agreement, but the rate at which it was fixed would no longer be so important. 'For, with a proper system of payments agreements which would prevent an unbalanced situation from developing, there would be no longer much object in depreciating the exchange. The method of depreciation is a bad method which one is driven to adopt failing something better. The currency system I have in view would be that something better. If USA inflates more than we do, we might even *appreciate* sterling.'

(d) The post-war sterling area could be extended to countries like Holland and Belgium. But even within the closed area it would still be necessary to guard against an 'unbalanced position' of a member country. 'There would have to be some arrangement by which an unbalanced position up to an agreed figure would have to be cared for by credit arrangements. But, if the maximum were reached, then the unbalanced debtor would have to restrict its purchases until it was in balance again.'

(e) The essence of the system was 'trading goods against goods'. If Argentina bought maize from Britain, it would have to spend its sterling in Britain or in the sterling area. Britain's role as the world's largest importer would give it a huge bargaining power to negotiate payments agreements with outside countries.

(f) 'The difficulty is to know quite how far it is safe to go in the direction of a complete freedom of transactions within the sterling area.' If Britain found itself with an adverse balance of payments as a result of countries like Argentina using their export earnings to Britain to buy too many goods from other sterling area countries then 'we should have to insist that the Argentine seller of maize must spend his sterling in the United Kingdom'.

(g) 'The necessity for some such plan as the above arises essentially from the unbalanced creditor position of the United States. It is a necessary condition of a return to free exchanges that the United States should find some permanent remedy for this unbalanced position. Sooner or later one can only suppose that she will have to do so. But it would be very optimistic to believe that she will find the solution in the immediate post-war period, even if she tries to mitigate her task by making large presents for the reconstruction of Europe.'[43]

Keynes's letter to Ashton-Gwatkin was a first, very uncertain bash at his own Clearing Union Plan, which he would draft that autumn. It is essentially what his Clearing Union might have looked like *without the United States in it*. The crucial point was the priority given to achieving trade balance. If trade between the sterling area and the United States was to be on a barter (bilateral clearing) basis, monetary issues like the sterling–dollar exchange rate and creditor versus debtor adjustment became secondary. Unlike Funk, though, Keynes did recognise the need for 'credit arrangements' to deal with short-run payments imbalances: Britain, unlike Germany, was in no position to plan the trade of its Empire.

It would be a mistake to believe that Keynes was *advocating* a 'Schachtian' world for Europe after the war, only one managed by Britain, not Germany. It is important to remember the context in which these ideas were put forward. Until America entered the war at the end of 1941, Keynes could not assume that it would play any part in constructing a new international economic order, one which would provide a 'permanent remedy' for its 'unbalanced position'. The Atlantic Charter was some months ahead; Russia was not yet involved in hostilities. If Britain 'won the war' in these circumstances, it would be left responsible for the 'economic reorganisation of Europe'; or, more realistically, it would be left *à deux* with a presumably post-Nazi Germany. An economic settlement would therefore of necessity have to build on the 'Schachtian' arrangements of the 1930s, as developed during the war itself; hence, too, the importance Keynes attached to the continuing '*economic* leadership [of Germany] in central Europe'.[44]

At the same time, Keynes never thought of the Schachtian system merely as a *pis aller*. That is to say, he did not put it on a par with what he would call 'failed experiments' like currency manipulation. In Lionel Robbins's view currency floating offered 'a complete solution to Britain's problem of external balance'.[45] But in Keynes's reading of inter-war history it was a weapon in the 'blind struggle' of countries to escape from the shackles of the gold standard, with a tendency to produce war.[46] By ensuring that 'goods exchanged for goods' the Schachtian system made possible trade which might not take place at all under *laissez-faire*. The doctrine that exchange controls were superior to currency depreciation became a permanent part of Keynes's thinking. It also became Treasury and Bank of England orthodoxy. And this created a favourable climate for Dr Schacht. Schachtianism might not be the best possible system, but it might easily be the best system possible.

IV

THE CLEARING UNION

One of the committees set up to consider post-war issues was an interdepartmental committee on post-war financial problems under Sir George Chrystal, permanent secretary at the Ministry of Health, and a bit of a wag: he had written a book before the First World War called *Memoirs of*

Prince Chlodwig of Hohenlohe Schillingsfuerst. Like most such committees, it rarely met. The work was done by the Treasury and the Bank of England. A composite document on 'Post-War Monetary, Financial and Trade Policy' – known as the 'Treasury sandwich' and later the 'Treasury Bible' – started to wend its portentous way through Whitehall in August 1941, gathering drafters and paragraphs on its journey. The British still hoped to avoid any definite commitments to 'Hullism'. This heavily influenced the approach of early drafts of the Treasury document, largely inspired by Hubert Henderson, Keynes's erstwhile ally, then resentful antagonist, now, like Keynes, at the Treasury. Henderson was a Schachtian. Commitment to Article VII, he argued, could not be reconciled with the prospective weakness of Britain's balance of payments; it was inconsistent with a system of national planning, of which exchange controls, centralised purchases of food and raw materials, and quantitative regulations of imports were an integral part. Such measures were not just for war; they represented 'an advance in the direction of a more ordered life'.[47] Henderson wrote: 'I am convinced that exchange control, and control of imports and exports, will have to continue for a prolonged period; and I'm not sure that I want *ever* to abolish the former *completely.*'[48] Henderson maintained this view right through the ensuing controversies on Britain's response to Article VII.

Henderson's views were heavily influenced by his reading of pre-war history, summed up in his paper 'The Nineteen Thirties'. Contrary to what he called the 'Chatham House' view, which blamed inter-war economic evils on economic nationalism, he viewed economic nationalism as an inevitable response to changes in the world economy. He did not believe that the old system of complementary international trade between manufacturing centres and primary producers, fuelled by rapid population growth and international lending, could be restored.* He thought it was illusory to suppose that, after the events of 1931, any 'self-respecting community' would ever again accept being placed 'at the mercy of . . . international speculators' and that it would be 'reckless in the extreme' to suppose that the USA would agree to liquidate voluntarily (for example, by reducing its tariffs) its 'unbalanced creditor position'. In his paper 'The British Balance of Payments', Henderson pointed out that Britain's post-war balance of payments was likely to be in deficit not just to the United States but to the sterling area. So it was madness to 'throw away the substantial portion of our exports which is dependent on the prefer-

---

* Henderson's view that the slump originated in agricultural surpluses has not worn well. Prices of raw materials collapsed before agricultural prices. This reflects reduced industrial demand following the downturns in the USA, Britain and Germany in 1929. More generally, agricultural surpluses in the 1920s were the counterpart of the heavy unemployment which persisted in industrial Europe right through the 1920s. The logic of this was that the problem would disappear if aggregate demand after the war was maintained at a high level.

ential favours we receive in Empire markets' or renounce the right to make barter agreements with foreign countries. Henderson was convinced that the system of planned trade pioneered by Schacht, and copied by Britain in the war, was tailor-made for both Britain's 'secular' and its short-term balance of payments problem.[49]

Henderson's views were a representative, though not uncontested, British reaction to the experiences of the inter-war years. Too proud to accept the position of a pensioner of the USA, too pessimistic to believe in the resilience of the British economy, Henderson believed that Britain needed to cling on at all costs to the imperial remnants of its once global position. His memoranda raised the issue of whether Britain could 'honestly' pledge itself to work with the United States to dismantle its protective systems in due course.

In point of theory, Hubert Henderson was a Schachtian because he was not a Keynesian. He believed that Britain's economic problems lay on the supply not the demand side. But, unlike the Thatcherites of the 1980s, he thought that very little could be done about them – that is, he had little faith in market mechanisms or the possibility of restoring them. This being so, Britain should grab as much of the world's supply as possible – by exploiting its imperial position to plan its trade to its advantage. This sounded very much like the 'rational' division of labour Funk planned for occupied Europe. Henderson accused Dennis Robertson of suffering from the 'Geneva complex' – a condition of guilt induced by reflection of his advantages which prevented him from any frank avowal of British interests.[50]

Had Henderson moved to the left or right since his collaboration with Keynes in the 1920s? Neither category fits his mixture of extreme scepticism about abstract reasoning and exaggerated faith in the efficacy of planning. He is accurately described as an Economic Nationalist – the British equivalent of Hjalmar Schacht.*

Keynes would have read Henderson's gloomy memoranda as he gathered his own thoughts on 'future currency arrangements' early in September. Where did he stand? Roy Harrod recalls running into him about this time in a Treasury corridor. He was leaning against a doorpost. ' "You must give up the bilateralist approach," I said, "and come down on the American side." "No," he said, "I must pursue both lines of thought . . . both." His expression was enigmatic. He seemed to be transfixed with a curious immobility that was unlike him. . . . Some deep inscrutable thoughts were proceeding. Even his great brain was baffled by this

---

* Economic Nationalists, too, can be divided into two camps – National Capitalists and National Socialists. Henderson fits the first, his protégé Thomas Balogh the second. One must, of course, distinguish the economic doctrines of the latter from the politics of Hitler's National Socialists.

problem'.[51] The problem, Keynes explained to Ernest Penrose, US Ambassador Winant's economic adviser, was that Britain would start off peace with a huge import surplus which couldn't be automatically liquidated by the price system. Bilateralism might be the only way to deal with it. Penrose believes that Keynes's attitude at this time was 'primarily a reflection of a temporary mood of despair regarding the chances of getting international agreement on a more enlightened solution than that of bilateral pressure and bargaining. A somewhat analogous situation had arisen in the early 1930s, when for a brief period he advocated tariffs as a remedy for British unemployment.'[52] A further piece of evidence comes from an exchange of letters with Richard Kahn. 'I believe that . . . the only fundamental issue', Kahn wrote to Keynes on 19 August 1941, 'is what degree of American co-operation would be necessary to justify a return to what might be called a liberal economic system and whether there is sufficient hope of persuading the Americans . . . to make the necessary concessions. . . .'[53] Keynes's perplexity is captured in his reply. He was not 'seriously worried by the rather unexpected strength of the *laissez-faire* school' which he had found in Washington. 'For . . . we shall start in practice *de facto* with a[n exchange] control and . . . what actually will be evolved from that is extremely unlikely to be *laissez-faire*.' The really interesting question was the 'technical problem' of adapting the *de facto* system to peacetime conditions.[54]

Keynes's wobble on Schachtianism in 1941 would encourage the *dirigistes* and dismay the liberals. 'The whole of Keynes's make-up, as I saw it, was in tune with free trade,' wrote that perceptive Keynes-watcher 'Foxy' Falk to Robert Boothby after Keynes's death. Boothby disagreed: 'I think there is no doubt that, at one time, he favoured a completely planned trade. The last time I saw him he said he regretted that I had not succeeded – as he had done – in "emancipating myself from bilateralism".'[55] Hubert Henderson concluded, after Keynes's death, that Keynes was 'an opportunist and eclectic to the end'.[56] This is almost, but not quite, right. Unlike Henderson, Keynes preferred internationalism. To the extent that he was a Schachtian, it was much more for practical reasons, to do with the situation Britain would find itself in when the war ended, and his scepticism concerning America's ability or willingness to step into Britain's shoes. This basic difference of outlook runs through their debates on both international and domestic policy. His internationalism, therefore, was contingent on getting the United States to do its duty as a creditor – by spending its surpluses, as Britain had done in the nineteenth century, and not hoarding them. He tried to work out a scheme for ensuring that it did so: this was his Clearing Union. If that failed he was ready to fall back on bilateralism.

Keynes returned to Tilton on Wednesday 3 September 1941 to spend, as he told his mother, 'several days in peace writing a heavy memorandum on post-war international currency plans'. Peace was the most elusive of his prizes. On Friday he was back in London for a meeting with Montagu Norman. The bomb explosion which killed Lord Stamp on 17 April had created a vacancy on the Court (board of directors) of the Bank of England. George Booth, a director, and son of Charles Booth the social reformer, had suggested Keynes to fill it, as being the most qualified person acceptable to Labour. Now Norman invited him to do so. As a director, he would have to buy £2000 of Bank of England stock for £7300. Having been assured that 'unofficially' he could continue to be at the disposal of the Chancellor and Treasury – that is continue exactly as he was – he decided to accept. The appointment was announced on 18 September.

Keynes wrote jokingly to Florence: 'Rather appalling, I feel, such respectability! Coming after a fellowship at Eton I feel it is only a matter of time before I become a Bishop or Dean of York. . . . My election to the Court may cause a bit of a stir . . . as . . . suggesting (more probably than is the truth) that my characteristic policies are becoming orthodox.' The appointment was largely honorific – the most important function of the Court being to appoint the governor – but it was also a seal of approval from the bastion of sound money. What did it signify? 'What rejoices all your friends', gushed Felix Frankfurter, 'is that the mountain has come to Mohammed and not the other way round'; Joan Robinson wrote: 'never mind, I will always say you were grand while you lasted'. The old leftie Walter Newbold, with whom Keynes had clashed on the Macmillan Committee in 1930–1, wrote to him shrewdly: 'You have never struck me at all as a terrible fellow. . . . You . . . have your place on the far outside left but you are part of one team indivisible & devoted to the perpetuation of the existing order.'[57] The governor had a more detached view. 'Keynes on a committee', he told Clapham, 'is rather like yeast.' Keynes was not sure who had captured whom. 'It remains to be seen', he wrote to Richard Kahn, 'which party is being made an honest woman of.'[58] Keynes now added Thursday morning meetings of the Court to his other duties. After one, he remarked to Booth, 'I do enjoy these lunches at the Bank: Montagu Norman, always absolutely charming, always absolutely wrong.'[59] The reconciliation was superficial. Shortly after Keynes's death, Norman wrote grudgingly, 'he must have been a great economist but was a bad banker'.[60]

After the excitement of his appointment, Keynes continued his drafting on Saturday. His memorandum was finished by Tuesday. He did it, he told Kahn, in an effort 'to make my ideas concrete' and 'to press others who have different ideas to do the same'. Keynes's method, as always, was to lead from the front and force others to make clear the nature of their disagreement.

The fruit of his weekend labour was two papers, 'Post War Currency

Policy' and 'Proposals for an International Currency Union'. The first of them was divided into four parts, 'The Secular International Problem', 'Our Contemporary British Problem', 'The Analysis of the Problem' and 'The Alternatives Facing Us'. This was mainly backward looking and was strongly influenced by Henderson's analysis. Then he jumped disconcertingly into his 'ideal scheme'.

The two questions Keynes set out to answer in his first paper were: what was wrong with the gold standard? And what were the special problems Britain would face after the war?

He started off by dismissing the classical theory of the gold standard. The flow of gold never did preserve equilibrium by adjusting relative price levels. Instead, Keynes claimed, provocatively, in the previous 500 years there had been only two periods, each of about fifty years, when the use of commodity money in international trade had 'worked' – the silver inflation period of the sixteenth century and the gold standard of the late nineteenth century, when 'the system of international investment pivoting on London transferred the *onus* of adjustment from the debtor to the creditor position'. This was a typical Keynesian sally. A market system did not work for the reasons economists said it worked. But it did work nevertheless, some of the time, for other reasons. If one could discover what these were, and build them into the design, it would work the whole time. Experience showed, he went on, that loans do not bring about a balanced position unless they create new sources of payments. Neither deflation nor depreciation produces a redistribution of trade through the adjustment of wages and prices. Tariffs, preferences and subsidies all fail. In the 1930s Schacht had 'stumbled in desperation on something new which had in it the germs of a good technical idea', namely, to cut the knot by substituting barter for the international use of money. Keynes quoted from Henderson's 'Nineteen Thirties' paper: 'If Germany had wished for butter instead of guns and aeroplanes, there is no reason to doubt that Dr. Schacht's expedients would have enabled her to obtain the butter instead of the metal from overseas.'

Why did the gold standard fail? Because it forced downward adjustment on the debtor. Adjustment, he wrote, was '*compulsory* for the debtor and *voluntary* for the creditor'. The debtor was generally a small country, least able to force its exports on the rest of the world by a one-sided change in its terms of trade. If the price of its exports had to be reduced to the same extent as their volume had to be increased, the problem was insoluble. So part of the initiative of adjustment had to come from the creditor. A further weakness was that since the last war money had failed to flow to where it was needed to develop new resources, but fled back to surplus countries. 'The flow of refugee and speculative funds, superimposed on [the favourable trade balance of the United States] brought the whole system to ruin.' There was no guarantee against a repetition of hot money flows after the war, when the position of wealth-owners would be threatened everywhere, and the 'whereabouts of "the better 'ole" will shift with the speed of a magic carpet'. Keynes echoed Henderson: 'Nothing is more certain than that the movement of capital funds must be regulated.'

After the war, Britain would need to re-establish equilibrium before it could maintain it. As a result of wartime losses, its prospective deficit would be between 50 and 100 per cent of its pre-war exports. Its best chance was to use its buyer's market in foodstuffs and raw materials to force open markets for its manufacturers. This involved bilateral negotiations which would, in any case, be needed to deal with sterling balances. To give up these weapons, in the absence of an American commitment to better alternatives, would be 'madness'. Anyone who agreed to such a surrender 'would be as great a traitor to this country as if he were to sign away the British navy before he had a firm assurance of an alternative means of protection'.

The United States might offer 'liberal relief' to Europe during the reconstruction period, some reduction of tariffs and restriction of agricultural exports, and 'New Deal' expedients to keep up employment. The first was a temporary measure, which would pass Britain by; the second would probably be inadequate, the third would offer 'great and perhaps adequate relief', but could not be relied on. If all that was on offer was 'currency disorders . . . mitigated and temporarily postponed by some liberal Red Cross work by the United States', Britain would have no alternative but to refine and improve 'the Schachtian device'. It would end the war with 'a well-developed' payments and clearing system which might evolve into a permanent peacetime system, mitigating the objectionable features of bilateralism. It could stabilise and balance its trade at a high volume by continuing to buy foodstuffs and raw materials in bulk from countries willing to take its exports.

So far it has been Schacht all the way. But now Keynes suddenly changed tack. He would prefer to challenge the Americans with an 'ideal' scheme, which would enable Britain to sign up honestly to the 'blessed word [non]-discrimination'; a scheme that was 'Utopian', not in the sense that it was impracticable, but 'in . . . that it assumes a higher degree of understanding, of the spirit of bold innovation, and of international co-operation and trust than it is safe or reasonable to assume'. None of this suggests any exaggerated hope that anyone would adopt this 'ideal' system. One can imagine him in his study at Tilton dusting down a copy of his *Treatise on Money* and looking up its pages on a 'supernational bank' issuing 'supernational bank money'. Like Jevons, he would flick his ideas at the world and hope they would fly.

The chief purpose of his International Currency Union (as he called

it) was to secure creditor adjustment without renouncing debtor discipline. Its method was to marry the Schacht–Funk 'clearing' approach with
the banking principle.

All residual international transactions – those giving rise to surpluses
and deficits in balance of payments positions – were to be settled through
'clearing accounts' held by member central banks in an International
Clearing Bank (ICB). Member central banks would buy and sell their own
currencies against debits and credits to their accounts at the Clearing
Bank. These balances would be held in 'bank money' (later called
'bancor'). Each member bank would have the right to an amount of bank
money (called its 'index quota') equal to half the average value of its
country's total trade for the five last pre-war years. This was its overdraft
facility. The ICB's total overdraft facilities came, therefore, to half the
value of pre-war international trade – about $25bn. Each national cur-
rency would have a fixed but adjustable relation to a unit of ICB's bank
money, which itself was expressed in terms of a unit of gold. But this link
with the gold standard was a fiction. Whereas bank money could be
bought with gold, it could not be sold for gold. Keynes called this 'one-
way convertibility'. 'A gold stock which can never be paid out to *anyone*
(except probably to the International Bank of Mars)' was an odd idea to
Dennis Robertson.[61] Keynes's long-run purpose was to de-monetise gold,
so that central banks would lose any incentive to hoard it. Bank money
would be the ultimate reserve asset of the system.

The object of the ICB was to maintain balance of payments equilibrium
between each member country and the rest of the world. Deposits of bank
money (credits and debits) would be created by surpluses and deficits and
extinguished by their liquidation. Keynes sought to bring a simultaneous
pressure on both surplus and deficit countries to 'clear' their accounts. A
bank whose annual 'overdraft' averaged more than a quarter of its index
quota would be designated a 'deficiency bank' and *allowed* to depreciate
its currency by not more than 5 per cent at the end of that year; if its
average overdraft over the year was more than half its quota it would be
designated a 'supervised bank', and might be *required* to reduce the value
of its currency by up to 5 per cent, to sell the ICB any free gold and to
prohibit capital exports. Interest would be charged on overdrafts, rising
in line with the debt–quota ratio. A persistently profligate member could
be expelled from the Union. There were similar provisions to liquidate
persisting surpluses: any member bank in persistent credit would be
allowed or required to revalue its currency (in steps of 5 per cent), be
required to unblock any foreign-owned balances and investments, and be
required to pay 5 or 10 per cent interest on credits running above a
quarter and half of its quota respectively to the Reserve Fund. Credit
balances exceeding quotas at the end of the year would be confiscated
and transferred to the Reserve Fund. If all countries were in perfect

balance at the end of the year the sum of bancor balances would be exactly zero.*

Attached to Keynes's Bank were a number of ancillary organisations: a supranational police force, a reconstruction and relief organisation, and buffer stocks. These would be financed by additional overdraft facilities, transfers from the ICB's Reserve Fund and direct contributions from surplus countries. As Treasury representative on Sir Frederick Leith-Ross's Export Surpluses Committee, Keynes was involved in the British policy of buying up stocks of primary commodities from sterling area neutrals like Portugal and Argentina to deny the enemy supplies. In his counterblast to the 'New Order' propaganda, he had advocated using these stocks – plus those being accumulated by the Americans – to feed and clothe Continental Europe after the war. He had also told Acheson in Washington that 'there might be found in this surplus scheme the beginnings of a comprehensive scheme for equalising the prices of the main commodities throughout the world'.[62] Placing the Commodity Control, as he called it, under the ICB was his way of avoiding producers' cartels.†

The ICB would be managed by a board of eight governors and a chairman. Britain, the Empire, the USA and the USSR would have one governor each, there would be two from Europe, one from Latin America, and one other. That Britain and its Empire could outvote the United States, which would be financing most of the overdrafts, was a felicitous touch.[63]

The choice Keynes presented in this paper was stark: either Schachtianism or the 'ideal' scheme. There was no Middle Way. But for Keynes there was always a middle way, once the action moved from theory to practice. Later he would abjure Schachtianism without the 'ideal' scheme, having persuaded himself that the American replacements – Bank and International Monetary Fund – were almost as good. To his left-wing

---

* These provisions can be illustrated by figures. The Bank of England's initial quota (overdraft facility) would have been $3.1bn, or £770m. at an exchange rate of $4.03 to the pound. It would have been allowed a maximum overdraft of £192.5m. over the year (a quarter of its quota) without any corrective measures being called for. If its overdraft averaged over £385m. a year it would have been declared a 'supervised' bank, required to devalue its currency by 5 per cent, stop exporting capital and hand over gold. It would also face rising interest charges on its debt. Conversely, if its credit balance averaged over £385m. a year, it would have been required to revalue its currency, release frozen foreign-owned balances and pay interest of 10 per cent on any amount over £385m. Any excess over the full quota of £770m. would have been confiscated.
† On 19 September 1941, Keynes proposed that Britain make a £25m. contribution to a Relief and Reconstruction Fund of £150m., with £75m. from the United States. Britain would sell its stocks to the Fund, and receive cash (dollars) in return. Whether or not it got more than it paid in, Britain (as well as the Dominions) would be exchanging sterling for hard currencies. He contrasted this approach with Leith-Ross's desire 'to give away as much as possible and to make sure that our contribution shall be as large and the contribution of others as small as he can manoeuvre to make them'. (CW, xxvii, 42–4.)

disciples, this was a betrayal based on self-delusion; to disciples like Harrod and Meade, it showed that Keynes's heart was always on the internationalist side. To the historian it seems as if Keynes (and Britain) had little choice.

The two papers which Keynes initialled on 9 September were the most important he ever wrote in terms of their direct influence on events. They were very uneven. The critique of the gold standard was sketched in an amazingly cursory and occasionally confused way, as though he was too tired – as he may well have been after his labours in Washington – to deploy the full case. But the problem was deeper. Technically it is right to say that a country may prefer liquidity to lending or investing abroad. But Keynes did not explain why this should normally be so, or why the nineteenth century, rather than the inter-war years, should be considered the 'accident'. To treat logical possibilities as assumptions was a good way of telling a story, but not of convincing those who started from different assumptions. The Americans were never as convinced as was Keynes that it was their 'liquidity preference' rather than mistaken or unsound British and European policies which had made the gold standard unviable.

The best part was the Plan itself. This shows Keynes doing best what he was best at: constructing a realisable utopia. But even here there was a critical ambiguity. Was the 'heart of the matter' to 'encourage balance of payments adjustment', as Professor Moggridge states?[64] Or was it to secure huge overdraft facilities for Britain and other debtors in the immediate post-war years? Also, although it was implied that some such monetary scheme would enable Britain to satisfy the requirements of 'Hullism', there was nothing about what it actually meant for Britain's imperial preference system, the sterling area and so on. So far, Keynes had produced merely a fragment of a Grand Design.

A more modern puzzle is posed by Keynes's rejection of floating exchange rates. The technical answer is that he did not believe that the Marshall–Lerner condition would, in general, be satisfied. This states that, for a change in the value of a country's currency to restore equilibrium in its balance of payments, the sum of the price elasticities for its exports and imports must be more than one. As Keynes explained to Henry Clay: 'A small country in particular may have to accept substantially worse terms for its exports in terms of its imports if it tries to force the former by means of exchange depreciation. If, therefore, we take account of the terms of trade effect there is an optimum level of exchange such that any movement either way would cause a deterioration of the country's merchandise balance.' Keynes was convinced that, for Britain, exchange depreciation would be disastrous, 'since there is a low elasticity in our demand for imports and a high elasticity in the demand of other countries for our exports'. The idea that the only way of improving a country's balance of payments was to change its terms of trade came out of the debates on German reparations in the 1920s, in which, of course, Keynes was heavily involved. It ignored the fact that changing the relative price of a currency changes the relative prices of tradeable and non-tradeable goods. If this was Keynes's blind spot, it was shared by most economists of his generation. It explains the low priority Keynes gave to exchange rate adjustment in his Clearing Union Plan.[65]

V

RUNNING THE WHITEHALL GAUNTLET

The Keynes Plan, as it was soon called, was contributed to the Treasury's planning exercise for dealing with Article VII of the Lend–Lease Agreement. This involved not just the core of financial experts from the Treasury, the Bank of England, and the Economic Section of the War Cabinet, but officials from the Board of Trade and the Colonial Office. Keynes had his own unofficial channels of consultation. His favourite 'first class critic' Richard Kahn left for the Middle East in October. His place was taken by Roy Harrod from the Prime Minister's Statistical Office. Though he was vain, petulant and tiresome, Harrod was also brilliant and imaginative, and has a strong claim to be regarded as joint author of the Clearing Union scheme in its final form.

The focal point of the early discussions was not the Keynes Plan but the thickening Treasury 'sandwich'. The Treasury approach sought to distinguish between the 'interim system' based on bilateralism and 'what we hope to come to as soon as may be'. The latter involved vague promises of co-operation with the Americans.[66] This approach was criticised both by the Schachtians and by the liberals.

Both Hubert Henderson and the Bank of England disliked the idea of making any promises for the future, however vague. The view which they represented was that countries, or groups of countries, should aim to balance their post-war trade by the wartime mixture of exchange controls and state trading agreements. This would enable them to maintain stable exchange rates with each other. Article VII, with its ban on discriminatory trading arrangements – those which favoured the exports of one country over another – struck at the heart of this philosophy. Henderson expressed a 'profound aversion' for the line that, while Britain's ultimate objectives were the same as those of the United States, it could not say 'when we shall be able to move in the direction of their objectives'. This reeked of hypocrisy. Far better, he added paradoxically, to offer to suspend some existing controls immediately after the war, when demand for British exports would be brisk, and make no undertakings for the further future.[67]

The Bank of England minuted:

it can surely be foreseen that we and others will refuse to limit our internal monetary policy by reference to any external standard; that we can never again tolerate conditions in which mass movements of capital are free to overwhelm the international exchanges; that we shall maintain exchange and import controls for an indefinite period; that we shall aim at maintaining the concept and structure of a sterling area; and that we shall retain the liberty to use bilateral negotiations as an instrument for promoting international trade.[68]

Like Henderson, the Bank of England believed that the 'cardinal mistake and the greatest admission of defeat which we can make is to put as a final objective something which we do not believe has a reasonable chance of coming about'. The Bank's hope of preserving London as a financial centre rested on maintaining the sterling area and using exchange controls to prevent gold and dollars from draining out of it.[69]

These memoranda reached Keynes, who was part of the consultative process. His criticisms of the Bank's strategy were polite, as befitted a newly appointed director, but devastating. Did the Bank really believe, he wrote on 22 October, that it could maintain the sterling area as a trading fortress after the war? Why should South Africa, able to pay in gold for American motor cars, want to restrict its imports of them? How did the Bank propose to prevent sterling area countries from using their sterling balances in London to pay for American goods? Whether Britain could afford to maintain the sterling area depended on the rest of the sterling area having a favourable balance with the United States 'in conditions of comparative freedom'.[70]

Henderson claimed that the moral of Keynes's critique was that 'we should seek to knit the sterling area more closely together than to break it up'. As long as Britain had an adverse balance of payments, the sterling area should be maintained as an important source of involuntary borrowing. If a sterling area country was running a deficit with the United States which Britain had to meet, Britain would be able to force it to restrict its imports from the United States. It was as important to think in terms of inter-imperial collaboration as of collaboration with the United States.

I have never understood [he wrote to Keynes on 23 October] the anti-Ottawa *motif* which I think forms part of your general outlook. It is true . . . that the present preferential arrangements are crude and anomalous in many ways . . . but the question [demanding fair consideration on its merits is] whether the basic facts of the post war problem do not call for an extension of mutual preferences. The best means of ensuring South Africans don't spend more dollars than we can afford on US motor cars is to give our motor cars increased preference in return for some *quid pro quo* in our markets.[71]

To Henderson the imperial preference system and the sterling area were mutually supporting. Strengthened imperial preference would help improve Britain's external accounts; improvement in Britain's external accounts would reduce its need to 'borrow' sterling balances. This, as we have seen, was not a very plausible 'lesson' to draw from the 1930s.

Keynes returned to the charge on 9 November. The Bank's memoranda implied that sterling area countries in surplus with the United States would make forced loans to deficit countries like Britain. This presupposed the 'whole apparatus of exchange controls within the Sterling Area'. The Bank attached great importance to import controls to 'balance trade'. But it did not make it clear whether import controls were to be applied between members of the sterling area or only between the sterling area and the rest of the world. If the latter, they were an extreme form of discrimination; if the former, the sterling area concept became very thin. The Bank's scheme presupposed a pooling of the sterling area's gold and dollar reserves. Under whose control was that reserve to be? Keynes denied that there was enough 'solidarity' within the sterling area for Britain to be entrusted with the pooling. It could only be done by an impartial international body. In any case, Keynes added in a further letter, America's special objection was to bilateral barter, which is what the Bank supported.[72]

Waley of the Treasury summed up against Henderson and the Bank on 8 November:

> The doctrine that exchange control and trade controls are good in themselves is one to which we shall never get everyone on this side and still less the Americans to agree, and it seems a pity to put it forward as a doctrine. The alternative doctrine that exchange control and trade controls are bad in themselves, but that we shall have to retain them unless and until we can get rid of them because the alternatives of exchange depreciation and deflation are worse, is one which we are much more likely to get general agreement for on both sides of the Atlantic.[73]

The Treasury 'sandwich' was also criticised by the free traders, on both political and economic grounds. Dennis Robertson at the Treasury found early drafts of the document 'very gloomy [and] fraught with the seeds of future international strife and (probably) wars'. He criticised Henderson for trying to maintain 'a value for our monetary unit which doesn't reflect our diminished power of export, and then trying to make up for that by driving clever bargains with people who will probably out-Schacht us in the end'.[74] Frederick Leith-Ross worried that calling something 'interim' might be an excuse for perpetuating bad practices for years.[75] Sir Horace Wilson, the Treasury's permanent secretary, dreaded a long period during which 'we shall only allow a ship to enter Liverpool Docks if we are quite certain that she will at once re-load there with manufactured goods and will go straight back to the port whence she sailed'.[76] Sir Arnold Overton, permanent secretary at the Board of Trade and a strong free trader, rejected the claims for the Schachtian system. He pointed out that Germany got advantage from Schachtian devices only by abusing them, for example, by reselling for cash goods it got on credit.[77] Waley also found it difficult to share Keynes's faith in barter, which 'having been in abeyance from the Stone Age till 1939, was then re-discovered by Dr. Schacht'.[78]

A powerful liberalising influence came from the Economic Section of the War Cabinet, headed by that redoubtable free trader Lionel Robbins. Its 'Note on Post-War Anglo-American Economic Relations', dated 18 August 1941, had pointed out the many flaws of bilateralism and discrimination: its tendency to diminish wealth creation, the threat of retaliation, the danger to Anglo-American relations, the inducement to political and economic frictions, the disruption of imperial relations, the entrenchment of vested interests. Robbins's assistant, James Meade, urged the insertion into the Treasury draft of these balancing arguments, together with a 'precise but conditional' commitment to take part in a 'non-discriminatory trading system'.[79] Sir Sydney Caine at the Colonial Office also took up a strongly free trade position.

In mid-November, Sir Richard Hopkins produced and circulated his own note on the Treasury 'sandwich'. The problem, he wrote, was that:

> We have to reconcile our desire to obtain the objectives of general prosperity and an expanding volume of international trade with our immediate necessity after the cessation of hostilities to attain equilibrium in our balance of payments with the rest of the world. . . . So far as can be foreseen, this will be a problem of the gravest difficulty. . . . When it [the war] is over, domestic reconstruction and reorganisation will have a prior claim on our productive resources and will entail various import requirements. . . . We must further bear in mind that our resources of gold, foreign exchange, and realisable foreign assets will have been greatly depleted by the war. . . . The degree and character of any help that we may receive from the United States . . . are entirely speculative questions.

The conclusion Hopkins drew from all this was that Britain could not risk 'large uncontrolled and involuntary deficits on current account'.[80]

Roy Harrod, at the Prime Minister's Statistical Branch of the War Cabinet, rejected Hopkins's 'ink-black pessimism'. Britain's external balance would be found not to have deteriorated by more than £100m. a year. He remarked pointedly that the Atlantic Charter – agreed by Churchill and Roosevelt in Newfoundland in August 1941 – was not signed to set up 'a system of a Schachtian kind run from London instead of Berlin. Yet how otherwise can one describe a widely ramifying system of payments agreements and bilateral arrangements?' Harrod then outlined his own scheme for creditor adjustment and buffer stocks.[81] Henderson reported sourly to Hopkins: '[Harrod's] general line was that as we could not afford to quarrel with the Americans after the war, we must agree to scrap everything in our economic arrangements that is objectionable to them, and repose our entire faith in Roosevelt. . . .'[82]

By mid-November 1941 the Henderson–Bank of England recipe for Britain's future had been undermined from various sides: barter bilateralism was economically inferior to multilateralism, it would not in fact solve Britain's post-war balance of payments problem, it would not preserve the sterling area, it would cause friction in the Empire, and it could not be sold to the United States. On the other hand, the free traders were equally opposed to the deflationary bias of the gold standard system which, in their understanding, had made free trade impossible. So they favoured new currency arrangements which would make the world safe for free trade. It was these considerations which brought Keynes's utopia into the foreground. Once again, getting in early with a worked-out scheme paid off. The Keynes Plan might be 'teased and nagged', as Harrod put it, but it was the only document on the table which went beyond the continuation of wartime arrangements, suggested a way of escaping from the gold standard trap, and offered a hope of enlisting US support.

From the start the Keynes Plan had received close attention from Bank of England officials. Catto wrote Keynes a note congratulating him on it, but warning him that it was premature in a world of mere mortals. Keynes came into his room with Catto's note in his hand and asked, 'How long?' Catto replied that it would be five years, maybe more, but that in the end the world would be driven to a plan along the lines he envisaged. Keynes looked at him with a wry smile: 'Ah, how sad to wait.'

The Bank viewed the Keynes Plan 'not only as unrealistically Utopian, but also a threat to the future of the sterling area'.[83] Harry Siepmann criticised it for assuming 'too readily that joint Anglo-American solutions can be usefully sought'.[84] Thompson-McCausland, Keynes's 'bag-boy' in Washington, feared that 'the Board of Trade and the Americans will be prone to believe that monetary devices alone will solve our post-war exchange problem. . . .'[85] He took the 'kernel' of Keynes's scheme to be provision for the 'automatic surrender of surpluses' and argued that 'we are surely a long way from a political world in which Surplus Countries would be content to go on paying taxes forever for the benefit of foreigners'. Keynes responded testily on 12 November that his criticism 'fundamentally misunderstands the nature of my proposals'. They were intended to prevent surpluses and deficits from developing. 'Your argument is like saying that if we admit the principle of capital punishment that can only end sooner or later in the entire depopulation of the country.'[86] George Bolton, another adviser, made technical objections: it would be almost impossible to determine an 'index quota' equal to a ratio of trade, a country might be forced to depreciate its currency on the basis of a four-month trade deficit, it was unclear how Russia would fit in, or how the ancillary organisations would be financed.[87]

Henry Clay, economic adviser to the Bank, was more enthusiastic. Ottawa had proved that Britain had no stomach for discrimination or exploiting its bargaining power. 'To cite the Schacht precedent without recognising the fundamental difference between the German and English governments is to miss the chief moral of his experiment.' Given the British situation, Keynes's 'automatic' system had great advantages. The problem which Keynes posed was not about the post-war difficulties of the sterling area, but about those of the UK. 'Even if we could discriminate against the United States it would be politically difficult to discriminate against India and Australia; yet unless the policy of discrimination covers the whole of the external trade of the United Kingdom it collapses.'[88]

Two conversations between Keynes and Siepmann and Bolton in the second week in November elucidated political and technical issues. Siepmann has Keynes explaining:

> Though the scheme is meant to be proof against criticism of its technical workmanship, it is primarily a contribution to the tactics of diplomacy in Whitehall and Washington. As regards Washington, the scheme caters for the professed devotion of Americans to progressive (idealist, liberal, expansionist) internationalism, and so diverts discussion from their own (entirely self-regarding) concrete demands. As regards Whitehall, it is meant to rally some of the supporters of appeasement or laissez-faire, who would otherwise join forces in opposition to the policies (e. g. bilateralism) which would suit our own interests better but which America would dislike. . . .
> The principles of the sterling area, offensive to America in an Imperial context, become acceptable, if they are universalised. . . . It is expected that while America would never agree to transfer her surplus to us, she would agree to transfer it to a country x (being us).

Keynes also explained that the sanctions on creditors were only on paper, the assumption being that no one would want to accumulate worthless bank money. He admitted that little thought had been given to how Continental Europe fitted in, beyond the vague suggestion that it might be divided into currency areas.[89]

The Keynes Plan was starting to attract comment from his Treasury colleagues. Ralph Hawtrey, still in the Treasury, with time on his hands, subjected it to several of his exhausting memoranda. Hawtrey, who remained what he had always been, an eclectic monetary economist, saw no real point in Keynes's super-bank, which provided no 'adequate safeguard against the abuse of the overdraft facility by a weak, reckless, misguided or corrupt country'. The business cycle, Hawtrey insisted, as he had done ever since 1908, was a monetary phenomenon. Inflation led to deflation. If all countries maintained internal price stability, both economies and exchange rates would be stable without the need for 'contractual' transfers. Post-war reconstruction should be financed on an *ad hoc* basis and not through the 'automatic credit facilities' provided by the ICB. Temporary shocks could be dealt with by inter-bank credits. More persistent disequilibria would have to be corrected by exchange rate changes. Hawtrey shrewdly noted that 'to limit the change [in exchange rates] to 5 per cent [as the Keynes Plan did] when the restoration of equilibrium calls for a bigger sum, is to shut the way of escape from the danger of [financial] panic'. As to policy, it would be better in the first instance to aim for an Anglo-American partnership, with the understanding that each country would maintain domestic price stability, and support each other's exchanges when required.[90] Through several redrafts of the Keynes Plan, Hawtrey persisted in his view that it had 'no stabilising principle at all . . . it not merely acquiesces in a general resort to exchange controls and import restrictions by all countries that cannot stand the deflationary pressure, but it is only too likely, by obstructing the devaluation of their currency units, to drive them to these expedients. Even the overdraft facilities may well be an aggravation.'[91] By this time Hawtrey's views were considered rather old-fashioned, and his memoranda were too lengthy and turgid to command much attention, but he made some shrewd points.

Brand sent Keynes pertinent criticisms from Washington. While 'entirely in agreement' with the 'general object' of Keynes's scheme, he foresaw a 'good many difficulties'. These centred on the problem of reconciling international co-operation with national sovereignty. Brand urged Keynes to drop any reference to an international police force, which involved a 'supranational government'. He raised the question of how an international organisation would have the authority to police the domestic policies on which the value of currencies depended as much as on trade conditions. He doubted whether the Clearing Union would have the authority to enforce changes in currency values. 'I remember during my education', he wrote, 'always learning that the control of currency was an especial attribute of sovereignty.' Finally, he questioned whether Keynes's scheme would meet Britain's particular problem, which was that it would be faced with a large balance of payments deficit after the war.

Did Keynes think that an initial depreciation of sterling would be the way to tackle this?[92]

Keynes's second draft of his Plan, dated 18 November, retained the charter and rules of the Bank virtually intact in an appendix (he now called ICB money 'grammor') but substituted for his previous first paper a glowing affirmation of the attractions of his scheme, which he had started to feel more intensely, and a robust reply to critics, actual and anticipated. Any plan put forward by Britain, Keynes explained, had to be of a general character, not a plea for special assistance, if it was to capture the 'interest and enthusiasm of the Americans'. The dismissal of the Henderson–Bank of England approach was restrained but unmistakable. The Schachtian devices, which he himself had lauded, were now described as a 'patched up contrivance, mainly based on abnormal war experience'. To insist on their continuation would be to risk isolating Britain from the United States without being able to construct a 'reliable economic union within the Empire'. *Au contraire*, the sterling area and the City of London needed the buttress of multilateral clearing. Keynes's love affair with Dr Schacht was over. It was the fallibility of the Bank's proposals which convinced him that Schachtianism could not be made to work for Britain. As he wrote a little later to an American correspondent: 'The more closely I have examined the details of bilateralism since I came home . . . the more firmly I have felt that [multilateralism] is the right [line] for all of us.'[93]

Keynes also rejected the Treasury's favourite distinction between interim and long-term arrangements. His Clearing Union was intended to secure both immediate (post-war) and permanent equilibrium in members' balance of payments. 'The plan aims', he wrote, 'at the substitution of an expansionist, in place of a contractionist, pressure on world trade, *especially in the first years*' (italics added). This might be achieved by voluntary United States help for European reconstruction. But 'particular arrangements' were likely to be influenced by 'extraneous, political reasons' and to put specific countries into a position of 'particular obligation'. In any case, Britain, as one of the war's victors, would be a poor claimant for American help. It would be better to persuade the United States to enter into a 'general and collective responsibility, applying to all countries alike, that a country finding itself in a creditor position *against the rest of the world as a whole* should enter into an obligation to dispose of this credit balance'.

Keynes next tried to meet actual and possible criticisms and misunderstandings. The main technical idea underlying his proposal 'was to generalise the essential principle of banking as it is exhibited within any closed system . . . [namely] the necessary equality between credits and debits'. Any increase in the Bank's liabilities (credits) would be exactly matched by an increase in its assets (debits). As a result, 'the Bank *itself* can never be in difficulties'. This implied that there was no limit to the amount of money Keynes's Bank could create.*

Keynes did not expect that credit balances would ever have to be consfiscated. 'The main point is that the creditor should not be allowed to remain passive.' Rules about exchange rate adjustments guarded against competitive currency depreciations. The discipline against persistent debtors was inadequate, but now there was no discipline at all, and 'a small expenditure of faith and a readiness to allow actual experience to decide are not too much to ask'. Keynes also emphasised the importance of transparency: the ICB would provide 'an automatic register of the size and whereabouts of the aggregate debtor and creditor positions respectively. The danger signal is shown to all concerned. . . .' On the question of national sovereignty, Keynes claimed that the surrender required by his scheme would be no greater than that presupposed by any commercial or military treaty, and that in any case a better world required a measure of 'financial disarmament'. If the ICB succeeded in maintaining balance of payments equilibrium between its members, there would be no need for discriminatory trade practices, exchange restrictions or impediments to private capital flows. The explicit repudiation of high tariffs, export subsidies, import quotas, barter agreements and blocked accounts would, he thought, 'enable us to give complete satisfaction to Mr Cordell Hull'. The satisfaction was less than it seemed. Imperial preference of up to 25 per cent could be retained under a formula allowing preferences between 'members of political and geographical groups'. Moreover the taboos against 'protective expedients' were not to apply for the first three to five years after the war.

James Meade had wanted Keynes to make clear that currency convertibility was to be the norm.[94] Keynes held fast to his conviction that member countries would need to establish and maintain the *machinery* of exchange controls. But this need not preclude freedom of remittance for current transactions, and 'open general licences of indefinite duration' for capital transactions.[95] It is important to notice that Keynes's Clearing Union scheme, unlike the Bretton Woods Agreement, envisaged free capital movements, except in specified circumstances. This was because its

---

* Keynes had explained the 'creation' of bank money in chapter 2 of his *Treatise on Money*. A bank 'creates' deposits in two ways: against value (cash or cheques) received and by making loans or advances. The first will constitute the bank's liabilities and the second its assets. 'It follows that the rate at which the bank can, with safety, *actively* create deposits by lending and investing has to be in a proper relation to the rate at which it is *passively* creating them against the receipt of liquid resources from its depositors.' But 'if we suppose a closed banking system . . . where all payments are made by cheque and . . . the banks . . . settle inter-bank indebtedness by the transfer of other assets, it is evident that there is no limit to the amount of bank money which the banks can safely create . . .' (vol. i, 20–3).

resources were considered large enough to finance temporary payments deficits, arising from either the current or the capital account.

Keynes bowed to the general feeling in Whitehall that the post-war order, whatever form it took, should start off with an Anglo-American agreement. The ICB was now to be founded as an Anglo-American club, which other countries would be invited to join. He nodded to the Bank of England's view that the post-war order should, evolve from, rather than supersede, existing economic blocs. Members of the ICB should, 'in some cases, be groups of countries rather than separate [national] units', bound together by customs, preference and currency unions. He even suggested eleven such economic groupings, including North America and four in Europe: the Germanic countries, the Scandinavian countries, the Latin Union, and Eastern Europe. Britain, centre of the sterling area, was, of course, 'outside' Europe. All this reflected his chats with Siepmann and Bolton. But part of Keynes's allure was his ability to seize a fleeting thought and invest it with his own fancy:

> A view of the post-war world which I find sympathetic and attractive and fruitful of good consequences is that we should encourage *small* political and cultural units, combined into larger, and more or less closely knit, economic units. It would be a fine thing to have thirty or forty capital cities in Europe, each the centre of a self-governing country entirely free from national minorities (who would be dealt with by migrations where necessary) and the seat of a government and parliament and university centre, each with their own pride and glory and their own characteristics and excellent gifts. But it would be ruinous to have thirty or forty entirely independent economic and currency unions.

This pleasing picture of a re-medievalised Europe did not survive in later drafts.

On 1 November two American economists, Alvin Hansen and Luther Gulick, had proposed a Joint Economic Declaration by which the US and British governments would pledge themselves to set up an International Development Corporation and International Economic Board to advise governments on how to co-ordinate full employment policies. Keynes had met them in London in September, and he now incorporated their proposals into his scheme. According to Penrose they were important in convincing Keynes that the US administration accepted that full employment was a requirement of free trade.[96] Keynes explained that the Development (or Investment) Board would be part of the mechanism for 'shifting the whole system of clearing credits and debits nearer to equilibrium'. The idea was taken up enthusiastically by Roy Harrod, who promised to work out a plan for it.

Keynes's careful balancing act worked its political magic in Whitehall.

For Meade it represented the only 'real hope of a generous and spacious economic collaboration after the war'. Robbins saw it as 'a real release of fresh air in this surcharged and stale atmosphere'.[97] 'I sat up last night reading your revised "proposal" with great excitement,' Dennis Robertson wrote to Keynes on 27 November, '– and a growing hope that the spirit of Burke and Adam Smith is on earth again.'[98] Robertson's coupling of Burke and Smith is a typically subtle tribute to Keynes's Middle Way. Bolton at the Bank was gratified that Keynes had 'absorbed most of our proposals in his remodelled plan'. Siepmann minuted that 'the only real difference is that we should like to complete the coach with four wheels, before fitting it with a fifth'.[99] The Treasury started to see the Plan as the basis for a consensus position to present to ministers.

The month between the second draft of 18 November and the third draft of 15 December was one of the busiest of Keynes's life. He put in sixty hours a week in Great George Street. He was involved in budget preparations, the end-play of the Lend–Lease negotiations and relief issues. But he mainly concentrated on remodelling his Plan in response to the intensive scrutiny it now started to receive.

Henderson was still in contention with a plan of his own (27 November). Its main points were that Britain should retain the complete mechanism of exchange control, offer to renounce barter agreements and discriminatory measures for an 'unspecified provisional period', propose an Anglo-American monetary ageement along the lines of the Tripartite Agreement of 1936 and suggest an Anglo-American board to promote mutual economic collaboration. Henderson's ideas were discussed at a Treasury meeting on 5 December. The officials present, who included Keynes, noticed the contradiction between Henderson's apparent reliance on US willingness to hold sterling and his refusal to give up bilateralism except temporarily. That put paid to the Henderson Plan.[100] He retained his position, though, as the chief thorn in Keynes's flesh. Lord Catto now suggested that Keynes's and the Bank's objectives were 'essentially' the same, only the Bank was more cautious. However, there was a world of difference between Keynes's bold leap into the future and the Bank's endorsement of an evolutionary development from the existing sterling area arrangements so slow as to be barely perceptible. Two inconclusive meetings took place between Treasury and Bank officials on 24 and 25 November.[101]

The debate was now captured by those who accepted the fundamental postulates of the Keynes Plan, but wanted to simplify, voluntarise and liberalise it. Catto, Waley and the indefatigable Hawtrey urged Keynes to place less emphasis on rules and leave more to the discretion of member countries, creditors and debtors. (Waley presciently remarked that the American New Dealers, with their suspicion of 'money lenders', would be much more likely to accept a 'stabilization fund' than a bank; Catto asked:

why give the Bank teeth it would not be able to use?) These officials saw
the ICB more like an informational and moral forum, establishing and
spreading norms of good-neighbourliness.[102]

Much the most ambitious attempt to reshape the Plan came from Roy
Harrod. Harrod was the most forthright critic of Schachtianism in Whitehall. He dubbed it a form of 'helotage' which could never be sustained in
peace. It 'rivets trade to politics and turns every new commercial development into an act of economic warfare. . . . By being too obdurate in
defence of Imperial Preference we might lose an Empire.'[103] Harrod's
reshaping took the form of producing a plan of his own. The most
important requirement was to get the United States committed to creditor
adjustment. Everything else was secondary. Creditor adjustment could be
secured most simply by an agreement that creditor countries would always
accept cheques from deficit countries in full discharge of their debts. No
pressure need be put on them to liquidate their balances with the Bank.
'So long as their credit position cannot cause pressure elsewhere, there is
no harm in allowing a further accumulation.' The Americans could either
spend their cheques or tear them up. Harrod did not mind very much
which they did, as long as they continued to accept them. Nor need
deficit countries be put under pressure, since 'debits would be automatically liquidated if and when the creditor countries took the necessary
measures', though Harrod admitted that some sanction was needed
against 'ultra debtors' – those countries whose deficits exceeded the
average of deficits. The Harrod Plan left everything else as before.
Countries were free to adhere to the gold standard. There would be no
need for exchange controls, capital controls, international bank money,
quotas or the other disciplinary paraphernalia of the Keynes Plan.

Harrod's concerns were different from Keynes's, despite a large over-
lap. Harrod combined extreme liberalism with extreme pessimism about
the sufficiency of global aggregate demand – an unusual, but not necessarily illogical, combination. He was primarily concerned not with short-
run adjustment problems, though he realised they could give rise to
deflationary pressure, but with the 'central problem' of global over-saving,
unemployment and 'poverty in the midst of plenty'. He wanted to convert
Keynes's Bank into an international investment engine, with the power to
create money as its main characteristic. In fact, he objected to the title
'Clearing Union', since it suggested a 'mere channel', whereas a bank
could 'make advances'. As his ideas developed he came to see in Keynes's
Bank a potential agent of an Anglo-American 'Condominium' or 'Service'
through which the greater part of world investment would be provided,
with its short-run adjustment functions as ancillary to this: an exact
reversal of Keynes's own priorities. This perspective made Harrod much
more of a free trader than Keynes, for with world full employment and
growth guaranteed by his 'Service' there would be no need for any form

of economic nationalism.[104] Politically, Harrod expected the Americans to swallow the pill of his ambitious 'Service' if it was coated with free trade.

Keynes was swayed by Harrod's arguments, but not bowled over by them. He discounted the possibility that the US would accept such a supranational agenda as Harrod's. He thought that maintenance of full employment would remain primarily a responsibility of national governments, which must therefore retain control over national interest rates. Despite Hull, he did not think that the US administration was nearly as committed to free trade as Harrod supposed. He thought that questions of commercial policy should be cautiously handled, though not as cautiously as Hubert Henderson wanted. Harrod's super-bank can be seen as a logical distillation of one strand of Keynesianism: the belief that rich economies were subject to 'secular stagnation' before they had exhausted their growth potential, and that a global institution had to be continually engaged to overcome depressive obstacles to full employment and growth. This led directly to the major flaw in Harrod's design. Potentially it was highly inflationary. Keynes worried about inflation and tried to guard against it by penalising both creditor and debtors. There was a wild unreality about Harrod's ardent conjectures from which he instinctively shrank.

On 1 December Keynes attended an inter-departmental meeting at the Treasury to discuss his Plan. Arnold Overton of the Board of Trade was 'much in favour' of Keynes's scheme 'if it were practicable'. Nigel Ronald, for the Foreign Office, said they would welcome anything constructive to put to the Americans in the Article VII conversations. Robbins and Meade agreed with Harrod that the USA should not be asked to set up the full machinery of exchange control. But, in contrast to Harrod, Meade wanted to maintain provision for the appreciation of surplus country currencies. Harrod insisted that any monetary plan should be be put into the Anglo-American negotiations as part of a broader package, including trade issues, customs unions, the Hansen and Gulick investment board proposals, and so on. Keynes stated the decisive objection to Harrod's own amendments: his (Keynes's) system would break down if overdrafts became unlimited at the USA's expense. He himself might have gone too far in disciplining deficit countries, but he would not go as far as Harrod in removing any discipline at all.[105] In the upshot, the Harrod Plan did not displace the Keynes Plan from the centre of the stage. It was too liberal for the *dirigistes*, too inflationary for the orthodox, and was thought to carry the principle of 'unlimited liability' much too far for the Americans to accept.

On 15 December Keynes sent Harrod a carbon copy of his third draft, calling him his 'most important critic'; he wrote to Catto, Hawtrey and Waley saying he had tried to deal with their points. On 19 December he sent a copy to Montagu Norman. He had, he said, received more encouragement for his Plan in Whitehall 'than for anything I have ever suggested'. In the simplified language he reserved for the technically challenged, he explained that his scheme was 'the extension to the international field of the essential principles of *banking* by which, when one chap wants to leave his resources idle, those resources are not therefore withdrawn from circulation but are made available to another chap who is prepared to use them – and to make this possible without the former losing his liquidity . . .'. He then addressed the Bank's chief concern:

> In particular, I believe that a multilateral plan is a necessary condition of the maintenance of the sterling area and the financial position of London. . . . From what Lord Catto tells me, I think you may have got the wrong impression of my proposals in this respect. So far from their endangering the sterling area, I claim it as one of their chief merits that they offer us the best chance of maintaining it in its traditional sense – i.e. that the British Commonwealth make London their financial headquarters. . . . A multilateral system, by giving us something similar to the gold standard in its best nineteenth-century days, allows international banking (apart from capital controls) to go on just as before. A series of bilateral agreements, to which all the members of the sterling area would have to be parties, seems to me quite impracticable – and very dangerous.[106]

The executive governor, Cameron Cobbold, assured Montagu Norman that Keynes's third draft was 'fairly innocuous, so long as it is regarded as a possible framework, given certain conditions. . . . Let it percolate where it will.' The Bank, though, spotted danger in the Dominions being given the option of banking with the new institution. Whatever the ultimate arrangement 'we should still wish the sterling area to bank and clear in *sterling* and regard *sterling* as their link with other currencies'.[107]

Keynes put forward the third draft of his Plan not as a 'cut and dried scheme' but as 'one variant of a central idea which is capable of being worked out in many ways'. To emphasise its *aide-mémoire* character, he omitted the appendix of the second draft, which had in fact been the whole Plan of the first draft, confining himself to exposition of fundamental principles. He explained the central idea as 'the establishment of a Currency Union, based on international money, called (let us say) bancor, fixed (but not unalterable) in terms of gold and accepted as the equivalent of gold by . . . all members of the Union for the purpose of settling international balances'. Keynes decided on 'bancor' after Hawtrey had rejected 'grammor'. Hawtrey's alternative was 'moy', deriving from 'moidore', an obsolete Portuguese coin, worth twenty-seven shillings. Pedantically, he gave the reference: Shakespeare's *Henry V*, Act IV, scene 4, where Pistol uses it as a play on the French 'moi'. But Keynes, like Pistol, decided that 'Moy shall not serve'. 'Bancor' encapsulated the idea of the 'bank money' to be created by his central bank.

In his second draft Keynes had felt the need to prescribe definite rules governing the maximum permitted balances and the sanctions for exceeding them. Now he wrote that 'the most difficult question to determine is how much to decide by rule and how much by discretion'. He opted for discretion. He weakened and postponed the interventions designed to deter or eliminate the excess balances of both creditors and debtors. In an important concession to Harrod he now allowed credit balances to pile up without limit. Instead, persistent creditors would 'discuss' with the Governing Board, retaining the final decision themselves, whether to expand their domestic economies, appreciate their currencies, reduce their tariffs or make foreign loans. For debtors no corrective measures would be started till the debit of a deficiency country reached half its quota, and these were now limited to currency depreciation. Excess credit and debit balances would still be charged interest, though this was 'not essential to the scheme'. The effect of these changes was to give the Bank a greater expansionist, but also inflationary, potential. However, the concessions were not all one way. Under pressure from the Board of Trade, Keynes made his prohibition of protective expedients more tentative. He now felt able to give Cordell Hull only 'substantial' rather than 'complete' satisfaction.

The third draft argued much more sharply than did the second that the Bank of England's proposals would break up, not preserve, the sterling area. Keynes also paid untypical homage to the gold standard – something he sometimes did to stress his conservative credentials – and made another concession to Harrod by not insisting on capital controls for all members of the Union. His praise of customs unions was much reduced, in length and enthusiasm, in deference to Hawtrey. After repeating his suggestions for ancillary institutions, and the joint management of the ICB by Britain and the United States, Keynes summarised the 'special merits' of his proposal. Britain would not be able to solve its prospective balance of payments problem or preserve the sterling area except through a scheme which provided for multilateral clearing and global market expansion. For the United States and others it offered a general framework for stable exchange rates and free trade, and attached institutions to promote post-war reconstruction, control of the trade cycle and the maintenance of active employment everywhere. Above all, it 'is capable of arousing enthusiasm because it makes a beginning at the construction of the future government of the world'.[108]

Keynes did not suffer from any undue pride in authorship. He tried to accommodate every possible point of view in an effort to maximise consent. It was a considerable feat to reshape the scheme in such a way as to preserve its central structure in the face of so many contradictory pressures. Inevitably some of the initial coherence was lost. In particular, the pressure on both creditors and debtors to balance their accounts was greatly weakened. In his usual subtle way, Robertson pointed out that the banking principle that assets and liabilities must balance did not of itself secure any particular quantum of purchasing power, since loans still had to be spent. He thought the scheme had been weakened by the dropping of provisions in the two earlier versions for the automatic surrender of credit balances above a certain sum. Keynes was bound to agree: the banking system made possible the continuation of purchasing power, it did not compel it. He had dropped the provision for the automatic surrender of credit balances with 'great reluctance' at the prodding of Harrod. Robertson scribbled on the margins of Keynes's reply: 'In substance I am really in danger of disagreement (as you might expect) on the grounds of the scheme not being strict enough on the deficiency countries, making it perhaps too easy for them to indulge in Forbidden Tricks, and ruling out (as I read it) by implication . . . the only real remedy, viz deflation of money incomes.'[109]

Buoyed up by some glorious winter weather, Keynes arranged his usual shoot at Tilton over Christmas. The 'bag' was twenty-eight pheasants, four rabbits, one hare, two woodcocks and a sparrowhawk. He followed it by a dinner for thirty-five, 'Lydia delivering from her hands beef of great antiquity'. His international currency plan, he reported to his mother on 21 December 1941, 'goes as well as I could hope – indeed in Whitehall amazingly well, but there are many hurdles yet'.

The main immediate one was the Treasury, which meant Sir Richard Hopkins, the second secretary. Harrod now became an enthusiastic advocate of the liberalised Keynes Plan. He wrote to Hopkins on 18 December that Keynes had 'greatly simplified his scheme . . . and gone very far to meet my criticisms'. It should be presented to ministers as a 'thoroughly workable and practical plan supported by the full weight of Treasury judgment'. Harrod was especially against giving ministers a choice between the Clearing Union and bilateralism, since, he added artlessly, they were bound to be 'rather at sea in these technical questions'. He shrewdly surmised that ministers would be much less willing to criticise a scheme put forward by 'the collective brains of the Treasury' than one emanating from the single brain of J. M. Keynes. Harrod insisted that the Keynes Plan be put to the Americans as an interlocking set of institutions including an international investment board, a buffer stock control, a nutritional standards board and a commercial union, or else the Americans would think it was designed solely to help Britain.[110] Hopkins replied on 24 December: 'I think the Keynes Plan is now in about as good a shape as it can be put and I don't believe there is any better alternative. . . .' He agreed that it should be put up to ministers as the 'best plan we can contrive'.[111] However, on 5 January 1942 he wrote to Phillips in Washington that he was not sure he liked utopia 'as much as I ought'. He found it all very perplexing.

After Christmas, Hopkins prepared to incorporate the Keynes Plan into the Treasury 'sandwich'. The status of his Plan was still in doubt, though. 'Whitehall in all its quarters has been surprisingly enthusiastic, and I have had quite a fan mail,' Keynes wrote to Kahn on 12 January 1942.

> The difficulties come from the Bank. But how serious they are going to be remains to be seen. My expectation is that the plan will at least be set up as cock-shy for the Americans, but with what ardour and conviction it will be advocated officially is less certain. On the whole, I am pretty well satisfied with the general tenor of the post-war discussions. My advocacy of multilateralism has brought concord and harmony again with your chaps at the Board of Trade: Overton very friendly about it; Stirling, who has now gone back to America, enthusiastic; and Shackle quite acquiescent.[112]

On the weekend of 24–25 January, Keynes undertook a final redraft. The scheme was now rechristened 'the International Clearing Union', which became its approved designation. He introduced important new touches. The suggestion that Lend–Lease and relief provision by the United States might take the place of the Clearing Union's 'quotas' in the first two years after the war pointed to the hiving off of relief and reconstruction functions to a separate organisation. Keynes removed the language of deficiency and surplus countries. He compensated for the weakening of sanctions on creditors and debtors by boosting the total of quotas. Instead of country quotas being set at *half* the sum of their average exports and imports over the five pre-war years (as in the first and second drafts) they would now be *equal* to that sum over the last three pre-war years, with certain exceptions. This would almost double the total over-draft facilities, from $26bn to $40bn. He retained interest charges, reduced to 1 per cent, on excess creditor and debtor balances. Countries whose debits exceeded a quarter of their quotas for more than a year were to be allowed to depreciate their currencies by 5 per cent without permission. If a country's debit balance exceeded three-quarters of its quota for more than a year 'it may be asked by the Governing Body to take measures to improve its position'; if it failed to remedy the position in two years it might be declared in default and prevented from drawing on its account. Member countries' trading arrangements should be the subject of a separate commercial treaty, with their credit and debit balances with the Union serving merely as indicators of what Forbidden Practices they might indulge in. This, he recognised, might give Cordell Hull only 'some' satisfaction.[113]

On 27 January 1942 Keynes could report to Phillips in Washington that 'Hoppy has now completed the draft of a general report on the whole business which we are to discuss in a few days'.[114] The Treasury had not, in fact, done what Harrod wanted, which was to put the Keynes scheme forward as its considered view. It was 'wrapped', as L. S. Pressnell writes, in the 'sombre swaddling clothes' of the eighty-four-page Treasury 'Memorandum on External Monetary and Economic Problems' whose pessimism threatened to smother the squeals of the lively infant.[115] Keynes thought the Treasury document 'very fine', but Robbins objected to its relentlessly pro and con approach. 'I think I can detect a slight sway of the argument in favour of the Keynes–Harrod–Hansen projects', but only a slight one.[116]

Much of the original 'sandwich' was rendered beside the point by Britain's signature of the Mutual Aid (Lend–Lease) Agreement on 23 February 1942. Negotiations over this had run in parallel with the evolution of Keynes's currency union, with Keynes's intermittent interventions directed to his familiar point that Britain should not promise anything it could not fulfil. With Churchill back in London, Roosevelt increased pressure on Britain to sign up. After much heated discussion in Whitehall and between the two Allies, Redvers Opie, economic adviser to the Washington Embassy, secured a form of words acceptable to the British. A commitment by both countries to eliminate discrimination and reduce tariffs was coupled with a commitment to expand production and employment. This could be taken to mean that moves to freer trade were predicated on measures to expand output and employment. The agreement called for an early conference between the two governments and 'other like-minded ones' to decide ways of implementing the commitment.*

By the New Year, news was filtering through to London that the US administration was having some ideas of its own on the post-war order. The expected imminence of Anglo-American conversations meant that the British government had to take a decision. The Treasury coalesced behind the Keynes scheme because of fears that the American plan would be too rigid and that the British had to come up with something other than opposition.[117] But unity on the British side had been achieved only at the expense of three considerable fudges. The Bank of England, while willing for the Keynes Plan to be thrown into the negotiating pot, was not

---

* Britain had tried to qualify its acceptance of non-discrimination by making it subject to its 'governing economic conditions'. The United States would have none of it; it did, however, insert some expansionist sentiments. The relevant passage of Article VII now read: 'To that end [the betterment of worldwide economic relations] the [benefits to be provided to the United States of America by the Government of the United Kingdom in return for aid] shall include provision for agreed action ... directed to the expansion ... of production, employment and the exchange and consumption of goods [and] to the elimination of all forms of discriminatory treatment in international commerce and to the reduction of tariffs and other trade barriers. ...' Also Roosevelt, as we have seen (p. 133 above), had assured Churchill that Article VII did not require the dismantling of imperial preferences.

committed to it. This 'was to . . . create dangerous gaps in perceptions and understanding that affected subsequent policy'.[118] A second gap in perception was between those like Keynes who thought that the ancillary institutions were 'in no way a necessary part' of the Clearing Union, and those like Harrod who wanted to promote the 'Keynes group of ideas' as a whole. The third area of unclarity was about whether the Clearing Union was expected to tide countries over the transition to peace or to maintain equilibrium on a permanent basis. Overdraft facilities required for the first might be too ample for the second. But this was the only way Keynes could hope to square the need to appease America with resistance to dismantling Britain's imperial preference/sterling area system.

The Treasury Memorandum on Post-War Economic Policy went to the War Cabinet Committee on Reconstruction Problems on 31 March 1942. Ernest Bevin, the Minister of Labour, was the last hurdle. 'Bevin comes in late,' Hugh Dalton, President of the Board of Trade, wrote in his diary, 'gives the appearance of being rather flushed, and proceeds to denounce the whole paper, saying it is an Anglo-American bankers' conspiracy against the working-class: it would doom us to two million unemployed. . . . And so on!' Dalton suggested they send for Hopkins and Keynes, who 'dealt cleverly' with Bevin's criticisms, which amounted to the assertion that the Keynes Plan represented a new gold standard. Keynes tried to allay Bevin's fears. The supply of bancor, he said, was 'absolutely elastic'. Gold could not in future limit the amount of money available for trade. After having heard them the Reconstruction Committee agreed to recommend to Cabinet that the Treasury paper 'might be put before the Americans' as the basis for Article VII discussions.

Bevin still needed to be squared. Keynes saw him privately on 22 April, and again reassured him that the International Clearing Bank could not possibly become an instrument of deflation and unemployment. Bevin said if this was made clear he would feel 'much happier about it'. Keynes redrafted once more to emphasise that the measures for debtor adjustment contemplated by his Plan 'do *not* include a deflationary policy, enforced by dear money . . . having the effect of causing unemployment'.

There also remained the question of the form in which the proposals should be presented to the Americans. Harrod revived his plan for an Anglo-American Economic Service, which would include an Investment Bank, a Buffer Stock scheme, and an agency for post-war relief and reconstruction. He wanted Britain to approach the United States as a 'potential joint victorious power planning a Pax Anglo-Saxonica . . . not as a mendicant, cap in hand'. He urged Keynes to drop capital controls, saying that outwitting foreign speculators had earned Britain's Exchange Equalisation Account £200m. in profits between 1932 and 1938. Harrod's silly side comes out in his rhetorical question: 'Are we really [by banning speculation] to reduce ourselves to the bread and butter level of ordinary mortals?' Keynes penned a magisterial put-down.[119] Henderson wanted Britain to propose 'a general regime of planned external economies' supplemented by the overdraft facilities of the Clearing Union. Keynes minuted that Henderson's ideas presupposed a world of barter agreements on Russian lines. 'There is the American bias and there is the Russian bias. I doubt if there is much between them which is likely to be practical politics. And whether or not we end up with the Russian bias, is there not much to be said for having a good try with the American bias first of all?.'[120]

Neither the Harrod nor Henderson modifications made headway. With the stipulation that the USSR become a founder member of the Union, the Treasury Memorandum – in effect the Keynes Plan – was approved by the War Cabinet on 7 May 1942 as the basis for Article VII conversations with the United States.[121] What had kept it alive, Keynes told Richard Kahn, was the unattractiveness of the alternatives. 'Now it is a question of capturing American sympathy'.[122]

APPENDIX 1

The Schachtian System

The Schachtian system developed out of the Payments (Standstill) Agreements, which Germany concluded with its creditors in 1931–3, themselves modelled on the Dawes and Young Plans for collecting reparations. These were designed to enable Germany to pay its debts out of its exports. Under these Agreements, made with countries like Britain, a proportion of Germany's export receipts were earmarked to settle with foreign bondholders.

The Agreements required that Germany run export surpluses. Between 1931 and 1934 Germany's balance of payments went into the red as first sterling then the dollar were devalued against the reichsmark. Germany rejected devaluation on four grounds: (a) because of its association with inflation going back to the early 1920s; (b) because part of its foreign debts were fixed in gold, so it benefited from having an overvalued currency; (c) because it feared retaliation in the form of competitive devaluation or tariffs; and (d) because it wanted to limit its exports of manufactured goods for political (that is, rearmament) reasons.

Under Schacht's New Plan of September 1934, bilateral clearing agreements were made with twenty-five countries in Europe and Latin America, designed to balance trade with Germany and each partner at fixed exchange rates. The partner was only allowed to sell as much to Germany as it bought from Germany. The aim of the system was to conduct foreign trade without foreign exchange. It was in effect a pure barter system between pairs of countries. By 1938, some 50 per cent of Germany's trade was conducted through bilateral clearings; only 20 per cent was settled through the 'free' foreign exchange market.

Under a bilateral clearing agreement, a German importer from, say, Hungary, instead of paying reichsmarks to the Hungarian exporter for exchange into pengos, would pay the reichsmarks into the Hungarian Central Bank's clearing account with the Reichsbank. German exporters to Hungary were paid reichsmarks from this account. The opposite process took place in Budapest. No actual exchange of national currencies took place. Credits which accumulated in the clearing of country A for its exports to country B could be used only to puchase imports from country B. The individual exporters in either country received payment in their own national currency from their central bank to the extent that importers made corresponding in-payments.

To make the system more flexible, a compensation agreement market in so-called 'Aski' (Ausländersonderkonten für Inlandszahlungen) marks grew up. An exporter to Germany could obtain a credit in 'Aski' marks, which he could sell at a discount to the importer of goods from Germany, who could thus pay the German price, the exporter raising his price in marks to compensate. This enabled the parties to negotiate the effective rate of exchange.

It was widely believed at the time that Germany set out to exploit its position as the chief market and leading supplier for countries in the Danubian basin by 'buying cheap and selling dear'. In fact, Germany often bought above, and sold below, the world market price: the terms of trade moved against Germany in the 1930s, and it failed to alter them in its favour till 1942, during the war itself. Germany was interested, not in exploiting its monopoly position, but in buying as much, and selling as little, of the materials it needed for rearmament. The bilateral clearing system, operated at an overvalued exchange rate, enabled it not to buy cheap and sell dear, but to buy more for less.

In the late 1930s, Germany exploited its power of seigniorage to run a balance of trade deficit with the Danubian countries. A Hungarian exporter who had accumulated claims in reichsmarks would offer them on the 'free exchange' for local currency (pengos). The Bank of Hungary would buy them to prevent the depreciation of the blocked reichsmarks relative to the official rate. This was equivalent to extending credit to Germany: its partners were, in effect, financing Germany's import surpluses. They did it to maintain the overvaluation of the reichmark and their own competitive advantage. But this was unintentionally advantageous to them. On the basis of foreign credits held by central banks in Germany, domestic credit could be issued which, in the prevailing conditions, raised employment rather than prices. (Ironically, Germany would finance the US balance of payments deficit in the 1960s by accumulating dollars. In 1960s terms, the US 'exported' inflation; in the depressed conditions of the 1930s, Germany 'exported' reflation.)

The domestic counterpart of the Schachtian system was the issue of state credits to German industry, which in four years restored full employment, with inflationary pressure being repressed by wage and price controls.

In toto the Schachtian system represented a way of escape from both the inflationary and balance of payments constraints on pursuing a full employment policy. The state paid money to businessmen to hire more workers and buy essential imports up to the level of full capacity, cutting off inflationary pressure through domestic wage and price controls and balance of payments pressure through bilateral clearing and payments agreements and issue of IOUs. As such it was certainly the most extreme version of Keynesian policy ever practised in peacetime, though probably devoid of any direct stimulus from Keynes himself.

This was the system that started to interest the Treasury in wartime. It is interesting that before then, Keynes paid no attention to this successful application of his ideas. His printed preface to the German edition of the *General Theory* (*CW*, vii, p. xxvi) makes no reference to, nor shows knowledge of, the 'Schachtian' system. As far as I know he made no reference to it, in public or private, between 1933 and 1940. It is highly unlikely that he knew nothing about it; and he could hardly have failed to be interested in what he read or heard. His silence has an obvious explanation. He did not want his ideas besmirched by associating them with fascism. He wrote in the German edition of the *General Theory*, omitted from the *Collected Writings* version referred to above, that his 'theory of output as a whole', while 'applicable' to German conditions, was 'worked out having the conditions of Anglo-Saxon countries in mind – where a great deal of laissez-faire still prevails'. It is a pity that he did not put the adjective 'rightly' or 'fortunately' after 'laissez-faire'. (See B. Schefold, 'The General Theory for a Totalitarian State? A Note on Keynes's Preface to the German Edition of 1936', reprinted from the *Cambridge Journal of Economics*, 4, no. 2, June 1980, in John Cunningham Wood (ed.), *John Maynard Keynes: Critical Assessments*, ii, 416–17; Larry Neal, 'The Economics and Finance of Bilateral Clearing Agreements: Germany 1934–8', *Economic History Review*, 2nd series, 36, 1986.)

APPENDIX 2

Changes in Keynes's Clearing Union Plan

1. First Draft (8 September 1941)

Multilateral clearing between central banks through International Clearing Bank. Payments can be settled in gold but in addition each CB has an 'index quota' (IQ) (overdraft facility) equal to half the five-year moving average of the value of imports + exports. (A world clearing union)

Fixed exchange rates. National currencies fixed against the international currency; international currency fixed against gold.

Ceiling to the annual penalty-free overdraft – a quarter of the IQ. Exceeding the ceiling for over a year means that the Central Bank in question is designated a 'Deficit bank' and a devaluation of not more than 5 per cent is *permitted*. Exceeding more than half of IQ triggers a *compulsory* 5 per cent devaluation and outward capital controls. The bank in question is designated a 'Supervised bank'. Interest charged for debit balances, which increases with the size of the balances. (Debtor adjustment)

If a bank's credit balances exceed a quarter of IQ then 5 per cent revaluation *permitted*. If it exceeds half of IQ then revaluation of 5 per cent *compulsory*. If surplus exceeds full value of IQ then excess amount confiscated. No interest received on credit balances. (Creditor adjustment)

Cross-border transactions control (optional for creditors, compulsory for persistent debtors). Capital account transactions to be controlled. Current account transactions can be controlled either voluntarily (for 'Deficit banks') or by compulsion (for 'Supervised banks').

Emergency finance. A Reserve Fund is to be established by the ICB funded by 5–10 per cent levy on surplus countries' credit balances. The ICB can use these funds to its discretion to help central banks in difficulties.

Several other post-war institutions suggested, which could be financed by the ICB: post-war Relief and Reconstruction Body; supranational policing body to ensure peace; Commodity Control Body (can hold stocks of commodities in order to stabilise their prices); International Economic Board (charged with trade cycle stabilisation).

Proposal for an eight-member Governing Body of the ICB. Great Powers each get their own representative; votes according to each country's IQ.

2. Second Draft (18 November 1941)

International currency to be called 'grammor'.

Limits on trade protectionism envisaged: ban on quotas, a 25 per cent limit to *ad valorem* taxes, ban on export subsidies.

'Deficit banks' to be renamed 'Deficiency banks'.

3. Third Draft (15 December 1941)

International currency to be called 'bancor' instead of 'grammor'.

Explicit discussion of the purpose of IQs. Intended to solve temporary problems, not as a long-term 'soft credit'. Emphasis on giving countries adequate room for non-deflationary adjustment.

The provision for the surrender of 'excessive' credit balances is dropped. Instead persistent creditors have the option voluntarily to adjust their surplus positions, using the measures outlined in previous drafts.

A charge of 1 per cent of IQ payable to the Reserve Fund when a state's account is in disequilibrium (credit or debit) by up to half of IQ. A charge of 2 per cent of IQ payable if the imbalance is in excess of half of IQ. The only way this charge can be avoided is by bilateral loans between member states.

4. Fourth Draft (March 1942)

IQs to be calculated on the basis of the three-year pre-war average of the value of imports + exports. Suggestion that IQ could be 'either equal to or in a determined *lesser* proportion to this amount'.

More stringent controls on debtors introduced: if a member state's debit balance exceeds three-quarters of its IQ for at least a year then the ICB can require it to reduce its overdraft to below that amount within a two-year period. Otherwise the country in question will be declared in default and its overdraft facility will be terminated. In the event of a default, all member states will be required to pay all debts to the country in question to the ICB. The Governing Body can require member states to leave the Union subject to one year's notice.

Explicit provisions for any gold that accumulates at the ICB to be redistributed to member states.

A new structure of Governing Body is proposed, whereby US and UK can outvote everyone else.

Outstanding credit balances by those who leave the Union can be used to pay existing Union members.

CHAPTER SEVEN

The Strange Case of Harry Dexter White

I

THE AMERICAN BIAS

Although the United States was now in the war, its 'sympathy' proved harder to capture. It was to be almost a year before British and American troops went into action together, in North Africa. In the first few months of 1942 the centre of the war shifted to the Far East, where the British suffered a string of military defeats at the hands of the Japanese. These not only damaged Britain's military reputation, but drew unwelcome attention to the existence of the British Empire. British imperialism made victory over Japan 'more difficult', in Walter Lippmann's view, 'because the United Nations are inhibited from appealing to the native populations as liberators'.

> The Asiatic War [Lippmann continued in his letter to Keynes on 18 April 1942] has revived the profound anti-imperialism of the American tradition, and this is the second of the controlling causes, I believe, of the anti-British sentiment which has appeared. Note that it did not exist when Mr Churchill was here in December and that it developed after the fall of Singapore. Obviously the popular feeling reflects the condition of military prestige. But that does not explain the popular feeling. British stock went up, not down, after the reverses in Europe (the Balkans, Crete). It went down after Singapore because the Americans saw that the imperialism they have always disliked was also inefficient.[1]

This was the context in which post-war economic planning by both sides got under way. Each Ally proceeded in isolation from the other. They were also at cross-purposes. The State Department was eager to get the trade talks, so rudely broken off by Keynes in Washington in July 1941, going again. The British wanted to start with the monetary talks. However, the US Treasury was not ready to start monetary talks; and the British Board of Trade was in no position to resume trade talks, in view of the Cabinet's refusal to contemplate any changes in the imperial preference system. As a result there were no official negotiations for eighteen months on either money or trade.

Keynes's International Clearing Union was conceived as a set of inter-locking regimes governing money, investment, commodities and trade. However, only the monetary scheme – the International Clearing Bank with its overdraft facilities – had been worked out in any detail. On Keynes's suggestion, Harrod had drawn up a scheme for an International Investment Bank 'in a few free evenings' at the end of 1941 and sent it to him.[2] A summary found its way into the 'Treasury Bible'. Little more was heard of it till the Americans themselves took it up. This was a great disappointment to Harrod. The reason is that Keynes himself did not press it. He saw no particular benefit to Britain, as Britain would be in no position to provide any capital for foreign investment for a long time to come.

However, at Roy Harrod's prodding Keynes did, on 20 January 1942, draft a memorandum on buffer stocks. Keynes's Buffer Stock Plan was the British attempt to meet the requirements of American agricultural producers, represented by Vice-President Henry Wallace, which, in some respects, cut across the State Department's free-trade perspective. Wallace had started talks with the main wheat producers in August 1941, aimed at imposing export quotas and excluding low-cost producers, acceptance of these stipulations to be a condition of post-war relief. Keynes had attacked these proposals as expressing 'discrimination' in extreme form. In his first paper on the Clearing Union, he noted that America proposed 'the enforcement of an agreement to restrict Europe's freedom to feed herself by compelling even the poorest Eastern European states . . . to eat pure white bread . . . all this for the purpose of maintaining on a profitable basis an export of wheat from the United States which, in the interests of . . . international equilibrium, ought to disappear altogether'.[3] However, with typical ingenuity he worked out a plan which aimed to secure for producers stable prices without involving the creation of a producers' cartel.

The Keynes Buffer Stock Plan set out to avoid the 'frightful' fluctuations in commodity prices, which caused or amplified the business cycle. Because of the difficulty of quickly adjusting output to demand, private stocks of commodities were either too large or too small, leading to prices which were either too high or too low. In a boom 'prices rush up, uneconomic and excessive output is stimulated and the seeds are sown of a subsequent collapse'. As Keynes put it, 'Our object should be to combine the long-period advantages of free competition with the short-period advantages of ensuring that the necessary changes in the scale and distribution of output should take place *steadily* and *slowly* in response to the steady and slow evolution of the underlying trends.'[4] Keynes's analysis was strictly Marshallian, in its distinction between short-period and long-period supply. And the policy he advocated was typical: to take a 'middle course between unfettered competition under *laissez-*

faire conditions and planned controls which try to freeze commerce into a fixed mould'.[5]

The centrepiece of the new Keynes scheme was a set of buffer stocks – or reserves – for the main internationally traded commodities. Each reserve would be managed by its own 'Control' capped by a General Council for Commodity Controls to ensure that individual schemes conformed to general principles. Each Control would set an initial 'basic' price for its 'commod', equal to its estimate of 'the long-period equilibrium costs of the most efficient producers', which it would vary from time to time 'by a process of trial and error based on the observed tendency of stocks to increase or decrease'. It would buy its 'commod' whenever prices fell 10 per cent below, and sell when they rose 10 per cent above, the 'basic' price. Its long-period pricing policy would aim to maintain a constant reserve, or what US Vice-President Henry Wallace had called an 'ever normal granary'.[6]

Buffer stocks would stabilise the incomes of primary producers:

It is an outstanding fault of the competitive system [Keynes wrote] that there is no sufficient incentive to the individual enterprise to store surplus stocks of materials beyond the normal reserves required to maintain continuity of output. The competitive system abhors the existence of buffer stocks . . . because such stocks yield a *negative* return in terms of themselves. It is ready without remorse to tear the structure of output to pieces . . . in the effort to rid itself of them; which should be no matter for surprise because the competitive system is in its ideal form the perfect mechanism for ensuring the quickest, but at the same time the most ruthless, adjustment of supply to demand to any change in conditions, however transitory. It is inherently opposed to stability and security, though, for the same reason, it has the great virtue of being also opposed to . . . stagnation. . . . If demand fluctuates, a divergence immediately ensues between the general interest in the holding of stocks and the course of action which is most advantageous for each producer acting independently.[7]

This difficult passage makes sense in the context of Keynes's economics. It is the existence of uncertainty which creates a speculative demand for stocks as well as for money. But this very uncertainty creates a problem for the commodity Controls, as long as private trading is allowed. For speculation may cause the Control to run out of stocks when prices are rising, and of money when they are falling. Keynes knew all about this as a speculator in stocks himself. Presumably he would have guarded against speculation by varying the overdraft facilities of the Clearing Bank contracyclically. But this was to give the Bank a role as manager of the global business-cycle which would strain it technically and overburden it politically. Similar arguments were used against the buffer stocks proposals of the 1970s.

There was another problem. Was the Buffer Stock Plan intended to stabilise prices which cleared markets or to stabilise producers' incomes at some 'adequate' level? Again Keynes tried for a Middle Way: it would do both. Wealthy countries would be left free to subsidise their higher-cost producers – but within 'moderate limits' to prevent the freezing of the existing distribution of production.[8] It was an ingenious compromise between producers' and consumers' interests, but it did not look too convincing. When the nations forming the EEC faced the same problem in the 1950s, they opted unequivocally for protecting the producer, in line with their history.

Keynes's Buffer Stock Plan never won the same degree of support in Whitehall as had his Clearing Union Plan. This time his Middle Way pleased neither the planners nor the free traders. The Bank of England was more interested in planned trade than in free trade. It condemned Keynes's mixture of private trading and price controls as a speculators' paradise.[9] Sir Donald Fergusson, permanent secretary of the Ministry of Agriculture, insisted that agriculture was a 'way of life, not an industry'. He wanted unconstrained freedom to protect British agriculture by import levies and subsidies.[10] On the other side Sir Frederick Leith-Ross at the Ministry of Economic Warfare took an extreme free-trade line. Once more Keynes was extraordinarily open-minded in drafting. But by the autumn of 1942 he had had enough. His Plan had been subjected to 'tens of thousands of minor or major criticisms from different Departments', he complained to Phillips.[11] 'Must I produce another stencil?' he exploded to Sir Wilfrid Eady. On Leith-Ross's amendments he commented caustically, 'it does not seem prudent tactics in a paper designed to protect the interests of primary producers generally to make its principal purpose appear to be the abolition of agriculture throughout the United States and most of Europe'. As for Fergusson, 'his contribution can only be described as barmy. . . . every paragraph of his letter and several of his detailed comments show an almost lunatic misunderstanding of what the paper says or is driving at. It is a frightful nuisance.'[12]

The first direct British response to Article VII's trade requirements was James Meade's plan for an 'International Commercial Union', dating from 4 August 1942. Hatched in the Economic Section of the War Cabinet, it went to the Overton Committee, which had been set up by Hugh Dalton, President of the Board of Trade. Meade proposed that all members of the Union would grant most-favoured-nation treatment to each other, with tariff preferences limited to 10 per cent; that quantitative import controls be outlawed except in emergencies; that export subsidies be limited to 10 per cent below domestic prices. His Plan was enthusiastically endorsed by the majority of the Overton Committee in December,

but furiously attacked by Hubert Henderson. For once Keynes sympa-
thised with Henderson's 'magnificent' critique, in contrast to Dennis
Robertson, who emitted a 'squeak of consternation' at the gale of protectionism blowing though the Treasury. He probably noticed that this
reinforced the gale of protectionism blowing through the Cabinet and
the Bank of England.

The war had had a double-edged effect on British thinking about post-
war possibilities. On the one hand, it was forcing Britain to live off
American largesse, thereby locking it into America's Article VII agenda.
On the other hand it seemed to make possible what Joseph Chamberlain
and his successors had only dreamt of: the organisation of the British
Empire and its satellites as an economic unit. It was the simultaneous
dwarfing of the British economy and the strengthening of imperial
organisation which made the nationalists and imperialists in the government look to the Empire as a guarantee of Britain's post-war independence – an independence which had now come to include the freedom
to pursue full employment policies. The battle between the 'American'
and the 'imperial' tendencies in British official thinking came to centre
on the elastic concept of the 'transition'. That a transitional period was
needed before any new post-war regime was put in place was common
ground, if only because Britain would face a large prospective balance of
payments deficit. However, a transition sufficiently prolonged might prove
to be permanent. Nationalists like Hubert Henderson wanted important
elements of the transitional arrangements built into the permanent
system. Liberals like Lionel Robbins, James Meade, Roy Harrod and
Dennis Robertson favoured a free-trade regime, but one underpinned by
global government, and modified by escape clauses. Keynes stood somewhere in the middle, with an inclination to the 'American bias'.

In correspondence with Treasury and Board of Trade officials and
Meade himself in the winter of 1942–3, Keynes sprayed the Overton
Report with criticisms. Some were technical: Meade, he thought, had not
worked out a non-discriminatory basis for state trading, though he
(Keynes) was attracted by his technique of auctioning import licences. He
had not allowed for customs unions. The Report was too abstract. It gave
no consideration to Britain's post-war position or to the question where
its self-interest lay. 'Ought we not to begin in a much more concrete
manner?' Keynes suggested it would be better to start with bilateral
agreements, into which a commercial code – like the old most-favoured-
nation clause – could be incorporated, rather than aiming for across-the-
board tariff reductions. Meade's Plan, Keynes thought, would be
unacceptable to Congress. 'We have to remember,' he wrote, 'that the
free trade element in the State Department . . . represents almost nothing
but themselves.' This was to prove a gross misjudgement. Keynes condemned as 'irresponsible' the Report's proposal that members of the

Union should give up quantitative restrictions on imports after a two-year transition. Quantitative controls were much less objectionable in principle than tariffs, preferences and subsidies, they fitted state trading arrangements which the Committee anyway proposed to allow (largely to make it possible for Russia to adhere to the Union), and Britain would in any case need to keep them in the foreseeable future for balance of payments reasons. Finally, Keynes resurrected the National Self-Sufficiency arguments of his 1933 articles.[13] 'One senses', he wrote to Waley, 'an excessive prejudice against autarky. A great many manufactured products can be produced with almost equal efficiency in any industrial country.' Britain could itself easily produce most of the £200m. worth of manufactured goods it imported before the war. There were strong arguments for establishing oil refining and additional smelting capacity at home. Only with difficulty was Keynes dissuaded from his conviction that turning pig iron into steel was the solution to Britain's balance of payments problem: it was typical of him that he should have sounded off on a technical matter with great assurance (while confessing he knew nothing of it) on the basis of a conversation with Old Wykehamist David Eccles, temporarily at the Ministry of Production.[14]

Announcing that he stood 'half way between Sir Hubert Henderson and the [Overton] Committee', he suggested approaching the United States with a bland statement of general principles, not a specific charter. 'If we were to take the initiative on the lines of the Overton Report,' he wrote on 15 January 1943,

> all the other parties concerned would then seek to modify the proposals to their own advantage. We should have already gone to the limit. We should have shot our bolt, leaving the rest of the world with its ammunition in hand. No-one will look after us if we do not look after ourselves. The solution of our balance of trade problem is the clue to our post-war economic prospects all along the line. It is not a thing to be handled so light-heartedly. Without a more robust – if you like, a more selfish – policy, we are sunk.[15]

Keynes's failure to endorse the Commercial Union delighted Henderson and disappointed Meade. His real reason was stated in the same paper: 'I am fearful of prejudicing our other post-war plans by associating them too closely with something as full of dangerous political dynamite as this.'[16] Without Keynes's support, the Overton Committee's proposals remained stuck in the corridors of Whitehall; and the trade talks with the Americans remained stalled.

A fifth draft of the Buffer Stock scheme was endorsed on 14 April 1943 as an official Treasury paper. 'What's this about Butter Scotch?' Churchill growled when it came before the Cabinet. The Cabinet agreed that both the Buffer Stock and Commercial Union Plans might be shown to the Dominions and 'mentioned' to the Americans in general terms. But unlike the Clearing Union they were never published as White Papers or put forward as British negotiating positions. The Keynes Plan shrank back to what it had been at the start: a Clearing Union with optional extras.

II

THE WHITE PLAN

What the British did not know was that on 14 December 1941, a week after Pearl Harbor had brought America into the war against both Japan and Germany, Morgenthau had instructed his director of monetary research, Harry Dexter White, to prepare a memorandum on an inter-Allied stabilisation fund which would 'provide the basis for post-war monetary stabilisation arrangements; and . . . provide a post-war "international currency"'. In giving him the status, though not title, of Assistant Secretary of the Treasury Morgenthau said: 'He will be in charge of all foreign affairs for me. . . . I want it in one brain and I want it in Harry White's brain.'[17] White would become the central figure in all Keynes's subsequent dealings with Washington. The battle between the two would become one of the grand *political* duels of the Second World War, though it was largely buried in financial minutiae. This did not exclude a wary comradeship developing between the two 'technicians'. Keynes also partly misunderstood the nature of the duel.

The speed of White's reaction to Morgenthau's request of 14 December 1941 suggests he already knew what he wanted to do. Indeed an initial outline of his proposals seems to have been prepared in the summer or early autumn of 1941.[18] On 30 December 1941 White handed a twelve-page memorandum to Morgenthau headed 'Suggestions for Inter-Allied Monetary and Banking Action'. This proposed two new institutions, an International Stabilisation Fund and an International Bank. Morgenthau's idea for a single international currency had been dropped, White convincing him that universal currency convertibility would be 'more realistic and just as effective'.[19]

In thinking about the post-war financial architecture, White, like Keynes, drew on the experience of the inter-war years, but as seen through American eyes. There was widespread agreement in Washington that any post-war regime should provide for fixed exchange rates, trade expansion and the end of discrimination. These were identified as necessary underpinnings for American and world prosperity and the prevention of war. The institutional innovations which White proposed had also been prefigured in American initiatives: the Exchange Equalisation Fund of 1933, the Tripartite Agreement of 1936, the proposal for an Inter-American Bank of 1940. If the Keynes Plan can be read as an attempt to 'universalise' the sterling area, so White's was an effort to project American power and responsibility beyond the two American continents. However, White's economic plans were mixed up with political aims which Keynes did not share. Partly these simply reflected the fact that the Americans held all the trumps and could design post-war arrangements to suit themselves. Partly they reflected a personal agenda which remains to this day a matter of controversy.

Born in Boston in 1892, Harry White – he added the Dexter later – was the youngest of seven children of Jacob Weit and Sarah Magilewski, who emigrated to America in 1885 to escape the tsarist pogroms in Lithuania. His father set up a small hardware business, for which Harry White worked for eight years after leaving high school, despite his efforts to continue his education. His school friends recall him as the 'smallest, smartest' student in his class. In 1917 he enlisted in the US Army, was commissioned as lieutenant, got married to Anne Terry, also Russian-born, in 1918, and was sent to France, though not to the front. After working at the family hardware store, an orphan asylum and a boys' summer camp, he enrolled at Columbia University in 1922, as a 'mature' student of government. A year later he switched to Stanford and econom-ics, where he graduated 'with great distinction', but not with the greatest. He had realised that 'most governmental problems are economic, so I stayed with economics'. A Stanford professor remembered him as 'aggressive and brilliant'. He supported the socialist candidate Robert La Follette in his Presidential bid of 1924. Graduate work at Harvard under Frank Taussig produced a prize-winning PhD dissertation, published in 1933 as *The French International Accounts 1880–1913*, which concluded that 'the orthodox attitude towards unrestricted capital exports is open to criticism'.[20] White's instructorship in economics at Harvard was renewed for six years, but like his friend and fellow instructor Lauchlin Currie, he failed to get tenure. People considered him able and quick, but some-what superficial. His arrogance also made him enemies. In 1932 he moved to a minor college in Wisconsin, as an assistant professor, becom-ing a full professor a year later. During the depression, he rejected protection in favour of 'centralized control over foreign exchanges and trade' and announced he was learning Russian in order to study the 'technique of planning' at Gosplan.[21] By this time, he was greatly attracted to the Soviet 'experiment'.

In 1934, Jacob Viner, then advising Morgenthau at the Treasury, directed White to Washington rather than to Moscow, by asking him to help him over the summer in a survey of banking legislation and insti-tutions. He was hired as a temporary economic analyst and stayed at the Treasury for eleven years. His report, 'Selection of a Monetary Standard for the US', was submitted on 22 September 1934. White's thesis in this, and other papers written round this time, was that the completion of domestic recovery required international monetary stabilisation, since American business needed trade expansion.[22] White became principal economic analyst in the Treasury's Division of Research and Statistics on 1 November 1934. In October 1936 he became assistant director of the Division; by March 1938, he had his own empire carved out of it when he became director of monetary research, with responsibility for the operation of the American Stabilisation Fund. A month later he became a member of Morgenthau's 9.30 group of senior officials, which met the Secretary every morning. By this time, White had become a 'Keynesian', favouring compensatory spending to fight the 1938 downturn, a redistribution of income from rich to poor, and the centralisation of monetary policy in the Treasury.[23]

In reaching the second position in the Treasury after only seven years, White had shown a 'remarkable talent . . . for acquiring and maintaining responsibility'.[24] He had established an intellectual ascendancy over Morgenthau, based mainly on his ability to explain things to him, not an easy matter, and an ability to channel Morgenthau's visions and obsessions into compact plans which enhanced the Secretary's standing in the administration; and he had filled the Treasury, especially the Monetary Division, with his own appointees.

Keynes had first met White in 1935 when he toured European capitals and more substantially in Washington in 1941, when he had suggested a way through the Lend–Lease imbroglio. He would have encountered a short, stocky man, with trim moustache, rimless spectacles and a rasping voice. No doubt he identified him as one of those able 'gritty' Jewish types in Morgenthau's entourage. In Washington, White had the reputation of being one of the pushiest, least agreeable men in town – and also for being anti-British. Keynes would surely have reinforced White's instinctive prejudices against the ruling class of a decaying empire. Keynes might have the style which he lacked, but he, White, had the power, and he knew it. Above all, Keynes's subtle intelligence was as much to be resisted as admired, because it could set all kinds of traps into which the unwary could fall. The fear of 'bamboozlement' was never far from the minds of those Americans who had read, as White would doubtless have read, Keynes's *Economic Consequences of the Peace*.

What Keynes never knew was that White was associated, politically and socially, with the American communist underground, and was passing confidential information to it which was being transmitted to Soviet intelligence; and that some of the Treasury people – including White's appointees – that he would have come across were also underground communists or agents or both. White did not believe that Soviet interests conflicted with American interests. The only matter in serious dispute is whether he knew, prior to 1944, whether the information he was providing was being handed to the Russians. (See Appendix to this chapter for review of the evidence.)

White was not a member of the American Communist Party – he was too independent to take orders from anyone – but like other fellow travellers of the 1930s he greatly admired Soviet planning and readily accepted the communist view that a powerful Soviet Union was the only reliable bulwark against Nazi anti-semitism and fascist expansionism. There was thus no conflict in White's mind between his hopes for a social democratic United States, a planned international economy and a US–Soviet condominium to guarantee the peace. That is why he could declare before the House of Representatives Committee on Un-American Activities in 1948 that he could not 'do a disloyal act or anything against the interests of our country'. In all this there was an astonishing naivety about the nature of Stalinism. But this was far from unusual on the left. J. K. Galbraith, who was neither a spy nor a communist, told James Meade that 'Russia should be permitted to absorb Poland, the Balkans and the whole of Eastern Europe in order to spread the benefits of Communism.'[25] Except for his clandestine activities, White's beliefs were not much different from those of Harry Hopkins or Vice-President Henry Wallace, who 'saw in the march of history a coming together of the Soviet experiment in Russia with the New Deal programmes of the United States' for the greater good of mankind.[26] Roosevelt also believed that US–Soviet co-operation offered the best hope of a peaceful and progressive world. Left-wingers in the New Deal much preferred the idea of an American partnership with 'progressive' Soviet Russia to one with reactionary, imperialist Britain.

Thus the 'universalism, legalism, and economism' of which Richard Gardner speaks as driving US post-war planning[27] was given by White and others a particular ideological slant which envisaged a 'new course' leading to the eventual convergence of the United States and Soviet Union in a single social democratic world system. A detailed study of the interrelationship between White's policy initiatives, the information he was passing to the underground, and the information he was receiving about Soviet desiderata is obviously out of place here. His activities encompassed the whole range of the US Treasury's external concerns, not least in the Far East. White was prolific in producing plans of wide geopolitical scope for settling the affairs of the planet, based on the use of American money power. But two points can be made.

First, he had to work through his Treasury Secretary. Although he was 'the beneficiary of some of the authority that fell by the osmosis of power from Roosevelt to Morgenthau',[28] his own policymaking power was necessarily circumscribed. In many ways, Morgenthau was an ideal instrument, sharing the same hatred of Germany (what it had become and what it might still be capable of), mistrust of bankers and Englishmen, and drive for American hegemony. He was dependent on White for technical expertise, and eager to challenge the State Department's claim to mono-polise foreign policy. However, no more than Roosevelt was Morgenthau an automatic supporter of the Soviet Union.

Secondly, despite White's long-standing technical interest in stabilisa-tion plans, the main aim of his personal policymaking was to secure a political and economic alliance with the Soviet Union by attaching it to a restored gold standard and through the instrument of large American loans. The thread of the large loan to Russia runs from White's first proposal in March 1939 to his last efforts in 1944–5 which envisaged a huge Marshall Aid programme for the Soviet Union.[29] This must be contrasted with his niggardly attitude to British requests for financial help. Lauchlin Currie, who was for two years *de facto* manager of the Lend–Lease programme, shared White's antipathy towards British imperialism.[30] Britain's importunities were inconvenient facts which had to be dealt with. But Britain was not part of the big picture, and White was scornful, though apprehensive, of Britain's Great Power pretensions. One must bear in mind that, for White and others in both Treasury and State, Britain was still considered an economic rival to the United States, whereas the Soviet Union, with its separate system, was not. Ostrander remembers Redvers Opie telling him that White was 'even more strongly anti-British than pro-Soviet'. White's Stabilisation Fund was just one fragment of a much larger design at whose centre lay American–Soviet condominium, not Anglo-American co-operation. The British examined and criticised White's schemes from the point of view of how they would help them. They never understood the particular nature of White's astigmatism, in which one eye focused on Washington, while the other swivelled on Moscow. Keynes, by contrast, rarely thought about Russia, and when he did it was usually disparagingly. In London he maintained friendly rela-tions with Ivan Maisky, the Soviet ambassador. The Maiskys even dined at Keynes's kitchen table in Gordon Square, which reminded Maisky of his Siberian childhood. But economically and politically, if not culturally, Russia remained for Keynes an alien country, which fitted uneasily into his Grand Design.

This then was the nature and outlook of Harry Dexter White, the man whom the British fondly imagined was working along lines parallel to their own. It helps explain why the American Treasury's reluctance to do private business with the British was not just due to unreadiness, fear of being outwitted by Keynes or departmental disputes in Washington, but stemmed from a reluctance to give the British a privileged place in what was clearly intended to be a Pax Americana.

In March 1942, White revised and expanded his December 1941 draft with the help of his assistant Edward Bernstein. When Keynes first saw it in July 1942 it had become a very bulky document, with a short preamble followed by eighty pages of text.

White called for the establishment of two institutions, an International Stabilisation Fund and a Bank for Reconstruction. He described their objects as (a) to prevent the disruption of foreign exchanges and the collapse of the monetary and credit system, (b) to assure restoration of foreign trade, and (c) to supply relief and reconstruction capital.[31] The Bank was a much more ambitious project than the Fund, its main purpose being 'to supply the huge volume of capital that will be needed virtually throughout the world for reconstruction, for relief, and for economic recovery'. It was to have a capital of $10bn (increased to $20bn in April 1943). Broadly speaking, it encompassed most of the work the ancillary institutions were designed to do in the Keynes Plan. Not surprisingly it was this aspect of White's Grand Design which most excited Harrod, then and subsequently, for it came closest to his own enthusiasms: 'it was to be a genuine international "Central Bank", with a right to issue notes and hold the deposits of other Central Banks. . . . It was to eliminate the danger of world-wide crises that are financial in origin, and reduce the likelihood, intensity and duration of world-wide economic depressions. . . . Alas, all these splendid features were in due course to be removed.' The Fund, on the other hand, had the 'limited objective of dealing with foreign exchange and balance of payments problems'.[32]

It was to be made up of levies of gold, domestic currency and interest-bearing securities totalling $5bn, each member's contribution based on a complex formula, in which gold holdings and gold production were heavily weighted. Suggested initial contributions were $3.2bn from the USA and $635m. from Britain. The ISF would lend foreign currencies to members in temporary balance of payments difficulties up to the limit of their contributions or 'quotas'. It would fix the par values of currencies in terms of gold, which could be altered only to correct a 'fundamental disequilibrium', and would require a four-fifths majority of the votes wielded by the Fund's directors. Drawing rights in excess of a member's gold contribution were subject to increasingly stringent conditions, which included correction of domestic policies. Membership of the Fund would be open to all countries which agreed to alter their exchange rates only with the Fund's approval, to abandon all exchange controls within one year of joining or the end of hostilities, and to reduce tariffs; which agreed not to make any bilateral clearing agreements or establish 'geographically preferential exchange rates', not to allow gold to circulate domestically, and not to inflate or deflate their currencies or default on foreign obligations without Fund approval. Freedom to move capital was qualified by a member having the right to refuse inward investment, and by the country exporting capital having the right to commandeer the foreign investments of its own nationals to meet capital flight. White also proposed an ingenious method of freeing blocked wartime balances.[33] Rigid in its insistence on exchange rate stability and elimination of exchange restrictions and discriminatory payments practices, the White Plan was niggardly in providing balance of payments assistance.

In conception, the ISF was an attempt to equip a restored gold standard with explicit and enforceable rules of the game and a balance of payments adjustment facility, the lack of which, in the American view, had brought the previous system crashing down. It was intended to outlaw both unilateral exchange-rate depreciation and discriminatory trading systems – the British offences against the United States in the 1930s – while recognising a limited responsibility of creditor countries to supply short-term finance to debtor countries. But all this was to be ancillary to the Bank, the real locomotive of the White Plan. It was the much greater opposition to the Bank, especially from the State and other departments and the banking community, which caused it to be replaced by the ISF as the centrepiece of the American Plan.

The White and Keynes Plans were based on different concepts. The Stabilisation Fund made loans out of subscribed capital; the Clearing Union created overdrafts out of nothing. In the Fund a member's maximum liability was fixed by its subscription; in the Clearing Union a member might be required to accept 'bancor' (in payment for its exports) up to the total of all the other members' overdraft facilities. Because the Fund's stock of foreign currencies ($5bn) was much smaller than the Bank's 'stock' of overdrafts ($26bn) it could run out of 'facilities' much sooner than could Keynes's Bank. Keynes's Bank ensured multilateral clearing; the Fund provided only particular foreign currencies. The Fund's principle of limited creditor liability put the onus on debtor adjustment, pressure for which started to apply as soon as a member had borrowed the gold equivalent of its subscription. The Clearing Union put the onus of adjustment on the creditor, by forcing the unadjusted creditor to give away a growing proportion of its exports for bancor. For the British, the White Plan spelled financial orthodoxy, the gold standard and deflation; for the Americans, the Keynes plan spelled reckless experiment and inflation.

On 8 May 1942, White gave Morgenthau his by now voluminous draft. He suggested a conference of finance ministers of all the United Nations, including Russa and China, to consider it. Morgenthau agreed to hit Roosevelt and Hull with this idea 'at the same time', promoting the scheme to his President as a 'New Deal in international economics'. Roosevelt rejected this as premature, ordering the White Plan to be discussed more extensively with the State Department and other agencies first. Morgenthau now saw the Plan as his 'own pet' and suspected that the State Department would want to kill it because they hadn't thought of it first. Hull told Sir Ronald Campbell of the British Embassy that he objected to 'long winded conversations' about post-war programmes, to the neglect of prosecuting the war.[34] However, his assistant Adolph Berle persuaded him that a monetary plan was an essential counterpart of any free trade agenda, and Hull nominated Leo Pasvolsky and Herbert Feis to represent his Department in the discussions. Inter-departmental meetings started on 25 May, with White chairing a technical committee. On 2 July Acheson pressed Morgenthau yet again to start informal conversations with the British. On 9 July, White, who was not on close terms with Phillips, handed Leith-Ross, who was in Washington to discuss inter-Allied relief matters, a copy of his plan, which Phillips immediately transmitted to the Treasury in London. (Presumably Morgenthau had authorised White to do this.) At the same time, Phillips urged London to give the Americans a copy of the Keynes Plan as the only means of starting a dialogue. Kingsley Wood agreed in mid-July. Each side finally found out what the other was hatching.

III

MUTUAL REACTIONS

Keynes took a copy of the 'leaked' White Plan down to Tilton on 24 July. He returned to London on 3 August with notes on the American proposal and redraft of his own Clearing Union. It is an exaggeration to say he was 'very favourably impressed' by White's handiwork.[35] 'It obviously won't work,' he told Hopkins. To Phillips he wrote: 'Seldom have I been simultaneously so much bored and so much interested.'[36] However, he found it 'striking and encouraging' that he and White had been working on parallel lines. 'The relationship between [the Stabilisation Fund and the Investment Bank] is obscure,' Keynes noted, 'especially in connection with gold and the position of the notes which the Bank is free to issue.' He also questioned voting arrangements which gave the minor states of Latin America twice as many votes as the British Empire.

His main criticism of the Stabilisation Fund proposal was that it 'makes no attempt to use the banking principle and one-way gold convertibility and is in fact not much more than a version of the gold standard, which simply aims at multiplying the effective volume of the gold base'. It would do little to help countries which started with only a little gold. On the other hand, he approved 'the extremely generous proposal for dealing with wholly or partly blocked balances at the end of the war' and discovered other helpful or suggestive proposals. He was pleased to note that the endorsement of 'Hullism' was only 'moderate'.[37] Keynes's redraft of his own Plan, which he now understood would be the version handed to the Americans, was shaped by his reading of the White Plan. He raised the possibility of determining quotas by 'other factors' than the value of a country's foreign trade; and of the Governing Body 'recommending' appropriate domestic policies to excess debtor members – 'surely something of a backtracking of the Bevin commitment of April'.[38] He added the suggestion that the Clearing Bank might provide bancor credits to liquify blocked (that is, sterling) balances. He conceded that post-war relief and reconstruction might be handled outside the Clearing Union, requiring a reduction or postponement of overdraft facilities during the transitional period. The process of hiving off the various functions envisaged for the Clearing Bank into separate bodies had started. Keynes also rewrote some of his arguments to bring out what he thought were the most attractive features of his scheme. He praised the miraculous properties of banking which turned hoarding into spending, or stones into bread. Admittedly, the power of money creation was open to abuse. But this was no reason for returning to the 'practices of the seventeenth century goldsmiths (which are what we are still following in the international field) and forgoing the vast expansion of production which banking principles have made possible'. He hoped to arouse the enthusiasm of his fellow technicians in Washington for the 'anonymous' and 'impersonal' character of the bancor mechanism, which obviated the need to apply to 'Parliaments and Congresses' for supply.[39]

Richard Law, Under-Secretary of State at the Foreign Office, took copies of the revised Keynes draft to Washington in August, and Phillips gave White a copy on the 28th. 'Everybody is now supporting it,' Keynes reported to Kahn, 'and (with the exception of the Bank of England) are really enthusiastic.'[40] In his covering note to White, Phillips wrote that the British proposals were drawn up specially to 'meet the threat of another world-wide post-war depression'.

The Keynes Plan was now intensively scrutinised in Washington. The State Department took the lead, Berle asking Phillips lots of questions, which he communicated to Keynes. The politically charged ones concerned the total of quotas, the potential liability of the United States, creditors' voting rights, discipline on debtors, and the inflationary potential of bancor creation.[41] The nub of the matter, Phillips wrote, was the American fear that 'the Union would have a Bank of Issue function which would have an adverse reaction on the position of the dollar, and that the plan might involve the United States in lending an indefinite amount to the rest of the world . . .'.[42] Keynes apart, London took surprisingly little interest in White's proposals – possibly because their status was as yet unclear.

The desultory nature of the long-distance contacts between Washington and London was briefly interrupted by the visit of Morgenthau and White to London in October 1942 to inspect armament factories and to discuss the currency arrangements to be implemented in North Africa following the impending, and presumably successful, Allied invasion. Winant, with Morgenthau's agreement, arranged a private meeting between Keynes and White. They met at the ambassador's residence on

23 October, with both American and British officials in attendance. Pen-rose, who was present, remembers a 'lively and at times somewhat acri-monious but exceedingly fruitful' discussion, dominated by Keynes and White. Keynes said the Fund wouldn't be large enough; White said it would be impossible to get more out of Congress. They discussed whether the capital of the new institution should be subscribed (White) or created (Keynes). Keynes vigorously attacked the idea of subscribed capital, but White said it was the only thing Congress would accept. He also said it would be politically impossible to use the Clearing Union for relief and reconstruction. Keynes said that the requirement for a four-fifths majority for changes in exchange rates was unacceptable to Britain, which would have to be free to act unilaterally if necessary. He argued 'heatedly' for direct talks with the United States in advance of an inter-national conference. White replied that this would give an impression of an Anglo-Saxon 'gang up'. With this barely tactful reminder of Britain's modest place in the big picture, the meeting ended. Both men agreed to modify their schemes on a number of points. Winant presided 'with his usual charm and skill'.[43]

Denied direct Anglo-American negotiations, Britain started to organise support for the Keynes Plan. Between 23 October and 9 November its various elements were discussed at the Treasury with representatives of the Dominions and India. Keynes judged the meetings to be 'an outstand-ing success – really a model of what sensible, constructive international discussion should be'.[44] He could not help noticing, though, that the Buffer Stock Plan and Commercial Union were less acceptable to them than the Clearing Bank. In the light of these encounters and his meeting with White, Keynes produced a sixth draft of the Clearing Union on 9 November. This time quotas were scaled down, and there was a provision for an agreed reduction of their total in inflationary conditions. The Bank might require collateral on debit balances in excess of 50 per cent of quotas. The Governing Body could reduce or remit interest rate charges on excess balances. Exchange rate changes became more difficult, the maximum allowed being 5 per cent rather than 5 per cent a year; however there was to be a long (five-year) transitional period before this took effect. The process of adapting the Keynes Plan to American requirements without abandoning the crucial 'banking principle' was under way.

In Washington, the game of cat and mouse continued. Keynes's revised draft was handed to the Americans, and new answers prepared for questions they raised. Keynes grew suspicious that the Americans were stringing the British along: the Washington exchanges were 'very harm-less, almost too harmless'. On 16 December he suggested to Phillips sending a British party to Washington for a 'more or less formal confer-ence' with a corresponding American group, and not just for a 'private tea party at the State Department'. Alternatively, why not revive his earlier suggestion for an Anglo-American Commission to prepare ideas for both governments? 'We have to bear it constantly in mind that, in the long run, large economic projects cannot possibly come into existence except with the aid of an instructed and educated public opinion.'[45] Phillips replied on 9 January 1943 that neither of Keynes's ideas was acceptable to the State Department, which wanted to consult experts from many countries. All this, Keynes noted, 'is far from fragrant in my nostrils'. The Americans were running away from anything concrete, and proposed to exhaust British energies boxing with 'a man of straw' – the Harry White Plan, to which they were in no way committed.[46]

Although nothing seemed to be going on in Washington, White was busy redrafting the Stabilisation Fund Plan, partly in response to Keynes's criticisms voiced at their London meeting. On 1 February 1943, without any further discussion of the Clearing Union or consultation with the British, the State Department sent the eighth draft of the White proposals – now without the Reconstruction Bank – to the British, Russians and Chinese as a 'basis of discussion'. The United States proposed to invite thirty-seven experts of the United Nations to Washington individually and separately to discuss monetary co-operation on White's 'or any other lines they may wish to suggest'.[47] The British Embassy in Washington arranged for the Latin American ministers invited to Washington to receive copies of the Clearing Union proposal.

In the game of tit-for-tat, the British government now sent copies of the Keynes Plan to Russia and China and opened discussions in London with the finance ministers of its West European allies on 26 February 1943. The Americans sent a representative but refused the British suggestion that the Stabilisation Fund proposal should also be circulated so that the two schemes might be compared. They wanted discussion of the White Plan to be stage-managed in Washington, not London. Keynes presented the British scheme as having four connected parts: monetary union, stabilisation of primary product prices, commercial policy and an international investment authority. He explained his Plan's novel feature – the application of the banking principle to a closed global system. Domestic banking had evolved from the Middle Ages (always a vague period for Keynes), but banking between countries was still medieval – that is, gold reserves were 'dead', like earlier deposits of coins. Keynes attacked the principle behind the White Plan:

We have not adopted another possible feature of banking by which you have capital, subscribed capital, which you can lend out. . . . It is perplexing to some people at first that that should not be necessary. In the first days of banking great stress was laid on the possession of capital but we have learned as time goes on that that is of insignificant importance. You need the capital if you are not in a closed system and have to meet liabilities for credit outside your system, but in a closed system you can reach your conclusion simply by offsetting the deposits of some members against the overdrafts of others. . . . As there is no liability to pay outside the system it involves no risk and therefore requires no capital.[48]

Keynes argued that centralising all foreign exchange transactions through central banks, leaving only final clearing by the Clearing Bank, would 'get rid of the whole element of exchange speculation which caused so much trouble after the last war'. He explained that quotas (overdraft facilities) would vary with the amount of foreign trade, so that – unlike under the gold standard – 'you are not fixing the quantity of international [money] irrespective of the amount of work which the international money has to do in the shape of financing trade; the two are connected together'.

At a party in London Keynes begged the Russian ambassador Maisky to send Russian experts to London. Maisky 'as usual grinned and said that all would be much easier if a second front was going on'.[49] Unlike White, Keynes thought it was not essential that Russia became a member of the Clearing Union, though it would be disappointing if it stayed out. The European Allies gave general support to the Clearing Union, but rejected any suggestion that the British and Americans should take all the main decisions. Keynes thought this lessened the need for prior Anglo-American agreement. 'With the Europeans and Dominions in sympathy with us, our position would be much stronger in a general than in a bilateral discussion.'[50]

He had meanwhile undertaken a further study of White's Plan. On 18 February 1943 he produced a first set of notes, complaining about the obscurity of the technical details, and said the only innovations compared to pre-war practice were provisions for controlling capital movements and for liquidating blocked balances.[51] On 1 March, he circulated a comparison between his scheme and White's. The quotas under the Fund were much smaller than under the Clearing Union; means of disciplining a creditor country were sadly lacking; exchange rate rigidity was excessive. While praising the proposal to unblock abnormal wartime balances, he pointed out that it would require much larger quotas than the Stabilisation Fund provided for. Under the voting system proposed by the Americans, the United States would have a *liberum veto*, but no 'positive power', so the initial rules would be, in effect, frozen. The fundamental difference was the 'subscribed capital versus the banking principle'. In the Stabilisation Fund quotas defined a right to buy currencies, in the Clearing Bank they were a claim for overdrafts. In the American Plan there would be a foreign exchange market, in the British Plan all foreign exchange transactions would be channelled through central banks. The Stabilisation Fund penalised debtors, the Clearing Bank creditors. The Americans intended to share a small part of their existing reserves; the Clearing Union's aim was expansionist.[52]

Two clauses in White's redrafts caused the British much trouble. The accounts of the Fund and the value of the currency of each member were expressed in 'unitas'. White saw unitas as a receipt for gold deposits, not as a tradeable instrument. The Fund itself would buy and sell currencies so as to keep them in a fixed relationship with each other. Keynes saw that if 'unitas' could be made into international 'money' it would have the double advantage of being a bridge between the subscription principle of the Fund and the banking principle of the Clearing Union and of promoting multilateral clearing. In the early months of 1943 the 'monetis-ation' of unitas emerged as the main British requirement for accepting a 'Fund' framework for monetary co-operation.

White's draft dated 16 December 1942 also introduced a 'scarce currency' clause, by which the Fund was empowered to 'ration' a currency for which there was an excess demand. This was designed to guard against the expected scarcity of dollars.[53] In effect, member states, deprived of dollars, would be allowed to restrict their purchases of American goods. The scarce-currency provision can be seen as White's attempt to supply the missing discipline on creditors. Keynes wrote dismissively that it 'seems unworkable'.

This is not how it struck Roy Harrod. Reading the revised White draft and Keynes's notes on the train to Oxford late at night, Harrod felt an 'exhilaration such as only comes once or twice in a lifetime' when he came to the scarce-currency clause. The Americans, he enthused, 'were admitting the principle of joint responsibility for disequilibrium . . .'. He wrote to Keynes at 2 a.m. on the morning of 4 March: 'The Americans offer us . . . what we could never have asked of them in the negotiations . . . that we (and other countries) should be allowed to discriminate against American goods if dollars are running short.' No deflation or general protection in the debit countries would be required. Moreover the American proposal avoided the danger inherent in the Clearing Union Plan, that the debtors as a body would exceed their quotas. It provided a mechanism for 'automatically sorting out what . . . I called "excess" debit countries from the general run of debit countries. Britain's main object should be to hold the Americans to SF 7' (the scarce-currency clause). Protesting against the 'tone and nuance' of Keynes's notes, he wrote: 'We need not bother about the proposals seeming "unworkable"; something could no doubt be worked out.'[54]

Keynes replied the same day:

I agree that, read literally, the interpretation you give to [SF, ii, 7] is the only one which makes any sense. Perhaps I ought to have attached more importance to it. I interpreted it as a half-baked suggestion, not fully thought through, which was certain to be dropped as soon as its full consequences were appreciated. I cannot imagine that the State Department really would [accept it]. You must remember that the evidence as to the extent to which the State Department have actually accepted this document of Harry White's is somewhat flimsy.[55]

Harrod came back on 6 March:

I suggest that the line we ought to take is that we assumed the rationing of scarce currency to be indissolubly linked to the limited credit quota proposal. We can point out that the latter is quite unworkable without the safety valve of rationing. . . . Then if they are determined to wriggle out of rationing, they would be thrown back onto the unlimited credit of the Clearing Union.

Keynes concluded (8 March) that 'from the tactical point of view [there is] a lot to be said for what you put forward. . . . I am sending Phillips a copy of our correspondence'. To Phillips, Keynes confided, 'There are those (e. g. Roy Harrod) who argue that this is a splendid, comprehending gesture by the USA to throw the whole burden on the shoulder of the creditor. . . . I find it difficult to take up so buoyant an attitude. It seems to me that at the most Harry White has put a quick one across the State Department and that the real significance of this provision has escaped notice.'[56] Keynes's coolness to the scarce-currency clause was due to the fact that he was thinking along different lines with the 'monetisation' of unitas. Harrod continued to bombard him with wild memoranda. Having been an enthusiastic expansionist in the early days of the Clearing Union, he now worried about inflation and urged Britain and the USA to insist that Russia and China slow down their industrialisation before admitting them into the Clearing Union. Keynes wearily replied: 'It is not wise to start hares of this kind unless there is a reasonable possibility of running them down.'[57] He regarded Harrod's enthusiasm for the scarce-currency clause as another of his hares. This time Harrod had a better grasp of what the Americans would find acceptable.

As copies of the two Plans had now been circulated to so many other countries, official publication could hardly be delayed. The British government suggested to the US administration that both Plans be published to stop garbled accounts of them appearing in the press. Morgenthau urged that publication be delayed till experts from the two sides had met in Washington, to avoid the risk of the British and American Plans being put forward as rivals. In March the British decided to go ahead any way and issue the Clearing Union proposals as a White Paper whatever the Americans did. The administration's hand was forced when an accurate account of the White Plan was leaked by Paul Einzig in the *Financial Times*.

The two Plans were published by their respective governments on 7 April 1943. Deprived of joint Anglo-American discussions, Keynes took comfort from the extensive circulation of the American proposals. The real risk was always that the USA would 'run away from their own plan, let alone ours'.[58] This had now become much more difficult. The US Treasury Plan 'represents a big advance, and if it turns out that this is the sort of set-up which appeals to people, it will not be too difficult to make something of it. But it is a long time too soon even to breathe a suggestion of compromise.'[59]

The proposals of the two groups of experts were widely discussed in the newspapers of the two Allies, as well as in the German press. Naturally enough, 'press comment tended to take a stand on patriotic ground rather than on the intrinsic merit of each plan'.[60] However, there was an undertow of criticism in both countries against setting up global institutions at all. The British Embassy reported New York banking and financial opinion 'unanimous against the White Plan and expressed with much bitterness. This does not mean that they favour the British plan. . . . What moved them is intense resentment at the idea of Latin American, Asiatic and other debtors becoming by right members of Governing Boards and presuming to lay down financial policies which may decide the economic welfare of all. . . .'[61] The influential Republican Senator Taft accused White of wanting to pour money 'down a rat-hole'.[62] In a widely publicised address delivered to the Los Angeles Chamber of Commerce on 11 May, Benjamin Anderson, a conservative professor of economics at California University, declared that 'both plans set up a super-national Brains Trust which is to think for the world and plan for the world, and to tell the governments of the world what to do'. They were both British plans, the professor thought, in that they both reflected trends in Keynesian thinking and British monetary policy. They both attacked symptoms, not causes. Exchange instability was a symptom of monetary instability which went back to unsound fundamentals – loose fiscal and monetary policy. The Keynes–Morgenthau Plans would encourage rather than check these tendencies. The conditions for exchange rate stability were sound domestic policies, assured peace and reduction of tariffs. If these conditions were met, Europe would get the loans it needed from private investors.

In a letter to Thomas Lamont, Russell Leffingwell attacked the capital controls envisaged by the Plans: 'One naturally thinks of stable exchanges as desirable not as an end in themselves but as a means to a freer movement of goods and services. It is disappointing to find that these experts intend merely to peg the exchange by policing them and preventing remittances not approved by the policeman.'[63] What the New York bankers would have preferred was close monetary co-operation between Britain and the United States, based on an agreement on exchange rates and credit facilities to re-establish sterling as a leading currency. This was crystallised in the so-called 'key currency' plan put forward by John Williams, a professor of economics at Harvard and vice-president of the Federal Reserve Bank of New York. It seemed to Williams inescapable that 'in a world practically all of whose trading is done in one or another of these currencies [dollars and pounds], the central fact must be the establishment between them of exchange rate stability around which other national currencies can be grouped'.[64]

Both Plans received unexpectedly conscientious coverage in the German press, a sign that intellectual independence was allowed in matters which did not directly interest the Nazi hierarchy. Not surprisingly the Germans much preferred the Keynes Plan to the White Plan, seeing it as an extension of the Funk Plan. Indeed 'the Germans maintain that the Keynes plan reaffirms what they have practised for more than a decade, namely that national economic policy should have priority over external currency policy and that the "external" value of a currency should be subordinate to the stability of its "internal" value'. The 'real daring of Keynes lies in the fact that he conceives of a clearing system as an international institution. But this may also be its weakness,' observed the *Frankfurter Zeitung* of 4 July 1943, since the establishment of economic stability within a region or *Grossraum* was more practical than a worldwide Clearing Union.[65]

Over the Easter holidays Keynes drafted a list of questions about the White Plan which he sent over to Phillips. 'The great majority of the difficulties', he wrote to Phillips on 4 May 'arise from not making unitas an effective international unit in the sense that bancor is. If the Fund dealt only in terms of unitas, instead of dealing in dozens of different currencies, many of these difficulties would be resolved.'[66] To Dennis Robertson, Keynes complained about its lack of multilateralism:

> The fact that the adverse balance has to be calculated with each country separately and does not relate to a net adverse balance with the world as a whole makes it even more unworkable and absurd. The result is that, even a country which has a favourable balance with the world as a whole cannot use the Fund for the purpose of multilateral clearing with any individual country with which, taken separately, it is out of balance. . . . this is outrageous rubbish and does not deserve even half-hearted defence.[67]

On 19 April 1943 Keynes wrote to his mother: 'My health is surprising – I do not know what has come over me. I have not been so steadily well for many years. This week I put my liver through its paces, lunching out every day and dining out several times on the richest and most indigestible food – without the slightest results.' One of the lunches was with the Spanish ambassador, the Duke of Alba, 'an old acquaintance of mine . . .

whose elegance I always respect'. A private dinner in London on 15 April with the former Governor of New York, Herbert Lehman, who had just been made director general of UNRRA (the United Nations Relief and Reconstruction Agency), provided a useful chance of getting American reactions to the British proposals. 'A full exchange of mind', he wrote to Lehman, 'is worth a cycle of Cathay in terms of telegrams.'[68] He was still hoping for a 'huddle with Harry White in Ottawa' in advance of a general conference.

At last Keynes was ready to use the House of Lords as a platform for his views. In his maiden speech on 18 May 1943 he once more mobilised the arguments in favour of his Plan in a language which he hoped that the 'educated public' to which he had always appealed would understand. Multilateral clearing – 'in English', Keynes said, 'a universal currency valid for all trade transactions in all the world' – was especially important for Britain, since 'the best markets for our goods are often different from our best sources of supply'. But if it was to be restored there must be a new money proportional to the trade it must carry and every country must have a supply of it proportional to its needs. Under his Plan every country would be allotted an additional reserve of bancor as a 'once for all endowment'. This was intended not to enable a country to live regularly beyond its means, but 'solely as a reserve with which to meet temporary emergencies'. The problems of the past had not always been caused by improvident debtors but by misers, 'hoarding beyond the reasonable requirements of caution'. The British proposals avoided the rigidity of the gold standard. There would be absolute freedom of remittance for current transactions, but 'unless the aggregate of the new investments which individuals are free to make overseas is kept within the amount which our favourable trade balance is capable of looking after, we lose control over the domestic rate of interest'. There was no intention to make the United States 'the milch cow of the world in general and of this country in particular'. His Plan did not require the United States or any other country to put up a single dollar which it would prefer to employ another way. Foreshadowing his very last article, Keynes hinted that the American surplus was a product of low world employment and would disappear in due course. He emphasised the 'significant [theoretical] difference ... between a liquid bank deposit which can be withdrawn at any time and a subscription to an institution's permanent capital'. Yet in practice this difference was not great, since the security demanded by the Americans was only to a small extent gold, and largely 'an IOU engraved on superior notepaper', so that a 'synthesis of the two schemes should be possible'.[69]

In Keynes's exposition it emerged that the only freedom which any member of his Union would have to give up was the *freedom not to spend*. What could be more reasonable! Yet who was to say what level of hoarding was prudent?

Keynes received many compliments on his speech. 'Of course the standard [in the Lords] is so fearfully low', he wrote to his mother, 'that any human utterance provokes special attention.' He was not as busy as he had been, but had 'more than enough to keep me amused'. He had received forty to fifty letters suggesting a name for the new international coin, 'most of them hopeless'. On 5 June Keynes celebrated his sixtieth birthday in Cambridge – 'I have the worst of both worlds, too old to be compos mentis, and too young to be venerable.' Had he been a paid civil servant, he would have been compulsorily pensioned off.

APPENDIX

Harry Dexter White: Guilty and Naive

The outline of the story of White's involvement with the Soviets is now reasonably clear, though some details remain obscure. It was first told by Whittaker Chambers, an underground communist controlled by Soviet military intelligence who deserted from the underground in 1938. On 2 September 1939, he named White (together with Alger Hiss at the State Department and Lauchlin Currie at the White House) as a Soviet agent to Adolph Berle, Assistant Secretary of State, and Roosevelt's adviser on internal security, who drew up a four-page memorandum which he passed to the President (Haynes and Klehr, *Venona*, 90–1). Roosevelt was not interested, dismissing the whole idea of espionage rings within his administration as absurd. Berle's report was pigeonholed. Chambers was interviewed by the FBI in 1942, when J. Edgar Hoover, its director, also dismissed his story as 'history, hypothesis or deduction', and he was not seen again for three years (Andrew and Gordievsky, *KGB*, p. 227). As Chambers told it, White, who had long been in touch with communists, was recruited in 1935–6. He passed over Treasury papers and handwritten information sheets to Chambers, who passed them to his 'control', 'Colonel' Boris Bykov. Chambers had kept a copy of one such sheet, written in 1938, which confirmed his story. According to Chambers, White was 'of but not in the Communist Party' – that is, not subject to its orders. He undertook to hand information over to Chambers voluntarily to strengthen global anti-fascism, most effectively represented by the Soviet Union. By the end of the 1930s Soviet agents were already implanted in some key departments of the Roosevelt administration, but espionage operations in America were given low priority by the KGB, which was chiefly interested in Whitehall. The question of whether White knew what use was being made of the information he was giving to Chambers is the point at issue.

There is a gap between 1938 and 1941. Chambers's defection evidently broke up Soviet intelligence's Washington operation: White and other agents 'abruptly ceased supplying information'. The disintegration of the Washington network may well have had something to do with the Nazi–Soviet Pact, which turned some communists and most fellow travellers temporarily against the Soviet Union. Normal service seems to have been restored after Hitler's invasion of Russia in June 1941. This led to the arrival in Washington of a new courier, Elizabeth Bentley. Her lover and control, Jacob Golos, had put her in touch with a new underground cell of Party members and sympathisers organised by Nathan Gregory Silvermaster, an idealistic communist, who had taken a PhD in economics at Berkeley, and who was employed by the Farm Security Administration. According to Miss Bentley, the Silvermaster group included not just White but present or past employees of the Treasury's Division of Monetary Research, recruited by White, including Frank Coe, Harold Glasser, William Ullmann and Sonia Gold. She also mentioned Lauchlin Currie, who worked in the White House as President Roosevelt's personal assistant on economic affairs. The Russians were particularly interested in political intelligence, like negotiations between Britain and the United States and loans to foreign and Allied countries (Rees, *Harry Dexter White*, 198). Members of the Silvermaster network brought secret material to the basement of the Silvermasters' house, where it was microfilmed, collected by Bentley and brought back to Golos in New York for encrypted transmission to Moscow by Soviet diplomatic telegraph. Unlike Chambers, Bentley did not claim to know White, but found out about him from Silvermaster and from documents labelled 'from Harry'. White was certainly in a position to supply extensive, high-quality information, as he represented the Treasury on eighteen inter-departmental committees. Furthermore, Bentley testified that in 1944 White had been put in direct contact with a Soviet agent (Rees, *Harry Dexter White*, 202). In August 1945, Bentley, like Chambers disillusioned with communism, went to the FBI.

Chambers and Bentley had *independently* identified White to the FBI as a Soviet agent, so had Katherine Perlo, the estranged wife of Victor Perlo, another government official who ran an independent espionage cell. There was also the circumstantial fact that most of the Silvermaster group mentioned by Bentley had secured positions at the US Treasury. Yet no further significant corroboration of their stories was brought to light publicly, although Hoover claimed that information on White which the FBI sent to the White House in February 1946 'came from a total of thirty sources, the reliability of which had previously been established' (Rees, *Harry Dexter White*, 381). White was never prosecuted, because the sources needed to be protected. Instead, he was, as ex-President Harry Truman put it in 1953, 'separated from the Government service promptly' – first from the Treasury, then from the IMF, to which he had briefly moved as a US director. Chambers and Bentley went public with their allegations against White before the House of Representatives Committee on

Un-American Activities in the summer of 1948. White himself appeared before the Committee on 13 August 1948, denying all their charges. Three days later he was dead, of a fatal heart attack. There was still no proof.

The declassification of the Venona decryptions in 1995 changed the position. Venona was the code name for the effort, started by the US Signals Intelligence in 1943, to decode and decrypt the text of KGB messages to and from the United States between 1942 and 1945. The significant breakthroughs date from late 1946. The fascinating story of how the Soviet code was partially broken, as well as the decrypts themselves, can be read on the Internet and in *Venona: Decoding Soviet Espionage in America* by Haynes and Klehr, published in 1999. Basically they corroborated the evidence of Chambers and Bentley about White and the other members of the 'spy rings'. Further corroboration came from partially released KGB archives, published by Allen Weinstein and Alexander Vassiliev (1999). The Venona files show that White was regarded as one of the Soviet Union's most valuable 'assets'. There are fifteen deciphered KGB messages in 1944–5 in which White was mentioned either as the source of information given by Silvermaster or as personally informing KGB officers of administration negotiating positions, including that at the San Francisco conference in May 1945. Venona confirms Elizabeth Bentley's claim that the crucial break between supplying information via Silvermaster and directly to Soviet intelligence officers took place in the summer of 1944, that is, about the time of the Bretton Woods negotiations. Venona confirms White meeting with a Soviet operative 'Koltsov'; the KGB files show him meeting Vladimir Pravdin, head of the KGB's New York station (Weinstein and Vassiliev, *The Haunted Wood*, 169).

The Venona decrypts identify 'assets' only by their cover-names, which themselves changed. (White was variously Jurist, Lawyer and Richard.) How were they matched up with real people? Klehr writes:

The identification of the cryptonyms came about in several ways. A number of people were given cryptonyms in a message itself. For example, a cable might say that 'we have signed on Theodore Hall, henceforth Youngster'. Although at first glance that seems an extraordinary breach of security, the KGB was confident that since its cables were both encrypted and enciphered (there was both a codebook and the use of a one-time pad to further protect the coded message) they were secure. More commonly, however, the identification was made by the FBI which would take the information in the cables provided by the NSA [National Security Agency] and try to match it with information it already had in its files or by following investigative leads. When it was unsure about an identification, it would note at the bottom of the Venona message that

STORM was possible or probably x or y' . . . the FBI identified Jurist as White around June 1950. (Personal communication to author, 9 September 1998)

An example of KGB carelessness is given by Haynes and Klehr on pp. 36–7 of their book. 'In April 1951, a newly decrypted Venona message noted that in June 1944 Homer was travelling back and forth between New York and Washington to see his pregnant wife, who was living with her mother. That settled it. There was only one name on the list [of suspects] that fit: Donald Maclean.' Kim Philby, as British liaison officer, was able to alert both Maclean and Burgess, who made their escape to the Soviet Union before they could be arrested (pp. 54–5). Eleven of the fourteen people Bentley identified to the FBI as agents (including White, Coe and Currie) were matched by Venona (p. 130). Venona's proved success in penetrating Soviet espionage networks and 'neutralising' scores of individual agents on the basis of its decrypts gave massive credibility to the reliability of its identifications.

The evidence which most clearly implicates White in direct involvement in espionage comes from a deciphered cable from Koltsov (the cover-name of an unidentified NKVD officer) on 4–5 August 1944 (Haynes and Klehr, *Venona*, 142):

As regards the technique of further work with us Jurist said that his wife was ready for any sacrifice . . . [but] he would have to be very cautious. He asked whether he should [unrecovered code groups] his work with us. I replied that he should refrain. Jurist has no suitable apartment for a permanent meeting place. . . . He proposes infrequent conversations lasting up to half a[n] hour while driving in his automobile.

White's role in the underground network seems to have been to provide Soviet intelligence officers with information about administration policies (some originating with him), thus enabling a better calibration between the timing of Soviet demands and policy proposals being discussed within the US government. Perhaps the most striking instance of this is the co-ordination of Soviet requests for an American loan in 1944–5 with White's attempts to get approval for such a loan in Washington. White was keeping Moscow informed of the progress of his own loan initiative in Washington, of those members of the administration who favoured it and of the reasons for the delay. (See the Venona decrypts of 29 April, 4–5 August 1944.) On 1 January 1945, Morgenthau wrote to Roosevelt that during the past year 'I have discussed several times with [US Ambassador to Moscow] Harriman a plan which we in the Treasury have been formulating for comprehensive aid to Russia during her reconstruction period . . . that will have definite and long range benefits for the United States and for Russia.' If Roosevelt was interested, Morgenthau would be glad to discuss it with him (Rees, *Harry Dexter White*, 301). Two days later, Soviet Foreign Minister Molotov asked Harriman for $6bn repayable over thirty years at 2.5 per cent. On 10 January 1945, White, assisted by Harold Glasser (a Soviet agent in the US Treasury's Department for Monetary Research), wrote a 'Memorandum for the President' from Morgenthau suggesting a $10bn loan to enable Russia to buy construction goods in the USA repayable at 2 per cent over thirty-five years (Haynes and Klehr, *Venona*, 142). On 18 January 1945 the Soviet control reported the following conversation: 'According to Robert's [Nathan Silvermaster's] information KAPITALIST [probably Harriman] advised the BANK [State Department] that we had requested a loan of 6 billion dollars . . . at 2½ percent annually. In RICHARD'S [White's] words we could get a loan under more favorable conditions.' If the loan project fell through, it was not for want of trying on White's part.

So what view should we take? That White promoted Soviet interests is clear, though these were not necessarily hostile to American interests. But there is a difference between trying to influence policy, or even placing Soviet sympathisers in strategic governmental posts, and knowingly passing classified information to the Russians without permission. In a careful and dispassionate biography of White, David Rees (1973) inclined to the view that he was knowingly a Soviet agent, but that the case was unproven. His own view is closest to that attributed to Silvermaster, that White didn't want his right hand to know what his left hand was doing (p. 200). Bruce Craig's study, written after the Venona evidence had become available, concludes that White was knowingly engaged in espionage, particularly after 1944, and that he lied about his involvement in 1948, but denies that he was part of 'an orchestrated Soviet-directed program' to subvert American policy. Not only did no such programme exist, but White 'legitimately advanced American governmental objectives' (ch. 13).

American liberals associated with the New Deal were reluctant to accept the view that White was a Soviet agent. For example, John Morton Blum, Morgenthau's friend and biographer, writes:

I spent far too long years ago trying to ascertain whether or not White was either a member of the C. P. or a Soviet spy. I concluded that there was no sure answer, though on balance I suspect neither. He was, as you say Keynes knew, an intolerable human being. When in the United States in the 1950s it became fashionable to consider all Communists sons of bitches, it also became usual to dismiss all sons of bitches as Communists. That helps to account for White's reputation then. . . . Henry Morgenthau, Jr. respected and trusted White, and in some measure shared White's reflexive distrust of Great Britain. . . . But when I showed Morgenthau that White had failed to carry out his orders about the transfer to the Chiang Kai Shek [Chinese Nationalist] government of [$200] millions of dollars worth of gold, the Secretary wondered, as I did, whether there had been Soviet influence in that failure. On no other account did Morgenthau suspect White's loyalty. (Private communication to author, 7 September 1998. For the Chinese gold episode, see Haynes and Klehr, *Venona*, 142–3)

Similarly Arthur Schlesinger doubts whether White was:

under Soviet discipline. The reasoning behind the identification of the VENONA cryptonyms has never been explained. . . . Of course Soviet intelligence gave everyone cryptonyms, even Walter Lippmann. An NKVD or GRU cryptonym is no proof *per se* of espionage. On the other hand, my impression is that White was of the no-enemy-to-the-left school. I would imagine that he knew that Silvermaster et al. were party members, and that he was quite eager to provide information to the Russians, as he no doubt presumed others in the administration were providing information to the British. My guess is that he took a certain pride in collaboration with Soviet intelligence. (Private communication to author, 1 September 1998)

James Boughton, a historian working at the IMF, goes further in exonerating White:

All of [the Venona cables mentioning White] fall within the period when White was meeting regularly and openly with Soviet delegations dealing with the Bretton Woods or San Francisco meetings. None suggests that White passed documents. They do suggest that he was indiscreet. . . . One cable suggests that the author (a still-unidentified GRU agent) had an ongoing relationship as White's handler, but it is impossible to verify whether he really was or was merely puffing himself up for his superiors in Moscow. And that is it. I draw three conclusions. First, no evidence exists against White that would stand up in court. It is entirely circumstantial, second-hand, or uncorroborated. If one is innocent until proven guilty, then White is innocent. Second, White supported friendship and cooperation between the US and the USSR because he believed that this relationship would be the key to post-war peace and prosperity. . . . Third, although he had a solid intellectual basis for his sympathies with the Soviet Union . . . he was also no doubt influenced by his ethnic background and his abhorrence of Nazi Germany. As a result, his policy advice occasionally seems naive and excessive in retrospect. (Private communication to author, 16 September 1999)

There is evidently much explaining of White's motives to be done. However, there is also the question of fact. To deny that White ever preferred Soviet to American interests, or to assert that he was working for the good of the planet, does not dispose of the question of whether in fact he passed information to the Russians. The wealth of converging evidence from many different sources strongly suggests that he knowingly did so. He would have had to be incredibly unworldly not to know to what use Silvermaster and his friends were putting his information, even before he was in direct touch with Soviet intelligence officers himself. On the other hand, Roger Sandilands argues that the case against Lauchlin Currie is unproved (*History of Political Economy*, 32, no. 3, 2000).

In the light of the charges against White, already made public by 1948, and which had implicitly been accepted as valid by the US administration, treatment of White's role by historians of the IMF and previous biographers of Keynes has, to say the least, been inadequate. The allegation of Soviet affiliations was not mentioned by Roy Harrod, Keynes's first biographer (1951), nor by by Keith Horsefield, the IMF's official historian (1969), nor by Richard Gardner in his classic account, *Sterling–Dollar Diplomacy* (1969). There is no hint of it in Charles Hession's life of Keynes (1984), and an incurious factual mention (p. 830) in Don Moggridge (1992). Armand van Dormael's detailed account of the origins of Bretton Woods (1978) mentions the charges against White in a short epilogue (pp. 306–7) but draws no conclusion, either as to their accuracy or as to what they might imply for White's policies. Harold James's book on the IMF (1996) is the first to suggest, briefly, that White's active Soviet connections may have influenced his policy advice (p. 69). These sins of omission may be contrasted with those of commission. Gabriel Kolko's *The Politics of War* (1968), a product of anti-Vietnam War radicalism, portrays Morgenthau and White as 'anti-Russian' agents of US business interests (p. 324), intent on 'de-Bolshevising' the USSR and integrating it 'into the capitalist world economy on a basis . . . [of] neo-colonialism' (p. 338). White's loan projects may of course be seen in this light; they may even, had they come to fruition, have had this effect. But it requires a rather advanced skill in fitting evidence to suit one's thesis, unfortunately characteristic of Marxist historiography, to believe that this was White's intention.

How to explain the silence? There was obviously a desire, early on, not to damage either Keynes or the IMF by association; also a revulsion againt McCarthyism. It was also assumed that White's Soviet connections were irrelevant to understanding the White Plan. Insofar as its sources were explained by non-technical considerations, it was in terms of American nationalism or New Dealism for the world or of a universalism, legalism and economism said to be characteristic of American thought. These understandings are all valid, or partly so. What is curious, though, is the incuriosity of historians about the possibility that White's pro-Soviet stance led him to advocate policies designed to boost the international position of the Soviet Union at the expense of Britain and Western Europe. This provides an indispensable context for understanding White's Grand Design, of which the Stabilisation Fund was just one fragment.

What is surely untenable is the view that White was merely passing on useful information to an ally. It would have been unthinkable for Keynes, anxious as he was for Anglo-American collaboration, to have taken classified Treasury or Cabinet papers away for filming, or to have had clandestine meetings with American intelligence officers.

A combination of naivety, superficiality and supreme confidence in his own judgement – together with his background – explains the course of action White took. There is no question of treachery, in the accepted sense of betraying one's country's secrets to an enemy. But there can be no doubt that, in passing classified information to the Soviets, White knew that he was betraying his trust, even if he did not thereby think he was betraying his country.

CHAPTER EIGHT

Building a Better Britain

I

Keynes used to say, ironically, that he used the calm of war to reflect on the turmoil of the coming peace. From 1942 an increasing part of his activity looked to beyond the war's end. His Clearing Union Plan had placed him at the centre of the search for an Anglo-American agreement on the post-war economic order. But he was also involved, though more tangentially, in the preparations for a domestic 'New Jerusalem', based on the Beveridge Plan for 'cradle to grave' social security and a full employment policy. And early in 1942 he became chairman of the Council for the Encouragement of Music and the Arts (CEMA), a wartime innovation which pointed to permanent state patronage of the arts. Keynes was never a passionate social reformer. But even he was caught up in the swing to the left which took place between Dunkirk and the British victory at El Alamein in November 1942. He endorsed the demand of William Temple, Archbishop of York, for a Christianised post-war capitalism, inviting the Archbishop to the Tuesday Club, helping him with his book *Christianity and the Social Order*, and pointing out that most early economists were churchmen and 'along the line of origin at least, economics – more properly called political economy – is a side of ethics'.[1] Thus far had Keynes travelled since the assertive atheism of his youth.

On 20 May 1942, Keynes received an honorary doctorate of laws from Manchester University, his first honorary degree in Britain. Next day he received a letter from Winston Churchill saying he was recommending him to the King for a barony. Florence's heart 'overflow[ed]' in her birthday letter to her 'darling son', written on 4 June. Maynard was fifty-nine. His name duly appeared on 11 June in the King's Birthday Honours List. That evening he dined at the Other Club, where Churchill proposed a toast to him. Next day there were 'dozens and dozens of letters and telegrams' from the people whose lives had intertwined with his at all phases of his life from Eton onwards – 'a telegram from LL. G, so I suppose we must regard the latest quarrel as made up, a very nice letter from Baldwin, a big kiss in the foyer of the Savoy from Margot [Asquith] ...'. Keynes reminded Lloyd George of the difference from

1918. Then everyone wanted to return to the pleasures of pre-1914. 'No-one to-day feels like that about pre-1939. *Everyone's* glance this time is forward and not back. . . .' Bloomsbury was predictably scathing. 'O-ah!' said Lydia, 'we come to be mocked,' as the newly ennobled couple braved the scorn of Charleston. 'No doubt they were,' Frances Partridge wrote in her diary, 'for Charleston cherishes what seems to me a totally irrational prejudice against titles earned by merit.'[2]

More profound was the reaction from his old and now gloomy friend Foxy Falk. Voltaire, he felt, had mistaken himself for Turgot, the thinker for the statesman. 'I won't say farewell, but I can't think of you within the walls of the B. of E. and the H. of L.' The trouble was, Keynes wrote back, that he was getting too old to have any fresh ideas well in advance of the times. 'I have run as fast as I could and am now out of breath. If practical forces catch up, what can one do about it? Certainly no help to transfer into monkish rumination.' That was the point: for the first time Keynes was in a position to shape policy according to his ideas. The 'capture' would not be all one way, but that too did not displease him. His radicalism had been on a limited front, on which he felt he was victorious. Just as when he had been at Eton, he enjoyed the honours which attested recognition of worth. His mocking tone, like the later Lytton Strachey's, was now maintained from habit rather than conviction. To be an intellectual in England is not easy, so great is the mistrust of ideas. The mountain and Mahomet met halfway: if Keynes was now 'respectable', he was respectable on his own terms, not theirs, the most satisfying kind of acceptance.

Keynes plied his delighted parents with the ancestral and ceremonial detail they loved. There would be a meeting with the Garter King of Arms, Sir Gerald Wollaston, to choose his title. His first idea was to call himself Lord Keynes of Tilton, but 'I am going to try Lord Keynes of Keynes on the Garter King – Keynes being Cahagnes (spelt like that if he insists) in Normandy.' Perhaps Garter King objected, or Keynes thought further about it. Viscount Gage agreed that he could take his territorial designation from the hamlet which belonged to him, and Lord Keynes of Tilton it was. Although it would have been natural for him to become a cross-bencher, he wrote to Herbert Samuel, the Liberal Leader in the Lords, 'In truth, I am still a Liberal, and, if you will agree, I should like to indicate that by sitting on your benches.'

He was introduced on 8 July, with Lord Bradbury, permanent secretary of the Treasury when Keynes had first joined in 1915, and Lord Catto as his sponsors and was 'placed at the lower end of the Barons' Bench'. He evaded early requests to intervene in debates, on the ground that he would not speak on matters on which he had inside information without being able to use it. Life in the Lords would not be devoid of comic incidents, typical of that dotty assembly. Lord Keynes and Lord Keyes –

the distinguished admiral – tended to get each other's post. The admiral, 'who never thinks twice before he acts', proved to be an affable guest at a lunch to which Keynes had been invited. He concocted 'a very polite and plausible reply' to a furious letter from Sir George Pirie, president of the Royal Society of Arts, addressed to the chairman of the Council for the Encouragement of Music and the Arts. 'I was very much puzzled as to why Sir George Pirie wrote to me,' Lord Keyes explained to Lord Keynes.

Outside the kitchen at Tilton, on a raised bed, grew a small fig-tree. It had never produced any fruit. Edgar Weller remembered Keynes standing beside it and saying ruefully, 'Barren fig-tree, Baron Keynes.'

II

THE BEVERIDGE REPORT

During the lull in the Anglo-American negotiations, Keynes had the leisure to consider the Beveridge Plan for recasting Britain's social security system. His interest in it, both personally and as a Treasury man, centred on its affordability. This depended partly on what post-war national income and unemployment were expected to be. That in turn led on to the question of what role policy might play in maintaining high aggregate demand after the war – a matter on which Whitehall was far from decided. An Economic Section paper on post-war employment policy, from the fertile brain of James Meade, was coming under Treasury scrutiny at the same time as the 'affordability' of Beveridge's ambitious schemes was becoming an issue. On the one hand there was a natural Treasury reluctance to sanction expensive social services when Britain's post-war external position was likely to be so shaky. On the other side, the process of wartime radicalisation, impressively documented in Paul Addison's *The Road to 1945*, made some 'New Jerusalem' promises a political necessity. Keynes was drawn into these discussions as an intermediary between Beveridge, Meade and the Treasury. He had no influence on the structure of the Beveridge Report, published in December 1942, but a decisive influence on the scale of finance the Treasury were willing to make available to start off Beveridge's Plan.

William Beveridge was an implausible people's hero. A rigid, monumentally self-assured social scientist, he was always a one-man band who nevertheless craved vast responsibilities and was convinced that his talents were much under-appreciated by his political masters. His famous Report came about by the accident that no one in government could stand him. The Minister of Labour, Ernest Bevin, therefore shunted him aside to a project where it was thought he could do no harm. He was told to produce a plan for rationalising the social security system. Beveridge accepted his appointment, and departure from Bevin's Ministry, with tears in his eyes. However, he soon decided to interpret his social security brief far more ambitiously than Bevin had intended – indeed to lay down a new direction for social policy, with himself as the 'prophet pointing the way to the Promised Land'.[3] His first two papers were ready in December 1941 and January 1942. Faced with their messianic tone and contentious political and financial implications, the Chancellor of the Exchequer insisted that Beveridge alone should take responsibility for them, with the committee of civil servants of which he had been made chairman, and which included a Treasury watchdog, Edward Hales, reduced to 'advisers and assessors'. This left him free to publish a report under his own name. Beveridge and his main idea, 'National Insurance', have labelled the British social security system to this day.

Building on three basic assumptions, a National Health Service, universal family allowances and full employment (by which he meant roughly 8 per cent unemployment), Beveridge proposed a system of national insurance for all citizens against retirement, unemployment and disability, centrally administered, and financed by equal contributions from employers, employees and the state, with equal benefits set at a physical subsistence level. This would replace the patchwork quilt of voluntary and compulsory insurance and charity, which, badly sewn and full of holes, made up Britain's social security arrangements. In March 1942 Beveridge sent Keynes copies of his two memoranda asking for his help in dealing with the financial implications of his proposals. They left Keynes in a state of 'wild enthusiasm for your general scheme. I think it is a vast constructive reform of real importance and am relieved to find it is so financially possible'. That single remark sums up Keynes's attitude to the Beveridge Plan. His chief concern was to limit start-up costs for the Exchequer. Beyond expressing justifiable scepticism that medical costs would be held down by improvements in the population's health,[4] he barely touched on its long-term economic and social consequences, taking the view that the 'future could look after itself'. His first, and last, instinct was to postpone as much of the scheme as possible. Beyond that he was indifferent to the principle of universality; and thought Beveridge's pension proposals the 'least interesting and least essential part' of his Plan.[5] This last comment is unsurprising. Keynes was not interested in pensions, but in unemployment insurance and family allowances and how they fitted into his general scheme of business-cycle management. Beveridge and Keynes met for lunch on 23 March, on the first of what Beveridge's biographer José Harris calls many convivial occasions in the Athenaeum and Gargoyle Club, though conviviality is not a word automatically conjured up by Beveridge's buttoned-up presence. Perhaps their conversations ranged more widely than the affordable scales of benefits.

With the cost of Beveridge's proposals causing alarm bells to ring in the Treasury, Keynes assumed the role of Beveridge's Treasury defender.

It seems that at lunch on 1 July 1942, the two men concocted the plan of appointing a small committee to consider the finance of Beveridge's proposals. Keynes got Hopkins to agree, and a committee of three consisting of Keynes, Lionel Robbins and the government actuary, Sir George Epps, met Beveridge several times over the summer and autumn to discuss ways of reducing the start-up costs of his proposals. The Committee's (for which read Keynes's) proposal at this stage was to reduce these costs by limiting the insurable categories to the 'employee class', reducing the increase in benefit rates, and excluding the first child from child benefit. This would produce a 'bedrock' scheme, lowering the initial cost from the £700m. a year envisaged by Beveridge to £450m., which would be only moderately above the existing cost (£315m.) of social security. The full scheme would be brought in gradually if and when it could be afforded. Keynes was particularly anxious to limit the additional budgetary charge to under £100m. a year. This turned out to be his principal reason for supporting the 'fiction' of insurance. By means of this device he hoped to keep some of the additional benefit payments 'off budget', even though he conceded that the fixed weekly contribution was a 'poll tax on the employed and an employment tax on the employer – both very bad kinds of taxes . . .'[6].

The Committee met Beveridge three times in August 1942, with a final meeting, in October, going over Keynes's draft point by point. At the first meeting, on 10 August, they saved £100m., a good day's work in Keynes's view. Beveridge accepted Keynes's suggestion to limit family allowances to second and subsequent children, though Keynes himself backtracked from this, judging it to be 'politically unstable'.[7] Pensions caused the most trouble, as they have done ever since. The problem was that to move from the existing contributory scheme, which covered only a fraction of workers, to a universal scheme, which also paid more than double the existing rate of pension, would be intolerably expensive, even allowing for the increased contributions. Beveridge had proposed some messy transitional arrangements, under which different scales of pensions would be paid to different groups of retirees on different conditions, and which Keynes attacked for maximising expenditure while minimising satisfaction. Keynes suggested instead that everyone be paid the same pension from the start, but at a much lower rate, the full Beveridge subsistence pension being phased in gradually.[8] Beveridge accepted the phasing-in, but still insisted that, during the transition, pensions be proportioned to contributions. By 24 August, following a further meeting with the Committee, Keynes reported that Beveridge's proposals were no longer open to serious financial criticism, though he doubted that they were 'politically stable'. 'The major part of the economy', Keynes claimed, 'has been achieved by accepting pensions at the greatly reduced rate of 14s single

and 25s double in the initial year.' In his final report to Hopkins on 13
October, Keynes restated his belief that it would be better to limit reform
'in the first instance' to consolidation and standardisation of the existing
system, but commended the Beveridge Report, nonetheless, as a 'grand
document'.[9]

It was published on 1 December 1942. The previous month the Allies
had landed in Africa; in January 1943 the German Sixth Army surrendered at Stalingrad. The race for post-war votes was on, and in the next
few weeks the Conservatives lost it, with Churchill and the Chancellor, Sir
Kingsley Wood, lukewarm in their response to the People's William. The
public bought 650,000 copies of the Beveridge Report, and swallowed
with enthusiasm the doctrine of 'cradle to grave' security. The Treasury
continued to fear that the additional taxes called for by the Beveridge
Plan would inhibit post-war recovery. Keynes wanted to make his maiden
speech in the Lords on the Report. He proposed to say, 'But there is
nothing, my Lords, in what we are discussing today which need frighten a
mouse.' In view of his colleagues' apprehensions, however, he felt this was
not tactful and stayed silent.

Keynes's largely technical response to Beveridge may be contrasted
with the reactions, enthusiastic or splenetic, of his friends and associates.
In the enthusiastic camp fell the Economic Section, which argued that
the disincentives to work of expanded unemployment and sickness benefits would be more than balanced by the positive effects on productivity
of a 'better fed, better housed, better clothed and better educated
population'; it commended the built-in stabilising properties of an unemployment fund based on receipts and contributions, and suggested that
these be reinforced by variations in contributions based on a 'normal'
unemployment percentage of 5 per cent.[10] James Meade would champion
this proposal with such persistence that it eventually found its way into
the Employment Policy White Paper of 1944. Hubert Henderson, who
had taken over Keynes's earlier role of Cassandra, was predictably
scathing. He warned that universal benefits would be much more expensive than targeted ones, that redistribution on this scale would reduce
economic efficiency, and condemned the 'insidious' suggestion in the
Report that 'a good time can be had by all when the last shot is fired'.[11]
Into the splenetic category came Keynes's old friend Foxy Falk, who wrote
in *The Times* on 3 December 1942 that the Beveridge Report was the 'road
to the moral ruin of the Nation . . . not a symptom of the vitality of our
civilization but of its approaching end'. Bob Brand agreed: 'it is the
obsession of all reformers that distribution is the whole show. I feel there
is some sort of dead weight being placed on this country. Perhaps it is
due to the sins of the fathers.'[12] The battle lines on social policy were
being drawn up which have raged ever since. Keynes's incuriosity about

this battle is itself curious. The truth seems to be that he was not interested in social policy as such, and never attended to it. The sole question in his mind was whether the Exchequer could 'afford' Beveridge.

III

FISCAL PHILOSOPHY AND EMPLOYMENT POLICY

One thing leads to another. Beveridge had started all sorts of hares, which gave intellectual entrepreneurs like Keynes and James Meade some meaty trails to follow. He had assumed a post-war unemployment average of about 8 per cent (which he thought of as 'full employment') as the actuarial basis of his National Insurance Fund. How plausible was this? Could it be improved on? A closely related question was the size of the immediate post-war national income: the higher it was the more generous the start-up benefits could afford to be. These questions were thrashed out at the Inter-Departmental Committee on Post-War Internal Economic Problems, set up in October 1941, where they merged insensibly with the question of what steps could be taken to encourage growth and maintain high employment after the war. James Meade's paper 'Internal Measures for the Prevention of General Unemployment', dated 8 July 1941, reached this Committee in November, and it never quite lost its place as front runner in the development of post-war employment policy. Meade was a Keynesian, and his paper focused on contracyclical demand management, though it dealt briefly with the frictional and structural elements in total unemployment, and the measures to be taken to deal with them.[13] The Treasury response, 'The Post-War Relation between Purchasing Power and Consumer Goods', came before the Committee in May 1942. It was mainly written by Sir Hubert Henderson, and was therefore suitably pessimistic. Drawing analogies with the period 1919–24, Henderson did not see how 'internal' measures could prevent a decline in employment in the exporting industries; since these were the source of Britain's problems, he took a gloomy view of the level of long-run demand. Keynes wrote scathingly of a preliminary draft of this paper, 'the author [seems to be] scared to death lest there might be some date at which the figure of unemployment would fall below three million'.[14] Henderson's views on this and other matters, strongly influenced the Treasury's new joint second secretary, Sir Wilfrid Eady. Apart from this, the Treasury had administrative and confidence objections to public works and unbalanced budgets going back to the 1920s.

Meade wanted Keynes to produce a Keynes Plan on post-war employment policy to complement the Beveridge Plan on post-war social policy. But Keynes desisted: yet another Keynes Plan might be one too many.[15] This is a great pity, because there never was a comprehensive Keynes plan for maintaining full employment after the war. Keynes's contribution to the famous White Paper on Employment Policy, issued in May 1944, was mainly by way of encouragement, commentary and criticism, even though parts of it clearly reflected his theories. However, the Whitehall debates stimulated by the Beveridge and Meade proposals provided Keynes with opportunities for his usual scatter of interventions, starting in 1942 and running through to his membership of the National Debt Enquiry of 1945. These point to a more or less coherent employment philosophy which is very different from what, after the war, passed for Keynesianism. They also strikingly bring out the *political* meaning which Keynes gave key terms like 'full employment', 'public sector' and 'capital budgeting'. In all these cases technical terms were being used for politically slippery concepts.

A good starting point is to ask what Keynes meant by full employment. He certainly did not mean by this zero or near zero unemployment; on the other hand he did not accept the 10 per cent unemployment average of the inter-war years as the best that could be achieved. Like Henderson, and indeed Meade, he distinguished between structural unemployment and demand-deficient unemployment. However, unlike Henderson, he believed that demand-deficient unemployment could persist – the *General Theory* had been written to explain why this was so – and also that improved demand conditions might improve the supply structure of the economy by increasing labour mobility. This was the basis for his optimism. He believed that governments now had the knowledge, experience and will to prevent a recurrence of the conditions of the 1930s.

In the wartime Treasury, Keynes and Henderson resumed the debates on employment they had been having in the 1930s. Basically, Keynes attributed the 'abnormal' levels of inter-war unemployment to demand-deficiency, with structural-adjustment problems as secondary. Henderson took exactly the opposite view. Keynes also looked back to the unemployment situation before 1914, whereas Henderson concentrated on what had happened to Britain's export industries in the 1920s. From his more extended backward glance Keynes came up with 5 per cent as the 'normal' rate of British unemployment, which had been disturbed by the excessively deflationary policies adopted to restore the gold standard.[16]

It is tempting to see this 5 per cent norm as a crude precursor of the 'natural rate' hypothesis developed much later by Milton Friedman. And there is a similarity, in the sense that the pre-1914 'norm' had reference to a cyclically adjusted price level. Indeed, the concept of 'low full employment' developed by Keynes's disciple A. P. Lerner in 1951, which is that unemployment level at which the price level is stable, is more or less identical to Friedman's 'natural rate of unemployment'.[17] There is no evidence that Keynes ever thought it possible to push unemployment below this institutionally given 'norm'. The difference is that Friedman thought this was the level to which the economy 'naturally' gravitates, whereas there is no such assumption in Keynes. He viewed the higher average level of unemployment experienced by Britain in the inter-war period not as evidence that the 'natural rate of unemployment' had gone up, but as evidence that monetary policy had been too deflationary.

The background to the optimistic scenario was the war itself. By 1942, unemployment was down to under 100,000, or less than 1 per cent. Between 1941 and 1945, the official price index rose at about 2 per cent a year. But this was not of course a normal peacetime performance, nor did Keynes regard it as such. The problem of unemployment was solved, Soviet-style, by a mixture of abnormally high government spending and a battery of controls, including price controls and labour conscription, but also compulsory arbitration, rationing and subsidies – and by Lend-Lease and the accumulation of sterling balances taking care of the balance of payments.

It was natural, therefore, that when Keynes started thinking about post-war employment prospects, his mind should revert to this 5 per cent. On 28 May 1942 he circulated estimates of post-war national income which he had prepared with Richard Stone. This *assumed* a post-war unemployment total of between 800,000 and 900,000, or between 5 and 6 per cent of the workforce. Together with other assumptions, Keynes and Stone calculated a 'standard' post-war national income of £6.5bn, or about 15 per cent higher, in real terms, than pre-war. Keynes himself thought this a bit conservative; but it was nothing as bleak as Henderson, who, in his rejoinder to the Keynes–Stone exercise, assumed two million unemployed (12.5 per cent), which implied a correspondingly lower (£5.7bn) national income.[18] An 'agreed' figure of 7.5 per cent was eventually settled in 1943 as the actuarial basis for Beveridge, which Keynes throught too high, and Henderson too low. As it turned out, Henderson was right about national income, but wrong about unemployment.[19]

Keynes did not, of course, say that unemployment would be 5 per cent after the war because it had been 5 per cent before 1914. In a note of 3 June 1942 he explained that he and Stone had arrived at their percentage 'chiefly on the grounds that it seemed to us that this was about the highest the public would stand in post-war conditions without demanding something very drastic to be done about it, coupled with the fact that it did not seem to us impracticable to take drastic steps which would bring down the figure to this total'.[20]

Full employment for Keynes is thus a politically determined variable. It is an estimate of the maximum unemployment the community will stand and the minimum that can be achieved without imposing on it an unwanted cost. The idea that a free society in peacetime might not be willing to pay the cost – in terms of either liberty or inflation – of a very high level of full employment escaped the hubristic Keynesians of the

1960s, who insisted that 'demand management' needed to be buttressed with 'additional instruments', like wage and price controls. Would Keynes have agreed? There is nothing, in either his pre-war or wartime writings, which suggests he would ever have gone beyond the attempt at a voluntary agreement on wage restraint. In 1940 he had drawn his own line between a 'free' and a 'totalitarian' society (see p. 68 above) and there is no reason to suppose that he would not have stuck to it.

Keynes never subsequently changed his mind about how much full employment was feasible. When Beveridge's *Full Employment in a Free Society* appeared in December 1944, with a much lower unemployment assumption than in the Beveridge Report itself, Keynes wrote to Beveridge: 'No harm in aiming at 3 per cent unemployment, but I shall be surprised if we succeed.'[21] Three months later he 'thought Beveridge went too far in setting an inviolable object of 3 per cent for unemployment'.[22]

After the war Keynesians had a simple answer to the question of how governments might maintain full employment, however defined. They would use national income statistics to calculate the prospective balance between aggregate supply and demand, and use fiscal policy to close any gap. If prospective demand exceeded prospective supply, threatening inflation, the government should run a budget surplus; in the opposite case, where unemployment was the danger, it should run a deficit. In either case, the state's budget was the balancing factor. Money was to be kept cheap under all circumstances.

When one looks at what Keynes said, both before and during the war, this neat fiscal package starts to dissolve. Keynes turns out to be as strong a believer in balanced budgets as Gladstone was! How did this square with using fiscal policy to 'balance the economy' at full employment? The answer to the riddle is that Keynes regarded public *investment* as the balancing factor, and treated the state's investment programmes as 'off-budget'. This view of things rested on his own peculiar definitions of 'public' and 'private' and on accounting conventions which drew a sharp distinction between 'current' and 'capital' spending. They both derive from the 1920s, and, in particular, from his contributions to the Liberal Yellow Book of 1928.[23] Whether they make much sense is another matter; Meade never thought they did.

Keynes's 'state' was defined, not by legal prerogative but by what we might call 'degree of publicness'.[24] By the 'state', he meant not the government and its servants, but that group of institutions, whether privately or publicly owned, which pursue public interest aims rather than short-term profits. In 1924, he gave as examples the Bank of England – then privately owned – the ancient universities, the public utility companies, *The Times* newspaper. (It is many years since the last example could be considered remotely plausible.) He believed that the state, in this sense, was a growing force in economic life, or, as he put it, that the economy was 'socialising' itself. The agents in this process were the divorce of management from ownership and the growing concentration of industry: in 1926 he wrote of the 'trend of the Joint Stock Institutions, when they have reached a certain size, to approximate to the status of the public corporation rather than that of individualistic private enterprise'. By this he meant that 'the general stability and reputation of the institution are more considered by the management than the maximum of profit for the shareholder'.[25] In modern language, they aimed to maximise 'stakeholder' value. Keynes was impressed by the fact that an increasing share of national investment was being done by quasi-public, semi-socialised institutions. In 1927 he estimated that two-thirds of the capital of large-scale undertakings could not be classed as private any more.[26] He regarded this 'socialised' investment as imparting much-needed stability to the investment market.[27] His demand in the *General Theory* for a 'somewhat comprehensive socialisation of investment'[28] was a demand not for greater public ownership – which he always opposed – but for an extension of 'publicness', with the government as leader rather than owner. It was the steady investment policies of this 'public sector' which he relied on to steady the economy, with government action on the margin to accelerate or delay public investment projects. Keynes's oft-repeated view was that prevention was better than cure. Typical is his remark to Robbins in 1943 that 'much less effort is required to prevent the ball rolling than would be required to stop it rolling once it has started. . . . After the slump has fully developed, the relevant figures get dreadfully large.'[29]

   This view of the 'state' helps explain why he treated public investment as 'off-budget'. In a contribution to the Treasury's budget enquiry, which Hopkins had started in May 1942, Keynes wrote (20 July) that the 'ordinary' budget, that of the government proper, 'should be balanced at all times. It is the capital budget which should fluctuate with the demand for employment.'[30] In fact, like the Victorians, Keynes favoured running a regular surplus on the 'ordinary' budget, which would be used to reduce debt in normal times, or be transferred to the capital budget in a downturn and used to replace dead-weight debt by productive or semi-productive debt. 'Deficit finance', in this concept, would mean 'reducing the normal sinking fund to zero' rather than budgeting for an actual deficit[31] – much as Churchill had done in his budgets of the 1920s. Keynes confusingly used the term 'capital budget' in several different senses. It was not till 1945 that he sorted them out. He now claimed that the term stood for three distinct budgetary concepts: (a) 'capital expenditure for the economy as a whole'; (b) '*all* capital expenditure under *public* control, including local authorities and public boards'; and (c) capital items 'paid for out of, and received into, the Exchequer': all estimated for the coming year. He called these the Investment, Public Capital and the Exchequer

Capital budgets respectively. Keynes's belief that government could control the level of investment rested on his conviction that (b) and (c) came to two-thirds or more of (a).

Keynes criticised his Treasury colleagues for mixing up capital budgeting with 'deficit finance'. The technique he was suggesting, whereby the Public Capital budget would correct any projected imbalance between aggregate saving and investment, had nothing to do with 'deficit finance'. Capital budgeting was a method of maintaining equilibrium, deficit budgeting a way of curing disequilibrium.[32]

Keynes related this way of treating the budget accounts to his general thesis of creeping 'socialisation':

> We need to extend, rather than curtail [Keynes wrote to Hopkins on 20 July 1942], the theory and practice of extra-budgetary funds for state operated or state supported functions. Whether it is the transport system, the Electricity Board, War Damage or Social Security. The more socialised we become, the more important it is to associate as closely as possible the cost of particular services with the sources out of which they are provided. . . . This is the only way by which to preserve sound accounting, to measure efficiency, to maintain economy and to keep the public aware of what things cost.

For Hopkins's benefit, Keynes sketched out a reform of the tax system, with contributions to a self-supporting social security fund replacing income tax. (Frank Field put forward a version of this idea in the 1990s.) This strained the patience of even Sir Richard Hopkins. He tartly commented on 21 July 1942: 'I do not feel equal to settling between now and the 15th August Lord Keynes' suggestions for a complete remodelling of the system of direct taxation in this country. . . .'[33]

Bifurcating the budget in this way enabled Keynes to divide the economic role of the state into two parts. The 'ordinary' budget would be concerned with issues of efficiency and equity; the capital budget with demand management. Critics, including most of Keynes's Treasury colleagues, saw it as a deliberate attempt at obfuscation. The public accounts were to be window-dressed to disguise budgeting for a deficit. Keynes himself would have claimed exactly the opposite: his aim was to introduce clarity into a confused discussion. The current–capital account distinction was also well understood in private business. However, there was bound to be an element of fiction in applying it to the public accounts. In the private sector, capital spending is spending which produces a cash return sufficient to service debt interest and repayment charges. Most of Keynes's 'public capital' spending does not qualify, though he thought it 'would, at least partially, if not wholly, pay for itself'.[34] Cash transfers to the unemployed might be justified as maintaining the stock of human 'capital'.[35] But it was hard to argue that it was as 'productive' as, say, investment in new technology, or that borrowing for the unemployment fund would not increase the National Debt.

Keynes was always conscious that new ideas had be 'dressed up' in familiar clothes to make them politically acceptable, especially to the business community. He criticised Abba Lerner's concept of 'functional finance' – a starkly logical application of the *General Theory* concepts of aggregate supply and demand to financial policy, shorn of any embellishment – on exactly this ground. Functional finance 'runs directly contrary to men's natural instincts . . . about what is sensible'. Lerner 'seemed to be spoiling a splendid idea [Keynes's own!] by pretending it can be crudely put into force, and then refusing to look in the face of all practical difficulties'. He distinguished between theories and policies. 'Economists have to be very careful, I think, to distinguish between the two.'[36]

What turned out to be the decisive practical objection to Keynes's 'capital budgeting' was the notion that investment programmes could, or should, be manipulated to meet the needs of countercyclical policy. As Professor Wilson writes: 'Unfortunately Keynes was sometimes inclined to treat investment as though its purpose was simply to act as a conduit for the transmission of purchasing power into the economy.'[37] For these reasons, post-war Keynesian governments (especially after 1951) came to discard 'investment budgeting' in favour of efforts to influence aggregate consumption by varying taxes and hire-purchase conditions.[38] With the reaction against discretionary fiscal policy in the 1980s and 1990s, the current–capital account distinction has come back into fashion, though how useful it will prove to be is still open to doubt.

There is very little in Keynes's writings about a topic which was to become of central interest in the 1970s and 1980s, namely, the effect of taxes on incentives, and the share of national income which the state could safely take in taxes before disincentive efforts and/or tax resistance became acute. He fiercely opposed the 100 per cent Excess Profits Tax, and tried hard to get it reduced. More interesting is his agreement with his former student Colin Clark that '25 per cent taxation is about the limit of what is easily borne . . .', though he doubted that Clark's statistics (drawn from inter-war data) proved, or could prove, his point. He arranged for the publication of Clark's findings in the *Economic Journal*.[39]

Many of Keynes's most characteristic fiscal attitudes are evident in his correspondence with James Meade. This came in two bursts – the first in 1942 while the Beveridge Report was germinating, the second in 1943 after it had been published – both triggered by Keynes's responses to Meade's employment-maintaining proposals. The Economic Section's evidence to the Beveridge Enquiry included Meade's suggestion for contra-cyclical variations in national insurance contributions. When unemployment rose, contributions would be lowered, when it fell, they would be raised. After initial scepticism, Keynes was 'converted to the idea', though he stressed its limited role in offsetting fluctuations in investment demand.[40] A more substantial correspondence started in 1943. Soon after the Beveridge Report was published, the Ministerial Reconstruction Priorities Committee, chaired by Sir John Anderson, asked the Economic Section for a study of measures which might be taken to realise Beveridge's full employment assumption. The Section produced Meade's much revised paper, 'The Maintenance of Employment', which Keynes found so indigestible that he thought only 'Pompous John' would be able to read it attentively. Keynes now pressed on Meade his suggestion for dividing the budget into a current and capital account. Meade did not agree. Controls on domestic investment would not be prompt enough, or in some circumstances sufficient. So consumption stabilisers were needed: variations in social security contributions linked to an unemployment index which act as an 'instantaneous automatic stabiliser', and planned tax reductions, leading to unbalanced budgets, to prevent unemployment from developing.[41] In both proposals, but especially the second, there is a naive belief, which Meade never shed, that statistics would tell economists – and politicians – what they needed to do.

In his reply, Keynes restated his preference for using investment as a stabiliser, though he supported the case for 'automatic' variations in social security contributions. Against the tax variation scheme, he argued that, as people had established standards of living, a remission of taxation which they could rely on only for an 'indefinitely short period' might not stimulate their consumption by much – an early statement of Milton Friedman's permanent income hypothesis. Moreover, it would be extraordinarily difficult to reimpose the tax again when employment had improved. Varying national insurance contributions avoided this objection, 'partly because it could be associated with a formula', and partly because it would be pumping purchasing power into the hands of a class which did not save much. (Technically, the 'multiplier' effect would be larger.) However, he insisted that the insurance contribution variations be applied only to employee contributions not to those of employers or the state. The state's contribution, from its own budget, should be held constant; reductions in employers' contributions would not lead to increased employment if they were seen as merely temporary.[42] Keynes deprecated trying to superimpose on the scheme to vary insurance contributions proposals 'to reduce taxation on drink and tobacco with a view to making people drink and smoke more when they were tending to be out of work, or to dealing with income-tax, where there is a huge time lag and short-run changes [are] most inconvenient'. Next, the idea of borrowing for capital spending in a slump would be understood much better by the 'common man' than encouraging consumption. The latter was 'a much more violent version of deficit budgeting' than the former. The fact that capital spending was 'capable of paying for itself' was much better in budgetary terms, since it did not involve a progressive increase in the National Debt. Finally, it was better to expedite investment spending whenever it was 'deficient' until the economy was saturated with capital goods.[43]

What emerges from this range of comments is a distinct bias against fiscal fine-tuning. The emphasis should be placed on prevention, not cure; on maintaining a steady stream of investment, not offsetting fluctuations. If – and here Keynes reverts to his ideas of the 1920s – 'two-thirds or three-quarters of total investment is carried out or can be influenced by public or semi-public bodies, a long-term programme of a stable character should be capable of reducing the range of fluctuation to much narrower limits than formerly. . . . If this is successful it should not be too difficult to offset small fluctuations by expediting or retarding some items in this long-term programme.'[44] This is far removed from the method of anxious interference, based on small fluctuations in spuriously precise forecasts, which became the hallmark of British Keynesian management.

In a memorandum of 25 May 1943 entitled 'The Long-Term Problem of Full Employment' Keynes, unusually for him, set his fiscal philosophy in a developmental perspective. The stimulus for this production was another monumentally gloomy paper by Hubert Henderson, who foresaw large-scale unemployment developing in the transition from wartime to peacetime production.[45] Keynes envisaged three phases after the war. In Phase I, which he thought might last five years, investment demand would exceed full employment saving, leading to inflation in the absence of rationing and other controls. In this phase, the emphasis should be on restricting consumption in order to reconstruct the war-damaged economy. In Phase II, which he thought might last between five and ten years, he foresaw a rough equilibrium between full employment saving and investment 'in conditions of freedom', with the state active in varying the pace of investment projects. In Phase III investment demand would be so saturated that it could not match full employment saving without the state having to embark on wasteful and unnecessary programmes. In this phase the aim of policy should be to encourage consumption and discourage saving, and so absorb some of the unwanted surplus by increasing leisure, with shorter hours and more frequent holidays. This would mark the entrance to the 'golden age', the age of capital saturation. Eventually, Keynes thought, 'depreciation funds should be almost sufficient to provide all the gross investment that is required'.[46] It is the age, foreshadowed in the *General Theory*, of the 'euthanasia of the rentier', since there will be no demand for new capital.

This is the Keynes of the 'Economic Possibilities for our Grandchildren', that remarkable, but misguided, essay in prophecy, published in 1930, which claimed that at root the economic problem was due to a *fear of consumption*. To achieve 'capital saturation' as quickly as possible, so that mankind could confront its permanent problem – 'how to live wisely and agreeably and well' – was the overriding aim of his economic statesmanship. Once societies were over the 'hump' of scarcity, all the economic 'dentistry' in which Keynes was so heavily involved could become redundant, and the heaven opened up by G. E. Moore's *Principia Ethica*, the bible of his youth, would be established on earth.[47] Little though Keynes dwelt on ultimate questions, it is characteristic of the man that he should have reverted to this optimistic vision of plenty during the most stringent period of scarcity. On 5 April 1945 he wrote to T. S. Eliot that the 'full employment policy by means of investment' was 'only one particular application of an intellectual theorem. You can produce the result just as well by consuming more or working less.'[48]

In July 1943, discussion of post-war employment policy moved into a higher gear. On the Reconstruction Priorities Committee, Kingsley Wood wanted to postpone discussion; the Labour members, Dalton and Morrison, wanted a government commitment on the lines sketched out by Meade. Sir John Anderson, Lord President of the Council, set up an inter-departmental Steering Committee on Post-War Employment to draft a report. Its terms of reference – to study means of controlling aggregate demand – leant in Meade's direction; its heavy Treasury membership, with Hopkins in the chair, flanked by Eady and Gilbert, and with Lionel Robbins, caught between supporting his Section's collective view and his own more conservative instincts, pointed the other way.[49] The Steering Committee's Report became the Employment White Paper, published on 26 May 1944. Not being on the Steering Committee himself, Keynes was not importantly involved in its preparation. Nor did he have time for continuous scrutiny of its work. When the Committee started business in September 1943, he was in the United States. Early in 1944 his time was taken up fighting for his currency plan in Whitehall; in March he fell ill. Hopkins, too, had a heart attack at a critical stage in the drafting. The absence of Keynes and Henderson had an anaesthetising effect on the White Paper's prose. It also made its compromise position possible.

Keynes shared some of the Treasury's objections to Meade's approach. As we have seen, he disliked Meade's emphasis on fine-tuning consumption and thought that the Economic Section underestimated structural problems. But he was even more worried by Eady's ignorance of even 'undergraduate' economics,[50] dismissed one of his papers as 'not much more than Neville Chamberlain disguised in a little modern dress',[51] and tried to reduce the influence of Henderson's destructive memoranda. Caught between two fires, Hopkins steered a middle course by dividing the unemployment problem into 'demand-deficient' and 'structural', the second being more important in the transitional period. He set out to ensure that the Steering Committee's Report contained the 'essential qualifications to the aggregate demand theory'.[52] 'It is important to maintain demand,' he wrote. 'But it is also important that the obstacles to mobility should be few.'[53] In the autumn, the Steering Committee pressed ahead with a draft in order to 'scoop' Beveridge, who, advised – or instructed – by Nicholas Kaldor, was writing his own report on employment policy.[54]

The Steering Committee's report, dated 11 January 1944, nodded skilfully in all directions. It endorsed the demand-management approach but did not sanction budget deficits and also emphasised the need for 'supply side' policies to secure a balanced distribution of labour. A full employment target, it believed, would become a 'political football'. It took account of external factors. Back from the United States, Keynes commended it, on 14 February 1944, as an 'outstanding State paper', representing a 'revolution in official opinion'. Economic analysis, he declared, 'has now reached the point where it is fit to be applied'. Unusually for him, he succumbed to an attack of arithmetical euphoria, proclaiming the dawn of an era of 'Joy through Statistics' when everything 'will all be obvious, and as clear as daylight with no room for argument'.[55] He had two criticisms. The first was the Report's gingerly approach to fiscal policy. It ignored his proposals for a capital budget. By neglecting to consider the 'multiplier' effects of injecting additional demand into the system, it was led to treat budget deficits as the price to be paid for maintaining employment, whereas 'measures to stabilise the national income are *ipso facto* measures to stabilise the national budget'. 'Is it supposed', he demanded, 'that slumps increase the national wealth?' Scornfully, yet wittily, he relived his pre-war battles with Sir Richard Hopkins:

> How slow dies the inbred fallacy that it is an act of financial imprudence to put men to work! If the Minister of Labour were found praising periods of cyclical unemployment on the ground that they gave the workers a much-needed rest and improved the nation's proficiency in the matter of darts, it should be for the Chancellor of the Exchequer to protest against such idling and to demand the present proposals for providing employment on the ground that they were essential to the solvency and stability of the Budget. This section has the air of having been written some years before the rest of the report.[56]

Secondly, there was the Report's hesitant approach to structural problems. Keynes regarded them as secondary – he was convinced that Britain had caught up substantially with American productivity levels during the war, by limiting restrictive practices and imitating mass-production methods[57] – but he was never mealy-mouthed about urging that they be vigorously tackled, accusing the Treasury of defeatism.[58] In his February 1944 comment, he strongly agreed with Lionel Robbins's 'Note of Dissent' on restrictive practices. Robbins had implied that policies of demand expansion would fail without sufficient labour mobility and wage restraint – a view also held by Meade. Keynes wrote:

> I feel confident that he speaks here – and most effectively, if I may say so – for the great majority of responsible economists in the whole of the Anglo-Saxon world. For those who believe that it will be the role of this country to develop a middle way of economic life which will preserve the liberty, the initiative and (what we are so rich in) the idiosyncrasy of the individual in a framework serving the public good and seeking equality of contentment amongst all, Professor Robbins' admonitions go to the heart of things. The Committee attempt no serious rebuttal of his arguments. The Report would be much enriched and its balanced effect on public opinion enhanced, if Ministers were to approve the substitution of his Note for the parched and desiccated passages of the Report which correspond to it.[59]

The final skirmishes came in March 1944. Enraged by Keynes's endorsement of the Steering Committee's Report, Henderson attacked it with a volley of papers, mocking Keynes's views and calling the Report 'a disgrace'. Any rise in unemployment, he insisted, would be associated with an adverse balance of payments. The policy of increasing domestic demand would worsen the balance of payments by leading to an increase in imports and a rise in costs. A depreciation of sterling would not correct the external deficit, because it would lead straight to compensating wage demands. The main effects of the Keynes–Meade policy of 'internal spending' would be a collapsing exchange, a flight from sterling and rising inflation. He was particularly scathing about Meade's 'automatic' variations in social security payments based on the movement of an unemployment index. This ignored the fact that there were many different types of unemployment (which Henderson spent much time classifying), which had different causes and required different remedies. 'The whole "automatic" approach', he wrote, 'is based on a laisser-faire-inspired distrust of governments. . . . not that I trust governments much more, but . . . I trust indices much less.'[60]

Keynes attempted a last rebuttal. Starting from the same premise ('I share his pessimistic view about our prospective external financial position'), he drew four opposite conclusions. First, since exporting 'is going to be a matter of life and death to us', the primary impulse to unemployment 'will not, and simply cannot be allowed to, come from that source'. (Eady's pertinent comment was that a categorical imperative would not itself increase exports.) Secondly, he agreed that import restrictions might be unavoidable, but this would increase the value of the 'multiplier'. Thirdly:

the view, to which he [Henderson] obviously attaches a good deal of importance, that it will be good for our external credit if we allow large-scale unemployment to develop . . . seems to me to be a plain delusion. There may have been a time when that sort of policy attracted the approval of foreign financiers. . . . But the world changes. It will improve our external credit if we are seen tackling the problem of internal unemployment vigorously. . . .

Finally, Henderson was oblivious to 'the social and political consequences of deliberately using domestic unemployment as a remedy for external disequilibrium', a policy which 'might easily mean the downfall of our present system of democratic government'. So 'we must discover some other way out'.[61]

The White Paper on Employment Policy (Cmd 6257) was published on 26 May 1944. Hopkins's final rewriting owed more to Henderson and Eady than to Keynes. There was nothing 'Keynesian' in the first three chapters, which dealt with the need to maintain export efficiency, transitional problems, and a 'balanced distribution of industry and labour'. How to deal with 'general unemployment', which it was emphasised would not arise for some time after the end of the war, was the subject of Chapter IV. Three co-equal conditions for success were stated: 'total expenditure on goods and services must be prevented from falling to a level where general unemployment occurs', 'the level of prices and wages must be kept reasonably stable', and 'there must be sufficient mobility of workers between occupations and localities'. The government's employment intentions would be 'frustrated' and 'fruitless' unless the second and third conditions held. In addition, the White Paper stated – three times – that those elements in general expenditure most likely to fluctuate – private investment and exports – were 'the most difficult to control', and also that 'an increase in one part of total expenditure can only within limits offset a decrease in another'.

Chapter V on 'Methods' promised that the government would '*supplement*' (italics added) a policy of varying interest rates to influence investment by accelerating or decelerating local authority and public utility investment programmes, though there were practical and political limits to how far this policy could be carried. If, despite these efforts, 'there are still swings in capital expenditure', the White Paper favoured, 'when settled conditions return', the 'automatic' method of varying national insurance contributions according to the movement of the unemployment index. However, no plan to legislate this was promised. Even more tentatively the White Paper thought it 'a matter of consideration' whether small variations in tax rates would be useful. In this mood of hopeful exploration it wondered whether tax increases in good times might take the form of 'deferred credits' to be returned to consumers in bad times. The government might also vary its orders for boots, clothes and furniture according to the general state of trade; but the White Paper rejected Hubert Henderson's suggestion for stockpiling such items. None of these suggestions, however, 'involves deliberate planning for a deficit in the National Budget in years of sub-normal trade'. At this point, the White Paper more or less endorsed Keynes's own proposals for capital budgeting, without using the phrase. In carefully balanced passages, it warned against increasing the National Debt, but saw merit in replacing dead-weight debt by 'productive or semi-productive debt'; it contemplated that this might sometimes unbalance the annual budget, but upheld the principle of balancing the budget 'over a longer period', and of holding the debt–GDP ratio constant; it insisted that 'any undue growth of national indebtedness will have quick results on confidence', but also that 'no less serious would be a budgetary deficit arising from a fall of revenue due to depressed industrial and commercial conditions'.

Moving on to easier ground, Chapter VI proposed a 'central staff' to analyse economic trends and submit appreciations based on 'exact quantitative information about current economic movements' – Keynes's 'Joy through Statistics'. By these methods governments would have a better chance of 'maintaining a high and stable level of employment without sacrificing the essential liberties of the subject'. Contrary to much myth, there was not even a commitment to full employment. The Foreword's famous opening sentence read: 'The Government accept as one of their primary aims and responsibilities the maintenance of a high and stable level of employment after the war.'

Keynes gave the White Paper a qualified benediction. In some notes he prepared for the Chancellor, he predictably criticised the section on monetary policy, but commended its budgetary philosophy:

As I have argued before now, the whole effect of stabilising employment will be on the receipt side to maintain the buoyancy of the revenue. Measures to increase investment and to maintain incomes will of course help the Budget on the receipt side. On the other hand it is the nature of our national accounting that practically nothing of the expenditure contemplated will fall on the normal Exchequer Budget. Neither modifications of the Social Security contributions, nor increased capital expenditure by Local Authorities and public bodies, nor inducements to Local Authorities, which will be spread over a period of years, will cost the Exchequer, narrowly interpreted in the budgetary sense, anything whatever. A forward employment policy is therefore entirely compatible with budgetary equilibrium; and not only so, but it is in fact the best way of ensuring budgetary equilibrium. Thus the criticism boils down to a complaint that proposals for taking off taxes in bad times have been rejected. These have been rejected for pretty good and obvious reasons.

He wrote to Austin Robinson that he thought it 'better to have got something, even if it is wrong in detail, because I believe the Civil Service has infinite power of making things work once it is clear that it intends to work it. My own feeling is that the first sentence is more valuable than the whole of the rest.'[62]

Keynes knew that there were loose ends. On 5 June 1945 he wrote to an Australian correspondent, S. G. McFarlane: 'I expect that both of our countries incline to under-estimate the difficulty of stabilising incomes where exports play so large a part. One is also, simply because one knows no solution, inclined to turn a blind eye to the wages problem in a full employment economy.'[63] How far would he have been willing to go to maintain full employment?

This question is of particular interest in light of his comments on Hayek's *Road to Serfdom*, that seminal anti-planning polemic, which was published almost simultaneously with the White Paper on Employment Policy, and which Keynes read on his sea voyage to Bretton Woods in June. Hayek's was a classic 'thin end of the wedge' argument, with Keynes at the thin end of an interventionist wedge which, if not checked, would lead to totalitarianism. Hayek rejected the political stability of any 'Middle Way' between *laissez-faire* and coercive central planning. In a passage which might have been aimed directly at the 'Keynesian' parts of the White Paper he wrote:

> Many economists hope indeed that the ultimate remedy [for general fluctuations in economic activity and recurrent waves of large-scale unemployment] may be found in the field of monetary policy, which would involve nothing incompatible even with nineteenth century liberalism. Others, it is true, believe that real success can be expected only from the skilful timing of public works undertaken on a very large scale. This might lead to much more serious restrictions on the competitive sphere, and in experimenting in this direction we shall have carefully to watch our step if we are to avoid making all economic activity progressively more dependent on the direction and volume of government expenditure.[64]

Those who already saw themselves in the Keynesian camp gave Hayek's book a very bad reception.[65] Keynes's response is unexpected. Hayek's was a 'grand book', he wrote, and 'we all have the greatest reason to be grateful to you for saying so well what needs so much to be said. . . . Morally and philosophically I find myself in agreement with virtually the whole of it; and not only in agreement, but in a deeply moved agreement.'

But – here is the weakness of the book and Keynes was on to it like a flash –

> You admit ... that it is a question of knowing where to draw the line. You agree that the line has to be drawn somewhere, and that the logical extreme is not possible. But you give us no guidance whatever as to where to draw it. It is true that you and I would probably draw it in different places. I should guess that according to my ideas you greatly under-estimate the practicability of the middle course. But as soon as you admit that the extreme is not possible ... you are, on your own argument, done for, since you are trying to persuade us that so soon as one moves an inch in the planned direction you are necessarily launched on the slippery path which will lead you in due course over the precipice.

Sure of his intellectual ground Keynes continued:

> I should therefore conclude your theme rather differently. I should say that what we want is not no planning, or even less planning, I should say that we almost certainly want more. But the planning should take place in a community in which, as many people as possible, both leaders and followers, share your own moral position. Moderate planning will be safe if those carrying it out are rightly orientated in their own minds and hearts to your own moral position. ...
>
> What we need therefore ... is not a change in our economic programmes, which would only lead in practice to disillusion with the results of your philosophy; but perhaps even ... an enlargement of them. ... I accuse you of perhaps confusing a little bit the moral and the material issues. Dangerous acts can be done safely in a community which thinks and feels rightly which would be the way to hell if they were executed by those who think and feel wrongly.[66]

On the first point, it is game, set and match to Keynes. Hayek never could draw the line between freedom and planning satisfactorily and had to rely on his own intuition and sympathies in judging where it should be drawn, as Keynes did. His distinction between general abstract laws and laws designed to benefit particular groups does not quite do the work he wants it to. Later in his life he tried to place constitutional obstacles in the way of majorities coercing minorities. Nor was Keynes much more successful in 'drawing the line'. In 1940 he had averred that prices were 'the indispensable elements of freedom' in an economic system. But an economy in which most investment is 'socialised', the capital market controlled and imports channelled through state trading agreements is free only in a somewhat peculiar sense.

The practical conclusions Keynes drew from Hayek's failure to draw the line are far from conclusive. His dictum that 'dangerous acts can be safely done in a community which thinks and feels rightly' is obviously correct. It was *safer* to have a Churchill running the war than a Hitler, even though the wartime organisation of the two countries was totalitarian. And one can multiply examples: it is safer that immigration laws be passed by liberals than by racists, that regulations be imposed by people who hate them than by people who love them. But this is a static argument. What the dictum ignores is Hayek's claim that the stock of 'right feeling' can be depleted by continuous governmental intervention: it is not, so to speak, independent of the acts being done. A society in which 'dangerous acts' by governments become continuous will lose its understanding of why they are dangerous – that is, its sense of what it is to be free. A good example is the way the extension of the social security system has eroded personal responsibility and charitable giving. It then becomes a matter of judgement as to which set of economic and social practices is most likely to preserve the moral values which Hayek and Keynes shared.

Much can be said on both sides, and Keynes was right to point out that policies which took no precautions against slumps were likely to produce 'disillusion' or, worse, hellish revolts against liberal values. On the other hand, no one who lived through the 1970s can fail to see a great pathos in Keynes's so English response to Hayek's warning – 'Don't worry, things will be perfectly all right here in England, because we're English and not crazy like the Continentals.' On this matter, at least, Keynes and Hayek fought each other to an honourable draw. The game is not over.

IV

MODEST PREPARATIONS FOR THE GOOD LIFE

On 1 April 1942, Keynes became chairman of the Council for the Encouragement of Music and the Arts (CEMA). He had been talked into taking it on by R. A. Butler, President of the Board of Education; his name may well have been suggested by his old friend Samuel Courtauld, Butler's father-in-law. Butler gilded his offer by suggesting that CEMA might evolve into 'something that might occupy a more permanent place in our social organisation'.[67] It had been set up in January 1940 on an initiative from Earl De La Warr, then President of the Board of Education, to help musicians, actors and artists whom air-raid precautions and bombing were likely to render unemployed, and to bring the 'solace' of music and the arts to the bored, bombed out, and evacuated. (According to David Webster it was formed 'very largely to meet the need for entertainment in air-raid shelters in London'.) The Pilgrim Trust put in £25,000 in the first year and provided the chairman Lord Macmillan and vice-chairman Thomas Jones; the Board of Education supplied matching funds, an office, and Mary Glasgow, the Council's secretary; there was an *ad hoc* committee.* By the time Keynes took over, CEMA was already 'an established national institution'; from its office at 9 Belgrave Square, London, it had organised 8000 concerts, mainly in factories, 600,000 had visited its 'Art for the People' exhibitions, 1.5m. had been to CEMA-sponsored plays. Tyrone Guthrie's productions of *King John* and *The Cherry Orchard* had been on long provincial tours, Sybil Thorndike and Lewis Casson had taken Shakespeare, Euripides and Shaw from the bombed-out Old Vic to County Durham and the Welsh mining villages.[68] CEMA had helped artists by securing their exemption from military service. At the end of 1941, the Pilgrim Trust had bowed out and CEMA was entirely Treasury financed. By 1946, CEMA had become the Arts Council of Great Britain. But before its charter could be incorporated, on 10 July 1946, Keynes, its chairman-designate, had died, with Sir Ernest Pooley taking his place.

Before he accepted his new job, Keynes warned Butler (on 24 December 1941) that he had been in 'only limited sympathy with the principles on which it [CEMA] has been carried on hitherto'. There was a wealth of meaning in this warning. CEMA had brought to its new tasks the tradition of the Pilgrim Trust's pre-war adult education work among the unemployed – what Thomas Jones, Lloyd George's old *éminence grise*, really loved best was amateur choral singing – and also a policy of directly financing drama tours itself. Both were anathema to Keynes, the first on artistic grounds, the second on financial grounds. In the summer of 1940 he had summoned Mary Glasgow to Gordon Square. 'He wanted to know why the Council was wasting so much money on amateur effort. . . . It was standards that mattered, and the preservation of serious professional enterprise, not obscure concerts in village halls.'[69] This debate about arts policy has gone on ever since.

Arts policy in Keynes's time at CEMA was closely bound up with his own personal philosophy. He brought to his new job a worshipful attitude to the arts, decided views on how they should be financed, and a strong but limited range of sympathies. The homage went back a long way: philosophically to G. E. Moore's *Principia Ethica*, which he had imbibed as an undergraduate, personally through his friendship with the painter Duncan Grant and membership of the Bloomsbury group.

Keynes, Clive Bell noted, was one of that class of benefactors 'who have devoted great powers of organisation to good purposes'. He had a

---

* The Pilgrim Trust was a body set up in 1930 to use a £2m. legacy from Stephen Harkness, a railway magnate of British descent living in America, for the purpose of sustaining and preserving 'culture' in Britain. Almost certainly it was Thomas Jones, secretary of the Pilgrim Trust, who put the idea of CEMA in De La Warr's head.

complex attitude to patronage. Between the wars he himself dispensed and organised largesse for the arts, not just by buying pictures himself, but by organising the London Artists' Association and by building the Arts Theatre in Cambridge. But he never believed in an open-ended purse. It was impossible, he thought, to go on getting support for something which presented itself as a 'bottomless sink' for originally enthusiastic backers. The purpose of patronage was to enable non-profit-making activities to take place – by way of capital endowment or loan, or guarantee against loss, not to provide permanent subsidies for loss-making enterprise. He wanted the London Artists' Association to be 'as nearly self-supporting as possible', and was pleased when the Cambridge Arts Theatre started to break even on its running costs.* He once said that if a subsidising body were 100 per cent successful it would end up by spending nothing except on its own administration. 'It would choose so well and back such uniformly certain winners that all its loans would be repaid in full and none of its guarantees ever called.'[70]

He was always intensely interested in the economics of the arts, including the material conditions for the production of great artists. He once remarked to Roger Fry that England could not have produced a Shakespeare a century earlier: Shakespearean drama was the joint out-come of genius and compound interest. His ideal was a mix of private and public patronage. 'The ancient world knew', he wrote in 1936, 'that the public needed circuses as well as bread. And, policy apart, its rulers for their own glory and satisfaction expended an important proportion of the national wealth on ceremony, works of art and magnificent buildings' – a tradition which continued into the eighteenth century. But then, Keynes continued, had come the penny-pinching Treasuries of the nine-teenth century, which regarded it 'as positively wicked for the state to spend a halfpenny on non-economic purposes', except, of course, for war.[71] Keynes's belief that the state should now resume its old tradition of spending money on the arts fitted his anti-depression policies. 'For with what we have spent on the dole in England since the war we could have made our cities the greatest works of man in the world,' he proclaimed in 1933.[72] The same thought would recur to him as the Luftwaffe dropped its bombs. He was always clear that state spending, in times of depression or boom, should be oriented to the beautiful as well as the useful. He gradually became convinced that state patronage would be the only way of saving arts from extinction when private patronage had been destroyed by economic egalitarianism.

In his own various artistic enterprises, Keynes's part was never just to

---

* The Cambridge Arts Theatre, which opened in 1936, cost £38,000, mostly raised by loan, including one from Keynes totalling £17,500. In ten years all loans had been repaid out of profits.

raise the cash. He was keenly interested in artistic policy, relying in part on advice from his wife Lydia Lopokova and his painter and writer friends, but also on his own judgement, especially in drama. His tastes and sympathies, however, were not wide. He had no innate feeling for the visual arts. 'Had he never met Duncan Grant he would never have taken much interest in painting,' says Clive Bell, who found his judgement of painters and works of art lamentable. He had only a moderate liking for music. He was unable to see foreign cultures from the inside: 'France, Italy, America even, he saw them all from the white cliffs of Dover, or, to be more exact, from Whitehall or King's combination room.' His own appreciation centred on literature, the dramatic arts (including ballet) and architecture; he was a fine and discriminating user of words himself. His homage was to the civilising mission of the arts, and he enjoyed the company of artists.[73]

Keynes adopted a suitably visionary tone in his first broadcast as chairman:

> I should like to see the war memorials of this tragic struggle take the shape of an enrichment of the civic life of every great centre of population. Why should we not set aside, let us say, £50 millions a year for the next twenty years to add in every substantial city of the realm the dignity of an ancient university town or a European capital to our local schools and their surroundings, to our local government and its offices, and above all perhaps to provide a local centre of refreshment and entertainment with an ample theatre, a concert hall, a dance hall, a gallery, a British restaurant, canteens, cafes and so forth.[74]

Keynes brought to his chairmanship qualities familiar to the Treasury: the drive to translate visions into plans, the urge to get to the bottom of things, a scatter of lively interventions, prodigious hard work, impatience with muddle and sloppiness. His deputy chairman, the art historian Kenneth Clark, thought that 'he displayed [his brilliance] too unsparingly . . . he never dimmed his headlights'. CEMA's secretary, Mary Glasgow, wrote: 'Supremely intelligent himself, he was impatient of anything less than clear thinking and well-defined aims. He knew what he wanted, and he liked to have his own way. He could be very rude on occasion, and he did antagonise a number of people. Faced with an issue on which he felt deeply – and there were many such – he never hesitated to declare war.'[75] At the same time, he gave CEMA an electrifying sense of direction:

> At a time when he was probably busier than at any other period of his life, often engaged in financial conferences in America and Canada, he wrote to me, the secretary, practically every day, some-times several times a day, as dictated missives flew into our head-

quarters, in Belgrave Square and later St James's Square, from the Treasury or across the Atlantic. And they *were* missives, long discourses, lists of questions, detailed comments on all that was happening in the theatre, concert halls and picture galleries. They were full of colourful, indiscreet talk about individuals and organizations. . . . It may well have been that he found relief in this way from the demands of his financial responsibilities. He said he gave about a twentieth part of his time to us at the Council . . . [but] that in order to run things properly a chairman ought to be devoting at least a quarter. . . . His praise was as heart-warming as his blame was cutting.

This was the paradox of Keynes: he wanted people to stand up to him, but he inspired such alarm in them that few took the chance. Mary Glasgow said that it took her three years to get over her 'paralyzing awe of him', then suddenly it evaporated.[76]

Keynes stated his own philosophy of the active life in a letter to Michael Macowen, whom he had invited to be drama director in 1945. Macowen did not feel he could combine producing plays with CEMA work. Keynes wrote to him:

My own experience of life is that, if a chap is personally able to combine the artistic life with other things, it is vastly to the good. One's artistic activities should not take up a very great amount of actual time. People who have nothing else to do run to seed. If you examine retrospectively the course of life of other people who have produced and have taken the high artistic line that they should do nothing else, you will find that they have been washed out in the end. . . . It is much better to have to struggle to find time to do . . . things than to have to take them to fill in the time. Forgive so long a sermon.[77]

His own positions were as clear-cut as any positions on arts policy can be. His first allegiance was to high professional standards; the question of whether a play or piece of music was high-brow or middle-brow was secondary. As Kenneth Clark put it, Keynes was not 'the man for wandering minstrels and amateur theatricals'. He steered CEMA towards the excellent, in the belief that the people deserved the best, and in the hope that they would enjoy it when they got it. His principles of finance were equally clear-cut: CEMA money was to be used not to subsidise performances but to guarantee them against loss. Under his chairmanship CEMA encouraged commercial companies to form non-profit-distributing subsidiaries, operating under Council guarantee, to avoid Entertainments Tax. CEMA failed to obtain automatic exemption from tax for the productions it sponsored, and much of Keynes's time was spent in exasperated correspondence with the 'illiterate' Plays Committee of Customs and Excise, trying to prove that Euripides and Ibsen were educational rather than entertaining.[78] In 1943, CEMA started supporting opera and ballet. Keynes saw his funding formula as a model for the way in which commercial companies after the war might be emboldened to woo audiences with a more demanding repertoire. There were grumblings that 'the commercial theatre was feathering its nest at the taxpayer's expense'; in fact, 'not a penny of CEMA money was spent on the . . . non-profit-sharing ventures. The managements took the risk, CEMA sponsored them, and the system of guarantee against loss came into its own'.[79]

Keynes was equally clear that it was CEMA's task to equip urban centres with what he called the 'material frame for the arts of civilisation and delight'. This boiled down to buildings. As a theatre-builder himself, Keynes's imagination was fired by the noble vision of each town having its own 'art centre'; less happily, as we have seen, he would have attached to each of these centres a 'British restaurant'. Throughout the war, he followed a trail of derelict warehouses or damaged buildings which might be turned into theatres. Most of these schemes foundered; the plan to rebuild the burnt-out Crystal Palace 'as a vast place of entertainment where the British citizen of the future can spend a whole day'[80] came to naught. But in one particular instance Keynes hit his target.

The historic Theatre Royal at Bristol, opened in 1766, was bombed in 1942, and its owners proposed to convert the site into a warehouse. Keynes was immediately on to Butler with the suggestion that CEMA lease it, restore it and put it back to work. Nine months later, on 11 May 1943, Bristol Theatre reopened, with Sybil Thorndike in Goldsmith's *She Stoops to Conquer*. Keynes went to Bristol for the opening, and was at his most playful and paradoxical in his pre-performance speech. He described how CEMA, possessed of an 'undefined independence, an anomalous constitution and no fixed rules' and therefore 'able to do by inadvertence what obviously no one in his official senses would do on purpose,' had 'accidentally slipped into getting mixed up with a theatre building'. He hoped that 'the precedent, having been once created . . . will . . . be officially improper not to repeat . . .'.[81] He was less playful a couple of years later when he heard that the director of education in Bristol had refused to allow children to see Lewis Casson's production of Shaw's *St Joan* in schooltime, because they weren't being examined in it that year. 'What is this thing that you call education?' he demanded of Butler.

Keynes's programme was not carried out without considerable internal dissension. By late 1942, CEMA had spawned a structure of expert panels for Music, Drama, Art, each with its own director, as well as Scottish and Welsh Committees, all full of prima donnas. Keynes expected to preside at quarterly meetings of the panels, whose decisions would be binding. But this proved one chore too many, and he soon handed the panels over to his deputy chairmen – Stanley Marchant for Music, Ivor Brown for

Drama, Kenneth Clark for Art – with their decisions having to be ratified by the full Council. Mary Glasgow remembers frequent dinners at Gordon Square, where the directors of the panels would discuss their plans in the basement dining room, with Lydia Keynes, dressed in woollens and high, fleece-lined boots, distributing carrots to help their vision in the black-out.[82]

There were demarcation disputes between the panels, disputes between the expert advisers and the Council and its officers, disputes over the distribution of funds (the Scottish Committee was especially 'tiresome', with Keynes contemplating wearing a kilt to pacify it). Much of the trouble came from the Drama Panel. Ivor Brown resigned as its chairman on 15 February 1943, complaining that the 'Industry of Entertainment' was full of 'cliques' and 'captious and cantankerous people'. Keynes himself was accused of favouritism. The playright Ashley Dukes, a Drama panellist, detected a conflict of interest when CEMA agreed to sponsor tours by Ballets Jooss and Norman Marshall's Repertory Company, both based in Cambridge, and connected, through interlocking directorships, with the Cambridge Arts Theatre Trust. His insinuations provoked Keynes to a wrathful response. 'What can I reply to your crazy letter', Keynes wrote him on 18 May 1943, 'except that you would do better justice to yourself and be a worthier inhabitant of the planet if you would discover the facts before circulating such a document. . . .'[83]

CEMA's exhibiting policy ran into predictable flak from the Royal Academy. It had been sending out exhibitions of Sickert, Wilson Steer and the Tate Gallery's wartime acquisitions on provincial tour. The Academicians complained about the lack of Old Masters in these exhibitions, and accused CEMA's Art Panel of dangerously 'modernist' tendencies. Keynes had put Henry Moore and Duncan Grant on the Panel. Why not balance them with Sir Edwin Lutyens, Butler suggested. 'I do not think he will do any harm.' 'Certainly old Lutyens [the famous architect was seventy-four] would do no harm,' Keynes responded warmly. 'But he would do no good. Is it wise to start so early in our life on the vicious practice of filling up with respectable dead heads?' Lutyens was successfully fought off, but Keynes returned from holiday in April 1943 to find that Butler had appointed a painter called Thomas Monnington, subsequently president of the Royal Academy, to balance the modernists. 'As I have never heard of Monnington, I cannot reasonably object to him,' Keynes told Butler. 'It will, I think, be of some assistance to be able to tell members of my Panel that I was not consulted.'[84] Butler's intervention proved usefully protective. When CEMA was publicly attacked by a group of Academicians for putting on exhibitions with a tendency to deprave the public taste, Keynes was able, in a letter to The Times on 12 March 1944, to cite Monnington, as well as Samuel Courtauld and the directors of the National and Tate Galleries, in support of his contention that his

Art Panel was 'as mixed a bunch of fogeys of repute as you could reasonably hope to collect'.[85]

Keynes's own ideas about the future of CEMA were slowly taking shape. Should CEMA be mainly concerned with subsidising buildings or subsidising performers? Should it aim to be a grant-distributing body, like the Universities Grants Committee, or an operating body, running its own concerns? Should it aim to encourage Art or encourage Audiences? What should it be called? 'Cema is a dreadful name,' he told Butler on 15 February 1943. '[The initials] convey nothing to anyone who does not know about it already and suggest something too much like Ensa [the organisation for entertaining troops] for our taste. . . . My own idea would be something like "The Royal Council for the Arts".' Butler agreed: 'Organisations which exist on their initials, I have repeatedly pointed out, end up by being second-rate.'[86] On 23 June 1943, Butler suggested setting up a small *ad hoc* committee to discuss CEMA's post-war future.

Nothing much happened, and early in 1944 Butler pressed Keynes to produce his thoughts. By this time, Keynes was so busy (and unwell) that he contemplated resigning. It was not till September 1944, in the interval between the Bretton Woods conference and the Stage II negotiations in Washington, that he managed to send Butler his memorandum on the future of CEMA, which was based on an earlier draft by a Council member, Ifor Evans. This proposed setting up a permanent Royal Council of the Arts of eleven members, five of whom would form an executive committee. This committee would chair the panels of outside experts. There would be a director-general and a small staff to service the panels. The Council would have two aims: to increase the accessibility of the arts to the public, and to improve standards of execution. It would receive an annual grant of £500,000. Keynes preferred the money to come from the Ministry of Education rather than directly from the Treasury, because 'to have a Minister to speak on our behalf who has not a direct responsibility for maximum economy may in future conditions be an advantage'.[87]

On 30 January 1945 CEMA's Council rejected Keynes's proposed title – it decided it wanted to call itself the Arts Council of Great Britain – but accepted the rest of his proposals. The first meeting of the new executive took place in Keynes's office in the Treasury on 14 February. Keynes now pressed for a royal charter to set up the new body as quickly as possible. In one of its last decisions, Churchill's coalition government agreed to continue CEMA, just as the European war was ending. On 12 June, the 'caretaker' Chancellor, Sir John Anderson, announced that the government intended to incorporate it as the Arts Council of Great Britain, with an initial annual grant of £320,000. 'Well it does look as if the Arts Council is now fairly launched,' Keynes wrote to Butler, now Minister of Labour, on 14 June, 'and we all owe you a great debt of gratitude for having carried this through to its conclusion just before we parted company. . . .'

Keynes's last broadcast as CEMA's chairman, on 12 July 1945, traced the transformation of CEMA into the Arts Council of Great Britain. His cultured, upper-class voice, preserved in the BBC archive, with its narrow range of modulation, drawling stresses ('Exchek*ar*'), slight hesitations ('initi-a-tive', 'Bee-Bee-See'), quick irony ('half-baked') and rather distant benevolence ('I hope you will call us the Arts Council for short. . . . We have carefully selected initials which we hope are unpronounceable') recalls that era of wise and good governors planning, with high serious-ness, the future happiness of their peoples. Having started with the idea of replacing what the war had taken away, 'we soon found', Keynes said, 'that we were providing what had never existed even in peacetime'.

> I do not believe it is yet realised what an important thing has happened [he continued]. State patronage of the arts has crept in. It has happened in a very English, informal, unostentatious way – half-baked if you like. A semi-independent body is provided with modest funds to stimulate, comfort and support any societies brought together on private or local initiative which are striving with serious purpose and a reasonable prospect of success to present for public enjoyment the arts of drama, music and painting.

But 'we do not intend to socialise this side of social endeavour' Keynes said.

> Whatever views may be held by the lately warring parties . . . about socialising industry, everyone, I fancy, recognises that the work of the artist in all its aspects is, of its nature, individual and free, undisciplined, unregimented, uncontrolled. The artist walks where the breath of the spirit blows him. He cannot be told his direction; he does not know it himself. But he leads the rest of us into fresh pastures and teaches us to love and to enjoy what we often begin by rejecting, enlarging our sensitivity and purifying our instincts. The task of an official body is not to teach or to censor, but to give courage, confidence, and opportunity.

Ultimately it will be the public which will decide what it gets.

> In so far as we instruct, it is a new game we are teaching you to play – and to which our wartime experience has led us already to one clear discovery: the unsatisfied demand and the enormous public for serious and fine entertainment. This certainly did not exist a few years ago. I do not believe that it is merely a wartime phenomenon. I fancy that the BBC has played . . . the predominant part in creating this public demand, by bringing everybody in the country the

possibility of learning these new games which only the few used to play, and by forming new tastes and habits and thus enlarging the desires of the listener and his capacity for enjoyment.

Turning to the need to provide the 'necessary bricks and mortar' all round the country in which these 'new games' can be played, Keynes tactfully finessed the tension which has dogged arts policy ever since:

We of the Arts Council are greatly concerned to decentralise and disperse the dramatic and musical and artistic life of the country. . . . How satisfactory it would be if the different parts of this country would again walk their several ways as they once did and learn to develop something different from their neighbours and characteristic of themselves. Nothing can be more damaging than the excessive prestige of metropolitan standards and fashions. Let every part of Merrie England be merry in its own way. Death to Hollywood. But it is also our business to make London a great artistic metropolis, a place to visit and wonder at. With the loss of the Queen's Hall there is no proper place for concerts. The Royal Opera House at Covent Garden has been diverted to other purposes throughout the war.[88]

As Mary Glasgow makes clear, Keynes's thoughts were really centred on his old dream of making London the artistic capital of Europe. The chance came when the lease of the Royal Opera House came up for renewal.

Even during the golden years of opera in the late nineteenth century, Covent Garden theatre had never consistently paid its way as an opera house, though until 1914 the successive lessees and sub-lessees of the Duke of Bedford who put on opera seasons there made an intermittent profit. Between the wars the situation worsened. A succession of syndicates took short leases from the new landlords, Covent Garden Properties, but none of them – not even the redoubtable Sir Thomas Beecham – could make the theatre pay, and once or twice it was on the point of being demolished. In 1939 Mecca Cafés acquired a five-year lease and during the war Covent Garden was used as a dance hall.

While Covent Garden faltered, a native school of British opera and ballet was growing up in the 1930s, based on the new Sadler's Wells in Rosebery Avenue, to which Ninette de Valois had transferred her ballet company in 1931. But Sadler's Wells was a modest theatre, serving mainly the residents of Finsbury, who had subscribed money for it, and was compelled by the terms of its charitable trust to provide seats cheap enough for 'artisans and labourers' to afford. It lacked the style, spaciousness and snob appeal to be a national or international house. It was also tied up with the Old Vic, whose managers regarded opera and ballet as an adjunct to Shakespeare.

This was the position when, on 1 April 1944, the music publishers Boosey and Hawkes were granted a five-year lease by Covent Garden Properties to 're-establish Covent Garden as a centre of opera and ballet worthy of the highest traditions'. In August 1944, Leslie Boosey appointed David Webster, a Liverpool draper with musical interests, to be managing director of the new venture. After Kenneth Clark, deputising for Keynes, had told Boosey that no CEMA grant would be available for Boosey and Hawkes to run the theatre directly, Keynes wired from the United States accepting the position of chairman of an Advisory Council (soon renamed the Covent Garden Committee) to be set up to run the theatre on a sub-lease from the music publishers. Lesley Boosey 'worshipped' Keynes. More significant in view of the need to raise money was the fact that Keynes was chairman of CEMA, on which Webster, too, had served as a financial adviser. As chairman of CEMA, chairman of the Covent Garden Committee *and* the dominant person in the Treasury, Keynes had in his hands all the instruments he needed for carrying out the policy he, Webster, Boosey and Philip Hill, chairman of Covent Garden Properties, were agreed on: to give opera and ballet a home worthy of their traditions, and a secure income.

He started to give Covent Garden business his full attention only when he returned from another long trip to the United States in December 1944. The rebirth of Covent Garden was essentially accomplished in the first half of 1945. His first and most easily accomplished task was to secure a Treasury stake in Covent Garden's future. His 'begging' letter to Sir Alan Barlow, the second secretary, dated 30 January 1945, is drafted with the practised skill of one insider talking to another:

> As you will see from the scheme, this is really a project to establish national opera and ballet by English performers at Covent Garden through building on the sound beginnings already made by Sadler's Wells. It is rather astonishing, I think, that it should be possible to plan something so big on such a very reasonable financial basis. The idea, as you will see, is that there should be a lump sum contribution of £25,000 during the financial year for production expenses [estimated at £75,000]. In subsequent financial years CEMA will no doubt be expected to give some guarantee against misfortune. But one would hope that the new institution would have a pretty good chance of covering its running expenses.[89]

The plan was for the Covent Garden Committee, consisting of Keynes, Leslie Boosey, Sir Kenneth Clark, Samuel Courtauld, Edward Dent, Ralph Hawkes, Stanley Marchant and William Walton, to become the board of a non-profit-making company or charitable trust, with Keynes as chairman. Keynes's reference to 'English performers' was not just tactful. The belief in developing an English 'national style' in opera was held on both patriotic and artistic grounds. Keynes, who knew little about opera, was heavily influenced by Edward Dent, a fellow of King's, who believed passionately in 'opera in English'. As a result anyone with any experience of producing opera before the war was excluded from the planning, management or artistic direction of the new venture: Beecham, Rudolf Bing, Carl Ebert, Eugene Goossens; Bing and Ebert because of their association with John Christie of Glyndebourne.

Throughout the war Christie had been agitating for government support, not just to reopen Glyndebourne after the war, but to make it a centre of Cultural Reconstruction. He had established a National Council of Music in 1940. He offered to form a Ministry of Economy to stop waste. He appealed to Sir Stafford Cripps, Minister of Aircraft Production, for money 'to crystallize the National Conscience by giving it a constitution and a home (Glyndebourne)'. There were signs, as his biographer Wilfrid Blunt writes, of megalomania in these projects.[90] Keynes had turned down several of Christie's applications for CEMA support to reopen Glyndebourne after the war, sometimes coupled with other projects, like establishing a National Opera School. Kenneth Clark believed that this was because 'Keynes had an ancient implacable hatred for John Christie, which Christie returned with interest.'[91] There is something in this. Christie felt that Keynes and CEMA had pirated his ideas for musical regeneration. When the two men travelled by the same train between London and Lewes, they pointedly went to different compartments. Eventually Christie was made a member of CEMA's Art (not Music) Panel; Keynes wrote to Mary Glasgow: 'Glad to hear that J.C. is to be incorporated. If only he could be transubstantiated at the same time. Could that be made a condition?' But the issue of principle, endorsed by CEMA's Music Panel, was that Glyndebourne 'was a rich man's pleasure, with no claim upon the tax-payer'.[92]

Early in 1944, Christie conceived the idea of buying Covent Garden, and making it the centre of a vast complex of cultural institutions, with Rudolf Bing as general manager. He 'believed, or came to believe' that his attempts to buy the freehold of Covent Garden in 1944 had been thwarted by 'hostility . . . in certain quarters'. In fact, there is no evidence that he made a serious offer. Boosey tried to get Christie on the Covent Garden Committee, 'but Keynes flatly refused . . . '. Keynes also refused his offer for a joint season at Covent Garden.[93] Hurtful though Keynes's rejection of Christie's grandiose schemes was, he unwittingly did him and Glyndebourne a great service. Glyndebourne remained Britain's one independent opera house. Disentangled from John Christie's wilder ambitions, the Glyndebourne Festival Opera would shine ever more brightly in the years ahead.

Keynes played an equally important part in securing for the Royal Opera House a resident ballet company – the first resident company in its history. This involved tough and complicated negotiations with Sadler's Wells, covering matters of policy, law and finance. Sadler's Wells was reluctant to lose its ballet and opera companies. There was the question of its contractual obligation to provide low-cost but high-quality entertainment, especially to the inhabitants of Finsbury. There was natural resentment at the prospect of a more glamorous house stealing the fruit of many years' labour. In a memorandum drawn up in October 1944, Tyrone Guthrie, administrator of Sadler's Wells, and Edward Dent, a governor, proposed that the resident companies should remain at Sadler's Wells, backed by a CEMA subsidy, while Covent Garden should be used by visiting companies only. This stand crumbled in the face of Ninette de Valois' determination to transfer her ballet company to Covent Garden. Keynes and Webster on their side were eager to acquire the strong ballet company, but did not much want its weaker operatic sister, preferring to build up their own resident opera company from scratch. Reading through the records of these negotiations in the archives of the Royal Opera House and in Keynes's papers at King's College, the decisive point which emerges is that Keynes's position as chairman of the Covent Garden Committee was backed throughout by his authority as chairman of CEMA. At crucial stages he was able to dangle the carrot of a CEMA subsidy, or the stick of its withdrawal, in support of his arguments.

Keynes's first opportunity to exert pressure came when the Earl of Lytton, chairman of the Sadler's Wells Board of Governors, solicited his support (2 March 1945) for an expensive new production of Benjamin Britten's *Peter Grimes*. Keynes's reply of 9 March is a neat example of 'linkage' politics: 'I understand from Webster that he and Guthrie will be consulting on various matters shortly and there is not, I think, much that I need to say until after they have made further progress. . . .' The message was plain: a CEMA subsidy hinged on a satisfactory outcome to the 'consultations' between Webster and Guthrie.

In a letter of 1 May 1945, Keynes made a 'clear-cut' proposal to the governors of Sadler's Wells, known as the 'Keynes Letter'. The Covent Garden Committee would take over the two Sadler's Wells companies, reserving the right to get rid of as many singers as it saw fit. In compensation Sadler's Wells would receive £2000 a year for four years. If the governors agreed to this idea, Keynes was 'very hopeful' that CEMA funds would be available to finance other activities at the Rosebery Avenue theatre, including an opera school. Discussions continued between Keynes, Webster and Sir George Dyson, who represented the Sadler's Wells governors. Dyson wanted Sadler's Wells to retain its opera company, which was readily agreed. He suggested that the two theatres be managed by a joint committee which would request and receive a single grant from CEMA, to be divided up in agreed proportions. He also wanted £30,000 from Covent Garden for the ballet company. These conditions were unacceptable, and the deadlock was not finally broken till August 1945 when Keynes, as chairman-designate of the newly formed Arts Council, offered Lord Lytton a guarantee of £5000 a year. Webster recalled that when negotiations with the Sadler's Wells trustees 'seemed almost at a standstill, he [Keynes] snatched a few minutes in the assembled House of Lords while waiting for the arrival of the King [to open the new Parliament] to secure the co-operation of Lord Lytton, followed the conversation with a brilliant memorandum and the transfer of the Ballet to Covent Garden came soon afterwards'.

The Covent Garden Charitable Trust was not set up till February 1946. Early that year Keynes was still struggling through a thicket of contracts with Boosey and Hawkes on the one hand, and Sadler's Wells on the other. Having tried to make sense of the trust deed, he wrote wearily to David Webster, 'This seems to be even more stuffed with lawyers' bunk than usual. If only it could be made illegal to employ the services of a solicitor, what a lot of trouble it would save!'[94]

CHAPTER NINE

The Great Compromise

I

ANGLO-AMERICAN SKIRMISHING

Maynard Keynes once told James Meade that whenever he read anything about nutritional issues 'my attention wanders'. In March 1943 Roosevelt suddenly proposed a United Nations conference on food and agriculture. When Penrose explained the President's nebulous ideas to Keynes, the great economist remarked glumly: 'What you are saying is that your President with his great political insight has decided that the best strategy for post-war reconstruction is to start with vitamins and then by a circuitous route work round to the international balance of payments!'[1] Delegates of the Allied and associated nations gathered at Hot Springs, Virginia in May and emitted a suitable blast of hot air. Lionel Robbins, a member of the British team, gave a speech on buffer stocks. He wrote in his diary: 'It is not difficult to agree that people should have more food, that agriculture should be widely balanced, that the economy should expand and that peace should be assured. It is very easy to be friendly in a luxury hotel with all expenses paid and no binding commitments on the agenda. When we did touch on bread and butter questions, as in the discussions on buffer stocks, opinion was by no means so united.'[2]

More important from the British point of view were the informal monetary conversations which had been taking place between the two Treasuries in Washington. Each side used the question-and-answer method to probe the technical merits and political acceptability of the other's plans. Berle had drawn up a list of questions about the Clearing Union the previous year. In May 1943, Keynes submitted his own questions about the Stabilisation Fund. Dennis Robertson, temporarily attached to the Washington Embassy, dubbed them the 'twenty-six distinct damnations / One sure if another fails'.

The insertion of Robertson into the financial negotiations added considerable intellectual firepower to the British team. If Keynes was the Impressionist of the new world order, Robertson was its pointillist, reducing Keynes's lyrical brushwork to exact relationships – much as Edward Bernstein did for White, which is probably why he and Robertson got on so well. Bernstein could not match Robertson's subtle wit; but they both had the type of mind which Keynes dubbed 'rabbinical', by which he meant a delight in precision for its own sake. What Keynes considered a defect when directed against his own theories was an invaluable asset when deployed against the 'Cherokee' of American draftsmen. Over the coming months Robertson and Bernstein would supply much of the detail by which the principles agreed by Keynes and White were made workable.

The one clear result of the summer discussions was to show that the Clearing Union was a non-starter in Washington. The United States would not budge on subscriptions and limited dollar liability. The European Allies who had enthused about the Clearing Union in London deserted to the Stabilisation Fund in Washington, influenced less by what Robertson called 'White's individual tuition hours' than by their realisation that Washington, not London, paid the piper and would therefore call the tune. There were also Canadian and French plans. The Canadian plan for an 'International Exchange Union', dubbed 'off White' in London, was a compromise between the British and American Plans. It adopted the Fund framework – it was 'not generally considered good banking', the Canadians told the British, 'to have the debtors control the bank' – but wanted an aggregate quota of $8bn not $5bn, and an international monetary unit based on gold. The French plan predictably looked like the gold standard. It was ignored.[3]

Robertson thought that the British had three options: to fight to the last for the Clearing Union principle, relying on the European Allies to back it, while ceding to the American desire for limiting US liability; to accept the Fund principle, and concentrate on enlarging its resources and entrenching the scarce-currency clause; or, while accepting the Fund, to preserve some of the elegance of the Clearing Union by turning 'unitas' into a real medium of exchange instead of a mere unit of account. Robertson believed that the tide of events was carrying them strongly towards the second, though it might be possible to deflect it towards the third. The first alternative would at some time be seen 'to have vanished quietly from the map'.[4]

Keynes in London could not disagree with this. He had told Harrod in April that the British would probably have to accept the American 'dress', but he insisted to Robertson that they should be 'as difficult and obstinate as possible' to gain real value for later concessions.[5] For Keynes the most important thing was to get the Americans committed to a scheme. If they preferred a Stabilisation Fund, the superior technical merits of the Clearing Union should not be allowed to stand in the way.

On 11 June 1943 he reported the state of play to Theodore Gregory in India:

The opinion of the European Allies and of South America as well as of the British Commonwealth is strongly and predominantly in favour of the Clearing Union. On the other hand, many of those concerned are extremely timid about opposing the USA, seeing that they have what I believe are known as 'expectations'. Moreover, Canada, whilst in fact preferring the principles of the Clearing Union, is showing a considerable inclination for a compromise very much on Stabilization Fund lines. Meanwhile, as I dare say you know, confused and desultory conversations go on in Washington, sometimes bilateral and sometimes semi-multilateral, and sometimes god knows what. The debates in both Houses of Parliament went off extremely well. But the main point is that in every quarter of the world it is now almost taken for granted that there has got to be some scheme. And when the time is at last ripe for effecting a compromise, I do not myself anticipate that undue difficulties will arise.[6]

The bilateral discussions with British officials concluded on 24 June in a 'friendly and extremely frank' atmosphere. The British Embassy telegraphed back to London: 'We stressed the absolute necessity of reassuring the British public that it [the British economy] would not be driven into deflation by inability to correct the initial error in fixing the [exchange] rate and White stressed the need for reassuring the American public that they would not be open to attack by competitive depreciation.' White told Phillips that the US Treasury must be able to satisfy Congress on four points: that the sterling–dollar peg be maintained at $4 to the pound, that America's liability be limited to $3bn, that Congress retain control over the gold value of the dollar, and that the monetary framework should be that of a fund and not a bank. The only idea which could be sold to the 'man in the street' was the idea of a 'fund into which all nations are being required to pay something, tempered to their individual capacities. Overdraft principle in spite of its intellectual attractions . . . would be regarded as abracadabra by the public and was fatally open . . . to the jibe that the United States would be left holding the bag'. Later on, if there was more than one surplus country, it might be possible to move in the Clearing Union direction.[7] Robbins left Washington in June agreeing with Keynes that 'the difference between our scheme as we should have to modify it and their scheme as they are prepared to modify it, ought not to constitute an insurmountable obstacle to men of goodwill'.[8]

In London, Keynes received yet another redraft of the White Plan, dated 10 July. While he thought it 'more logical and self-consistent' than previous drafts, it showed 'no increase in political wisdom and not much in technical capacity', while some provisions were drafted 'with great selfishness in the interests of a country possessing unlimited gold'. Keynes recommended that Britain accept the 'substance of White's essential conditions', subject to three British requirements: that members should have more control over their exchange rates, that the Fund should not deal in a 'mixed bag of currencies', but only in international money (unitas), and that gold subscriptions should be no more than 12.5 per cent of quotas, the balance in non-negotiable government securities.[9]

Unitas still lurked in the White Plan as a unit of account 'after the original reason for its existence [as a money to be issued by White's Bank] had disappeared'.[10] Keynes regarded making it 'a true medium of international exchange' the 'most fundamental condition of a satisfactory compromise'.[11] His insistence on this became an obsession, and for many months proved the main stumbling block to an agreement. His most complete statement of the case comes out from a letter he wrote to Sir Wilfrid Eady on 19 July:

> This condition means that, in turn for their initial subscription in terms of gold and securities, members would be credited with corresponding amounts of unitas on the books of the Fund which they would be free to transfer to one another in exchange for needed foreign currencies. Thus the Fund would become passive so far as exchange dealings are concerned, just as the CU would be passive. Under the alternative proposed by Dr. White, the Fund would possess a mixed bag of currencies. . . . It would exercise its discretion whether or not to accept or supply particular currencies. It would purchase only those currencies which it decided (on no clear criterion) to be 'in good standing', and (also on no clear criterion) the sale of which 'is required to meet an adverse balance of payments predominantly on current account'; and it would ration scarce currencies. Moreover it would not assure multilateral clearing, since it would not undertake to buy any foreign currency and supply any other needed currency in exchange. The Bank of England maintain, and with reason, that such a system could be so worked as seriously to jeopardise the international position of sterling. . . . More turns on this than appears on the surface, since, otherwise, thare are no clear limits to the active banking function which the Fund might assume and its power to exercise a discriminatory discretion against certain currencies.

To the American economist Jacob Viner Keynes explained: 'If members of the Fund were to acquire a holding of unitas in exchange for their initial contributions and then, as a result of clearing operations, exchange these holdings of unitas between one another, there would be very much less difference between the basic structures of the two schemes [CU and SF] than there is at present.'[12] In addition, Keynes hoped that unitas would enable the Fund at some future date 'to become a credit-creating agency'.[13]

Keynes's correspondence with Viner brings out the thinking behind the other British and American requirements. Early experimentation in determining exchange rates was needed, Keynes told Viner, but in general he was in favour of stable exchange rates. Exchange rate depreciation was no longer as popular as it was, as the European Allies would want to protect the value of pre-war savings in terms of money. 'My own feeling about exchange rates is that we should aim at as great a stability as possible and that exchange rate depreciation is not at all a good way of balancing trade unless the lack of balance is due to . . . the movement of efficiency wages in one country [being] out of step with what it is in others.' He added, 'All this needs a good deal of further thought.' Viner replied that relative trends in efficiency wages would not suffice as a criterion of exchange rate changes. 'The wage criterion . . . accepts . . . powerful trade unions as the ultimate and unlimited sovereign over monetary policy.'

Keynes agreed that countries were unlikely to accept an 'unlimited liability to be net creditors', but argued that under the Clearing Union 'a country is completely controlled in this respect as soon as it seeks to increase its debit by above half of its quota. Perhaps you mean that these provisions ought to come into force sooner in the rake's progress. . . .' Viner wrote back that 'the absence in the CU of a rigid limit to creditor obligation is of course very attractive *per se* to those who are debtor-minded but it is literally terrifying to those who anticipate being creditors'. The difficulty under both Plans was that members had an unconditional right to borrow up to a certain point regardless of creditworthiness. 'In this respect, I believe, neither plan has any historical counterpart whether in private or in public finance.' Viner would try to get the best of both worlds by limiting unconditional credit more narrowly, but making conditional credit larger than in the American Plan.

Viner accused Keynes of being blind to the inflationary potential of his scheme.

> Not at all [Keynes responded]. Assuredly I share your concern about the possible menace of inflation, or rather, what is not quite the same, but is perhaps what you mean in this context, the possibility of redundancy of gold. Experience shows that what happens is always the thing against which one has not made provision in advance. These currency schemes are providing against the danger of an insufficiency of international money. For my own part, I should not be at all surprised if, in fact, the danger which meets us turns out to be just the opposite, namely, an excess of international currency. Everyone seems to me to be assuming, without sufficient reason, that the United States is going to run after the war an enormous credit balance. . . . I regard this as quite uncertain. Sup-

pose the opposite takes place, and the United States begins to export its gold holdings. Suppose at the same time Russia is using some part of her now quite gigantic hoards to pay for her imports of capital goods, and suppose simultaneously with this the normal gold output of the world is helped by scientific progress to increase. Nothing highly improbable in any of these possibilities. Between them they might certainly create the state of affairs about which you rightly feel concerned.

Keynes has reverted here to his recurrent fear, first voiced before the First World War, that the gold standard could be as inflationary as deflationary. An internationally managed money loosely, not rigidly, linked to gold had long been his preferred alternative to the classic gold standard.

Viner's most telling criticism of both Plans was that they failed to distinguish between the problems of the transition and the problems of peace, between Britain's immediate need for dollars, which should be met by the United States, and the transactions proper to a Stabilisation Fund. A cogent distinction between 'how much of the transition period problem the new monetary agency is intended to handle and what type of provision is to be made for the part of the problem to be handled otherwise ... would not only clarify thinking, but would also promote agreement'.[14] The problem of the transition to peace was starting to cast its long shadow over the Article VII negotiations. Britain's debts to the sterling area were mounting up alarmingly, while the US administration, in British eyes, was managing Lend–Lease so as to prevent the British from building up an adequate post-war reserve. Given the niggardliness of adjustment finance offered by White's Fund, how soon would Britain be able to meet its Article VII commitment to abandon its discriminatory trade and payments system?

Early in August Halifax suggested to Hull that Britain send a strong delegation to Washington in September to initiate informal discussions on the whole field covered by Article VII. He emphasised the importance of Britain and the United States reaching prior agreement before these matters were negotiated internationally. On 12 August the Embassy cabled London: 'White agrees that the next step should be Anglo-American discussions on the basis of fundamental principles.' Having got most countries to agree to his Plan, White was at last prepared to confront the British. Keynes was delighted. Shortly before his departure for Washington, he told Winant that 'he believed that in a weekend of conversations Dr. White and he could reach agreement on most basic points of the currency proposals'.[15]

Keynes spent as much of August as he could at Tilton, relaxing over his mother's history of the High Stewardship of Cambridge, which he found 'most fascinating and interesting'. His health was no longer as perfect as it had been in June, but by the end of the month he had benefited greatly from his rest and the course of frictional tepid baths which the Ogre was giving him in London.

II

On 3 September Maynard sailed from Glasgow with Lydia on the *Queen Mary*, bound for 'preliminary, informal, non-committal, purely unofficial' discussions with the Americans on Article VII. He was part of a strong British delegation headed by Richard Law, now Minister of State at the Foreign Office. It included David Waley and Frank Lee of the Treasury, Lionel Robbins of the Economic Section of the War Cabinet, Nigel Ronald of the Foreign Office, Gerald Clauson of the Colonial Office, Percivale Liesching, James Meade and Robert Shackle representing the Board of Trade, and P. W. Martin from the Ministry of Food. Lucius Thompson-McCausland came along as Keynes's personal assistant with a watching brief from the Bank of England. In Washington they would be joined by Dennis Robertson and Redvers Opie from the Embassy. Sir Frederick Phillips would not be there. His unstinting labours for Britain's cause were over. In July he had returned to London for consultation. Already mortally ill with cancer, he died on 14 August. His passing was universally mourned. In June, Berle had told Robbins, 'Phillips is worth his weight in gold to the British Empire. If you recalled Phillips, Morgie would almost call off the war. They sit and talk to one another, about ten sentences to the hour; and everything is grand.'[16] Phillips's silences would no longer be available to soothe Anglo-American relations.

The instructions from the War Cabinet, drafted by Hugh Dalton, President of the Board of Trade, were based on Keynes's minimum requirements, noted above, with the significant addition that sterling balances should not be included in any monetary scheme. As late as 22 June Keynes had approved White's suggestion that these balances should be funded – that is, blocked by Britain, and paid back over a long period through the Fund. In effect, White was offering to put US dollars – though not very many – behind Britain's wartime liabilities. In the Bank of England's view, the blocking of sterling balances would spell the end of the sterling area, which may also have been White's motive in putting forward his proposal. It persuaded the War Cabinet to veto the deal.[17]

Before boarding the *Queen Mary*, 'the whole party took breakfast at a large table in a private room at the Central Hotel, Glasgow, Keynes making the unseemly witticism that "it looks more like the last supper than the first breakfast"'. On the launch carrying them out to the ship, James Meade encountered Lydia 'ordering her distinguished husband to lie down and rest'. Once on board, the captain, a 'bluff and hearty sadist', threatened to clap them in irons if they broke any of the rules. One of the rules was to wear life-belts continuously. 'To have seen them [Maynard and Lydia] thus was a precious and unforgettable memory,' gushes Roy Harrod.

The experts hoped that the two sides would be able to hammer out agreed proposals on the main elements of the Grand Design – money, investment, trade, buffer stocks, employment. These could then be put to the two governments, and, if they agreed, an international conference would follow to endorse the rules and set up the institutions of the post-war system. But there was a large snag. Only the two monetary Plans had reached a relatively advanced stage of technical development, possible compromise and political support. All the rest were ideas floating round departments in the two governments. They were all Article VII matters; to Meade they were all interdependent. But, if they were all expected to go forward together, the risk was that the monetary Plan would fall by the wayside.

The British had with them not just White's revised proposal for the Stabilisation Fund, dated 10 July, but also an eviscerated version of his plan for a Reconstruction and Development Bank, which Opie had forwarded from Washington just before they sailed. Modelled on the US Reconstruction Finance Corporation, it aimed to reconstruct the war-shattered economies and provide or guarantee capital for industrial development at low interest rates. Attached to it would be an Essential Raw Materials Development Corporation and an International Commodity Stabilisation Corporation. Oscar Robson, who had got hold of a leaked copy, wrote enthusiastically in the *News Chronicle* of 11 September, 'This is world planning on a grand scale.' But the crucial money-creating powers which had so excited Roy Harrod had been omitted; and the administration was split on the merits of what remained, though Morgenthau favoured it.[18] On the voyage over, Keynes approved its spirit, but savaged its mechanics as 'Bedlam' and its drafting as 'positively Sumerian'. He objected strongly to two features – that debtor countries should contribute as much as creditor countries to the Bank's capital, and the severity of sanctions on defaulters. He 'gave us by way of a digression a marvellous proof of the fact that international investment always had been and always would be defaulted'.[19] The British delegates agreed not to bring up the Bank until the Americans did, but to press independently for an International Development Corporation.

Keynes noted that White's 10 July draft of the Stabilisation Fund had already been circulated to Congress. The increased Fund resources and greater flexibility for exchange rate adjustment apparently agreed with the British in June had been cancelled and the gold element in the subscription upped to between 25 and 50 per cent, depending on size of reserves, 'although they are aware that this provision is not acceptable to anyone'. All this would reduce the American team's negotiating flexibility.[20] Fighting off seasickness, the delegation met frequently during the voyage to concert its negotiating strategy. Meade was much encouraged by the line Keynes took: 'He enthusiastically supported the view that we should press for a consideration of all these projects as forming a single whole. I had feared that he might consider it his . . . job to fight with the Americans toughly on the details of the monetary arrangement, and disassociate himself and the Treasury . . . from other parts such as the Commercial Union.'[21] In fact, this is exactly what Keynes did.

Before they sailed for America, Meade had been arguing for 'automatic' variations in social security contributions (see p. 227 above). Now he tried to persuade Keynes that what was needed was an 'automatic test' for currency depreciation and/or quantitative regulation of imports. Keynes was sceptical that such a test could be found. At dinner, Meade found the Keyneses 'a quite perfect couple', combining 'the best qualities of a devoted Darby and Joan with the airs and graces of intellectualism and the arts'.[22]

Meade's awe-struck diary continues to give glimpses of Keynes in action. On the train journey from New York to Washington on Saturday 11 September, 'Keynes was in first-class form. The first part he spent reading the newspapers and periodicals at a fantastic rate. His great enjoyment was Hitler's speech on the defection of Italy which he continually asserted he was enjoying so much because Hitler was enjoying it all so much' – a somewhat obscure remark. 'There was a flow of acid comment on the American country-side, their air-raid precautions, lack of birds and the sterility of the land! He and Lydia and Ronald indulged in a tremendous discussion on modern painting; and the whole journey was rounded off by Lydia singing the Casse-Noisette music at the top of her voice and dancing it with her hands.'[23]

This time Maynard and Lydia checked in at the Statler Hotel. They preferred it to the Mayflower, because it had a Coffee Shop, where Keynes could take light meals. They did not expect to stay long. Keynes, as already noted, thought that he and White could settle all outstanding issues in a weekend's discussion; White thought it might take 'a week or so'. In fact, Keynes remained in America for six weeks, and the joint statement of experts was not finalised and published till April 1944.

Both sides agreed to set up groups to discuss the different elements of the Grand Design – money, investment, buffer stocks and commercial policy – with plenary sessions to 'stress the interdependence of all the subjects'. The first of these plenaries took place on 20 September, with Law leading off for the British 'in a most moving speech'. Keynes wound up for Britain when it continued a day later. 'I have never heard him better,' wrote Meade enthusiastically, 'more brilliant, more persuasive, more witty or more truly moving in his appeal . . . that we should treat the whole economic problem as a unity and be prepared to present to the public a total solution of the problems of unemployment and of raising standards of living.'[24] Keynes had indulged in one of those flights of fancy which so endeared him to the technicians. Recalling the main theme of his essay 'The Economic Possibilities for our Grandchildren', he claimed the world was in transition 'from an era of scarcity to an era of abundance', which would require a change in 'all our habits and traditions'. The problem would be one of maintaining sufficient demand; the difficulty of agreeing a global plan was that 'different countries were moving through the period of transition at different speeds'. The rich countries would need to invest in the poor ones, but the notion that they could expect full repayment of their investments was out of date, hence the need for new investment institutions.[25] All this was music to the idealistic James Meade. He was soon to discover an alarming gap between Keynes's rhetoric and his negotiating style.

Keynes naturally led for Britain on the Monetary Group, where he was normally flanked by Robbins, Robertson, Waley, Opie and Thompson-McCausland. (Meade joined the group later.) Keynes had started the monetary discussions privately with White on 13 September in a 'friendly and uncontroversial' way. He was soon able to report that they were 'going very well'.[26] White readily agreed that the Fund's resources should be increased: he was much more concerned that US liability should be limited. They circled round the transitional problem. Keynes said that the Stabilisation Fund could not meet Britain's 'immediate post-war adverse balance', and that Britain might have to continue with its wartime controls. White apparently made no objection. Britain, he said, would be free to keep its sterling area arrangements for an indefinite period. He thought that Lend–Lease would continue till after the end of the Japanese war, now expected to last longer than the European one. They both thought that an international conference of ministers to approve their handiwork might be held in December or January. Keynes was impressed by White's willingness to take 'a high intellectual interest in all these questions and approach . . . them on that plane and not on official or bureaucratic lines'.[27] The impression that all would be sweetness and light was soon dispelled.

On 15 September, the Anglo-American monetary group held the first of eight meetings. Detailed minutes were kept by both sides. Supplemented by James Meade's diary and Thompson-McCausland's reports to the Bank of England they give a full, and sometimes vivid, account of the experts at work. The matter was often forbiddingly technical. Fifty years later there would have been overhead projectors, computer print-outs, graphs. As it was the meetings were dominated by verbal duels between Keynes and White – the rapier versus the blunderbuss. Richard Gardner

says 'they were not unlike two vain and rather jealous economics profes-
sors striving to impress a university seminar'. Keynes was the intellectual
superior, but White held the better cards.[28] Meade wrote: 'Ten years ago
at Oxford I should never have dreamed that an economist could live in
such a heaven of practical application of *real* economic analysis!'[29] The
willingness to engage in argument on the merits of the case was what
distinguished this seminar from the normal political pow-pow. But Keynes,
White and the others were also Englishmen and Americans, representatives of their countries, negotiating under the authority of their governments, and therefore spokesmen of their countries' national interests.
Both sides were prepared to say, when it suited them, that the other's
proposals would be unacceptable to their governments – or, in the
American case, to Congress and the 'American people'.

The seminars tended to follow a set pattern: the British proposed, the
Americans disposed. This was the inevitable consequence of the asymmetry of power. The British were seeking to modify an American plan to
their advantage. They punched: the Americans counter-punched. Both
Keynes and White found the confrontations nervously exhausting. Keynes
was 'sorely tried by White's rasping truculence', White, terrified by open
debate with Keynes, 'tended to over-react, to the point that it affected his
health'.[30] White used to get sick arguing with Keynes, because he was
outgunned, sending, whenever possible, Bernstein in his place.[31]

Keynes's hope of settling the outstanding disagreements over a weekend of discussions proved wildly over-optimistic, because the technical
questions masked large political differences. The British position was that
the smaller the resources of the Fund, the larger must be the latitude
given to members to do what they wanted. The British negotiators
insisted on members' right to devalue and retain exchange and import
restrictions. This was reinforced by a practical consideration. With the
war going so well, the 'transition to peace' could not be long delayed.
Britain would face huge bills for imported reconstruction materials and
expensive social programmes, with its export trade shattered, its overseas
investments largely liquidated, and with a mountain of sterling debts.
The Fund would be useless for all this; but agreement with America to
create it might well be a precondition of American support during the
transition.

The main quarrels were about the size of the Fund's resources, the
conditions of access to them, determination of exhange rates and the
monetisation of unitas.

White had set the Fund's aggregate resources at $5bn, in contrast to
the Clearing Union's $26bn. He wanted the US liability limited to $2bn.
Before the monetary conversations opened, he agreed to increase the
capital of the Fund from $5bn to $8bn–$10bn (depending on how many

nations joined), with a US contribution of $3bn rather than $2bn. This was to be balanced, though, by increased gold subscriptions.

These issues were argued out in the meetings of 17, 24 and 28 September. Keynes insisted that no member be 'required' to subscribe more than 12.5 per cent of its quota in gold. The US formula of 25 to 50 per cent gave a 'gold complexion to the scheme which we should find it hard to accept'. He suggested instead that countries with increasing gold stocks might be requested to increase the gold fraction of their subscriptions. This would gradually equip the Fund with the 'ample gold reserves' the American wanted. Bernstein explained that the White formula should be understood to mean that a member's minimum gold subscription to the Fund should be 25 per cent of its quota or 10 per cent of its gold and foreign exchange reserves, whichever was smaller. Keynes was eventually convinced – though not till he got back to London – that this would actually reduce the amount of gold Britain would be required to pay in.

In the White draft, contributed quotas and borrowing quotas were the same. If a country paid in $100m. in gold and $400m. in securities, its borrowing power would be $500m. It was obvious that the total borrowings could not exceed the Fund's total holdings. But there was no reason why an individual country's maximum borrowing quota should be exactly the same as its contribution. At the 24 September meeting, Keynes proposed that a country's maximum lending commitment should be set at 120 per cent of its quota, and that a country should be allowed to borrow up to 150 per cent of its quota. The first proposal implied that the Fund itself should be able to borrow additional quantities of 'scarce' currencies, using its gold and tradeable securities as collateral. The second meant that with $8bn of subscriptions, aggregate borrowing powers would amount to $12bn, 'though it was not possible that everyone should be using their full powers at once'. Bernstein replied that the Stabilisation Fund scheme did not insist on precise equality between contributed and borrowing quotas, but the inequality should not be too great, or the Fund would run out of available currencies. When the discussion was resumed on 28 September, White pointed out that subscribed quotas were not the limiting factor in borrowing, since the Fund would be able to supply small countries with foreign currencies up to three or four times their quotas. This was more flexible than the British proposal, which, in order to provide for exceptional needs of individual members, would increase facilities available to all members. However, the Americans made important concessions to the British view. The Fund would be allowed to borrow additional currency from a member; and it would be allowed to increase its holdings of a (deficit) member's currency to up to 200 per cent of its quota. This represented a sizeable increase in the Fund's lending facilities over and above its subscribed capital.

But the Americans insisted that any money the Fund lent to a member in excess of its gold subscription would be at its own discretion. As they saw it, the only way to reconcile limited liability to supply currencies with exceptional demands for currencies was to police the supply. In White's 10 July draft, a member's unconditional right to borrow a currency was limited to the amount of its gold subscription. Above this credit would be conditional on 'satisfactory measures' by the borrowing country to 'correct the disequilibrium in the country's balance of payments'. The British wanted the Fund to sell members foreign currency on demand up to an agreed limit. As Keynes had put it to Viner, the issue was 'at what stage in the rake's progress' conditionality would start to apply. It dominated the meeting of 17 September and debate was resumed on 24 September and 4 October. It was never satisfactorily resolved.

At the 17 September meeting Keynes insisted that 'discretionary policing' should not apply to the quotas themselves, only to borrowings which exceeded the quotas. Otherwise drawing rights could never be established as a central bank reserve in competition with gold. The British argued that the Fund should be a 'passive transfer agent' not an 'active discretionary authority'. Keynes remarked, further, that any discretionary rights of the Fund should be framed so as to distinguish between a 'developed country managing its affairs prudently' and an 'irresponsible country anxious to exploit a new source of borrowing'. White replied that it would be irresponsible to expose the Fund to abuse. He explained that his aim was to prevent the Fund's facilities being used to finance capital flight or the issue of foreign loans by a country which couldn't afford to.[32] Thompson-McCausland takes up the story:

> 'The trouble is [Keynes explained] that the Fund is there to be drawn on but you look on yourselves as never likely to draw on it. Neither will we draw on it.' An incredulous gasp from the Americans followed by Harry White with 'Do you mean that England will never have to draw on the Fund?' 'We should never let ourselves draw on terms like that.' This answer from Keynes drew appreciative smiles and applause from Pasvolsky and Berle, the two State Department representatives. It is clear already that the State Department are pressing for a liberal constitution.[33]

At the meeting of 24 September, Berle was in the chair, White was away ill and Bernstein took the US Treasury part. Bernstein insisted that, beyond the drawing right guaranteed by the gold subscription, the Fund would supply foreign currencies at its discretion, having the power to refuse supply 'if its resources were being abused'. Keynes 'doubted whether this proposal would meet his objections. The real function of reserves is to give confidence and Mr Bernstein's proposals seemed to cut at the root of confidence.' Emmanuel Goldenweiser of the Federal

Reserve Board agreed that large countries would find Bernstein's procedure 'intolerable'.[34]

The Americans were prepared to soften the wording, but not the substance. In the 4 October meeting White restated his view that the Fund's facilities were a privilege not a right, and were therefore rightly subject to a behaviour test. Keynes replied that the US proposals 'did not get over the objection that a member's actions would be subject to scrutiny the moment its currency in the Fund equalled its [gold] quota' and that he thought there was only a remote chance that the British government would accept it.

Keynes summarised his views to Jacob Viner on 17 October:

Our view has been very strongly that if countries are to be given sufficient confidence they must be able to rely in all normal circumstances on drawing a substantial part of their quota without policing or facing unforeseen obstacles.... the Clearing Union may have been too strict on this, though this was actually balanced ... by the much greater size of the quotas.... No doubt it is a difficult issue. But I am sure that it would be very unwise to try to make an untried institution too grandmotherly.[35]

The debate over the 'nuances of uncertainty'[36] attached to drawing rights continued beyond Washington.

An equally contentious issue was exchange rates. In the White draft of 10 July par values of members' currencies were fixed in terms of gold (by reference to the Fund's unit of account, unitas). As under the gold standard, this fixed the exchange rates of national currencies – the rates at which they could be bought by and sold for other currencies. But it was not a gold standard, merely a conditional fixed exchange rate system, since membership of the Fund entailed no requirement to pay out gold in settling international accounts. However, the White draft did presuppose that, with the help of the Fund's facilities, members would be able to maintain fixed exchange rates without recourse to 'foreign exchange restrictions, bilateral clearing arrangements, multiple currency devices, and discriminatory foreign exchange practices...'.[37] It erected barriers against unilateral changes in exchange rates. For the first 'uncertain' three years after the war members were allowed to change their initial rates by 10 per cent without Fund approval, and by more than that with majority approval. Thereafter, rates could be altered only to correct a 'fundamental disequilibrium' and with the approval of three-quarters of the member votes.*

* The White draft also stipulated that the Fund itself could not change the value of all currencies against gold without the approval of 85 per cent of the member votes. This provision was dropped. It reflected the fear that, by this means, the Fund could vote itself

The Clearing Union had also envisaged fixed exchange rates, but it made a difference to the British that the monetary scheme would be White's and not Keynes's. In the Keynes Plan the United States was liable, in theory, to 'give away' up to $23bn of its exports – in other words, to accept other countries' paper in payment; in the White Plan, this was whittled down to $3bn. The British thus placed increasing weight on a country's freedom to devalue its currency or refuse to accept a surplus country's goods.

In its instructions to the British team the Cabinet had insisted on retaining national sovereignty over exchange rates with the possibility of an 'objective test' for exchange rate changes. Meade had been advocating 'some objective statistical test' for allowing quantitative import restrictions in his Commercial Union scheme.[38]

Keynes claimed that the only suitable test was if the production costs of one country were inflating faster than those of another. This expressed his long-standing view that a country's monetary 'standard' should adjust to its 'labour standard'. Meade thought that this 'won't do' and worked out an 'objective test' of his own, based on trends in a country's balance of payments and reserve position.* Unlike Viner, Meade was not against handing over 'monetary sovereignty' to the trade unions. He was simply arguing that an objective test based on reserve movements would cover relative wage movements, as well as other causes of disequilibrium.

Keynes was unconvinced. But he commissioned, and endorsed, a note by Meade on 'The Problem of Securing Sufficient Elasticity for Changing the Exchange Rates',[39] which steered a tortuous path between the American demand for fixed rates and the British demand for flexibility. Exchange rates should be changed only to correct a 'fundamental disequilibrium'. Approval of 10 per cent changes over a ten-year period would be automatic. Larger changes would require Fund approval. In deciding whether to give such approval, the Fund should take into account changes in relative costs and changes in the balance of payments (combining the Keynes and Meade 'tests'), but not the social or political policies which had led to the disequilibrium. If Fund approval was withheld, the member could leave the Fund.

---

larger quotas, that is, be able to borrow larger amounts of American dollars. 'It would be impossible', White explained, 'to submit to Congress a plan giving other countries the power to determine the gold value of the dollar.'

* Meade's test was that 'a country would be permitted to depreciate its currency by x per cent in any year if during the preceding year the fall in its net holding of International Currency, of Gold and of quick assets in the currencies of countries which were members of the Monetary Union (after deducting corresponding quick liabilities) was more than y per cent of its total international trade'. Slightly modified, this would also give a test for quantitative import restrictions.

Keynes introduced what became known as the 'Keynes–Waley' proposal at the first meeting of the joint monetary group on 15 September. White was sceptical about the possibility of an objective test. 'Would not reliance on the Fund's discretion be more satisfactory in a matter so full of politics?' Objecting to the procedure of the American proposal, Keynes said that discussing exchange rate changes in 'mixed company' would give rise to speculation; a devaluation must come about as a sudden act on a certain date after secret discussions. White thought that a unilateral emergency change would not be needed if there was continual contact between the three or four major Treasuries, and that speculation would be held in check by exchange controls.

Keynes's negotiating position was undermined by the British Treasury's refusal of his proposal. It would not accept surrender by treaty of its 'right to protect employment by exchange adjustment', and wanted a general promise to consult about exchange rate changes substituted for Keynes's formula. Keynes cabled back that 'it would be a very drastic change to propose that every country should be free to make unlimited unilateral alterations in its exchange merely after consultation. All of us here think that [our] proposals give sufficient elasticity and independence. We would be sorry to have to go back so completely on the idea of having some definite rules to preserve exchange stability.' Dalton in London surmised that 'while the cats are away, the mice, led by the rump of the Treasury and the bloody Bank of England', were seizing the chance to sabotage agreement with the United States. He persuaded the War Cabinet to tone down the instructions.[40]

At the joint monetary meeting of 4 October White suggested that a country should have the right to change its rate once by up to 10 per cent; if it wanted a further 10 per cent it should be entitled to an answer from the Fund within forty-eight hours. Discussion then turned on 'whether an undertaking to consult the Fund before changing the exchange rate should replace an obligation to obtain the Fund's approval for changes'. They also discussed whether a member whose request had been refused should be able to withdraw from the Fund immediately. The Americans dropped the 75 per cent majority approval for a change in exchange rates and conceded Keynes's proposal that a country's domestic policies should not be a ground for refusing a devaluation. In the end the only difference which remained was by how much, and under what conditions, a member would be allowed to devalue its currency during the three-year transition period.

The British also extracted concessions on 'scarce currencies'. The White draft of 10 July only provided for the 'rationing' of scarce currencies by the Fund, but without indicating how this would work. Kyriakos Varvaressos, the governor of the Greek Central Bank, had pointed to the lack of Fund discipline on persistent creditors. At the 28 September meeting Keynes took up this argument: if, when a country's currency was declared scarce, other members were expected to maintain their exchange rates against the scarce currency, they must be allowed to restrict payments in that currency. On 4 October the United States group accepted this, but hoped that it would lead to import, not exchange, controls.[41] Meade, who was simultaneously engaged in the trade negotiations, could not believe that 'Hawkins and the other people in the State Department realise what their Treasury people are suggesting'.[42] Keynes reported to the Chancellor of the Exchequer that the new scarce-currency clause 'puts the creditor country on the spot so acutely that in the view of us all, the creditor country simply cannot afford to let such a situation arise'.[43]

Keynes's main effort to get the Stabilisation Fund to put on the clothes of the Clearing Union was his proposal to monetise unitas. The crucial structural difference between the Clearing Bank and the Stabilisation Fund set-ups was that in the Keynes Plan member central banks banked with the Clearing Bank, whereas in the White Plan the Fund banked with member central banks. Member central banks would subscribe gold, domestic currencies and securities to the Fund's account with them, from which the Fund could make payments to any other central bank, whenever that country's currency 'cannot be disposed of in the foreign exchange markets within the range established by the Fund'. If, for example, the Bank of England needed more francs it could be instructed by the Fund to transfer gold or cash from the Fund's acount at the Bank of England to the Bank of France as collateral for a franc loan from the Fund. In Keynes's view, this had a threefold defect. A member bank was subject to a potential drain of its gold reserves through the Fund's account with it, the Fund was the active agent in currency dealings, and multilateral clearing was not assured, since the Fund, at its discretion, could refuse to buy sterling with its francs, even though sterling was not, in general, in over-supply. The Fund's prospective hyper-activism was also anathema to the Bank of England, which feared it could use its discretion to discriminate against sterling and thus undermine the sterling area. The Bank instructed Thompson-McCausland that on 'no account' must the Fund be allowed to 'buy or sell currencies or gold'.[44]

Keynes's proposal for a unitas-based Stabilisation Fund, designed to overcome these defects, was sent to White on 21 September. Subscriptions would be sterilised – the Fund could not transfer them to other members. In return for their deposits, member banks would receive 'credits' of unitas which they could trade with each other. If now the Bank of England needed more francs (or any other currency) it could buy them with unitas, its own reserves being unaffected. This achieved two main purposes. It ensured that inter-Fund settlements were multilateral: 'a monetised unitas [would] express a generalised . . . claim on the world at large'.

rather than a claim on a particular currency. And it assured the prized British goal of Fund 'passivity'.[45]

'In a brilliant speech' to the joint monetary group on 24 September, Keynes 'expounded the case for making Unitas into a real transferable money'. The bluntness of Bernstein's rejection of the idea is apparent even in the bland language of the minutes: the United States, he said, would want an assurance that 'a share in their production was not claimable by tender of a new "trick" currency, and that the economic power represented by the United States gold reserves would not be substantially diminished'. More pertinently, he stressed that 'no magic could disguise the fact that the Fund might be short or long in particular currencies even in unitas terms'.[46]

The meeting on 28 September was largely 'a duet between White and Keynes'. White rejected Keynes's proposal because it would give every country a claim on dollars, leading to the possibility that the US would have to supply the Fund with dollars equal to the total drawing rights of all the other members. 'It would, he felt, be bringing in the clearing-union principle by the back door.'[47] White however made important concessions to the British position. The Fund's accounts were to be inter-convertible, and dealings in currencies take place only 'on the member's initiative'.[48] Most of the British monetary group thought these concessions were enough, but not Keynes, who continued to fight for his pet. Meade was horrified. It would be 'criminally foolish' to break on this matter. If Keynes persisted 'we must organise a revolt'. Meade went through the roof when he heard that the Bank of England from London was insisting on the monetisation of unitas: 'all the other elements in these talks – our Commercial Union, the Commodity proposals, Investment, Full Employment, Cartels – all hang upon a successful outcome of the monetary talks; in the monetary talks we look like obtaining every point of substance – and there is talk of the Bank of England making agreement impossible on something which doesn't matter a tinker's cuss. Who governs England?'

When the point came up at a meeting of the British currency group at the Willard Hotel on 2 October, Robbins urged that they give way. Ministers in London would not consider this a breaking point. Keynes then intervened: 'You have forgotten the Governor of the Bank of England.' Meade wrote in his diary: 'What a wonderful foolish remark! Lionel made a questioning gesture, Waley looked extremely uncomfortable.' Meade was convinced that Keynes remained intransigent 'merely on grounds of bargaining now. He is convinced, I believe, that it is not really a point of substance.'[49]

For Keynes it was more than a drafting issue. He saw a monetised unitas as a technically elegant or *aesthetic* way of achieving the purposes of his Bank: credit creation, multilateral clearing, passivity, protection of members' gold reserves, protection of sterling's position. He was also much more alive than was Meade to the power of the Bank of England to sabotage an international currency scheme if it joined opponents of it in the government. So Keynes reserved Britain's position. He noted ruefully that 'there is nothing more difficult than to continue a controversy with people who admit that your proposal is immeasurably better than theirs but nevertheless hold out on the ground that for obscure psychological reasons only theirs is practical politics'.[50] Ironically, it was the British insistence on multilateral clearing which led the United States to make currency convertibility on current account a condition of receiving Fund assistance, which in turn led the British to the concept of an indefinite transition period.

Throughout the negotiations Whitehall had wobbled between supporting Keynes's efforts to make the Fund more like the Clearing Union and preserving Britain's freedom on the assumption that it would not be. One particularly unfortunate consequence of this uncertainty of aim was the deletion of that section of the White draft dealing with the funding of 'abnormal' wartime balances. The idea was that the Fund would gradually buy the temporarily 'blocked' sterling balances from Britain, Britain repaying the Fund 40 per cent of their value over a period of twenty years. Bound by his instructions, Keynes told White that Britain was anxious to postpone any serious discussion on 'abnormal' (sterling) balances. This momentous decision ensured that sterling debts remained unfunded for thirty years, the disproportion between reserves and liabilities leading to a succession of sterling crises in the post-war era.

By early October, the technicians had got as far as they could get, and the atmosphere was not improving. The carefully calculated British strategy to reduce the areas of disagreement had clearly expired by the time of the following entry in Meade's diary, dated 4 October:

What absolute Bedlam these discussions are! Keynes and White sit next each other, each flanked by a long row of his own supporters. Without any agenda or any prepared idea of what is going to be discussed they go for each other in a strident duet of discord which after a crescendo of abuse on either side leads up to a chaotic adjournment. . . . Today we first discussed the problem of policing the use of the fund, on which some compromise may be found. Incidentally it became crystal clear that White believes that discriminatory exchange or import restrictions should be imposed against scarce currency countries rather than that exchange rates should be allowed to go. . . . We then discussed flexibility of exchange rates. The Americans insist on great stability, and we oppose with a demand for almost unilateral freedom to depreciate. Everyone seems to have forgotten the possibility of an objective test . . . which should logically provide the solution of allowing the Americans to say to *their* public that unnecessary competitive exchange depreciation had been ruled out and us to say to *our* public that we could not be prevented from depreciating if and when it became really necessary.[51]

When discussion turned to procedure, there were more explosions. Morgenthau himself had put White's plan for a Reconstruction and Development Bank officially on the conference agenda at a lunch he gave for Keynes on 14 September.[52] At the final meeting of the Plenary Conference on 30 September, from which Keynes was absent, White suddenly anounced that his scheme – minus the Commodity Stabilisation Corporation – having received the President's approval, was about to be presented to Congress and published, without any consultation with the British or, apparently, the State Department. The next day Keynes got White round to see him and told him 'frankly and crudely' what they thought of him. This wigging, according to Keynes, entirely restored his good humour and he promised to postpone publication. The document itself, Keynes thought, was 'extremely odd'. There were some 'very genuine motives' behind it, but these were 'so wrapped up and camouflaged' that it looked like the work of a 'near lunatic'.[53] Meade was sunk in despair. 'Keynes is now calling White's investment plan loony,' he wrote in his diary. 'That man is a menace in international negotiations.'[54]

Keynes's bad temper did not end there. At the meeting of the joint monetary group on 6 October, both sides agreed to prepare a directive for the Drafting Committee, which would be charged with fleshing out the principles which the experts wanted their governments to accept, as a prelude to an international monetary conference. The final meeting on Saturday 9 October, called to consider drafts of the directive prepared separately by British and American teams, was explosive:

> Keynes [wrote Meade, who was not there] has been storming and saying (when Bernstein in place of a short note ... produced yet another typically Bernstein document), 'This is intolerable. It is yet another Talmud. We had better simply break off negotiations,' Harry White has replied 'We will try to produce something which Your Highness *can* understand.' Negotiations *were* apparently broken off at lunch time. Then the Americans produced a more reasonable draft. ... This was discussed at 4.30 and the scene ended with love, kisses and compliments all round. But it augurs ill for the future unless these negotiations can somehow or another be got out of the hands of two such prima donnas as White and Keynes.

Keynes believed his 'explosion' had led to the 'breakthrough'. Bernstein had tried to get the British to sign an interpretation of the Stabilisation

Fund 'which the Talmudist wrote many months ago and has never been willing to alter, if he could help it, by one iota'. The other members of the Group 'thought I had overdone it, but after we had left the meeting a telephone message came along . . . that the paper was withdrawn. . . . It is one example, in my judgment, of how important it is in this country to react strenuously.'[55]

Harry White's summary of what had been achieved in Washington is just: 'It is a part compromise, but much more like the American plan.'[56] The two sides managed to produce an 'Anglo-American Draft Statement of Principles' calling for the setting up of 'an international stabilisation fund'. The essential feature of the Anglo-American compromise was that, in return for accepting the US principle of limited liability, Britain won a small increase in Fund resources, a greater freedom to devalue, without reference to 'the domestic social or political policies which may have led to the application', a promise of passivity and the right 'temporarily to restrict the freedom of exchange operations' in a currency which the Fund had declared 'scarce'. Remaining disagreements were covered by rival statements. The two sides continued to dispute the proportion of gold subscriptions, the conditionality attached to drawings, the latitude for exchange rate depreciation, provisions for repaying borrowings, and the degree to which the Fund might finance capital transactions. There was a general British reservation about a non-unitas Stabilisation Fund and Keynes – or rather Thompson-McCausland – produced a unitas version of the Joint Statement.[57] There was no clear acknowledgement of a transition period before the Fund would come into operation. One clear gain, soon to be lost, was the translation of the Principles from 'Cherokee' into English.

It was typical, Keynes thought, of the American way of doing business that White refused to sign the agreed document, which therefore bore Keynes's signature alone. 'During the war', he wrote in some exasperation to the Chancellor, 'I have altogether spent five months in close negotiations with the United States Treasury and on no single occasion have they answered any communication of mine in writing, or confirmed in writing anything which has passed in conversation.'

Keynes continued to be baffled by how public business *was* done in America. He always tended to believe that the administration was guarding against phantom dangers; or, if they were real dangers, this was only because of poor presentation. Morgenthau had spent ten years at the Treasury trying to appease a 'non existent public sentiment'. After Morgenthau had shown the experts' schemes to Congress, he mused: 'The difficulty is, of course, that these plans are presented to Congress in just about the most unattractive manner and with just about the most unattractive faces and unattractive voices that human nature can compass.' (The Senators' confusion had been compounded by the fact that 'Harry has chosen to call his Bank a fund and his fund a Bank.') He deplored the absence of the 'arts of government as we understand them. It may be that some other art, which we have difficulty in apprehending, is being employed.'[58] Keynes could never quite accept that manner of presentation, so important in a parliamentary regime, mattered little in the American system; the black arts were those of jaw-boning, arm-twisting and cutting deals.

Keynes gave his usual upbeat report on the performance of the British delegation. 'We have been a very happy party, with great concord all round.' This is not entirely borne out by Meade's diary. Keynes started very well, eloquent, lucid, witty and enthusiastic, but got steadily more bad-tempered the further the negotiations progressed and the tireder he got. Meade was eventually made distraught by the way his 'ill-manners' in the monetary seminars jeopardised the progress he, Meade, was making with the Americans on commercial policy. Keynes, as Meade rightly surmised, had no 'fire in his belly' for free trade. He talked of the need to 'unleash and unshackle' monetary from commercial policy – a pun on the names of Liesching and Shackle who, together with Meade, were the Board of Trade officials conducting the negotiations on the latter. 'As you know', he wrote to Liesching on 8 October, 'I am . . . a hopeless sceptic about this return to nineteenth century *laissez-faire*, for which you and the State Department seem to have such a nostalgia. I believe that the future lies with – (i) State trading for commodities; (ii) International cartels for necessary manufactures; and (iii) Quantitative import restrictions for non-essential manufactures. Yet all these . . . instrumentalities for orderly economic life in the future you seek to outlaw.' Harrod, who quotes this letter, writes that it was 'partly meant to tease'.[59] There was more to it than that. First, Keynes was determined to get a monetary agreement accepted by the British government; hence his determination to 'unleash and unshackle' it from imperial preference, to which the Cabinet was firmly committed. Secondly, to the extent that White's Stabilisation Fund fell short of his much more grandiose Clearing Union, Keynes became more protective of national sovereignty and the right to indulge in what Robertson called 'Forbidden Tricks'. Thirdly, he doubted whether there was much enthusiasm in America, outside the State Department, for 'Hullism'. On this matter he was influenced by the bitter disputes which had been taking place in Washington that summer between British and American officials over the administration of Lend–Lease, and what these showed about America's post-war intentions.

Limiting Britain's gold and dollar reserves had become official US policy at the end of 1942. This, together with the limitations on its exports which Britain had accepted in September 1941 in return for Lend–Lease, meant that Britain would start the peace with a massively adverse balance of payments deficit, and reserves which fell far short of its rapidly

accumulating debts. Without some alleviation, it would be in no early
position either to honour a commitment to currency convertibility or to
scrap its imperial preference system and wartime controls on imports.
Dean Acheson of the State Department understood most clearly that a
policy of restricting British exports and reserves during the war was
inconsistent with the Article VII agenda. He therefore pressed for policies
which would allow Britain to build up its reserves. He was defeated,
however, by an alliance between Harry Dexter White of the US Treasury
and Leo Crowley, who had been appointed head of the Foreign Economic
Administration (successor of the Office of Lend–Lease Administration
(OLLA)) in July 1943. Crowley was an anti-British American of Irish
extraction, close to business interests in Congress. But Harry White was
the real author of the policy of manipulating the Lend–Lease Agreement
to limit the growth of British reserves. He was the chairman of an inter-
departmental committee which recommended in December 1942 that
they be kept within the range of $600m. to $1bn, a policy endorsed by
Roosevelt on 11 January 1943. He had two instruments to hand: extending
US requirements for free deliveries from Britain under Reciprocal Aid
(Reverse Lend–Lease), and reducing the volume of American Lend–Lease
supplies. Both policies were put into operation in the course of 1943,
under Lauchlin Currie, who was OLLA's (and later FEA's) chief administrative officer; under him was Frank Coe, another White–Currie protégé.
Keynes knew that White and Currie were in favour of limiting Britain's
balances, though probably not that White initiated the strategy. He
assumed that their aim was to limit Britain's independence; Currie
(retrospectively) claimed that his only purpose was 'to defend Lend–Lease
from scandal or attack'.[60]

Keynes was only peripherally involved in the Lend–Lease battles, but
he left the Americans in no doubt about his attitude. At a lunch he gave
for officials of the Foreign Economic Administration at the Statler on 24
September 1943 he asserted Britain's determination to launch a 'frontal
attack on the existing policy of limitation [of reserves]'. The Americans,
he told his luncheon guests, 'must dismiss from their minds that any
Chancellor could get up in the House of Commons and explain that we
had accepted any limit to our balances. The financial sacrifices which we
had made for the common cause were incomparably greater than those
of any other of the United Nations. . . . Why, moreover, should the poverty
test be applied to us alone? It was not applied to Russia nor, in the case
of Reciprocal Aid, to America herself. . . .' If the Americans had decided
it was time to reduce Lend–Lease, that was up to them. Keynes's remarks
had no effect. At a US Treasury meeting on 29 September, White stated
that 'the time had come to take a strong line to reduce the lend–leasing
of non-military goods'. As to 'the deeper reason' for Britain being treated
differently from the Soviet Union (or China), Bernard Knollenberg, one

of the FEA officials present at the Keynes lunch, pointed out that neither 'is a great traditional competitor of ours in international trade'.[61]

Despite these undercurrents, Keynes found the post-Pearl Harbor atmosphere in Washington more congenial than when he had last been there in 1941. 'People in Washingon are extraordinarily kind.' Lord Halifax was in England, so he and Lydia were spared Embassy receptions; they relaxed in the 'high-brow' circle of the Lippmanns, Frankfurters, Chatfield-Taylors and Archibald MacLeish, who was a poet and the librarian of Congress. Keynes gave a rare interview, to *Fortune Magazine*, whose feature on him appeared in March 1944. He had the *frisson* of being rung up by the Duke of Windsor. The Duke, who had been made Governor of Bermuda, was trying to get a Cambridge job for his economic adviser, John Henry Richardson. Rather more excitement was caused by the sudden resignation of Under-Secretary of State Sumner Welles. 'Remind me when I get back to tell you the full story,' Keynes wrote to Eady. Welles resigned on grounds of ill-health, but Keynes would have known all about the homosexual scandals.

Keynes did not notice people as a novelist does, and his judgement of them was based on pseudo-scientific clues (like the shape or condition of their hands) rather than on close observation. Nevertheless, within these limitations, he recorded some acute impressions of the Washington scene. Adolph Berle was 'a queer attractive, unattractive figure in disequilibrium with himself and the world'. Lauchlin Currie was 'an old friend of mine and I know him well, but there is no one more difficult to handle. He is extremely suspicious and jealous, very anti-British on such issues as India, and always inclined to assume the worst'. Keynes's keen sense of the Jewishness of both White and Bernstein did not blind him to distinctions between the two. His depiction of Bernstein as a 'regular little rabbi, a reader out of the Talmud, to Harry's political high rabbidom' is astute. Out of his rows, and progress, with White, a wary admiration had developed:

With Harry White, as you may suppose, we have been spending a vast amount of time. Any reserves we may have about him are a pale reflection of what his colleagues feel. He is over-bearing, a bad colleague, always trying to bounce you, with a harsh rasping voice, aesthetically oppressive in mind and manner; he has not the faintest conception how to behave or observe the rules of civilised inter- course. At the same time, I have a very great respect and even liking for him. A very able and devoted public servant, carrying an immense burden of responsibility and initiative, of high integrity and of clear sighted idealistic international purpose, genuinely intending to do his best for the world. Moreover, his over-powering will combined with the fact that he has constructive ideas mean that he does get things done, which few else here do. The way to reach him is to respect his purpose, arouse his intellectual interest (it is a great softener to intercourse that it is easy to arouse his genuine interest in the merits of any issue) and to tell him off very frankly and firmly without finesse when he has gone off the rails of relevant argument or appropriate behaviour.[62]

A little later Harry White told Roosevelt that Keynes was 'an extremely able and tough negotiator with, of course, a thorough understanding of the problems that confronted us, but when not negotiating or discussing points of difference . . . he was quite friendly'.[63]

Before he left Washington Keynes provided his parents with his usual summary:

> I doubt if I have ever in my life spent a more strenuous month. 42 lunch and dinner engagements, endless meetings . . . countless speeches. . . .
>
> I end up in excellent health, after having been near exhaustion once or twice. Assuredly this is due to the attendant conditions – Lydia always comforting and ruling, a first class staff in Lucius Thompson and my Secretary Miss Macey, great comfort in the hotel (the rent of our rooms, where we have done most of our entertaining, £40 a week!), a large Packard with a knowing chauffeur at our disposal. . . .
>
> And we are very content indeed with what we have accomplished – greatly in excess of our expectations . . . a great *will to agree*, and a remarkable comradeship growing up between the British and American civil servants with almost emotional scenes on parting. We all really are trying to make good economic bricks for the world after the war – however hopelessly difficult the political problems may be.

Maynard and Lydia spent a few days in New York, he using his 'best arts of persuasion on the more obdurate bankers' and arranging for a show of American pictures for CEMA, she seeing old ballet friends like Leonid Massine. Her mother had died in Leningrad, still under German siege, while she was in America. After returning to Washington for further Lend–Lease discussions, they flew back by Clipper, arriving in London on 28 October.

Christmas at Tilton followed its now usual pattern. There was a shoot, in which Maynard took part. On Christmas Day, thirty-five sat down to lunch, for which 'Roma' had prepared six rabbit pies. For the Charlestonians, Vanessa Bell and Duncan Grant, Keynes had written out his forecasts for 1944. The European war, he thought, would end between August and October, after a crushing Allied offensive on both fronts. This date 'will suit President Roosevelt and he has not overlooked this'. The last stages of the Japanese war 'may be long or short but will remain as boring as they are now'. With Germany's capitulation 'new and harassing anxieties will arise. The fact that no-one has a good solution will make it difficult to resist bad ones.' This time it was not just Maynard's usual over-optimism. Few doubted that Germany would be beaten in 1944. Safeguarding Britain's economic survival in the post-Lend–Lease world had become a matter of urgency.

Early in January 1944, Keynes drafted some 'Notes on External Finance in the Post-Japanese Armistice Transitional Period'. This raised the issues which would occupy an increasing fraction of his time and energy in the last two years of his life: the problem of Britain's post-war balance of payments, the problem of the sterling balances, the pros and cons of seeking American assistance in a post-Lend–Lease world.[64] But the war was still too clamant for Britain's post-war needs to command much attention in Whitehall. The future would take care of itself.

III

CONVINCING WHITEHALL

Two steps were now required to clinch the Washington agreement. The experts themselves had to resolve their remaining differences, and the two governments had to endorse their work. The first was more easily done than the second; and the second more easily done in Washington than in London. White, having got most of what he wanted from Britain – and the rest of the Allies – was now the pursuer rather than the pursued. He was supported by Morgenthau, and Morgenthau was supported by the President. Washington politics dictated speed, not delay. There was a Presidential election due in November 1944. An international treaty setting up Fund and Bank, signed, sealed and delivered and, if possible approved by Congress, would form part of Roosevelt's re-election campaign, enabling him to brand the Republicans as isolationists.

White got into action first, sending Keynes a letter with a revised draft statement of principles on 19 November. He wanted this to be published in the near future; they could then proceed with an international conference in March or April and the treaty submitted to Congress in May. Keynes took a month to reply. He had been working through the text trying to rub away outstanding differences. The trivial issues were quickly disposed of, in exchanges between Keynes and White, and in discussions between White and Opie in Washington. Keynes accepted the American formula for gold subscriptions, and abandoned his insistence on gold sterilisation. On his suggestion, the International Stabilisation Fund now started to be called the 'International Monetary Fund'.[65] White thought that trivial technical details could be settled at the conference itself.

Keynes pointed out that some of the details might be technical, but they were not trivial. In a letter to Opie in Washington on 7 December, he said that the main points being stressed in London were the monetisation of unitas and the need to secure Britain 'an entirely free hand' during the transition period. Keynes told White on 17 December that deficits incurred during the transition period were 'outside the true scope of the new institution' and inserted a new section on transitional arrangements giving countries the right to maintain exchange controls and exempting them from the obligations of convertibility for an indefinite period after the war. There was no date for setting up the Fund. On unitas, he told Opie that 'whilst I have every natural reason for vastly preferring this set up, I cannot persuade myself that the difference between the two versions [justifies] an ultimate breach'.[66]

Morgenthau and White could not understand the reason for the British delay in agreeing to publication of the experts' report, since they did not think it would commit the British government. They failed to appreciate that a government White Paper in Britain was more than an invitation to negotiate with Parliament. And the British government was far from ready to make any commitments on the range of topics negotiated by the experts in Washington. Keynes noted that there were those who, having been foiled in their hope that 'these plans would die a natural death', now saw no need 'officiously to keep alive any international currency scheme at all'.

Keynes had to fight for the survival of the Joint Statement in the Treasury itself. The Chancellor, Sir Kingsley Wood, had died suddenly on 21 September, Sir John Anderson succeeding him. Anderson carried more weight in the Cabinet than Wood had done. But Keynes hardly knew him, and Anderson immediately came under other influences, notably that of Sir Wilfrid Eady. Eady had taken charge of overseas finance in the summer of 1943. Unfortunately for Keynes his promotion coincided with the illness of Sir Richard Hopkins, another victim of heart troubles. Eady, who had not enjoyed being on the receiving end of Keynes's witticisms on domestic employment policy, mistrusted flights into the international stratosphere. Keynes should have been – perhaps was – alerted to the changed mood in the Treasury by the flavour of the instructions he received in Washington. These placed less emphasis on trying to reach agreement with the United States, more on escaping from commitments. What had happened was that, while Keynes was abroad, Eady had teamed up with Henderson and the Bank of England to block the monetary deal. Dalton, with his acute political antennae, sniffed 'a high-powered intrigue to lessen [Keynes's] influence'.[67]

The alliance of a section of the Treasury with the Bank of England gave opponents of the Article VII agenda in the Cabinet their chance. These included Bevin, Beaverbrook, Brendan Bracken, Amery and Hudson.

Opposition to Article VII had been strengthened by the Beveridge and full employment commitments. These, in conjunction with more familiar desires to defend imperial preference and British farming, led, early in 1944, 'Hudson, Amery and Beaverbrook, with widespread Labour support, to send a spate of papers to the Cabinet and to Churchill opposing British entry into commercial talks with the State Department of the kind which had been envisaged by the Law Mission talks of September and October 1943'.[68] Prominent in the campaign was Churchill's court favourite Lord Beaverbrook, now Lord Privy Seal, a Canadian by birth, who had long espoused imperial economic union as a counterweight to American power. A Canadian observer wrote of an 'extraordinary harlequinade of colours', made up of 'old-fashioned Imperialists and old-fashioned protectionists, of doctrinaire socialists wedded in principle to planning and opposed in principle to gold and to international bankers, and finally of new-fangled economists (many of them at the Oxford Institute of Statistics) who favoured bilateralism on theoretical grounds'.[69] Churchill let the battle rage. Like Bevin he hated any suggestion of a gold standard, but was an instinctive free trader. However, on economic matters, he now spoke from memory. Addressing a meeting of the Party faithful in April, he declared in ringing tones: 'It's all about dear food; we beat you on that before and we'll beat you again' – forgetting that he was now the leader of the Conservative Party, not the liberal free trader of 1906.[70]

Having received Law's Report on the Washington conversations, the War Cabinet asked him, on 21 December, to prepare a report on the matters on which ministers would have to decide. These covered the whole field of the Article VII negotiations. Keynes and other members of the Treasury and the Economic Section drafted the monetary section of Law's Report, and tried to answer questions put by ministers. The most hostile were by Bevin, Leo Amery and Robert Hudson, the Minister of Agriculture. In a note of 19 January, Eady presented a picture of a Treasury 'riven on the subject', with Keynes and Robertson emphatic in support of the Stabilisation Fund, Hubert Henderson hostile, Waley sceptical, and a Bank of England full of technical objections.[71] For his part, Keynes longed for the return of 'Hoppy', still convalescing. 'It would make an enormous difference if we could get him back again in reasonably good health,' he told his mother.

Henderson still believed that the real issue was not the structure of the proposed organisation but 'whether we can afford to renounce so much of our power to regulate our external economy'.[72] The Bank's two main worries – as expressed in a memorandum by Catto – were over-rigid provision for exchange rates and 'the passivity problem which is more acute in the "mixed bag" draft than in the "unitas" draft'. If Keynes's Clearing Union, which had 'never been bettered' (the Bank now said!), was ruled out, the Fund should be put into cold storage. Above all, Britain should not go to America 'on our knees, creating an impression that only their wealth can save us. We can, if need be, save ourselves.'[73] Keynes's rejection of the Bank's argument, frequently repeated, was twofold: Britain's debts to the sterling area were too large for it to remain its banker without American support; and the Bank's 'going it alone' would mean throwing over the welfare state. 'We are not going to win the war', he said, 'and put on a hairshirt.'

The monetary section of Law's Report to the War Cabinet outlined two options, the first drafted by Keynes recommending acceptance of the Joint Statement, the second by Henderson recommending rejection. These mirrored the two factions, as described by Lord Cherwell: 'The one is headed by Lord Keynes, and supported by most of the Treasury, the Economic Section of War Cabinet and officials of the Board of Trade. The other acts under the aegis of the Bank of England and consists of Sir Hubert Henderson, an economist with Schachtian aspirations, and Sir Wilfrid Eady, who after a variegated Civil Service experience, has only recently joined the Treasury.'[74] Once again, Keynes marshalled his arguments. Multilateral clearing was enormously to Britain's advantage, since 'our best sources of supply are not always our best markets'. The Washington Plan enabled countries to resume multilateral clearing by correcting the maldistribution of gold; the Plan was likely to 'double our resources to meet contingencies . . . not to be lightly rejected'.

On the question of creditor adjustment, Keynes summed up:

> Put shortly in terms of the US as an example, what the Americans are offering the rest of the world is as follows. Up to £750 million they put at the disposal of the Fund the equivalent of any dollars which may accrue to them from a favourable balance of payments as a result of their neither consuming nor investing what they earn from their imports. If it appears that the cumulative balance thus built up is in danger of exceeding this total, they have the option of getting rid of their surplus on imports or overseas investment, of increasing their contribution to the Fund . . . or accepting the conditions which become applicable when the Fund has declared dollars to be a 'scarce' currency. The conditions under this third alternative mean in effect that . . . all the other countries of the world become entitled forthwith to put any form of restrictions they choose in the way of accepting American goods and in the way of paying for any they do accept. . . . This proposal represents, therefore, a revolutionary change for the better compared with the position in the inter-war period.

Keynes argued that the compromise on exchange rates combined 'an orderly procedure for change with retaining a sufficient ultimate freedom of action to individual members'. Although monetisation of unitas was greatly to be preferred from the technical point of view, the Americans had objected that it could not pass Congress, and the experts thought the British should defer to the Americans on this point. On the transitional arrangements, the Treasury had sent a new clause to Washington, reserving for Britain full freedom in the transitional period. Britain should tell the United States frankly that it could not enter the proposed scheme unless America helped Britain after the end of Lend–Lease. The balance of advantage lay, not in postponing the scheme, but in clinching the deal as quickly as possible, because even in the interim period, when its provisions would be suspended, 'an authoritative organ of international discussion and consultation can play a specially significant part in finding the way out of the transition, where we would sit as equals, instead of waiting on the mat outside the US Treasury'.[75]

The Law Report was circulated to the War Cabinet on 9 February 1944, with Law, in attendance, strongly supporting the monetary compromise. A decision on what to do was needed, since Dominion representatives were coming to London to be briefed on the outcome of the Washington talks. The majority favoured the monetary proposals, despite 'a ludicrous paper' from Beaverbrook saying they meant a new gold standard, but the Cabinet did not know what to do about the other parts of the Grand Design. So it decided to set up a Committee on External Economic Policy to consider the Report further, consisting of the Chancellor, Oliver Lyttelton, Beaverbrook, Dalton, Law and Cherwell.

In this, and the subsequent Cabinet discussions, Churchill refused to give a lead. He complained that he did not understand complex economic issues, and anyway was too busy to study the papers. He was indifferent to anything except winning the war. Naturally enough, his mind was concentrated on the planned D-Day landings in Normandy. Still, with the war now more or less won, this attitude of detachment from post-war problems made less and less sense. It was to contribute greatly to the heavy Conservative defeat in 1945.

The Cabinet Committee met six times between 14 and 17 February, with Keynes attending the meeting on the 15th. Briefed by Cherwell about its goings-on, he reported to Waley on 17 February that it 'has been complete bedlam, which only Hoppy's hand keeps in any sort of order. Ministers are in perpetual session, driving one another crazy with their mutual ravings, the Beaver being mainly responsible, his approach being nothing short of criminal. All the same, a certain amount of progress is being made, not all of it in the wrong direction. . . . Ministers have now left Currency for Commercial Policy, and, as you may suppose, confusion is still worse confounded.'[76]

In a note submitted to the Committee, the Bank of England argued that the Fund's mechanism was inconsistent with the maintenance of the sterling area in two respects: (1) 'The Fund as drafted is basically a gold fund – the whole suggestion is that gold-convertible currencies are better than other currencies,' and (2) 'The Fund contemplates settlement of international trade payments in the currency of each country and not international currencies.' Public acceptance of Fund principles would mean that 'we say publicly that we are working towards a system where sterling will be less useful. This can only make our transitional arrangements, where we are largely dependent on the credit of sterling, more difficult.'

Dormael's comment is just: 'Thus, the Bank which had prospered for more than a century on the generally accepted idea that sterling was preferable to other currencies because it was gold-convertible, did not accept the theory any more, because only the dollar was now gold-convertible.'[77] Once Britain forsook the gold standard for a 'labour standard', sterling was doomed as an international currency. The Bank of England accepted the premise while rejecting the conclusion. Keynes had tried to disguise this unpalatable truth by putting the dollar behind sterling in the form of 'bancor' or 'unitas'. America's rejection of a 'bancor' or 'unitas' standard removed the fig-leaf: any post-war monetary order which allowed for multilateral clearing was bound to be based on the dollar. The desperate alternative, to which the Bank was driven, was to use Britain's sterling debts to force its creditors to accept payment in British goods. But this ignored both imperial and domestic realities. India, Britain's main creditor, was about to throw off British rule; and Britain itself was unprepared for the austerity which the Bank solution would have forced on it.

Dalton was far from impressed by the performance of the Bank's representatives, Cobbold and Catterns, before the Committee on External Policy:

> They obviously hated the very idea of any kind of international bank. Its assets, they asserted, 'must inevitably deteriorate', until it was all filled up with levas and dinars – and perhaps that would be the intention. The proposed fund could not possibly be 'passive' because no active-minded banker could disinterest himself in the fate of his assets. Therefore, it was inevitable that people would ring up on the telephone and advise sales or purchases of sterling. It would all, they thought, be under the influence of foreigners. . . . Anderson thought, and Lyttelton and I agreed, that the Bank were totally unconscious of post-war realities, and in particular of our need to get very substantial assistance from the U.S. during the transitional period. The wretched Beaver is tolerated by all because he has this queer influence over the PM.[78]

Although he was a director of the Bank, Keynes's own dismissal of the Bank's stand, in a letter to the Chancellor dated 23 February, was equally scathing:

The Bank is not facing any of the realities. They do not allow for the fact that our post-war domestic policies are impossible without further American assistance. They do not allow for the fact that the Americans are strong enough to offer inducements to many or most of our friends to walk out on us, if we ostentatiously set out to start up an independent shop. They do not allow for the fact that vast debts and exiguous reserves are not, by themselves, the best qualification for renewing old-time international banking.

He accused the Bank of wanting to lead the country down the road which led to disaster in 1931 – 'reckless gambling in the shape of assuming banking undertakings beyond what we have any means to support as soon as anything goes wrong, coupled with a policy which . . . pays no regard to the inescapable requirements of domestic policies'.[79] Keynes's relentless exposure of the Bank's pretensions did eventually have an effect. 'It is sheer madness to think the Empire can create a cave where we take in one another's washing and ignore the rest of the world! . . . The countries we sell to are not necessarily the countries from which we buy, and if we begin unilateral trading we return to *barter, the survival of the fittest* and *more war.*' The words were Catto's, but the thought is Keynes's.[80]

On 18 February, the Cabinet Committee recommended that discussions with Dominion experts on the monetary Plan should proceed 'on the basis that, while no commitment will be entered into, our expectation is that at the appropriate time we shall find it to our advantage to participate in these schemes . . .'. It worried though about whether the Fund would be passive in exchange markets, the position of the sterling area, and arrangements for the transition period. It also recommended that, in the commercial negotiations, imperial preference should be traded only in return for general tariff reductions, and that state purchasing and subsidies were preferable to tariffs for agricultural products. Beaverbrook produced a note of dissent: 'The Financial Plan', he declared, 'restores the Gold Standard in the form of a "Gold Fund". . . . If we accept the "Gold Fund" we lay ourselves down to die.'

At the Cabinet on 24 February, Anderson expounded the case for a monetary agreement 'with heavy over-emphasised lucidity'. Beaverbrook railed against it, supported by Brendan Bracken and 'dull, deaf, boring' Hudson. Pandemonium broke out with everyone shouting at the same time. 'The PM . . . deliberately allows the thing to get out of hand, explaining he hasn't had time to read the papers . . . and why anyway should we be hustled, "just because a few officials from the Dominions are here; they can be entertained for a few days, and given drinks, and taken round to see the bomb craters".' After three hours, 'the PM said that it was clear we could reach no decision that night but he saw no harm in this Cabinet paper being given to their officials on the clear understanding that the Cabinet had reached no decision on it'. Churchill's understanding of what *had* been decided was that there should be no return to the gold standard, no abolition or reduction of imperial preferences except in return for tariff reductions elsewhere, and no taxation of food.[81] This was about the limit of his, and the Cabinet's, understanding of the three topics – monetary arrangements, commercial policy and buffer stocks – which had dominated the technicians' discussion of post-war economic problems over the previous year.

Keynes briefed the Dominion experts in February and March, making an introductory statement at the first meeting on monetary policy, and more detailed follow-ups. They also discussed White's Bank Plan, of which Keynes had now written a critique.[82] The Australians pressed hard for greater exchange rate flexibility, which Keynes resisted on his usual technical grounds. He failed to see how an alteration in the exchange rates could be the right remedy for a catastrophic fall in the demand for some export commodity like wool. Such a policy was like 'burning down the house for roast pork'.[83] The situation, he reported to White on 16 March, was that he could not yet convey to him official British acceptance of the Joint Agreement, but 'personally, I think it is most unlikely that we shall make unitas a condition of acceptance'. (The Cabinet conceded this in April.) He would shortly be sending White suggestions he had received from representatives of the Dominions and India. They were mainly 'improvements in drafting', though they would also want larger quotas. He gave White no account of the Cabinet battles.[84] White refused to budge on the quotas, and they remained a matter to be bargained.

The politics of the battle only partially overlapped with the economic issues. Although the monetary plan could be attacked as a 'new gold standard', Keynes realised that the main political hostility to the Article VII programme was to its free-trade flavour. Specifically, the banning of 'discrimination' might bring together imperialists who wanted to strengthen commercial ties with the Empire and socialists who wanted state trading, particularly with the Soviet Union. So the only way to save the monetary plan was to detach it from the rest of the Grand Design. His line became that 'whilst the commercial scheme would find it difficult to function without the monetary scheme, the monetary scheme in no way needs the commercial proposals as an aid or support'. Beaverbrook, on the other hand, emphasised the interdependence of all the objectionable features. His tactic was to convince Churchill that the International Monetary Fund stood for the gold standard, hoping to discredit, 'by association in the PM's mind, the proposals that might affect Imperial Preference'.[85] 'The monetary plan', the Beaver wrote to Keynes, 'leads us on to the commercial plan which, in turn, is linked to the commodity scheme. This is an expression of praise for the project as a logical, self-consistent entity. But it will explain to you why I find myself in disagreement with each portion of it. I am at variance with the underlying doctrine because it is essentially international and free-trade, and because my own beliefs are neither the one nor the other.'[86]

The British were coming under increasing pressure from the US Treasury to get cracking. Early in April, Keynes persuaded Hopkins that the Fund should be allowed to 'go it alone'. Hopkins persuaded the Chancellor. At a typically confused meeting of the Cabinet on 14 April, Anderson proposed that the government publish the revised Joint Statement without official commitment, and with several riders: the principles of the Fund would not apply to the transitional period, it would come into operation in stages, it would need supplementing by provisions for reconstruction, and Britain would not agree to join until its transitional problems had found a solution. They then discussed whether they should say they were in favour of the 'broad objective'. Churchill suggested some broad objectives of an innocuous kind, which Dalton pointed out applied to commercial, not monetary, policy. Beaverbrook 'keeps on shouting that he wants the Commercial Plan published as well', Bevin remarking, 'You want to strangle the one plan at birth and do an abortion on the other.' Everyone thought this was very funny.[87] In essence, the Cabinet ordered a stop to all economic planning talks with the United States except for those to do with the Fund. Churchill told the Commons in April that Article VII no more committed Britain to abandoning imperial preference than the USA to scrapping its tariffs.[88]

There were last-minute hitches, but the deed was done. On 22 April, the Joint Statement was published simultaneously in Washington, London, Moscow and Chungking. The London version had an explanatory preface by Keynes saying that the Stabilisation Fund's purposes were the same as those set forth in the Clearing Union; when it was published, Keynes briefed the financial press and Members of Parliament.

He had returned to the Treasury only four days before, after recovering from a severe collapse of health. He had been working in the government for almost four years without any significant problems under the kind of strain which caused his colleagues to drop like ninepins – a monument to the strength of his constitution, Plesch's ministrations and Lydia's *ukases*. On 17 February he explained to Margot Asquith why he could not come to see her at the Savoy:

> Although extremely recovered and being able, apparently to the outside world, to do a full day's work, this is not quite the full truth of the position. I am only able to get through the overwhelming work which I have by spending in bed practically the whole time when I am not in the office, and cutting off practically all social engagements. . . .

Winter and early spring were always bad periods for weather and work, made worse by the battle to save the Fund, and on 6 March Maynard experienced the premonitory 'heart flutters' which had preceded his collapse in 1937. He regarded them as 'primarily nervous and due to cumulative overwork and requiring nothing but rest'. He struggled on part-time at the Treasury for another few days, but they intensified, and on 17 March the Ogre prescribed complete bed rest for a month. Florence hoped that after it her son's engine 'will be like that of a car which has been de-carbonised'. He wrote to Dadie Rylands on 19 April: 'I have really been rather a long time in my ogre's hands, but at least for the last three weeks I should say that I have been suffering more from excess of drugs and all kinds of medicine than from anything else. I am now trying to get clear of these lowering intakes, and am going back to the Treasury to-day.' He added: 'What very good reviews Noël Annan has been writing in the New Statesman. Don't you think we might find some way of electing him a Fellow?' His health was now on a declining curve.

Early in May Keynes explained the Statement of Principles to experts of the Allied governments in London – among them Keilhau of Norway, Beyen of Holland, Varvaressos of Greece. In his brief to the Chancellor for the forthcoming House of Commons debate, sent through Eady, he urged him to concentrate on the differences between the Joint Statement and the gold standard: under the gold standard currencies were rigidly fixed to gold by a 'moral contract', the Fund allowed changes in currency values 'whenever there is a good and sufficient reason'; under the gold standard currencies were convertible into gold, the Fund imposed no such obligation.[89] The Treasury still needed stiffening. Waley had become a convert to John Williams's 'key currency' proposal. It was far more important, he wrote to Keynes on 16 May, that Britain get a loan from the New York bankers of about $3bn than sign up to post-transitional arrangements to which the American bankers were deeply opposed. Keynes, sure of his ground, replied robustly the same day: 'What strings would there be to the $3 billion? A great many I should expect.' It was better to run with the US Treasury than with its disgruntled critics, 'who . . . do not know their own mind and have no power whatever to implement their promises'.[90]

The tenth of May found Keynes in the Peers' Gallery of the House of Commons 'lacerated in mind and body' as speaker after speaker denounced the monetary plan for no other reason than that the Americans had agreed with it.[91] The leading critics were Richard Stokes (Labour), P. C. Loftus (Conservative), G. Strauss (Labour), Emanuel Shinwell (Labour), Robert Boothby (Conservative) and Sir George Schuster (Liberal). Some had been briefed, or had their speeches written, by the Hungarian economists Thomas Balogh and Nicholas Kaldor.[92] Keynes likened currency debates in the House to 'a loonies' picnic or an idiots' day out, where lunatic Members who on other occasions would be doomed to a decent restraint have a chance, for once, of catching the Speaker's eye'.[93]

Balogh's letter in *The Times* denouncing the experts' plan as 'highly dangerous' had appeared earlier that day. It concentrated on the insufficiency of the Fund's liquid resources, the unjustified hopes attached to devaluation, and the damage to the sterling area of the convertibility requirement. The spirit of the monetary plan was hostile to the imperial preference system and to trade agreements 'between countries desiring a planned production'. The scarce-currency clause would be inoperative so long as 'the United States is willing to purchase capital assets in the British Empire and the United Kingdom and thus provide Britain with dollars'. In a reply to Balogh, Keynes wrote that 'Schachtian minds ill consort with great Empires.'[94] He readily forgot his own past heresies when he had moved on. To an American correspondent he attributed the anti-American mood to the 'great anxiety that we should not be cutting ourselves off from conceivable expedients before we really know what expedients we are likely to need', to irritation at the 'completely untruthful charges that we are trying to take improper advantages' of Lend–Lease, and to annoyance at the apparently 'concerted effort' by America 'to prevent us doing anything at all to improve our export prospects after the war' – all of which, he did not add, he shared.[95]

Keynes himself took part in the debate in the Lords on 23 May. As a piece of rhetoric his speech reads wonderfully well. He adduced five main advantages of the monetary plan. First, it gave Britain complete freedom during a transitional period of 'uncertain duration' to retain its wartime system. Secondly, it offered currency convertibility. Without this, London would lose its pre-eminence and the sterling area would fall to pieces. 'To suppose', he said, 'that a system of bilateral and barter agreements, with no one who owns sterling knowing what he can do with it – to suppose that this is the best way of encouraging the Dominions to concentrate their financial system on London seems to me pretty near frenzy.' On the contrary, 'with our own resources so greatly impaired and encumbered, it is only if sterling is firmly placed in an international setting that the necessary confidence in it can be sustained'. Thirdly, it offered 'a great addition to the world's stock of monetary reserves' – in Britain's case worth about £325m. Fourthly, the scarce currency clause would prevent 'the draining of reserves out of the rest of the world to pay a country which was obstinately borrowing and exporting on a scale immensely greater than it was lending and importing'. Finally, the plan set up international rules to provide orderly changes in exchange rates.

Keynes vehemently rejected the suggestion that the scheme represented a return to the gold standard – or a repudiation of his own theories. How could someone, he asked their lordships, who had attacked the gold standard as a 'barbarous relic' be accused of forging 'new chains to hold us fast to the old dungeon'? The new monetary scheme maintained the three principles he had fought twenty years to achieve:

> We are determined that, in future, the external value of sterling shall conform to its internal value as set by our own domestic policies, and not the other way round. Secondly, we intend to retain control of our domestic rate of interest, so that we can keep it as low as suits our own purposes, without interference from the ebb and flow of international capital movements or flights of hot money. Thirdly, whilst we intend to prevent inflation at home, we will not accept deflation at the dictate of influences from outside.[96]

A critic of Keynes's exposition might well wonder what obligations Britain had in fact assumed in return for the benefits so enticingly displayed. He seemed to advocate the monetary plan as a way of maintaining the sterling area and imperial preference system, whereas the Americans all too clearly wanted to dismantle both. He claimed Britain's right to determine its own exchange rate, when the Americans wanted a fixed exchange rate system. When told in Washington a little later that his line of defence had greatly embarrassed White and others, Keynes replied that it had been the only way to save the Fund from political extinction at Westminster.[97] A disconsolate Robert Boothby sadly admitted 'that the plan he had thought to be dead was very much alive'.[98]

In the first five months of 1944 Keynes had fought virtually single-handed to protect the Joint Statement agreed in Washington from Treasury scepticism, Bank of England opposition and widespread political hostility. If ambiguous language was the price of success, then it was a price he was willing to pay, so great was the importance he attached to keeping America constructively involved in Europe's post-war life. And in this judgement he was right, although he could not foresee what precise form that involvement would eventually take. Had America and Britain fallen out on the whole range of Article VII issues, had the relations between the two closest wartime Allies been seriously soured in 1944–5, who knows what the balance of forces would have been in the US administration, or what opportunities the Soviet Union would have had to exploit Anglo-American quarrels.

CHAPTER TEN

The American Way of Business

I

As the European war entered what it was hoped would be its final year, the United States stepped up pressure on Britain to honour Article VII of the Lend–Lease Agreement. This called on it to negotiate a liberal international trading order with the United States. The Americans expected the monetary agreement to be followed by a commercial agreement. But the British were stalling. The Morgenthau–Crowley policy of using Lend–Lease to control Britain's reserves cut across the State Department's aim of getting it to promise to liberalise its trade. A country whose 'quick assets' were about a tenth of the size of its 'quick debts' and whose export trade had been reduced to under 30 per cent of its pre-war level was an unlikely early candidate for Cordell Hull's free-trade world.

Like everyone else in Whitehall, Keynes deeply resented the way the administration of Lend–Lease seemed designed to weaken Britain's ability to survive without it; and he said as much to Edward Stettinius, Sumner Welles's successor as Assistant Secretary of State, when Stettinius visited London in April 1944. Stettinius's book, *Lend Lease: Weapon for Victory*, had just been published. After congratulating the American on 'a most splendid effort', Keynes revealed his frustration at being in the trap which 'the most unsordid' act had sprung:

> The greatest cause of friction over a very long period was the problem of what we used to call the old commitments, arising out of the fact that lend lease did not come into anything like full operation for some nine months after it had come legally into force. The whole episode of the Viscose transaction, the Jesse Jones loan, the process of what we called scraping the barrel, you leave in complete obscurity. You do not emphasise the point that the US Administration was very careful to take every possible precaution to see that the British were as near as possible bankrupt before any assistance was given. Nor do you recur at the end of the volume to the recent recrudescence of these same standards, according to which lend lease ought to be appropriately abated whenever there seems the

slightest prospect that leaving things as they are might possibly result in leaving the British at the end of the war otherwise than hopelessly insolvent.[1]

Keynes did not interpret American policy as a deliberate attempt to destroy Britain's independence. He remained convinced of America's fundamental goodwill. Rather he attributed it to the narrow legalism of the US government and its fear of Congress. Nor was he blind to the divisions in the British government on post-war financial and commercial policy, or to the fact that the British had been cheating on the Export White Paper. But his dominant view, universally shared in Whitehall, was that the British had made much greater sacrifices for the common cause than had the United States, and that this asymmetry should be rectified as a *matter of justice*. This view was to determine his approach to Anglo-American negotiations for the rest of his life.

Keynes's persistent aim, pursued whenever opportunity offered, was 'the retention by us of enough assets to leave us capable of independent action'. This thread runs from his attempt in 1941 to narrow the scope of Lend–Lease through to his continuing efforts to economise on war expenses so as to minimise Britain's external debt and hence its need for US aid after the war. His efforts to keep down sterling debts to India and the Middle East were vigorous but largely unavailing.[2] Early in 1944 he started to prepare a strategy for breaking the American embargo on increased reserves and exports. This was to feed into the Treasury's strategy for securing a continuation of Lend–Lease in Stage II, as it was now called – the period between the defeat of Germany and the defeat of Japan. He minuted Hopkins on 13 March: 'We have allowed the Americans, in their recent depredations on lend lease and extension of reciprocal aid, to trade too extensively on our large current and immediately prospective receipts from American troops without allowing sufficiently for the fact that this is anything but a permanent source of income.'[3]

The state of the Article VII negotiations had been left as follows. The 'Joint Statement by Experts' on 21 April 1944 had finalised the principles on which an International Monetary Fund would be set up. The US administration was committed to it, the British government was not. But it still had to be translated into the language of a treaty and approved by the US Congress and the British Parliament. There would be minor hurdles on the way, but, barring a political veto from either side, none that seemed likely to derail the through-train to a higher-level agreement.

The International Bank for Reconstruction and Development had not been through a comparable process of bilateral or multilateral scrutiny, and remained, at this stage, merely a US Treasury proposal. Keynes had made a number of cogent criticisms in a memorandum of 21 February, redrafted early in March. It is plain from this that he was thinking of the

Bank chiefly as an agent of reconstruction rather than development. Since Britain could not expect to receive much 'reconstruction' money, his main purpose was to minimise the British contribution, ensure that the Bank operated mainly by way of guaranteeing rather than making loans, and see to it that borrowers could spend the proceeds of a loan anywhere – that is, they were not to be tied to buying the lending country's goods. Until these principles were agreed, 'it would be a mistake to consider drafting amendments or detailed points, or attempt to draw up the outlines of an alternative'. These comments were communicated to Washington. Keynes was starting to become an advocate of the Bank in London.

Frank Lee of the British Treasury had come to Washington in September 1943 prepared to discuss 'Commod', as Keynes's Buffer Stock Plan was known. Robbins thought it was worth pursuing for the 'purchasing power which it distributes in times of depression and mops up in times of inflation'. But the Americans dismissed the Plan as a speculators' paradise, and it dropped out of the Article VII picture.

As already mentioned, the British had stalled on the trade talks. Harry Hawkins of the US State Department and James Meade of the Economic Section had made progress in Washington the previous autumn. The US proposal for a 'multilateral convention' (rules of the game) on commercial policy was in close harmony with Meade's proposal for a Commercial Union. The British placed more emphasis on maintaining high levels of employment as a condition for trade liberalisation; the Americans looked to trade liberalisation to create high levels of employment. The Americans' main goal was the elimination of imperial preference; the British were after reductions in the US tariff. An obvious opportunity to trade preferences for tariffs existed. However, little attempt had been made to dovetail the principles of the IMF with those of the commercial treaty. And within weeks of the Washington conversations, protectionists and subsidisers on both sides had raised a barrage of objections. A British Cabinet Committee on Commercial Policy was finally set up in July 1944. It was soon locked in battle with the Ministry of Agriculture. All this left the main matter of the Article VII agenda unresolved. But the State Department had not given up on it.

Morgenthau had hoped to have an inter-governmental conference in Washington at the end of May to ratify the Joint Statement of Experts. He wanted to offer a treaty setting up the Fund as his present to Roosevelt at the Democratic convention in July. But with the British government still uncommitted, the most Anderson would agree to was to send experts to an international monetary conference as soon as they got an invitation. Keynes begged Harry White not to 'take us to Washington in July, which should surely be a most unfriendly act'. Morgenthau told White: 'Have it in Maine or New Hampshire, some place up in the mountains there.' On 25 May, Secretary of State Cordell Hull invited forty-four nations to attend a conference in July at Bretton Woods, New Hampshire, 'for formulating definite proposals for an International Monetary Fund and possibly a Bank for Reconstruction and Development'. Before the conference, a smaller drafting committee would meet in Atlantic City, New Jersey. There was much Anglo-American bickering about arrangements for Atlantic City, partly connected with the rigid timetable for the main conference (the delegates had to be out of their hotel at Bretton Woods by July 21), partly to do with which countries should be on the drafting committee. Keynes thought it outrageous to put Cuba on and exclude Holland. White brutally remarked that Cuba's function was merely to provide cigars. The British wanted to put on Greece and India. 'The Greek [Varvaressos]', White said, 'is nothing but a British stooge'; he would accept Indian delegates, but only as members of the British team. After Morgenthau had received a snooty letter from the Chancellor of the Exchequer, White exclaimed: 'God, how they must treat their colonies!'

Keynes himself found the proposed arrangements 'curiouser and curiouser'. The main conference itself would have no power of committing governments. But it would have no work either, since all the main decisions would have been taken. It was hard to see how the 'monkeyhouse' would occupy itself. 'Acute alcohol poisoning would set in before the end.'[4] White had no intention of allowing anyone to do serious work. His own hand-picked team would stage-manage the drafting committee and conference to produce the result the US Treasury wanted.

Running parallel with these preparations, the British government had finally turned its mind to 'transitional' problems. With the war against Germany expected to end a year or so before the war against Japan, semi-peace (Stage II) might start quite soon, and with it the problem of reconverting the British economy to peacetime production. When Stage II became Stage III (the end of the Japanese war) Britain would come face to face with the stark economic realities from which Lend–Lease had shielded it: a huge import surplus, lavish overseas cash spending, and a mountain of unfunded sterling debt. The need was so to manage Stage II that Britain started Stage III as little dependent on American help as possible.

Keynes's mildly alarmist January 1944 paper dealing with transitional finance (see p. 325 above) had fallen foul of Treasury complacency and Bank hostility.[5] Alarmed by Stettinius's hint that Lend–Lease might be replaced by a loan for Stage II, Keynes resumed the attack in mid-May with a memorandum on 'The Problem of our External Finance in the Transition', a final version of which was dated 12 June. Eady called it 'one of the most readable 10,000 official words of recent times'. Certainly, it was Keynes's last major state paper written at the full height of his powers – well balanced, urgent, scornful and much tauter than most of his late productions. The section on the sterling area (paras 12–28) is a model of lucid exposition. Keynes's main point was that, without a change of policy, Britain could expect a financial disaster once Lend–Lease stopped. The government's assumption that after the war Britain could import all it needed to provide full employment and improved standards of living was 'blind faith'. He 'aimed to support faith with works'.

Keynes estimated a deficit on the balance of payments of between £1.5bn ($6bn) and £2.25bn ($9bn) over the first three post-war years. This included excess of imports over exports (£750m.–£1bn), excess of overseas spending over overseas income (£250m.–£500m.) and repayment of between £500m. and £750m. of abnormal sterling balances. 'Better statistics' from the Ministries of Supply and Food and the Board of Trade, he added tartly, 'would be helpful'. His solution was fourfold.

First, Britain should fund the abnormal balances at zero interest and a long repayment period, though tied exports of capital goods might mean that some creditors got paid off quicker; further, during the transition it should limit access to sterling area reserves to members' current dollar earnings. By these measures repayment of the balances could be reduced to £50m. a year or even eliminated during the transitional period. (He added a typically ingenious countercyclical twist: capital exports and repayments should be speeded up when unemployment was rising and vice versa. This would fill an important gap in the White Paper on Employment Policy, which had nothing to say about unemployment caused by a fall in export demand.)

Secondly, Keynes aimed to raise Britain's *net* end-war reserves to £500m. by stopping the United States 'chiselling at lend lease either currently or at the end of the German war', by getting it to finance more of Britain's Middle and Far Eastern war spending, and by ending the 'financial appeasement' of Sweden and Switzerland. Thirdly, Britain should end its 'Lady Bountiful' attitude to the West Europeans and Russia. They should pay Britain gold, not IOUs, for post-war relief and reconstruction exports. Fourthly, Britain should prepare vigorously for an export drive, even if it meant stinting the consumer. Restrictions on British exports should be dropped in Stage II, without abatement of Lend–Lease. None of the argument hinged on getting American money or supplies post-Lend–Lease. Pressnell's contention that the 'aid from the United States' was at this stage a 'crucial' element in Keynes's policy[6] is misleading. American help in Stage III should be treated as a 'residual', to encourage self-reliance, independence and capacity to repay debt earlier. 'We must reduce our own requirements for American aid to the least possible – say, $2 to $3 billions . . . and even be prepared, if the worst befalls, to do without it altogether.'[7] There was no talk of a gift; but any American loan should start off interest-free. The scale of the residual help needed depended entirely on the vigour with which Britain pursued the main objectives. Unfortunately:

Our own habits are the greatest obstacle in the way of carrying out almost every one of the above recommendations. All our reflex actions are those of a rich man, so we promise others too much. Our longings for relaxation from the war are so intense that we promise ourselves too much. As a proud and great Power, we disdain to chaffer with others smaller and more exorbitant than ourselves. Having been so recently in dire extremity, our financial policy is rooted in appeasement. Above all, the financial problems of the war have been surmounted so easily and so silently that the average man sees no reason to suppose that the financial problems of the peace will be any more difficult. The Supply Departments have demanded of the Treasury that money should be no object. And the Treasury has so contrived that it has been no object. This success is the greatest obstacle of all to getting the problems of this memorandum taken seriously. And when we come to exports, no one ever seems to suppose that we need expect to be paid cash for them in full. . . .[8]

The success of Keynes's strategy depended crucially on Stage II arrangements. Britain must ensure the continuation of Lend–Lease, but in such a manner that it was allowed to build up its reserves and start reconverting its economy for exports. This demanded a break with the 'marginal principle' – that only so much Lend–Lease supplies would be given that Britain's fully mobilised war economy could not produce for itself.

Anderson circulated this explosively alarmist brief to selected colleagues. It was a sign of Keynes's authority that it was immediately regarded as the definitive statement of the problem. Its implication, Waley argued, was that 'we shall have to practise a much greater degree of austerity than anyone has yet dreamed of'. Admiring and disturbed comments flowed in. Cherwell and Hubert Henderson thought that Britain's prospective post-war deficit would require a partial cancellation of the wartime sterling balances. Keynes rejected this: 'however much we may talk about doing such a thing', he remarked presciently, 'I doubt if we shall actually do it when it comes to it'. This did not stop him himself proposing partial cancellation in 1945.

The Chancellor held a meeting with the relevant ministers on 14 June, with Keynes, Hopkins and Eady in attendance. Keynes dominated the discussion, repeating the main points in his memorandum. In July the Cabinet authorised early Stage II negotiations with the Americans and immediate steps to prepare an export drive.

The British line in the forthcoming monetary discussions was thrashed out at two meetings between Anderson and Keynes on 8 and 16 June. The first agreed that the delegation should press on the Americans the 'Catto' formula on exchange rate rules. Catto had succeeded Montagu Norman as governor of the Bank of England in April. The Bank's aim was to preserve the sovereign right of nations to change their exchange rates; Catto's formula provided that members should have to consult the Fund, but not obtain its permission, before devaluing their currencies, reserving to the Fund simply the *ex post* sanction of cutting off the offending member from the use of its facilities. Further, it was agreed that British membership of the Fund should be conditional on a satisfactory solution to its transitional difficulties; that the convertibility obligation would exclude wartime sterling balances; that the Fund would start only when Britain and America both agreed it should; and that, in any event, no agreement reached at the conference would bind the British government and Parliament. Britain's negotiating position on White's Bank Plan followed Keynes's redraft in March: loans should be untied, the Bank should concentrate on guaranteeing not making loans, British liabilities should be small.

II

AN INTERLUDE IN NEW HAMPSHIRE

On the evening of 16 June, Maynard and Lydia sailed on the *Queen Mary* from Southampton, accompanied by Eady, Robbins, Ronald and Bolton (Bank of England adviser). This time the delegation was accompanied by a lawyer, William Beckett, also from the Bank. Brand, Lee, Opie and Robinson, already in Washington, would join them. Travelling with the British team were 'experts' from Holland, Belgium, Greece, Norway, Czechoslovakia, India and China, most of whom were on the Drafting Committee.

On board, the British held seven team meetings, and six with the Allies. These resulted in two 'boat drafts' on both the Fund and the Bank. Robbins, having been excluded from the Treasury discussions prior to embarkation, was disturbed to hear that the British were under instructions to press the 'Catto clause', but was delighted that 'the Treasury are at last completely sold on the Bank'.[9] Keynes found the voyage 'a most peaceful and also a most busy time. . . . I have often had the ambition of doing work on a ship, but this is the first time it has really come off.' He had not been in better health for a long time.[10] He relaxed by reading Trevelyan's life of Macaulay and dipping into a new edition of Plato. More importantly, he read Friedrich Hayek's *Road to Serfdom*, on which he wrote him an important and challenging letter (see pp. 284–6 above).

The experts were met by Brand and Frank Lee in New York on 23 June, then whisked off by train to Atlantic City, where they booked into the Claridge Hotel. This was a 'wretched skyscraper' of twenty storeys, which they were to share for the next week with the annual convention of the Homeopathic Institute. The Americans and others were already installed, but serious drafting awaited 'Anglo-US elucidations'.[11] Keynes immediately had a private meeting with White, at which he handed him the 'boat drafts'. White had divided the seventy-five experts from seventeen countries into four specialist groups which would go through all the suggested amendments to the Joint Statement, reporting back once a day to a general meeting. Parallel to this would run Anglo-American meetings. Having resolved all their disagreements, they would then proceed to the 'monkey-house' at Bretton Woods.

At the first joint session with the Americans, on Saturday 24 June, Keynes waxed eloquent on the subject of the Bank. Robbins wrote:

> This went very well indeed. Keynes was in his most lucid and persuasive mood; and the effect was irresistible. At such moments, I often find myself thinking that Keynes must be one of the most remarkable men that have ever lived – the quick logic, the birdlike swoop of intuition, the vivid fancy, the wide vision, above all the incomparable sense of the fitness of words, all combine to make something several degrees beyond the limit of ordinary human achievement. Certainly, in our own age, only the Prime Minister is of comparable stature. He, of course, surpasses him. But the greatness of the Prime Minister is something much easier to understand than the genius of Keynes. For in the last analysis, the special qualities of the Prime Minister are the traditional qualities of our race raised to the scale of grandeur. Whereas the special qualities of Keynes are something outside all that. He uses the classical style of our life and language, it is true, but it is shot through with something which is not traditional, a unique unearthly quality of which one can only say that it is pure genius. The Americans sat entranced as the God-like visitor sang and the golden light played around.[12]

By the time he had finished recasting White's draft, Keynes had developed keen enthusiasm for the Bank, which he saw as a more rational investment engine than the 'ill-conceived racket' which had followed the last war, and one that would relieve Britain from the 'pressure . . . to make advances . . . far beyond what we can reasonably afford'. He still saw it, though, more as an agency for post-war European reconstruction than for long-term development.[13] However, there was no response from the US Treasury. The Bank was barely discussed. It was left to Emilio Collado to take up the Bank's cause at the State Department for a somewhat different motive – as a way of binding Latin American countries into supporting American positions on the Fund and elsewhere.

Keynes's tactics in Atlantic City were straightforward. White, he explained in a letter to Hopkins on 25 June, was anxious to avoid any appearance of a stitch-up between the British and American Treasuries.

So he and White would try to agree a text behind the scenes, but present alternatives to the monkey-house, having agreed which alternatives they would drop or press. 'Harry White', he reported to 'Hoppy', is 'wreathed in smiles and amiability, hospitable, benevolent and complacent. I doubt if Sigi [Waley] would recognise him.'[14] White's attitude had changed markedly as a result of the Washington conversations the previous autumn. He realised that, without British support, nothing would get through. And Britain meant Keynes. So White set out to conciliate Keynes, to the extent that his abrasive nature allowed. They were also starting to click as human beings.

The search for a 'prior' Anglo-American agreement was only partially successful. The chief stumbling block was the 'Catto clause'. Keynes insisted that the Articles of Agreement must explicitly recognise national sovereignty in monetary matters. In presenting the case, he was driven to the despised tactic of pleading political difficulties back home.[15] The debate proceeded along familiar lines, Keynes emphasising the need for each country to preserve 'ultimate control' over its exchange rate, White retorting that the cardinal point of the Fund was to secure stable exchange rates. The British tabled a less provocative draft, which Keynes thought White and Bernstein would accept, unless sabotaged by the lawyers. 'The essence of our plan is that there is no absolute obligation to obey the Fund in the matter of exchanges and that a member in the last resort has the power to take the matter into his own hands without having to go through the prior act of formally withdrawing from the Fund.'[16] The Americans recognised the force of Keynes's assertion that nations like Britain would not obey Fund rules unless they wanted to, and gave way. In the opinion of Harold James, 'The desire to conciliate the Soviet Union helped to make the United States more flexible on the general issue of sovereignty.'[17]

There were problems over the transitional arrangements. The Joint Statement had envisaged a transitional period of three years, with 'any restrictions which impede multilateral clearing on current account' being progressively withdrawn. Keynes said a three-year transitional period was 'Utopian': every country must be free to decide the length of its own transition, and during that period to continue wartime exchange controls: 'the time when approval is required [to continue with them] will never come for the United Kingdom'. He thought White would agree, if pressed. He was right.

The Indians and Australians pressed for larger quotas, but White refused to discuss quotas till Bretton Woods. The issue of automatic versus discretionary access to the Fund's borrowing facilities once more raised its head. Keynes was asked if 'the British recognized that in joining the Fund they were accepting some obligation to modify their domestic policy in the light of its international effects on stability'. He replied that they did – but at their own discretion. Connected with this, the British urged that Fund directors be part-time to safeguard their conception of the Fund as passive, whereas the Americans demanded full-time executive management. The British also pressed for the headquarters of either the Fund or Bank or both to be in London, while the Americans made it clear that they were to be in Washington.[18] These matters were left over for the full conference.

The Drafting Committee spent the week going through the suggested amendments clause by clause. There were far too many to be considered in the allotted time, so most of them – seventy in total – were remitted to the Bretton Woods conference, against the wishes of Keynes, who wanted the conference to be presented with a streamlined Anglo-American text. In Robbins's view, the main achievement at Atlantic City had been to consolidate 'the friendly understanding between ourselves and the American technical experts', with most of the issues of principle resolved.[19] As Bretton Woods was to show, agreement on principle could easily be undermined by disagreement on detail – especially once the legal draftsmen had got to work.

Keynes himself rarely attended the plenary sessions, which White controlled in masterly fashion from the chair. Nor did he see, or approve, the set of documents which would go forward to the main conference. Ensconced with Lydia on the tenth floor of the Claridge, overlooking the Atlantic, he had found the conditions 'most comfortable and endurable'. However, exhaustion was setting in. After one day spent in meetings without rest, his system gave 'ominous signs of conking out'. He recovered quickly, but incessant work, meetings and nervous excitement were once more starting to affect his damaged heart muscle. Apart from one conversation with Pasvolsky, Keynes did not raise with the Americans the issue of financial help after the end of the German war.

On 30 June Maynard and Lydia travelled by overnight train from Atlantic City to Bretton Woods, New Hampshire, 'a wide basin of woods and meadows, surrounded by low mountains',[20] set in the White Mountain National Forest, a nature reserve of one million acres. Lydia described it as 'a cross between Switzerland and Scotland', temperate in climate, with trout in the river, 'an ideal place for a holiday, alas it is not so for Jemkins'. Today one drives up Highway No. 93 from Boston, but in 1944 the 730 delegates and clerical staff from forty-four countries and numerous international organisations – far more than expected – had arrived at the Bretton Woods railway station on special trains, their multilingual chatter producing a 'tower of Babel on wheels'. The delegates booked into the Mount Washington Hotel, the clerks were scattered in nearby lodgings.

'Reserve Your Place in History' in 'one of America's last grand hotels' beckons today's hotel brochure. 'Experience the days and remaining

THE AMERICAN WAY OF BUSINESS

nights of this legendary valley . . . the service, style and elegance of a bygone era . . . and the gentle majesty and serenity of the White Mountains.' Mount Washington Hotel was built by the railroad magnate Joseph Stickney in 1902. Designed by the architect Charles Alling Gifford in a Western version of Spanish Renaissance, it stands in the centre of the valley, its Y-shaped construction featuring two red-roofed turrets, a granite foundation and a white stucco exterior. There were 350 bedrooms, most with bathrooms, an indoor swimming pool, a giant ballroom at one end, an equally large dining room at the other, and a cupolar conservatory decorated with Tiffany glass where tea could be had with palm-court orchestra accompaniment. A broad wooden verandah ran all the way round the hotel's spine, where guests could sip their cocktails. The Stickneys (widow and nephew) ran it as a summer resort till 1943, when it was sold to a Boston syndicate. As the new owners prepared to open for the 1944 season, the State Department requested the use of the hotel for an international monetary conference. The hotel is proud of its role in giving the post-war world 'a badly needed currency stability for the next 25 years'. From the turrets flutter two pennants, one with the American flag, the other the IMF's. The Gold Room where the Agreement was signed is cordoned off, with its original furniture in place. The suites and bedrooms have brass plaques on their doors indicating their conference occupants. Maynard and Lydia were in No. 129, overlooking the River Ammonoosuc and the Cog railway winding up to Mount Washington. It was next door to the grander suite occupied by the Conference President, Henry Morgenthau. Lydia's bedroom adjoined that of Mrs Morgenthau, who complained of being kept awake by Lydia's balletic exercises.

The hotel had been less than fully prepared for its reopening. It was the mixture of luxury, chaos and inefficiency which impressed Lydia: 'the taps run all day, the windows do not close or open, the pipes mend and unmend and no one can get anywhere'. Despite its beauty, Bretton Woods was a 'madhouse', Lydia wrote on 12 July, 'with most people . . . working more than humanly possible'. It must have reminded Maynard of the Majestic Hotel in Paris at the Peace Conference – that other grand monkey-house which had left him exhausted and ill in 1919.

The difference was that this time he was one of the masters of ceremony, victimised at innumerable cocktail parties and photo-sessions: 'Lord Keynes conversing earnestly with the Chairman of the Russian delegation [Stepanov] (neither of whom know each other's language); Lord Keynes warmly clasping Dr Kung, the Chinese banker, by the hand; Lord Keynes sitting down; Lord Keynes standing up. . . .' He avoided the tedious opening ceremonies, but hosted a small party in his drawing room to celebrate an esoteric academic occasion – the 500th anniversary of the 'concordat' between King's College, Cambridge and New College, Oxford.

He had looked forward to the event as 'excitedly as a schoolboy' and delivered an 'exquisite allocution', explaining to the guests that ancient academic corporations constituted the core of 'much that is most precious in the world's civilisation'. Robbins, who represented New College, was driven to muse, not for the first time, on the 'curiously complex nature of this extraordinary man. So radical in outlook in matters purely intellectual, in matters of culture he is true Burkean conservative'.[21]

At Bretton Woods, the problems of peace were discussed in the shadow of a war about to end. It was a war, moreover, which the Soviet Union was doing most to win, and this was reflected in the number of honorary posts its delegates were assigned. It was the first time Keynes had encountered the Commissars *en masse* since his visits to the Soviet Union in the late 1920s. He used the opportunity to try to persuade them to send the Bolshoi Ballet over to Covent Garden the following year. The Foreign Office took up the idea, but nothing came of it. There would be no Russian ballet in London till 1956. The reason, it turned out, was that the Russians had a well-founded fear of defections.

The Normandy landings had just started, and from Western Europe ghostly allies, their nations about to recover independence, were clamouring for a share in the spoils of peace. In the circumstances, it was just as well that the Americans and British had stitched things up beforehand. The main unfinished business was the allocation of quotas which White had cleverly reserved for the conference itself, in the correct expectation that this would be the only matter of interest to most delegates.

White had planned two main commissions, Commission I on the Fund, which he would chair, and Commission II on the Bank, which Keynes would head. (There was also a 'residual rag-bag,' Commission III, called 'Other Means of International Cooperation'.) Commission I would consider the composite draft prepared in Atlantic City, which included all the amendments left over from that meeting; Commission II, it was hoped, would knock the constitution of the Bank into shape. White was determined to maintain control of the outcome, while creating the impression of participation in the process. A Commission chairman, he explained to Morgenthau, must be someone 'who knows the complete matter', who would 'prevent a vote' on anything he did not want voted on, and who would 'arrange the discussion' so as to stop agreement 'on something we don't want'.[22] His own Commission would be equipped with four committees (as well as *ad hoc* sub-committees) which could be relied on to keep most delegates uselessly active. Although the chairmen of these committees were non-Americans, they had American rapporteurs and secretaries, appointed and briefed by White. Unresolved issues would be referred to a Special Committee on Unsettled Problems chaired by Morgenthau. As decisions came through they were to be turned into 'Articles of Agreement' by lawyers on a Drafting Committee headed by the Canadian Treasury official Louis Rasminsky. As the lawyers got down to the drafting, the Agreement got longer and longer and more intricate.

It was becoming a document of 'incredible complexity' Robbins noted in his diary on 11 July, and the 'utmost vigilance' is necessary to ensure that the differences between ourselves and the United States . . . do not once more become active'.

Goldenweiser's golden rule was to 'let anybody talk as long as he pleases provided he doesn't say anything'. This was not too difficult. Most delegates were assertive without being competent. The conference language was English, which many did not speak or understand. This made it easy for the Americans, backed up by the British and Canadians, to control the agenda. Away from the 'cordial cacophony' of 'overcrowded and acoustically unsuitable hotel rooms',[23] the important decisions were made behind closed doors, between the Americans and the foreign country involved. While Harry White and his small group of 'technical advisers' kept absolute control over the text of the articles to be included in the agreement, 'the powerhouse of the conference was in Morgenthau's office . . .'.[24]

White's aim in making Keynes chairman of the Bank Commission was to neutralise him. He was well aware of Keynes's failing stamina. If he could keep him occupied on Bank business, he would have no energy or time left over for Fund business. This strategy worked. Keynes was head of the British delegation, and unofficial leader of the much larger Commonwealth group. Although the Commonwealth teams looked to Britain for leadership, they did not always follow it. In particular, the Indians and Egyptians tried hard, but unsuccessfully, to secure Fund involvement in making the sterling balances, of which they held by far the largest amount, convertible. Keynes had to intervene on Commission I on 10 July to state that, while Britain would settle the debts 'honourably', 'the settlement . . . must be . . . a matter between those directly concerned'.[25] This commitment, known as the 'Keynes pledge', ruled out unilateral repudiation. The British were also the main conduit through which the smaller European Allies could put their suggestions to the Americans. Through meetings of the British group and 'bilaterals' with Empire and European countries Keynes just about kept abreast of what was going on in Commission I. These meetings usually took place in his suite of rooms, 'to which everybody went for inspiration and guidance and compromise'.[26]

Britain's conference organisation was far from ideal. Its team, while of the highest quality, was too lean – technically, legally and administratively understaffed and therefore overworked. At one point, Keynes complained that he had had barely five minutes with his 'technicians' in three days; by the end he was writing to the Chancellor, 'all of us from the top to the bottom . . . are all in'. Keynes doubted – not for the first time – whether he had 'ever worked so continuously hard' in his life. Apart from presiding at his Commission and sitting at committees, he looked through a thousand documents, composed nearly a hundred long telegrams to the Treasury describing progress and asking for instructions, and as leader of the delegation had to 'make the full dress speeches and proceed to the attack with all guns blazing whenever there was trouble'. But he had a less gruelling time than the others, because Lydia, with rare exceptions, refused to allow him to attend committees after dinner, whereas the others, night after night, sat on committees till 3.30 a.m. and then started up again at 9.30 a.m.

> I certainly shouldn't have survived without [Lydia] [he wrote to his mother on 25 July]. After a little experience it became clear that what was really dangerous was for me to talk business or near-business at meal times with polyglot companions. . . . So we made it a rule to refuse all cocktail parties (which are a vile abuse for the busy) [and] to have our meals alone, and increasingly, as time went on, in our rooms. And she cherished and comforted me in all other ways also.

Because of Keynes's need to rest, Robbins and Robertson were given virtually a free hand on the Fund Commission to uphold British government instructions on such matters as exchange rate adjustment, convertibility obligations, conditions attached to drawing rights, and so on. Reporting back to Keynes was done by Sir Wilfrid Eady, who sometimes floundered in the technicalities. The Bernstein–Robertson axis proved crucial in getting Commission I business done, and Keynes was fulsome in his praise of Robertson. 'Dennis . . . has been absolutely indispensable. He alone had the intellectual subtlety and patience of mind and tenacity of character to hold on to all details and fight them through Bernstein (who adores Dennis), so that I . . . could feel completely happy about the situation.'[27] He wrote to his mother, 'Absolutely first-class brains do help.' However, in the drafting of Article VIII, communication between Keynes and Robertson, via Eady, broke down completely, and this was to cause immense trouble later.

White had stage-managed other aspects of the conference. He arranged for a conference journal to be produced every day to keep everyone informed of the main decisions. He also arranged daily press briefings, at which he displayed an efficient charm. Keynes appeared at only one of these, on 6 July, somewhat dampening the cheerful effect White was trying to create by saying that the Fund could be easily criticised, but all the alternatives were worse. Goldenweiser's record brings out the atmosphere of the madding crowd: the mass of stenographers working day and night, the boy scouts acting as pages and distributors of papers, the legal language which made everything difficult to understand, the great many varieties of unintelligible tongues, the Russians 'struggling between the firing squad . . . and the English language'.[28] A controlled Bedlam was what White wanted. It would make easier the imposition of the *fait accompli*.

What the delegates did understand was that there was a cache of American dollars available, of which they wanted as many as possible for themselves. Raymond Mikesell, who served under White in the US Treasury, had worked out a complicated formula for allocating 90 per cent of the available money, leaving $800m. 'to be added to any place we wanted to'. White had told him that the formula should yield a quota of $2.5bn for the USA, about half that for Britain and its colonies, with the Soviet Union and China assured third and fourth places. To 'cook' the results White wanted, Mikesell had to introduce data for national income. 'These last had to be approximated, and their uncertainty afforded opportunities for making minor adjustments to the suggested quotas when these did not conform to political realities.'[29] The quotas were made public for the first time at Bretton Woods, but the basis of their calculation remained secret. When the figures became known, there were explosions of affronted pride. Russia, which wanted quotas to reflect military as well as economic prowess, said it would not accept a quota smaller than Britain's. Britain said that if Russia got a larger quota, so should India. India wanted equality with China. France would accept a smaller quota than China 'for political reasons', but insisted on a larger quota than India. The Americans, with an eye on voting strength in the Fund, took up the demand for larger quotas for the Latin Americans. Chile insisted on equality with Cuba, Bolivia wanted equality with Chile. Australia also wanted more. White responded by setting up a Quota Committee, chaired by Judge Frederick Vinson, vice-chairman of the US delegation, to which countries could bring their complaints. Professor Mosse, a member of the French delegation, remembers that the quotas were established 'more or less arbitrarily by the United States in a series of deals'.[30] On one occasion, Pierre Mendès-France, for France, turned up in Morgenthau's room, apologising in broken English for being early, 'because it is very expensive . . . when I come too late'. When Stepanov the Russian was told that Soviet national income statistics did not justify a quota of $1.2bn, he replied cheerfully that he would produce new statistics. He got his way. (By this time, White was almost certainly in direct contact with Soviet military intelligence.) Morgenthau, White and Vinson agreed a final distribution of their spare millions on 14 July. 'See, Fred, that is why I am Secretary of the Treasury,' Morgenthau told Judge Vinson waggishly after doing some back-of-envelope calculations. 'I can add and subtract.'[31] The largest quota holders, the USA, Britain, the USSR, China and France, became permanent members of the Security Council of the United Nations a year later, affirming the world's political as well as financial pecking order.

Keynes confined his efforts to getting the Indian quota raised from

$300m. to $400m. His success was not received with much satisfaction. 'Indian *amour propre* in connection with ... China', wrote Robbins, 'was still far from satisfied; and it was very vocal. Moreover, they are still ambitious for a permanent seat on the Executive. Keynes, who received them, lying on his couch – he is now very exhausted and has to rest whenever he can – railed them on their ingratitude and urged with much force that they now had an excellent case to present at home, which he proceeded to outline in the form of an imaginary speech which might be delivered by Mr Shroff [an Indian delegate to the conference]. All this was without much visible effect.'[32]

Anglo-American agreement on exchange rate rules was confirmed on 8 July. The Fund was bound to accept a change in a member currency's exchange rate up to 10 per cent; and changes above this if satisfied they were necessary to correct a 'fundamental disequilibrium', the Fund being barred from objecting on the ground of the proposing member's 'domestic social or political policies'. If changes of above 10 per cent were unauthorised, the country concerned could still remain a member, though without use of the Fund's facilities. This became Article IV (sections 5 and 6). Robbins privately agreed with the Americans that the British insistence on preserving monetary sovereignty was making the Fund a toothless tiger, without any powers to 'control the Latin Americans'.[33] A little-noticed amendment to Article IV (section 1) laid down that the par values of currencies should be expressed in terms of gold 'or in terms of the US dollar of the weight and fineness in effect on 1 July 1944'. This made the dollar, the only gold-convertible currency, the key currency of the new system. While every other currency could devalue against the dollar, the US dollar could be devalued only against gold.

The British also got their way on the transitional period, the only obligation on members being to consult the Fund if they wanted to continue payments restrictions after five years (Article XIV, section 4). They still hoped to have the Fund offices in London, not America. Keynes wrote Morgenthau a 'long-winded letter' asking for the decision to be postponed, which the Treasury Secretary read out at an American group meeting on 13 July. White commented, 'We are putting in twice as much money as anybody else, three times as much ... it is preposterous that the head office should be any place else. We can vote it any place we want ... that is why they don't want it to come to a vote.' White correctly surmised that the British would not break off negotiations because 'they don't like where the head office is. ... If they don't like it, it is too bad. ... New York has become the financial center of the world. These British are just fighting up-hill.'[34] Keynes reserved the right to reopen both this question and the issue of whether the Fund should have full-time or part-time executive directors.

Goldenweiser wrote that Keynes was the 'outstanding personality. ...

He shone in two respects – in the fact that he is, of course, one of the brightest lights of mankind ... and also by being the world's worst chairman.'

The Bank Commission met for the first time on 3 July, but didn't get to work till the 11th, with an American draft produced by J. W. Angell and Emilio Collado, based on the principles of the 'boat draft' prepared by the British. Collado later described the Bank as a 'sort of stepchild at the beginning days of Bretton Woods'. But as a result of belated State Department work it seemed as if agreement might be reached on this as well.

Soon Morgenthau was declaring that he had 'never had so many complaints in my life' about Keynes's chairmanship of the Bank Commission. On 13 July Dean Acheson, America's representative, told the Treasury Secretary that Keynes was rushing it 'in a perfectly impossible and outrageous way. . . . He knows this thing inside out so that when anybody says Section 15-C he knows what it is. Nobody else in the room knows. So before you have an opportunity to turn to Section 15-C and see what he is talking about, he says, "I hear no objection to that", and it is passed. Well, everybody is trying to find Section 15-C. He then says, we are talking about Section 26-D. Then they begin fiddling around with their papers, and before you find that, it is passed.' More than at Keynes, Acheson's complaints were directed at poor American preparations. On the Fund there had been a 'very close-knit, effective group' in the American Secretariat. On the Bank Commission, Acheson was not receiving the 'party line'. White explained that 'What we wanted Keynes to do was to give the stuff to the four committees to stall until we were through with the Fund and then we could come in. Instead ... he has short-cut all that. . . .' Morgenthau was given what he ironically called 'the pleasantest task, as President of the Conference', to see Keynes and 'ask him would he please go slow and talk louder, and have his papers in better arrangement . . .'.[35] Despite the complaints, Keynes's methods got the business done. In seconding the report on the work of Commission II by George Theunis of Belgium to the Plenary Session, Keynes remarked that he and Theunis were the only Bretton Woods delegates who had been at the Paris Peace Conference twenty-five years before.

Keynes's haste was partly dictated by a determination to escape as soon as possible. He was growing steadily more exhausted. 'He is not the easiest of men to control, and the eagerness of his mind is such that it is intolerable for him to go slow,' Robbins wrote on 6 July. He had hoped to get away on Wednesday 19 July. In any case, the hotel had only been booked till the 21st. On 17 July Morgenthau summoned a meeting of the Steering Committee to discuss the 'Extension of the Conference'. He gave the floor to Keynes, who said he had reluctantly concluded that the conference should go on till Saturday or Sunday to give the technicians time to clear up the loose ends, the lawyers to draft the the Final Act, and all the delegations a bit of time to scrutinise it. But as 'some of my people . . . are quite breaking up under the strain' he urged that from now on there should be no official committees or commissions after dinner, and that Morgenthau as 'headmaster' should declare that day to be a 'whole holiday'. The whole holiday was duly proclaimed.

There was a last-minute Keynes explosion over the Bank for International Settlements. Set up as a club for central bankers in Basle, Switzerland in 1930, it had maintained contacts with both sides during the war: it had accepted the transfer of Czech gold to Germany, it had a German director, and Emil Pühl, deputy president of the Reichsbank, was a frequent visitor to Basle. A resolution proposed by Keilhau of Norway and supported by other Europeans demanded its immediate liquidation. The Americans and British had agreed to support a milder version recommending eventual liquidation, but at a meeting of Commission III on 18 July, the American representative Luxford put forward a resolution making membership of the BIS and IMF incompatible. This passed over British and Dutch objections. Keynes heard about it that evening, and it put him into a towering rage. He stormed into Morgenthau's room, accused the Americans of double-crossing the British, and said that unless the American resolution was withdrawn he would quit the conference. Mrs Morgenthau, who was present, reported Keynes as 'quivering, he was so excited about it'. Morgenthau quietened him down, and Keynes left with a promise to send him a new resolution next morning. The eventual agreement was to call for liquidation of the BIS 'at the earliest possible moment'. This moment never arrived, and the BIS continues to this day. Keynes's intervention probably saved it. He thought that the American action was part of a US Treasury sub-plot to discredit New York bankers opposed to the IMF who had had associations with the BIS.[36] Kept in existence, the BIS revived in the late 1940s as a centre for intra-European financial co-operation when the IMF was dormant.

Significantly, Morgenthau took Keynes's side against his own legal adviser, Luxford. 'B. M. Baruch has fed me full of this stuff that you can't believe Keynes, and Keynes double-crossed him at Versailles, and so forth and so on, and I have been looking for it, but I have seen no evidence of it.'[37] Relations between the two men were certainly warmer than they had ever been. Keynes explained to the Chancellor that 'until Bretton Woods I had never spent a minute with him that was not sticky. Now all that is completely changed. . . . He could not have been more consistently kind and friendly, and even expansive.'[38] Harry White, too, was 'all smiles, kindness and geniality. The position definitely is that we are allies and the common foe is without' – by which Keynes meant the Congressmen and bankers on the US delegation.[39]

The excitement over the Bank for International Settlements made

Keynes ill. Late in the evening of 19 July word spread that he had had a heart attack. Following an item to that effect in the newspapers, telegrams flowed in wishing him speedy recovery; the German press published suitably adulatory obituaries. Keynes made light of it. Forgetfully he had run up the stairs to keep an engagement, had been 'knocked out' for a quarter of an hour, a distressed Lydia had blurted out the news to a lady who had a son working for Reuters . . . 'In fact', he wrote to Catto, 'I have been exceptionally well. . . .' The last remark was certainly not true. 'As regards Keynes's health,' Robbins noted in his diary on 20 July, 'we were on the edge of a precipice. There was one evening of prostration at Atlantic City, two the first week here, three last week; and I now feel that it is a race between the exhaustion of his powers and the termination of the conference.'

The conference ended with a grand banquet on the evening of Saturday 22 July. Keynes came in a little late 'and as he moved slowly towards the high table, stooping a little more than usual, white with tiredness, but not unpleased at what had been done, the whole meeting spontaneously stood up and waited, silent, until he had taken his place. Someone of more than ordinary stature had entered the room.'[40]

As the dinner ended, Keynes moved to accept the Final Act, clothing his address with a mixture of literary and theological language, so expressive of the way his mind worked and of the civilisation from which he sprang. He remarked that 'we have had to perform at one and the same time the tasks appropriate to the economist, to the financier, to the politician, to the journalist, to the propagandist, to the lawyer, to the statesman – even, I think, to the prophet and soothsayer'. Had he not written of Marshall twenty years earlier that the 'master economist . . . must be mathematician, historian, statesman, philosopher – in some degree . . . as aloof and incorruptible as an artist, yet sometimes as near the earth as a politician'? He paid a tribute to the messenger boys – 'Puck coming to the aid of Bottom' – and to the 'indomitable will and energy, always governed by good temper and humour, of Harry White'. He even managed – the tongue is rather prominent in the cheek – to praise the lawyers 'who have turned our jargon into prose and our prose into poetry', though he would have wished that 'they had not covered so large a part of our birth certificate with such very detailed provision for our burial service, hymns and lessons and all'. Nor could the 'critical, sceptical and even carping spirit' evinced by the press disturb his benediction. 'How much better that our projects should *begin* in disillusion than that they should *end* in it,' he said. Forty-four nations had been learning to work together. 'If we can so continue, this nightmare, in which most of us present have spent too much of our lives, will be over. The brotherhood of man will have become more than a phrase.' The delegates applauded wildly. 'The Star Spangled Banner' was played. As Keynes left the dinner

8

JOHN MAYNARD KEYNES

some of the delegates – presumably those from the Anglo-Saxon world – started singing 'For He's a Jolly Good Fellow'. The Soviet reaction to these strange rites is not recorded.

Keynes set down his impressions of the results to Catto:

In the Fund we have in truth got both in substance and in phrasing all that we could reasonably hope for. The Bank really has, in my judgment, grand possibilities. We are not taking on ourselves any significant liability, yet the Americans are virtually pledging themselves to quite gigantic untied loans for reconstruction and development.

. . .

The Russians by stonewalling tactics have got everything they wanted – 1. Too large a quota in the Fund. 2. Too small a contribution to the Bank. 3. Reduced gold subscriptions. 4. Provisions by which even gold they put up can probably never leave Moscow. 5. Virtually contracting out of the exchange fixing clauses and so forth. Nearly all the concession, however, have been at the Americans' expense. It has been the concern of the American policy to appease the Russians and get them in. For my own part, I think this was wise.

. . .

You may be interested to know that the star performer amongst the American delegation has been Edward Eagle Brown, President of the First National Bank of Chicago. He is an enormous man of 20 stone who lives exclusively on beef, beginning with beef-steak at breakfast, and nods his big head like a bull in a stall. But . . . his mental grasp and force of character are altogether unusual. It is a long time since I met a more competent or distinguished banker; he has a complete intellectual understanding.[41]

Bretton Woods produced an agreement because agreement on money was easier to reach than agreement on trade, because the main work had already been done in the bilateral Anglo-American negotiations, because the conference itself had been carefully managed by White and the US Treasury, and because both Morgenthau and Keynes, for different reasons, were desperately anxious to sign a document – Morgenthau to deliver a re-election present to Roosevelt, Keynes to lock the United States into a rule-based post-war financial order.

The magic of Keynes contributed as much to the success of Bretton Woods as did the efficient logistics of White. In retrospect one official considered it had been a mistake 'to combine, especially in so frail though furiously hard-working a person as Lord Keynes, the burdens of being both leader of the delegation, in constant demand from leading representatives of other countries, and also its principal expert.'[42] But the magic would have been incomplete had he been cast in a ceremonial role. He was the Churchill of this world, and no one could have taken his place.

Roy Harrod summed up Keynes's contribution as follows:

> To have devised in the quiet of one's study a new economic theory which determined the nature of the economic thinking of the younger generation in two great nations, to have gone further and devised practical proposals for international co-operation to implement that theory, to have gone still further and won acceptance for those proposals by persuasion, first among officials and politicians at home and then in a wide international arena, was surely an accomplishment for which it would be difficult to find a parallel. The combination of the purely scientific aptitude for intellectual construction with a keen sense of realities and power of adapting theory to practice, and the combination of these again with persuasive and diplomatic faculties, were surely unique.[43]

This is well put, but only partly right. Keynes gave the Bretton Woods Agreement its distinction not its substance. The Agreement reflected the views of the American, not the British, Treasury, of White not Keynes. The British contribution tended, finally, towards the negotiation of derogations, postponements and escape clauses. The Agreement was shaped not by Keynes's *General Theory*, but by the US desire for an updated gold standard as a means of liberalising trade. If there was an underlying ideology, it was Morgenthau's determination to concentrate financial power in Washington. As the *Commercial and Financial Chronicle* pointed out 'The delegates did not reach an "agreement". They merely signed a paper which looked like an agreement.' There was a transition period of indeterminate length.

Some of the ambiguities which had made the Agreement possible were immediately exposed. Keynes had not had time to read the complete text of the ninety-six-page document – covering both Fund and Bank – before he signed it. 'Our only excuse', he later explained, 'is that our hosts had made final arrangements to throw us out of the hotel, unhousseled, disappointed, unanealed, within a few hours'.* A worrying discrepancy emerged between two clauses in Article VIII, which seemed to suggest

---

* Ghost:

> Thus was I, sleeping, by a brother's hand
> Of life, of crown, of queen, at once dispatch'd:
> Cut off even in the blossoms of my sin,
> Unhousel'd, disappointed, unaneled;
> No reckoning made, but sent to my account
> With all my imperfections on my head.
>
> (*Hamlet*, Act I, scene 5, lines 74–9)

that members had renounced their right to suspend convertibility in certain circumstances. Keynes was up in arms; he blamed Dennis Robertson for not spotting the offending clause; Robertson replied that Keynes himself had authorised it; Keynes said he had no recollection of having done so. He concluded that Britain might have to repudiate the Agreement. The point turned out to have no practical importance. But its passage into oblivion took up an inordinate amount of time and energy, and soured – yet again – relations between Keynes and Robertson. Robertson accepted responsibility for the 'blunder', but 'carried the wound with him to the grave'.[44]

The Bretton Woods Agreement still had to be ratified by the US Congress and approved by the House of Commons. In Britain, the Whitehall and Parliamentary 'Schachtians' were unreconciled. They had gone along with the Clearing Union because they were convinced the Americans would turn it down. They had not banked on Britain signing up to multilateralism with far less financial protection than the Clearing Union offered. A year later, Henry Siepmann of the Bank of England told Emmanuel Goldenweiser, who was visiting London, that Bretton Woods was 'a swindle . . . Keynes started the swindle by proposing to shift all the burden on the United States. He did not get away with it – and all kinds of compromises were made – but the whole thing still is dishonest. . . .' Henry Clay, also from the Bank, called Bretton Woods 'the greatest blow to Britain next to the war'. Their argument was that convertibility of sterling into gold and dollars would remove the incentive for sterling area countries to buy British goods and hold balances in London. 'What seems to worry them – and quite understandably –', Goldenweiser shrewdly noted, 'is that Bretton Woods is an acknowledgment of the fact that London has lost its position as the financial center of the world. I think that's the emotional basis of their reaction.'[45]

After Bretton Woods, Keynes and Eady went to Ottawa to negotiate an increase in Canadian Mutual Aid. For Keynes the Canadian trip was a relaxing break. Not having to work more than half a day, it was the nearest he had had to a holiday since the war started. He and Lydia were driven from Bretton Woods to Canada in a car provided by the high commissioner, Malcolm MacDonald, dawdling in brilliant summer weather. From Montreal they flew to Ottawa. The high commissioner and the Minister of Finance with their officials, in black jackets and pinstriped trousers, waited on the runway to receive them. Emerging first, sumptuously wrapped in a brown fur coat and hat, Lydia rushed towards Malcolm MacDonald, whom she had never met, flung her arms round him, and before he could say a word exclaimed in a loud voice: 'Oh, my dear High Commissar, how are you? I dreamed zat I was lying in bed, and zat you were lying in my arms.' Keynes followed behind her with cordial, though more conventional, greetings. MacDonald was duly captivated.

They drove to the Chateau Laurier Hotel, where the Keyneses were given the Moorish suite of nine rooms. ('It will be a great come-down to return to the basement kitchen,' Maynard gossiped to his mother.) Lydia's performances continued when, an hour later, MacDonald and his advisers called on him to hold a preliminary talk about the financial negotiations due to start in the afternoon. Keynes had misplaced the key to his official red box, and he and Lydia hunted about for it in their luggage. Eventually, the conference began in a private study with Keynes, the High Commissar and his officials sitting round a table. There was a knock on the door, and Lydia slipped in.

> She wore nothing but a short white chemise (presumably with a pair of brief drawers below) which hung flimsily round her otherwise bare body. In that state of near nudity she stood in apologetic manner casting a half-guilty, half-mischievous look at Keynes as she said, 'Oh Maynard darling, I am so sorry. You did give me ze key; and I forgot zat I hit it for safety between my little bosoms.' At that she clutched in her hands a ribbon hanging round her neck, and as she lifted it over her head raised from between her breasts – which so far as we could detect were not quite so small as she suggested – the lost article. . . . She blew him a kiss, turned in a ballerina's pirouette on her toes, glided through the door, and closed it behind her.[46]

After these *hors d'oeuvres*, the main meal started. The Mutual Aid Agreement had been signed in 1943, with Canada agreeing to advance Britain war supplies equal in value to the sterling area's deficit with Canada. In March 1944, the expected 1944–5 deficit was estimated at $1.475bn, while the Canadian appropriation under Mutual Aid was only $450m. Another $250m. had been wrung from the Canadians at Bretton Woods, and the British War Departments had started restricting their purchases. In a fortnight's negotiations, Keynes and Eady succeeded in extracting a further $655m., which covered the gap then estimated for the remainder of the financial year. Keynes also gave the Canadians a summary of the memorandum on Britain's External Financial Prospects he had prepared in May. On 27 July he gave a dinner party to celebrate the 250th anniversary of the Bank of England, at which he made a suitably indiscreet speech, reminiscing affectionately about 'Monty' Norman, who had just quit as governor.[47]

Their visit was adjudged highly successful. Keynes made or cemented important political friendships – notably with Graham Towers, governor of the Bank of Canada, and Clifford Clark, the Deputy Finance Minister – as well as renewing contact with his former students Bob Bryce and Wynne Plumptre. He reported that 'Malcolm MacDonald (Ramsay's son) looks after us like a brother and arranges picnics for us in the hills, forests and lakes such as we had forgotten could exist.' On these outings and also at the ballet, the three of them recalled the performances of Tchaikovsky's *Sleeping Princess** at the Alhambra in 1921, when MacDonald and Keynes, unbeknown to each other, had both been in the audience watching Lydia dance. Lydia added her own inimitable commentary: 'What a relief to be away from Bretton Woods! I do not scream, or hysteria or lunatic asylum any more. . . . Your Johnny looks well, and although he always has difficult matters to deal with (he is born for that) he has his reprieves in his meals, or sitting in the park watching the statues before or after dinner.' The temperature was often over 100 degrees Fahrenheit, and one day Keynes swore to MacDonald that in the early hours of that morning he had followed Lydia to their kitchen, and saw her disappearing into the large ice-box 'like Alice in Wonderland disappearing down the White Rabbit's tunnel'.

The contrast between North American affluence and British penury could not have been greater. 'On this continent,' Keynes noted, 'the war is a time of immense prosperity for everyone.' They often ate beefsteaks, and Lydia went on a shopping spree, buying 'deersucker' dresses and shoes every day, presumably out of their foreign exchange allowance. Keynes was struck by the unfairness of it. Britain would end the war bankrupt, North America flush. Surely some retrospective rebalancing of the sacrifice was only just? Keynes loved Canada: 'if one ever had to emigrate, this should be the destination, not the USA'.[48]

An agreement on extending Lend–Lease to Stage II still had to be struck with Washington. Disturbing indications had emerged that the State Department was applying pressure to substitute interest-bearing loans for Lend–Lease or to link its continuation to a commercial agreement.[49] Keynes had expected the Chancellor to come over to take charge of the Stage II negotiations after Bretton Woods. Instead Morgenthau and White flew to London early in August to discuss financial help for a liberated France, and Roosevelt and Churchill decided to confer on grand strategy for the Japanese war in Quebec in September. Keynes and Eady hung around Washington for a few days, before being called back to London, Keynes re-establishing contact with Halifax, whom he had not seen since 1941. 'Keynes asked me a lot about Linky [Quickswood] and was sorry to hear what I told him of his mental disturbance and annoyance with Jasper Ridley. He was very sorry that Linky proposed to give up the Provostship . . . he brought a distinction to Eton that few others would.' Lord Halifax added: 'I like Keynes very much.'[50] Maynard and Lydia flew back to England with Eady by Clipper on 20 August. It was the last time his state of health allowed him to fly across the Atlantic.

---

* Diaghilev had changed the name of the ballet (see Skidelsky, *Keynes*, ii, 98–100).

III

MORGENTHAU TO THE RESCUE

Just over a month later Keynes was on the *Île de France* bound for Halifax, Nova Scotia, to negotiate an extension of Lend–Lease into Stage II. He saw it as 'the most important (and perhaps the most difficult) of all my missions. . . . I am substituting for the Chancellor of the Exchequer for a job which, on a point of form, is his.' In fact, it proved the easiest of his assignments. Keynes loved sea travel, and to him the voyage was a 'magnificent holiday'. The Atlantic was still. He and Lydia had a comfortable cabin and sitting room, were attentively looked after and excellently fed. In the mornings he 'worked and wrote leisurely at different papers'. In the afternoon they sat out near the bridge reading, with 'sailor boys to move our chairs whenever the sun and wind change'. He found Abba Lerner's *The Economics of Control* a 'grand book', deploring only its reliance on 'Benthamite arithmetic', which led Lerner to advocate income equality. 'The whole complication and fascination (and truth) of the ethical doctrine of organic unity passes you by . . .' he wrote to him, in a half-remembered echo of the debates of his youth.[51]

The parameters of the financial negotiation were set by the 'Octagon' Conference between Roosevelt and Churchill at Quebec from 13 to 16 September. The war against Japan was then expected to continue for at least a year after the defeat of Germany; Churchill was determined that Britain should take part in the final assault on Japan. Both prestige and finance were involved in this decision. The prestige of the British Empire in the Far East needed restoring after earlier disastrous defeats. And if Britain dropped out of the war Lend–Lease would stop. The Treasury saw in this double imperative an opportunity to scale down Britain's war production by more than the reduction in Lend–Lease supplies, creating a margin to increase exports and rebuild its reserves. Its other objective was to end American manipulation of Lend–Lease to keep reserves low and to revise the terms of the Export White Paper of 1941.

The State Department also saw its opportunity to nail Britain to its policy of the 'Open Door'. It had been having trouble with the British over meat supplies from Argentina, oil rights in the Middle East, civil aviation rights in the British Empire. In return for an extension of Lend–Lease to Stage II, Britain should pledge itself to end 'discrimination' against American interests and resume commercial negotiations. However, Roosevelt, for reasons still obscure, decided to exclude the State Department from the Quebec meeting. Churchill then excluded the Foreign Office, but insisted on bringing over Lord Cherwell, and asked for Morgenthau's presence. In London Morgenthau had got on well with Sir John Anderson, who, briefed by Keynes, had persuaded him of the grimness of Britain's financial prospects. He promised to do all he could to help, provided he were in charge and the British did not lobby Stettinius and Acheson. The British shrewdly surmised that they would get what they wanted from Morgenthau without commercial strings attached. Morgenthau was in a benevolent mood. The British had co-operated at Bretton Woods. They had appealed to him for help. And he needed their help for a scheme of his own.

The famous Morgenthau Plan for the pastoralisation of Germany was hatched, as one might have expected, by Harry White. On their aeroplane journey to London on 6 August, White pulled from his briefcase a State Department paper on German reparations, which 'envisaged the eventual reintegration of Germany into the world economy'. The fiercely anti-German Morgenthau was aghast, and this gave White his chance to press an alternative scheme. At a conference of American officials in Redrice, Hampshire, on 12 August, Morgenthau outlined a plan for destroying Germany's capacity to wage war in the future. Its industries would be eliminated, it would be broken up into little bits, and it would be converted into an agricultural territory. Destruction of German industry would enable Britain to take over Germany's export trade. Now it was the State Department's turn to be aghast. When Penrose from the American Embassy pointed out that Germany's population was too big to be supported by agriculture, Morgenthau replied easily that any excess could be dumped in North Africa. Ambassador Winant's political adviser, Philip Moseley, expostulated that White's proposed treatment of Germany would 'replace a German hegemony on the Continent by a Russian one'. This was White's aim. David Rees sums up his attitude as follows: 'Drawn toward the Soviet Union by an emotional sympathy at the very least . . . White may have felt in the late summer of 1944 that the irreversible crushing of the Reich would help to lead to post-war Soviet–American understanding. If the Russians achieved a dominant position in Europe as a result, this might be a price worth paying. . . .'[52] By 4 September the US Treasury had prepared a memorandum entitled 'Program to Prevent Germany from Starting World War III', which Morgenthau pressed on Roosevelt in advance of Octagon.

Keynes first heard of the Morgenthau Plan from White just before he left Washington in August. He and White had lunch on the 20th, as a result of which White reported to Morgenthau that Keynes was 'heartily in agreement with our view of the desirability of dismembering Germany and as to the relative unimportance of reparations'. Keynes, it seemed, was 'wholly in our corner'. White was wrong. Keynes, while 'much tempted' by the proposal for a temporary break-up of Germany, was never in favour of its de-industrialisation.[53] He had been Treasury representative on an inter-departmental committee chaired by Sir William Malkin of the Foreign Office to consider Germany's economic future. Its Report of 1943 advocated reparations in kind, not money, and limited to a few years – so as to avoid the 'transfer problem' which followed the last war. Germany would be prohibited from producing armaments of any kind, but in lieu of defence expenditures it should make a long-term financial contribution to peace-keeping, from a levy on export earnings. 'This, the most novel of the Committee's recommendations, was clearly attributable to Keynes. It ultimately found expression in Germany's financial contribution to NATO.'[54] Like his colleagues, Keynes aimed to 'normalise' Germany, not destroy its means of livelihood. When the Report came before a meeting of ministers on 29 September 1943, it was attacked by Lord Cherwell, who wanted Britain to take over Germany's export markets, especially in steel and machine tools.

Roosevelt, who had told Cardinal Spellman the same month that Russian domination of Europe was inevitable,[55] brought Morgenthau's ideas (and Morgenthau himself) to Quebec, against strong opposition from his own State Department, which opposed not just the substance of the Morgenthau Plan, but Morgenthau's attempt to take over US foreign policy. On the first day of the conference, Roosevelt overruled his military advisers and accepted Churchill's offer of extensive naval and military help in the Pacific. When Morgenthau expounded the Morgenthau Plan at a dinner with Churchill and Roosevelt on 12 September, he received from Churchill, slumped in his chair, 'a verbal lashing' such as he had never had in his life; Churchill's condemnation of it as 'un-Christian' was 'one of the less sensitive of the epithets he used'.[56] However, next day Morgenthau won over Cherwell; Cherwell then sold it to Churchill by parading the benefits it would bestow on Britain's export trade. The same day Churchill dictated the final draft of the Plan, which he and Roosevelt then signed. This committed the leaders to the 'closing down' of German heavy industry, and envisaged 'a country primarily agricultural and pastoral in character'.[57] Here was another grand design. Germany would be de-industrialised; Britain would take over Germany's export business; Morgenthau would secure a generous Lend–Lease settlement for Britain in Stage II. There is no conclusive evidence of the linkage. White certainly believed that Morgenthau and Cherwell agreed a *quid pro quo*: British support for German pastoralisation in return for US support for British aims.[58] The fact remains that the Morgenthau Plan decision preceded the discussion of Britain's needs.

On 14 September, a directive on Lend–Lease was agreed almost perfunctorily. A Joint Committee, chaired by Morgenthau, would be set up to determine Britain's Lend–Lease requirements in the light of an 'agreed record of a conversation between the Prime Minister and the President'. The record, of course, omits the fact that at one point in the 'conversation' Churchill was driven to expostulate: 'What do you want me to do ... stand up and beg like Fala [the President's dog]?' Churchill proposed that Lend–Lease supplies would continue 'on a proportional basis after Germany's defeat, even though this would enable the United Kingdom to set free labour for rebuilding, exports, etc'. Morgenthau suggested that fixed amounts were better. The British had indicated that they wanted $3.5bn for munitions and $3bn for civilian expenditure, and they should proceed from these. Roosevelt agreed. He also agreed that Britain should be allowed to start exporting all goods except those 'obtained on lend lease or identical thereto'. This implied a relaxation of the terms of the Export White Paper, which had forbidden the export of goods 'similar' to those obtained under Lend–Lease. These new arrangements would apply to Stage II – after Germany had been defeated. In September it looked as though they would be in force by the end of the year.

The Quebec conference was a triumph for Churchill. He had got exactly what the Treasury had asked for. It also seemed a triumph for Morgenthau. He had got the leaders to endorse his Plan. And he had been restored to his favourite role as Britain's sugar-daddy. But Roosevelt was left exposed. Cordell Hull was furious that no commercial *quid pro quo* had been obtained from the British; the US military, who wanted to finish off the Japanese war on their own, were angry at having to divert supplies to Britain. Within a few weeks, Roosevelt started to retreat from the Quebec spirit. On 3 October, he told Secretary of War Stimson that Morgenthau had 'pulled a boner' on Germany. Quebec turned out to be the high-water mark of the Morgenthau Plan – and indeed of the Morgenthau–White axis. After it, Morgenthau's influence waned, and White's with it. The British Foreign Office, too, lobbied successfully against the Plan. Churchill, with an economy of truth, notes briefly in his memoirs that 'with my full accord, the idea of "pastoralising" Germany did not survive'.[59]

The Cabinet in London nominated Keynes and Sir Robert Sinclair to serve on Morgenthau's Joint Committee, Keynes representing the Chancellor and Sinclair Oliver Lyttelton, Minister of Production. But Churchill had already asked Cherwell to start off the implementation negotiations in Washington.[60] Morgenthau expressed himself 'delighted to have Lord Keynes over', but insisted 'the thing got down to Lord Cherwell and myself. That is what the President and Mr Churchill wanted.' But Morgenthau wanted details which Cherwell could not supply. On 22 September Cherwell was told to delay the presentation of the British case till Keynes came.

Maynard and Lydia arrived in Washington on 2 October. They had travelled from Ottawa in a private railway car provided by the president of the Canadian Railway 'with bedrooms, drawing room, dining room [and] a special chef ... called Romeo [who] cooked in a heavenly fashion'. They had an air-conditioned suite on the top (fourteenth) floor of the

Statler, 'with windows as big as the walls, so you never get sad or bored, the whole of Washington is at your feet'. Keynes was given a room in the British Delegation offices at the Willard Hotel on Pennsylvania Avenue, next door to the Treasury.

The situation into which he stepped was distinctly ticklish. The State Department were sore that the Lend–Lease negotiations had been entrusted to Morgenthau rather than to them. Work on preparing the British requirements had been held up by the Cherwell 'delusion' that 'if only Mr Morgenthau and he could be left in a room together for about five minutes . . . he (Lord Cherwell) would emerge with a definite promise of $5-$6 billion and no questions asked'. As a result, 'until [Keynes] came we were little better than a disorganised rabble'.[61] Keynes rejected the Cherwell approach. He knew, from his 1941 experience, that Morgenthau was likely to promise more than he could deliver, and that 'all the decisions will have to be implemented by *other* Departments [the Military and Supply Departments, the State Department and the Foreign Economic Administration] and none by the Treasury'.[62] Realistically he argued that if, as he expected, the Morgenthau Plan for Germany was defeated by the State Department 'an agreement between M[orgenthau] and Cherwell . . . may not assist elsewhere as much as one might have hoped'. Cherwell should stay long enough to get the proceedings properly launched and then find 'some good excuse for going home. . . .'[63]

For Stage II, Keynes was instructed to obtain Lend–Lease supplies equal to 75 per cent of Britain's existing Lend–Lease requirements, about $7bn. He was also to negotiate a drastic easing of restrictions on Britain's export trade. When he called in on Morgenthau and White for a preliminary talk, he found they were considerably more interested in their 'mad' plan for de-industrialising Germany than in the details of Lend–Lease. Fearful of getting involved in Washington in-fighting, Keynes was driven to preserve an 'unwonted and uncomfortable silence'. He did ask White how the inhabitants of the Ruhr were to be kept from starving. White replied that there would have to be bread lines. When Keynes asked whether the British would be expected to provide the bread in their zone of occupation, White said the US Treasury would pay for it, provided it was on 'a very low level of subsistence'. 'So whilst the hills are being turned into a sheep run, the valleys will be filled . . . with a closely packed bread line. . . . How I am to keep a straight face . . . I cannot imagine.'[64]

The British group met at 11 a.m. on Tuesday 3 October. Keynes started off with his suggestions. He would try to persuade the Americans to accept three principles for Stage II: that Britain should be allowed to release manpower for civilian purposes, to export more freely, and to build up reserves. It was hopeless trying 'to do a deal largely with Morgenthau himself' as 'Morgenthau could not give a directive that would be carried out in detail'. Cherwell's assistant, Donald MacDougall, noted in his diary that Keynes 'was evidently not aware that the Prime Minister had directed Cherwell, against his will, to come down to Washington to carry on the negotiations'.

While Morgenthau went off electioneering, and Cherwell went off on a scientific tour (that is, to learn about the atomic bomb), Keynes and his colleagues prepared their 'book of words', otherwise 'British Requirements for the First Year of Stage II'. Keynes presided daily at the Steering Committee, which spawned sub-committees dealing respectively with military and civilian supplies. To Keynes, Bob Brand (the Treasury's permanent representative in Washington) and Frank Lee (Brand's Treasury assistant) fell the task of relating the detailed programmes to the financial arrangements for Stage II.

The 'book of words' took ten days to compile. Trying to penetrate the Washington thicket, Keynes had a private talk with Leo Crowley, the head of FEA, whom he found 'very well disposed'. Crowley had confirmed that 'we must work closely with Morgenthau, who is playing the leading part. He also said that Currie, Harry White and Acheson would in fact settle the whole thing. Their Ministers would do what they told them.'[65] On 13 October Halifax wrote in his diary: 'My admiration of [Keynes] and his mind grows. He came up to tell me that all his business was going very well and the only snag on the horizon was if Llewellyn [the Minister of Food] went ahead with his Argentine Meat Contract at this moment and cast Hull into open or covert opposition. He accordingly sent John Anderson a telegram on this topic.' On Saturday 14 October, Cherwell and Keynes agreed to scale down the British munition demands from $3.75bn to just over $3bn. After receiving a cable from London, indicating a prospective drop in gold and dollar reserves in 1945, Keynes added a 'Chapter 3' of additional requirements to the tune of $500m. These were to be met by a combination of additional shipments of tobacco and sugar, and money which the British claimed the Americans owed them from pre-Lend–Lease contracts, dubbed 'half-dead cats' by British officials.

On 17 October, Keynes sent six copies of the 'book of words' to the US Treasury. He and Cherwell followed this up with a visit, to find Morgenthau, worn out from West Coast electioneering, uneasily fingering what he thought was a three-volume document, three copies having been left on his desk.

Formal negotiations started on 19 October in a Main Committee in Morgenthau's office, over which the Secretary presided, with two subordinate committees on munitions and non-munitions. Keynes soon realised it would be impossible to make any oral presentation at these chaotic gatherings. Morgenthau himself had only the vaguest idea of what was going on. 'At the Main Committee', Keynes noted, 'any continuous argument or indeed more than a dozen simple sentences were always out of place.' After a week, Morgenthau was reluctantly persuaded to set up a joint sub-committee under White. This helped, but only to some extent. Although White proved an efficient chairman, the Americans found it hard to field the same team for more than ten minutes at a stretch, since members were always running out to take telephone calls. Its secretary, Frank Coe, who took the minutes, kept falling asleep.[66]

In Washington, the British always had to adapt themselves to the American habits of business, with small teams facing seemingly anarchic battalions of lawyers, academics, researchers, statisticians, pressmen, photographers. When it was all over, Keynes wrote that if there was one thing he had learnt after spending almost one year out of the last four 'stepping like a cat over the hot tiles of Washington' it was that the situation was 'fluid up to almost the last moment'. 'I liken them to bees who for weeks will fly round in all directions ... providing both the menace of stings and the hope of honey; and at last, perhaps because the queen in the White Hive has emitted some faint, indistinguishable odour, suddenly swarm to a single spot. ...'[67] Keynes saw the Queen Bee only once, for tea on 26 November. Lydia bought herself a new dress for the occasion. Keynes reported the re-elected Roosevelt in 'grand form', though unchanged about how to treat Germany.

The British found the Americans amazingly cordial. Morgenthau was keen to shovel his billions into Britain's empty purse. The munitions programme was agreed 'with remarkable ease and celerity', despite objections from the War Departments, who saw no need for a British 'Blücher' in the Pacific. The civilian programme took longer to agree, but eventually the British got most of what they wanted on this as well. The main hitch, as Keynes had foreseen, was meat. The British had offered to buy Argentine beef on a four-year contract. This cut across the State Department policy of enforcing a blockade to punish Argentina for its 'pro-fascist' neutrality. The British had given them promises on which they now seemed to be reneging. On 31 October Morgenthau threatened to break off negotiations. It was an awkward moment. The British minister in Buenos Aires locked himself in his bathroom so as not to receive the Argentine acceptance of the British offer. 'How reasonable people can lend themselves to such monkey tricks, beats me,' wrote Keynes. The British cancelled the contract, but not the imports.[68]

Keynes was less interested in the details of the programmes than in their impact on Britain's prospects for Stage III. This depended on how far Britain would be allowed to increase its reserves and expand its exports during the Japanese war. Roosevelt had accepted the case for increased exports at Quebec. But reserves had not been mentioned, and the Americans were reluctant to yield control over them. Indeed, 'White gave Keynes his own personal opinion – completely off the record – that it would be better for us to run down our gold and dollar reserves to a dangerously low level in Stage II, since this would make it easier for the

Americans to give us very generous assistance in Stage III. Keynes very properly resisted this suggestion since it would put us at the mercy of the Americans in Stage III.'[69]

To augment Britain's reserves of gold and dollars, Keynes had put in the Chapter 3 of additional requirements (they rose from $500m. to $750m. in the course of the negotiations) to be made up of certain civilian supplies which it currently paid for and by US cash payments for aircraft contracts, which Britain had ordered for itself but 'sold' to the Americans before reciprocal aid had been formalised in September 1942. These were the 'half-dead cats'. Their revival made Morgenthau 'hopping mad', and his reaction made Keynes nervous. Lydia intervened. She went to see the reserved Secretary in his office and told him: 'Mr Morgenthau, *Maynar'* cannot sleep at night. He says he wants sixpence from you: only sixpence more. Why, Mr Morgenthau, why cannot you give *Maynar'* sixpence?' At which, according to her own account, Morgenthau promised her the sixpence and congratulated her on being one of the ablest and most skilful negotiators he had ever met.[70] He told Keynes he would find 'a large lump sum of new money'. 'We are agreeing with him', Keynes reported to Anderson, 'that it would be vastly better to replace half-dead cats with a new live dog. But in what kennel is he to be found?'[71]

Negotiations on Chapter 3 matters and exports were broken off during the week preceding the Presidential election on 7 November. Keynes took the opportunity to give an informal talk in the State Department on the sterling area, stressing the voluntary and informal character of the arrangement, and trying to disabuse American officials of their conviction that the sterling–dollar pool was a nefarious conspiracy to deprive US exporters of markets. 'I guess it would have done some good,' noted the ambassador, who had gone to hear him. 'He made them laugh by saying that the U-boats had always been the best friend of the British Treasury by making it impossible for people to buy things for which they would have had to pay dollars.' However, Keynes refused the State Department's request to liberalise the sterling area's dollar pool as a *quid pro quo* for Stage II help, telling Currie that 'he was not prepared to enter into any sort of bargain on this point as part of the present discussions'.[72]

Keynes and Halifax were getting on well. Keynes often came to see him on what the ambassador called 'Keynes's business', Halifax's understanding but detached charm providing a calming influence in moments of stress. More stimulating to Halifax was the gossip they had on the Eton Provostship. 'Linky' Quickswood had resigned. 'He wants me to accept the Provostship,' Halifax noted on 2 November, 'but I do not think it is quite my cup of tea. . . . He [Keynes] was depressed about getting decisions on post-war stuff in England and about the immersion of Ministers in day to day work. He evidently hopes that John Anderson will be Prime Minister rather than Anthony if and when Winston goes.' On the night of the Presidential election Maynard and Lydia joined the Halifaxes, the David Bowes Lyons and Isaiah Berlin for dinner in the Embassy. Bored with the election results coming in over the radio, Lydia suddenly said to Berlin: 'Do you like Lord Halifax?' Halifax was sitting a few chairs away. Berlin emitted a neighing sound. Keynes did not stop her. She went on, 'He is quite popular, but it was not always so. Do you remember appeasement? It was terrible. Munich . . .' Nothing from Maynard. Halifax looked embarrassed and got up and patted his dog. 'Now Frankie enough of this politics.' After telephoning Harry Hopkins, Halifax came back and announced the election was 'in the bag'. Keynes was thrilled with Roosevelt's victory, writing with unnecessary asperity that his republican opponent Thomas E. Dewey 'is one of the most miserable rats ever brought to birth'.[73]

The Russians have a word for Lydia's behaviour – *stoochki*, roughly 'tricks'. 'Naughtiness', recalled Berlin, 'Keynes rather liked, especially against the pompous.' Lydia's remarks, like Keynes's, started the rounds of Washington. At a dinner given by Cordell Hull, she was heard, in a lull in the conversation, to say to a neighbour, 'Two men – yes – I can see they've got something to take hold of. But two women – that's impossible. You can't have two insides having an affair.'[74] Lydia was both unselfconscious and contrived; and part of what people took to be her lack of self-consciousness was simply an exploitation of her most endearing feature.

Despite the incessant work, Keynes remained in good form and good health for the whole of his two months on North American soil. Washington was at its autumnal best, with unbroken sun, a temperature between 65 and 70 degrees Fahrenheit, the leafy trees changing their colour to golden brown in its spacious streets and squares. Although it seemed to Keynes that the 'paradisical' climate made everyone ill, his only complaint was a toothache. While Maynard was at work, Lydia did her Christmas shopping in Connecticut Avenue, the Bond Street of Washington. Among the clothes she bought for herself was a new dressing gown, which made her look like an old-fashioned coachman from *Petrushka*. Lydia thought that it was best for Maynard, in the evenings, 'to be alone in my whimsical silent company', but they often dined out, or went to the ballet. The Lippmanns gave a dinner party for Lydia's birthday on 21 October. Maynard's nephew Richard, who was in Washington working for the Admiralty, wrote to his fiancée Anne Adrian: 'We got Maynard talking about the history of the theatre in England. Shakespeare as seen by his contemporaries, and several other fascinating subjects – he was quite brilliant. Only politics was banned. . . .'[75] Maynard was worried by his nephew Quentin, whom, he told Richard, 'must be firmly jolted out of his easy existence here'. For her birthday, Maynard gave Lydia a new dress and 'lots of pocket money' – which, he told Sir Richard Hopkins, she had amply earned. At the end of October they took Austin Robinson – 'looking like a little boy in blue' – on a drive to Mount Vernon. 'For three or four hours', Robinson remembered, Keynes 'forgot everything except the exquisite perfection of that lovely house, and the shock of beauty of the view from its terrace, while he engaged in light-hearted and completely preposterous arguments about George Washington and modern America'.

Having agreed to find an extra $400m.–$500m. to replenish the British reserves, Morgenthau asked for extra figures which he could use to justify it. Keynes sent White and Morgenthau revised versions of his Chapter 3 arguments on 13 and 16 November. They give an impression of how he would have conducted his oral persuasion, had it not been vetoed by the telephones. It would have been a story of unstinted sacrifice for the common cause. The British had conducted themselves with a 'wartime imprudence which has no parallel in history'. But this very imprudence which had enabled Britain 'to save ourselves, and [help] save the world' had bankrupted it. Britain would be left with net gold and dollar reserves of $1.5bn against overseas gold and dollar liabilities of $12bn.[76]

Morgenthau did his best, but the President was unpersuaded, and 'Mr Morgenthau', Keynes shrewdly noted, 'has easier access to [the President's] presence than to his mind.' Morgenthau tried to find a way of paying off the American aircraft debts, but the US Air Force was opposed to reopening the contracts. The new dog turned out to be a scrawny animal, worth only about $250m. Crowley of the FEA refused to put tobacco and sugar back on to the civilian list, from whence he had removed them in 1943. In place of cigarettes, the British were offered prefabricated houses, better for health, although worse for the reserves.

However, the nub of the matter, and the point on which the British failed to get real satisfaction, was freedom to resume exporting. They had been led to believe that the Export White Paper's restrictions on exporting would be scrapped on 1 January 1945. But at the wind-up meeting of Morgenthau's Committee on 22 November Crowley declared that they must stand till the end of the German war, whenever that was, and reserved administrative discretion even after that. Keynes was infuriated, calling Crowley a 'Tammany Polonius' whose 'ear [was] so close to the ground that he was out of range of persons speaking from an erect position'.[77] The best Keynes could secure was a promise of some administrative easement from 1 January 1945, and increased export freedom when the German war was finished. Putting the best face on it, he told Dalton on his return that this had given Britain 'all the export freedom we can use'.[78]

Frank Lee had no doubt that Keynes stood out as the hero of the negotiations:

THE AMERICAN WAY OF BUSINESS 371

Maynard's performance [he wrote] was truly wonderful. I think that
occasionally he overplayed his hand and occasionally wore himself
out struggling for points which were not worth winning. But in
general he was an inspiration to us all.... we felt like Lucifer's
followers in Milton, 'Rejoicing in their matchless chief'. His industry
was prodigious, his resilience and continual optimism constant
wonder to those of us more inclined to pessimism, while I doubt
whether he has ever written or spoken with more lucidity and charm.
And, of course, the impression he makes on the Americans gives us
an enormous initial advantage in any negotiation in which he
participates. Take Harry White, for instance – that difficult nature
unfolds like a flower when Maynard is there, and he is quite different
to deal with when under the spell than he is in our normal day to
day relations with him. I think that everyone on the United Kingdom
side would agree that we could not have hoped to get anywhere near
the results which have actually been achieved had it not been for
Maynard's genius and inspired leadership.[79]

What were the results? On the military side of Lend–Lease the British
got $2.838bn having asked for $3bn, and on the non-military side
$2.569m. having requested $3bn. Morgenthau had promised to find
another $250m.–$300m. of miscellaneous items to help the reserves.
Amazingly, all this turned out to be more, not less, Lend–Lease than the
British had been getting before, even though it would now support a
smaller war effort. The Americans, Keynes thought, had abandoned the
'marginal theory' for good.

In fact, the agreement proved much more shaky than it seemed.
Morgenthau had done his best, but American opinion had turned anti-
British again, partly in response to British military intervention to put
down a communist uprising in Greece. The American press screamed that
Lend–Lease should not be used to shore up British imperialism. With
American public opinion swinging against the British, and under pressure
from Admiral Leahy and the military, Roosevelt reneged on his Quebec
commitments. Britain would get no right to export goods 'similar' to
those being lend–leased till the victory over Germany. It failed to secure a
promise that Lend–Lease would continue for a year after VE Day. Above
all, on Roosevelt's orders, nothing agreed in Washington was signed. This
meant that there was no assurance that the $5.5bn would actually be
forthcoming, or that Britain's reserves would not continue to be used as a
criterion of Lend–Lease management. In his press announcement on 30
November, Crowley said that 'the amount and types of supplies would
continue to be subject, as always, to adjustment from time to time....' As
Dobson comments, 'It was as if the Quebec conversations had never
been.'[80]

On 27 November Maynard and Lydia flew to Ottawa in a private aeroplane with Stage II proposals to put to Canadian ministers. But a conscription crisis deprived Keynes of their attention, further talks were scheduled for 1945, and on 6 December he and Lydia sailed back to England from New York on the *Nieuw Amsterdam.*

On board, he drafted a huge letter to the Chancellor summarising his achievements. On the whole it was upbeat. Keynes comforted himself with the thought that the United States was now wholly committed to Britain's restoration as a Great Power. American illusions about all its other allies had faded or were fading. 'There is nothing to be found reliable or homely in the habitable globe outside Britain and the British Commonwealth. This, today, is America's deepest, least alterable conviction – a sure rock upon which, whatever may appear on the surface, we can build with safety.' However, there were sombre lessons to be learnt for Stage III. The chief of these was to avoid 'inconvenient strings' being attached to further American help after the Japanese war had ended. He urged 'with vehemence' that 'financial independence of the United States at the earliest possible opportunity should be a major aim of British policy. . . . A mighty Empire in financial leading strings to others will not be mighty at all. . . .' Britain 'must stand unpropped, or be laid low'.[81]

Maynard and Lydia landed at Southampton on 12 December. They had been away for eight days short of three months.

PART THREE

THE LAST
BATTLE

There can be no Greater Error than to Expect or Calculate Upon Real Favors from Nation to Nation. George Washington

CHAPTER ELEVEN

Temptation

I

USURY

From the point of view of the British Treasury it would have been ideal if Germany had surrendered at the end of 1944 and Japan had fought on till the end of 1945. This would have given Britain a year partially to demobilise its war economy and restart its export trade; this, in turn, would have made it less dependent on American help when peace finally broke out. But it was not to be. On 16 December 1944 Hitler launched his last counterattack in the Ardennes. It was soon contained but, together with Russian inaction in the east, it delayed the end of the European war by several months. The second factor, of which Keynes had no inkling, was that the atomic bomb was on the point of becoming operational. Keynes hoped that 'the Japanese would not let us down by surrendering too soon'. In the event, the use of atomic weapons abruptly terminated the Pacific war in August 1945. The Stage II arrangements, on which rested Britain's hopes of recovering a measure of financial independence before the war ended, were thus not only postponed till May 1945, but were then compressed into three months. Britain's last hope of avoiding a 'financial Dunkirk' was scuppered when Lend–Lease was suddenly cancelled after Japan's surrender instead of being tapered off. Peace started, therefore, with a balance of payments deficit of wartime proportions. This meant that Britain would have to go back to Washington cap in hand – exactly the situation Keynes had hoped to avoid. Thus was the plot set whose outcome was the humiliation of the American loan which Keynes negotiated in Washington in December 1945.

While the Allied armies prepared for their final assault on Germany, Keynes's energies were temporarily absorbed by the less pressing problem of post-war domestic finance. Sir Richard Hopkins had set up the National Debt Enquiry the previous autumn, and Keynes was put on its Committee, together with officials from the Treasury, the Inland Revenue Department and the Economic Section. Evidently the National Debt would be hugely enlarged by the war, and the Treasury was looking for an authoritative financing doctrine, consonant with modern thought. Keynes expounded his views on savings and investment, interest rates and capital budgeting at three meetings, on 8, 22 and 27 March 1945. According to Meade's diary, he was in erratic form – 'perverse, brilliant and wayward': extreme in the statement of his liquidity-preference theory, incredibly rude to a senior Treasury official Sir Herbert Brittain (he called him 'intellectually contemptible'), cautious and sensible in his policy suggestions. At the first meeting on 8 March, Keynes 'gave an academic lecture on the whole of the *General Theory*'. Saving and investment, he said, were kept equal by changes in income, not interest rates; the interest rate was simply the price demanded for parting with money. This being so, 'authorities make rate what they like by allowing the public to be as liquid as they wish'. Meade felt it must have been 'terribly hard' for the Treasury officials present to follow the lecture – 'Bridges very able and competent but without much technical knowledge of these subjects; Hoppy very wise and learned as the elder statesman making way for new blood.... Eady muddled and uncertain'.[1] Hopkins, at any rate, caught the drift in favour of cheap money, and now went off to read the *General Theory* himself for the first time.

Keynes 'leaves out all qualifications of the Liquidity Preference idea so as to assert unequivocally that neither thrift nor the productivity of capital have any influence over the rate of interest'.[2] This brought him into conflict with Meade, who argued that variations in interest rates had a part to play in influencing the level of investment.* By contrast, Keynes argued that the complex of interest rates should be set with sole regard to the different liquidity preferences of savers. To make this possible, the Treasury had to rid itself of the 'Funding Complex'. Only if 'they are indifferent to funding ... can [they] make both the short- and long-term [rate] whatever they like ...'. For 'social reasons' '*de facto* illiquidity' should be rewarded by the offer of long-term securities set at a maximum of 3 per cent, in the hope that as few people as possible would invest in them. Below this ceiling, the Treasury should offer tap issues of intermediate and short-term debt at decreasing rates. Bank rate should be set at 1 per cent. This amounted to a permanent policy of cheap money, though Keynes did not exclude the possibility of raising both long-term and short-term rates if an inflationary boom developed.[3] Keynes's advocacy of a continuation of the cheap-money policy after the war fitted the Treasury's concern to service its vastly expanded debt charges as inexpensively as possible. Hopkins's report of the National Debt Enquiry, which broadly endorsed Keynes's line, set the course of post-war monetary policy. In Sayers's summary: 'the fascinations of technical possibilities of reducing the burden of National Debt took over, but the practical effect accorded with the latest doctrines and everyone was happy ...'.[4]

---

* In advocating a 2 per cent rate of inflation to guard against the technical impossibility of having zero or negative nominal interest rates, Meade was anticipating modern discussions.

Keynes's view that low interest rates should be maintained after the war made a good deal of sense in light of the actual situation which faced the Treasury. But the extremism of the theoretical position from which it was argued illustrates the perverse streak in his make-up. To say that an increase in the desire to save reduces the amount saved, and that (therefore) if you want to increase saving you should reduce the rate of interest was a paradox too profound to convince even the adequately intelligent. It also had the disadvantage of being wrong, outside the special circumstances of depression. Further, Keynes seemed to be arguing that the *only* reason for postponing the 'euthanasia of the rentier' was that 'public psychology' was not yet ready for it. To be 'revolutionary in thought but very cautious in policy'[5] is all very well, but what happens when mortality removes the caution, leaving only the revolutionary theory? Dennis Robertson had tried to rid Keynes of the idea that the rate of interest had *no* connection with productivity and thrift, that to set a rate of interest permanently below the profit rate was bound to produce an inflationary boom. In certain moods, Keynes seemed to accept this; but when Robertson was not there to argue with him he reverted to his extreme views. His hatred of the rentier was proof against economic arguments, because at bottom it was theological, not scientific. The bondholder was, in his mind, nothing but the medieval usurer, or Shylock, someone who sought to make a profit out of lending money. To Sir Cornelius Gregg, chairman of the Board of Inland Revenue, Keynes wrote on 9 April: 'In other words, it is usury to extract from the borrower some amount additional to the true sacrifice of the lender which the weakness of the borrower's bargaining position or his extremity of need ... make[s] ... feasible. ... I find it interesting to put it this way because it really amounts to exactly the same thing as my theory of liquidity preference.'[6]

It is important to notice that these thoughts were in Keynes's mind as he plotted his appeal to the Americans for a grant or interest-free loan to carry Britain into Stage III. To charge interest to Britain in its 'extremity of need' would be *usury*, especially after Britain's disproportionate sacrifice for the Allied cause.[7]

On 28 March Keynes wrote his first letter for five years to his now ancient French friend Marcel Labordère, with whom he had happily discussed gold movements and investment psychology in the 1920s, and who had always revered him as a poet rather than as a scientist. Addressing him as 'My dear Alchemist', Keynes wrote: 'Another matter which will have interested you is our large sales of gold in the Middle East countries, but more particularly India, not so much to realise a large premium on the gold as deliberately to provide a means of hoarding and thus damning inflationary pressure.' His light-hearted tone in the continuation could not disguise the decline in his health: 'I am well, in the sense of being able to do my work with my brain for as many, or more hours a day as ever [sic]. But my heart is very deficient in strength (lungs, liver and kidneys beyond reproach fortunately) and I cannot walk. I find it profitable to spend 12 hours in every 24 in a horizontal position in bed.'[8]

II

PREPARING FOR STAGE III

On 4 January 1945, informal commercial talks between Britain and the United States had started up again in London, involving Liesching, Robbins and Eady on the British side and Harry Hawkins and Ernest Penrose of the US Embassy on the American side. The American draft of a 'multilateral convention' covered such topics as tariffs, imperial preferences, cartels, agricultural subsidies, blocked balances and procedure. The British said they favoured the American aims, but wanted to liberalise trade more cautiously; by June they had only got so far as to give the Americans a 'specimen draft of a possible statement of principles'. In a personal conversation with Hawkins and Penrose on 7 February, Keynes affirmed that Britain had 'a fundamental and inescapable interest in the multilateral organization of trade'. He and others would shortly launch a 'counter-offensive' against the 'nonsense' of bilateral bargaining, which was supported by a 'vocal minority' outside government. However, he said he was 'heretical' about the most-favoured nation principle for generalising tariff reductions favoured by the Board of Trade, pointing out that industrialising countries might want to retain high tariffs to protect their 'infant industries'. It might be better for the British Empire and the United States 'together with whatever countries might care to join' to form a 'sort of customs union'. He also emphasised the dependence of liberal trading policies on 'the maintenance of a high level of employment in the United States'.[9]

Although post-war financial prospects were discussed in 'grave terms' in January 1945,[10] the British lacked a defining document on which to base their strategy for a post-Lend–Lease world. Keynes had his own ideas. A new Roosevelt 'brainwave', he told Brand on 15 February 1945, should provide for a 'reconsideration of the sharing of the costs of the war'.[11] The Americans might agree to repay pre-Lend–Lease costs Britain had incurred in the United States; and part of the sterling debts might be cancelled. What this boiled down to was a post-war grant from the United States to repay part of the costs of the war. Keynes aired these thoughts to Judge Rosenman and Lauchlin Currie when they visited London in March and April respectively, knowing they would get back to Roosevelt.[12] At this stage the British were unwilling to contemplate 'direct loans' from the

United States 'either to facilitate unblocking [of sterling balances] or even to finance essential imports any further than might be temporarily required by inability to obtain them by alternative means'.[13] Unfortunately, Roosevelt died before Keynes's ideas could reach his brain. It is unlikely that they would have lodged there.

It was the Canadians who prodded the British into more positive action. Alarmed by remarks made by the visiting British Minister of Agriculture, Robert Hudson, to the effect that the British would stand no 'multilateral nonsense', Graham Towers, the governor of the Bank of Canada, prepared a policy statement, dated 8 January 1945, called 'Post-war Commercial Policy Prospect: A Proposal for Averting a Breakdown in International Trade Relationships'. The Canadian government accepted Towers's suggestions and, in a telegram to London on 23 February, offered to replace Mutual Aid – the Canadian version of Lend–Lease – with a loan of $1.2bn at 2 per cent for three years after the war, repayment not to start till after ten years, and with a waiver clause on balance of payments grounds. With a corresponding line of credit from the United State, Britain, it suggested, should be able to drop restrictive and discriminatory commercial policies. The Canadians also proposed that the US and Canada should assume some of the sterling debts, with remaining balances being scaled down. They wanted to come to London to discuss these ideas. Churchill accepted the proposal for a Canadian visit. 'I think this is the very least we can do to meet the Canadian government's wishes,' he told his Cabinet. So the visit was fixed for early summer.[14] With hindsight, it seems odd that the Canadian plan failed to suggest to the British the likely form in which assistance from the United States would be offered. What it did do was to elicit a response from Keynes. In an effort to give the British officials something to discuss with the Canadians, Keynes took ten days' 'rest' in Cambridge in the second week in March to produce a memorandum entitled 'Overseas Financial Arrangements in Stage III'. Initialled on 18 March 1945, it was extensively discussed and revised before going to the Cabinet on 15 May. It provided the intellectual and mythical foundation of the American loan negotiations later in the year.

What Keynes proposed, in short, was that Britain should offer two post-war financial 'trades': to the Americans, a return to the convertibility of currently earned sterling in return for a gift of $5bn; and, to sterling area countries, immediate convertibility of part of their balances, in return for cancellation and funding agreements covering the rest. Underlying these trades was the concept of a retrospective redistribution of the costs of the war he had mentioned to Brand. If the USA and sterling area countries would compensate Britain for disproportionate war sacrifices, Britain, with higher reserves and fewer debts, could agree to enter a multilateral trade and payments system. A 'just' accounting of the war would thus make possible a liberal resumption of the peace. There was a beautiful moral balance in this design, as well as a blend of morality and self-interest, which made Keynes's memorandum intuitively attractive to all those who read it.

Another typical Keynesian feature was the tripartite division of possible remedies for Britain's prospective balance of payments problem into ideal, worst-case and intermediate solutions. This was not just Keynes being a good civil servant, setting out the options. It was his way of providing a framework for discussion which could be accepted by the two main warring Whitehall factions, the internationalists and the Schachtians. He had done roughly the same thing in his very first paper on the Clearing Union. The categories, once announced, stuck. Everyone involved, thereafter, discussed the question of American financial assistance in Keynes's intellectual framework. This was not the only possible framework, and it is far from clear that it was the best. But it was undeniably seductive, and Keynes was Whitehall's greatest intellectual charmer.

The move to the moral plane, while de-emphasising the need for British self-help, was the most striking of the departures from the cold lucidity of Keynes's 1944 attack on the problem (see pp. 341–2 above). It reflected the fact that it now looked likely that the peace would start without any real progress having been made on reconverting the British economy from war production to exports. The new memorandum was also wordier, more self-indulgent than Keynes of old. It suggests a certain slackening of the intellectual coil which was Keynes's brain, perhaps due to the merging of fatigue with his long-established habit of self-confident pontification.

The theme of the opening recital of facts was that Britain had spent its treasure profligately and imprudently to ensure Allied victory. On the plus side, Britain would end the war without debts in foreign currencies (the debts were to the sterling area), with a reserve not far short of what it had been when the war started, and with a competitive exchange rate. That it owed large sums to sterling area countries was also not without advantage. 'Owe your banker £1000 and you are at his mercy; owe him £1 million and the position is reversed.' On the minus side were the bloated cash spending of the Service Departments in Africa, the Middle East and South Asia, the slowness of reconverting production to exports, and the obligations for relief and reconstruction Britain had assumed under UNRRA. The first and last points echoed Keynes's now familiar attack on 'Lady Bountiful'; the second, Keynes's export pessimism, which went beyond the immediate problem of reconversion. Whereas in May 1944 Keynes had been optimistic about short-term export prospects – Germany and Japan knocked out, the rest of Europe handicapped, a huge cost advantage vis-à-vis the United States, Empire countries demanding capital goods which Britain could supply – he now reverted to an attitude of Hendersonian gloom. To maintain its pre-war living standards, Britain would have to export 50 per cent more than pre-war to pay off debt and compensate for wartime disinvestment. Yet in the transition period he doubted whether Britain could do much more than regain its pre-war export volume.

In this, the last full year of the war, Britain was balancing its accounts by a combination of American Lend–Lease and Canadian Mutual Aid (together running at about £800m. or $3.2bn a year) and by accumulating debt to the sterling area at the rate of almost £700m. (or $2.8bn) a year. Without a change of policy, therefore, Britain would enter the post-war period with a prospective balance of payments deficit which Keynes estimated at about £1.4bn or $5.6bn annually. Strenuous efforts to reduce overseas military spending and increase exports might reduce this to £1bn. But a cumulative deficit of £2bn or $8bn was likely over three to five years. This deficit had to be financed somehow.

Keynes dubbed his three policy alternatives Austerity, Temptation and Justice. (In the second draft, Austerity became Starvation Corner.) The first would be the consequence of rejecting any American help. It was Keynes's name for the policy of bilateralism advocated by Hubert Henderson, the imperialists, the Bank of England and left-wing socialists – those he now indiscriminately labelled 'Schachtians'. It would require the continuation and intensification of rationing and wartime controls, national planning and the direction of foreign trade on Soviet lines, the postponement of social projects at home and colonial reconstruction and development abroad, and the virtual abandonment by Britain of any overseas activity, military or diplomatic, that cost money. It would risk 'serious political and social disruption and our withdrawal, for the time being, from the position of a first-class Power'. The more Keynes thought about Austerity the less he liked it. In economic terms bilateralism made no sense, since Britain bought too much from countries it did not sell to. The attempt to negotiate bilateral agreements would break up the sterling area, which required sterling to be 'freely convertible'. However, its chief objection was that it would encounter the active hostility of the United States, thus breaking up the liberal front. The US could also offer much more attractive inducements to sterling area countries than could Britain. 'In short, the moment at which we have for the time being lost our financial strength and owe vast sums all round the world is scarcely the bright and brilliant occasion for asking all our creditors to join up with us against where the financial power now lies, not for the purpose of getting paid, but for the purpose of obliging us with a little more.'[15]

Keynes saw this 'disastrous' alternative as a 'bluff' to elicit an American offer 'not so much generous as just'.[16] American help of $8bn would 'give us real liberty of action' and allow Britain to offer 'the full multilateralism of trade and exchange'. America, he thought, would be willing, even eager, to lend Britain this kind of money as a commercial loan, with interest as low as 2 per cent, easy terms of repayment postponed for ten years, with provisions for deferral of repayment, and on condition that Britain made sterling area earnings convertible and signed up fully to the Article VII agenda. This was the policy of Temptation. The objection to it was not just, or mainly, because it would force Britain into possibly unsupportable debt bondage, but because it would be 'an outrageous crown and conclusion of all that has happened'. It was particularly intolerable that Britain should start the peace owing over $20bn (sterling debts plus American loan) – roughly what the Allies proposed to exact in reparation from Germany. Keynes fulminated: 'The fundamental reasons for rejection are incommensurable in cash terms.' Temptation might be transformed into something approaching Justice if the United States lightened the annual service and repayment conditions on the loan, allowed the release of blocked sterling balances to be deferred and desisted from financial pressure in commercial negotiations. But these mitigations would not be enough. 'The sweet breath of Justice between partners . . . would have been sacrificed to some false analogy of "business".' Justice required a 'general re-consideration of the proper burden of the costs of the war'.[17]

The just solution was for the USA to reimburse Britain the $3bn it had spent in the United States before Lend–Lease started, and open a credit line of up to $5bn for ten years, at a token interest rate and on easy repayment terms. Canada would write off $500m. of debt and advance $500m. at nominal interest. In return Britain would accept 'de facto convertibility of sterling' within a year after the end of the war.[18] This deal was the cornerstone of Keynes's plan from the start. He also proposed a tripartite division of sterling claims: a quarter would be cancelled, a half funded, and a quarter made freely available for buying dollar goods, but not adding to creditors' reserves. Of the funded part, 2 per cent a year would be released, starting five years after the war, for buying British capital goods. This solution was designed to reflect the fact that no Lend–Lease had been forthcoming to Britain from its Empire. Keynes's solution of the sterling balances problem survived all subsequent revisions, though the proportions were changed. Initially at least, there was a pleasing symmetry between the two sets of contributions to Justice: the US and the sterling area would contribute $3bn and $4bn retrospectively to Britain's war costs, the US by way of a gift, the sterling area by way of cancellation of its claims. South Africa would be specially penalised for its 'notoriously inadequate contribution' to war costs by being asked to make a retrospective payment of £50m. or $200m. in gold.

These contributions to the cost of the war would come to £1.83bn or $7.2bn. Of this, $3.2bn would be 'new' money to go into Britain's reserves, the rest being relief from debt. With this injection, Britain would start the peace with a reserve of £1.25bn, roughly double that of 1939, as against outstanding debts of £1.5bn, having sold about £1.5bn of overseas assets on the way. It would still be the only country in the United Nations to end the war with its overseas earnings heavily mortgaged. Nevertheless, with such a settlement the only anxiety it would face was 'knocking some energy and enterprise into our third-generation export industries and of organising the new industries which our first generation is well qualified to conduct'.[19]

Keynes had something to say about tactics. Britain could hope to reach such an outcome only by 'robust and unyielding negotiation'. He thought there might well be a breakdown at the end of the first round. Britain should present its case to the US in the form of an appeal to Justice, pointing out that never again would it 'have a better chance of a wise act at so modest a cost'.[20] Negotiations should start at the earliest in September – after the end of the German war, the last Congressional appropriation for Lend–Lease and the ratification of the Bretton Woods Agreement by Congress. This timetable reflected the expectation that the war would still be going on.

As 'Otto' Clarke, who was with Keynes in the Treasury at the time, later wrote, 'the [memorandum's] immense breadth of concept and mastery of detail made a great impression on those who read it, especially when one realizes it was all done in Stage I, with the expectation of another eighteen months' war'. He also recalls that 'From the beginning he showed a total optimism that "Justice" would be accepted. . . .'[21] This has been disputed, and Keynes certainly did not ignore the possibility of breakdown and the need for tough negotiation.

Before entering into the detail of the coming financial battles, it is worth looking both backwards and forwards. It cannot be said that Keynes's – or Britain's – tune had changed much since the Article VII issue had arisen in the summer of 1941. Britain would accept the obligations of multilateralism only if guaranteed a large credit line to the United States. In the Clearing Union scheme this had been a generalised overdraft facility. When America evaded the trap, Keynes turned to bilateral assistance. That the gift was to be in payment of a moral debt was also familiar: it was simply the revival of the British claim, renewed at different times through the war, for reimbursement for the 'old commitments', or 'half-dead cats'. The British view that the Empire should be retrospectively taxed on its 'windfall profits' was also long-standing, though less universally shared.

Experience in Washington should have taught Keynes that the Americans had never accepted that they owed Britain a moral debt, and it was unlikely that the Empire would recognise one. There was an ivory-tower quality to the argument, which made parts of it remote from practical possibilities. But it was remote in another sense. Keynes's 'feel' for Washington politics was unduly influenced by his double triumph of 1944 in getting the Bretton Woods Agreement through and negotiating an exceptionally favourable Lend–Lease settlement for Stage II. His expectations for Stage III were based on the continuation in power of the duumvirate of Roosevelt and Morgenthau, and, on the British side, of Winston Churchill, with his unparalleled prestige. All these figures toppled in 1945 – through death, resignation or electoral defeat. Yet by the time all this came to pass, Keynes's Grand Design had taken root in Whitehall and could not be dislodged. When he eventually got to Washington in September his plan was unchanged, but he found that everything else had changed.

It was Keynes's ability to lift his subject on to a higher plane which made him, in Lydia's words, 'more than economist'. But this could be a weakness. The coherence of his memorandum lay in the realm of morals rather than finance. Keynes was using Justice in its classic Aristotelian sense of just desert. Britain had sacrificed disproportionately more of its treasure than the United States or its Empire in a cause of equal value to all three: it deserved to be compensated by the other two; and certainly not to be left with bills equivalent to what Germany might justly be required to pay. It was hard to make this argument seem compelling outside Britain, since Britain had a much more direct interest in the defeat of Nazi Germany than did America, while India, Britain's largest creditor, had to be 'protected' against Japan mainly because it was part of the British Empire. A former member of the Indian Finance Council said that if Britain mentioned 'Justice' to Indians 'we should never get another word in edgeways'.[22]

Although Keynes was always fighting Britain's corner, it would be wrong to see his moral arguments simply as a mask for British self-interest. For Keynes, as for all public men of his generation, Britain was a 'good' Great Power, which had fought a 'good' war in a 'good' cause. Justice demanded that Virtue be rewarded. That Britain alone of the belligerents should face the future encumbered by vast debts seemed to Keynes to be an overthrow of the moral order. His categories were ultimately moral, not power political. But, if morality was not just a cloak for self-interest, it was certainly a vehicle for illusion. The hope for gifts to rescue Britain from the consequences of policy had become by 1945 a necessary illusion – the only way of averting the eyes of British policymakers from the truth that in fighting a 'just' war Britain had lost its position as a Great Power.

Keynes gave vent to his export pessimism in an outburst against the inefficiency of British industry:

> The available statistics suggest that, provided we have never made the product before, we have the rest of the world licked on cost. For a Mosquito, a Lancaster, Radar, we should have the business at our feet in conditions of fair and free competition. It is when it comes

to making a shirt or a steel billet that we have to admit ourselves to be beaten both by the dear labour of America and by the cheap labour of Asia and Europe. Shipbuilding seems to be the only traditional industry where we fully hold our own. If by some sad geographical slip the American Air Force (it is too late now to hope for much from the enemy) were to destroy every factory on the North-East coast and in Lancashire (at an hour when the directors were sitting there and no one else), we should have nothing to fear. How else we are to regain the exuberant inexperience which is necessary . . . for success, I cannot surmise.[23]

Probably, by this time, the deepest objection felt by Keynes to Schachtian methods was political. Technically, he did not believe that an imperial solution could be made to work. This being so, what 'Schachtianism' meant in practice was Britain's withdrawal to a Stalinist island fortress, with bilateral trade agreements made with whomsoever could be induced to enter into them. We have already noted his resistance to comprehensive rationing early in the war. Barter trade, he now averred – having forgotten his own earlier advocacy of it – was the 'antithesis of free enterprise' and was only being advocated by 'near Communists'. He wrote, 'We would have to retire, as Russia did between the wars to starve and reconstruct. We might, like Russia, emerge in good health half a generation later, but nothing much less than Russian methods would have served our turn meanwhile.'[24] In claiming that even a mind as lucid as Keynes's quailed before the prospect of Britain retiring as a Great Power, Correlli Barnett[25] misses the point that such retirement was linked in Keynes's mind with the adoption of communist methods. Keynes was nostalgic not for imperialism, as Barnett suggests, but for freedom. The imperialist strategy would lead to communism in practice, if not in intention, while the left-wing strategy intended communism under the guise of cementing an Empire bloc. What Keynes wanted to recreate was a modified version of the Britain in which he had grown up – a liberal world power set in a liberal world. And for this American help was essential.

There was still of course the question of how to get American help on the best terms, and here Keynes's tactical approach, with its emphasis on past services, was at fault. Great Powers are kept going not by gratitude, but by the incentives – carrots and sticks – they can deploy to induce other Powers to do what they want. In the war this had been clear. The Americans were finally convinced that the defeat of Britain would be a disaster for the United States. And Britain could draw on reserves of both sympathy and power to run up overdrafts with the Empire – power much more than sympathy in the case of its two largest creditors, India and Egypt.

Keynes partly understood this. He thought that Britain still had the whip-hand in the matter of sterling balances. He also knew that it could disrupt American hopes for a liberal post-war order. But with regard to the former he was constrained by the 'Keynes pledge' against unilateral repudiation of sterling debts given at Bretton Woods, and more generally by the concept of *noblesse oblige* which still governed the attitudes of the gentlemanly capitalists running the sterling area system; while he was diverted from making the threat of rupture with America credible by his hatred of what it would mean. Although he talked about Britain's 'temporary' retirement as a first-class power, he never brought into the bargaining frame a credible threat by Britain to withdraw from all its military responsibilities in Europe and the Middle East and leave the United States to pick up the pieces.

Like every other official, Keynes was compelled to work within the political limits set by the government of the day. But he himself occupied a unique position in 1945, his already immense authority enormously buttressed by the three-month political interregnum which followed the break-up of Churchill's coalition government at the end of the German war. Within broad limits Keynes could have got the British government to do anything he wanted on external financial policy. Where he was at fault in this period was not in lack of preparation for negotiations with the United States, but in presenting the prospects of US help to the Cabinet through rose-tinted spectacles. He held fast to the illusion that what Britain deserved could be made to happen and, as we shall see, infected the Labour government with his optimism. The effect of this was to leave the defence of British interests dangerously dependent on his magical arts of persuasion.

III

PERSUADING WHITEHALL

Before they could become British policy, Keynes's ideas had to be accepted by Whitehall. This time he got no input from his previous 'first class critics': Henderson, Robertson, Kahn and Harrod were not on the scene. More surprisingly, Robbins and Meade were not shown early drafts. 'Hoppy' too was in semi-retirement, his successor Bridges was unversed in financial technicalities. That left Sir Wilfrid Eady, the joint second secretary. Eady was a Schachtian. In the drama which followed he was the leading opponent of a settlement with the United States on anything but British terms. Keynes had written in his memorandum: 'Most of us would, when we are up against it, prefer ... Temptation to Starvation Corner. ...'[26] Not Sir Wilfrid Eady. In his first comment on the Keynes Plan, he wrote that it had to be 'an all or nothing business' – that is, Justice or Austerity. He thought Keynes's suggestion of a credit-line of $5bn additional to the $3bn of retrospective Lend–Lease 'plain Temptation and . . . dangerous Temptation'. A loan would only sour Anglo-American relations. Apart from this, Eady injected three notable dollops of realism. He doubted whether Britain should offer '*de facto* convertibility' one year after the end of the war, since he did not foresee exports expanding sufficiently to make this a proper risk. He urged the elimination of the formula 'redistribution of the costs of the war', which he foresaw would antagonise Britain's sterling area creditors. And he warned that Keynes's 'extraordinarily difficult financial diplomacy' would make no progress unless Britain was prepared to take 'a definitely forthcoming attitude on Article VII' of the Lend–Lease Agreement.

This being so, Eady naturally regretted the absence in Keynes's memorandum of a serious consideration of the Austerity alternative:

> What are the exact consequences to us either of failure or of a decision not to proceed along your lines? You discuss them rather gingerly. I suppose we would begin by programming imports from North America in the first three years to reduce them to a minimum. . . . We could then try to arrange suitable credit terms for those imports, and meanwhile should be attempting to switch to other sources. . . . The next step would be a real examination of the problem of organising exports so as to secure for them not only the necessary drive, but the accepted priority of export demand over the satisfaction of civilian home demand.
>
> Then we should call in aid the principle of Article 14 of the Bretton Woods document, and try to adapt our exchange clearing arrangements as best we can. We must not overlook the real bargaining value of our market, or the equal wish on the part of our Sterling creditors to go on doing business with us. . . .
>
> But I feel that even if it is to enforce an ultimate conclusion of the inevitability of your line of approach, we must be prepared with a fairly detailed presentation of the alternative policy.

In effect, Eady accused Keynes of eliding the choice between Justice and Temptation, and making both seem too rosy and easily attainable. His alternative was to borrow for necessary purchases from the United States, while redirecting the flow of trade to sterling area and 'payments agreement' countries.[27]

Early in April, Keynes got an opportunity to try out his ideas at a dinner party hosted by Churchill for the American financier Bernard Baruch, with the Chancellor, Cherwell and Beaverbrook as fellow guests. Baruch agreed with Cherwell that Germany and Japan should be stopped from exporting manufactured goods. This was the basis for his 'extreme optimism' about Britain's post-war position. When Keynes said that the only way out was a 'general reconsideration of our indebtedness, the United States facilitating this by a contribution', Baruch had great difficulty in grasping the point, perhaps because he was 'stone deaf'. Churchill 'was quite magnificent throughout, in his very best form, taking a profound interest in our Treasury's problems for once'.[28] Following this dinner, Keynes got permission to show his memorandum to both Beaverbrook and Cherwell. The Beaver wrote back congratulating him on its 'vigour and grace. You make exciting literature out of finance, which nobody but yourself has done for a long time.'[29] Beaverbrook's comments led to a meeting on 19 April, at which he conceded that 'if we could get such a plan, he would favour it', but doubting whether any satisfactory bargain with the United States was available. Keynes wrote back in his seductive mode: 'Do you really favour a barter system of trade which would mean, in practice, something very near a state monopoly of imports and exports a la Russe? Do you welcome an indefinite continuance of strict controls and (probably) severer rationing than we have now? Will you applaud the retrenchment of colonial development?'[30] Keynes had never shown the slightest interest in colonial development. But it seemed a good tactic of persuasion to use on an imperialist.

Both the Treasury and the Bank of England raised objections to points which were to cause trouble later. The first concerned the treatment of sterling balances. Keynes had suggested that if sterling area countries refused his plan for a tripartite 'settlement' of their balances, Britain should simply freeze the lot. Ernest Rowe-Dutton pointed out the weakness of this so-called sanction. It would be impossible to apply to those balances which were privately owned. Blocking all the balances would break up the sterling area. The second problem had to do with the riskiness of sterling convertibility, Keynes's *quid pro quo* for American help. Waley, the deputy head of the Treasury's Overseas Finance Division, rejected the possibility of 'full convertibility' at 'any foreseeable future'. The third problem, as Rowe-Dutton put it, was to find an alternative to 'unconditional surrender' if Justice were refused. The Bank of England's position was forcefully stated by Cobbold and Bolton: a loan was no solution, but a grant looked like charity. This might be acceptable. But the Bank, like Eady, would prefer to borrow dollars commercially to buy necessary American goods, and keep the 'dollar pool' intact. Cobbold felt confident that with British spending in America covered, Britain could finance its deficits elsewhere by continuing to run up balances with the sterling area.

Waley found it almost impossible to present an agreed Treasury position for the Chancellor's consideration. He summed up in a note of 12 April. They could all agree to ask the United States for retrospective Lend–Lease of $3bn. They had to decide on whether they needed to adopt 'Ministry of Production' methods for expanding exports. They were not to offer any commitments on convertibility. They should try to get voluntary Indian and Egyptian contributions to the cost of the war. They would have to hesitate about blocking sterling. The Bank disagreed with the option of borrowing a further $5bn from the United States. 'But the alternative is a degree of austerity which is not within practical politics,' wailed Waley. The Overseas Finance Division met in Keynes's room on 18 April. Keynes insisted that Britain should obtain enough to allow sterling convertibility: $3bn would be too low, $8bn would be too high. On the question of sanctioning the sterling area, he said there was no intention of using sanctions, it was only a weapon for arriving at a desired end – that is, another bluff.[31]

Stringent criticism of Keynes's approach came, as one might have expected, from the British financial team in Washington, headed by Brand and Lee, whose ears were much closer to the American ground. In renewing Lend–Lease in March 1945, Congress attached the proviso that Lend–Lease funds should not be used for reconstruction or relief and that the programme should terminate with the war. In the last period of the war, Lend–Lease supplies to Britain were unilaterally curtailed by Leo Crowley, the 'faithless' Irish-American head of the Foreign Economic Administration. Keynes did not mind much, since he thought the demands of the British Service Departments were 'largely phoney' anyway.[32] But it did mean that the Morgenthau–Keynes agreement of November 1944 was dead and 'the level of Britain's external reserves had become a bargaining point again'.[33] Roosevelt's death on 21 April ended Keynes's hope of a *coup de théâtre* to replace Lend–Lease; the surrender of Germany on 7 May 1945 meant that Stage II had arrived.

The mini-Whitehall in Washington was much quicker to sense the chill blowing through Anglo-American financial relations than its parent in London. Brand scotched any hope of getting a free gift: it would require an 'atmosphere totally different from anything like the present one'.[34] Nor did he recommend any appeal for a gift on grounds of restitution. 'What we cannot put to the American people is that it is justice that they should give us a free grant on the ground that they should have entered the war before they did and therefore they owe us the $3 billion we spent here.'[35] The British should appeal for a free gift on grounds not of justice but of generosity: Britain needed help, but could not repay. To disguise the fact of bankruptcy, Brand would like a free gift 'dressed up' as far as possible to look unlike a free gift.[36] Brand also foresaw that the US would insist on linking any aid to a settlement of sterling debts. Keynes's proposal, he thought, was like 'the drastic reconstruction of a company and the putting in of new money'. The USA would need to know how Britain intended to deal with its other creditors.[37] This business analogy came naturally to a banker: Keynes would hate it when Marriner Eccles, chairman of the Federal Reserve Board, used the same argument in Washington in the autumn.

In his various replies, Keynes resisted Brand's attempt to 'omit the appeal of Justice'. If Britain did not use the Justice argument with America, how could it do so with its Empire? However, he agreed that if the Americans offered $5bn on 'easy terms' it would be 'extremely difficult to know whether it is wise to meet them'.[38] More realistically, Brand suggested that it might be best to patch up 'some temporary interim arrangement to carry us on for a year or more after lend–lease.' pending a campaign of education, and the crystallisation of anti-Russian feeling.[39]

This last point suggested an alternative strategy which should have merited serious consideration. Keynes never apparently considered the geopolitical context in which aid from the United States might be sol-icited. Churchill understood the politics, but failed to link it to finance. Using the phrase the 'iron curtain' for the first time, he cabled Truman on 12 May 1945, 'Anyone can see that in a very short space of time our armed power on the Continent will have vanished . . . [leaving it] open to the Russians . . . to advance if they chose to the waters of the North Sea and the Atlantic.' He countermanded the running down of British forces on the Continent.[40] But the connection between Churchill's fear of the Soviet threat and Keynes's hope for a gift was never made. It would have required a political context for the financial negotiation. Perhaps in 1945 this was premature: a good reason for Brand's 'interim' arrangement. The financial and political trains moved along separate tracks. They came together only with the announcement of Marshall Aid in June 1947 – which *was* the post-war version of Lend–Lease. But by then it was too late.

Brand's other suggestion, that to insure against the abrupt cancellation of Lend–Lease Britain should cut down its purchases of US food, substi-tuting for these long-term contracts with non-dollar countries,[41] chimed in with Eady's idea of exploring the potential of Austerity. In this, he found a powerful ally in Richard ('Otto') Clarke, who had joined the Overseas Finance Division in 1944 after a career in financial journalism. On 11 May, Clarke produced the first of a number of memoranda arguing for a serious fall-back position should Justice fail. Clarke started from a Hendersonian export pessimism, projecting an annual payments deficit in 1950 still running at between $500m. and $600m. a year, even in the unlikely event of a world boom. The main reason, he thought, lay in a lack of 'will to export', though an overvalued pound was a subsidiary factor. To get itself back into balance, Britain should reduce its imports and export capital equipment to its colonies to develop their agriculture, transport and electrity, using the funded portion of sterling balances to pay for such 'development plans'. (The Tanzania groundnuts scheme of 1948 was a bizarre offshoot of this approach.) Clarke favoured a 'just' settlement with the United States, but warned against being a permanent borrower or pensioner, and insisted that 'we should maintain the power and apparatus to enable us to be bilateral if events prove this to be

"DO I UNDERSTAND YOU WISH TO OMIT THE WORD 'OBEY'?"

JMK congratulated Low on capturing Morgenthau's 'dreadful smirk'.

JMK and Harry White at the Claridge Hotel, Atlantic City, June 1944

JMK and Lydia at Bretton Woods, July 1944

Morgenthau, Mrs Morganthau and Dr H. H. Kung (China) on the verandah at Mount Washington Hotel, Bretton Woods. Kung never missed a
photo opportunity.

Above. The start of the Loan Negotiations: JMK and Halifax at Press Conference, Washington, 12 September 1945

Below. Signing the Loan Agreement, 6 December 1945 (*from left to right*): JMK, Halifax, Byrnes (US Secretary of State), and 'Judge' Vinson

JMK, with Lydia, 'rushes from Southampton to the House of Lords', 17 December 1945

JMK and Bob Strand at Savannah, March 1946

JMK speaking at Savannah. He hoped no 'malicious fairy' would spoil the christening of the IMF. Vinson was heard to say 'I don't mind being called malicious, but I do mind being called a fairy'.

necessary'. By bilateralism he meant 'having a UK-based multilateral group of less than world size'. This required 'currency and import discrimination' until Britain got back into balance.[42]

After some criticism from Keynes, Clarke developed what he called a Plan II. He pointed out that Plan I (Keynes's Justice) was 'very closely integrated; if any important part of it fails or is largely modified, the balance is broken'. He doubted whether Justice would succeed. Clarke's crucial move, though, was to reject Temptation, on the ground that a loan (with likely accompanying conditions) carried too many risks. This left Plan II. Shorn of its complications, Plan II envisaged enlarging the sterling–dollar pool to include the countries of Western Europe, together with their colonial empires. It would not be hostile to the USA, but would be bound to discriminate against the dollar, because all the members of the pool would be short of dollars. Clarke proposed a directive from the Chancellor to departments to work out a viable Plan II as a 'fall back'.[43] In a gloss, Eady suggested that 'an expanded non-Dollar block' (which he called an 'Association'), based on sterling and managed by London, could earn enough dollars to puchase all it required from the United States. He wanted this developed as something 'to which events may force us to' and not just put forward as a 'bluff'.[44]

Keynes dismissed Clarke's paper as fantasy. He minuted: 'What these figures show is that if a tidal wave were to overwhelm North and South America . . . nothing worse than starvation would supervene.' There would still be a residual deficit of 25–30 per cent with the United States, which Britain could not meet by borrowing from an enlarged sterling area, since 'they also will have a large adverse balance with the Americas'. He asked 'What motive have they to rupture trade relations with USA in order to lend us money they have not got?' Keynes then committed himself to one of his rashest predictions: taking into account American contributions to UNRRA, the Export-Import Bank and the two Bretton Woods institutions, 'I do nor think there is any serious risk of an overall shortage of gold and dollars in the first three years [after the war].'[45] Brand reinforced Keynes: 'However [Plan II] is dressed up the US would regard it as a "ganging up" of the countries concerned against them.'[46] These dismissive phrases ended the first semi-serious discussion in Whitehall of a European economic policy. Keynes's hostile reaction was not just based on technical considerations. To him the Channel had become wider than the Atlantic; perhaps it always had been.

At a meeting with officials in the Treasury on 29 May, Keynes was still confident that Lend–Lease would be allowed to taper off gradually, though the others doubted this. Frank Lee, who had just flown in from Washington, thought that Keynes's Starvation Corner alternative would 'prove effective with the State Department, but not with Congress and he doubted the possibility of Justice as a solution to Britain's problem'.

Thompson-McClausland of the Bank of England also thought that a gift from America was a non-starter.[47]

The next day, Waley continued to wonder whether the Chancellor had accepted Keynes's revised memorandum. If there was still room for discussion, he wanted to restate his view that the proposals on the sterling balances were 'either a fairy story or a nightmare'. To block the balances would be 'politically impossible . . . destroy any confidence in sterling . . . disturb our relations with the rest of the sterling area in a quite impossible way'. It was a fairy story to expect South Africa, India and Egypt to make gifts to Britain. Virtue was rewarded only in the theatre. There was no alternative but to 'fix targets of expenditure in non-sterling currencies', that is, continue to discriminate against US imports.[48]

There the matter rested. It was assumed that Stage III negotiations with the Americans would start some time in September. But no decision on Keynes's Plan was taken by Churchill's government. Clarke has left as acute an account as one is likely to get of Keynes's over-optimism – and sense of urgency. The explanation of both, he suggests,

> is that Keynes regarded this agreement with the United States as the capstone of the great constructive effort on which he embarked in 1941 to create a world-wide multilateral financial system. To see sterling convertible at an early date was a major objective – perhaps, apart from getting the money, his most important objective. He could not tolerate that after he had overcome for three years all these obstacles which were intrinsic in the task, the edifice would collapse – and because the British had not played their part. So of course he had to believe that the Americans would help him to complete this masterpiece of his public service. He may well have felt that his health would not stand a negotiation in 1946 or 1947; and he had more mistrust than he probably should have had of the ability and willingness of Ministers, Treasury and Bank to carry the project along.[49]

IV

AMERICAN PRESSURE

On 7 May 1945, Germany surrendered, and Britain entered Stage II. No reflection by Keynes, profound or trivial, on the end or meaning of this catastrophic episode in world history has survived. If he made any to his Bloomsbury friends, Virginia Woolf was no longer alive to record it. Maynard and Lydia reopened the dining room at 46 Gordon Square. Two days after VE Day, a young official at the Canadian High Commission, Douglas LePan, caught a glimpse of Keynes at the reopening of the

National Gallery, of which he was a Trustee, by King George VI and Queen Elizabeth. Keynes was standing between E. M. Forster and Henry Moore. 'I was surprised that Keynes seemed to have such bulk and mass. Formally but unobtrusively dressed in a double-breasted dark suit, he loomed benignly above his two friends, large and protective, almost avuncular.'[50]

Keynes was deeply depressed about what to do with Germany. He hoped that 'history and the course of events will provide something better for us than we are capable of inventing ourselves'.[51] After the Yalta Conference in February, he protested at the decision to divide Germany into occupation zones. A dismembered Germany with a Russian zone was inferior to a 'buffer state in the shape of a unitary Germany'. The dismembered parts would be 'seed-beds of social revolution', which would be preliminary to a 'German USSR'. He pointed out the contradiction between dismemberment and reparations. Who was going to pay to maintain a minimum standard of life in Germany? Britain must not be put in the position of sending supplies to relieve Germany which were then delivered as reparations to Russia.[52] Put on a Committee on Reparations chaired by Eady, Keynes told Brand, 'We have been spending recently an inordinate amount of time talking nonsense about reparations. Not that we should be blamed for it. We talk nonsense because there is no sense available to Ministers. Ministers still have to exercise their prerogative of adding or subtracting nonsense.'[53] In the autumn of 1945 when he was in Washington, the economist Calvin Hoover sent him a report he had just written saying that Germany could not pay reparations and maintain its pre-war living standard. Keynes's last recorded comment on Germany was to agree with Hoover. He had disengaged from the discussions because the subject had become 'so distasteful'.[54]

The highlight of Keynes's May was a colloquium at King's College, Cambridge with the Canadians. It was the impending Canadian visit that had prompted Keynes to write his memorandum on Stage III and it was on the Canadian delegation which arrived in May that he first tried out his ideas outside Whitehall, even though the Cabinet had not seen, much less approved, them. The occasion was a Whitsun weekend at King's College on 19 and 20 May 1945. An account of Keynes in action on this occasion has been left by the Canadian Douglas LePan, who came to Cambridge to take notes. A poet and novelist, LePan was highly sensitive to the atmosphere of the occasion, as well as recording the substance. He depicts Keynes 'displaying all his marvellous gifts – intellectual, forensic, social, cultural, personal – outspread like a spangled train'.

Although Keynes's homosexuality had long been purely sentimental, he could still exert a formidable charm on the young when stimulated to do so. At dinner on Friday evening, he took LePan, then in his twenties, 'slim and almost handsome' with golden hair, by the arm and guided him to sit on his right. He seemed to sense that LePan – secretly at that time – shared his tastes. Realising that he knew little economics, Keynes tactfully shifted the conversation to ballet. The impression of weight and gravity which LePan had noticed at the National Gallery persisted; 'but as he turned and lifted his head to look down the Hall, I was also conscious of fun and sweetness and of an amused and wayward and playful spirit'.

The plenary meetings took place in the Audit Room at King's. Keynes presided, flanked on his left by Hopkins and Eady from the Treasury, Cobbold the executive director of the Bank of England, Gordon Munro from the UK High Commission in Ottawa, Alec Clutterbuck from the Dominions Office and Freddie Harmer, a junior Treasury official whom Keynes had taught economics at King's in the late 1920s. On the right sat three senior Canadian officials, Bill Mackintosh, acting Deputy Minister of Finance in his chief's absence through illness, Graham Towers, governor of the Bank of Canada, and Hector Mackinnon, chairman of the Canadian Tariff Board.

Keynes opened the meeting like 'a great conductor' taking over an orchestra. He had before him a Treasury brief containing not just his own revised memorandum on the choices facing the UK but much supporting material. 'This was his score for the meeting, but he very rarely consulted it.' He spoke for almost a day and a half. LePan said he had 'never listened to such a fine forensic performance', it 'often soared and fluttered and hovered, was bright with fancy, was variously inflected'. Like Dr Johnson, Keynes did not practise the art of accommodating himself to different sorts of people. So his personality either attracted or repelled you. 'Towers . . . felt deep and fundamental sympathy towards him,' Mackintosh thought he was a 'spoilt brat'.

Keynes outlined Britain's choices – Starvation Corner, Temptation and Justice. The Treasury, he said, had decided to stake everything on Justice. Opinion had been shifting, and it now felt there was less need for a long transitional period, not more than one year. Multilateralism was in Britain's interest. 'You can't be an international banker if you keep too many strings on your customers' cheques,' Keynes said. Most ministers, he thought, agreed with the Treasury policy. Keynes then summarised British financial policy during the war, stressing that Britain's financial recklessness was the price of victory. Hopkins intervened to emphasise two points about the sterling balances: 'They had been incurred as the result of a strategic decision as to how the War should be fought; and they had built installations which would contribute to the prosecution of the War against Japan as well.' Hopkins and Eady also intervened to soften the effect of Keynes's attacks on the 'dud directors' who ran British industry.

Saturday Whitsun lunch was given by Keynes and Lydia in the Combination Room. It was attended by Provost Sheppard, the heads of many colleges and colleagues like John Clapham, Dennis Robertson and Austin and Joan Robinson. LePan met Lydia for the first time. 'Lively, vivacious, amusing, with eyes that readily turned to mischief, with lips that were now pert, now prim, with an idiom that was always unpredictable but always piquant, she was the perfect hostess for a lunch that otherwise might have been rather heavy in spite of all her husband's gifts. It was obvious that she was fascinated by Maynard and that he was fascinated by her.' For all their independence, their marriage, LePan thought, was old-fashioned – and good. Similarly LePan noticed that for all Keynes's 'speculative daring, for all his scepticism, for all his willingness to follow the argument wherever it might lead', he was 'deeply attached to many of the ancient sanctities, and wanted us to share in an intimate, almost family, way his pride in Cambridge and in its traditions'. In the seating plan, the host was described as 'High Steward of the Borough of Cambridge', and other eminent guests given their full pedigrees. 'It was a *very* Cambridge occasion.' Lionel Robbins had noticed the same contrast between Keynes's speculative intellect and his reverence for tradition.

After lunch, Keynes talked about the policy of Temptation and the danger of being sucked into it by the Americans. He admitted that the policy of Justice was separated from Temptation by 'no very strict dividing line'. The Americans might offer a large loan on easy terms. Gradually, by the introduction of modifications on both sides, the two positions might approach each other. But this was the wrong way to go about the matter. Supporting him, Eady said the proper course was for Britain to present 'clear-cut suggestions and to add that if these suggestions, without essential modification, were not acceptable to the United States, the United Kingdom would have to embark on a much more restrictive and self-sufficing policy'.

Keynes then put forward a package of proposals – an American gift of $3bn, plus a credit line of $5bn, cancellation of about $3bn of sterling balances, lesser contributions from Canada and South Africa – which constituted Justice and which would enable Britain to make currently earned sterling plus £750m. or $3bn of the 'abnormal' balances convertible into other currencies. If his package were accepted, 'the sweet breath of justice would be felt to be blowing'. 'I had no difficulty', LePan wrote,

in remembering that sentence. Nor in remembering Keynes' look as he said it. His nature was protean, and his range of expression. He could be magisterial, analytic, scornful, withering, contemptuous, insinuating, persuasive. But as he lifted his head to speak of the 'sweet breath of justice', I was reminded of the sweetness and youthfulness I had noticed in his expression that first evening in

Hall when I was sitting beside him. There was something cherubic, almost seraphic, about his smile. And there was something else that is difficult to speak about, the word has been so debased. His charm.

The discussion turned from poetry to prose. Towers said it might be easier to get a loan of $8bn from the USA than a grant plus a credit line. Keynes said that would be unacceptable, and Eady supported him even more vehemently. The Canadians suggested that the approach to the US should emphasise their self-interest in restoring a multilateral system since the Americans were 'shy of acting as a permanent Christmas tree'. Towers emphasised that, if the British did not succeed in reaching an agreement with the US on multilateralism, Canada would inevitably be sucked into the US orbit.

The Cambridge interlude included a play and a concert at the Arts Theatre. LePan's last recollection of that weekend was walking down the Backs to the river. Bill Mackintosh said, 'How beautiful it is.' Keynes, a step or two behind, hesitated for only a moment. 'Yes, it is beautiful, isn't it? And we want to keep it, you know. That's why you're here.' On the young Canadian official Keynes made an undying impression: 'I am spellbound. This is the most extraordinary creature I have ever listened to. Does he belong to our species? Or is he from some other order? There is something mythic and fabulous about him. I sense in him something massive and sphinx-like, and yet also a hint of wings. One of the later and more elegant Greek sphinxes, then, it must be.'

There were a number of further meetings between the British and the Canadians: Sir John Anderson hosted a lunch for them at Claridge's on 25 May and there was a final conference in Keynes's room at the Treasury three days later. This resulted in a letter from Keynes to Mackintosh promising that, during Stage II, Britain would not discriminate against traditional or essential Canadian exports to Britain while Mutual Aid lasted.[55]

Official scrutiny of Keynes's proposals took place against a dissolving political background. Labour ministers had resigned from the coalition government on 20 May. Churchill formed a 'caretaker' administration. Parliament was dissolved on 15 June, the general election took place on 5 July. But the results were not to be announced for three weeks when all the servicemen's votes were in. In the interim the Big Three were scheduled to meet at Potsdam to settle the future of Germany and Poland. Keynes concluded that this timetable would give the Cabinet no time to consider his memorandum till 1 August. Like most 'insiders', Keynes expected a Conservative victory.

Meanwhile, President Truman's new administration was working out its own response to the expected British request for post-war aid. The agreed

American position was summed up in a letter of 25 June 1945 from William Clayton, the new Assistant Secretary of State, to Frederick Vinson, about to become Secretary of the Treasury: 'It would be quite unwise . . . to consider making Britain an outright gift. . . . It would be unwise even to supply the funds as credit without laying down conditions that would insure a sound advance towards our post-war objectives.' Clayton had in mind a credit of 'as much as $2 billion or $3 billion', at low interest rates, repayable over thirty years and with a 'waiver' in the event of a world slump. The conditions would be: elimination of the 'Sterling Area dollar pool', funding and probable write-down of sterling balances, and elimination (or at least 'substantial reduction') of Empire Preferences.[56]

On a fact-finding visit to London early in July, Emmanuel Goldenweiser of the Federal Reserve Board, found Keynes depressed about Germany ('no workable plan'), about the slow pace of demobilisation ('Bevin's formula is not to release anyone until all can be released. As a result no labour is released for the export trade . . .'), and wondering what was going to happen to Harry White now Morgenthau had gone.[57] Goldenweiser's impression of Keynes's depressed state is confirmed in a letter Keynes wrote to Brand on 11 July. So far 'all efforts towards reasonable economy . . . have had the smallest possible result'. Except when he was feeling 'exceptionally buoyant' he doubted whether Britain could be trusted with $3bn. 'We would just run through it in the first year or two and then where would we be? . . . If we do not pull ourselves together, there will be a financial Dunkirk anyway. If we do, then the projected plan is a good one.' Keynes felt that the 'art of government all round seems at the moment to be at its lowest ebb'. The general election was a 'ghastly even a shameful business. . . . Beaverbrook and the PM between them have done their damnedest to lose it.'[58]

Keynes's bad luck with electoral predictions continued. The result, announced on 26 July, was a landslide swing to Labour, which secured an overall majority of 140. Attlee became Prime Minister, with Ernest Bevin as Foreign Secretary and Hugh Dalton of the booming voice and Keynes's not-too-friendly Cambridge student as Chancellor of the Exchequer. Dalton promptly reappointed Keynes as his chief economic adviser, but was wary of him. His principal private secretary, Burke Trend, told Dalton's biographer Ben Pimlott that 'Dalton realised that he wasn't one of his buddies out hunting in the jungle; but he also realised that you didn't offend that sort of animal unnecessarily.'[59] Hunting in the jungle, though, is just what the two wary Kingsmen were about to embark on.

Keynes initialled a further revision of his March memorandum on 23 July. As always he had tried to incorporate all the suggestions he had received in order to make possible an agreed Treasury position. The main change was to leave out Temptation. There were now only two

alternatives. The 'austere' one, rechristened an 'essay in cunctation', was
to go on borrowing from the sterling area and make a bilateral payments
agreement between the sterling area and the United States. In deference
to Eady and Cobbold this was now portrayed in somewhat more winning
colours. But Keynes's preferred alternative was to settle the sterling
balances problem on the basis of cancellation and funding, the USA
providing a 'grant-in-aid' of $5bn over three years. In return Britain would
make post-war sterling area earnings immediately convertible, and release
the blocked balances by instalments. Britain should not be prepared to
borrow 'new money' from the USA, whose repayment came ahead of
debts owed to its sterling creditors, nor could it contemplate using a
dollar loan to pay off sterling debt. These were 'final decisions'. The main
argument Britain should put to the United States was that only with a
grant of this size could it commit itself to the Article VII agenda. But
Justice still lurked in the background in the form of an appeal to the
'immaterial' element of wartime sacrifice and feelings of fairness.[60] Presumably Keynes hoped to meet the gap between the $7bn-plus deficit he
still projected over three years and the $5bn American grant he solicited
by receiving help from Canada and by running down reserves. It was on
the basis of this document that the final Treasury approach to the Stage
III discussions was thrashed out at meetings on 20, 23 and 30 July. Keynes
reluctantly accepted Brand's suggestion that it be left to the Americans to
propose a grant after hearing the British case. However, the idea of a
grant might be tried out on them in 'absolute privacy' if the occasion
offered.[61]

The chance to do so came when Clayton came to London for a meeting
of the UNRRA Council, at which Britain, still playing the role of 'Lady
Bountiful', agreed to contribute $320m. to the reconstruction of Europe.
The American Assistant Secretary of State and his team had two days of
financial conversations, on 3 and 14 August, with Keynes, Eady and Brand
(back from Washington), and also a couple of meetings at the Board of
Trade. Except for details of the sterling balances settlement, Keynes
exposed the complete case he would put in Washington the following
month. and got the American response. The British position was not
unfairly summarised by Harold Glasser of the US Treasury as follows:

> they would like to have a 'gift' of about $5 billion or $6 billion in
> cash plus settlement of all outstanding obligations including lend–
> lease; in return they will co-operate in Bretton Woods, liberalize
> Empire trade and institute free foreign exchange. If the 'gift' is not
> forthcoming, the British will be forced to maintain – and expand –
> the sterling bloc, trade controls, and government sponsorship of
> export expansion. The position of the British is fully elaborated in

the *Economist* article of August 4, which expressed the ideas of Keynes so well, and in such similar language that Keynes might have played a primary role in the writing of the article.[62]

Clayton indicated that a $3bn credit would be possible, on condition that Britain dismantled the dollar pool which was 'anathema' to US exporters, agreed a 'satisfactory' (that is, non-discriminatory) commercial policy, and scaled down and funded the sterling balances. Keynes commented that he would prefer a 'more meaningless phrase' than 'credits', and that $3bn might not be enough to give confidence: if Britain was left 'but a shilling better than bust, we shall be bust'.[63]

On 11 and 15 August Keynes attended two meetings with the Americans at the Board of Trade on commercial policy, at which Clayton made it clear that the financial and commercial negotiations would have to be linked, since 'the collectibility of international credits depended on . . . liberal and multilateral measures' to expand trade.[64]

A very full – and at times dramatic – record of the second financial meeting, on 14 August, was transmitted by Clayton to the State Department 'to indicate the type of thinking of Keynes and the considerable difficulties which may be anticipated in our further trade and financial discussions with the British'. It opened with Keynes expressing the hope that there would be no hasty cut-off of Lend–Lease. Keynes then urged that the Americans accept a British delegation to Washington as soon as possible, using the urgency of the financial question as a reason for delaying the commercial talks. The British would like to take up first 'the problems of Lend–Lease wind up and settlement, then the question of financing the British balance of payments, and finally matters concerning trade policy'. The last discussions would take 'many months'. Clayton did not fall for that gambit, retorting that it was up to the British to decide how long they wanted to spend on trade matters, but that without a trade agreement they would get no money. The US would extend 'liberal credits on moderate terms of interest and amortization with proper regard to cyclical fluctuations in the balance of payments'. Keynes 'with typical abruptness' then said that allocating the entire British availability to servicing new United States obligations would be 'an *indecent* solution of the problem'. If America insisted on this, Britain would be 'forced to choose' bilateralism. Clayton said Britain would have to abandon that position if it wanted new money. Eady asked whether Britain might still avail itself of the transitional protections allowed by the Bretton Woods Agreement. Clayton said that the purpose of financial aid was to enable Britain to discontinue the dollar pool and Empire preferences, and make sterling fully convertible straight away. To 'soften the impression which Keynes had made', Brand urged the administration not to 'crystallise' its position until the British had had the chance to make a full presentation of the facts.

The discussion continued:

> [Keynes] said that the *realistic* mind is an awful thing, and to work out an *inspired* solution to the problems which face the world requires a person with a *crazy* mind. To this Clayton made reply that the view that bankers' solutions were impracticable had his considerable sympathy but that he (and he believed the American people) was essentially *realistic* and that in saying that the British should not expect to get financial assistance in the form of free grants, he would be only frank with Keynes.

Clayton summarised the meeting as follows:

> Of course, we realize that the British attitude is being presented by Keynes in his usual extreme manner. My personal opinion is that to cover a basically very weak financial position with a very serious outlook the British are putting up a very determined front. Under these circumstances it would be easy for the British to go the route of bilateral trade. It is my belief that the British will press for types of financial assistance which we may not find it desirable or possible to offer and that our discussion with them will be very difficult.[65]

Clayton also reported to Secretary of State Byrnes that:

> the British recognize that we will insist on discussion of commercial, cartel and commodity policy in connection with . . . financial discussions but are trying to maneuver us into discussing finance without requiring full trade discussions at the same time. Keynes would probably readily agree that problems of exchange convertibility and the sterling dollar pool would have to be discussed at once but Empire preferences, reduction of tariffs and other trade barriers and commodity policy he would like to put off into next year as much as possible. I have indicated that it . . . will be necessary for us to come to a broad understanding as to postwar trading methods and policy before we can ask Congress for any large scale financial aid to Britain.[66]

There is very little doubt, Keynes wrote to Halifax on 17 August,

> that the financial discussions will very soon become entangled with Article VII, Commercial Policy and Bretton Woods. But I am anxious to start off with the technical problems arising out of the wind-up of Lend–Lease and with our financial proposals as to what should come next, and leave it to the Americans to take the initiative in raising

the other matters, as they doubtless will as part of the price of their assistance.[67]

Both sides knew what to expect. The British would ask for a gift of $5bn, offering a *quid pro quo* of sterling convertibility on current account, and nothing else. If they did not get it, or something like it, they would be 'forced' to choose bilateralism. The Americans would offer them a credit of $3bn conditional on clearing up the sterling debt position, 'liberalising' Empire trade, and making sterling convertible into dollars. But these could be regarded as opening shots in a prolonged bargaining game.

Keynes's request for urgent financial conversations was precipitated by the military resolution of the Pacific war. On 6 August the Americans dropped their first atomic bomb on Hiroshima, followed by another on Nagasaki three days later. On 10 August Emperor Hirohito broadcast the Japanese offer of surrender. With the imminent arrival of Stage III, everything speeded up. Keynes now had to persuade the government to send him to Washington straight away. On 15 August, he saw the Foreign Secretary, Ernest Bevin. Bevin told him that he would prefer to postpone financial or commercial arrangements 'until we could see our way more clearly'.[68] Dalton was more amenable. He had received Keynes's alarmist paper 'Our Overseas Financial Prospects' the previous day, in which Keynes predicted a 'financial Dunkirk' unless Britain got immediate help. Clayton, too, urged Washington to receive the British, with a view to reaching agreement on the Lend–Lease wind-up, financial assistance and trade policy in October.

On 17 August President Truman decided to terminate Lend–Lease immediately, on the advice of Crowley and after Vinson had advised a taper. On the 20th Crowley informed Brand of the President's decision. No new goods would be supplied; all goods already ordered would have to be paid for. This news sent the Whitehall machine into overdrive. On 20 August Dalton told Bevin that 'we should open discussions [with the Americans] at once'. The next day Bevin and Dalton saw Clayton, for the first time. Clayton confirmed that there was no hope of the British getting anything but 'credit on very liberal terms', but said that he would try to 'continue the flow of supplies for the present without prejudice to the terms of the settlement'.* Bob Dixon of the Foreign Office telephoned

---

* The abrupt cancellation of Lend–Lease, without warning or consultation, was deeply resented in Britain. As Attlee pointed out to the House of Commons on 24 August, while Lend–Lease had made it possible for Britain to mobilise on an unsurpassed scale, its cancellation left Britain far worse off 'than it leaves those who have been affording us the assistance'. President Truman subsequently came to see it as his worst mistake. Vinson and Clayton were both furious at being 'double-crossed' by Crowley. The British plight was worsened by the fact that it lacked a 3(c) agreement – the section in the Lend–Lease Act of

Halifax at Garrowby in Yorkshire, telling him that he would have to cut short his holiday, as Bevin wanted him to lead the British delegation in Washington. 'This is an awful bore, and completely wrecks my plans,' wrote the disgruntled ambassador.

March 1945 which enabled other Allies – the newly liberated ones – to borrow for Lend–Lease supplies, by this time mainly civilian, in the pipeline. Britain was faced with the immediate need to pay cash. It took over a fortnight, and a resolute letter from Attlee, to ensure that these supplies continued, with terms of payment to be agreed later. A further American concession allowed Britain to place new orders, for cash or credit, for two months. (See R. S. Sayers, *Financial Policy 1939–1945*, 378–483; *FRUS*, 1945, vi, 102–3, 113–15.)

CHAPTER TWELVE

Averting a Financial Dunkirk

I

At 10.15 p.m. on Thursday 23 August 1945 an emergency meeting was held in the Cabinet Room at No. 10 Downing Street. It was chaired by the Prime Minister, Clement Attlee, flanked by the senior ministers of his government: the Lord President of the Council Herbert Morrison, the Chancellor of the Exchequer Hugh Dalton, the Foreign Secretary Ernest Bevin, and the President of the Board of Trade Sir Stafford Cripps. On the opposite side of the table were Halifax, Keynes, Bridges, Eady, Brand, Sinclair and Hall-Patch. There was one item only on the agenda: how to avert the 'financial Dunkirk' which Keynes had predicted in his paper 'Our Overseas Financial Prospects', circulated a few days previously. Lend–Lease and borrowing from the sterling area had been plugging a gap in the balance of payments, which in 1945 was estimated at £2.1bn or just over $8bn. Lend–Lease running at £1.35bn would stop forthwith; borrowing from the sterling area might continue, but on a greatly reduced scale. By increasing exports, eliminating imports of munitions, and cutting down overseas expenditure the deficit for 1946 could be reduced to just under £1bn or $4bn. In 1947 it might fall to £550m. and in 1948 to £200m., leaving Britain in balance by 1949. Over these three years, though, it would have to finance a total deficit of £1.7bn or about $7bn. 'Where is all this money to come from?' Keynes asked. Gold and dollar reserves, which in 1945 stood at £500m., might be run down by £250m. Britain might be able to borrow £150m. net from the sterling area in 1947 and 1948. This would reduce the cumulative deficit over the three years to £1.3bn (Keynes wrote £1.25bn) or $5bn. 'The conclusion is inescapable', Keynes wrote, 'that aid of the order of $5bn is required from the United States' if Britain was to 'spend on the scale we contemplate'. The United States would probably make available between $3bn and $5bn, but the British would have to bargain hard on terms and conditions. Britain must refuse a loan. But if 'the term *credit* is no more than a camouflage for what would be in effect a grant-in-aid, that is another matter'. In return for this, Britain should 'not seek to escape our obligations under Article VII of the Mutual Aid Agreement'. Keynes warned that 'no arrangement which we can properly accept is yet

in sight; and that, until such an arrangement is in sight, we are . . . virtually
bankrupt and the economic basis for the hopes of the public non-existent'.
He ended: 'In practice, of course, we shall in the end accept the best terms
we can get.'[1]

The main difficulties of the subsequent negotiations are encapsulated
in this contradictory document. Britain should refuse a loan, but not a
grant 'dressed up' as a loan. What did this mean? Some conditions would
apparently be unacceptable; but in the end Britain would accept any
conditions. No wonder Eady had referred to Keynes's 'extraordinarily
difficult financial diplomacy'.

Halifax wrote in his diary of 23 August: 'Keynes gave a good exposition
of the business, ending on a rather optimistic note, and we all said our
say, Ministers agreeing to turn Keynes loose but without authority to settle
except on reference home. This Keynes himself wanted, to strengthen his
hand.'

Dalton confirms Keynes's optimism:

> Keynes, in his talks with Ministers just before leaving for Washington,
> was almost starry-eyed. He was very confident that, in the coming
> negotiations, he could obtain American aid that was ample in
> amount, and on most satisfactory conditions. He told us that he
> thought he could get £1500 millions (six billion dollars) as a free
> gift. There would be no question of a loan to be repaid, or of a rate
> of interest on a loan. Nor did he, at this stage, say much to us about
> 'strings'. . . . This undue optimism, as it soon proved to be, naturally
> predisposed us against concessions, which Keynes proposed later, to
> the Americans.[2]

Ernest Bevin, the Foreign Secretary, thought that he could almost hear
the money jingling in Keynes's pocket as he spoke, though he wondered
whether it was really there.

There is testimony in the same sense from the financial journalist Paul
Bareau, who came with Keynes to Washington as press officer of the
British Mission. Keynes, Bareau wrote,

> was utterly convinced that 'justice' would prevail. Not only was he
> himself filled with the righteousness of our cause, but had he not
> expounded it with success in the Stage 2 negotiations? He had
> carried conviction then and had obtained from the Americans the
> main substance – and very generous substance it was – of his
> requirements. The success of Stage 2 did a great deal to predeter-
> mine strategy for the Stage 3 negotiations.[3]

On the other hand, Keynes wrote to his old friend Molly McCarthy on 26
August: 'I am off on the toughest mission yet with very moderate hopes
indeed of sufficient success.'[4]

The official record of the Cabinet discussion does not suggest that Keynes was unduly optimistic. He told ministers that the 'terms offered might vary from an out and out grant in aid to a commercial credit'. His insistence that 'he should not be authorised to agree to anything except an out and out grant', that help 'on any less favourable terms should not be accepted except after very long thought on the part of Ministers in London', that the 'financial terms . . . would constitute the greatest stumbling block', do not suggest undue confidence in the outcome. Nor did Keynes promise $6bn. He told ministers that the Americans were thinking in terms of $3bn, 'rising possibly to 5'. The only *quid pro quo* Keynes asked for authorisation to offer was a promise 'to go to the sterling area and ask them to cancel part of our indebtedness to them and agree that the remainder should be made fully convertible by instalments'. He thought 'this was the only constructive proposal which he should put forward at the outset'. The next step was more ambiguous. Keynes thought that Britain 'could undertake the obligations' contained in the Bretton Woods Agreement, provided they were not coupled with 'dangerous concessions on commercial policy'. By this he meant chiefly making sterling convertible on current account. How much money would Britain need to accept this obligation? This was not made clear, though the implication was that it would have to be $5bn. On only one point did Keynes mislead Ministers. This was in de-emphasising the linkage between financial help and a commercial agreement. On the contrary, 'Lord Keynes emphasised that there was no question of our being asked to agree to a detailed commercial treaty at this stage.' True enough: but the Americans were certainly expecting something more than a 'joint invitation to 15 other countries to attend an international conference next year'. Even worse, Keynes discussed the two countries' differences on commercial policy without pointing out that the outcome of the financial negotiations would depend on their resolution.

The Cabinet Committee accepted Brand's suggestion that the British should not ask outright for a grant-in-aid, but allow the case for it to develop irresistibly from their presentation, leaving it to the Americans to propose it. Attlee summed up that the negotiations be left to 'Lord Keynes and his colleagues on the basis that he had outlined . . . and that negotiations should be *ad referendum*, reports being made to Ministers in London as and when necessary'.[5]

Pressnell claims that Keynes did not leave ministers unduly optimistic about the chances of obtaining a grant or an interest-free loan.[6] Nor does the contemporary record show them to have been very optimistic. On 22 August – the day before the Cabinet discussion – John Balfour, the minister in charge of the Washington Embassy, had telegraphed Bevin that 'The dollar sign is back in the Anglo-American equation and the

ghost of Mr Coolidge seems to be hovering near the White House'; the
same day Bevin, Dalton and Cripps minuted Attlee that 'it is quite clear
that what the United States will ask us for is a credit with a fairly high rate
of interest and also acquiescence in Bretton Woods and their commercial
policy.... At present, however, we have no bargaining counter....'[7]
Perhaps, at that meeting of 23 August, Keynes impressed himself on them
as their bargaining counter. Nothing in what Keynes is *reported* to have
said suggests that he was over-optimistic. But what the official record of
the 23 August meeting does not give us is Keynes's tone of voice, his
emphases, his hesitations, his asides, his inflections – all those things
which determine the impression a speaker leaves. That it is incomplete is
clear from the remarks attributed to Brand. Brand said he was 'less
hopeful' than Keynes was of getting a grant.

The nub of the matter is that Keynes's presentation of the alternatives
had been seriously undermined by the Treasury–Bank refusal to have
anything to do with Temptation. This middle way between Austerity and
Justice was therefore unexplored before Keynes set out for Washington.
He left, that is, without an agreed fall-back position. Since he disliked
Austerity so much, he probably exaggerated the chances of getting Justice.
Eady and the Bank of England were more than willing to see Keynes's
mission fail, leaving Austerity as the sole alternative. The Labour ministers
were caught in this cross-fire. They therefore pinned their hopes on
Justice, and persuaded themselves that Keynes had promised it.

Keynes's mission to the United States was announced in the House of
Commons on 24 August. The news that no Board of Trade officials would
go out dismayed the Americans, since it implied that the British were not
prepared for serious commercial discussions. Under pressure from Clayton and Hawkins, ministers agreed, on 31 August, that Lionel Helmore of
the Board of Trade should accompany the Mission as an 'observer', with
a separate Board of Trade mission to be sent out 'as soon as practicable'.[8]
Robbins was soon to comment, 'If . . . anybody had told me that it would
have been possible for high personages in Whitehall to believe blithely
. . . that we could get away with a financial settlement . . . with no
commitments on commercial policy, I just would not have believed him.'[9]
Keynes's tactic was to avoid detailed trade discussions by the simple device
of not including in the Washington Mission anyone competent to conduct
them.[10] The experts concerned – Sir Percivale Liesching of the Board of
Trade and Lionel Robbins of the Economic Section – protested angrily,
but were overruled on Keynes's insistence. 'Lord Keynes took the view
that if he had the opportunity to explain our financial position and our
difficulties this would influence the Americans in their approach to
commercial questions. Lord Keynes would therefore wish to develop the
financial side at some length and in detail in the expectation that as a
result of his explanation the American position on commercial questions

would change. . . . The Foreign Secretary expressed some doubt as to whether Lord Keynes might not be optimistic in his assumptions. . . .'[11] Robbins later explained Keynes's attitude as less a deliberate snub to the Board of Trade than a 'brainstorm in which he [Keynes] was carried away by over-confidence in his own ability and a vision of what it might accomplish'.[12]

The announcement of the Keynes Mission produced disconcerted reactions from across the Atlantic. The conservative banker Leffingwell, Keynes's old sparring partner from Paris Peace Conference days, thought that the dispatch of Keynes to America was a bad move: 'There is nothing more disturbing, I think, than the sending of Lord Keynes here. Brilliant man that he is, he is too brilliant to be persuasive with us Americans. Many Americans admire him. . . . But, rightly or wrongly, how many trust him? How many will accept his sales talk? No one.'[13]

Leffingwell thought that the British should make their post-war economic plans on the assumption of no help from abroad whatever, just as Churchill had made his war plans in 1940. This would do more to elicit a spontaneous American offer of help than 'a thousand Keyneses'. In other words, a 'financial Dunkirk' was needed to loosen America's purse-strings just as the actual Dunkirk had. There was much psychological shrewdness in this assessment.

II

OPENING MOVES IN WASHINGTON

Maynard and Lydia Keynes left Southampton by sea on the Canadian troopship *Pasteur* on 27 August bound for Quebec City. Accompanying them were Frederic Harmer of the Treasury, Edward Hall-Patch of the Foreign Office and Lionel Helmore of the Board of Trade. Halifax and Brand had already returned to Washington. Even by British standards it was an extraordinarily lean mission, to be headed by a man who was not only frail, but had started to look old. Keynes's hair and moustache had turned white, the whiteness emphasising his now habitual pallor. His medically ordered loss of weight was good for the heart but left his tall frame looking curiously under-supported. He now needed thick glasses to read. Only when they were taken off could one see that his eyes still burnt with brightness and amusement. And as the negotiations were to show he had lost none of his power for wit and rudeness.

The sea voyage had its usual tonic effect. Keynes wrote to his parents that he had had his 'best holiday for a long time'. This did not exclude writing a 'boat paper', which was a yet further revision of the memorandum which had started life in March. A notable feature of the latest revision was a scaling down of Britain's prospective balance of payments deficit to the reduced scale of anticipated American assistance. The estimated deficit in the first year of peace was now $3.2bn, instead of the $4bn projected as late as August, and it might be possible to keep it to $2.5bn. The projected cumulative deficit over three years had shrunk from $6.8bn to between $4bn and $6bn.[14] These different estimates, of course, were based on different assumptions about policy. But they do raise the question of how much American help Britain actually needed to survive the first post-war years.

Maynard and Lydia arrived in North America 'fat and blooming'. Maynard's enjoyment of the voyage reinforced his optimism that he would find a good atmosphere in Washington, which Harmer doubted. From Quebec, they flew to Ottawa, the pilot keeping the plane low to avoid straining Keynes's heart. In Ottawa, he and Lydia reoccupied the Moorish suite at the Chateau Laurier they had stayed in in 1944. Negotiations on the Mutual Aid wind-up were arduous 'but they are all so friendly that there is no pain or grief'. The upshot was that the British got $300m. more than they expected.[15] On 4 September Keynes wrote to Eady that he was 'increasingly doubtful about the prospects of a straight grant-in-aid [from the United States]'. But a conversation with Graham Towers raised his hopes. Towers urged Keynes to tell the Americans that with a grant plus some borrowing power the British would be able to take far more risks in liberalising trade than if they were burdened with a commercial loan.[16] Neither dwelt on the possibility that the Americans would insist on the risks as the price for a loan.

On Thursday 6 September Maynard and Lydia took the train for Washington, where 'the pain and grief will begin. . . . However I start in extremely good health and nerves,' Keynes told his mother. They booked again into the Statler Hotel.

He was in fine fettle when he stepped off the train in Washington. Asked by British officials what conditions were like back home, he quipped that they were not too bad – 'but don't let on here in Washington; we must fill our mouths with false teeth and yell as each one is pulled out'. Paul Bareau, the delegation's scribe, noted 'that infectious, that dangerously infectious optimism' with which Keynes approached his negotiations. Harry White told Keynes that he was working out a plan which would get Britain $5bn interest-free.[17]

At the first formal meeting of the Anglo-American Top Committee on 11 September, it was agreed to set up sub-committees covering Finance, the Lend–Lease wind-up, Surplus Property Disposal (mainly military) and Commercial Policy. The British would be led by Halifax and Keynes on Finance opposite Vinson and Clayton, and Keynes would lead for the British on the Lend–Lease wind-up or clean-up negotiations, as they were known, opposite Crowley, with Sir Henry Self, deputy chairman of the British Supply Council, representing Britain on Surplus Property.*

The State Department's insistence on setting up a parallel Commercial Policy Committee came as a nasty surprise to Keynes – and to London. It was the first defeat for the British negotiating strategy. However, Keynes took comfort from Clayton's apparent willingness to keep the discussions general, and proposed that he and Halifax lead for Britain on commercial policy. Meade was dismayed at the thought of Keynes in action without the 'commercial policy boys', and gripped by 'crazy, lunatic and self-contradictory' ideas on commercial policy.[18] Keynes was instructed to postpone the first meeting, scheduled for 17 September, till the arrival of Board of Trade reinforcements from London. Though both he and Halifax protested, the decision was confirmed.[19]

The key players on the American side were William Clayton, acting as chairman in place of Byrnes, the Secretary of State away in London, and Fred Vinson, who had succeeded Morgenthau as Secretary of the Treasury. This was an advantage, for both were pro-British. Clayton, a six-foot-six self-made cotton manufacturer from Texas, with a soft southern drawl, was an ardent internationalist. The problem was not his internationalism, but his free trade agenda, which he was determined to force through; and, as Keynes would remark, he was also 'deeply imbued with business analogies'. Vinson, a former professional baseball player and conservative Democrat Congressman from Kentucky, was a genial lawyer of provincial outlook, much addicted to the humbugging school of public oratory and, it is now generally agreed, somewhat over-promoted. He too wanted to help Britain, within the limits of Congressional opinion and that of the 'folks back home'. Sixty per cent of the folks, polled by Gallup, opposed the idea of a loan to Britain.[20] It would have been too much to expect him and Keynes to strike an instant rapport. (It had taken several years for Morgenthau and Keynes to thaw out.) In fact, Keynes liked Vinson, but Vinson did not like Keynes: he was too often on the receiving end of slashing remarks. The other Americans had little influence. Marriner Eccles, chairman of the Federal Reserve Board, had one idea, which he would expound in a stentorian bellow at inordinate length: that Britain was a bankrupt company, and America must get paid back ahead of any

---

* The Lend–Lease wind-up negotiations (together with those on surplus military property) were designed to establish what Britain owed the United States for civilian supplies in the pipeline when Lend–Lease was cancelled, together with unused American military equipment 'leased' to Britain, offset against British counterclaims under reciprocal Lend–Lease and resurrected 'dead cats'. The balance of the claims and counterclaims seemed likely to net out in a British debt of between $500m. and $800m., which would be included in the overall financial settlement.

other creditors. Henry Wallace, now Secretary of Commerce, struck Keynes as 'completely gaga. He seems to pass out within five minutes of the beginning of any meeting.' Leo Crowley, the unfriendly Lend–Lease czar, was on his way to political oblivion. His facial characteristics made him the butt of some of Keynes's unkindest jokes. They reminded him, Keynes said, of the 'buttocks of a baboon'. The nickname stuck, inspiring the 'BABOON' code name for British telegrams from the Treasury during the Loan negotiations, whose counterparts from Washington were code-named 'NABOB'. On 28 September Keynes was happy to report that 'the Baboon is dead, deader than the cats we were trying to revive and he to bury, and the worms have got him'. Keynes was quick to renew his friendship with Harry White, who advised him 'not to lose his temper except at the right moments'. However, with Morgenthau's departure from the Treasury, White was plainly in eclipse, though Keynes was not to know that Elizabeth Bentley had, on 21 August 1945, denounced him to the FBI as a Soviet agent. White himself was convinced that he would soon be dismissed from the Treasury, and was looking for a new job in the IMF or World Bank.[21] Keynes retained some illusions not only about White's influence with the new Secretary, but also about White's support for the British position.

The Halifax–Keynes axis was central to the British negotiating effort. Keynes quickly re-established close relations with the languid charmer and, as he later wrote, they worked together 'like brothers'. The ambassador's part in the loan negotiations has been seriously underplayed. He greatly preferred tennis, hunting and gossiping with old friends (Lady 'Baba' Metcalfe was staying at the Embassy for much of the autumn) to financial work, or indeed to most forms of work. He did not pretend to understand technicalities. Having attended a discussion on the Commercial Policy Committee on the merits of export and import taxes, he observed wearily that it was 'not one of the subjects that I find stimulating'. After a long discussion about how much the discounted value of the American offer worked out at, he noted: 'This is one of the subjects that I made up my mind long ago I should never understand, and so do not make any attempt.' Halifax's main role was to calm the increasingly frayed nerves of the Mission, and relate their concerns to the big picture of Anglo-American relations. When Keynes was abrasive he was emollient. Late at night he would tone down Keynes's increasingly angry telegrams to London, and talk him out of resignation. He was constantly entertained by Lydia, and developed almost unstinted admiration for Keynes. At the conclusion of the negotiation he wrote in his diary:

> Keynes has been a perfect tower of strength: ingenious, resilient, patient and I think always distinguishing very surely between the points that really mattered and points that could be compromised.

It is unjust but not unintelligible that people in London should have been from time to time irritated with him and no doubt with me, for it has been quite impossible to judge these things as they have been going along unless you were soaked from day to day in the unavoidable discussion of the technicalities. (5 December)

Apart from personal affinity, Keynes and Halifax were both convinced that a collapse of the negotiations would be a major catastrophe. But Halifax could also show steel, when required, and on one notable occasion his firmness almost certainly prevented a breakdown.

Keynes's relationship with Bob Brand might have been difficult. As in 1941 when Sir Frederick Phillips was in charge, Keynes had come to take over from Britain's permanent Treasury representative in Washington. Brand had both the ability and technical knowledge to question Keynes's judgement. But he had almost unlimited trust in Keynes's intelligence and persuasive ability, and like Halifax was committed to Anglo-American partnership. His unwillingness to stand up to Keynes was a weak spot in the negotiations. Lionel Robbins joined the inner group when he came out in October to take over the commercial negotiations. He was certainly formidable, and not uncritical. But, being a strong internationalist, he was determined to make a success of the negotiations, more so perhaps than even Keynes was. His attitude to Keynes had also undergone a complete transformation. Wracked with guilt over his opposition to Keynes's theories in the 1930s, he had come to regard him as an incomparable advocate for views he now shared.

The rest of the British team were not on a level with the top four. Hall-Patch represented the Foreign Office ('A lovely name for a man seeking a reconstruction loan', gossiped a Washington journalist). Frank Lee and Roger Stevens were joint secretaries. Frederic Harmer, Harry Goschen and Paul Bareau were junior Treasury officials. Harmer was, in effect, Keynes's personal assistant, as that other 'nice boy', Lucius Thompson-McCausland of the Bank of England, had been in 1941. Paul Bareau, a financial journalist working at the *News Chronicle*, had been temporarily seconded to the Treasury to handle the press. Keynes liked him, but did not rate his economic expertise highly. After trying to explain something complicated, he burst out, 'My advice to you, Paul, is to go back to honest journalism.' Bareau was allowed to attend all official meetings and kept an informal record of them, which he later used as the basis for a series of lectures at the London School of Economics. Harmer kept a more intimate diary, which illuminates Keynes's state of mind – and nerves – as the negotiations proceeded.

On 12 September Keynes and Halifax held a press conference at the Embassy. In his prepared statement, which he delivered on his feet, Keynes started spinning the web in which he hoped to entangle the

Americans, expatiating on Britain's war-weariness, the way that Lend–Lease, while essential to Britain's full mobilisation, had led it to sacrifice two-thirds of its export trade, the transitional balance of payments deficit, the problem of the sterling balances, the advantages of a liberal trading world. He emphasised the disadvantages of a commercial loan, and said that, rather than accept it, Britain would try to 'do what we can to get on as best we can on any other lines which are open to us'. One must try to imagine that tall, stooped, by now bespectacled and rather ill-looking figure, glancing up from time to time from his hand-held text to deliver his statement in his refined voice to a room full of tough, hard-bitten and surprisingly well-informed American reporters. Harmer thought that he contrived to make it sound 'both dramatic and spontaneous'. Bareau was less impressed. 'It did not appear to create any great enthusiasm and typically Keynesian phrases like "Our pains, ours and yours, are more likely to be due to our stomachs being fuller than our heads and our appetite weaker than our opportunity" caused no amusement at all.' Under stiff questioning – including some from Robert Boothby, who was covering the negotiations for the *News of the World*, not a newspaper even then noted for its coverage of financial topics – Keynes adopted evasive tactics. He was repeatedly asked to quantify the advantages which would accrue to America – 'what the sales point' would be – of a grant or non-interest-bearing loan. At one point he said, 'You can't, of course, sum it up and say it is worth so many dollars. I should say that to get the world's economy going on the right lines is worth immensely more than any of the figures which may be mentioned.'

After an hour and a quarter, Halifax suggested drinks. He thought that 'Keynes got himself pressed a bit more than was wise when it came to questions.' Bareau, however, thought he dealt with them 'in a masterly fashion'.

At three long opening sessions of the Top Committee, on 13, 14 and 17 September, held in the board room of the Federal Reserve Building, Keynes gave a revised version of the allocution LePan had heard in Cambridge in May. 'I thought he did this quite well,' wrote the ambassador after the first lecture, which lasted about two hours. In giving facts and figures about Britain's prospective deficit for the first year of peace, Keynes emphasised the exceptional weight of British government spending abroad, and the time-lags as well as degree of consumer 'stinting' involved in channelling output into exports. The cumulative balance of payments deficit was likely to be $6bn or more over three to five years. At one point, when Keynes was talking about the frightful destruction caused by the blitz, Harry White provided the appropriate backstage effects by knocking over an enormous tripod ashtray. 'One of the lighter touches he [Keynes] introduced', noted the ambassador, 'was to say that the housebuilding programme was being held up by a lack of lawyers to complete the legal preliminaries. Glancing at the legal forces behind him, Vinson joked that there would be no difficulty about lend–leasing the required supply of lawyers to Britain. But, as he was to show, Vinson was sensitive to jokes about lawyers not made by himself.

The second session, on Friday 14 September, was devoted to sterling balances. Keynes explained how sterling debt had been built up through the sterling area system. Clayton 'came into the open' when he said that the American people would find it hard to understand why Britain had got war supplies from America free but owed money to Empire countries for the same kind of goods. Should not these countries be got to scale down their debts? Keynes replied evasively that the British were thinking along similar lines, but that the 'problems had not yet been tackled' with the countries concerned.

On Monday 17 September, recalls Bareau, Keynes worked up his presentation with a magnificent development of the theme that though the Germans had invented the concept of Total War it was the British who had applied it most thoroughly in their everyday lives. It was reflected in the reckless profligacy with which Britain had thrown its overseas assets and export trade away in the common cause. 'Was not that recklessness the factor that tipped the scale and brought victory? The exposition ended with this question – and without any specific mention of that massive American grant which Keynes hoped to obtain. Keynes expected the offer to come from the other side. It never came.'[22] When the negotiations were done, an American gossip columnist, Paul Edison, wrote: 'Lord Keynes opened the conversations . . . and he talked for three days in a row. That was to explain the British position. It must have been bad.'[23]

The British had made a tactical mistake by circulating a document comparing the British and American war efforts, to the latter's disadvantage. Keynes later admitted that 'showing our medals' had been an error. It was leaked by the Americans, John Crider published an account of it in the *New York Times*, and it led to caustic comments in the press.

On 19 and 20 September Keynes expounded further to the Joint Finance Committee. He put forward the two alternative solutions to Britain's problem – what he had called Starvation Corner and Justice – being careful to say that they were extremes within the range of which many compromises were possible. Keynes clearly indicated that he disapproved of the austere alternative, which would inevitably lead to bilateralism and a contraction of trade. His second alternative was one which envisaged 'liquidating as far as possible the financial consequences of the war'. Without referring to any American contribution, Keynes outlined his tripartite scheme for dealing with the abnormal sterling balances, involving cancellation, funding and release, without attaching figures. This would enable Britain to make currently earned sterling (plus the

released portion of the abnormal balances) convertible and bring into
force the 'major part' of the permanent Bretton Woods Agreement by the
end of 1946. What did the Americans think? asked Keynes, fishing for an
offer. Paul Bareau's account continues:

> Vinson expressed the deepest disappointment in Keynes's statement
> which he said had not crystallised the situation in any way. . . .
> Keynes, said Vinson, had left so many blanks in his description of
> the second alternative that it was more or less meaningless to the
> Americans. What Vinson clearly had in mind was that the second
> alternative demanded American help and he was disappointed that
> Keynes had not mentioned that fact and had not specified the
> magnitude of the aid which would be required. . . .

Under further prompting from Clayton, Keynes said that, while the
British wanted the sterling debts reduced, it could not be done on a
uniform basis, or by unilateral action, but would require individual
settlements with Britain's creditors, according to the circumstances of
each case. At this point, Henry Wallace, who had fallen asleep, woke up
to ask why Britain could not trade Indian independence for a write-down
of Indian debt – a suggestion which horrified both Keynes and Halifax.
Marriner Eccles bellowed above the noise that all former ideas of honour
and financial rectitude must be readjusted to the cataclysm which the war
had caused. Britain was like a bankrupt company which had to be
reconstructed, and the creditors must take the rap. This was one business
analogy too far. The suggestion that countries like India and Egypt should
be thought of as part of a consortium of creditors to refinance Britain's
busted imperial enterprise was too dramatic a reversal of the normal
order of things to be contemplated. 'These people will never be able to
run an Empire,' Frank Lee remarked icily as they left the room.[24]

Keynes was being forced out into the open. At the 20 September
meeting he said that Britain might cancel $4bn of the estimated $12bn of
sterling debt, fund $7.2bn and release $800m. over the transitional period.
It would need at least $5bn, plus a Lend–Lease wind-up, from the US over
three to five years to cover its adverse balance of trade, finance sterling
withdrawals and pay back a number of smaller non-sterling debts. 'The
Americans did not bat an eyelid and accepted the figure [of $5bn]
without any demur.' In return, Britain would make currently earned
sterling (plus the released portion of the balances) freely convertible into
dollars and remove the 'discriminatory aspects of the sterling system' by
the end of 1946. Vinson said that the American officials would go off and
study the matter. Meetings were then suspended for a few days.[25]

Sensing that the British team's inability to disclose their hand on the
sterling balances had irritated the Americans, Keynes asked London for
permission to discuss debt cancellation in more detail. Worried by the

prospect of leaks to sterling area countries, London refused. Keynes should try to get the Americans to make proposals. It would help if the Americans could state 'in a form which could be used' that help from them was conditional on 'an adjustment of our sterling indebtedness'.[26] Appalled at the thought of unilateral default, London clearly wanted to use the Americans to put pressure on its sterling creditors.

The first crisis of the negotiations had arrived. Keynes was giving his usual brilliant interpretation of his own score, but the orchestra obstinately refused to follow his baton. In particular, Vinson's trumpet refused to come in on cue. It was clear that Britain's initial negotiating strategy had completely misfired. The British had assumed that Keynes's eloquence in stating British importunities would elicit a generous offer from the United States. Instead, as Paul Bareau noted, 'the United States did not in any way regard assistance to us as reward for good behaviour in the past but as the means to enable us again to dispense with the protective devices of inconvertibility of sterling, licensing of imports and bilateral payments agreements'.[27] In lieu of an American response, Keynes had been forced to disclose his hand. In doing so, he had hinted at *quid pro quos* on sterling balances and commercial policy beyond his brief. Professor Moggridge, following Pressnell, believes that London had made a serious tactical mistake in 'not including commercial policy specialists in the original team'.[28] This is certainly true. There is this defence of Keynes, though. He believed that the principles (as opposed to the details) of a commercial convention could be swiftly agreed, giving him an important bargaining counter in the financial talks. But London was clearly frightened by the thought of Keynes being set free to agree commercial principles with the Americans on his own. They were especially alarmed that he would offer unauthorised concessions on imperial preference to get the grant-in-aid. So it was not Amerian pressure but a desire to safeguard Britain's commercial bargaining position which led to the decision, on 14 September, to send out a Board of Trade team. As 'principal advisers to HM Ambassador on commercial policy' they would restrict Keynes's role in the trade negotiations.[29] Eight officials headed by Sir Percivale Liesching and Lionel Robbins sailed out on 21 September and arrived on the 27th. Keynes, who had been 'very angry' at their coming, greeted Robbins cordially and invited him on to the Financial Committee.

As Keynes had anticipated, the commercial negotiations, starting on 1 October, went smoothly after all the preparatory work in London, with Keynes playing second fiddle to Robbins and Liesching. The two sides worked to an American draft constitution – known as Com/Trade 1 – of an International Trade Organisation, covering preferences, subsidies, state trading, export taxes, exchange controls and cartels. Differences surfaced between the American and British approaches to eliminating

Forbidden Tricks, the Americans favouring outright prohibitions, the British preferring a case-by-case approach. Keynes made his own typical contribution. At one point when they were discussing the control of cartels, he interjected: 'Isn't our scheme intended to get things done, whereas yours will merely provide a living for a large number of lawyers?' Vinson exploded, 'That is just the kind of statement you would make' – which makes one wonder how well Keynes would have done had he been left in sole charge of the negotiations. After eleven days the only substantial obstacle which remained was imperial preferences. The Americans insisted, from the outset, that a unilateral elimination of preferences must be a condition of financial aid. The British were prepared to trade reduction in preferences for all-round tariff reductions, and resisted any explicit link between commercial concessions and financial assistance. However, two precious weeks had been lost – one of them at sea. Keynes came to believe that this delay dissipated the atmosphere he had created in his oral presentations, prejudicing the eventual outcome.

Robbins soon sniffed out what was happening on the financial side. 'It is clear', he wrote in his diary on 29 September,

> that a pure grant-in-aid is right out of the picture. It is clear, too, that Maynard accepts this completely and is beginning to be inclined to think it is absurd to believe otherwise. I had no difficulty in refraining from saying I told you so. But I perceive that we shall have great difficulty in dehypnotising London; and I think that Maynard will have to be told that, having himself made the magic passes that now hold the King's Treasurers entranced in rapturous contemplation of ideal 'justice', it will be up to him . . . to reverse the process.[30]

III

RETREAT TO TEMPTATION

Two informal meetings between Halifax and Keynes and Clayton and Vinson at Blair Lee House on 25 and 27 September made the position clear. Both sides 'understood that some amount in the neighbourhood of $5bn was in their minds as well as ours'. So far so good. But, wrote the ambassador in his diary, just 'when I thought it had been going well, we ran into trouble'. The Americans made it plain that they could not contemplate either a grant or an interest-free loan. 'We said we could not contemplate paying interest because we could not see our way to do it. And so there we were.'[31] At the second meeting, the American pair did not 'recoil too violently' from Keynes's suggestion of a combined grant-in-aid and low-interest loan, but doubted that they could get it through

Congress. Halifax and Keynes left it that they would report to London and meet the following week.

Keynes now asked London permission to discuss 'the acceptability of a loan without interest', which annual payments limited to $100m. Reversing his previous arguments, he told Dalton that he could think of no 'plausible reason' for any gift at all, since 'retrospective lend lease corresponding to what we spent here is, most certainly, not a good starter' – as Brand had told him all along. He had, in Bareau's words, 'consigned his earlier concepts of Justice to a limbo amid the ghosts and skeletons of which only fools and dullards would roam and search'.[32] An interest-free loan might well be attainable. Harry White was apparently advising Vinson to offer one. (For details of White's scheme, see p. 424 below) Keynes now urged that Britain could afford to accept a $5bn loan, repayable in fifty instalments, with the first instalment postponed for five or ten years. In return Britain would be expected to liberalise sterling area arrangements, accept the Bretton Woods plan and scale down sterling debts. On the basis of fifty instalments, the repayment would amount to $100m. a year. 'Release' of accumulated sterling balances at $150m. a year would bring the annual charge to $250m. This would come to less than 5 per cent of the 'break even' export target of $6500m. 'Either we can manage this or we are sunk anyway.' As part of this approach, Britain should accept an escape clause based 'not on our ability to pay but on the willingness of the creditor country to receive'.[33]

This was Keynes's personal fall-back position – the version of Temptation he had always been willing to accept. 'My advice would be to accept a settlement on these terms . . .' if nothing 'better' was available, he cabled Dalton on 1 October, and he requested 'discretion' – though rather obliquely – to negotiate a deal. But he had not yet completely given up hope that something 'better' might turn up.[34] Not surprisingly, Dalton cabled back the next day: 'My present inclination is to decline any loan which carries interest, however it is dressed up, because I do not believe that that principle is appropriate to the circumstances.'[35] Dalton's biographer writes that 'Keynes's steady retreat from optimism was regarded . . . with incomprehension' by the ministerial team of Dalton, Bevin and Cripps which was handling the London end of the negotiations.[36] A gap had started to open up between the expectations Keynes had aroused in London and the realities of Washington. Keynes's efforts to scale down London's hopes coincided with a hardening of Labour's attitude towards the negotiations. Eady warned him on 28 September that the new government would be much less frightened by austerity than its predecessor, indeed might positively welcome it 'partly as a more noble way of life, partly as a psychological sublimation of disappointment'. Many ministers would be loath to be 'under a loan obligation of enormous amount to one of our two major Allies'. Eady, himself a hardliner, still hankered for a grant based on retrospective Lend–Lease. If this was not forthcoming, he felt that it might be best to go for a two-stage agreement, to assure supplies for the following year, and leave a more comprehensive settlement till the financial Dunkirk which would follow.[37]

Keynes summed up the position to Lippmann on 6 October. The negotiations were seriously being held up by two matters: (a) the extent to which the British should pledge themselves to give up imperal preference, and (b) whether American financial help should take the form of a grant-in-aid or a non-interest loan or an interest loan on liberal but nevertheless semi-commercial terms. On the former he was confident that London 'can be persuaded to give away the substance'. On the latter 'there is room for endless sitting around and a variety of compromises'.[38]

During the first bout of sitting around Keynes gave a talk to the Overseas Writers' Club, briefed both British and Dominion journalists, and tried his persuasive arts on the first of the dinner groups of American Senators and Congressmen Halifax had arranged for him. Halifax thought that Keynes handled these occasions 'admirably well', though they were 'pretty gruelling'. The American politicians worried about Harold Laski's influence on the British government, feared that American help would be used to 'finance socialism', and wondered what benefits the Americans would gain from 'getting us up on our feet and liberalising the sterling area' and whether 'we could . . . make ourselves efficient'.[39] Harmer, who attended a couple of these occasions, made a shrewd comment in his diary of 9 October:

> The pro-British line always needs defending in this country; the anti-British never. This is psychological, and need not be taken too seriously: but it is a fact which always needs remembering in handling any important issue here. It isn't that there is underlying hostility to Britain: on the contrary, there is very great friendliness. But their history starts with the War of Independence and that colours all their thinking. They must always be able to show that they haven't been outsmarted.

On Saturday 6 October the ambassador had 'Keynes to dinner with Roger Makins [of the Foreign Office] and his wife. Lady Keynes was in grand form and kept us all vastly entertained. We got Keynes going on the subject of Monty Norman, whom he liked very much, but who he said on some sides of life was a somewhat dangerous mixture of imp and charlatan. The high moment of his power he judged to have been Snowden as Chancellor who was completely mesmerised by him.'

The first fortnight in October was the happiest part of Keynes's last Washington trip. The negotiations had not yet got too tense, Washington had cooled down from the semi-tropical summer heat, with clear blue skies and fresh breezes every day.

We get up early [Lydia wrote to Florence Keynes on 13 October]. I ring for our breakfast, the Lord sips tea with a bun and jelly. I inhale coffee, but before I drink it I cover it with an angora scarf to keep it very hot: sometimes we get a wrong paper, I walk in the passage and steal the right paper from someone who is still asleep, but on the whole the Americans get up early – by 8 o'clock the lift is full of businessmen with a cigar.

After breakfast I dress, go into the lobby to get New York papers, sniff the air, come back, wait till Maynard has cleaned his teeth and go out with him in the car to his office [at the Willard Hotel] which is in the shopping centre (F Street). If the weather is nice I get out of the car and begin examinations of the windows, in the end I am driven with desire to enter and re-examine the shape of things to come. . . . I do that for about two hours and walk back home and wait for the telephone if Maynard is coming to the coffee shop, run ahead to reserve a table, then he joins me . . . in drinking tomato juice, etc. I have described a quarter of the day, no more to-night. . . .

'Today is Lydia's birthday,' Maynard wrote to his mother on 21 October,

> she hopes to shop on a big foot next week. Not that her foot has been so small as it looks. In the last five weeks some two hundred objects purchased, including eighteen pairs of shoes, forty pairs of stockings, between twelve and twenty costumes, a new suit and a tie for me (the suit costing a thousand times as much as the tie), a new raincoat for me, a large trunkful of food, five safety razors, ten ferocious jewels, half a dozen headgear and in addition enough odds and ends to fix up a shop. . . . But from tomorrow, having had a satisfactory birthday present, she proposes to shop seriously.

Entering Keynes's drawing room on the top floor of the Statler to draft telegrams, the ambassador encountered a 'jumble sale of bright colours', reflecting Lady Keynes's 'bohemian tendencies'.

Keynes at last received new instructions from the Chancellor on 8 October. 'If best offer is large loan at 2 per cent interest we would not accept it,' Dalton cabled. 'We remain firm that we will not accept obligations which we do not see reasonable certainty of discharging. Also such a commercial settlement would be regarded as an inequitable conclusion to our mutual effort.' Dalton was lobbing back Keynes's poetry to him. If the worst came, they would borrow for necessary imports through the Export–Import Bank, and restrict purchases from the United States. What sort of settlement would be acceptable? Dalton allowed two alternatives. London would accept a grant of $2bn 'as partial repayment of what we had to spend in America during cash and carry period', plus a credit of $3bn to $4bn on which they would pay 1 per cent interest on the drawings made. If this failed, it would accept an interest-free $5bn loan repayable over fifty years, provided the 'background conditions' were right. Dalton emphasised two requirements: (a) an 'undisputed right to restrict Britain's total imports' and (b) a waiver clause of the kind Keynes had suggested. But Keynes himself was to make no offer along these lines for the time being, leaving the Americans to take the initiative.[40]

Keynes could now feel that London had accepted his version of Temptation, and what remained to be done was to put forward Dalton's first alternative in the hope of eliciting his second. When Keynes and Halifax saw Vinson and Clayton again on 9 October, Keynes urged that $2bn of American help should come in the form of a grant, but failed to shift the American view that this was politically impossible. Vinson and Clayton also repeated that an interest-free loan was politically impossible. But what the British negotiators did get from Clayton was a suggestion that the Americans might provide a loan of $5bn, repayable in fifty annual instalments starting in five years, with an additional annuity of $50m. a year to cover interest at 2 per cent. Interest might be 'finally waived (repeat waived) and not deferred' if in any year Britain could not pay, Clayton inviting Keynes to draft a waiver clause. At his press conference the same day Clayton 'actually mentioned $5bn as the agreed figure'.[41]

This was the best offer the British got, though it was not entirely firm. Keynes clearly thought it offered the basis for a settlement. He immediately asked Dalton for permission to explore possible waiver formulae based on that offer. The first would allow Britain to waive payment on interest in three contingencies: a breakdown of multilateral clearing, an international depression and a scarcity of dollars, the last certified by the IMF. This became known as the 'London waiver', though it actually originated with Clayton. Although 'we do not want to have the bailiffs in the house for two generations sizing up the position', Keynes also suggested a second waiver of interest – known as the 'Washington waiver' – based on Britain's capacity to pay. He suggested it might be invoked in any year in which 'our visible exports failed to reach six billion dollars reckoned in current prices'. The thrust behind these suggestions was to limit Britain's obligation to $100m. a year, or even less, in any years in which Britain could not afford to pay more.[42]

In these days, when the first stage of the negotiations hung in the balance, Keynes made two important tactical mistakes. What he needed to send London was a short telegram outlining the American offer, and asking for authority to accept it – as a matter of urgency – subject to satisfactory background conditions, including a liability limited to $100m. a year. Instead, in his two telegrams of 9 and 11 October he muddied the water by over-complicated discussion of possible waiver formulae. Partly this was because he was still not convinced that the Americans had made their 'final best offer'.[43] Partly it was because he got fascinated by the mathematical complexities of the waiver conditions. His second mistake was to get diverted by what he called a 'fascinating contraption' by Harry White for settling the sterling balances question, which he intruded into the main negotiation, unsettling London. (See p. 424 below.) In short, he took his eye off the ball. Nevertheless, Halifax thought that 'it does look as if we are moving to a settlement with a bit of luck', and Harmer talked of trying 'to force the whole thing to a settlement in a couple of weeks or so'.[44]

The let-down was swift and brutal. Dalton cabled him bluntly on 13 October that 'we do not find a loan on these terms acceptable'. It failed 'two tests of principle'. First, it lacked the 'sweet breath of justice'. Secondly, there was no 'reasonable certainty' that Britain would be able to discharge the debt. In return for Britain's wartime sacrifice, 'we are offered still further indebtedness and in the case of the sterling area the partial conversion of a widely distributed sterling debt owed to those who normally trade with us . . . into a canalised dollar debt, to a country whose visible balance of trade with us is so onesided'. Dalton then enumerated the various 'stages in the development of this affair'. First they had hoped for a grant-in-aid. When that was said to be impossible they had hoped for a repayment of pre-Lend–Lease spending in the United States, plus a loan at nominal interest. If that failed they had said they would consider an interest-free loan. 'Now we are offered a loan larger than our own needs require . . . and we are to pay interest on it.' To Clayton and Vinson, the difference between $100m. and $150m. might be 'peanuts', but 'unfortunately it cannot be so to us'. To add to this annual liability, repayments to the sterling area as part of the deal were 'the last straw'. Dalton rejected the 'Washington waiver' based on Britain's capacity to pay, because it suggested default. 'We do not want high liabilities with ample escape clauses. . . . manageable liabilities can be our only safe guide. . . .'[45] Dalton instructed the British negotiators to continue to seek 'a complete or partial interest-free grant, and to resist annual payments exceeding $100 million'.[46]

The lack of an agreed fall-back position now started to have a deadly effect. Had Keynes been authorised to accept a $5bn loan carrying 2 per cent interest, with a suitable waiver, he might have clinched a deal there and then. If Britain could not pay 2 per cent interest after five years, it was, in Keynes's own words, 'sunk anyway'. Keynes's time of suffering was about to start. He had insisted in London on not being allowed to accept anything but a grant. Now when he asked for flexibility to negotiate a loan, it was being denied him.

IV

DESCENT INTO HORROR

Keynes and Halifax dutifully tried out Dalton's now exploded formula on Clayton and Vinson on 15 and 16 October. They asked for a grant-in-aid of $2bn and a credit line of up to $3bn at 2 per cent interest, capital repayment and interest starting in five years' time. But they 'made no progress whatsoever', with the atmosphere 'gloomy and unconstructive'. Moreover, Clayton's mind also seemed to be moving in the 'unpleasant direction of proposing a reduction in the credit below 5 billion whilst keeping the annual service charge at $100 million'.[47]

On Wednesday 17 October, Keynes drafted NABOB 177 to London, dispatched at 1 a.m. the following morning. 'I thought it was quite brilliantly done,' the ambassador wrote in his diary that day, 'with pleasant touches of wit redeeming the atmosphere of official telegrams. He certainly has got an extraordinarily good mind.' The telegram 'is after consultation with the Ambassador, Brand, Self, Liesching, Robbins and Hall-Patch and represents our collective opinion'. In essence, it was a plea to London to authorise Keynes to accept the Clayton offer, with two waiver clauses, relating both to America's capacity to receive payments and to Britain's capacity to supply them (the Washington and London waivers respectively). Keynes admitted that the British had failed to achieve any of their objectives: 'at best a free grant, failing that a partial grant, and at the worst an interest-free loan'. This was because the American negotiators believed that Congress would not stand for any of these, and there was no leadership such as would have been provided by the 'gay, generous and brilliant spirit' of the late President to find a way round Congressional opposition. 'In this business country', Keynes wrote ironically, 'where it is a moral duty ... to make ... money ... some imitation of a normal banking transaction is necessary if the moral principles of the country are not to be affronted.'

But was that a reason for breaking off negotiations? Clayton had been leading the British down the treacherous path of Temptation, and Keynes now tried the same tactic on London, using Clayton as his mouthpiece:

> Clayton frankly admits the force of our case. His point is that he must dress the thing up to look as ordinary as possible, to escape notice wearing a business suit.... What really scares us is the possibility of owing to the US an amount of money which is enormous in relation to our prospective exports to them in conditions where, for all we know now, multilateral clearings may have broken down. Very well, says Clayton, draft a clause to protect yourself against this possibility. We admit that commerce in the post-

war world either goes all right from our point of view or it does not. In the first case 150 millions may be practicable and in the second case 100 millions may be scarcely possible. Nevertheless failing the solution of a free grant one has to draw the line somewhere and they must not try to involve us in the fallacy of sorites. Very well says Clayton, draft a clause under which your liability will be related to your capacity. . . .

You will be aware how reluctant I have been to enter on the slippery path of escape clauses. But we all think that the time has come when we cannot reasonably excuse ourselves from making some response to Clayton's generous and not unreasonable suggestions. In refusing to do so we are in truth still grasping at the ineluctable poetry and refusing to come to earth in well-reasoned prose. . . . If you had sat as many hours as the Ambassador and I have sat declaiming all our best poetry before an audience, not indeed unresponsive to those strains in their own hearts, but never deviating from the rejoinder that Congress . . . will be deaf to them, you would see our difficulty in persisting with a refusal to come down to earth.

The mask of poetry having been torn to shreds, Keynes came to the point. He wanted authority to negotiate a settlement on the basis of a loan of $5bn at 2 per cent interest, payable over fifty years, in which the interest portion would be waived whenever 'home-produced exports' were insufficient to finance the pre-war volume of imports.

The last weapon in his persuasive armoury was the threat of isolation:

Can anyone honestly argue [he went on] that the difference between this and a loan which is interest-free in all circumstances is so material than even in the last resort we should prefer a breakdown of the present discussions with all that means to our standard of life, to our hopes of recovery, to our position in the world and to Anglo-American friendship?[48]

Thus Keynes used his seductive arts on Whitehall. What he did not realise when he dispatched this telegram was that the Clayton offer had been withdrawn. Keynes's 'friend' Harry White had stabbed him in the back, and he never realised it. A US Treasury committee headed by White concluded that Britain's prospective balance of payments difficulties had been exaggerated and that Britain would not need as much as $5bn to get it through the transition. Keynes first got wind that the Americans were considering a smaller loan when he saw Harry White on 12 October. The Treasury, White told Keynes, had been arguing for $5bn but had failed to get it, and 'he warned me about getting a nasty surprise. . . . Nevertheless, I think he must be wrong.'[49]

Harry White's role in the British loan negotiations is, like almost everything else in his career, mystifying. He was plainly out of favour, but not yet without influence. In his testimony on the Bretton Woods Agreement before the Senate Banking Committee in June 1945, he had denied that Britain needed any special transitional help after the war. He was convinced that it would quickly recover its productive power, and that the £3bn of accumulated sterling balances would give it an unfair advantage in exporting to those countries which held the balances; he also feared that Britain might devalue sterling and thus add to its competitive advantage in world markets.[50] He excluded Bernstein and Luxford from the Treasury's technical committee, set up to consider Britain's requirements. 'I do not believe that White was opposed to a British loan,' Luxford told White's biographer David Rees, 'although definitely he was on the low side. . . . My friendly criticism is that he did not fight as hard as he should have for a proper figure and deluded Vinson and others into believing the loan figure [eventually decided] was adequate.'[51] In fact, White's position was more complicated. It is true that he thought a $3bn credit (which he suggested should be free of interest) would suffice for Britain's own current account needs; at the same time, he offered what Keynes called a 'rather fascinating contraption' for liberalising the sterling area and reducing Britain's sterling debt. When Dalton, in his telegram of 8 October, rejected the notion of 'a partial conversion of a widely distributed sterling debt . . . into a canalised dollar debt', the reference was to White's 'fascinating contraption' of which Keynes had apprised him on 5 October.

The essence of White's scheme was that Britain should exchange part of its debt to the sterling area for a reduced debt to the United States. Keynes had envisaged cancelling $4bn of sterling balances, funding $8bn and releasing $1bn. White suggested that the US Treasury buy $5bn of the funded portion from sterling area countries for $2.5bn in cash, this being its present discounted value at 3 per cent interest over fifty years. Thus Britain would end up owing the US $5.5bn ($3bn plus $2.5bn) altogether, free of interest, and the sterling area $4bn, instead of owing the United States (under the Clayton proposals) $5bn at 2 per cent interest and the sterling area $9bn. Keynes thought White's scheme 'extremely generous', though he understood it would herald the break-up of the sterling area.[52] This was no doubt White's intention.

The White Plan cut across, and indeed undermined, the main negotiation which Keynes and Halifax were pursuing with Vinson and Clayton. Keynes should never even have flirted with it. It was received with horror in the Bank and the Treasury. Vinson also rejected it as 'too fancy'[53] – the very reason, of course, it attracted Keynes. But the legacy of White's 'contraption' was dire. It eroded London's confidence in Keynes as a negotiator; and it convinced Vinson that Britain was exaggerating its needs.

The 'nasty surprise' of which White warned Keynes on 12 October came at the meeting on the 18th, when Vinson told Keynes, Halifax and Brand that the 'best offer' they could make was a loan of $3.5bn at 2 per cent, repayable over fifty years, plus whatever was needed to clean up Lend–Lease at 2⅜ per cent, repayable over thirty years. The total in the round figures then being bandied around came to about $4bn altogether. Asked how they had arrived at the lower figure, Clayton said that it assumed that Britain would run down its gold and dollar reserves to $1bn at the end of the transition – a replay, it seemed, of the previous American management of Lend–Lease. Britain's commitment to liberalising sterling area payments would remain unchanged.

Keynes treated the American proposals 'very roughly', wrote Halifax, 'and at one time the argument became strained. I thought of interrupting Keynes in one of his explosions. On second thoughts I was not sure that the explosion was not doing good and so let it run.' Keynes said that their proposal would certainly be quite unacceptable to London, and therefore he would like their advice as to whether it would not really be better for him to break off and to go back to London, with 'dangerous and even tragic consequences'. Vinson demurred: 'In Kentucky we never ask our guests to leave.' This restored them to good humour.[54]

Too late, Keynes now returned to Clayton's proposal of a $5bn loan. It seemed that the Americans might, after all, agree to go up to $4bn plus the Lend–Lease clean-up. They then started talking about waiver conditions, with Keynes stressing that he was going 'quite beyond my instructions' in reverting to the 'capacity to pay' criterion, rejected by Dalton. Clayton insisted that 'the criterion of our external income must include our net invisible income'. Keynes reported that the Americans might agree to forgive interest in any year when British exports and net invisible income failed to reach $7bn at post-war prices. With a five-year deferment, the annual sum required to yield 2 per cent interest came to $159m. In a year when the waiver operated it would come to $109m. – barely above Dalton's requirement.[55]

To his mother Keynes wrote on 21 October, 'We have reached a point in our negotiations where we can get no further without instructions from London. . . . On the face of it things don't look too good. But it is almost essential for them as for us to reach an acceptable conclusion. So I remain fairly optimistic and, with the onset of senility, don't worry anything like as much as I used to. . . .' Dalton was due to present his budget on 23 October, so another period of waiting began.*

---

* In an effort to break the logjam Catto suggested to Keynes on 20 October that in return for $5bn free of interest Britain offer to repay $1bn of the First World War loan 'in final

The ball was now in London's court. The *ad hoc* negotiations between Halifax and Keynes and Vinson and Clayton were broken off for nearly three weeks while NABOBs and BABOONs flew between Washington and London.

In the previous seven weeks, the attitudes of the principals in London and their agents in Washington had come distressingly apart. To simplify matters, Britain's negotiators in Washington were instinctively pro-American; their masters in London were instinctively anti-American. Conservative (or in Keynes's case Liberal) envoys were negotiating on behalf of a Labour government committed to large-scale nationalisation. Keynes's preference for the 'American' to the 'Russian' bias had hardened with the advent of a Labour government in Britain and the first rumblings of the Cold War. The very reasons which were making the Labour Cabinet hesitate to tie Britain to America's coat-tails were, for Keynes, increasingly important arguments for doing so.

As in the negotiations leading up to the Bretton Woods Agreement, Keynes often railed against the United States, and sometimes talked of breaking off negotiations. But he would never have done so unless he had been convinced that America positively meant Britain harm. As it was, there was always enough 'give' in the American position to reassure him of America's underlying goodwill. So it was easy for him to fall back on such second-order explanations of Anglo-American conflicts as misunderstandings arising from the different British and American ways of doing business, and, above all, from the need for the administration to pacify Congress.

Keynes was also conscious of the timetable. The Bretton Woods Agreement had to be ratified by Parliament by the end of the year. A financial agreement had to be in the bag by then, or it could well lapse. This was, for Keynes, a decisive argument against breaking off: the whole edifice of post-war reconstruction was at stake. Vinson and Clayton also had a tight timetable. They wanted Congress to ratify the loan before it adjourned in mid-December, fearing a build-up of opposition. The Americans, Keynes was convinced, would never force the British to break off. This gave him what little leverage he had.

A further factor which made Keynes increasingly anxious to force the pace of agreement was the precarious state of his health. In letters home, he insisted that he felt 'pretty well and equal to one more push'. Lydia was exercising 'iron discipline about diet, ice-bags, rests and sleeping'. As often as they could they had supper alone in their suite in the Statler, and retired early, with Lydia removing the ice crystals from their salads to put into the icebag on Keynes's chest. However, Keynes had already had a

---

settlement'. Keynes wrote back politely that it was better to let 'this deeply sleeping dog . . . lie' (*CW*, xxiv, 564n. and 565).

'slight heart attack' on 7 October, 'due to over-eating on top of over-working'.[56] As the negotiations lengthened, his heart pains returned, and he started taking sodium amytal capsules to relieve them. A fully fit man might have flown back to London to obtain more flexible instructions. But Keynes was trapped in Washington by his infirmities. He could not risk air travel. Instead, he begged Sir Edward Bridges, the Cabinet secretary, to come out, so that he could confirm the Mission's account of the Washington atmosphere. But this was vetoed by Attlee, who didn't want 'crossed wires on finance'.[57] So, as Robbins put it, Keynes would 'spend hours late at night drafting telegrams, superb in literary style and wit, which had better been left to small fry, both because of the labour saved and because of the palpable unsuitability of many of his flourishes for the persuasion of bewildered ministers who felt they had once already been taken in by his eloquence'.[58] This last point is important. Keynes was eloquent, not terse. He needed to create an atmosphere for his persuasion. Today, one can enjoy the atmospherics of his NABOBs, but also understand why hard-pressed ministers and officials back in London found them rather confusing.

While worsening American terms made Keynes more, rather than less, eager to finish off the negotiations quickly, this had the opposite effect in London. Some still clung to the hope of ideal Justice. Others worried about Britain's capacity to repay debt. Ministers also foresaw another trap: that Britain would be forced to commit itself to making sterling convertible before it had recovered its solvency.

Keynes was starting to come to a more optimistic view of post-war possibilities. Conventional wisdom in Whitehall was that dollars would be scarce after the war, that is, that America would export more than it imported, as it had done between the wars. Both White and Clayton pooh-poohed these fears. Their fears were the opposite: that Britain – and Germany – would soon recover their exporting power. Keynes reported Clayton predicting 'that America's over-seas expenditure . . . will overtake her exports'.[59] Keynes thought Clayton might be right. In between the meetings and the telegrams, he started a note forecasting the end of the dollar shortage, which was published posthumously as 'The Balance of Payments of the United States'.

There were other powerful pressures working against an agreement. The Bank of England's position was the most intransigent – and politically hopeless. Determined to maintain the sterling area, it opposed debt cancellation, premature convertibility, and borrowing from America. If it had a policy, it was to enforce Starvation Corner on Britain and use the sterling debts as a lever to impose British exports on sterling area countries. This raised the question of commercial policy. Here imperialists and state-trading socialists united in demanding an escape from the Article VII commitment. Eady at the Treasury and Cobbold at the Bank

were against any agreement that tied Britain's hands in any way. This
struck a responsive chord in the Labour Cabinet, which feared that an
American loan, with all its strings, would limit the possibility of insular
socialism.

Exponents of *Realpolitik* will say that Keynes was blind to the real
conflicts of interest between the two powers. But his London critics failed
to offer a plausible alternative. In the last resort, no one was really ready
for Starvation Corner. England was a democratic, not Soviet, state. Instead,
as Freddie Harmer noted, London clung to the 'lunatic idea that we
could break with the Americans on anything they really care about and
still get enough finance on some terms or other to get us through'.[60]

The divided counsels in London were reflected in the BABOONs
Dalton sent on 27 October in reply to Keynes's NABOBs of 19 and 20
October. Meade thought these were 'the lowest point of Eady's and
Cobbold's efforts'.[61] They were based on the idea – logical in itself – of a
trade-off between assistance and obligations. Two alternatives, Dalton
cabled, might satisfy Parliament. Alternative A envisaged a $2.5bn loan,
for fifty years at 1 per cent, repayment starting after five years, plus an
option of an interest-free $2bn credit to make currently earned sterling
freely available for spending outside the sterling area. This would be
subject to the London waiver only, involving America's capacity to receive
rather than Britain's capacity to pay. If this was accepted Britain would
seek a settlement with its sterling creditors, would sponsor an International Trade Conference and would recommend Parliament to accept
the Bretton Woods Agreement. If it failed, the negotiators should fall
back on Alternative B. Britain would seek to borrow $2.5bn on commercial
terms, plus whatever amount was needed to settle the Lend–Lease
account, the whole at 2 per cent interest, without any policy commitments
whatsoever. In an explanatory cable, BABOON 156, Dalton explained that
Alternative A assumed that Britain's net debit on the Lend–Lease clean-
up would not exceed $500m., which would be included in the loan at 1
per cent, and that Britain would be able to cover essential imports from
the United States in 1946 and 1947 with $2bn, allowing for a 'vigorous
switching' of exports and imports to Empire markets.[62]

Before the telegrams had gone off, Meade attended:

> a meeting in the Treasury with Eady and Clarke from the Treasury,
> Cobbold from the Bank of England and Helmore from the Board of
> Trade. They all ... seemed to delight in the proposed solution
> because the time had come to show the Americans that we could be
> tough. But it was not until I heard Cobbold on this occasion that I
> realised that he really delighted in a wrecking proposal of this kind.
> Clearly he does not want any general settlement on the lines
> contemplated with the Americans. He would like us to snap our

fingers at the Americans and to develop the Sterling Area – though God knows how we could get on in this way. He is a clever ass.[63]

Dalton's BABOONs left Keynes 'white with rage and talking about resigning'. But by the next day, Harmer noted, 'M. had thought it out very well and after writing and destroying one or two vitriolic drafts produced very good ones'. Alternative B, he told Dalton, was a non-starter: the commercial rate of borrowing was 3 per cent and would involve immediate repayment of capital. As to the first plan, 1 per cent was equally out of the question. (London agreed to substitute 2 per cent.) In a longer reply on 30 October, Halifax and Keynes wrote that 'the realities of the position B are fatally misunderstood in London'. Joint loans from the Lend–Lease Administration and the Export-Import Bank would cost Britain $228m. a year starting in 1946, assuming, which was doubtful, that the sums requested were available from these sources. Moreover, if Alternative B were raised, 'we must expect a dangerous hardening in all quarters here. In American eyes we would be deliberately preferring the policy of separate economic blocs. Their first reaction might be just to sit, content to allow the financial pressure against us to develop under its own steam.' On the other hand, Alternative A might run, with the Washington rather than the London waiver.[64]

Keynes's parallel efforts to clear up the question of the sterling balances also ran into trouble. When he had indicated, on 20 September, how Britain planned to deal with the balances, Vinson and Clayton asked for further details. On 24 October he sent London a draft of the proposals he wanted to table: these stated the quantities of the balances to be cancelled, funded and released, together with a timetable for securing agreements with Britain's creditors. 'As you already know,' he cabled Dalton on 23 October, 'large concessions by the sterling area are of course an absolute essential and, we think, not unreasonable conditions for American assistance. They started this way and are most unlikely to change their position.'[65] The Americans wanted the sterling balances dealt with because their existence affected British ability to service any American debt, and impacted on the question of the conditions of the waiver. When Keynes's proposals reached London, 'Cobbold and Eady threw a fit saying we could in effect give the Americans no assurances about getting our sterling creditors to scale down their balances or about the amount to which we could release sterling balances for conversion into dollars.'[66] A heated exchange with Rowe-Dutton and Eady followed about the nature of the sterling area. Eventually Keynes was moved to a jibe at the Bank's expense: 'Some fig leaves which may pass muster with old ladies in London wilt in a harsher climate.'[67] Keynes received permission to pass on his suggestions for scaling down balances to Harry White, but minus quantities, commitments or dates. In his BABOON 156, Dalton explained that, had American aid taken the form of a grant, the 'moral impetus' created would have enabled Britain to secure a 'large cancellation' of sterling balances. Without this 'moral impetus' no results at all could be guaranteed, and if the Americans made any attempt to tie down the British to figures 'the whole negotiations must break down'.[68]

With the commercial negotiations also threatening to founder on the rock of Dominion objections to the elimination of trade preferences, Robbins and Hall-Patch flew back to London on 28 October 'ostensibly to discuss Anglo-American differences over Imperial Preference'[69] but in fact to remove misunderstandings about the sterling area proposals and also to secure London's support for the Washington waiver. Robbins carried a letter from Keynes to Dalton, complaining that 'dangerous and, indeed, demented advice is abroad', and warning that the government was risking a financial débâcle as in 1931. 'There is no way out remotely compatible with the present domestic policy of the Government except on the basis of substantial American aid.'[70] Keynes and Halifax decided to put off trying even Dalton's Alternative A on the Americans until Robbins had secured further elucidations.

On Sunday 4 November Keynes wrote to his mother:

> Before the end of this week I shall know where I am. The crisis will come in the next few days. On the whole I am not unhopeful. But my difficulties in bringing London along to a reasonable compromise are not less than those in moving Washington. . . . Last week was very worrying and I could not see how I was to extricate myself from all the nets of obstinacy and misunderstanding which were closing in from all quarters. But now it looks much better. . . .
>
> The team here has pulled grandly together. Halifax and I work like brothers. A week ago we sent two faithful ones to London to handle the situation there. Obstinate and tiresome though the Americans are, they are full of good will and good intentions and kind nature. What a country of optimists!

Robbins and Hall-Patch returned from London on 7 November. They reported Ministers in a frightful muddle. They spent all their time discussing the theory of nationalisation; most of the senior officials were working to the verge of collapse. Stafford Cripps understood what was going on and Bevin was starting to; but Dalton was quite unable to read any of the papers and had not even consulted the Prime Minster. Keynes commented, 'When I first knew Dalton as an undergraduate at King's he was a passionate supporter of Joe Chamberlain and his room was plastered with placards about Imperial Preference. Then one night when he was drunk he was converted to Fabianism by Rupert Brooke. Hence all our present troubles.' The Robbins–Hall-Patch visit to London had its effect. The dispute over imperial preference was resolved – or at least shelved –

making it possible for the Cabinet to accept a 'United States Proposal to Establish an International Trade Organisation' on 6 November.* And Dalton's Alternative B was scrapped, the Mission being told to press on with Alternative A. If that failed, the negotiators could accept a new Alternative B – $4bn at 2 per cent interest, repayable over fifty years, with an option for a further $1bn on the same terms. London also agreed that the negotiators could accept the Washington waiver.[71] Little by little London was conceding ground.

The ambassador's diary of 6 November takes up the story:

> From the State Department I went on to the Treasury, where Keynes, Bob Brand and I tried the first of the two London alternatives on the Americans. They did not like it too much, as I expected. . . . They are to think about it. . . . It looks to me more and more as if Vinson was the sticking point rather than Clayton. We did our business in a very much over-heated room with all the Venetian blinds down, although the sun was shining brightly outside. That the Americans should like living this way is a constant puzzle to me.

The British plan – presented as a draft agreement – which the American Top Committee went off to consider envisaged an American credit in two parts: $2bn plus an amount (which the British still hoped could be limited to $500m.) for cleaning up Lend–Lease, and a further sum up to $2bn for making current sterling 'available without discrimination' for non-sterling transactions and for partial release of accumulated sterling balances. The $2.5bn would carry 2 per cent interest and would be repayable in fifty equal instalments starting in 1951. The remaining credit facilities, also repayable in fifty instalments starting in 1951, would be interest free. In any year in which British visible and invisible exports fell short of the $7bn needed to finance the pre-war volume of imports, interest would be waived. Capital repayment could be deferred in the event of a breakdown in multilateral clearing ('less than 75 per cent of British exports being sold to countries of which the currencies are freely convertible into dollars'), an international depression, or the dollar having been declared a 'scarce currency' by the IMF.[72]

After considering Alternative A for three days, Vinson and Clayton rejected it on Friday 9 November. Keynes then activated the fall-back position. Talks proceeded 'on the assumption that the loan will be increased to 4½ billion inclusive of lend–lease clean-up', the whole at 2 per cent interest. But this concession on amount was accompanied by an avalanche of new and old demands. The Americans knew they had

---

* The Cabinet finally accepted a formula, presented by the Americans, but actually drafted by the British negotiators, the gist of which was that preferences rates were not to be reduced until general tariff rates had been reduced to the preferential rate.

the British on the rack and were determined to press home their advantage. They wanted interest postponed, but not waived; the test for activating the deferment should include the state of Britain's reserves; currently earned sterling should be made convertible not just for sterling area countries but for the non-sterling area countries with which Britain had payments agreements; and repaying the American loan should have priority over other debts.

Keynes couldn't stand it any longer. Bareau's semi-official note – he was not present – cannot altogether hide the drama of the occasion:

> Lord Keynes ... appeared to lose both patience and interest in further conduct of the negotiations, and wished to settle with the Americans roughly on their terms and using the wide discretionary powers which London had given the Delegation. On Saturday morning he was talking of settling the deal and seeing the press in the course of the afternoon. He was, however, dissuaded from following this plan.[73]

The meeting which followed on Saturday 10 November was 'tense and painful'. The Americans turned the screw tighter, by demanding a scrapping of the Anglo-American Petroleum Agreements, signed as recently as 24 September, which reserved Britain's right, under Article XIV(2) of the Bretton Woods Agreement, to discriminate against foreign imports. 'We had a great deal of trouble particularly over this oil question,' Harmer noted, 'and only a good deal of firmness and tact (with Lionel R. preeminent) got [Maynard] to face it properly and not side-step.' The American demand that Britain give up its transitional rights under the Bretton Woods Agreement was destined to become London's last sticking point. Bareau wrote that 'strenuous efforts had to be made later in the day [10 November] to prevent the dispatch to London of certain telegrams which might well have precipitated the immediate breakdown of the negotiations'.

On Monday 12 November, the technicians from the two sides argued technically, while Keynes and the ambassador had another meeting with Vinson and Clayton, which went no better. At one moment, Keynes burst out: 'Why do you persecute us like this?' Clayton was at his most doctrinaire, haranguing them on the theme that Britain's greatness had been built on free trade and convertibility. Coming out of the explosive confrontation, Keynes remarked: 'At one time I had come to believe that the Mayflower came over to this country filled with lawyers. I am now inclined to go back to my original belief that it was filled with theologians.' Harmer reported 'M. nervy and difficult to deal with. He is quite exhausted and the effects are not easy for the rest of us. ... everything is rather a nightmare.' The Americans promised a counter-draft by 15 November. 'I am becoming steadily more worried,' wrote Hall-Patch. 'The "smoke-filled" room technique with no witnesses and no record is a form of negotiation which is only possible if you are supremely confident that the people with whom you are dealing are powerful enough to put through what they agree with you is reasonable. With the rabbits with whom we are dealing I am not sure it is the right technique. . . .'[74]

Attlee's brief visit to Washington did nothing to help. He had arrived on another vain mission: to get President Truman to share atomic secrets with Britain. 'Ineffective' in his speech to Congress, 'stiff and unsociable' at an Embassy reception,[75] he declined to take up the financial question in Washington, as Churchill might well have done, weaving financial assistance, free trade, the Soviet menace, atomic weapons, and naval bases, into a grand design for post-war Anglo-American partnership. This was quite beyond Attlee's scope. The electrifying effect of Churchill's speech at Fulton, Missouri, only four months later shows what a fillip a Churchillian speech to Congress in November 1945 might have given to the stagnant financial negotiation.

Nevertheless, Keynes was 'moderately hopeful' that the revised American draft agreement would take into account the comments of the British experts, and that he could sail home on the *Queen Mary* on 30 November. The American text arrived at the Statler Hotel at 9 a.m. on Thursday 15 November. Freddie Harmer 'went up [to Maynard's room] and found M. in bed looking very shaken and white; and all he could say was that we had better pack up and go home'. Their technicians, Harmer felt, 'had been at work and every kind of silly and insulting technicality had been written into the draft: together with several major new points which would have caused an explosion of fury if sent home'. At ten o'clock they all met at the Embassy. Halifax 'took charge very firmly of the position. It was decided that we should refuse to discuss the draft and merely offer to send it to London for instructions, warning them of possible consequences. M. very nervy and finding it difficult to control his feelings. (The personal aspect of all this to him is obvious.)' When Harry White rang up offering to see Keynes for technical discussions, 'M was appallingly rude to him on the telephone – just what we wanted to avoid.'

The 'most momentous' meeting of the Joint Finance Committee took place that afternoon at three o'clock, with Halifax, Keynes, Brand, Robbins, Hall-Patch, Lee and Harmer representing Britain, and Vinson, Clayton, Eccles, McCabe, Thomas, White and Collado for the Americans.

Halifax opened 'in plain language of rather melancholy menace' that the American proposals had brought them to the precipice of failure. The American draft included suggestions which would be quite unacceptable to London. If these suggestions represented the Americans' last word, the British delegation would have no choice but to go home. Perhaps after a year or so they might be able to resume with better hope of success. Meanwhile, there could be no question of Britain ratifying the Bretton

Woods Agreement or taking part in the International Trade Organisation discussions.[76]

> This statement [wrote Bareau, who was present] caused very visible shock to the Americans. Vinson immediately began to urge how completely at a loss he was to understand the Ambassador's contention that parts of the American document did not even offer a basis for discussion. While Eccles was droning on . . . Vinson and Clayton had a whispered conversation at the end of which Vinson said that nothing which the Ambassador had indicated suggested that we must face breakdown. This document and the clauses which gave offence to us must be discussed over again. We must not remit the document to London. . . . The Ambassador picked up the ball admirably. 'We are all friends in this room,' he said, 'and we all want to serve the same cause.'

Keynes then went through the American memorandum clause by clause, in his most mocking style. No waiver, the Americans said, could be given if Britain's gold and foreign exchange reserves were above 15 per cent of its imports. Its effect, he said would be 'to keep Britain on the breadline'. It may well have been on this occasion that he was provoked into one of his famous repartees. He was arguing that Britain's gold reserve was already far too low, when an official of the Federal Reserve Board chipped in: 'Your gold reserves must be an essential criterion. You might find a great deal of gold hidden in a cave'. Keynes immediately turned to Frank Lee: 'Gold in a cave, Frank, put that down in the Agreement. We accept that.'* He tore into the clause deferring rather than cancelling interest payments. 'The Americans accepted that for 55 years we should not pay if we could not pay, but after that period we should pay even if we could not do so.' Finally, Keynes rejected prioritising the American debt. Eccles argued that, if America was asked to refinance a bankrupt concern, it had a right to insist on an upper limit on repayments to previous creditors. Keynes exploded: 'You cannot treat a great nation as if it were a bankrupt company.'[77] Harmer thought 'M. not at all in good form – far too worked up, and the whole atmosphere was very trying. But as a result they decided to have a further meeting immediately, with a view to technical discussion of the less important points in the morning.'

The first of these took place on Friday 16 November with Keynes and White as the principals. 'Some very trying discussions ensued with M. almost uncontrollable,' noted Harmer. The Saturday meeting was a replica of the first, only worse. Harmer wrote: 'We were all thoroughly

* The story was told to me by the late Paul Bareau, in this form. There have been several variants.

worried by now. M.'s health cannot stand this strain. . . . One of the first essentials is to give him somehow or other a rest next week, and we must hope that after Monday's meeting there will be a lull while we wait to hear from London. Meanwhile we must somehow or other get through Monday without explosions.'

Keynes and the others spent Sunday drafting a batch of telegrams to London setting out the points at issue. The Mission prefaced this series with the statement: 'We should warn you that . . . we are having heavy going and there may be further troubles ahead.' The ambassador's journal on Sunday 18 November for the first time mentioned 'internal friction' in the British ranks. 'Keynes, who has a good many of the defects of genius, is not an easy member of a team. I get on very well with him and I think everybody has immense admiration for his qualities. But most people whose minds do not work as quickly as he does are a bit apprehensive of his ingenuity in producing new suggestions they have not had time fully to consider. Bob Brand is very sane and I rely greatly on his judgment.' Bareau confirms that a 'Mutiny on the Bounty' took place that day. In preparation for Monday's meeting, the British team decided that as much of the talking as possible was to be left to the ambassador and kept 'away from the Lord'. Technical matters were to be referred to Brand, the cautious banker.

The British were expecting the Americans to table formal proposals at the Finance Committee on Monday 19 November, which they could transmit to London. But instead 'they offered for discussion a provisional text which still included our amendments and proposed omissions in square brackets'.[78] Vinson 'brusquely' proposed that they go through them. Since the matter was highly technical, and the ambassador and Brand could not cope, the British had no choice, in Bareau's words, but to 'pass the ball to Lord Keynes'. There then began a 'long and at times very tedious discussion of the various points of difference in the draft scheme'. Eccles, who held forth at length, still insisted on treating Britain as a bankrupt company. After the meeting, Keynes, who according to Harmer was 'much more himself', remarked that he and Harry White had agreed that Bretton Woods and $4bn were too high a price to pay for having to listen to Marriner Eccles. Keynes added 'No wonder that man is a Mormon. No single woman could stand him.' Such moments of levity were getting fewer.

Little though it looked like it at the time, the three meetings of 16, 17 and 19 November once more brought the two sides to the brink of an agreement. The subsequent nightmares were the result of London's attempt to impose vetoes on what Keynes had negotiated.

When the revised American draft, together with the Mission's comments on it, was sent to London on 21 November, the position was as follows:

(a) The Amount of the Loan. The British would accept $4bn of 'new money' and borrow up to $500m. more to pay off Lend–Lease supplies 'in the pipeline', both at 2 per cent. The Americans had offered $3.5bn, and they calculated Britain's net Lend–Lease debt at $750m., to be serviced at 2¾ per cent.

(b). The Waiver. The Americans had dropped the proposal for deferral, rather than waiver, of interest. 'After a prolonged struggle,' the Mission reported, 'we have failed to retain any part of the London waiver ... [and] we do not feel very strongly about carrying the dispute any further.' On the Washington waiver, the Mission wanted to accept the American proposal that 'the critical figure of our external income relates to a moving average of five years instead of a single year', but to alter the reserve criterion to net, rather than gross, reserves.

(c) Liberalisation of Sterling. The revised American clause was 'much more satisfactory than at one time we would have ventured to hope'. The British were expected to 'complete arrangements ... not later than the end of 1946' under which all sterling receipts from the current transactions of sterling area countries be made available for currency transactions in any currency area without discrimination. This would achieve the American aim of eliminating discrimination arising from the 'so-called dollar sterling pool' and would confirm Keynes's own *quid pro quo* for the loan.

(d) Payments Agreements. The Americans wanted Britain to make all currently earned sterling – that is, not just sterling earned by sterling area countries – convertible by the end of 1946. The 'insuperable' objection to this was 'that it commits us to grant convertibility to future non-resident balances irrespective of whether the other country accords us reciprocity'. The British team were willing to agree a text committing Britain to start negotiations to free current transactions with payments agreement countries.

(e) Discrimination. The Americans wanted Britain to give up any right to discriminate against US imports, except for the purpose of utilising blocked balances or helping war-destroyed countries. The British team recommended acceptance.

(f) Priority of American Debt. Clayton had suggested a compromise which would limit to $175m. British repayment of sterling balances or other loans after 1945 in any year in which the waiver was being claimed. If the British accelerated repayment to other debtors, it should accelerate payments on the principal of the American loan as well. The British wanted to limit this to loans taken out after 1945, and exclude colonies from the accelerated payment restrictions.

(g) Wartime Sterling Balances. The British had managed to restrict references to these to an undated intention to settle along Keynes's original tripartite basis – immediate release, funding and cancellation.[79]

Foreseeing trouble in London, Keynes warned that the State Department attached 'first class importance' to Britain's complete renunciation of its transitional rights under Article XIV of the Bretton Woods Agreement.[80]

While London pondered, Keynes wrote several 'atmospheric' letters. To Eady, 21 November:

> As you may have surmised, life here for the past three weeks or longer has been absolute hell; though I doubt if you can have guessed quite how bad it has been.
>
> Everything that we think we have settled with the Top Committee is then transmitted by them inaccurately to experts and lawyers, who have not been present at the discussion. The latter work without consultation with us and produce to their own top lads something which bears not the slightest resemblance to what we have agreed. This is then adopted by the American Top Committee and hurled at us in what looks very like an ultimatum. We then in a series of exasperated meetings have to throw out as much as possible to bring the text, not completely, but as nearly back as we can. This sort of thing does not happen just once but time after time after time.[81]

To Catto, 22 November:

> You must appreciate that the long delays have caused a steady deterioration of the position. After I had made my initial exposition of our case the atmosphere both with the American group and with the Press and Congress was at its best. For more than a fortnight after that we had to mark time waiting for the arrival of the commercial party. And when they arrived we naturally concentrated on their business. You know how quickly things go stale in this country. Then there was another gap of more than a fortnight whilst we were awaiting instructions from the Cabinet. . . . The consequences were that the initial atmosphere was completely lost. . . . All the old wiseacres and bogus elder statesmen are now shaking their heavy locks to our disadvantage. Baruch, Jesse Jones, Crowley and the like are inserting insidious words.[82]

To Richard Kahn, 23 November:

> This has been the most harassing and exhausting negotiation you can imagine. All of us are stale and exhausted and have outstayed our welcome. There is nothing more to be said on either side. So we must find some means in the next five days of hustling to a conclusion, if ever we are to reach one. . . . If I can turn up back home in time for the Annual Congregation [of King's College, Cambridge, 8 December] it will be a great happiness.[83]

To Florence Keynes, 21 November:

> They mean us no harm – but their minds are so small, their prospect
> so restricted, their knowledge so inadequate, their obstinacy so
> boundless and their legal pedantries so infuriating. May it never fall
> to my lot to have to *persuade* anyone to do what I want, with so few
> cards in my hand.
>   As you may suppose I am beginning to use up my physical
> reserves. . . .

Lydia was by now desperately worried by the deterioration in her
husband's health. In public she kept up her amusing front. At an Embassy
dinner on 23 November, she suddenly announced that it was a well-known
scientific fact that there was much more heat in women's bodies than in
men's bodies. Accordingly, the latest scientific invention of the Americans
had been to have an electric blanket for a double bed that was able to
generate a different temperature on each side. But, like Maynard, she was
longing to get back. 'We are still here isn't it awful?' she wrote to Florence
on 25 November. 'Meetings go on and on, officials collapse from sheer
exhaustion on either side. It does seem mad'.
    After his return from Washington, Keynes gave the Ogre a detailed
account of the collapse of his health:

> For the first eight or nine weeks I was extremely well, – provided I
> did not walk anywhere, scarcely conscious of physical
> deficiencies. . . . In the last few weeks, however, when I was conduct-
> ing a war on two fronts and suffering the greatest responsibilities
> and irritations, I began to give way. Every two or three days, when
> there was something particularly annoying or tiring, symptoms would
> appear which made Lydia very cross. Whenever my emotions caused
> a discharge of adrenalin, it was more than the old heart could
> comfortably manage. So, in addition to the ice-bag, I took to
> spending as many hours out of the twenty-four as practicable in a
> horizontal position. What really got me through, however, was the
> marvellous effect of the sodium amytol. . . .[84]

London did not like the American draft at all. Following a tense
Cabinet meeting on 23 November, notable for Herbert Morrison's attack
on the Treasury for not giving Keynes enough elbow room, the Mission
received, this time from the Prime Minister, new instructions. The government would be willing to accept a credit 'of not less than $4bn including
Lend/Lease at 2 per cent, to be repaid over 50 years beginning after 5
years'. In return, it would be willing to 'liberalise' sterling area arrangements, recommend Parliament to accept the Bretton Woods Agreement
and endorse the 'principles of commercial policy' agreed on 6 November.
But it would not – 'repeat not' – agree to complete the negotiations with

creditor countries by the end of 1946, abrogate its transitional rights under Bretton Woods or formally rank the American debt above others. It wanted the Washington and London waivers in their original form, without the reserve criterion; if this was not possible it would substitute an anodyne clause committing the two governments to consult. The Prime Minister was 'dismayed' that 'legal and controversial' conditions should be holding up the agreement.[85] He was, however, dissuaded by Halifax from intervening directly with President Truman to expedite matters.

Keynes was slow to see danger. On receipt of this telegram, he and Halifax handed a version of it to Vinson and Clayton as their formal comment on the US draft of 18 November. Keynes cabled Dalton encouragingly on 25 November:

> Subject to certain comments below we were well satisfied with the line of instructions in the Prime Minister's telegram. . . . Vinson and Clayton were considerably taken aback. Nevertheless they did not react too violently against the change in the general approach for which we were pleading. One lives on a see-saw here and there are several indications recently that we may have reached bottom point. There are quite a few on the American side who . . . are experiencing some revulsion . . . against the legalistic binding provisions which they have been pressing on us lately.

The only thing which disturbed Keynes was the 'relatively small importance London now seems to attach to the waiver'.[86] No alarm bell had yet started to ring at Attlee's refusal to complete negotiations with creditor countries by the end of 1946. The American draft, as we have seen (Point (c) on p. 436) referred only to the release of *currently earned* sterling: no time limit was attached to 'negotiation with creditor countries'. London was apparently conflating the current earnings of the sterling area with their accumulated sterling balances. Keynes probably thought this was simply a mistake. At any rate, in his reworking of the Attlee telegram for presentation to the Americans, he wrote, 'In particular, they [the UK government] cannot accept a time limit for completing the negotiations on the *accumulated sterling balances* . . .'[87] (italics added).

Clayton had now succumbed to influenza, but on Monday 26 November, at meetings friendlier than at any other time, Vinson remarked significantly, or perhaps merely wearily, that whatever was put in the draft, 'they would have to trust the good faith of the British Government just as we would have to trust theirs'. This seemed to open the way to a rout of the lawyers. Keynes asked for authority to exploit the 'last-minute opportunity', drafting a series of compromise clauses covering the gold reserve test, priority of American debt and convertibility which he thought the Americans would accept. On the reserve criterion for a waiver, the British would now offer merely 'to take due account of the . . . adequacy of their available reserves'. The Americans, Keynes thought, were now prepared to abandon the 'ceiling' of $175m. for waiver-year repayments of other liabilities. He attempted to meet American concerns about discriminatory exchange regulations and import controls directed against the USA, without entirely abandoning the transitional rights of Article XIV of the Bretton Woods Agreement.[88]

The result, according to Harmer, was 'swift and disturbing'. London objected 'to our having maintained a fixed date [end of 1946] for the liberalisation of the sterling area. This had been a cardinal point hitherto in our whole proposals, and had been as we understood reaffirmed by the most recent instruction which London now wanted to go back on.' Keynes, Harmer noted, was 'profoundly upset – not only because he thought it quite wrong on merits, but because he was committed, it was an integral part of the whole plan as he saw it, and he did not see how he could retract. Some very troubled days followed. M. at the point of extreme nervous tension and on the verge of physical collapse; Lydia in floods of tears at almost every occasion. . . . Telegrams passed to and fro: M's getting more desperate. . . . London getting more and more curt, and completely uninformative.'

The trouble started with Dalton's BABOON 303 of 26 November, refusing any 'formal and public promise' to make current sterling area earnings convertible into dollars, on the ground that they must be treated as part of the 'general negotiations with each creditor'.[89] A NABOB flew back from the whole Mission at 1.19 a.m. on 27 November (purged of its insulting passages by the ambassador in another late-night drafting session), pointing out that London had completely misunderstood the difference between sterling which would be earned by British exports after the war and the sterling balances or debts which Britain had piled up during the war. Right from the start the British had offered to make the former convertible into dollars at an 'early defined date': it had, in fact, been 'the most attractive offer we were in a position to make'. But the Mission had always 'reserved' Dalton's position on the latter.[90] Dalton now replied disingenuously that he 'did not know of any long-standing undertaking' to release current earnings in advance of negotiations over blocked balances.[91] He may not have read the telegrams from Washington, but his Treasury officials certainly did. Keynes (rightly) saw the hand of Eady in his new discomfiture. 'The trouble about these telegrams', he fumed, 'is that they are all drafted either by Sir Wilfrid Eady or by the Treasury messenger boys except that the Treasury haven't got any messenger boys.'[92] Eady, who could well imagine the verbal lashings he was getting from Keynes in Washington, since he had often been a direct recipient of them in London, assured Keynes that 'we are not trying to sabotage your efforts or being more stupid than nature has made us. To settle such an important document in a hurry by cable is very difficult for both sides, and we must be patient with each other.' Keynes was long past patience: 'We thought we were in sight of home and were, and indeed still are, dismayed at the revival of what must wreck things here when we believed it had been disposed of long ago.'[93]

But it was not just a misunderstanding. The convertibility pledge was never seen by London – nor indeed initially by Keynes – as an absolute promise, rather as one contingent on the size and terms of American assistance. As the amount shrank below the magic $5bn, so did the *quid pro quos* which the government in London felt it was obliged to offer in return. It seems that, at the last minute, Eady – and possibly Dalton – alarmed at the enormity of the British commitment to sterling convertibility on current account, especially in view of the shrinkage in the resources which the Americans were willing to make available, was trying to impose on it the degree of 'vagueness' they had reserved for settlement of the accumulated balances.[94] The events of 1947 would show that they were not wrong to be frightened about honouring the Keynes pledge. But they should not have sprung it on the Mission at the last moment. As for Keynes, an agreement with the Americans had clearly become an end in itself, almost irrespective of the terms. Perhaps it had always been so.

While this drama with London was being played out, Keynes was finally clinching a settlement with Vinson & Co. in Washington. On 26 November Vinson withdrew the reserve criterion for the waiver clause. He accepted that Britain could borrow money for the Lend–Lease clean-up at 2 per cent. Keynes now proposed a final concession: in return for '$4½ billions including Lend–Lease' Britain would give up all its transitional rights under the Bretton Woods Agreement. He wrote to Eady, 'Once granted the inevitable that we have to pay 2 per cent., the rest . . . is not too bad.' To Dalton he pleaded on 27 November: 'A quick OK . . . and we might be home in both senses of the word.'[95]

London refused. The crucial Cabinet discussion took place on Thursday morning 29 November. Both Shinwell and Bevan attacked the terms. The agreed Cabinet draft, sent to Washington at 4.40 p.m., and arriving on the morning of the 29th, Washington time, stuck out for transitional protection and 'vagueness' on the date of convertibility. Furthermore, the government wanted to be able to postpone repayment of principal as well as to waive interest, and refused to accept any linkage between its obligations to the Americans and other creditors.[96]

On receipt, the Mission went into a huddle. NABOB 419, sent at 3.17 a.m. on 30 November, declared its 'unanimous conviction that the course we are told to take must be disastrous'.[97] Attlee and Dalton sent a curt note back to Halifax: 'It is now our firm opinion that you should put [our] text to the Americans as soon as possible with the supporting arguments which we have supplied to you.'[98] Faced with the Mission's mutiny, Dalton decided to send Edward Bridges – together with another

Treasury official, A. T. K. Grant – to Washington immediately to carry out
the Cabinet's instructions. Robbins's terse note for that morning reads:
'Complete slap in face. Arrival Bridges telegram. Meeting Ambassador.
Dramatic moment – Maynard threatens to resign. Lunch Ambassador.'[99]
Bridges arrived at lunchtime on Saturday 1 December and immediately
went into conference with the Mission. Bareau writes:

> Although Bridges handled the situation *vis-à-vis* his colleagues here
> extremely tactful [sic] it very soon became evident from the tone of
> London messages that he was intended to supersede Keynes as the
> effective operational head in the financial negotiations. All the
> telegrams started to come in addressed 'personally' to him. It
> became quite evident from this behaviour ... and remarks of
> AG[rant] that Keynes in effect had lost the confidence of his
> ministers in London some time ago, and that they had all been
> surprised in London not to have had his resignation before now. It
> had certainly not been for want of trying on their part.[100]

What Bridges discovered on that Saturday was that the Mission was
united behind their sick and embattled chief. On Sunday 2 December,
the British and Americans went into all-day discussions at the Joint
Finance Committee. Vinson, realising what had happened, generously
went out of his way to praise Keynes's conduct of the negotiations. By the
end of the day, a number of British officials were near collapse; so was
Clayton, who had got up from his sickbed to be there.

The predictable result, as Robbins put it, was 'exactly as anticipated,
humiliation'.[101] The British submitted their Cabinet draft which the
'Americans plainly did not view ... with any favour'. The Americans
produced their draft, and the British team spent most of the day trying to
modify it as London wanted. They had a few successes. The American
offer of $3.75bn of 'new money', coupled with $650m. for the Lend–
Lease clean-up, made a total of $4.4bn, more than London had been
willing to accept. On the waiver, the Americans rejected the proposal that
the principal might be postponed, but accepted a modification of their
claim to priority. In the new formula, no waiver of interest would be
allowed unless releases or payments of sterling balances were reduced
proportionately and interest on new Commonwealth loans waived as well.
Bridges did not think that the Americans could be budged from this.
There was a small American concession on the timing of the release of
the sterling area's current earnings. Keynes had promised this for December 1946. 'After hard fighting' the British were given till a year after
Congress ratified the Agreement (that is, till mid-1947) to 'complete
arrangements' for 'eliminating the Dollar pool'. On the transitional
protection for the current account granted by the Bretton Woods Agreement, the Americans refused to budge, repeating their argument that the

loan was a substitute for this. The British government had to agree not to apply exchange controls against imports from the United States or to limit the convertibility of sterling earned by the US for current transactions; more generally, all restrictions on current account transactions, with a couple of exceptions, were to be removed not later than a year after Congressional ratification. Bridges's conclusion was that 'there is not much left to argue about', and he asked for discretion to settle 'without further reference back'. In other words, having sniffed out the Washington atmosphere, he was telling London politely to back off. He did so with decisive brevity. When told that a new BABOON had arrived, he said, 'Let them Baboon away. If the buggers give the right answers they will save the timetable.' The conversion of Bridges, noted Bareau, had been complete. 'Not however that of Alec Grant who to the end remained sour and dissatisfied, and convinced that the negotiations had . . . been handled with gross carelessness and laxity on our part.'[102]

London did continue to baboon away on Britain's transitional rights, without effect. The government came close to breaking off the negotiations on this 'clear and limited issue'. Dalton wrote in his diary: 'They [the Americans] would almost certainly, we thought, have to come back to the negotiations in a month or two.'[103] More wishful thinking! There was a bizarre final touch. The British officials assembled at the Willard after dinner on Tuesday 4 December to await a message 'at the very highest level' from the Prime Minister to the President, who was duly informed that a telegram was on its way. When it arrived it turned out to be from Attlee to Bridges, demanding a last stand on transitional protection. Halifax rang up Truman and told him he could go to bed. Keynes proposed that they all go to bed. But Bridges said they had to find Vinson and put to him the formula suggested by London. But where was Vinson? After much telephoning, he was tracked down to a nightclub – at the Willard Hotel itself. He eventually arrived in Brand's room, 'well primed with liquor', but sufficiently sober to reject the British démarche out of hand. He then telephoned Dean Acheson, whose reaction was even more unfavourable. NABOB 463 from Bridges to the Prime Minister went out at 5.41 a.m. the next morning: 'We fear that you must take it that there is no chance of getting the decision reversed and that no appeal to the President would affect this. If we are to reach agreement we believe we must accept the American formula. . . . This telegram has been seen by and has the full agreement of the Ambassador, Brand and Keynes.'[104] At ten o'clock that morning London's capitulation was received. 'They told us to have another go but not to make ourselves a bore by pressing it,' wrote the ambassador. 'So after a chat among ourselves we went off, as Keynes said, "to fire a blank cartridge at Vinson".'

And so it was done. The Anglo-American Financial Agreement was signed by Halifax and Clayton at the State Department on Thursday morning 6 December. (For the text of the Agreement, see Appendix to this chapter.) In the group photograph taken at the signing, Keynes sits on Halifax's right at the glass table, detached and lifeless, no spark of animation lighting up his features. He is desperately tired, but the day has only begun. There is a press conference for British and Commonwealth journalists, then a cocktail party for American commentators and editorial writers. Finally, there is his own dinner party for the whole delegation at the Statler Hotel 'in honour of a job finished by a team'. He nibbles at his food, then is up on his feet with a tongue-in-cheek tribute to Vinson and Clayton, warning the guests never to think of Americans as peculiar kinds of Englishmen. The ambassador is suitably light and amusing. He feels sure that, with Lydia's departure, Washington's retail stores will suffer a trade recession. Brand repeats his familiar tale that working with Keynes always makes him feel the bottom boy in the class. Frank Lee wittily pulls Maynard's leg. Robbins, full of eloquence, talks of an escape from the dark ages. Lydia bubbles with delight at Maynard still being alive.

On Friday 7 December, Keynes called in on President Truman to say goodbye. Then he and Lydia went to New York, saw some banking friends, collected a silver tankard bequeathed by J. P. Morgan to the Bank of England, and caught the *Queen Elizabeth* on 11 December, leaving a Mission ' "lapsed in time and passion" without your inspiration and fire'.[105]

V

KEYNES'S DEFENCE

While Keynes was still at sea, the government whipped both the Loan and Bretton Woods Agreements through the House of Commons with a large majority (343–100), but a lame defence. Twenty-nine Labour MPs voted against; so did seventy Conservatives, mainly imperialists, although they had been told to abstain. Even supporters of the loan thought it was a bad business. The *Economist* summed up the general reaction: 'We are not compelled to say we like it. . . . Our present needs are the direct consequences of the fact that we fought earlier, that we fought longest and that we fought hardest.'[106]

Robbins recalls that, 'grey with anxiety, Keynes sat in his cabin receiving, with growing anger and contempt, the misrepresentations, as they came from the wireless operators, of *his* efforts and *his* loan, and polishing the periods of the defence which he was gathering all his remaining forces to make'.[107] He got back to England on 17 December. With the briefest stopover at Gordon Square, he went straight from Southampton to the Lords, where the peers' debate on Bretton Woods and the loan had started, and sat through five hours of it.

Keynes himself opened the second day's debate. His aim was to dispel the ignorance and mistrust which had enveloped the speeches in both Houses. Even supporters of the loan treated it as a humiliating imposition, and directed their wrath at its source – the United States.

Both political parties [Keynes wrote to Edward Halifax on 1 January 1946] were split on issues which had nothing to do with the technical details; and both sets of party leaders decided that a complete abdication of leadership would be the happiest way out. A section of the Socialists thought they detected too definite a smell of *laissez-faire* in the American conception of international affairs. This is only half true; but the doctrine of non-discrimination does commit us to abjure Schachtian methods, which their Jewish economic advisers (who, like many Jews, are either Nazi or Communist at heart and have no notion of how the British Commonwealth was founded or is sustained) were hankering after. . . .*

A section of the Conservatives, led by Max [Beaverbrook] and supported by others too near Winston, were convinced, with some reason, that the proposed commercial policy . . . taken in conjunction with the opening up of the sterling area, doomed the idea of an Empire economic bloc. . . .

The general public was upset solely because they were being told by those who ought to know, that, after all their past and *present* sufferings, they were being given a raw deal by their old comrades in the US.

At the centre of Keynes's defence of the loan was the assertion that the deals with the Americans, embracing the Loan and Bretton Woods Agreements and Commercial Policy, were interlinked parts of a coherent design, each of which, and the whole together, represented not an assertion of American power but a reasonable compromise between two great nations with the same goal: to restore a liberal world economy. Far from being humiliated, Britain stood to gain substantially. Moreover it had received unique loan terms, in recognition of its unique contribution to the Allied victory. Thus were the desperate wrangles in Washington glossed over and polished for public consumption.

Keynes finessed the issue of unequal bargaining power and clashing national interests. America and Britain were pursuing the same goals by different methods, born from different national characteristics. It was in terms of the 'complex politics of Congress', the 'remoteness' of public opinion, the contractual and commercial basis of American life that

---

* Presumed reference is to Thomas Balogh; possibly Keynes also had in mind Nicholas Kaldor. Lord Balogh subsequently wrote: 'I was against Bretton Woods, I was against the US loan terms, and I said so, and I wrote so' (in A. P. Thirlwall (ed.), *Keynes and International Monetary Relations*, 66).

Keynes explained the characteristic American approach to negotiating with the British. The Americans wanted everything cut and dried, the British preferred things left 'vaguer'; the package of deals represented a 'workable compromise between the certainty they wanted and the measure of elasticity we wanted'. But basically they both wanted the same thing. It turned out that the Americans and the English were two types of Englishmen after all. The British, he admitted, should not have placed so much reliance on extracting help by parading their 'war medals'. 'Our American friends were interested not in our wounds, though incurred in a common cause, but in our convalescence. They wanted . . . to be told that we intended to walk without bandages as soon as possible.' This too had its positive side: the Americans wanted to endow future prospects, not past sacrifices.

As we can see, Keynes was engaged in a delicate balancing act between what Britain had a right to expect and what America could reasonably be expected to give. Only in regard to one particular did his benevolence break down, and a hint of passion break through: 'On the matter of interest, I shall never so long as I live cease to regret that this is not an interest-free loan. The charging of interest is out of tune with the underlying realities. It is based on a false analogy.' It was inconsistent with the unique character of Britain's contribution. But even on the question of interest the Americans had offered substantial mitigations. 'The balm and sweet simplicity of no per cent is not admitted, but we are not asked to pay interest except in conditions where we can reasonably afford to do so, and the capital instalments are so spread that our minimum obligation in the early years is actually less than it would be with a loan free of interest repayable by equal instalments.'

Keynes ran through all the advantages the Grand Design offered Britain. He was not worried about the size of the loan: it was as much as was good for Britain to accept. He emphasised the 'unprecedented liberality' of the Lend–Lease settlement. 'No part of the loan which is applied to this settlement relates to the cost of lend lease supplies consumed during the war, but is entirely devoted to supplies received by us through the lend lease machinery, but available for our consumption or use after the end of the war.' Thus it was not a war debt but in effect a reconstruction loan.

Keynes next rounded on the critics of the loan agreement, starting with those who had denounced the convertibility obligation. His sharpest weapons now came into play. He pointed out that convertibility would not apply to balances accumulated before the spring of 1947. In any case, there was little hope of *voluntary* accumulation of balances after 1947. India and South Africa, which had gold or dollar surpluses, would probably have made 'their own arrangements' anyway, 'leaving us with a dollar pool which is a deficit pool'. Two-thirds of the sterling debts were owed to India, Egypt and Ireland: Britain could not force these countries to buy goods which it could not supply. Keynes then pointed out that the loan could not have been secured without the convertibility condition. 'The very object of . . . half of the loan is to provide us with dollars mainly for the sterling area. We are given not only the condition but the means to satisfy it.' Keynes would have found it beyond his 'forensic powers' to ask the Americans for so many dollars in order to impound the earnings of the sterling area.

Warming to his theme he continued: 'The way to remain an international banker is to allow cheques to be drawn upon you; the way to destroy the sterling area is to prey on it and try to live on it.' He would have preferred 'more than fifteen months to handle the situation', but had the critics grasped the nature of the alternative? 'The alternative is to build up a separate economic bloc which excludes Canada and consists of countries to which we already owe more money than we can pay, on the basis of their agreeing to lend us money they have not got and buy from us . . . goods we are unable to supply.' So much for the Bank of England.

Next, Keynes defended himself against the charge that the 'long-term commercial and currency policy' represented a return to *laissez-faire*. He denied that it prevented state trading and bulk purchasing, or planning for a balanced trade. It was an attempt 'to use what we have learnt from modern experience and analysis, not to defeat, but to implement the wisdom of Adam Smith. . . . We are attempting a great step forward towards the goal of international economic order amidst national diversities of policies. . . . Proposals which the authors hope to see accepted both by the United States and by Soviet Russia must clearly conform to this condition.' But there was another balancing act to perform. Like any human bridge between eras, Keynes found himself in the position of being denounced as a revolutionary by the old while being acccused of betraying the revolution by the young. 'Not so. Fresh tasks now invite. Opinions have been successfully changed. The work of destruction has been accomplished, and the site has been cleared for a new structure.'

Despite his having drafted the London waiver, Keynes was not worried about American willingness to receive British goods. The United States had changed its spots. It no longer had a high-tariff, export-subsidy outlook. American costs were rising relative to those of its competitors. 'These are the historical, classic methods by which in the long run international equilibrium will be restored.'

By this route Keynes approached his peroration:

The separate economic blocs and all the friction and loss of friendship they must bring with them are expedients to which one may be driven in a hostile world. . . . But it is surely crazy to prefer that. Above all, this determination to make trade truly international and to avoid the establishment of economic blocs ... is plainly an essential condition of the world's best hope, an Anglo-American understanding. ... Some of us, in the tasks of war and more lately in those of peace, have learnt by experience that our two countries can work together. Yet it would be only too easy for us to walk apart. I beg those who look askance at these plans to ponder deeply and responsibly where it is they think they want to go.

After five more hours of discussion, the House approved the the financial resolution by 90 votes to 8, about 100 peers abstaining. The Bretton Woods Agreement was approved without a division.[108]

There was much myth-making in Keynes's speech. But against the background of a hostile public opinion and his own extreme exhaustion, Keynes's defence of his handiwork ranks as the most courageous and skilful public speech of his life. He knew the case he wanted to present and he found fit music for his vision. The prose of Washington had – almost – been turned back into poetry. Perhaps it is in the realm of rhetoric that his true greatness lies, using that word in its classic sense of the 'art of persuasion'. 'How much easier', James Meade lamented, 'affairs of state would be if rational men having agreed on a rational course of action were then permitted to give a rational account of it!'[109] Keynes sometimes talked in this way, but his sense and use of language – the words and phrases which came into his mind naturally, because of the kind of person he was and the culture which he breathed – demanded and commanded assent at some different level. He continued his letter to Edward Halifax:

My strong belief is (though you may all be justified, as usual, in saying I am too optimistic) that the line I took in my speech met with an immediate response from genuine public opinion ... and a lot of people quickly became rather ashamed of the way they had been talking. This was certainly so in the House of Lords. ... Mingling in the division lobby and as the House broke up, it seemed to me clear that practically everyone was voting Aye out of conviction, and not merely to avoid a constitutional crisis.

. . .

Cranborne, by the way, made a most masterly speech. A pure Cecilian utterance. ... He helped to give Max, who was sitting next to him on the front bench, one of the most humiliating days of his life. ... Cranborne, in my opinion, is worth ten times Anthony [Eden]. The combination of his diffidence and unimpressive appearance with some inherent quality of dignity and authority ... produces a remarkable effect. Old Lord Salisbury, as beautiful and pure a picture as ever, was there to hear him. However, I am prejudiced. I have never in my life been able to resist a Cecil.

. . .

> For me, I think the time has come . . . to slip out of the Treasury, if not suddenly, at least steadily. . . . Being of a resigning tempera- ment, I shall not last long in this galere in any case; so I had better go when I go quietly and friendly.[110]

The magic of Keynes's words is still potent more than half a century later, yet we also have the knowledge of distance to ask the question: was his vision fit to the circumstances? Or was it 'demented counsel abroad'?

Much of this chapter has necessarily been concerned with Keynes's negotiating style. On this, his penultimate mission to the United States, he was engaged in two sets of negotiations – with Americans in Washing- ton and British in London. How are we to judge his performance? On the Washington side, his crucial failure was to get on terms with Vinson. The Kentucky lawyer and the waspish Bloomsbury intellectual were like chalk and cheese. Keynes's old Washington network was broken, and he was too tired and ill to build a new one. He was not the ideal negotiator for the long grind which developed in Washington. Bareau's summary stands for many: 'He was too brilliant, too crushing and, towards the end, too exhausted.'

But none of this is to say that he failed as a negotiator. Although he succumbed to moods of despair, he was extremely resilient and – as the ambassador rightly discerned – both tenacious and fertile. He had the quality of waking up every morning full of fight. No other British representative in Washington in the autumn of 1945 had the technical competence and confidence to handle a complex financial negotiation. Vinson and Clayton were no match for Keynes in argument. But they always held the whip-hand. It was a case of brains pitted against power. No doubt Keynes frequently bewildered them. But many of the technical complications which developed in November – and particularly the fre- quent backsliding of the two top Americans – were not his fault, but a consequence of their ignorance, and saying things which their 'tech- nicians' – off stage in the informal sessions – then made them withdraw.

It is also misleading to see Keynes in isolation from the rest of the Mission. Halifax, Brand, Robbins and Liesching all played key roles in moving things along – on some occasions when Keynes might have broken down under the strain. The most warming revelation of the Washington negotiations is the support which these men and their juniors gave Keynes. They respected, admired and in some cases loved him for his genius, his wit, his resilience, his buoyancy, his gaiety of spirit and his sheer persistence, and became increasingly protective of him as his health declined.

Keynes was less successful with London. He himself must be held mainly responsible for the overestimation of what was possible, and Whitehall's corollary reliance on his 'magic' to achieve unrealisable goals. Contemporary opinion is unanimous that Keynes hypnotised Whitehall into believing what, of course, it wanted to believe – that it could get the best of all possible worlds. It is not enough to point to qualifications and doubts in his pre-Washington advice; to say that he did not hide from ministers the probability of having to slide down the slippery slope of Temptation. The hypnotism lay not in the arguments, but in the choice of language. The phrase 'sweet breath of Justice' set the standard by which the outcome of the negotiation would be judged, and 'Starvation Corner', 'financial Dunkirk', the penalties of failure. All the decisions were taken within the emotional framework Keynes established.

Having bamboozled Whitehall before he left, he had to de-bamboozle it when he got to Washington. But his arts of communication were not attuned to the medium of the telegram. He needed room to develop spacious, subtle arguments, when what harassed ministers required were terse statements of pros and cons, with clear-cut recommendations. These Bridges was able to provide in the last week of the negotiation. Keynes was right to want him over earlier, though his eventual arrival was humiliating. Douglas Jay, Attlee's personal assistant, recalls endless late-evening meetings of the Ministerial Group, in which 'shoals of telegrams passed to and fro daily. . . . On one occasion quoting from one of them, Dalton said peremptorily to Bevin: "Foreign Secretary, have you got the telegram?" "I've got 'undreds," replied Bevin, and Bridges trotted round the table to reshuffle the cards for him.'[111] Not till 17 October did Keynes clearly state that only a loan of 2 per cent was available, and even then held out hopes that better might be forthcoming. Almost nowhere in the long series of NABOBs and other messages did Keynes flatly say that this or that was all that was on offer. Ministers were thus left in a continuous state of surprise, which eventually turned to loss of confidence in Keynes's negotiating skills. In the final stages they deprived him of virtually all negotiating discretion.

But the problems were not just of Keynes's making. The death of Sir Frederick Phillips and the illness, and then semi-retirement, of Sir Richard Hopkins had seriously undermined his position at the Treasury. The new triumvirate of Eady, Clarke and Grant at Overseas Finance never approved of the loan, and would not have been sorry to see the negotiations fail. Although Dalton wrote Keynes a gracious note after the Cabinet's last concession – 'My dear Maynard, Thank you from the bottom of my heart for all you have accomplished in this long, hard fight – against great odds. . . . You have got us the dollars . . .' – he did not really trust Keynes, and had a different agenda. What also coloured Dalton's attitude was an antipathy to Halifax – the man of Munich – a leftover from Churchill's machinations, and, like Keynes, with no place in the new 'galere'.

Had Churchill and Roosevelt still been in power, or even Churchill alone, it is possible that Britain might have got at least an interest-free loan, with fewer strings. Vinson and Clayton repeatedly pointed out that domestic politics would not allow it. It must never be forgotten that Keynes negotiated in the autumn of 1945 with people who were highly suspicious of giving money to a socialist government, with a Congress behind them which was even more suspicious. A Churchill in power would not only have made this irrelevant, but would have been able – and probably willing – to play the Soviet card. Whether this would have worked in the autumn of 1945 is doubtful. The Soviet decision not to ratify the Bretton Woods Agreement, which Harold James has called the real start of the Cold War, came on 29 December 1945. George Kennan's famous long telegram, sent from Moscow on 22 February 1946, was the first major analysis which identified the Soviet Union as an enemy of the United States.[112] But these developments came too late to influence the outcome of the Keynes Mission.

All of this raises the question of whether Keynes had set out the alternatives rightly in his memorandum of 18 March 1945. The Austerity option, with its unpleasant combination of stinting and Schachtianism, left out two choices which Britain had involving neither starvation nor anti-Americanism.

The first was devaluation. Britain was driven to this in 1949. But it was not unthinkable in 1945. As we have seen, expectation of a British devaluation was one reason Harry White gave to the Senate Banking Committee in the summer of 1945 for denying that Britain would need extensive transitional assistance. Keynes had a long-standing objection to this line of thought. He feared that currency depreciation would drive Britain further from equilibrium by producing a fall in export prices larger than an increase in export volume. To this was added a pessimistic appraisal of the speed of reconversion. Both strands were present in Keynes's reply to a question at his Washington press conference on 12 September 1945:

There are certain conditions in which it [devaluation] certainly helps a country. The right level [of the exchange rate] depends on the real wages in the respective countries, and if wages are on a real competitive basis, as I believe ours are, I think countries can very easily make their positions worse, and not better, by altering their exchange. You see, it simply means paying more for your imports and [receiving] less for your exports. Now, if you are in great difficulty about markets, you may be driven to that. That is not our position today. . . . We can sell anything we can produce. Our problem is to reconvert our industry quick enough . . . to have the exports, and in those circumstances you can't imagine anything more foolish than to be trying to sell those exports at quite unnecessarily low prices.

Thus in 1945 Keynes thought that Britain was competitive on price, and that the export problem was due to lack of supply. Meade of the Economic Section pooh-poohed this argument when Keynes produced it at the National Debt Enquiry earlier that year, pointing out that 'as we produced manufactured goods in competition with many other exporting countries and in competition with the home industries of many of our customers it seemed to me highly improbable that a decline in our export prices relatively to others would not cause a very substantial expansion of our exports'. Meade might have added that the main impact of a decline in sterling would have been to increase the *profitability* of exporting, thus producing a supply response. But Keynes would not be budged.[113]

The second omitted choice was simply to wait till the post-war position had become clearer, borrowing short-term to cover necessary imports. Keynes was right to believe that a breakdown in negotiations for the loan after they had started would have been very damaging to Anglo-American relations. But this would not have been the case had they never been started – or at least on such a grand scale. It is hard not to agree with Clarke's (retrospective) judgement on the whole affair:

> The simplest plan . . . for which [sic] nobody could have persuaded Keynes . . . was to abandon the concept of a 'Grand Design' negotiation in autumn 1945. . . . We could easily have said 'We are willing to sign the Bretton Woods Agreement and participate in the International Commercial Policy conference; but we are not willing to accept any prior commitments at all until we see how the new world develops: we would be willing to negotiate in 1947.' We would have borrowed, say $1,000 millions . . . and would have undertaken to accept a loan for the residue of Lend–Lease at the rate of any ultimate major loan. After the abrupt end of the war and the cessation of Lend–Lease, the Americans could not have refused or tried to impose strings. In fact events by 1947 showed that the multilateral theologians' concepts of the course of events had been utterly wrong, and that the doctrines of the 1945 negotiations had fallen into the background of US policy, and that the combination of the Communist threat to Europe together with the world dollar shortage had persuaded the Americans to grant millions of dollars in pursuit of European discrimination against the USA! So the idea of postponing the 'Grand Design' negotiation, and borrowing relatively small amounts, if necessarily expensively, would have been well justified by events.[114]

This is not just hindsight: Brand, Bevin, Eady, the Bank of England suggested it at the time, though often in passing. Had Keynes advocated it, there wouldn't have been much opposition. In retrospect, one can see why it was ruled out. It was a combination of Keynes's eagerness to launch his internationalist ship before he died and Labour's 'New Jerusalem' hopes which conspired to get an unworkable agreement. Hopes triumphed over reality.

Financial Agreement between His Majesty's Government in the United Kingdom and the Government of the United States

Washington, 6th December, 1945

It is hereby agreed between the Government of the United States of America and the Government of the United Kingdom of Great Britain and Northern Ireland as follows:

1. *Effective Date of the Agreement*

The effective date of this Agreement shall be the date on which the Government of the United States notifies the Government of the United Kingdom that the Congress of the United States has made available the funds necessary to extend to the Government of the United Kingdom the line of credit in accordance with the provisions of this Agreement.[1]

2. *Line of Credit*

The Government of the United States will extend to the Government of the United Kingdom a line of credit of $3,750,000,000 which may be drawn upon at any time between the effective date of this Agreement and 31st December, 1951, inclusive.

3. *Purpose of the Line of Credit*

The purpose of the line of credit is to facilitate purchases by the United Kingdom of goods and services in the United States, to assist the United Kingdom to meet transitional post-war deficits in its current balance of payments, to help the United Kingdom to maintain adequate reserves of gold and dollars and to assist the Government of the United Kingdom to assume the obligations of multilateral trade, as defined in this and other agreements.

[1] Effective date, 15th July, 1946.

4. Amortisation and Interest

(i) The amount of the line of credit drawn by 31st December, 1951, shall be repaid in 50 annual instalments beginning on 31st December, 1951, with interest at the rate of 2 per cent per annum.

Interest for the year 1951 shall be computed on the amount outstanding on 31st December, 1951, and for each year thereafter interest shall be computed on the amount outstanding on 1st January of each such year.

49 annual instalments of principal repayments and interest shall be equal, calculated at the rate of $31,823,000 for each $1,000,000,000 of the line of credit drawn by 31st December, 1951, and the fiftieth annual instalment shall be at the rate of $31,840,736.65 for each such $1,000,000,000.

Each instalment shall consist of the full amount of the interest due and the remainder of the instalment shall be the principal to be repaid in that year. Payments required by this section are subject to the provisions of Section 5.

(ii) The Government of the United Kingdom may accelerate repayment of the amount drawn under this line of credit.

5. Waiver of Interest Payments

In any year in which the Government of the United Kingdom requests the Government of the United States to waive the amount of the interest due in the instalment of that year, the Government of the United States will grant the waiver if:

(a) the Government of the United Kingdom finds that a waiver is necessary in view of the present and prospective conditions of international exchange and the level of its gold and foreign exchange reserves, *and*

(b) the International Monetary Fund certifies that the income of the United Kingdom from home-produced exports plus its net income from invisible current transactions in its balance of payments was on the average over the five preceding calendar years less than the average annual amount of United Kingdom imports during 1938–38 fixed at £866,000,000, as such figure may be adjusted for changes in the price level of these imports. Any amount in excess of £43,750,000 released or paid in any year on account of sterling balances accumulated to the credit of overseas governments, monetary authorities and banks before the effective date of this Agreement shall be regarded as a capital transaction and therefore shall not be included in the above calculation of the net income from invisible current transactions for that year. If waiver is requested for an interest payment prior to that due in 1955, the average income shall be computed for the calendar years from 1950 through the year preceding that in which the request is made.

6. *Relation of This Line of Credit to Other Obligations*

(i) It is understood that any amounts required to discharge obligations of the United Kingdom to third countries outstanding on the effective date of this Agreement will be found from resources other than this line of credit.

(ii) The Government of the United Kingdom will not arrange any long-term loans from Governments within the British Commonwealth after 6th December, 1945, and before the end of 1951 on terms more favourable to the lender than the terms of this line of credit.

(iii) Waiver of interest will not be requested or allowed under Section 5 in any year unless the aggregate of the releases or payments in that year of sterling balances accumulated to the credit of overseas Governments, monetary authorities and banks (except in the case of colonial dependencies) before the effective date of this Agreement, is reduced proportionately, and unless interest payments due in that year on loans referred to in (ii) above are waived. The proportionate reduction of the releases or payments of sterling balances shall be calculated in relation to the aggregate released and paid in the most recent year in which waiver of interest was not requested.

(iv) The application of the principles set forth in this section shall be the subject of full consultation between the two Governments as occasion may arise.

7. *Sterling Area Exchange Arrangements*

The Government of the United Kingdom will complete arrangements as early as practicable and in any case not later than one year after the effective date of this Agreement, unless in exceptional cases a later date is agreed upon after consultation, under which immediately after the completion of such arrangements the sterling receipts from current transactions of all sterling area countries (apart from any receipts arising out of military expenditure by the Government of the United Kingdom prior to 31st December, 1948, to the extent to which they are treated by agreement with the countries concerned on the same basis as the balances accumulated during the war) will be freely available for current transactions in any currency area without discrimination with the result that any discrimination arising from the so-called sterling area dollar pool will be entirely removed and that each member of the sterling area will have its current sterling and dollar receipts at its free disposition for current transactions anywhere.

8. *Other Exchange Arrangements*

(i) The Government of the United Kingdom agrees that after the effective date of this Agreement it will not apply exchange controls in such a manner as to restrict:

(*a*) payments or transfers in respect of products of the United States permitted to be imported into the United Kingdom or other current transactions between the two countries; or

(*b*) the use of sterling balances to the credit of residents of the United States arising out of current transactions.

Nothing in this paragraph (i) shall affect the provisions of Article VII of the Articles of Agreement of the International Monetary Fund when those Articles have come into force.

(ii) The Governments of the United States and the United Kingdom agree that not later than one year after the effective date of this Agreement, unless in exceptional cases a later date is agreed upon after consultation, they will impose no restrictions on payments and transfers for current transactions. The obligations of this paragraph (ii) shall not apply:

(*a*) to balances of third countries and their nationals accumulated before this paragraph (ii) becomes effective; or

(*b*) to restrictions imposed in conformity with the Articles of Agreement of the International Monetary Fund, provided that the Governments of the United Kingdom and the United States will not continue to invoke the provisions of Article XIV, Secton 2, of those Articles after this paragraph (ii) becomes effective unless in exceptional cases after consultation they agree otherwise; or

(*c*) to restrictions imposed in connection with measures designed to uncover and dispose of assets of Germany and Japan.

(iii) This Section and Section 9 which are in anticipation of more comprehensive arrangements by multilateral agreement shall operate until 31st December, 1951.

9. *Import Arrangements*

If either the Government of the United States or the Government of the United Kingdom imposes or maintains quantitative import restrictions, such restrictions shall be administered on a basis which does not discriminate against imports from the other country in respect of any product; provided that this undertaking shall not apply in cases in which:

(*a*) its application would have the effect of preventing the country imposing such restrictions from utilising, for the purchase of needed imports, inconvertible currencies accumulated up to 31st December, 1946; or (*b*) there may be special necessity for the country imposing such restrictions to assist, by measures not involving a substantial departure from the general rule of non-discrimination, a country whose economy has been disrupted by war; or

(*c*) either Government imposes quantitative restrictions having equivalent effect to any exchange restrictions which that Government is authorised to impose in conformity with Article VII of the Articles of Agreement of the International Monetary Fund.

The provisions of this Section shall become effective as soon as practicable, but not later than 31st December, 1946.

10. *Accumulated Sterling Balances*

(i) The Government of the United Kingdom intends to make agreements with the countries concerned, varying according to the circumstances of each case, for an early settlement covering the sterling balances accumulated by sterling area and other countries prior to such settlement (together with any future receipts arising out of military expenditure by the Government of the United Kingdom to the extent to which they are treated on the same basis by agreement with the countries concerned). The settlements with the sterling area countries will be on the basis of dividing these accumulated balances into three categories:

(*a*) balances to be released at once and convertible into any currency for current transactions;

(*b*) balances to be similarly released by instalments over a period of years beginning in 1951; and

(*c*) balances to be adjusted as a contribution to the settlement of war and post-war indebtedness and in recognition of the benefits which the countries might be expected to gain from such a settlement.

The Government of the United Kingdom will make every endeavour to secure the early completion of these arrangements.

(ii) In consideration of the fact that an important purpose of the present line of credit is to promote the development of multilateral trade and facilitate its early resumption on a non-discriminatory basis, the Government of the United Kingdom agrees that any sterling balances released or otherwise available for current payments will, not later than one year after the effective date of this Agreement, unless in special cases a later date is agreed upon after consultation, be freely available for current transactions in any currency area without discrimination.

11. *Definitions*

For the purposes of this Agreement:
(i) The term 'current transactions' shall have the meaning prescribed

in Article XIX (*i*) of the Articles of Agreement of the International Monetary Fund.

(ii) The term 'sterling area' means the United Kingdom and the other territories declared by the Defence (Finance) (Definition of Sterling Area) (No. 2) Order, 1944, to be included in the sterling area, namely, 'the following Territories, excluding Canada and Newfoundland, that is to say:

(*a*) any Dominion,

(*b*) any other part of His Majesty's dominions,

(*c*) any territory in respect of which a mandate on behalf of the League of Nations has been accepted by His Majesty and is being exercised by His Majesty's Government in the United Kingdom, or in any Dominion,

(*d*) any British Protectorate or Protected State,

(*e*) Egypt, the Anglo-Egyptian Sudan and Iraq,

(*f*) Iceland and the Faroe Islands.'

12. *Consultation on Agreement*

Either Government shall be entitled to approach the other for a reconsideration of any of the provisions of this Agreement, if in its opinion the prevailing conditions of international exchange justify such reconsideration with a view to agreeing upon modifications for presentation to their respective Legislatures.

Signed in duplicate at Washington, District of Columbia, this 6th day of December, 1945.

For the Government of the United States of America:
FRED M. VINSON,
Secretary of the Treasury of the United States of America.

For the Government of the United Kingdom of Great Britain and Northern Ireland:
HALIFAX,
His Majesty's Ambassador Extraordinary and Plenipotentiary at Washington.

CHAPTER THIRTEEN

'The Light is Gone'

When he got back from America Keynes was half dead with fatigue. At a dinner given by Dalton for the loan delegation at the Savoy, he had been 'forced to lie on a sofa and rest throughout most of the evening'.[1] For the last time his amazing powers of recuperation saved him. By the time Leonard Woolf came for his usual Christmas dinner at Tilton, he had already started to feel better, though Lydia was exhausted. They talked about Virginia: Keynes suggested to Leonard that he read excerpts from her diaries at the next meeting of the Memoir Club, which he duly did at 46 Gordon Square in February. On Boxing Day, Lydia distributed her 'Washington booty on a lavish scale' at a party for the farm labourers and their families, with 'the usual sketches and songs and beer and refreshments, with the children of the hamlet exceptionally attractive and well-behaved. The Charlestonians joined us. We feel that we have our own little rural civilisation down here.'[2] Charleston's contribution to civilisation was a skit on the popular radio programme *The Brains Trust*, with Duncan Grant taking the part of a bishop. On 28 December, Maynard's nephews, Richard and Stephen Keynes and Maurice Hill, came for the shoot. Maynard 'very much enjoyed having the boys' and Stephen shot his first pheasant.

On 1 January 1946 Mrs Stephens arrived 'and work begins again'. But it was work he enjoyed – 'free from worry'. Much of it had to do with plans for the reopening of the Royal Opera House. There was a minute to Dennis Proctor of the Treasury warning against inflationary wage settlements.[3] He also resumed work on a paper 'Will the Dollar Be Scarce?' which he had sketched out with Freddie Harmer of the Treasury and David McCurrach of the Bank of England during a lull in the Washington loan negotiations. By 5 January, a couple of days before his return to London and Treasury work, the 'perfect weather' had made him feel 'wonderfully well' again. An American Treasury official who saw him in his Treasury room on 18 January found him looking 'remarkably well and rested'.

The Canadian economist the late Harry Johnson, a Jesus College, Cambridge undergraduate in 1945–6, remembered Keynes reading a version of his 'Will the Dollar Be Scarce?' paper at the Political Economy

Club on 2 February 1946. This club, which Keynes had founded in 1909 for invited economics faculty and bright students, had been taken over by Dennis Robertson, and now met on Thursday evenings in his chilly drawing room at Trinity College. Johnson remembers Keynes in an armchair by a fire which glowed but gave out little heat, with his legs 'slumped out in front of him'. Barely glancing at the notes beside him, he gave a 'a very elegant talk, beautifully constructed, every sentence a piece of good English prose and every paragraph cadenced – just a wonderful performance'. Its theme was rather 'anti-Keynesian', his negative answer to the question he asked depending very heavily on the 'long-run classical mechanism, basically the influence of balance-of-payments surpluses on money, wages, and so forth'. In a phrase which his radical followers hated – and which, according to some, suggested malign neo-classical influences – he said:

> I find myself moved, not for the first time, to remind contemporary economists that the classical teaching embodied some permanent truths of great significance, which we are liable to-day to overlook because we associate them with other doctrines which we cannot now accept without much qualification. There are in these matters deep undercurrents at work, natural forces, one may call them, even the invisible hand, which are operating towards equilibrium.[4]

After his talk Johnson went through the same experience recorded by Michael Straight in 1937.[5] Called on to comment on Keynes's paper, he stumbled through a 'rather lame' argument, to the effect that given the availability of lots of farm labour it would take some time before the pressure of demand for industrial products forced up American wages.

> [Keynes] was very kind, and he picked up the point and made something of it. And I noticed that this is what he did. One of the secrets of his charm was that he would go out of his way to make something flattering out of what a student had said. If the student had made an absolute ass of himself, Keynes would still find something in it which he would transform into a good point. It might well be the very opposite of what the student had said; but the student was so relieved to find that he was not being cut to pieces that he was really impressed by the brilliance of what he was told he *had* said. On the other hand, when a faculty member got up . . . and at that time Joan Robinson stood up and attempted to argue with him . . . he simply cut their heads off. . . . And that, again, flattered the students, because they had been told that they were really incisive and then someone they knew was really clever was reduced to rubble before their eyes. . . . I think this has something to do with the various well-known reactions to Keynes as a personality. When

he was out of the public eye, he could . . . make somebody glad to be alive. On the other hand, when the chips were really down, he could be quite ruthless in the way he dealt with people.

Afterwards Johnson told Dennis Robertson how much he had enjoyed the paper. Robertson replied 'Ah, but you missed something that used to be there – the impishness of his mind.'[6]

Dadie Rylands hoped that in 1946 Keynes would not be entirely sacrificed to the welfare of his country and would find time to 'turn over the leaves of Jacobean play-books with a decanter of claret by your side'.[7] It was certainly Keynes's intention to cut down his Treasury work, both for health reasons and because he was out of sympathy with the new regime. He did not click with Dalton; he mistrusted Labour's *dirigiste* tendencies. Socially, he got on much better with left-leaning Conservatives than with right-leaning socialists. But set against his inclination to resign was the continuing opportunity to 'avert evils', which 'is as much as one can plausibly hope for in this world'.[8] The financial problems of peace, while not so dire, seemed no less urgent than those Keynes had confronted in the war. Also, like all those who have had a commanding influence on affairs, Keynes felt that the work he had started would be ill done if he were not there to continue it.

Above all, there was the task of making a success of the loan. He had no doubt that it could be done. The great obstacle, he told Lippmann, was 'the inner reluctance [in England] to accept a situation so utterly reversed from what she is used to and to find herself asking for financial aid instead of giving it'.[9] Making the loan work meant cutting out extravagance at home and abroad, and settling the sterling balances problem. Although, as a member of the Budget Committee, Keynes took part, as usual, in the pre-Budget discussions, most of his Whitehall time was taken up with loan-related matters.

To Brand he wrote on 29 January: 'The mixed chauvinism and universal benevolence of the FO and other departments and the weakness of the Chancellor in these matters are slopping away on everything and everybody in the world except the poor Englishman the fruits of our American loan.'[10] A 'hair-raising' paper[11] on Britain's overseas financial commitments was rushed to the Cabinet in February. Britain, Keynes warned, stood ready to squander the loan 'to cut a dash in the world'. Echoing the memoranda he wrote in the First World War, he minuted: 'Our resources are strictly limited. Any one of them is, therefore, *alternative* and not *additional* to some other use.'[12] The cost of keeping an army of Poles in Italy should be weighed against the cost of the bacon ration. Britain should cease all political loans. It should drastically reduce its overseas military forces in Greece, Egypt and elsewhere: 'We simply cannot afford to make our plans on the basis of being half and half-heartedly

ready for war with Russia.... We are spending twice too much for
solvency, and twice (or four times) too little for safety. . . .' The policy, by
which Britain would be left alone responsible for feeding a de-industrialised
and bankrupt Germany, was 'the craziest ever – if one did not remember
last time'. And so on.[13]

A couple of powerful papers on 'Sterling Area Negotiations' showed
that his fertility had not deserted him. Cancellation of part of the
accumulated sterling balances might be achieved without mentioning the
'ill-sounding' word itself, through the operation of 'compound discount-
ing'.[14] At a 12 February meeting at the Treasury, Keynes claimed that with
their overvalued exchange rates India, Egypt and some colonies would be
a 'sink for imports and would be able to export little or nothing', thus
causing a drain of their balances from London. He wanted to bring these
countries 'brutally up against the need for them either to devalue or to
restrict imports by simply blocking a large part of their balances . . .'.[15]
These were tough words, but in the end even Keynes's resolve failed
before the complexity of the problem.

Keynes was also preparing for the inaugural meeting of the International Monetary Fund and World Bank. His appointment as British
governor of both institutions was announced on 19 February. After some
negotiations, the meeting was fixed early in March at Savannah, in
Georgia. 'I remain dreadfully in two minds about going,' Keynes wrote to
Bridges on 12 February. But he longed to be in at the birth, there were
still issues to settle about the location of the Fund and the Bank and the
role of the executive directors, and Plesch and Lydia thought a holiday in
warm weather, without too much work, would be good for him. What
turned the decision in favour may well have been his love of sea travel. 'It
is in fact a holiday jaunt,' he told Sheppard.[16]

Keynes's good health did not last. Covent Garden was due to reopen
on 20 February with a gala performance of *The Sleeping Beauty*. It would be
danced by Sadler's Wells Ballet, with new sets by Oliver Messel, conducted
by Constant Lambert, and with Margot Fonteyn as Aurora – one of the
parts Lydia had danced when Keynes was courting her during the run of
Diaghilev's magnificent but ill-fated production at the Alhambra in 1921
– and Robert Helpmann doubling as Prince Florimund and the evil fairy
Carabosse. As chairman of the Covent Garden Trustees it would be
Keynes's duty to greet the King and Queen, and lead them to the Royal
Box. He was thrilled to have engineered the reopening. 'It is a rather
symbolic occasion,' he wrote to Lippmann on 29 January. 'We shall be
over a limited field declaring peace, so to speak, by restoring again this
fragment of civilisation.' There was much work to be done to transform
the wartime dance hall to its former grandeur. 'The Opera House', wrote
Margot Fonteyn, 'had been dormant as a theatre for so long that it might
have been Sleeping Beauty's palace in need of cleaning up and refurbish-

ing. . . .'[17] The wooden floors were taken up, the bandstands removed, the red seats brought out of store, and the whole theatre repainted. In the two or three weeks before the gala performance Keynes visited Covent Garden several times. 'I just thought I would come and find out if there was anything I could do,' he told David Webster. Webster recalled that 'his knowledge of theatrical affairs was vast, and he met one half-way by knowing before one had made a point exactly what one was about to say'. A particular pleasure was arranging for his ninety-four-year-old father to attend a matinée performance in the directors' box later in the month.

Keynes told his mother that the opening night went off 'in great glory'. The Royal Family and Cabinet attended. Unluckily, Keynes had had 'a rather severe day at the Treasury, and the weather was cold, so that I was rather shaky by the evening and could not perform all my duties'. This was an understatement. He rushed to the theatre after a difficult three-hour pre-budget meeting with Dalton, and a few minutes before the royal party arrived he had a small heart attack. Lydia received King George VI, Queen Elizabeth and the other royals on his behalf. He forced himself to entertain a party of people in the first interval and to make presentations to the King and Queen in the second. The Queen Mother, well briefed or with a prodigious memory, told Keynes she had remembered with great pleasure meeting his mother, Florence Keynes, at Papworth some years previously. Keynes received many letters afterwards saying how emotionally the occasion had struck them. 'The explanation, I think, is that many people had come to fear in their hearts . . . that all the grace and elegant things from the old world had passed permanently away, and it caused an extraordinary feeling of uplift when it was suddenly appreciated that perhaps they had not entirely vanished.'[18]

Once again there was that miraculous power of recovery. The next day he felt perfectly all right, and Plesch renewed his permission to travel. On 24 February Maynard and Lydia sailed to America for the last time on the *Queen Mary*, accompanied by Rowe-Dutton from the Treasury and Roy Bridge and Cameron Cobbold from the Bank of England. They arrived in New York on 1 March. Despite a rough crossing he had not missed a single meal. Their week in New York was crowded with ballet activities, as well as Keynes's discussions with officials of the Federal Reserve Bank. He and Lydia concocted a letter of ballet gossip to Ninette de Valois, who ran the Sadler's Wells Ballet Company. They had had tea with Balanchine and Danilova, whose Ballet Russe de Monte Carlo 'was the only serious artistic enterprise in the country'. Balanchine's *Ballet Imperial*, set to the music of Tchaikovsky's 2nd piano concerto, 'quite took our breath away . . . rich, intricate and fertile beyond imagination. Lydia thought you and Fred [Ashton] would have been madly excited by it. . . . I am sure that we ought to aim at them [for Covent Garden] sometime next year.' Practical as ever, Keynes noticed the ballet's shabby scenery, which he attributed to the gigantic cost of building sets in the United States. Covent Garden could build them new sets which would count as part of their remuneration. This would equip them for a season at the Met.[19]

By 5 March they were back at the Statler Hotel in Washington. Keynes saw both Morgenthau and his successor, Vinson. He told Morgenthau that Bevin was 'a great guy', but answered with his usual brusqueness when Morgenthau asked him what Britain would do if America imposed economic sanctions on 'fascist' Argentina: 'Nothing. We just can't be bothered with that sort of thing. We are too dependent on the Argentine for beef.' He told Morgenthau that Winston Churchill was in Washington to head off Bernard Baruch's opposition to the Anglo-American loan.[20] Churchill did better than that. Three days before the Savannah conference opened he made his famous speech at Fulton, Missouri, Truman's home state, warning of the 'iron curtain' which had descended across Europe, and linking it to centrally directed communist expansionism working through fifth columnists. One of those agents, Harry Dexter White, noted that the future of the world would depend much more on friendly relations between the USA and the Soviet Union than between the USA and Britain.[21]

Keynes's meeting with 'Judge' Vinson suggested that Savannah would not be quite the holiday he was expecting. He was told bluntly that the Fund and Bank would both be located in Washington, rather than New York as the British wanted. This decision was to keep them free from the taint of 'international finance'. Keynes, by his own account, reacted 'very vehemently'. They also talked about Harry Dexter White. White had been approved by the Senate as executive director of the Fund, and Keynes hoped he would be made its managing director. But Vinson told him the latter idea had been dropped. The Americans wanted an American as head of the Bank, and therefore a European would have to head the Fund.[22] Keynes did not know that White's nomination as managing director had been dropped as a result of an FBI report on him received by Truman on 4 February. The administration decided that the best way to ease White, who was under FBI surveillance, out of the Treasury without alerting the Soviets to the fact that he had been rumbled was to allow him to take up the low-security-risk job of Fund executive director. Savannah was the last time he and Keynes met, and clashed, on the international stage.

In Savannah, 750 miles south of New York, Maynard and Lydia stayed at the General Oglethorpe Hotel on Wilmington Island, where the meetings were held. The usual huge collection of bodies had assembled – nominated governors, their alternates, observers, secretaries and reporters. Keynes fell in love with this gracious nineteenth-century city on to which had been superimposed a busy twentieth-century port. On arrival he issued a press statement in which he called Savannah 'a beautiful woman . . . whose face was concealed behind a veil of delicate lace'. To Halifax he wrote of the American South, 'It is quite a different nation here, and in many ways a preferable one.'[23]

Unfortunately the cast of American negotiators assembled at Savannah, headed by Vinson and Clayton, was the same Keynes had recently encountered in Washington. At the inaugural meeting of governors on Saturday 9 March, 'Vinson', wrote Bareau, 'made a long and turgid speech full of emotional and fundamentally insincere expressions of hope. He was followed very much in the same strain by the Chinese, Czechoslovakian, French and the Mexicans. A breath of fresh air was introduced into the proceedings by Keynes' speech with its fairy tale metaphors. . . .'[24] In Keynes's mind, and language, the birth of the twins 'Master Fund and Miss Bank' – whose names, he wished, had been reversed – fused with the great first-act christening party in *The Sleeping Beauty* which he had just seen danced, when the fairy godmothers showered their gifts on the newly born Princess Aurora. The gifts bestowed by Keynes's godmothers were to be Universalism, Courage and Wisdom. Having playfully embroidered this theme, Keynes expressed the hope that there was 'no malicious fairy, no Carabosse' whom the organisers had forgotten to ask to the financial christening. 'For if so', he went on, 'the curses which that bad fairy will pronounce will, I feel sure, run as follows: – "You two brats shall grow up politicians; your every thought and act shall have an *arrière-pensée*; everything you determine shall be not for its own sake or on its own merits but because of something else."' If the twins ever became political, their best fate would be to fall into 'eternal slumber'.[25] Whether the delegates quite followed the thread Keynes was so expertly spinning may be doubted. After he had finished, Collado and Clayton leant over to Brand and said, 'Keynes is really much too clever for us.' Vinson sensed that Keynes's barbed words might be directed against him. 'I don't mind being called malicious, but I do mind being called a fairy,' he growled.[26]

Two main issues divided the British and Americans: the location of the Fund and Bank and the Fund's *modus operandi*. The British, following Keynes's original design of the Clearing Union, wanted the two institutions to be a-political, deciding matters on technical criteria. To this end they wanted them located outside Washington; and wanted the Fund, in particular, to be under the unencumbered control of the managing director and his staff, with the twelve executive directors and their alternates representing their countries or regions on a part-time basis, and at part-time salaries. The Americans wanted the Fund and Bank to be located in Washington; they wanted the executive directors to be full time, and lavishly reimbursed. They also envisaged a staff of 300 technicians, whereas Keynes thought thirty would be 'more than adequate to handle the business of the Fund'.

The two questions were thrashed out on 13 March. Paul Bareau's note runs: 'The Committee on the Site met in the afternoon and all oppo-sition to Washington was brushed aside with complete brutality by the Americans.' Keynes put forward four reasons for having the Fund and Bank in New York: they would be seen as international, no single govern-ment would have undue influence over them, it was technically advan-tageous to be close to a financial centre, and co-operation with the UN's Social and Economic Council would be easier. Clayton countered that the loans would be governmental, not private, and Washington was the source of the statistics the Fund would need. Keynes was supported by Mendès-France and the Indian governor-designate, Sir Chintaman Desh-muck, but the Latin Americans toed the State Department line. Keynes decided to concede graciously, but felt a grave mistake was being made. The decision, he said, was *nem. con.* – nobody opposing, but by no means all supporting.

The main battle took place on the Committee on the Functions and Remuneration of the Executive Directors. Clayton based his case for full-time executives on Article XII, Section 3(g) of the Final Act, which provided that executive directors should 'function in continuous session at the principal office of the Fund'. Keynes put up a last-ditch fight for a passive Fund. He argued the case for part-time directors on three grounds: that the executive directors should be men who normally took part in formulating the policies of their countries; that the managing director must have and act on information – such as on exchange rate policy – which could not be shared with a dozen executive directors; and that full-time executive directors would not have enough work. All governments, he said, liked to have positions available where they could pension off people past their prime, but it would not make the institution efficient to have these people hanging around.

Keynes's main purpose was to protect the Fund from preponderant US political control. He saw the managing director as analogous to the governor of a central bank, ultimately accountable to his board, but not under its day-to-day control. The main function of the executive directors was not to manage the Fund, but to be the link between the Fund and the national treasuries and central banks from which they were seconded. They would imbibe the internationalist outlook from their sojourns at Fund headquarters; and they would bring to the Fund intimate knowledge of their own governments' policies and objectives. In this way national could be made to yield to international perspectives through a process of learning and mutual accommodation. Keynes also believed that this kind of set-up would cut down on the need for the Fund to amass statistical information centrally, and thus enable it to make do with a lean staff.

By contrast, American conception of the Fund was hegemonic. Clayton insisted that it needed a strong, full-time executive board and a large specialist bureaucracy to police the policies of its members. Clayton produced a further argument: the executive directors would have more than enough work to do in Washington following the 'trends', a point dutifully, if monotonously, echoed by Harry White. He said this so often that Graham Towers of Canada, who supported the British line, told Keynes that he had a nightmare of being pursued by a trend in a vicious circle. Support for the American position came from Guatemala, Mexico, Honduras, Ethiopia and Greece, which perhaps looked forward to having their pensioners maintained at American expense.

That evening Keynes wrote a couple of gloomy letters to Richard Kahn at King's College and Edward Bridges at the Treasury. The Americans, he told Kahn, planned to equip his twins with huge staffs, and railroad through their proposals. They had no idea of international co-operation: 'since they are the biggest partners they think they have the right to call the tune on practically every point. If they knew the music that would not matter so much; but unfortunately they don't.' To Bridges Keynes conceded that Vinson has 'enough stooges . . . to feel able to act independently of the views of the rest of us . . .'. For the first time in international negotiations Keynes found himself faced not by arguments, but by voting battalions. The Latin Americans could be depended on to read, in broken English, speeches prepared for them by the State Department. 'The lobbying for votes, the mobilisation of supporters, the politics of the lunch and the dinner table, were not arts in which Keynes excelled or indeed which he attempted to cultivate,' noted Bareau.

On 14 March, Clayton offered a compromise which Keynes reluctantly accepted: though both executive directors and their alternates would be full-time, only one of them would need to be 'continually available'.[27] But Keynes balked at the tax-free salaries proposed for both of them, and other staff, set at American standards, arguing that it would be wrong 'to load the budgets of these bodies with such high emoluments for such a large body of officials'. Had the British foreseen the problem, they would have insisted on salaries being paid by the member governments.[28] On Dalton's instructions, Keynes voted against 'life in Washington with no defined or onerous duties and a grand, tax-free salary'.[29] Not surprisingly, he was the sole critic of this rosy prospect: and his was the only negative vote recorded at the conference.

The salaries issue crystallised what White saw as the fundamental difference between the British and American positions ever since the gestation of the two countries' schemes back in 1941: the British wanted an automatic source of credit, the Americans a financial policeman.[30] With Harry White vetoed for the managing directorship of the Fund, Keynes sounded out Camille Gutt – 'an old trusted friend and a successful former Finance Minister of Belgium (though no longer young or very vigorous)'[31] – on whether he would take it on. Gutt agreed, and was formally elected on 6 May. The two twins had been duly christened and equipped with homes and minders.

Although Keynes said afterwards that 'I went to Savannah to meet the world and all I met was a tyrant,' the acrimony of the Savannah meeting has been exaggerated. Keynes kept himself well in hand, and in truth did not have much to do: the substantive arguments took place over two days only. If, as Harrod claims, he fought to the 'full limit of his strength'[32] this only shows how limited his strength had become. His memories were benign. He and Lydia left on a 'lovely middle March evening, with a full moon over the rivers and lakes of this delta, and the sea, with a temperature of about 70 at 10 o'clock in the evening'.[33] At their closing dinner, Harry White led a 'Bacchic rout of satyrs and Silenuses' from Latin America into the dining room, with 'vine leaves' – or perhaps cocktail sticks – in his hair and loudly bellowing 'Onward Christian Soldiers'.

Nevertheless, the strain was still too much. On the morning of 19 March, Keynes started off for breakfast down the interminably long corridor of the swaying special train taking them from Savannah to Washington. Walking, by his own account too fast, he ran out of breath. He struggled to the dining car, feeling completely 'knocked out' and 'winded', as if at the end of a long race.[34] After an hour he seemed better, and started on the long walk back to his compartment. He never made it. Fighting for breath and life, he was carried back to the dining car and laid on a table. Lydia was by his side, Bob Brand and Harry White hovered anxiously. After two hours he had recovered. Somehow or other he managed to get to the taxi taking them to the Statler. After a good night's rest, he felt 'competely as usual'. He and Lydia booked into the Waldorf Astoria in New York next day, and sailed for Southampton on the *Queen Mary* early on 21 March.

By all accounts, it was a difficult voyage. Although Jacob Viner was good company at the captain's table, the part of the ship occupied by returning members of the British team was filthy from troopship days, and many passengers, including Keynes, became sick with a stomach bug.[35] George Bolton, who travelled back with him, recalled in 1972 that Keynes spent much of the voyage 'writing an article for publication condemning American policy with extraordinary ferocity and passionately recommending H.M. Government to refuse to ratify the Fund and Bank agreement. . . . Eventually, he agreed to destroy the paper.'[36] For reasons which Donald Moggridge has explained, this is all muddled misrecollection.* Keynes's now familiar 'boat draft' was a sober, and indeed appreci-

---

* Moggridge (p. 834) suggests that Bolton's memory was at fault: Britain had already ratified the Bretton Woods Agreement in December 1945, Keynes's report to the Cabinet on the Savannah conference was circulated much as it was written. He suggests that the paper to whose publication Bolton and Rowe-Dutton objected was the one on 'The US Balance of

ative, report on 'The Savannah Conference on the Bretton Woods Final Act' which was circulated as a Cabinet paper on 29 March. Without disguising his disappointments, Keynes took a more hopeful view of the outcome. In particular he now understood Clayton's insistence on a strong Fund executive as an administration attempt to insulate American foreign economic policy from Congressional politics, conceding that 'some of our criticism and opposition may have seemed churlish and a little off the point. But we were not handled in a way which made apprehension easy'.[37]

Keynes's final reflections on his last American trip were contained in a note he wrote for Dalton in London on 4 April. He was confident that the American loan would get through Congress owing to the 'changed situation in relation to Russia'. He now advised a policy of 'drift' for six months on the sterling balances, since it paid Britain to go on accumulating them. This was surely Temptation with knobs on. He repeated his conviction that the United States was now a high-cost country, whose competitive advantage – and with it, by implication, the dollar-shortage – would drain away.[38]

Eady was shocked by Keynes's appearance on his return to the Treasury on 27 March: 'he was not only very white, but he slumped in his chair, and very gentle as though he found it very difficult to revive interest in all the many daily things on which he guided us'.[39] But he was soon back to form, reducing James Meade to tears with 'the whole battery of . . . wit, petulance, rudeness and quick unscrupulousness in argument' directed against Meade's economic forecasts. Meade had worked out a plan to bring the national income and expenditure estimates into the same financial year as the budget estimates of revenue, so that planning policy and fiscal policy could operate with the same set of figures. Keynes was furious. He wanted wartime planning to die away, and thought it would if it was kept as far away from budgetary preparations as possible. It was Meade's last encounter with him, which did not affect his judgement that he was 'the greatest genius I have ever met'. He would always refer to him as 'My God'.[40]

Keynes managed to snatch two weekends at Tilton before the start of his Easter holiday. On one of them, he wrote a 3000-word essay on 'Bernard Shaw and Isaac Newton'. 'Pitiably old' at ninety, GBS had written to Keynes in January, following his speech on the loan, commenting on the 'tragic spectacle' of their Lordships 'talking vociferously – and oh!

Payments' for the *Economic Journal*, then still in draft (see pp. 459–60 above). The main interest of this memory lapse – if such it was – is the assumption by Bolton in 1972, which Kahn accepted two years later (A.P. Thirlwall (ed.), *Keynes and International Monetary Relations*, 28–9), that anything Keynes wrote was bound to have a decisive effect on the policy of the British government. It is symptomatic of the veneration in which Keynes was held for many years after his death, which was far from being complete while he was still alive.

how earnestly – without understanding a single one of the substantives they were throwing about. And the strange figure of Maynard Keynes rising and chilling them with a cold blast of knowledge and reality.'[41] Keynes had been asked to contribute to a volume of tributes to GBS on the occasion of his ninetieth birthday. He spent Sunday 7 April writing it, apologising to the editor for 'such a poor and perfunctory thing'. His essay twitted Shaw on minor errors and anachronisms in his play *In Good King Charles's Golden Days*, which was set in Newton's non-existent Cambridge house. It ends: 'Wishing not to be absent from this volume of tribute but still deprived of leisure of mind and pen by vain pre-occupation with the perplexed business of the world, I write in haste these scanty lines. They do little justice to the love and honour in which I hold GBS'.[42]

On Thursday 11 April he had lunch at the Bank after the regular meeting of the Court. He sat next to Henry Clay; they discussed the American loan. Keynes said that he relied on Adam Smith's 'invisible hand' to get Britain out of the mess it was in, and went on: 'I find myself more and more relying for a solution of our problems on the invisible hand which I tried to eject from economic thinking twenty years ago.' 'An interesting confession for our arch-planner,' Henry Clay noted. The now-retired Montagu Norman, the recipient of Clay's letter, wrote back: 'About Keynes . . . I think he relied on intellect, which perhaps means that he ignored the "invisible hand", and I guess he was led astray by Harry White. But surely it is easy to arrange a loan if you ignore its repayment, and is there any hope of that, unless there is to be such an inflation across the Atlantic as will affect their claims and provide an easy way out?'[43]

Keynes's Easter holiday started the next day, on 12 April. It was a glorious spring – 'definitely not the old England. . . . Is it sunspots?'[44] He did a couple of hours' Treasury work each morning. He sat in the garden reading his latest purchases of Elizabethan and Jacobean authors. His mother had come to stay and they wandered round the farm together. One morning clad in straw hat and light-blue jacket bought in America, he took her to see veal being carved into joints for the Easter feast for the families on the estate.

Keynes was exhausted, but he was not ready to die. On Thursday 18 April he had tea with Clive and Vanessa Bell and Duncan Grant at Charleston. He went without Lydia and stayed almost till dinner. It was like old times.

I have seldom known him in better spirits [wrote Clive Bell to Mary Hutchinson]. He was extremely gay and full of projects. We talked of Roger [Fry] – about whom I happened to have written something for the Americans – and the fine show at the Tate, and plans for future shows of French painting. He was delighted with Kingsley Martin's misadventures in the Russian zone, abused the government, and took more than half seriously a wild project of Duncan's for a gala performance at Covent Garden in honour of Shaw's ninetieth birthday, to end with a laurel crowning by a pretty young actress (not Dame Sybil Thorndike) in the manner of Voltaire. Probably he would have realised it triumphantly. I have some reason to think he had been given, and was much pleased to have been given, an OM [he had]. . . . The last thing he said to me was that he had something in mind to write about Lytton [Strachey], and that if he could get it done he would read it at the next meeting of the Memoir Club.[45]

Clive Bell told Roy Harrod that Maynard was furious with the government's decision to nationalise the road-hauliers, which he regarded as an unnecessary act of regimentation.[46]

On Saturday 20 April he made his third ascent of the week – by car – to Firle Beacon, with Lydia and his mother. He decided to return with Lydia by the footpath. He had not walked down the path for years, not since his illness. He felt quite fit to do it again. 'I watched the two of them,' Florence wrote later, 'as they disappeared gradually below the brow of the hill – he, bending down to her in animated talk, she looking up in eager response.' He had been describing a poem by Thomas Parnell, a friend of Pope and Swift, the first edition of which had just reached him. He had ended his explanation with the words: 'And the meaning of it all is: don't worry, there is always divine justice.'[47]

Keynes died in his bed on the morning of Easter Sunday, 21 April. There is some dispute about the details. Roy Harrod writes: 'Early next morning his mother heard a sound of coughing in his room. She went to seek Lydia, who was with him in a flash. An attack, such as he had often endured before, had just come on, but this time there could be no recovery. In a few minutes it was all over. His features assumed an expression of beautiful peacefulness.'

Clive Bell's account (written two days later fom Charleston) is different: 'Maynard died as suddenly as possible. Lydia had brought him a cup of tea at ten o'clock in the morning: he made a grimace and collapsed. . . .' Moggridge writes: 'But next morning there was another attack. This time there was no recovery: in Lydia's presence, he died within three minutes.'[48] Lydia was present at his death, and so was Florence. Clive's account is to be preferred: Logan Thomson brought Charleston the news the same morning. Were there any last words? If so, they were not recorded.

This time there was no weeping and wailing from Lydia. When Vanessa and Duncan dined with Lydia, at her request, that evening, she was calm and collected. Dozens of letters of condolence arrived, from the eminent, from former students, from economists and from old friends. Most of them were beautifully, even arrestingly, phrased. 'He taught us', Hugh Dalton wrote, 'to unite Reason with Hope.' A common theme was that

Keynes was unique and irreplaceable. Lionel Robbins said that 'he has given his life for his country, as surely as if he had fallen on the field of battle'; his most intransigent intellectual opponent, Friedrich Hayek, wrote that 'he was the one really great man I ever knew, and for whom I had unbounded admiration. The world will be a very much poorer place without him.' The historian Charles Webster, whom Keynes scarcely knew, offered the best succinct summary: 'He was the greatest intellectual force of our generation and one of the greatest of its men of action.' His brother Geoffrey had glimpsed another truth, no less important: that Maynard and Lydia were an inseparable team: 'I always enjoyed enormously seeing [them] together. They were both so vital, and each so continuously amused by the other's company. There was never a trace of staleness in their married life.'[49]

Sir Richard 'Otto' Clarke wrote in his diary on 22 April:

> Appalling news of death of Keynes. Felt bereft, as on the death of Roosevelt. He is the man whose abilities I would soonest have [wanted] to match. The extraordinary thing about him was his intellectual attraction and zing – always fresh and interesting and original and provocative. . . . His death leaves the Treasury in a terrible hole. . . . Now, at the beginning of a period of far-reaching negotiations, the controller of the basic strategy (and of 75% of the tactics) has gone. A frightful gap is left in Bretton Woods; another in the sterling balances.
>
>   . . .
>
> But what a wonderful career! Aged 31 in 1914; finished the war as Treasury representative at the Peace Conference; then the 'Economic Consequences' (one of the greatest and most influential books of our time); then 15 years in academic life culminating in 'The General Theory'; back to the Treasury with the masterly war-time Budgets, the conception of Bretton Woods, and the gradual domination of overseas financial policy.[50]

The Times obituary of the same day wrote: 'To find an economist of comparable influence one would have to go back to Adam Smith. . . . And finally there is the man himself – radiant, brilliant, effervescent, gay, full of impish jokes. . . . He was a humane man genuinely devoted to the cause of the common good.' Catto, for four years his Treasury neighbour, wrote: 'More and more I came to admire his brilliant intellectual gifts, his vivid and exhilarating imagination, amounting to genius; and that facility of expression in speech and in writing that was so fascinating. . . . He was tenacious in his beliefs, yet, among those whom he liked, he could differ with a curious and delightful gentleness and, contrary to the general idea of him, he could readily accept constructive criticism.' His Treasury colleague David Waley singled him out for 'foresight, breadth of vision and courage'. Keynes, he wrote, 'always saw many moves ahead in the game'. Also, he never wrote a dull paragraph. 'It was impossible for him to be boring because it was impossible for him to be bored. Everything interested him because everything in his mind fitted instantaneously into its place in the conflict between Wisdom and Folly.... He had in Whitehall no enemies. Those who knew him best loved him most deeply.' Eady wrote: 'When we came back to the Treasury after Maynard's death, the drab corridors were grey and silent, the files were strangely heavy and lifeless. The kindly light had gone out.'

Keynes was cremated in Brighton on 24 April. He had wanted the urn containing his ashes to be deposited in the vault of the chapel of King's College. His brother Geoffrey forgot all about this clause in Keynes's will and scattered his ashes from the point halfway up the Downs above Tilton which Maynard had loved so well. Memorial services were held in the Bethlehem Chapel of Washington Cathedral on 25 April, attended by Vinson and Clayton, and with the lesson read by Bob Brand, at Westminster Abbey on 2 May, and at King's College Chapel on 4 May.

The memorial service in Westminster Abbey was an extraordinary occasion in which all the many lives of Keynes were represented. The mourners were led by his widow, parents and family. Most of the senior members of the Cabinet, led by the Prime Minister, were present, though Winston Churchill was unavoidably absent in the United States. The Court of the Bank of England were there, minus Catto, also abroad, but plus Montagu Norman. The surviving members of the wartime Treasury turned out in force, as well as the American ambassador John Winant, the Australian Prime Minister and the high commissioners of the Commonwealth. The Provost and Fellows of King's College, the Provost and Vice-Provost of Eton, the leading British economists, his colleagues on the Arts Council and a generous sprinkling of peers turned out to pay him their last tribute. Duncan Grant, Vanessa Bell, Clive Bell and Leonard Woolf, survivors from Old Bloomsbury, were there, as were many former students and artists, including Margot Fonteyn and Robert Helpmann, who had so recently danced in *The Sleeping Beauty*.

That Keynes should be mourned in death by a governing class he had often derided, and enfolded by a religion whose tenets he had dismissed as 'hocus-pocus', was not inappropriate. Keynes's world had been that of the British Establishment, at no time more than in the last six years of life. He was tethered to it by upbringing, inclination, aptitude, language and, above all, by his Englishness. By Establishment we mean here not a closed order or corporation but an elastic governing class with an instinctive sense of self-preservation, and therefore an exceptional capacity for self-renewal. This expressed itself in the meritocratic selection of its elite, and the authority and honour given to exceptional ability. In England it was not necessary for rebels to become revolutionaries in order to 'get on'. They were absorbed by the established order and used to strengthen its defences. A harsher Continental tradition is apt to understand this process of absorption as one of betrayal and co-option. This was certainly how some of the intransigent Keynesians interpreted the Master's shift back to economic liberalism in the last years of his life. Keynes of course never saw it in this way: Mahomet may have gone to the hill, but the hill had also come to Mahomet. In the world of economics and finance Keynes had come to occupy the same position as Churchill in the world of politics: he *was*, in fact, the Churchill of his domain. Both had been called on by their country in its hour of need, previous sins forgiven.

The elasticity of this order depended on a shared sense of Englishness, which in turn expressed itself in a rather uncomplicated patriotism: the complications in the use of these terms came later. Virtually anything could be forgiven provided one's patriotism was not in doubt. Schumpeter was penetrating when he wrote that Keynes's advice was in the first instance 'always English advice, born of English problems even when being addressed to other nations', that 'barring some of his artistic tastes, he was surprisingly insular, even in philosophy, but nowhere so much as in economics', and that his 'patriotism ... was so genuine as to be subconscious and therefore all the more powerful to impart a bias to his thought and to exclude full understanding of foreign (also American) viewpoints, conditions, interests, and especially creeds'.[51] There are two caveats to this view of Keynes. Schumpeter never accepted the generality of the *General Theory*. He also left out the imaginative quality of Keynes's utterance. Both gave Keynes a universal appeal; both still have the power to provoke and move the economist and layman the world over.

That Keynes should be honoured at Westminster Abbey and in an Anglican ceremony was also fitting. It was not just that the proximity of Westminster Abbey to Parliament and Whitehall symbolised the Erastian character of the British state; it was also that Keynes was steeped in the culture of Christianity. Moore's *Principia Ethica*, which remained his 'religion under the surface', was a secularised version of monasticism, whose unworldliness, Keynes once said, made the New Testament, by comparison, a 'handbook for politicians'. As his worldly concerns multiplied – for Maynard Keynes was not by nature destined for the cloister – he came to realise that it was not Christianity which was the enemy, but the 'Benthamite calculus' or, more mundanely, materialism. As he became older, the atheism of his youth – the rejection of Christian dogma – ceased to define his attitude to Christianity. He had come to value it for social and moral reasons.

Yet there was too much recalcitrant material in his make-up for the Christian categories of the memorial service quite to fit Keynes. Take the opening hymn, 'The King of Love my Shepherd Is', which has the verse:

> Perverse and foolish oft I strayed,
> But yet in love he sought me,
> And on his shoulder gently laid,
> And home, rejoicing, brought me

in which the Divine Shepherd receives back, with love and forgiveness, the repentant human sheep who has strayed from the fold. Conventional opinion often portrayed Keynes as 'perverse and foolish' and believed, or hoped, that in later life his 'straying' had ended. Yet this view of him begs too many questions.

In one sense, he never strayed far from the fold. His parents outlived him, and were, with his widow, his main, certainly his oldest, mourners. Florence and Neville Keynes kept him loosely attached to the 'presuppositions of Harvey Road'. He was bound to his parents by love, which if anything grew stronger on his side as the years went by; and by values which were flexible enough to accommodate the twentieth century without breaking up into incoherence.

On the other hand, Keynes was no saint. As a young man, he seemed to epitomise to D. H. Lawrence a kind of unclean brilliance. To Russell Leffingwell, he was, till late in life, 'always perverse, Puckish . . . a bright boy, shocking his admiring elders by questioning the existence of God and the Ten Commandments'. Dennis Robertson saw him as an imp; to Hubert Henderson this impishness was almost a professional badge, put on to attract the young. It is difficult to dissociate the younger Keynes from Lytton Strachey, the arch-Bloomsbury scoffer and 'immoralist'.

Keynes's 'straying' was part of his make-up. But he was never an outlaw; nor did he repent. It is wrong to portray him as an antinomian, repudiating conventional rules, claiming unfettered discretion for his own judgement or inclinations. The truth is that, both in his own life and in his economics, Keynes bent the rules, he did not break them. His radicalism was contained within the conventions and expectations of his time and class. Predominantly homosexual by temperament, he made a marriage built on love, not convenience. Without Lydia there would have been no 'public' Keynes, probably no *General Theory*. But one gets no sense that in marrying Lydia Keynes was sacrificing something essential to his self-fulfilment. She was the indispensable means to his self-fulfilment, and his emotions redirected themselves accordingly.

In his economic and philosophical reasoning, he was much more radical in thought than in action; and his first thoughts were more iconoclastic than his second or third ones. His method was often fiercely confrontational, or dialetical. He could be a wounding opponent in argument. To the end of his life there was an unsparing quality about his brilliance, except to the young and the ignorant. The words 'barmy', 'crazy' and 'lunatic' tripped too easily off his tongue. The concessions to his opponents' positions would come later – which was perhaps a poor recompense for their having been lashed by him. Yet at heart he was a constitutionalist, not a revolutionary, a synthesiser, not a knocker. He shrank from the revolutionary consequences of his own theory, which suggested a world in which no equilibrium was possible. A chaotic universe which could nevertheless be forecast sufficiently to be stabilised – here surely was a supreme paradox. Yet it was the necessary premise of the Keynesian Revolution. Throughout this volume we have seen his Middle Way approach vigorously at work. Typical was his willingness to have his radical ideas on wartime and post-war finance 'dressed up' in familiar clothes, so as not to alarm the traditionalists. This was not just tactical: he also understood the strength of the traditionalists' case. As he grew older Keynes became more attached to appearances. He liked the thought of pouring new wine into old bottles. Classical economics was strengthened, though altered, by its encounter with Keynes. With the more spacious perspective which time brings, we can now say about Keynes what Marshall said about Jevons: 'His success was aided even by his faults ... he led many to think he was correcting great errors; whereas he was really only adding important explanations.'

In another sense it was fitting for Keynes to be remembered in the words of this hymn. His economics were much more New Testament than Old. It was an economics of love and forgiveness rather than Justice; or rather it was an economics in which Justice was modified by generous escape clauses. Keynes did not expect or demand a standard of behaviour which presumed prodigious calculating powers based on perfect information about the future. He agreed with Locke, who wrote that 'in the greatest part of our concernment, God has afforded only the Twilight ....'. To err is human; all endurable human arrangements have to be merciful.

Yet, when all allowances are made, the words of the hymn do not really fit Keynes. For he did not repent his straying from the orthodox fold: rather, he enlarged what was meant by orthodoxy. One could say that he evolved back towards the values in which he was brought up, but he did so without any sense of repudiating a journey through life which had made those values more elastic. His 'straying' was part of his development, not an aberration. He was a prodigiously successful prodigal son, and in some sense he realised the virtues of this: that in order to be of any use to the fold a person has to do some straying.

Other thoughts and phrases less central to Christian dogma capture him better. In the lovely words of Psalm 15, the choir asked: 'Lord, who shall dwell in thy tabernacle: or who shall rest upon thy holy hill?' And answered: 'Even he, that leadeth an uncorrupt life: and doeth the thing which is right, and speaketh the truth from his heart.' Keynes was a political economist, though not a political animal. He aimed always for what was achievable, and was happy to compromise. But he knew how to speak out. When he resigned from the Treasury on 5 June 1919 in order to publish his denunciation of the Paris Peace Treaty, he chose to 'speak the truth from his heart'. It was the first defining moment of his life, and the source of his subsequent moral authority. He chose then to do the difficult, unpopular thing; and repeated the performance, on an intellectual plane, in the *General Theory*. On both occasions voices were not lacking advising him to 'tone down' the attack, to take account of 'political reality'. Ruthless truth-telling first, the compromise between truth and politics later: this was Keynes's credo, and on the whole he lived by it.

The famous passage from Ecclesiasticus which starts 'Let us now praise famous men' continues in words peculiarly apt for Keynes: 'Leaders of the people by their counsels, and by their knowledge of learning meet for the people, wise and eloquent in their instructions'. Like Marshall and the other great nineteenth-century economists, Keynes was a 'leader of the people', not an economist's economist, using scientific mumbo-jumbo. He used his learning to educate and elevate the public, and his communications to it were 'wise and eloquent', never more so than in his last speech in the House of Lords defending the American loan and the Bretton Woods Agreement.

Then came the famous quotation from Corinthians – 'Death, where is thy sting? Grave, where is thy victory?' – which John Bunyan puts in the mouth of Mr Valiant-for-Truth in *Pilgrim's Progress*. These would have recalled to those who had followed and shared Keynes's pilgrimage his own legacy of Truth, Courage and Skill. This was the sword Keynes bequeathed to those 'who shall succeed me in my pilgrimage'. For the thousands of economists the world over, proud to call themselves Keynesians, he left the conception of economics as a tool to lighten the material cares of mankind and hasten the day when, as he himself put it, people could 'sing' again – as they had in the Garden of Eden. Nicholas Kaldor expressed what Keynes had meant for his generation of economists in a letter he wrote to Lydia the day Keynes died:

> There is no one to whom I owe so much in the formation of my thoughts and ideas; and this must be just as true of most economists of my generation. In the truest sense of the world he was our master who for many years exerted a magic influence on us all. He created an intellectual revolution in economics the like of which only occurs once in a century, if at all; and if the world after the war will prove a happier and more prosperous place for the ordinary man and woman, it will be very largely due to the fact that his ideas had caught fire.

The memorial service continued with a prayer which opened: 'Oh God, the physician of men and nations, the restorer of the years that have been destroyed; look upon the distractions of the world and complete the work of thy healing hand; draw all men unto thee and one to another by the bands of thy love. . . .' Keynes was destined to spend most of his life trying to repair the damage which others had wrought, to restore that promise of civilisation he had fitfully glimpsed before 1914. He was always a man of peace. He spent his own last years, and even hours, trying to build a peace that would last.

The memorial service ended with the familiar climax of Blake's 'Jerusalem':

> I will not cease from mental fight,
> Nor shall my sword sleep in my hand,
> Till we have built Jerusalem
> In England's green and pleasant land.

Keynes was not a socialist. But like Blake he strove to realise a utopia beyond the economics of industrialism, when 'we shall once more value ends above means and prefer the good to the useful. We shall honour those who can teach us how to pluck the hour and the day virtuously and well, the delightful people who are capable of taking direct enjoyment in things, the lilies of the field who toil not, neither do they spin.'

Like Odysseus, Keynes was a successful, not a tragic, hero. He heard the beautiful singing of the Sirens, but took precautions against being shipwrecked, keeping to the course for which his talents and the state of the world predestined him. Artfully, he strove for the best of all worlds, in his life and his work, and, miraculously, came close to achieving it.

So Keynes went to his eternal rest. Lydia wrote: 'And now I am so utterly alone without him. The light is gone. I grieve and weep.'

EPILOGUE

Keynes's Legacy

I

MAYNARD'S BEQUESTS

Maynard Keynes cared most for his family and friends, the arts, his College and his country. He died in the knowledge, or expectation, that he had left them all well provided for. 'In the long run', he famously wrote, 'we are all dead.' But Keynes cast such a long shadow that it would be a bold author, even now, who would want to apply this dictum to him. In the nearest reaches of that shadow were his testamentary dispositions, and their effect on his widow, his family and friends, and his College. Beyond that stretched the influence of his life, achievements and ideas. The modern world cannot do without Keynes, any more than it can do without Marx – though both have been repeatedly declared dead and buried. Both men expressed permanent truths about the human condition, even though these were not necessarily central to what they thought would happen or wanted to happen.

Keynes's will was probated on 19 September 1946. He left £479,529, roughly equivalent to £12m. or $19m. today. Of this just over £400,000 was in securities, most of the rest in pictures and rare books and manuscripts. The two executors of his will and trustees of his estate were his brother Geoffrey Keynes and his 'favourite student' Richard Kahn. After bequests of £40,000 (which included £4000 to each of his eight nephews and nieces, and smaller sums to Duncan Grant, Logan Thomson, Norman Higgins, Frederick Woollard, farmhands and servants), Keynes directed that a trust fund be set up, the income of which (apart from annuities to Duncan Grant and his secretary, Mrs Stephens) was to go to his widow Lydia during her lifetime, with the stipulation that her post-tax income should never fall below £1500, a curiously pessimistic assessment of her financial prospects. After her death, the capital sum would revert to King's College, Cambridge, together with his pictures, books and manuscript collections, notably the Newton MSS.

Keynes divided his private papers into two. His personal papers and contributions to the Memoir Club, which he left to Geoffrey Keynes, were to become the property of King's College after Lydia's death; his economic papers were left to Richard Kahn and were to be deposited in the Marshall Library, at Cambridge.

Typically, Keynes left his trustees and ultimate legatee, King's College, a wide discretion. The trustees were to invest the capital as they saw fit. He nevertheless hoped 'without imposing any obligation to that effect', that his College would apply the money it would eventually receive 'for buildings of greater amenity and beauty' on sites it owned and to make grants or advances to the Cambridge Arts Theatre. Interestingly, he 'requested' (rather than 'directed') his brother to 'destroy the greater part' of his personal papers, and Richard Kahn to do the same to his economic papers; he wanted none of his papers published except his two talks to Bloomsbury's Memoir Club.

When Roy Harrod had finished writing his biography, he returned Keynes's wartime papers to the Treasury, much to Kahn's annoyance. The rest of the economic papers were preserved. Possibly some of the personal papers were destroyed by Geoffrey Keynes. The personal papers have, of course, been extensively used by biographers, but the only part to have been published so far are the *Two Memoirs* – 'Dr Melchior' and 'My Early Beliefs' – in 1949, and three years of Keynes's correspondence with Lydia Lopokova before they got married.[1] About one-third of Keynes's economic papers have been published as part of the Royal Economic Society's edition of the *Collected Writings of John Maynard Keynes* in thirty volumes (1971–89). This was successively edited by Elizabeth Johnson and Donald Moggridge.

Then there was Keynes's public legacy. His chief gifts to the arts were the Cambridge Arts Theatre, paid for out of his own pocket, the Arts Council of Great Britain, which started its official life in August 1946 under Sir Ernest Pooley, and with an annual Treasury grant of £320,000, and the reborn Royal Opera House, Covent Garden. All three institutions survive, though none has quite fulfilled Keynes's hopes.

His economic bequests were more controversial. Most tangible was the American loan of $3.75bn he had negotiated in 1945 to see Britain through the immediate post-war years. This proved the least durable of his legacies, quickly dissipated – though, without its false promise, the British welfare state might never have taken root. The Bretton Woods Agreement was partly his invention, Britain's acceptance of it largely the result of his untiring advocacy. The International Monetary Fund and World Bank – the 'twins' he christened at Savannah a month before he died – are still with us, though other elements of that Agreement, notably fixed exchange rates and capital controls, are gone. Beyond all this stretched the 'Keynesian Revolution' – the logic and practice of managing economies so as to maintain full employment and avoid depressions like that of 1929–33. In the form Keynes left it, his Revolution was never wholly accepted; and the debate about its value and relevance, and its author's place in the pantheon of thought and statesmanship, continues. We still live in the shadow of Keynes, not because his legacy has been assimilated, but because it is still disputed.

II

LYDIA'S WORLD

Lydia Keynes was fifty-three when Maynard died, and lived another thirty-six years.[2] A week after his death, his nephew Richard Keynes reported her 'wonderfully cheerful; and quite in her old form most of the time' at Sunday lunch at 6 Harvey Road, Cambridge, 'and then she remembers, and bursts into tears for a moment. But it is soon over.' Lydia was not one to mope. 'I used to think of [Maynard] every day, but now I don't think about him at all,' she told the choreographer Fred Ashton a few years later. The truth was that, while she and Maynard had been extraordinarily happy together, a huge part of his life had been beyond her reach, interest and understanding. As for the rest, she kept her silence. No one could coax her into revealing reminiscence. This is surprising only to those who live by the pen. She was not a gossip or a writer. Her significant memories were, in any case, too intimate for circulation. She had done her duty by Maynard, and was now entitled to her privacy. When journalists rang for comments, she would pick up the telephone, pretend to be her own secretary, and say in a thick Russian accent, 'No, Madam does not give interviews.'

Above all, she no longer had Maynard to protect her. So she withdrew into the world of ballet, where she had been a star in her own right, and on which subject she could speak as an expert. Even here, though, she needed support on public occasions. In 1947 she asked Provost Sheppard of King's College, Cambridge for help in making a speech to honour Ninette de Valois. 'Please do scribble something to me in typewriting, put yourself in my shoes and spread your general wits across my nervous system.' She signed herself 'your uneconomic geisha'.

At the same time, she inherited Maynard's income, his homes, his staff, his pictures, his family and many of his friends, his routines. She kept up, and expanded, that part of their married life which had been most closely connected with the stage. She was a member of the Arts Council Drama Panel and Trustee of the Cambridge Arts Theatre, though she soon resigned from the former. She divided her time, as they had both done, between Tilton, Gordon Square and St Edward's Passage. For ten years after his death she remained an enthusiastic theatregoer in Brighton, London and Cambridge.

She continued to come up to Cambridge to see her 'dear old characters', whom she also had to stay at Tilton. These included Jack Sheppard, Provost of King's, 'Dedy' as she called Dadie Rylands, a new friend Noël Annan, who succeeded Sheppard as Provost in 1956 at the early age of thirty-nine, and, of course, Maynard's parents, the 'starychki'. Neville Keynes died in 1949, aged ninety-seven, but Lydia's bond with Florence

('Mil') continued unbroken till Florence's death in 1958, at the age of ninety-six. Florence's lucid and loving letters to her 'Lyddy' continued till the end. Two years before her death she wrote: 'I always think of you & the happiness you gave him.' In Cambridge, Lydia usually took her meals at the Theatre Restaurant, opposite her flat, attended by the head waiter, Mr Schurch. She had a natural affinity with the more theatrical King's College dons, her quick wit and mastery of the *double entendre* perfectly fitting their camp style. She once told Noël Annan that Englishmen were either 'boys or old boys'; it was less of a complaint than a typically sharp observation. Lydia's visits to Cambridge tailed off in the later 1950s. The flat in St Edward's Passage, having been largely unoccupied for some years, was given up in 1965. In 1967, by which time she was seventy-five, she refused to come up to the opening of the new Keynes Building.

In London, Lady Keynes was still invited to some of the official receptions she and her husband might have graced. She refused most of them, but exceptionally turned up, in 1950, at a party at the American Embassy for the Achesons: she thought the Foreign Secretary, Ernest Bevin, looked far from well. Mostly, though, she stuck to her own world. Her 'boyfriends' were homosexuals like Richard Buckle, Fred Ashton, Cecil Beaton, Raymond Mortimer, Eddie Sackville-West. These men, particularly the ballet critic 'Dicky' Buckle, had the advantage of being available as escorts. Lydia was also 'thick', as she put it, with Laurence Olivier and Vivien Leigh. Number 47 Gordon Square was sub-let. At Number 46, Lydia herself occupied less and less space, driven from most of the house by the cold as well as by the expense. The basement was let out to a caretaker; the upper floors to a society for Christian aid. She liked them as tenants because they were clean. Lydia herself often answered the doorbell. 'Are you Christian?' she would teasingly ask a likely looking stranger. She now camped out in the ground-floor front room – their old dining room – which had her bed, a large mirror and barre; she entertained in a small, high back room at a table covered with oilcloth, 'where among the piles of books and tins of food, one was surprised', Buckle wrote, 'to find a Cubist Picasso and Delacroix's sketch for the mural of "Jacob Wrestling with the Angel" in the church of Saint-Sulpice'. Milo Keynes, a favourite escort for Covent Garden, would sometimes come back with her for supper. 'What do you want to eat,' Lydia would ask him, 'cold chicken or hamburger?' But, he recalls, he never had a hamburger. 'She gave memorable meals, at which she would tear off hunks of chicken with her hands to place beside the cold salad, putting the carcass on her own plate. We would all laugh and talk endlessly, and get wittier, happier and more profound as the wine flowed. . . . Once, she and Balanchine jumped up in turn to dance and explain a passage from *The Firebird*.' Lydia had been told by Maynard to warm the red wine, so she always left it too long by the fire, where it turned into mulled claret. She took daily meals at Antoine's in Charlotte Street.

Asked by *Newsweek* in 1955 to compare contemporary dancing with that of her youth, Lydia answered sensibly: 'Why confuse the standards of to-day with those of 30 years ago? To-day is to-day and yesterday is history. The great thing is that Ballet flourishes.' History reappeared when Pablo Picasso visited London in November 1950. She asked him for the drawing of her with Massine dancing the can-can from *La Boutique Fantasque* in the early 1920s. He promised to send it, could not find it, and sent her the photograph inscribed 'pour Lydia en attendant l'original'. The original never did arrive: the photograph today hangs in Richard Keynes's dining room. Lydia retained her fine discrimination. She was pleased, she told David Webster in 1947, that the critics 'at last recognise how sublime [Margot Fonteyn] is'. On 21 March 1949 she told him: 'The costumes and decor of Coppelia must be drowned – it is disgrace for Covent Garden, not Surbiton.' On 13 April she took Maynard's old friends Duncan Grant, Vanessa, Clive and Quentin Bell to Fred Ashton's new production of *Cinderella*. It was 'glorious', she reported. 'Fred has achieved "magnum opus". I laughed and cried. . . .' However, his choreography in *Tiresias* was 'not strong enough' to match Constant Lambert's 'wonderful score'. By the early 1950s, she felt Ashton was 'stale', and needed to get away from Sadler's Wells. She was out of sympathy with modern ballet, feeling that it had become purely technical and acrobatic. The glory days of Covent Garden in the 1960s, made memorable by the partnership of Margot Fonteyn and Rudolf Nureyev and by the superb ballets of a revived Fred Ashton and Kenneth Macmillan, largely passed Lydia by. In 1965 she gave up Gordon Square as well. By then she had started to live in contented seclusion in her beloved Tilton.*

Lydia once told Ninette de Valois that whenever she and Maynard returned to Tilton after their travels 'we were like two children setting out on a long, long holiday'. As she grew older she became increasingly reluctant to leave what had been their joint refuge from the world. After Maynard's death she never went abroad, not even to Russia, though she maintained a correspondence with her brother, Fyodor Lopukov, the choreographer at the Maryinsky Theatre in Leningrad. 'Tilton community suits me,' she told Richard Kahn, 'no diplomacy, "gentleman's agree-ments" or prima donnas.' She was remarkably self-contained, she never suffered from loneliness or boredom. 'The world is full of nightmares, but Tilton woods are full of beauty,' she wrote. And when the summer sun came to turn her into a 'Red Indian', '24 hours is just not enough to

---

* Lydia retained the sub-tenancies of both 17a St Edward's Passage and 46 Gordon Square till her death. After 1965, King's College took responsibility for rent and outgoings, and sub-let. In London, her new landlord, from 1949, was London University.

be happy. I wish for 48.' Her enjoyment of country life, especially in summer, was rhapsodic: surrounded by 'broad beans, green peas and weeds', her skin 'rattled' from the sun, 'so rewarding and sudorous'; she became 'like a plant with two arms'; life was a 'melody, away from Oxford Street'. On top of the Downs with her farmers' boots, she became 'celestial . . . gliding through the ridges and sweating out my fibrositis'. But winter, too, had its special quality, with the apples in her orchard 'who still hang like a hangover' in December.

Once Lydia no longer had to play the great man's wife, her natural bohemianism asserted itself. Her clothes had always been eccentric, now they became bizarre. She relied on woolly hats and brightly coloured boots to adorn – and protect – the extremities, and was not much interested in anything in between, provided it kept her warm. She treated the English climate as an extension of Russia's, arctic for most of the year, but interspersed with precious intervals of sunshine. She dressed accordingly. For much of the year she would be heavily bundled up against the cold, both inside and outside the house. When the sun shone, she would strip almost naked, to thaw out her body under its health-giving rays. Tilton saw her in both aspects – trundling up the flinty private lane wrapped up in old scarves and Maynard's pullovers, or flitting half naked among the broad beans and cabbages in the garden, or sunbathing fully naked in the redcurrant bushes within a few yards of a footpath. Once asked if this habit might not cause embarrassment, Maynard replied, 'No – passers-by simply can't believe their eyes.'

Lydia accepted the coming of old age without fuss, and preferred to be comfortable rather than smart. On being asked for a photograph by the choreographer Walter Gore in the mid-1950s she replied, 'Would you like me as I am or as I was? There is quite a difference.' When Cecil Beaton visited her in July 1951, she greeted him 'wearing a mercerized silk skirt of cream leaf pattern, cocoa-coloured stockings, woollen socks, straw boots, an apron, and about three different sweaters over a silk blouse. Her head was tied in a maize-coloured handkerchief: a pale grey, shiny face without make-up, but freckled and sunburnt at back of neck.'

At Tilton, she bustled round the house, with headscarf round her hair, a cigarette dangling from her mouth, looking like a charlady, though she never did much cleaning. Nor did she bother much with cleaning herself. When she arrived to stay with the Oliviers without her toothbrush, and Vivien Leigh offered to lend her one, she said: 'Oh my dear, do not worry. What's the point of cleaning your teeth? You have to lose them some time.' In 1965 she told Jack Peters, the bursar's clerk at King's – an unusual recipient for such news – that 'I have now removed my few remaining teeth, all very painless and successful. I am now relieved of the task of cleaning my teeth with a toothbrush, it is all done scientifically by a special detergent, supplied by the dentist.' What she enjoyed most was relaxing with the newspapers and magazines Maynard had loved to read, and which continued, uncancelled, to be delivered; being driven, by the farm manager Logan Thomson, to Lewes or Eastbourne for lunch and a shopping expedition, or to a theatre in Brighton; and wandering on the Downs, learning poetry and taking in the 'melodies' of the countryside.

Most of Tilton, like 46 Gordon Square, was abandoned, Lydia concentrating her living in a small space on the ground floor, like a bird making its nest. She never cooked, and kept clear of the kitchen at the rear of the house. She took her meals in the small dining room on the left of the front door. Logan Thomson would often join her, as she liked a 'man at the table'. To the right of the front door was the 'boot room', where Maynard had died, and in which Lydia now slept, with a bathroom beyond in the 'wing' which Maynard had built. Behind the dining room was the large apple-green drawing room, with its overstuffed grey sofas and armchairs in the 1930s style, with two hexagonal tables with shelves for books, an old upright piano out of a junk shop, and windows hung with thick beige curtains. This was used mainly in the evenings, or when she had guests to stay. As the years went by, Lydia lived increasingly in the front part of the entrance hall, separated from the panelled rear by an arched entrance which could be closed off. Here she would sit surrounded by her impedimenta: tins of food and powdered milk, originally bought to survive the wartime blockade, and still unemptied from their shelves, perhaps for fear of future poverty; and rows of tiny boots, shoes and ballet slippers on the floor. At the back of the enclosed courtyard behind the main house, Maynard's old study stood dank and abandoned. The garden, so expertly created by Edgar Weller, was increasingly unkempt, the flowerbeds and lawn tennis court reverting to rough grass, the vegetable gardens, their wiring broken, overrun by rabbits.

The dilapidated house was still thickly hung with pictures, the best ones – the Seurat, the two Cézannes, the Picassos – in the drawing room. Lydia said, 'Cézanne painted hundreds of apples and I have five of them.' Maynard's pictures were so valuable that a huge burglar alarm was attached to an outer garden wall of the house to protect them. Lord Gage contributed to the defence by leaving the private road off the main road so full of holes as to deter the most intrepid burglar. Every so often the bell would start ringing loudly when a branch fell on the telephone line, or when someone touched a picture accidentally. The police would then roar up the drive. The pictures came to be hung higher and higher to avoid setting off the alarm accidentally. Eventually Lydia could stand it no longer and insisted that they be removed. After a year of nagging at Richard Kahn (who excused himself from action on the ground that he was 'terribly tied up in Important Government Business') she managed, in 1967, to get them transferred to King's, and then to the Fitzwillian, where they are on permanent loan. 'Now I can once again live in the drawing room without disturbance . . .' she told her laggard trustee. 'I have filled all the empty spaces with Duncan, Vanessa, Matthew Smith, Gore and Quentin Bell and the effect is most pleasing, in fact one or two I prefer to the old ones.'

Lydia enjoyed visitors, but, as in the days of Maynard's illness, got rid of them abruptly if they showed signs of staying too long. 'And now good bye, my dear . . .' she would say suddenly in the middle of a conversation. The Provost (Sheppard) arrived after Christmas in 1949, looking 'like a Panda, reading the life of John Knox, who hated women'. The Noël Annans came for Easter 1951 'and we gorged ourselves with veal, it . . . made us brisk and lively for three days and nights'. Sir John and Ava Anderson came to lunch: 'a good man', she thought he was, 'with . . . Scotch solidity'. In July 1951 'we had a lovely week-end with Munbys & Buckle, Vanessa, Duncan, broad beans, string beans, raspberries and veal'.

Lydia was never malicious. But she distinguished acutely between people who were worthy and people who were fun, and greatly preferred the company of the latter. Best of all were those with whom she could gossip about the ballet, though she did not like to be contradicted in her reminiscences, for which she had an excellent memory. Richard Buckle has left this rare glimpse of post-Keynesian life at Tilton in the early 1950s:

> Maynard's principles were strictly adhered to. Gin and whisky were therefore not provided, though a glass of sherry was permitted before meals and wine was plentiful. . . . The hall was stacked with tins of food, tribute from America, and with innumerable pairs of shoes. . . . The furniture was as characterless as in the London flat . . . but the pictures were . . . by Sickert, Picasso, Braque, Cézanne, Renoir, Degas and Seurat. . . . Lydia and I would meet for a jolly lunch . . . then I walked on the Downs while Lydia rested and learned the poems of Shakespeare and Eliot by heart. . . . After dinner with Lydia and Logan Thomson . . . I would settle down by the log fire in the apple-green drawing room to talk about the ballet. Lydia, with a big box of cigarettes beside her, and wrapped in rugs and jackets against the 'curly winds', would describe how she used to steal Pavlova's shoes in the old days in St. Petersburg . . . then, filled with nostalgia for her Imperial past, she would run eagerly across to the upright piano and play a tinkling tune she had danced to in Theatre Street over forty years ago.

As time went on, and 'staff problems' mounted, she became less inclined to have guests to stay at all, and put them up, at her expense, at the White Hart Hotel in Lewes. 'I do hope you will not think this very rude of me,' she wrote to Richard Kahn in 1967, 'but nowadays I enjoy people for a few hours during the day, but hate to have them sitting on my doorstep. Forgive me.' She was just as decided with Geoffrey Keynes: 'I love you and long to see you but not, my dear, at breakfast.'

Lydia had inherited a staff reduced by wartime labour shortages, and it never recovered to its former ample dimensions. At Gordon Square, Mrs Turtle came in to clean, and Mrs Beaumont cooked. At Tilton, the chauffeur Fred Woollard went when the Rolls was sold. Edgar Weller now had a full-time job, but he and Ruby stayed on at Tilton Cottage (Ruby as cleaner). There were the Carters to cook and garden. Servant problems were not long in coming. In 1949, Mrs Beaumont said she wanted to sleep out and have Fridays to Mondays off, at which Lydia told her 'the sooner we part company the better'. Mrs Carter (Rosie) had to go to hospital to be 'de-warted, inside of a nostril'. Then in 1956 the Carters left her with one week's notice after twelve years. 'It's all the full employment,' Kahn commiserated, 'Maynard is to blame.' Their place was taken by the Taylors. Mrs Taylor had a part-time job in a lunatic asylum in Eastbourne, and did not much differentiate between Lydia and her other customers. Lydia disliked Mrs Taylor intensely, but it never occurred to her to sack her. Instead she had the doorways connecting the servants' quarters to the main house bricked up, so she would not be driven mad by the cook's chattering proximity. Traffic between the two parts of the house had to pass through the front door, except for meals, which came through a hatch. On the cook's days off, Lydia and Logan took lunch at the White Hart Hotel.

Her third 'cooking couple', the Lessiters, stayed from 1962 to 1966. Mavis Lessiter, now Hicks, remembers Lydia as a lady of routine. Every morning she made her breakfast, washed some dishes in the pantry, fed the cat and took a walk down the lane. Ruby would arrive to clean. Logan would come to lunch and often to dinner before going off for a pint at Berwick. By this time Lydia rarely went to London. The Lessiters had two sons, of whom Lydia was very fond. 'She treated us like family,' Mavis Hicks said, and was hurt and upset when they emigrated to New Zealand. There was then a year's interregnum before the Whiters arrived. Jean Whiter found everything in an advanced state of decay. She restored the first-floor bedrooms, so that the Keynes family could come to stay. She found the bedclothes and sheets full of burns and had to confiscate Lydia's cigarettes when she went to bed. She and Ruby bickered endlessly.

Relations with Charleston thawed, though Lydia was too hurt by earlier snubs, and by now too self-contained, to pass much time with the ageing Bloomsberries. She still had to summon up courage to see the forbidding Vanessa Bell, though she found Leonard Woolf 'sweet and noble'. The Charlestonians were sometimes asked to help entertain Maynard's nephews when they came to stay. But Angelica Garnett's daughter, Henrietta, remembers relations between the two houses as distant, if no longer frosty. One summer afternoon, when she was ten – this was in 1955 – Henrietta went boldly up to the front door of Tilton, knocked and was greeted affectionately by a tiny lady, much muffled up with pullovers and head-scarves, looking 'rather like an old tea-cosy, except for her feet, which were delicate and beautiful, and for her hands, which were very graceful'. She sat Henrietta down in the drawing room, offered her a glass of sweet Sauterne, and talked about the ballet in St Petersburg before the First World War. After a number of such visits over the years, Henrietta thought 'how queer it was that, at tea with Lydia, there was never any tea'. Lydia outlived all the original Bloomsberries, Vanessa Bell dying in 1961, Clive Bell in 1964, Leonard Woolf in 1969, and finally Duncan Grant in 1978.

It was Logan Thomson who replaced Maynard as the man in the house, possibly as the man in Lydia's life, though there is no evidence that she was emotionally involved with him. Logan still ran the Tilton and Charleston Farms, whose profits he shared with Lydia. His parents had died; he lived in the pink bailiff's house at Tilton with his aunt. One day, the aunt 'dropped a boiling bottle on her leg, with one wooden leg already, she has no ... leg to stand on, most painful, poor old thing'. Mavis Lessiter remembers the aunt limping down the lane, followed by the wicked farm boys copying her gait. Logan was devoted to Lydia, and she came to depend increasingly on him – to write her letters, to handle her money, to keep her company, to take her out. He tried to keep the house and grounds in order:

> The fire in the spare room [he wrote to her in London on 1 July 1956] shall be like the Olympic flame. . . . Your garden is blooming, the first time since before the war, the drive is weeded, the cage is weeded and the lawns cut. The cat is a very good mother, we murdered all her children but one which will in good time be transported to Charleston. . . . Ruby is away in France, due back I think next weekend. Jurinac and her husband are living in Alciston for the Glyndebourne season. . . .

When the aunt died and Logan gave up the farms in 1966, he moved into Tilton. He was a man of few words, but he and Lydia enjoyed their silences together, like Morgenthau and Sir Frederick Phillips had done in the war.

Lydia's relations with Logan, and also with Ruby Weller, were a strange mixture of democracy and formality. They would all go to plays in Brighton, eating fish and chips before the shows. But Ruby always called her 'Your Ladyship' and Logan called her 'Madam'. Ruby, too, stayed with Lydia till the end of her days at Tilton. They quarrelled endlessly, but 'You can't help being fond of her, can you?' Ruby said.

To Richard Kahn fell the unpromising job of controlling Lydia's overdraft. The income she inherited was not far short of what she and Maynard had jointly enjoyed in their last years. But she also inherited the punitive tax rates imposed to pay for the war, and which now served to finance Labour's 'New Jerusalem'. She also had personal securities of her own, which came to £24,000 by 1956. Had he not sold 'a considerable part' of her original holding of Hawker Siddeley, they would have been worth much more, her trustee informed her gloomily.

Lydia complained to Kahn of being home rich, cash poor. 'The big houses to-day are a liability,' she wrote to him on 23 October 1949, 'and well-off people like me live like paupers.' At 46 Gordon Square, dry rot spread, and the pipes were continually bursting. 'My teeth are troubling me, I get swollen cheeks, colds, I feel I cannot go out, and I stay in, without comforts, except bed and electric fire.'

Lydia was not extravagant with money, she was careless. Whenever she needed cash, she wrote out cheques, and never kept the stubs, or looked at her statements. Often she just signed the cheques, leaving it up to Logan and others to fill in the amounts. She was a mixture of generosity and peasant habits. She always responded to appeals from old dancers in need like Karsavina, Baranova, Larionov and Goncharova, and in 1950 set up a charitable trust fund to help them. 'I know Maynard would have done something immediately to relieve their worries,' she told Richard Kahn. She financed a play by Richard Buckle. But she cut up newspapers for lavatory paper.

Lydia wrote to Kahn guiltily about her purchases, and slyly about her need for cash to make more. On 18 March 1949: 'I bought a new hat, a scarf and pair of shoes. I wanted to refurbish myself.' On 14 September 1950: 'If I don't buy [my coat] now the price of wool will be unsupportable later.' On 11 October 1950: 'I do long for cash, and I want to get rid of some furniture, if I don't I'll get frustrated.' She was particularly keen on purchasing what she called 'electrical appliances' to satisfy her insatiable need for more heat. On 27 May 1951 she informed her trustee that 'I am going to London, must buy something, otherwise there will be unemployment.' She justified her habits by her late husband's theories: 'Maynard always said "Money's for spending, it goes round and round".'

Kahn ponderously rebutted Lydia's economic dicta:

It seems to me [he wrote on 26 June 1952] that you are being somewhat premature in applying the ideas associated with the name of the late Lord Keynes to the hints dropped by the Chancellor of the Exchequer, that the country is in for a touch of unemployment. We paid £500 into your account in March and another £500 as recently as the middle of May, on each occasion the account having become overdrawn. By the 21st June it had become overdrawn again and another £500 has been paid in. This means that in the past quarter you have been spending at more than twice the proper rate. I am afraid it is my duty to warn you that this cannot go on.

It's not quite clear why Lydia was going through so much money at this time. She thanked Kahn for his 'innumerable scriptures', which seemed 'Chinese' to her. In 1959 she wrote him: 'Dear Richard, It appears that I ought to be redecorated. I look in the mirror and think it's long overdue. I should be glad of your opinion.' After Lydia gave up her properties, her cash position improved and by the late 1960s she was underspending.

Richard Kahn was devoted to Lydia, not just for her own sake, but because of the part she had played in the life of his hero. But he was not an entirely satisfactory trustee. He lacked Maynard's speed in transacting business; he also suffered from bouts of depression during which he was incapable of conducting business at all. So in good peasant fashion Lydia would sell her furniture and other personal possessions to meet her expenses. In 1956 she needed to get the roof at Tilton repaired, but Kahn was too busy to reply to her letters. So she sold a cast of a Degas ballerina given to her by Samuel Courtauld for £5000. In 1958, she wrote to Dadie Rylands, 'no letter from Kahn, constipation'.

Kahn generally came down to Tilton after each Christmas to discuss farm accounts with Logan Thomson. Lydia dreaded these bursarial visitations, though she kept up a cheerful front, promising him 'Tilton's speciality, well prepared electric blankets', and assuring him that with '80 degrees hot water', there would be 'not a dull moment in the bathroom'. Once she wrote: 'How would you feel about endowing your bed with a couple of pairs of sheets (and perhaps some pillow slips if you are feeling generous).' She was fiercely protective of Logan, though: 'Logan is a farmer, not a bursar or civil servant who writes memorandums all day long. . . .' She mocked her trustee for his forgetfulness ('We screamed with laughter, especially when you signed [yourself] Logan'), for his illegible handwriting ('It is a dream to read your typed letter'), and for his bureaucratic habits: 'Yesterday we went to see a film which was your cup of tea, a life story of a civil servant in the Treasury. . . .' She accused him of addressing her as though she were a 'chart or a trade cycle', and handed his article on tariffs to Logan, unread. She forwarded to him enquiries from Japan, saying that 'I really [am] incapable of dealing with Oriental economics.' After receiving a further batch of technical papers, she asked him: 'Would it cause unemployment if I sent a circular letter to the effect that Maynard is no more alive for 5 years?'

But Lydia was tied to Kahn, not just by Maynard's will, but by his love for Maynard. She tried to thaw out his frozen feelings: 'You sound so tired and hurried in your letter; if only you pick broad beans you'd forget all about index of prices. . . .' And having once scolded him for acting like 'Oliver Cromwell', she concluded, 'Still, all in all, you are noble and good, and I am very fond of you.'

Kahn struggled on doggedly to fulfil his Master's trust, despite increasing deafness and oddness. In 1959, he converted her life interest into an annuity to release capital for a new 'Keynes Building' at King's College. He assured her that her position would be fully safeguarded. Lydia was (rightly) worried by the thought of a fixed annuity. 'What happens to me if I live to one hundred and you economists let inflation run away again?' She poured out her worries to Maynard's nephew Maurice Hill, who was staying with her. Geoffrey Keynes wrote to her reprovingly: 'I don't know what you have been telling Maurice about your affairs, but he has come back to Cambridge spreading slanders about your trustees. This is really quite serious, and I have had to demand an apology. Richard is much distressed. Maurice is a notorious spreader of malicious stories, and it would be wiser not to talk to him of affairs which don't concern him.' Lydia was quick to defend Maurice: 'I am very fond of him, he has a kick, even if it is gossip, which he and I have in common, but I deny that it is malicious. There are times when it is good that these things are talked off. There is too much closed shop in the world already.'

In 1970, Lydia informed her trustee that she was eighty. Kahn disagreed (10 April 1970):

You will remember that when Jack Peters and I negotiated your annuity with the insurance company we had to try to estimate your age. The evidence before us were various passports, a marriage certificate, a statement from your brother and, for what it was worth, a statement from you. . . . It became apparent that in your young days you were seriously understating your age and that as you got less and less young you began more and more to overstate it.

We did our best to arrive at a fair estimate and the insurance company accepted it. According to this estimate your age at present is 78½.

III

HARROD'S PURPOSE

The first major assessment of Keynes's personality and contribution to economic theory and statecraft came with the publication of Roy Harrod's official *Life of John Maynard Keynes* in 1951. There had already been some chipping away at the icon. Etienne Mantoux's *The Carthaginian Peace*, subtitled *The Economic Consequences of Mr. Keynes* and published within a few weeks of Maynard's death, attacked both the economics and sympathies of his anti-Versailles Treaty polemic, *The Economic Consequences of the Peace*. The publication, in 1949, of *Two Memoirs* gave ammunition to critics of Keynesian economics by revealing their author to be a self-confessed 'immoralist'. More seriously, Keynes's reputation for economic statesmanship had been compromised by the predictable failure of the American Loan Agreement. The convertibility of the pound into dollars, started on 15 July 1947, had to be suspended six weeks later, as Britain's, and the world's, hunger for dollars caused a flight of sterling from London. The IMF was put in cold storage, its co-founder Harry White dying in 1948, under suspicion of being a Russian spy. The Cold War had arrived, and with it the McCarthyite witch-hunt to extirpate 'communists' from American life.

However, Keynesian theory, in the form bequeathed in *How to Pay for the War*, was increasingly accepted as the basis for macroeconomic policy. In 1947 it became clear that the British economy was suffering from suppressed inflation. The budget of November 1947 marked a shift in anti-inflationary policy from physical planning and price controls to fiscal policy: presumably Keynes would have approved. The cheap-money policy was maintained, despite rumblings from Dennis Robertson. Robertson pointed out that fiscal policy was relatively ineffective against wage-induced inflation, since higher taxation would tend to be included in wage demands. The only remedy was dearer money.[3] However, bank rate remained at 2 per cent till 1951.

As in the war, British prospects depended on American policy. The grant-in-aid which Keynes had failed to win in Washington in 1945 eventually came in the form of $13bn worth of Marshall Aid, of which Britain's share was $2.7bn, and which, between 1948 and 1951, helped finance Britain's, and Europe's, dollar deficits. Isolationism and Anglophobia had been finally overcome by the Cold War. However, at the time, America's long-term commitment to Western Europe looked as insecure as did the continuation of the US boom. If depressive forces reappeared, how Keynesian would American policy be? In 1946, Congress had passed a 'high' but not 'full' employment act. There was strong conservative opposition to active fiscal policy.

Part of the purpose of Harrod's book was to clinch the success of the Keynesian Revolution in Britain and the United States – the two countries in the world which mattered to him. He was quite clear that this involved suppression of anything in Keynes's life which might set Americans against him. When the two trustees, Geoffrey Keynes and Richard Kahn, proceeded, on Keynes's instructions, to organise the publication of the *Two Memoirs*, Harrod urged that certain remarks, which might be construed as having a homosexual flavour, be omitted. 'Such passages, if seized on,' he wrote to Geoffrey Keynes on 10 January 1949, 'might greatly undermine Maynard's reputation . . . and that in turn might damage his influence. In a sense he still lives on. It is still in the balance whether his policies will be adopted or not and that means much for the welfare of the world. Maynard was always most critical about his reputation outside a narrow circle. . . . He wanted to conserve his power of exerting public influence.

And he still would. . . .' To this conservation, Harrod's biography was dedicated.

Commissioned by Sir Geoffrey Keynes, it was a labour of love, passion and projection, researched and written in an astonishingly short time. Harrod started work in 1947. Almost immediately he had to resist Sir Geoffrey's determination to burn all 'incriminating' Keynes letters before Maynard's official biographer had time to see them. Harrod enlisted the Bloomsberries and John Sparrow on behalf of preserving the 'great correspondence' with Lytton Strachey, for publication in '100 years' time'.[4] This campaign was successful, because Harrod convinced Geoffrey Keynes of his 'discretion'. In 1955, the correspondence was deposited at King's College, but not listed in the catalogue of Keynes's Papers. No one was supposed to know that it was there.

For writing the book Harrod relied on the Keynes Papers (which then included much fuller wartime files), many interviews, and personal knowledge. He got nothing out of Lydia. 'Roy comes every day and works with Mrs Stephens,' Lydia wrote to Kahn from 46 Gordon Square on 31 January 1949. But she refused to discuss Maynard with him. 'She herself does *not* want to pick over the old memories *at all,*' Harrod told Sir Geoffrey Keynes on 28 November 1948. After Harrod's book was published, she commented: 'Well, Roy got wonderful press. I am so glad. Robbins in the Times was exhilarating.' But Lydia never read it. Harrod spent 'very pleasant weekends' with Vanessa, Clive and Duncan discussing Maynard's personality. He went on a research trip to the United States, where he found that 'they had all – or almost all – evidently fallen in love with Maynard'. By the end of 1948 he had polished off the pre-First World War chapters. In June 1949 he was finishing the 1939–46 section, but still had the inter-war years to do. By February 1950, he was sending galleys round for comment.

His book was published in January 1951. Reviewing the English reviewers, the German émigré economist Edward Rosenbaum wrote: 'It was not so much the controversial views of Keynes that were discussed as the question of whether the author had succeeded in creating for posterity a convincing picture of Keynes.'[5] This is true, and unsurprising: Harrod's book was after all a biography, not an economic treatise. Discussion of Harrod's achievement as a biographer was given particular point by what more hostile reviewers called his own 'intrusiveness'. The biographer himself was one of the prominent *dramatis personae*, powerfully present, not just in the flesh, so to speak ('Keynes was staying with me in Christ Church some time after that . . .'), but through a marked idiosyncrasy of style and tone. Geoffrey Keynes had urged him to cut out the 'Ands' and 'Buts', with only limited success.

The theme of the reviews in the 'tabloids' was Keynes's success in making money. Someone who left a fortune must know a thing or two!

With a few exceptions, like Malcolm Muggeridge in the *Daily Telegraph* of 26 January, the tone of the serious reviews was one of considerable veneration for the subject, much less so for the biographer, and some doubt about the intellectual legacy. Harrod may be judged to have succeeded in his main purpose, which was to portray Keynes as a brilliant thinker, an entrancing personality and a great world benefactor.

Harold Nicolson in the *Observer* of 28 January 1951 praised Harrod's biographical method for giving immediacy and colour to his portrait of Keynes. Henry Phelps Brown in *Economica* (May 1951) also detected 'a glowing Boswellian joy . . . that is very moving'. Lionel Robbins in *The Times* of 26 January 1951 was Olympian both about the man and about the biographer. Keynes was the many-sided genius who 'shook age-long error and prejudice, but . . . also sometimes shook essential foundations'. As for Harrod, he had made of Keynes's life a book which 'whether it commands agreement or not, it is exceedingly difficult to stop reading'. The same sense of balance, though with much more personal engagement, and at many times the length, was conveyed by the magisterial (though anonymous) reviewer in the *Times Literary Supplement* of 23 February. (It was, in fact, Noël Annan.) Keynes was the outstanding product of the Cambridge civilisation of his day; his Achilles' heel was his lack of political sense: 'he never studied the sources of power nor how society is affected by social stratification or the forces of social control'. Harrod is praised for 'pace, proportion, sanity, and regard for truth', criticised for style and tone of voice. The truth discerned by Annan was that Harrod was an adequate writer who aspired to the artistry of his subject. 'The spirit which inspired Keynes to write the great set-pieces of Clemenceau, Lloyd George and Wilson beckons; but to all but masters of prose this spirit is an *ignis fatuus.*' Furthermore, Harrod radiated a 'moist light'. 'The photograph is accurate but tinted; and this is inappropriate to a landscape which should be exceptionally precise, hard, angular and clearly defined.'

The mistakes of style and tone were also noticed by Leonard Woolf in the *Listener* of 25 January and Anthony Crosland in *Tribune* on 23 February. To Woolf, Harrod's style oscillated 'between inappropriate intimacy and strings of rhetorical questions. He could have greatly improved it if he had reduced its length by a hundred pages, cutting out ninety per cent of his own reflections, the Stracheyean reconstruction of Keynes's reflections, and all the sentences ending with an interrogation mark.' To Crosland, Harrod 'has, I think, the most irritating style of any man now writing' – a style overladen with purple passages, rhetorical questions, arch exclamations, archaisms, and interior monologues. It 'reached a nadir in his description of Keynes falling in love; it is to be hoped that Mr Harrod will do one last service to his subject by cutting this passage out of future editions'.

Criticism of Harrod's eulogistic treatment of Keynes's last phase came, as one might expect, from Hubert Henderson in the *Spectator* of 26 January 1951. Henderson pointed out that Harrod's idea that the future of Anglo-American relations turned on the fate of the IMF and World Bank 'would be a grotesque exaggeration even if it had not become clear meanwhile that the crux of Anglo-American relations in our time will be the measure of unity that can be maintained in handling the very different problems raised by Stalin'.

A fair generalisation would be that those reviewers who knew Keynes best liked the biography least. Those who knew Keynes not at all, or only in his last heroic years, found Harrod's account of his hero's progression from youthful iconoclasm to conservative statesmanship moving and convincing. Bloomsbury and Cambridge (the latter excluding the family) believed that Harrod underplayed Keynes's iconoclasm in all phases of his life – in other words, that he made out Keynes to be too much like Harrod. Kingsley Martin wrote in the *New Statesman*: 'This is the biography of Lord Keynes, someone else must write the life of Maynard.'

Harrod was deeply hurt by Bloomsbury's critical reception of his work. In a letter to Clive Bell dated 28 February 1951, he conceded that he had not done 'my best to get you all to talk about *Maynard*'. Still, Bloomsbury was also to blame. 'They were a little reluctant in going the whole way with one on the ground that all this narrative would be executed later by a more competent . . . hand. But where *is* that hand? . . . You have got to find someone who *can* write. You can publish letters long after the event, but without interpretation they will not convey the original impression. I think the presence in the minds of some of this mythical interpreter, destined to come forward at the right hour & write the inspired account, has hampered me a little in achieving quite all I might have.' By far the most perceptive contemporary Keynes-watcher was Foxy Falk, but he never attempted the penetrating memoir which he could have written.

Rosenbaum's view that the reviewers of Harrod's biography discussed his success in evoking Keynes's personality rather than the validity of his theories is, nevertheless, incomplete. It would be more accurate to say that their assessment of Keynes's personality led most of the economically literate reviewers (Crosland is an exception here) to be sceptical of the general validity of Keynesian theory. The link lies in Keynes's well-known changeability, expressed in the joke that two of the theories, whenever a group of economists were assembled, would be Keynes's. The fundamental criticism of his economics, many times repeated since, was that Keynes substituted creativity for rules. Yet a system which depends on a continuing *tour de force* is no system, but a set of temporary expedients, which cannot be indefinitely prolonged. Keynes destroyed the old wisdom, and left only his own capacity for self-correction in its place. An American economist called him the 'Kerensky of the Keynesian Revolution'.[6]

This line of thought can be traced in a number of assessments of Keynes's economics arising from Harrod's book. Hubert Henderson, in the review cited above, made the point that Keynes's influence was too varied to be captured by a single production like the *General Theory*: 'He was an opportunist and eclectic to the end. He was far too prone to extract cosmic generalisations from practical prescriptions adapted to the passing scene to make a really satisfactory job of the grand new synthesis of economic thought for which he strove.'

John Hefferman, writing in *City Press* on 2 February 1951, called Keynes a 'man of short views and brilliant expedients' who didn't realise that 'his measures for dealing with immediate unemployment would inevitably result in deeper processes, which would make even that problem more serious in the long run'. The bankers were right, and Keynes was wrong. He overlooked the fact that raising bank rate:

> was designed to correct a situation which was made the more difficult by the rigidity of the economy and the refusal of trade unions and others to accept adjustment. . . . Instead of spending his time pointing out the evils of rigidity and the disadvantages of it to the peoples, Keynes accepted rigidity as inevitable and hoped that it would be overcome by the depreciation of the currency. . . . He failed to appreciate that the time would come when he would no longer be here to provide the next answer. His friends will doubtless endeavour to excuse this by saying that Keynes would not have allowed such things as are developing to take place without counter-action. That is always the disaster which results from policies of mere expediency and in forgetting the great truths.

The anonymous reviewer in the *Glasgow Herald* of 27 January 1951, who sounds like Hayek, wrote that 'the brilliance of his own mind allowed Keynes to assume too readily that his own – frequently changing – judgments were always right, and that opposition was due to mental sloth and incomprehension'. The review continued:

> There is a great deal of Faust in Keynes, and a good deal of Mephistopheles; the belief in the vast range of his own knowledge, the distrust of inherited learning, the thirst for action, the willingness to take supreme risks, the continuous striving. As Mephistopheles monetised dormant buried Treasure, so Keynes urged the issue of money against unutilised resources. Like Faust, he was a greatly admired teacher, but like Mephistopheles, he was apt to make fun of other teachers. Like Faust, he died surveying the improvement of his own acres, but, more fortunate than Faust, he married and retained his Helena.

Of Keynes's economic theories, the *Economist* wrote on 27 January 1951: 'They display the essential connections existing at a moment of time, and in given conditions, between various economic magnitudes, but not the dynamic laws governing change in those conditions themselves.' Keynes left a permanent legacy: 'The study of economic aggregates has taken its place in the centre of economic science, and can never again be pushed away to the periphery where pre-Keynesian economists left it. . . . one does not undiscover America.' But it was dangerous to rely confidently on Keynesian economics as a guide to practical policy. This was due not just to the static nature of Keynes's analysis, but to something deeper,

> from the very readiness to change, adapt, reformulate, which was part of Keynes's strength. Whatever he wrote, said, and advocated was always . . . related to current conditions and circumstances, its emphasis coloured by the needs of the moment. . . . The difficulty was that he always assumed a similar adaptability on the part of his disciples and converts – and always in vain. To adapt his own famous phrase about Wilson, it was harder to de-bamboozle them than to bamboozle them in the first place. . . . His influence . . . was such as could be safely wielded only by an immortal who would always be there to correct himself when necessary.

This was especially true since much of his doctrine had a powerful appeal to 'two pernicious types of mind – the illiberal and the irresponsible'.

To all of this the correct answer was surely given by the economist Alan Peacock in *Liberal News* of 23 February 1951. Peacock thought that what would survive was not Keynes's unemployment theory but 'his general method of approach, which is equally applicable to conditions of deflation and inflation'. Keynes bequeathed a style of thinking about economic problems, supported by a technique of stabilisation, which certainly made demands on the judgement of policymakers (unlike automatic rules), but was certainly not the eclectic, or even worse anarchic, procedure depicted by his critics. If a criticism is to be made of his outlook, it is that anything left to the judgement of politicians is likely to go wrong.

Reviewers' difficulty in summing up Keynes's economic doctrines was matched by their inability to agree on his political position. Harrod, who himself stood as a Conservative candidate in the general election of 1945 and was later Macmillan's 'favourite economist', depicted Keynes as a radical who became a liberal Conservative as he grew older. According to the *Guardian* of 20 April 1951, 'the paradox of Keynes's career is that he was fundamentally a Man of the Right who, by the accident of time and circumstance, had strayed into the Left Wing intellectual camp of the generation into which he grew up'. The *Financial Times* reviewer of 29 January 1951 thought that the *General Theory* provided a 'theoretical excuse for Socialist extravagance'; but to Anthony Crosland it was Keynes's

achievement to have demolished Marx and shown how a private property
system could be made to avoid unemployment 'through its metamorpho-
sis into a reformed, planned neo-capitalism'. Crosland attacked the Conservative whitewash in which Harrod painted Keynes, remarking
perceptively: 'The truth is that Keynes was strongly hostile to capitalism
loosely defined as a system of *laisser-faire*. But he was not opposed to
capitalism, defined as a system of private property and enterprise.'

IV

A MAN FOR ALL SEASONS?

In the thirty years following his death, Keynes's reputation soared and
then crashed. The magic seemed to work, then suddenly it faded. The
years of success were the so-called 'golden age' lasting roughly from 1950
to the early 1970s, when the 'mixed economies' of Western nations
achieved a stability and rates of economic growth unequalled in economic
history. Then came the time of troubles, when the economic machine
stuttered and stalled, and familiar patterns of boom and slump reasserted
themselves. The Keynesian age – as the golden age is often known –
ended in 'stagflation' – a combination of rising inflation *and* rising
unemployment. New magicians appeared who talked about the need to
return to 'market disciplines' and 'Victorian values' and who said that the
government was the problem, not the solution. In the golden age most
economists would have called themselves Keynesian; by the early 1990s,
only a minority. How much had Keynes to do both with the golden age
and with its collapse?

There were four important elements in the Keynesian mindset. The
first was that, for various different, and largely unexplained, reasons,
economies were sticky, not fluid. They would only adjust sluggishly, if at
all, to 'shocks'. So, Keynes said, governments must intervene to stop
unemployment developing; because, if they did not, unemployment might
persist for a long time.

Secondly, there was a powerful political economy argument: free
societies could not stand heavy, persisting unemployment. In the long run
we may have full employment. But in the long run we are dead; and in
the short run we may have revolution if we allow mass unemployment to
develop. This, as we have seen, was Keynes's answer to Hayek.

Thirdly, although most economists rejected any simple idea of 'secular
stagnation', they were powerfully influenced by Keynes's thought that
investment opportunities would flag in rich societies, while saving habits
continued unchanged. So they were continually haunted by the prospect
of depression even when economies were booming. The boom, Keynes
himself had predicted, could not last.

These were all backward-looking ideas. The fourth, which looked to the future, was summed up in Keynes's phrase 'Joy through Statistics'. With Keynes this was something of a wisecrack. He was always deeply sceptical about statistical forecasting. But his followers took it seriously. From the crude beginnings of national income accounts they developed a faith that Keynesian policy could be made completely scientific, or 'automatic' as James Meade put it. This faith enabled them to finesse the problem to which anti-Keynesians constantly directed unwelcome attention: the fact that economic policy was bound to be run by politicians, with political aims and ambitions. These pre-scientific disturbances were simply removed from the Keynesian picture, their place taken by forecasting models, with more and more equations.

In time, all these assumptions, faiths, hopes, started to break down. Some of the problems started with the theory itself; others in the way it was accepted; others in the way it was applied. Some had nothing to do with Keynes or Keynesianism at all, though he got blamed nonetheless. All contributed to a 'counter-revolution' in both theory and policy which got under way in the late 1960s. In the course of it, some old truths were properly rediscovered, some new truths improperly ignored.

Keynes's 'general theory of employment' was not quite as general as he believed. For one thing, it left out the many causes of unemployment apart from demand-deficiency, particularly those to do with labour immobility and slowness of adaptation to change. Unemployment can occur even when there is enough aggregate demand. Hubert Henderson always emphasised the structural character of Britain's inter-war unemployment problem. Keynes was aware of 'structural unemployment', but it was not the subject of his theory. In that sense the *General Theory* was an unbalanced book, and it left an unbalanced legacy. This meant that little attention was paid to 'supply side problems' in the golden age; and they tended to cumulate. It is inconceivable that Keynes would not have wanted to attack them. But he was no longer there, and his book was.

The deeper problem was with his theory itself. What Keynes meant by 'general theory' was 'generalised theory'. He saw his theory as of a higher order of generality than was the classical theory. A 'general' theory of employment, in this sense, allows the possibility of many equilibria. For Keynes mass unemployment, or underutilisation of available resources, was a logical possibility rooted in uncertain expectations. But economists had never understood how unemployment could persist, even occur, if workers were always willing to price themselves into jobs, and they felt that Keynes had not properly explained how this might be so, even though the fact could not be gainsaid. So the mainstream in the profession fell back on traditional reasons. Powerful unions and social legislation prevented the required wage flexibility and worker mobility which would have enabled economies to adjust fairly painlessly to shocks. 'Classical theory' was right after all in its claim that unemployment could not occur if wages and prices were perfectly flexible; it just happened not to be terribly relevant. The so-called 'neo-classical synthesis' of the 1950s thus reaffirmed 'classical theory' as the 'general case', with Keynesian theory as a 'special case of Classical theory where wages are rigid'.[7] However, the special case was the actual case in the modern world. So there remained a substantial role for Keynesian *policy* in moving the economy from an inferior to superior equilibrium, or preventing the emergence of an inferior equilibrium.

This compromise with classical theory seemed to leave economics in a mess. The unexplained assumption of sticky wages and prices seemed to contradict the much more powerful axiom on which economics itself rested – that economic agents were rational maximisers. There was evidently a deal of theoretical clearing up to do. This clearing up took an anti-Keynesian form once the promise of Keynesian policy started to fade.

The second Keynesian thesis which ran aground was that of the long-run tendency to stagnation and unemployment. The post-war boom proved exceptionally strong and was prolonged all over the 'free' world, even after post-war reconstruction was finished. At the time this was attributed to Keynesian policies themselves, but this turns out to be unproven. True enough, both the British and US governments 'targeted' unemployment. But the targets were repeatedly revised downwards as actual results exceeded the targets. Low unemployment, it seemed, was not caused by the pursuit of low unemployment targets; the low unemployment targets were caused by low unemployment.

What then was it that made the 1950s and 1960s so 'golden'? A large part of the explanation is 'catch-up'. Keynes tended to lump all the rich societies together as suffering from incipient sclerosis. In fact, economies, rich and poor, were on an ascending ladder of richness with America at the top. After the Second World War, writes Moses Abramovitz, 'the countries of the industrialized "West" were able to bring into production a large backlog of unexploited technology. The principal part of this backlog ... consisted of methods of production and of industrial and commercial organization already in use in the United States at the end of the war, but not yet employed in the other countries of the West.'[8] The opportunities for technological 'catch-up' gave capital a high marginal productivity, leading to high private investment demand. A high rate of productivity growth allowed a sufficient rise in real incomes to satisfy workers' aspirations while keeping unit costs fairly stable. (Britain, whose productivity growth lagged behind that of all developed countries except the USA, is a partial exception.)

'Catch-up' is a potential; its exploitation depends on such factors as opportunities for diffusion of technology, social capacity, industrial adaptability and the state of aggregate demand. In the inter-war years 'catch-up' was 'frustrated by the irregular effects of the Great War and of the years of disturbed political and financial conditions that followed, by the uneven impacts of the Great Depression itself and of the restrictions on international trade'. During the Second World War, the productivity gap between the United States and the rest of the world widened. After the war 'the three elements required for rapid growth by catching up came together . . . large technological gaps; enlarged social competence . . . and conditions favoring rapid realization of potential'. Of the last, Abramovitz writes:

> There was *on this occasion* . . . a strong reaction to the experience of defeat in war, and a chance for political reconstruction. The postwar political and economic reorganization and reform weakened the power of monopolistic groups, brought new men to the fore, and focused the attention of governments on the tasks of recovery and reform. . . . The facilities for the diffusion of technology improved. International markets were opened. Large labor reserves in home agriculture and immigration from Southern and Eastern Europe provided a flexible and mobile labor supply. Government support, technological opportunity, and an environment of stable international money favored heavy and sustained capital investment. The outcome was the great speed and strength of the post-war catch-up process.[9]

To what extent were the 'conditions' which facilitated 'catch-up' put in place by the Keynesian Revolution? Apparently, not much. The reconstruction of industries and industrial relations on the Continent of Europe were the products of defeat, not of Keynesian policy. The victorious nations, Britain and the United States, which were also most influenced by Keynesian ideas, exhibited the weakest tendency to structural reform.

To be sure, governments consumed a larger share of the national income than before the war and this contributed to stability. But this was because of the extensive post-war nationalisations and expansion of the social services. Neither had an explicit warrant in Keynesian theory; neither was undertaken for Keynesian reasons. Nor for that matter was America's recession-proof military spending. As John Hicks put it in 1974: 'The combination of more rapid technical progress (surely a fact) with the socialist tendencies which increased demand for collective goods (surely also a fact) could have produced such a boom without the added stimulus of Keynesian policies. It is still unclear how much is to be attributed to the one and how much to the other.'[10]

The post-war trading and monetary regimes undoubtedly facilitated the diffusion of best-practice technology. Keynes's handiwork can be found in the setting up of both, but the ideas which inspired them – trade liberalisation, fixed exchange rates, currency convertibility – were not of specific Keynesian provenance. They go back to Adam Smith, David Ricardo and the gold standard. What was intended to be restored was the nineteenth-century gold standard/free-trade system, improved by experience of the inter-war years. This reflected the American conviction that the troubles of the inter-war years had been brought about by currency and trade wars.

Keynes's own specific, the doctrine of 'creditor adjustment', was not accepted at Bretton Woods. This meant that the 1944 Agreement provided no mechanism for dealing with the 'dollar gap', which most Americans were anyway inclined to regard as fictional. For example, the J. P. Morgan partner Russell Leffingwell dismissed it in 1949 as a euphemism for 'living beyond one's means'; Keynes's defeated 'bancor' proposal was simply an attempt to 'create an international currency without limit and thus enable the British to consume American products without paying for them'.[11] Following the failure of the bilateral loans to Britain and France in 1945, the Bretton Woods Agreement was put into cold storage for almost fifteen years; the International Trade Organisation was similarly aborted. Far from being the 'foundation upon which [post-war] world trade, production, employment and investment were gradually built', as one historian has claimed,[12] the Bretton Woods rules and institutions played little part in the golden-age experience. Their cornerstone, currency convertibility at fixed exchange rates, was not restored in the main European countries till 1959, by which time the golden age was in full flower.

The 'dollar gap' of which Leffingwell spoke in 1949 was eliminated, not by the 'invisible hand', which was Keynes's somewhat despairing alternative to 'bancor', but by the very visible US commitment to keep Western Europe and Japan free of communism. This led the United States to acquiesce in the large sterling, franc and deutschmark devaluations against the dollar in 1949; it led to the huge outflow of American dollars on government account, later supplemented by large private outflows; it led the USA to promote a European Payments Union and to allow it to discriminate against American goods which it had sought to deny Britain. The trend in the balance of payments in turn enabled exchange rates to be gradually stabilised and currency convertibility re-established. This promoted trade liberalisation, which in turn fuelled economic growth. By 1960 Leffingwell, in the last year of his life, was singing a different tune:

> Wisely we undertook to set the world to rights. We gave money and know-how to our foreign friends, we made fixed foreign investments, and we policed the world against the Russians and Communist Chinese with foreign bases and foreign based troops and ships and planes. All this involved spending immense sums of dollars abroad.
> We and our friends abroad had been so obsessed by the thought

of the ... dollar gap ... that until recently few noticed that the dollar shortage had disappeared and a dollar glut had taken its place. Our foreign aid has been successful beyond our dreams. Western Europe and Japan had fully recovered and were in hot competition with us here and abroad. So our favorable trade balance had dwindled to little or nothing.

We are still spending abroad billions more than our income from abroad, and the resulting deficit is reflected in our loss of gold and increased short term debt to abroad. . . . For the first time in more than a quarter of a century we are being subjected, willy nilly, to the discipline of the gold standard.[13]

Any influence of Keynes in all this? These American policies, we may say, had Keynesian effects; they were not undertaken for Keynesian reasons.

But there is more to be said. The Keynesian background became more important as the great boom continued through the 1950s. In 1937 Keynes had sketched his technique of 'boom control'. Governments should run fiscal surpluses while avoiding dear money 'like hellfire'. In 1941 he had written to the American economist Mordecai Ezekiel: 'But I am quite unconvinced that low interest rates cannot play an enormous part in *sustaining* investment at a given figure. . . .' This strategy of cheap money and fiscal surpluses was pursued by most governments in the first fifteen years after the war. It might well have sustained the post-war boom over a far longer period than would otherwise have happened. By the early 1960s it had started to break down.

In 1945, Keynes had confessed himself baffled by the wages problem in a full-employment economy. Full-employment policy seemed to have the unpleasant by-product of handing over power to determine money wages – and with it the rate of inflation – to the trade unions. This had been a worry when Keynes wrote *How to Pay for the War* in 1940. The 1944 Employment Policy White Paper had insisted that full-employment policy would founder in the absence of 'wage moderation'. But the contract – full employment in return for wage restraint – was, in Britain at least, only implicit. In Continental non-communist Europe it was promoted through more formal institutional arrangements. By the early 1960s it was showing signs of strain.

The Keynesians thought they had an answer: incomes policy. The government would keep aggregate demand high, but only if trade unions accepted controls on wages. This deal had not been possible in the Second World War and it was even more unlikely to work after two decades of full employment. In Britain, it proved impossible to replicate the neo-corporatist wage-bargaining systems of the Continent. 'Declarations of intent', 'wage freezes', 'statutory incomes policies', 'social contracts' followed in rapid succession from the early 1960s to the late 1970s, without solving the 'wages problem' at full employment. Keynes's bafflement was inherited by his closest disciples. I once asked Richard Kahn – this would have been in the mid-1970s – why Keynesian policy seemed to be breaking down. His reply sticks in my memory: 'We never thought the leaders of the trade unions could behave so stupidly.'

Having said this, it is far from clear that trade-union-led 'wage push' was the driving force behind inflation and subsequent breakdown of Keynesian policy. Pride of place here must be given to the mishandling of fiscal policy – the jewel in the Keynesian crown. This takes us back to the debates of 1942–3 about the 'affordability' of the welfare state planned by Beveridge, translated into a setting of rising expectations produced by full employment and relatively rapid growth. Economists have always known that, beyond a certain point, taxes encounter tax resistance. In 1945, Colin Clark had suggested that 25 per cent was the taxable limit for free societies of the British type. Keynes was inclined to agree. This turned out to be too low, but not much too low. What became clear in the 1960s was that tax resistance developed much sooner in the working class than in the middle and upper classes, for whom it was mitigated by guilt and *noblesse oblige*. As the tax take started to 'bite' lower and lower down the income scale to finance improvements in the social services, tax resistance took the form of demanding compensating increases in 'take home' pay. As Labour's Social Services Secretary Richard Crossman was driven to remark in 1968: 'The trade unionists want to see us spending less on social services so there will be more for wage packets.'[14] Compensating wage-push was not the only result. With a public spending momentum unmatched by a comparable expansion of tax tolerance, budget deficits started to develop unrelated to any macroeconomic rationale. This destroyed the usefulness of the Keynesian technique of 'boom control'.

However, it was the breakdown of the Keynesian strategy of boom control in the United States which proved fatal to the golden age.

The fiscal 'rule' approved by the influential American Committee for Economic Development in 1947 was to 'Set tax rates to balance the budget and provide a surplus for debt retirement at an agreed high level of employment and national income. Having set these rates, leave them alone unless there is some major change in national policy or conditions of national life.' The agreed unemployment rate was 4 per cent, which the Committee reckoned was the non-inflationary rate. The budget surplus would automatically increase when unemployment fell below 4 per cent, and a deficit would automatically develop if unemployment rose much above 4 per cent. Herbert Stein writes that 'CED's 1947 statement profoundly influenced fiscal discussion, fiscal thinking and fiscal policy in the two decades that followed it.'[15] In the fourteen years from 1947 to 1960 inclusive, the US budget was in surplus for half the time, in deficit for the other half. Interest rate changes, though, were given a larger share in stabilisation policy than Keynes had recommended. Since, under the fixed exchange rate regime of the 1950s and 1960s, US financial policy determined the inflation rate of the whole system, it must be given the main credit for keeping inflation under control for most of the golden age.

The fiscal conservatism of the Truman–Eisenhower years was dubbed non-Keynesian by the generation of Keynesians who came into power in the 1960s. But this was a misreading of the Keynesian Revolution. Setting tax rates to achieve an employment target consistent with a low rate of inflation was properly Keynesian; it marked a radical departure from pre-Keynesian fiscal orthodoxy which paid no attention to the 'state of trade'. Ironically, the real contribution of Keynesian policy to the golden age was not to stimulate aggregate demand. It was to keep inflation under control by methods which did not bring about the collapse of the secular boom.

However, US fiscal restraint broke down in the 1960s. In 1962, the second-generation Keynesian economists who came in to office with President Kennedy were convinced that the long-predicted slump was at hand. A further stimulus to action was the quite unwarranted fear that the Soviet Union would win the Cold War economically and politically, without any need for a hot war. So the scene was set for the big Kennedy–Johnson tax cuts and 'Great Society' programmes. Furthermore, it turned out that the $35 an ounce gold conversion price was not the constraint Leffingwell had thought it would be in 1960, since the USA could use the privileged position of the dollar to export its deficit rather than its surplus. Not only had the dollar long replaced sterling as the world's chief reserve asset, but the existing arrangement, whereby European countries accumulated dollars in return for America protecting the free world from communism, suited both the United States and its Cold War partners.

The American economist Robert Triffin invented the famous 'Triffin paradox': the world needed the growth in reserves which only dollars could provide; but, in splaying convertible dollars round the system, the US government was not only igniting world inflation but undermining confidence in its own currency. The unfolding of the 'paradox' might have been postponed had America not got involved in the Vietnam War. But vast military expenditure overseas, coming on top of the 'Great Society' programmes, started a haemorrhage of gold from Fort Knox in the late 1960s. Once inflationary expectations got built into the global system, fiscal policy was disabled. Raising taxes could no longer be used to fight inflation, since unions would ask for higher wage increases to compensate for reductions in take-home pay; reducing taxes to stimulate the economy would only ratchet up prices. When the US's short debt came to exceed its gold reserves, it was forced to suspend dollar convertibility into gold and float the dollar in 1971. The Bretton Woods system collapsed, inflation was let loose, and the long boom ended.

With it collapsed the reputation of the Keynesian Mandarinate and the serviceability of the Keynesian political formula. It was not capitalist economies but the Keynesian cardinals who were growing sclerotic. No one understood their theology – indeed it was of the essence that it should be highly esoteric – but it was expected to deliver, if not secular salvation, at least continuous progress to some version of it. It took credit for the progress when it occurred, and got the blame when it faltered.

By a supreme irony, the inheritor of the Keynesian Revolution turned out to be its. arch-critic, Milton Friedman. Theoretical revisions would have come anyway. There were too many loose ends. Keynes had left an unfinished masterpiece, and he surely would have modified much of the detail and given different emphases had he lived. But the revision took the form of 'monetarism' because of growing policy failures from the mid-1960s onwards. Friedman's own attacks were launched from within Keynes's own macroeconomic citadel, but, by ruthlessly applying the maximising logic to individual behaviour, he gave two of the Keynesian 'functions' – the consumption function and the demand for money function – properties of stability which they had lacked in their Keynesian form. One conclusion he drew from his analysis was that market economies were more cyclically stable than Keynes had believed: the built-in stabilisers were present in market exchanges, so to speak, and did not have to be imported from outside. What emerged from this line of thought was the notion that market economies fluctuated round their 'natural rate of unemployment', which Friedman thought of as the rate consistent with stable prices. The second conclusion, which followed from the first, was that government interventions of the Keynesian type could improve upon a pre-existing equilibrium only in the very short term, and might well make matters worse. It was only a short step from this to the rational expectations models associated with Richard Sargent and Robert Lucas, according to which monetary and fiscal policy is completely ineffective in altering output and employment unless people are caught by 'surprise'. The circle had come right round; it was as though Keynes had never been. The scene was set for the revival of faith in markets, and the deregulating 'supply-side' policies of the 1980s. At the end of that decade the collapse of communism completed the triumph of free-market liberalism.

Yet there was something incomplete in the new magic. The contractionary fiscal and monetary policies adopted in the early 1980s to eliminate inflation left in their wake heavy and persisting unemployment – just as Keynes would have predicted. The regime of floating exchange rates and increasingly liberated private capital flows which followed the collapse of the Bretton Woods system in 1971 led to short-run currency volatility and prolonged currency misalignments which inflicted heavy losses on many countries, though the currency wars of the 1930s did not repeat themselves. In response to these unexpected consequences of the 'counter-revolution', Keynesianism started to revive – in new theories to explain sticky prices and in the renewed attention policymakers paid to 'output gaps'.

V

LIFE AFTER DEATH

The successes and failures of Keynes's prescriptions for diseased economies were outside his widow's interests and beyond her understanding. She now lived entirely in the past. Angelica Garnett describes going to see her with Duncan Grant early in January 1972, in her seventy-ninth year: 'The light was on, and Lydia came out at once peering out of the door exactly like Mrs Mole – tiny and round, with an extraordinary knitted helmet on her head of a tawny colour. As soon as she saw Duncan making his way towards her she was delighted, and warmly embraced him – a couple of lamp-lit old moles hugging each other.' At eighty she could still lift each leg straight as high as her head. But, a couple of years after this, she was knocked out by a severe bout of viral pneumonia. Following this, she started to lose both her memory and her mobility. She and Logan would sit for hours in Tilton's spacious hall, facing the front door. Lydia sipped wine most of the day. Anglica Garnett's daughter Henrietta visited her on 1 May 1975:

> Lydia and Logan were sitting opposite one another on sturdy armchairs, beneath an over-hanging electric element. . . . She was more shrivelled and more shrunken. Her head was wrapped, as always, in several scarves; her tiny feet were thrust into a pair of short orange rubber boots. She wore a dark-green nylon jacket, buttoned to her chin, which made her look even more Russian than ever. . . . We exchanged several kisses. Logan levered himself up from his chair: his leg had grown gammy.
>
> As usual, I was offered a glass of Sauterne, and, as usual, I accepted it. As usual, too, the conversation rattled swiftly to the subject of ballet.
>
> '. . . it was a good school, my dear. We were taught. They do not teach you now. Not like that. And the food was good: that is so important.'

One of the last sightings of Lydia at Tilton was by Maynard's grand-nephew Simon Keynes, who, coming down for the night with his parents, met Lydia for the first time in September 1975. He found her and Logan

Thomson sitting, as always, in the hall, which was now 'very tidy'. She was 'dressed in the most extraordinary clothes – a greyish woollen suit of skirt and jacket, with loose rings of wool dangling (intentionally) from every part of its area; an odd woollen hat; a pair of boots, coming about 9 inches up her legs'. She boasted that the outfit had cost only £20, and removed her jacket to show off the lining. Logan feared there would be nothing underneath; mischievously aware of the general anticipation, Lydia tried to engage Anne Keynes in discussion about the fullness of her (Lydia's) breasts. In disconnected fragments, and with much repetition, Lydia talked about Diaghilev and Nijinsky and Massine and about Blooms-bury, particularly Leonard Woolf. She did not mention Maynard. She was very keen to give them a meal and at 6.15 fetched a melon and tried to lead them into the dining room. Simon Keynes was sad not to have seen Lydia when she was completely *compos mentis*. 'But her unique character is quite plainly evident – her sense of mischievousness . . . her devotion to ballet and the arts . . . her good but not perfect grasp of English which produces highly original expressions curiously supported by magnificent gesture with her hands and face.'[16]

Lydia was transferred to a nursing home in Seaford in 1976. That October, James Callaghan, Labour Prime Minister of Britain, made a speech to the Party Conference, announcing the end of Keynesian economics. 'The option of spending our way out of recession no longer exists.' It had worked in the past only by 'injecting bigger and bigger doses of inflation into the economy'. By 1984, Britain's Conservative Chancellor of the Exchequer Nigel Lawson was stating the new orthodoxy in his Mais Lecture: the job of macroeconomic policy was to fight inflation; unemployment was to be handled by microeconomic policy – the reverse of what Keynesians had come to believe, though Keynes himself might, by then, have had some sympathy with it.

Lydia survived into the Thatcherite era, dying on 8 June 1981, at the age of eighty-nine. Her ashes were scattered by Richard Keynes from the same spot on the Downs where his father Geoffrey Keynes had scattered Maynard's ashes thirty-five years earlier. But ideas do not die so quickly; and Keynes's will live so long as the world has need of them. That depends on whether our new global economy has enough natural stability to be politically acceptable. Only events will give us the answer.

Bibliography and Sources

(1) MANUSCRIPT COLLECTIONS CONSULTED

I have followed the procedure, adopted in the first two volumes of this biography, of listing the manuscript collections consulted by location. Where I have cited papers consulted, the reference is to the collection alone; for example, references to the Keynes Papers, located at King's College, Cambridge, will be to KP. (See References, after the Bibliography, for the code.) Only those papers consulted for this volume are listed. For other papers at these locations used for earlier volumes, see Robert Skidelsky, *John Maynard Keynes*, i, 403–5; ii, 636–8.

KING'S COLLEGE, CAMBRIDGE

Keynes Papers, Lydia Lopokova Keynes Papers, Charleston Papers, Kahn Papers, Sheppard Papers.

The Keynes Papers contain both his 'personal papers' and his 'economic papers'. The latter were deposited at the Marshall Library till 1986, when they were transferred to King's College to join the 'personal papers'. A fraction of the 'economic papers' have been published in *The Collected Writings of John Maynard Keynes* (see next section). The personal papers are now all classified as PP. Any other reference to the Keynes Papers will be to the unpublished economic papers.

After JMK's illness in 1937 there is hardly any further correspondence between JMK and Lydia Keynes, as they were almost never apart again. There will be no reference to the source for JMK's and Lydia's letters to JMK's parents (almost always to his mother). They are in KP, PP/45 and LLK 5.

BANK OF ENGLAND

Thompson-MacCausland Papers (ADMIN 14).

BODLEIAN LIBRARY, OXFORD

Brand Papers.

BRITISH LIBRARY, LONDON

(1) The JMK–Duncan Grant correspondence 1908–46, Add. MSS 57930–1, (2) JMK and Macmillan & Co., Add. MSS 55201–4, (3) the Christabel Maclaren Papers (letters from Samuel Courtauld), Add. MSS 52432–5, (4) JMK's letters to O. T. Falk, Add. MSS 57923.

COLUMBIA UNIVERSITY, NEW YORK

Herbert H. Lehman Papers.

HARVARD UNIVERSITY

Thomas Lamont Papers; J. A. Schumpeter Papers.

UNIVERSITY OF KENTUCKY

Vinson Papers.

HOUSE OF LORDS

Lloyd George Papers.

HUMANITIES RESEARCH CENTER, AUSTIN, TEXAS

Contains letters from JMK and Clive Bell to Barbara Bagenal, J. L. Garvin, Mary Hutchinson and Mary McCarthy.

LIBRARY OF CONGRESS

Felix Frankfurter Papers; Emmanuel Goldenweiser Papers.

NUFFIELD COLLEGE, OXFORD

Henry Clay Papers; Hubert Henderson Papers.

PRINCETON UNIVERSITY

Harry Dexter White Papers.

PUBLIC RECORD OFFICE, KEW

Treasury Papers, Foreign Office Papers, Cabinet Papers. T247 contains the collection of papers from Keynes's private office; most of the others dealing with Keynes are to be found in the T160 and T236 classes.

ROOSEVELT LIBRARY, HYDE PARK, NEW YORK

Morgenthau Diaries.

ROYAL OPERA HOUSE, COVENT GARDEN

Archive.

TRINITY COLLEGE, CAMBRIDGE

Pethick-Lawrence Papers; R. C. Trevelyan Papers.

STIRLING MEMORIAL LIBRARY, YALE UNIVERSITY
Leffingwell Papers; Lippmann Papers.

BORTHWICK INSTITUTE OF HISTORICAL RESEARCH, UNIVERSITY OF YORK
Halifax Diary.

PRIVATE SOURCES

A collection of O. T. Falk papers is held by Mrs Roland Falk. The diary of Sir Frederic Harmer, August–December 1945, is in the possession of his widow, Lady Harmer. A collection of Paul Bareau papers is held by Peter Bareau. Sir Donald MacDougall's wartime diary, covering part of the Stage II negotiations in 1944, is with Sir Donald MacDougall. 'Few Excuses, No Regrets' is an unpublished biography by Peter Plesch, which has much in it about his father Janos Plesch, Keynes's doctor, who brought him back to 'active life' after his illness. Professor Richard and Mrs Anne Keynes have shown me some wartime letters with glimpses of Keynes in Washington in 1944, and Professor Simon Keynes a note of his visit to Tilton in 1975.

(2) PUBLISHED PRIMARY SOURCES

The main published source is *The Collected Writings of John Maynard Keynes*, 30 volumes, including Bibliography and Index, published by Macmillan/CUP for the Royal Economic Society, 1971–89. They include practically all Keynes's published writings, including journalism, as well as a generous proportion of his unpublished economic correspondence, notes, memoranda, lectures and speeches. They do not include his personal papers, except for a few excerpts from his letters to his parents and his wife. All references to Keynes's published writings are to this edition, though the text is not always identical to the originals – for example, capital letters are used more sparingly. References will also be given to the published versions of the manuscript materials, rather than to the originals. Where reference is given to the Keynes Papers themselves, this is to material which has not been published.

The volumes which have been most relevant to the writing of this book, all edited by Donald Moggridge, are:

XXI. *Activities 1931–1939: World Crises and Policies in Britain and America*, 1982
XXII. *Activities 1939–1945: Internal War Finance*, 1978
XXIII. *Activities 1940–1943: External War Finance*, 1979
XXIV. *Activities 1944–1946: The Transition to Peace*, 1979
XXV. *Activities 1940–1944: Shaping the Post-War World: The Clearing Union*, 1980
XXVI. *Activities 1941–1946: Shaping the Post-War World: Bretton Woods and Reparations*, 1980
XXVII. *Activities 1940–1946: Shaping the Post-War World: Employment and Commodities*, 1980
XXVIII. *Social, Political and Literary Writings*, 1982
XXX. *Bibliography and Index*, 1989

The other main published primary sources are:

A. O. Bell (ed.), *The Diary of Virginia Woolf*, v: *1936–1941*, Hogarth Press, 1984

Roger Bullen and M. E. Pelly (eds) *Documents on British Policy Overseas*, Series 1, iii: *Britain and America: Negotiation of the United States Loan 3 August–7 December 1945*, HMSO, 1986

Foreign Relations of the United States, 1941, iii; 1945, vi

John Harvey (ed.), *The Diplomatic Diaries of Oliver Harvey*, i: *1937–1940*, ii: *1941–1945*, Collins, 1970, 1978

Polly Hill and Richard Keynes (eds), *Lydia and Maynard: Letters between Lydia Lopokova and John Maynard Keynes*, André Deutsch, 1989

Susan Howson and Donald Moggridge (eds), *The Wartime Diaries of Lionel Robbins and James Meade, 1943–45*, Macmillan, 1990

——(eds), *The Collected Papers of James Meade*, iv: *The Cabinet Office Diary 1944–46*, Unwin Hyman, 1990

Nigel Nicolson (ed.), *Harold Nicolson: Diaries and Letters*, i: *1930–1939*, ii: *1939–1945*, Collins, 1966, 1967

——(ed.), *The Letters of Virginia Woolf*, vi: *1936–1941*, Chatto & Windus, 1980

Ben Pimlott (ed.), *The Second World War Diary of Hugh Dalton 1940–45*, Jonathan Cape/LSE, 1986

Frederic Spotts (ed.), *The Letters of Leonard Woolf*, Weidenfeld & Nicolson, 1989

White Paper on *Employment Policy*, Cmd 6527, HMSO, May 1944

(3) SECONDARY SOURCES

BOOKS AND CHAPTERS IN BOOKS

Dean Acheson, *Present at the Creation: My Years in the State Department*, Hamish Hamilton, 1970

Paul Addison, *The Road to 1945: British Politics and the Second Wold War*, Jonathan Cape, 1975

Christopher Andrew and Oleg Gordievsky, *KGB: The Inside Story of its Foreign Operations from Lenin to Gorbachev*, Hodder & Stoughton, 1990

Noël Annan, *The Dons: Mentors, Eccentrics and Geniuses*, HarperCollins, 1999

Thomas Balogh, *Unequal Partners*, ii, Basil Blackwell, 1963

John Barnes and David Nicolson (eds), *The Empire at Bay: The Leo Amery Diaries 1929–1945*, Hutchinson, 1988

Correlli Barnett, *The Audit of War: The Illusion & Reality of Britain as a Great Nation*, Macmillan, 1986

——, *The Lost Victory: British Dreams, British Realities 1945–1950*, Macmillan, 1995

Charles A. Beard, *President Roosevelt and the Coming of the War 1941*, Yale University Press, 1948

Clive Bell, *Old Friends*, Cassell, 1956 (1988 edn)

Quentin Bell, *Elders and Betters*, John Murray, 1995

William H. Beveridge, *Full Employment in a Free Society*, Allen & Unwin, 1944

Leonard Bickel, *Rise up to Life: A Biography of Howard Walter Florey*, Angus & Robertson, 1972

The Earl of Birkenhead, *The Prof in Two Worlds*, Collins, 1961

J. Morton Blum (ed.), *From the Morgenthau Diaries*, i: *Years of Crisis 1928–1938*, ii:

Years of Urgency 1938–1941, iii: *Years of Achievement 1941–1945*, Boston: Houghton Mifflin, 1959, 1965, 1967

Wilfrid Blunt, *John Christie of Glyndebourne*, Geoffrey Bles, 1968

George Borrow, *Wild Wales*, Fontana/Collins, n.d.

Lord Bridges, *The Treasury*, Allen & Unwin, 1964

Stephen Broadberry and Peter Howlett, 'The United Kingdom: "Victory at all Costs"', in Mark Harrison (ed.), *The Economics of World War II: Six Great Powers in International Comparison*, Cambridge University Press, 1998

Alan Bullock, *The Life and Times of Ernest Bevin*, ii: *Minister of Labour 1940–5*, William Heinemann, 1967

J. MacGregor Burns, *Roosevelt: The Soldier of Freedom 1940–1945*, Weidenfeld & Nicolson, 1971

Alec Cairncross, *The Price of War: British Policy on German Reparations 1941–1949*, Basil Blackwell, 1986

——, *The Years of Recovery: British Economic Policy 1945–51*, Methuen, 1985

Alec Cairncross and Nina Watts, *The Economic Section 1939–1961: A Study in Economic Advising*, Routledge, 1989

David Carlton, *Anthony Eden*, Allen Lane, 1981

W. Carr, 'John Maynard Keynes and the Treaty of Versailles', in A. P. Thirlwall (ed.), *Keynes as a Policy Adviser*, Macmillan Press, 1982

James Chace, *Acheson: The Secretary of State who Created the American World*, Simon & Schuster, 1998

John Charmley, *Churchill: The End of Glory: A Political Biography*, Harcourt Brace, 1993

D. N. Chester (ed.), *Lessons of the British War Economy*, Cambridge University Press, 1951

Rupert Christiansen (ed.), *Cambridge Arts Theatre*, Granta Editions, 1998

Winston S. Churchill, *The Second World War*, 6 vols, Cassell, 1948–1954

Kenneth Clark, *The Other Half: A Self-Portrait*, John Murray, 1977

Sir Richard Clarke, *Anglo-American Economic Collaboration in War and Peace 1942–49*, ed. Alec Cairncross, Clarendon Press, 1982

Derek Crabtree and A. P. Thirlwall (eds), *Keynes and the Bloomsbury Group*, Macmillan Press, 1980

N. J. Crowson (ed.), *Fleet Street, Press Barons and Politics: The Journals of Collin Brooks 1932–1940*, Royal Historical Society, 1998

Robert Dallek, *Franklin D. Roosevelt and American Foreign Policy*, Oxford University Press, 1979

Hugh Dalton, *High Tide and After: Memoirs 1945–60*, Frederick Muller, 1962

Nicholas Davenport, *Memoirs of a City Radical*, Weidenfeld & Nicolson, 1974

Alan P. Dobson, *US Wartime Aid to Britain*, Croom Helm, 1986

Frances Donaldson, *The Royal Opera House in the Twentieth Century*, Weidenfeld & Nicolson, 1988

Armand van Dormael, *Bretton Woods: Birth of a Monetary System*, Macmillan, 1978

Ian M. Drummond, *The Floating Pound and the Sterling Area 1931–1939*, Cambridge University Press, 1981

Elizabeth Durbin, *New Jerusalems: The Labour Party and the Economics of Democratic Socialism*, Routledge & Kegan Paul, 1985

Barry Eichengreen, *Golden Fetters: The Gold Standard and the Great Depression 1919–1939*, Oxford University Press, 1992

Paul Einzig, *Hitler's New Order in Europe*, Macmillan, 1941

C. H. Feinstein, *National Income, Expenditure and Output of the United Kingdom 1865–1965*, Cambridge University Press, 1972

Herbert Feis, *1933: Characters in Crisis*, Boston/Toronto: Little, Brown, 1966

David Felix, *Keynes: A Critical Life*, Westport, Connecticut/London: Greenwood Press, 1999

John Fforde, *The Bank of England and Public Policy 1941–1958*, Cambridge University Press, 1992

Margot Fonteyn, *Autobiography*, W. H. Allen, 1975

Michael Foot, *Aneurin Bevan 1897–1945*, MacGibbon & Kee, 1962

James Fox, *Five Sisters: The Langhornes of Virginia*, Simon & Schuster, 2000

M. Friedman and A. J. Schwartz, *The Great Contraction 1929–1933*, Princeton University Press, 1965

J. K. Galbraith, *A Life in Our Times*, André Deutsch, 1981

——*Money: Whence It Came, Where It Went*, André Deutsch, 1975

R. N. Gardner, *Sterling–Dollar Diplomacy*, Oxford University Press, 1969 edn

Mary Glasgow, *The Nineteen Hundreds: A Diary in Retrospect*, Oxford University Press, 1986

Sean Glynn and Alan Booth, *The Road to Full Employment*, Allen & Unwin, 1987

Claude Guillebaud, *The Economic Recovery of Germany 1933–8*, Macmillan, 1938

W. A. Hancock and M. M. Gowing, *British War Economy*, HMSO, 1949

José Harris, *William Beveridge: A Biography*, Clarendon Press, 1977

R. F. Harrod, *The Life of John Maynard Keynes*, Macmillan, 1951

——, *The Prof: A Personal Memoir of Lord Cherwell*, Macmillan, 1959

F. A. Hayek, *The Road to Serfdom*, Routledge & Kegan Paul, 1944 (paperback edn 1962)

John Earl Haynes and Harvey Klehr, *Venona: Decoding Soviet Espionage in America*, Yale University Press, 1999

Hubert Douglas Henderson, *The Inter-War Years and Other Papers*, ed. Henry Clay, Clarendon Press, 1955

Charles H. Hession, *John Maynard Keynes: A Personal Biography of the Man who Revolutionized Capitalism and the Way We Live*, New York: Macmillan, 1984

J. R. Hicks, *The Crisis in Keynesian Economics*, Basil Blackwell, 1974

Michaela Honicke, ' "Prevent World War III": An Historiographical Appraisal of Morgenthau's Programme for Germany', in Robert A. Garson and Stuart S. Kidd (eds), *The Roosevelt Years: New Perspectives on American History 1933–1945*, Edinburgh University Press, 1999

J. Keith Horsefield, *The International Monetary Fund 1945–1965*, vols i and ii, Washington DC: IMF, 1969

Susan Howson, 'Cheap Money and Debt Management in Britain 1932–1952,' in P. L. Cottrell and D. E. Moggridge (eds), *Money and Power: Essays in Honour of L. S. Pressnell*, Macmillan Press, 1988, 227–89

Susan Howson, *British Monetary Policy 1945–51*, Clarendon Press, 1993

Susan Howson and Donald Winch, *The Economic Advisory Council 1930–1939*, Cambridge University Press, 1977

Cordell Hull, *The Memoirs of Cordell Hull*, New York: Macmillan, 1948

Harold James, *International Monetary Cooperation since Bretton Woods*, IMF, Oxford University Press, 1996

Harold James, 'Post-War German Currency Plans', in Christoph Buchheim, Michael Hutter, Harold James (eds), *Zerrissene Zwisschenkriegszeit: Wirtschafthistorische Beiträge*, Knut Borchardt, 1994

Douglas Jay, *Change and Fortune: A Political Record*, Hutchinson, 1980

Elizabeth Johnson and Harry G. Johnson, *The Shadow of Keynes*, Basil Blackwell, 1978

Milo Keynes (ed.), *Essays on John Maynard Keynes*, Cambridge University Press, 1975

——(ed.), *Lydia Lopokova*, Weidenfeld & Nicolson, 1983

Warren F. Kimball, *The Most Unsordid Act: Lend–Lease 1939–1941*, Baltimore: Johns Hopkins University Press, 1969

——, *The Juggler: Franklin Roosevelt as Wartime Statesman*, Princeton University Press, 1991

Charles P. Kindleberger, *The World in Depression 1929–1939*, Allen Lane, 1973

Gabriel Kolko, *The Politics of War: The World and the United States Foreign Policy 1943–1945*, New York: Random House, 1968

David Kynaston, *The City of London*, iii, *Illusions of Gold 1914–1945*, Chatto & Windus, 1999

John Laughland, *The Tainted Source: The Undemocratic Origins of the European Idea*, Little, Brown, 1997

Dan. H. Laurence (ed.), *Bernard Shaw: Collected Letters 1926–50*, Max Reinhart, 1988

Sir Frederick Leith-Ross, *Money Talks: Fifty Years of International Finance*, Hutchinson, 1968

Douglas LePan, *Bright Glass of Memory: Memoirs*, McGraw-Hill Ryerson, 1979

A. P. Lerner, *The Economics of Employment*, McGraw-Hill, 1951

Wm Roger Louis, *In the Name of God, Go: Leo Amery and the British Empire in the Age of Churchill*, W. W. Norton, 1992

Sir Donald MacDougall, *Don and Mandarin*, John Murray, 1987

B. J. C. McKercher, *Transition of Power: Britain's Loss of Global Pre-Eminence to the United States 1930–1945*, Cambridge University Press, 1999

David S. McLellan, *Dean Acheson: The State Department Years*, New York: Dodd, Mead, 1976

Kingsley Martin, *Editor: A Volume of Autobiography 1931–1945*, Hutchinson, 1968

D. E. Moggridge (ed.), *Keynes: Aspects of the Man and his Work*, Macmillan Press, 1974

——, *Maynard Keynes: An Economist's Biography*, Routledge, 1992

——, 'Keynes and the International Monetary System 1909–1946,' in J. S. Cohen and G. C. Harcourt (eds), *International Monetary Problems and Supply-Side Economics: Essays in Honour of Lorie Tarshis*, Macmillan, 1986

John E. Moser, *Twisting the Lion's Tail: Anglophobia in the United States 1921–48*, Macmillan Press, 1999

H. G. Nicholas (ed.), *Washington Despatches 1941–1945*, Weidenfeld & Nicolson, 1981

Walter Nimocks, *Milner's Young Men: The 'Kindergarten' in Edwardian Imperial Affairs*, Hodder & Stoughton, 1968

R. W. Oliver, *International Economic Cooperation and the World Bank*, Macmillan, 1975

Frances Partridge, *A Pacifist's War*, Hogarth Press, 1978

G. C. Peden, *British Rearmament and the Treasury 1932–1939*, Scottish Academic Press, 1979

——, *Keynes, the Treasury and British Economic Policy*, Macmillan, 1986

——, *The Treasury and British Public Policy 1906–1959*, Oxford University Press, 2000

E. F. Penrose, *Economic Planning for Peace*, Princeton University Press, 1953

Ben Pimlott, *Hugh Dalton*, Jonathan Cape, 1985

John Plesch, *Janos: The Story of a Doctor*, Victor Gollancz, 1947

L. S. Pressnell, *External Economic Policy since the War*, i: *The Post-War Financial Settlement*, HMSO, 1986

David Rees, *Harry Dexter White: A Study in Paradox*, Macmillan, 1973

Lord Robbins, *Autobiography of an Economist*, Macmillan, 1971

——, *The Economic Problem in Peace and War*, Macmillan, 1947

Andrew Roberts, *Holy Fox*, Weidenfeld & Nicolson, 1991

C. H. Rolph, *Kingsley: The Life, Letters and Diaries of Kingsley Martin*, Victor Gollancz, 1973

Benjamin M. Rowland (ed.), *Balance of Power or Hegemony: The Interwar Monetary System*, Lehrman Institute, New York University Press, 1976

R. S. Sayers, *The Bank of England 1891–1944*, 2 vols, Cambridge University Press, 1976

——, *Financial Policy 1939–1945*, HMSO, 1956

B. Schefold, 'The General Theory for a Totalitarian State? A Note on Keynes's Preface to the German Edition of 1936', repr. in John Cunningham Wood (ed.), *John Maynard Keynes: Critical Assessments*, ii, 416–17, Croom Helm, 1983

Arthur J. Schlesinger Jr, *The Coming of the New Deal*, William Heinemann, 1959

J. A. Schumpeter, *Ten Great Economists*, Allen & Unwin, 1952

Robert E. Sherwood, *The White House Papers of Harry L. Hopkins: An Intimate History*, 2 vols, Eyre & Spottiswode, 1948

Robert Skidelsky, *John Maynard Keynes: Hopes Betrayed 1883–1920*, Macmillan, 1983, Viking, 1986; *John Maynard Keynes: The Economist as Saviour 1920–1937*, Macmillan, 1992, Allen Lane, The Penguin Press, 1995

——, 'Keynes and the State', in D. Helm (ed.), *The Economic Boundaries of the State*, Oxford University Press, 1989

——, 'The Role of Ethics in Keynes's Economics', in Samuel Brittan and Alan Hamlin (eds), *Market Capitalism and Moral Values*, Edward Elgar, 1995

——, 'Keynes and the Quantity Theory of Money', in *The Quantity Theory of Money from Keynes to Locke and Friedman*, intro. by Mark Blaug, Edward Elgar, 1995

——, *Keynes*, Oxford University Press, 1996 (Past Masters)

——, 'Thinking about the State and the Economy', in S. J. D. Green and R. C. Whiting (eds), *The Boundaries of the State in Modern Britain*, Cambridge University Press, 1996

——, 'Keynes's "Concluding Notes"', in G. C. Harcourt and P. A. Rich (eds), *A 'Second Edition' of The General Theory*, i, Routledge, 1997

——, 'The Conditions for the Reinstatement of Keynesian Policy', in Luigi Pasinetti and Bertram Schefold (eds), *The Impact of Keynes on Economics in the 20th Century*, Edward Elgar, 1999

Boris Sokoloff, *The Story of Penicillin*, New York: Ziff Publishing 1945

Frances Spalding, *Vanessa Bell*, Weidenfeld & Nicolson, 1983

——, *Duncan Grant: A Biography*, Chatto & Windus, 1997

Bartholomew H. Sparrow, *From the Outside In: World War II and the American State*, Princeton University Press, 1996

Ronald Steel, *Walter Lippmann and the American Century*, Little, Brown, 1980

Herbert Stein, *The Fiscal Revolution in America*, University of Chicago Press, 1969

David Sutton, *Simon: A Political Biography of John Simon* Auren Press, 1992

A. J. P. Taylor, *The Origins of the Second World War*, Penguin edn, 1964

Peter Temin, *Did Monetary Forces Cause the Great Depression?*, W. W. Norton, 1976

A. P. Thirlwall, *Nicholas Kaldor*, Wheatsheaf, 1987

——(ed.), *Keynes and International Monetary Relations*, Macmillan Press, 1976
——(ed.), *Keynes as a Policy Adviser*, Macmillan Press, 1982
Nicholas Timmins, *The Five Giants: A Biography of the Welfare State*, HarperCollins, 1995
Jim Tomlinson, *Employment Policy: The Crucial Years 1939–1955*, Clarendon Press, 1987
Keith Tribe, *Strategies of Economic Order: German Economic Discourse 1750–1950*, Cambridge University Press, 1995
Allen Weinstein and Alexander Vassiliev, *The Haunted Wood: Soviet Espionage in America – The Stalin Era*, Random House, 1999
Benjamin Welles, *Sumner Welles: FDR's Global Strategist*, Macmillan, 1997
John Williamson, 'Keynes and the International Economic Order', in G. D. N. Worswick and J. Trevithick (eds), *Keynes and the Modern World*, Cambridge University Press, 1983
David Wilson, *Penicillin in Perspective*, Faber & Faber, 1976
Thomas Wilson, *Churchill and the Prof*, Cassell, 1995
John G. Winant, *A Letter from Grosvenor Square*, Hodder & Stoughton, 1947
E.L. Woodward, *British Foreign Policy in the Second World War*, HMSO, 1971

ARTICLES, MONOGRAPHS

Moses Abramovitz, 'Catching up, Forging Ahead, and Falling Behind', *Journal of Economic History*, 46, June 1986
Sir George Bolton, 'Where the Critics Are as Wrong as Keynes Was', *Banker*, November 1972
Alan Booth, 'Simple Keynesianism and Whitehall, 1936–1947', *Economy and Society*, 15, 1986
——'The "Keynesian Revolution" in Economic Policy-Making', *Economic History Review*, 2nd series, 36, 1983
Colin Clark, 'Public Finance and Changes in the Value of Money', *Economic Journal*, 55, December 1945
Thomas F. Cooley and Lee E. Ohanian, 'Postwar Economic Growth and the Legacy of Keynes', *Journal of Political Economy*, 105, no. 3, 1996
L. Cuyvers, 'Keynes's Collaboration with Erwin Rothbarth', *Economic Journal*, September 1983
Sir Wilfrid Eady, 'Maynard Keynes at the Treasury', *Listener*, 7 June 1951
B. Eichengreen, 'Sterling and the Tariff 1929–1932', *Princeton Studies in International Finance*, no. 48, September 1981
C. W. Guillebaud, 'Hitler's New Economic Order for Europe', *Economic Journal*, 50, December 1940
George C. Herring Jr, 'The United States and British Bankruptcy 1944–1945', *Political Science Quarterly*, 86, 1971
Sir Richard Hopkins, *Tributes*, Church [of England] Information Board, 1957
Susan Howson, 'The Management of Sterling 1932–1939', *Journal of Economic History*, 40, 1975
David Hubback, 'Sir Richard Clarke, 1910–1975: A Most Unusual Civil Servant', *Public Policy and Administration*, 3, no. 1, Spring 1988
Byrd L. Jones, 'The Role of Keynesians in Wartime Policy and Postwar Planning 1940–46', in 'The Second Crisis of Economic Theory and Other Selected

Papers', from the Annual Meeting of the American Economic Association, 27–29 December, 1971

John Maynard Keynes, 1883–1946: Fellow and Bursar, King's College, Cambridge, 1949

Warren F. Kimball, 'Lend–Lease and the Open Door: The Temptation of British Opulence 1937–1942', *Political Science Quarterly*, 86, 1971

Axel Leijonhufvud, *Keynes and the Classics*, Institute of Economic Affairs, 1969

A. P. Lerner, 'Functional Finance and the Federal Debt', *Social Research*, 10, no. 1, February 1943

Bruce Littleboy, 'The Wider Significance of "How to Pay for the War"', *History of Economics Review*, 25, Winter–Summer 1996

Raymond F. Mikesell, 'The Bretton Woods Debates: A Memoir', *Princeton Essays in International Finance*, 192, March 1994

Larry Neal, 'The Economics and Finance of Bilateral Clearing Agreements: Germany 1934–8', *Economic History Review*, 2nd series, 32, 1979

G. C. Peden, 'Sir Richard Hopkins and the "Keynesian Revolution" in Employment Policy 1929–45', *Economic History Review*, 2nd series, 36, 1983

——, 'The Treasury and Unemployment Policy in the later Nineteen-Thirties', *Oxford Economic Papers*, 32, no. 1, March 1980

E. A. G. Robinson, 'John Maynard Keynes 1883–1946', *Economic Journal*, 57, March 1947, 1–68

——, 'Keynes', *Dictionary of National Biography 1941–50*, 452–7

Joan Robinson, 'The International Currency Proposals', *Economic Journal*, 53, June 1943

Roger J. Sandilands, 'Guilt by Association? Lauchlin Currie's Alleged Involvement with Washington Economists in Soviet Espionage', *History of Political Economy*, 32, no. 3, 2000

Richard Toye, 'Keynes and the Labour Movement, and "How to Pay for the War"', *Twentieth Century British History*, 10, no. 3, 1999

J. A. Trevithick, 'Keynes, Inflation and Money Illusion', *Economic Journal*, 86, March 1975

Sean Turnell, 'A Clearing Union or a Stabilising Fund? Australian Economists and the Creation of the IMF', Macquarie Economics Research Papers, no. 11/98

UNPUBLISHED

Paul Bareau, 'Anglo-American Financial Relations during and since the War', four lectures delivered at the LSE, 1951. In the possession of Peter Bareau

Edward M. Bernstein, 'Reflections on Bretton Woods', first of three papers on 'The Fortieth Anniversary of the Bretton Woods Conference', 18 May 1984

Bruce Craig, 'Treasonable Doubt: The Harry Dexter White Case', PhD, American University, 1999

Donald Markwell, 'John Maynard Keynes and International Relations: Idealism, Economic Paths to War and Peace, and Post-war Reconstruction', DPhil, Oxford University, 1995

VENONA: http://www.nsa.gov:8080/docs/venona

References

These reference notes are intended to be used in conjunction with the Bibliography. Books and articles referred to are cited by author and short title. The following abbreviations have been used:

BE: Bank of England Papers
RBP: Robert Brand Papers
CAB: Cabinet Papers
HCP: Henry Clay Papers
CW: *Collected Writings*, followed by relevant volume
OTFP1: O. T. Falk Papers (British Library)
OTFP2: O. T. Falk Papers (in possession of Mrs Roland Falk)
FO: Foreign Office Papers
FRUS: *Foreign Relations of the United States*
FFP: Felix Frankfurter Papers
EGP: Emmanuel Goldenweiser Papers
HDHP: Hubert Henderson Papers

RFKP: Richard Kahn Papers
KP: Keynes Papers
LLKP: Lydia Lopokova Keynes Papers
RLP: Russell Leffingwell Papers
WLP: Walter Lippmann Papers
CMP: Christabel Maclaren Papers
MPP: Macmillan Publishers Papers
MD: Morgenthau Diaries
PLP: Pethick-Lawrence Papers
PREM: Premier's Papers
JASP: Schumpeter Papers
JTSP: Sheppard Papers
T: Treasury Papers

Chapter 1: Curing Invalidism

1. Borrow, *Wild Wales*, 76.
2. Lorie Tarshis, q. Skidelsky, *Keynes*, ii, 574.
3. JASP: Box 2, JAS to O. Lange, 24 February 1937.
4. *CW*, xxi, 426, JMK to HDH, 14 November 1937.
5. *CW*, xxviii, 87, JMK to K. Martin, 29 September 1937.
6. Milo Keynes (ed.), *Lydia Lopokova*, 34.
7. HDHP: 21, JMK to Lord Stamp, 7 November 1937.
8. Nicolson (ed.), *Letters of Virginia Woolf*, vi, Virginia Woolf to Vanessa Bell, 6 October 1937.
9. Quentin Bell, *Elders and Betters*, 102.
10. Nicolson (ed.), *Letters of Virginia Woolf*, vi, Virginia Woolf to JMK, 23 December 1937.
11. Keynes's review is reproduced in *CW*, xi, 439–44.
12. The review appeared in the *Economic Journal* in February 1938; it is reproduced in *CW*, xi, 542–58.
13. *CW*, xxi, 426.
14. *CW*, xii, 28.
15. Nicolson (ed.), *Letters of Virginia Woolf*, vi, Virginia Woolf to Angelica Bell, Christmas Day 1937.
16. LK to RFK, 20 February 1938.
17. A. O. Bell (ed.), *Diary of Virginia Woolf*, v, 129.
18. JMK to RFK, 5 March 1938.
19. *CW*, xii, 38; see Skidelsky, *Keynes*, ii, 525–6, for Keynes's investment philosophy.
20. *CW*, xii, 47.
21. CMP: S. Courtauld to Christabel Aberconway, 27 June 1938.
22. Q. Bell, in Crabtree and Thirlwall (eds), *Keynes and the Bloomsbury Group*, 82, 83. For other reminiscences by Quentin Bell of Tilton, see his *Elders and Betters*, ch. 6.
23. R. C. Trevelyan Papers: 18, 96–8.
24. A. O. Bell (ed.), *Diary of Virginia Woolf*, v, 168–9.
25. *CW*, x, 433–50. For discussion of

this paper, see Skidelsky, *Keynes*, i, ch. 6.

26. KP: GTE/1.6.
27. *CW*, xxi, 390–1, 393.
28. *Ibid.*, 385.
29. *Ibid.*, 407.
30. *Ibid.*, 479.
31. *Ibid.*, 394, 408–9.
32. OTFP2 (unclassified).
33. *CW*, xxi, 408, 409.
34. *Ibid.*, 481.
35. *CW*, xiv, 207–10, 229.
36. *CW*, xxi, 449, 453.
37. *Ibid.*, 402–3.
38. *Ibid.* See especially *ibid.*, 513–17 and 535–46.
39. *Ibid.*, 483, JMK letter to *The Times*, 5 October 1938.
40. *Ibid.*, 456–70; see also *ibid.*, 505–8 for his wheat plan.
41. KP: PP/21, N Wedd to JMK, 26 August 1938. For the main threads of Keynes's arguments see *CW*, xxi, 509–18, 535–46, 551–64.
42. Howson and Winch, *Economic Advisory Council*, 109, 140–2.
43. *Ibid.*, 343–55.
44. Howson, *British Monetary Policy*, 29.
45. JASP: 4.8, Box 2, JAS to K. Bode, 19 May 1937.
46. Harrod, *Keynes*, 485.
47. Moggridge, *Keynes: An Economist's Biography*, 620–4.
48. Rolph, *Kingsley*, 249, 244–5.
49. Carr, 'John Maynard Keynes and the Treaty of Versailles', in Thirlwall (ed.), *Keynes as a Policy Adviser*, 102.
50. OTFP2 (unclassified): OTF to R. Boothby, 4 March 1947.
51. Markwell, 'Keynes and International Relations', 227.
52. Taylor, *Origins of the Second World War*, 50.
53. Markwell, 'Keynes and International Relations', 227.
54. *CW*, vii, 382.
55. q. Skidelsky, *Keynes*, ii, 62.
56. *CW*, xxviii, 100, 102.
57. *CW*, xxi, 499.

58. So Halifax told Hitler on 19 November 1937 at Berchtesgaden: Taylor, *Origins of the Second World War*, 176.
59. *CW*, xxi, 370–2.
60. *CW*, xxviii, 55; see also his letter to Gladwyn Jebb, 12 July 1937, *ibid.*, 65–6.
61. Carlton, *Eden*, 59.
62. *CW*, xxviii, 48–50, *NS*, 8 August 1936.
63. *Ibid.*, 47, JMK letter to *NS*, 13 July 1936.
64. *Ibid.*, 54–6.
65. *Ibid.*, 55.
66. *Ibid.*, 62–4.
67. *Ibid.*, 72–3.
68. *Ibid.*, 82–3.
69. Carlton, *Eden*, 120–1.
70. *CW*, xxviii, 92–3, 81.
71. *Ibid.*, 93–4.
72. KP: PP/5, JMK to Margaret Keynes, 16 October 1937.
73. For an excellent account of American Anglophobia see Moser, *Twisting the Lion's Tail*, esp. chs 4 and 5. The comment on the Nye Committee is at *ibid.*, 91.
74. *CW*, xxviii, 99–104.
75. *Ibid.*, 117, 119, letters to K. Martin.
76. This letter is misdated by Keynes 29 August 1938. It should be 29 September 1938.
77. *CW*, xxviii, 122–3.
78. Nicolson (ed.), *Letters of Virginia Woolf*, vi, 280.
79. *CW*, xxviii, 126, *NS*, 'Mr. Chamberlain's Foreign Policy'.
80. Taylor, *Origins of the Second World War*, 219–20.
81. KP: PP/80, T.S. Eliot to JMK, 15 November 1938.
82. *CW*, xxi, 491–500, 'Democracy and Efficiency'.
83. KP: PP/45, JMK to B. G. Catterns, 30 April 1942.
84. Plesch, *Janos*, 424–5, 459–60, 504, 453–6.
85. RBP: File 198.
86. Sokoloff, *Story of Penicillin*, 69.
87. *CW*, xxi, 528–32, *Listener*, 1 June 1939.
88. *Ibid.*, 564, 'Borrowing by the State'.

Chapter 2: The Middle Way in War

1. KP: HP/3, JMK to R. H. Brand, 22 October 1939.
2. RFKP: 13/57/434, JMK to RFK, 1 September 1939; *CW*, xxii, 3, letters to Roy Harrod and Lord Stamp, 7, 15 September 1939.

3. *CW*, xxii, 7.
4. *Ibid.*, 13.
5. KP: W/2, JMK to HDH, 21 September 1939.
6. *Ibid.*, JMK to Clough William-Ellis, 16 September 1939.

7. *Ibid.*, JMK to W. Beveridge, 30 September 1939.
8. *Ibid.*, JMK to Sir F. Leith-Ross, 10 October 1939.
9. OTFP1: JMK to OTF, 24 September 1939.
10. KP: W/2, JMK to W. Beveridge, 15 October 1939. See also *CW*, xxii, 20–2. JMK was urging on the Treasury (without success) the 'temptation policy' – removing certain items from the contraband list in order to tempt Germany to squander foreign exchange on buying inessential items.
11. KP: W/2, JMK to Sir G. Schuster, 16 October 1939.
12. See Laurence (ed.), *Bernard Shaw: Collected Letters 1926–50*, 537.
13. *CW*, xxviii, 132.
14. Laurence (ed.), *Bernard Shaw: Collected Letters 1926–50*, G. B. Shaw to JMK, 5 October 1939; see also KP: PP/45.
15. *CW*, xxii, 36–7.
16. CMP: S. Courtauld to Christabel Aberconway, 20 October 1939; KP: HP/3, R. H. Brand to JMK, 17 October 1939.
17. *CW*, xxii, 37.
18. *CW*, xii, 74, JMK to F. C. Scott, 20 September 1940: see also correspondence with Leonard Elmhirst, 1939–40, in KP: W/2.
19. KP: PP/45, correspondence between JMK and Lord Macmillan, 14–19 December 1939; Keynes tried again with John Reith, director-general of the BBC, in March 1940, with equal lack of success.
20. WLP: MS 326/82: 1217, JMK to WL, 6 January 1940.
21. KP: PP/80.7, JMK to Fred Ashton, 8 December 1939; R. A. Butler to JMK, 29 February 1940; JMK to Raymond Mortimer, 14 January 1940.
22. KP: PP/80.7.
23. *CW*, xxii, 38, JMK to A. B. Ramsay, 24 November 1939.
24. KP: L/39, HDH to JMK, 26 November 1939.
25. *CW*, xxii, 31, letter to *The Times*, 28 September 1939.
26. *Ibid.*, 32–3.
27. Trevithick argues that the lag was due to sticky contracts, not money illusion. See J. A. Trevithick, 'Keynes, Inflation and Money Illusion', *Economic Journal*, 85, March 1975, 104.
28. *CW*, xxii, 6, 30–2.
29. *Ibid.*, J. R. Hicks to JMK, 4 October 1939. For the exchange of letters see *ibid.*, 31–6.
30. KP: HP/1, HDH to JMK, 15 October 1939.
31. *CW*, xxii, 33, JMK to J. R. Hicks, 7 October 1939; KP: HP/1, JMK to HDH, 17 October 1939.
32. Moggridge (*Keynes: An Economist's Biography*, 629) writes that Keynes discussed it at 'a dinner meeting of officials, MPs and Ministers' on 27 October, but gives no reference.
33. KP: HP/6, JMK to G. Dawson, 11 December 1939.
34. *CW*, xxii, 50–1. The articles are reproduced at *ibid.*, 41–51.
35. KP: HP/6, G. Dawson to JMK, 20 November 1939.
36. KP: HP/4, F. A. Hayek to JMK, 3 March 1940.
37. KP: HP/3, HDH to JMK, 29 October 1939; Lord Stamp to JMK, 30 October 1939; H. Clay to JMK, 9 November 1939. See also Sayers, *Financial Policy*, 60.
38. KP: HP/3, JMK to HDH, 31 October 1939.
39. *Ibid.*, R. H. Brand to JMK, 1 November 1939; JMK to R. H. Brand, 3 November 1939.
40. HDHP: Box 22/A/1, R. H. Brand to HDH, 26 December 1939.
41. KP: HP/3, JMK to R. H. Brand, 27 November 1939.
42. *Ibid.*, JMK to R. H. Brand, 5 January 1940.
43. RBP: File 198, JMK to R. H. Brand, 27 April, 3 May 1940; R. H. Brand to JMK, 2 May 1940; Sayers, *Financial Policy*, 194.
44. KP: HP/3, Lord Stamp to JMK, 30 October 1939.
45. KP: HP/2, correspondence between JMK and C. R. Attlee, 24–31 October 1939.
46. *Daily Express*, 17 November 1939.
47. *Manchester Guardian*, 17 November 1939; KP: HP/2, Ernest Bevin to Seebohm Rowntree, 29 December 1939.
48. KP: HP/3, JMK to Lord Stamp, 12 January 1940.
49. Sayers, *Financial Policy*, 34.
50. PLP: 2/216, JMK to F. Pethick-Lawrence, 19 November 1939; see also *CW*, xxii, 82.
51. KP: HP/2, JMK to Arthur Greenwood, 19 November 1939.
52. *CW*, xxii, 81.

53. PLP: 2/217, JMK to F. Pethick-Lawrence, 11 December 1939.
54. *CW*, xxii, 84.
55. KP: HP/2, correspondence between JMK and H. Laski, 5–29 December 1939.
56. Howson, *British Monetary Policy*, 74–7.
57. See Skidelsky, *Keynes*, i, 346.
58. KP: W/2, JMK to S. Courtauld, 10 December 1939.
59. A. O. Bell (ed.), *The Diary of Virginia Woolf*, iii, 255–6.
60. KP: HP/1, G. Warnborough to JMK, 11 December 1939; JMK to G. Warnborough, 14 December 1939.
61. KP:L/39, correspondence between JMK and Polly Hill, 7, 11, 15 July 1939.
62. See Cooley and Ohanian, 'Postwar British Economic Growth and the Legacy of Keynes', 439–72.
63. *CW*, xxii, 82, letter to *The Times*, 29 November 1939.
64. *CW*, ix, 406, JMK, *How to Pay for the War*.
65. KP: HP/3/75–84, 160–3; 4/32–3 for details of these suggestions, and Keynes's responses.
66. *Spectator*, 24 November 1939.
67. *CW*, xii, 93; KP: HP/2. JMK to Lord Stamp, 29 January 1939.
68. *CW*, xxii, 97–8, JMK to H. Laski, 28 January 1940.
69. KP: HP/3, JMK to R. McKenna, 28 January 1940.
70. KP: HP/2/88–100; 3/176–88.
71. KP: HP/2/60–63, JMK Notes, 16 January 1940, on memo 'On Wages, Prices and Standards of Living during the War' prepared by the TU members of the National Advisory Council, Ministry of Labour.
72. KP: HP/3, R. H. Brand to JMK, 17 January 1940.
73. KP: HP/4, JMK to V. H. Mottram, 21 March 1940.
74. MPP: JMK to R. Heath, 18 February 1940.
75. *CW*, ix, 394–6, JMK, *How to Pay for the War*.
76. *Ibid.*, 406–8.
77. *Ibid.*, 412–13.
78. *Ibid.*, 399–402.
79. *Ibid.*, 407.
80. MPP: JMK to Harold Macmillan, 8 March, 4 and 11 April 1940.
81. KP: HP/4, D. H. Robertson to JMK, 6 March 1940.
82. *Ibid.*, J. L. Garvin to JMK, 6 March 1940.
83. KP: HP/5, JMK to D. Tyerman, 19 March 1940.
84. KP: HP/4, A. L. Hobhouse to JMK, 28 February 1940.
85. KP: PP/45.
86. A. O. Bell (ed.), *Diary of Virginia Woolf*, iii, 283.
87. Quentin Bell, *Elders and Betters*, 101.
88. Cairncross and Watts, *Economic Section*, 22–3.
89. Robbins, *Economic Problem in Peace and War*, 31–50.
90. *Ibid.*, 33–4.
91. Chester (ed.), *Lessons of the British War Economy*, 57.
92. See Harrod, *Keynes*, 490–4; Moggridge, *Keynes: an Economist's Biography*, 630–3.
93. *CW*, ix, 410, JMK, *How to Pay for the War*.
94. *CW*, xxii, 122–3, letter to *The Times*, 18 April 1940.
95. Reproduced in *ibid.*, 155.
96. *CW*, xxii, 101–4, JMK to G. Dawson, 11 March 1940.
97. T175/17.Pt 1, unsigned note dated 15 March 1933.
98. Kynaston, *City of London*, iii, 464.
99. Sayers, *Financial Policy*, 68.
100. *CW*, ix, 381, JMK, *How to Pay for the War*.
101. For a discussion, see Peden, *Keynes, the Treasury and British Economic Policy*, 39. Peden points out that Hawtrey, the Treasury's one trained economist, rejected Keynes's aggregative approach.
102. *CW*, xxii, 66–73, for JMK's *Economic Journal* article, March 1940; for correspondence with Rothbarth and Kaldor on this matter, see KP: W/4.
103. KP: W/4, E. Rothbarth to JMK, 29 November 1939; JMK to E. Rothbarth, 21 January 1940. Readers interested in the development of the concepts underlying the accounting identities, and how they diverged from those of Colin Clark, are referred to the discussion in Cuyvers, 'Keynes's Collaboration with Erwin Rothbarth', 629–36.
104. There are many versions of these calculations which do not tally exactly; Keynes also habitually rounded up figures by £50m. to emphasise the inexact nature of the calculations. The figures above are summarised from *CW*, ix, 381–93, JMK, *How to Pay for the War*, and from *CW*, xxii, 60–1.
105. Sayers, *Financial Policy*, 33–4.
106. The phrase comes from Sir Richard Hopkins's 'Draft Statement on War

Finance for the National Joint Advisory Council, 6 December 1939.
107. Sayers, *Financial Policy*, 35 and n.

108. KP: L/40, JMK to V. Gollancz, 25 April 1940.
109. *CW*, xxii, 133.

Chapter 3: The Dragons of War

1. KP: A/40, JMK to Bruce Bliven, 29 June 1940.
2. *CW*, xxii, 181–3, JMK to Brendan Bracken, 12 June 1940.
3. KP: PP/57, JMK to Sterling S. Lamprecht, 19 June 1940.
4. Sayers, *Financial Policy*, 233.
5. KP: W/3, JMK to Lord Stamp, 22 February 1940; JMK to Sir F. Phillips, 22 February, 4 March 1940.
6. *CW*, xxii, 162.
7. *Parliamentary Debates* (HC), 9 April 1940, vol. 359, no. 50 col. 465.
8. KP: W/3, JMK to R. Boothby, 11 April 1940.
9. RFKP: 13/57/441, JMK to RFK, 9 May 1940; BE: G1/15, 9 May 1940; Kynaston, *City of London*, iii, 469–70.
10. For details see *CW*, xxii, 156–82.
11. RFKP: 13/57/460, 462, JMK to RFK, 27 May, 2 June 1940.
12. See *CW*, xxii 156–82, for Keynes's involvement in the foreign exchange crisis, together with Sayers, *Financial Policy*, ch. 8. See also KP: W/3 for Brendan Bracken to JMK, 13 June 1940, E. Monick to JMK, 17 July 1940, JMK to Lord Stamp, 22 February 1940, and to Sir F. Phillips, 4 March 1940.
13. *CW*, xxii, 143, JKM to Clement Davies, 3 May 1940.
14. RFKP: 13/57/462, JMK to RFK, 2 June 1940. See also *CW*, xxii, 184–7.
15. KP: PP/45, A. C. Pigou to JMK, ? June 1940; JMK to A. C. Pigou, 18 June 1940.
16. *CW*, xxii, 191, JMK to F. C. Scott, 23 July 1940.
17. KP: PP/45, JMK to A. C. Pigou, 3 July 1940.
18. JMK to Florence Keynes, 28 June 1940.
19. *Ibid.*, 5 July 1940.
20. *CW*, xxii, 432–54, 197–212, 394–401; *CW*, xxiii, 2–10.
21. *CW*, xxii, 398–9.
22. *Ibid.*, 197–215.
23. A. O. Bell (ed.), *Diary of Virginia Woolf*, v, 314.
24. The British version is reproduced in *CW*, xxii, 240–5. Reference to American aid is from the American version. His optimistic assessment differs markedly from the later one of Sayers, *Finan-*

cial Policy, 56–7, who wrote that 'the inflationary pressure in the economy was being appreciably aggravated in this period by the inadequacy of taxation'.
25. KP: L/K/127, RFK to JMK, 25 September 1940.
26. *CW*, xxii, 218–22, 223–7, 234–40.
27. *Ibid.*, 273, 'Revised Proposal for a War Surcharge', 5 January 1941.
28. Sayers, *Financial Policy*, 77.
29. *CW*, xxii, 276.
30. T171/355, Sir H. Wilson, 'The Next Budget', 10 January 1941.
31. *Ibid.*, Sir K. Wood to Sir H. Wilson, 'The Next Budget', 14 January 1941.
32. *Ibid.* 'Note by the Board of Inland Revenue on Mr. Keynes's revised proposal for a war surcharge', 15 January 1941; *CW*, xxii, JMK to Sir R. Hopkins, 19 January 1941.
33. *CW*, xxii, 277–9, JMK to Sir R. Hopkins, 19 January 1941.
34. T171/355, Sir K. Wood, 'The Next Budget', 1 February 1941.
35. Sir Richard Hopkins, 'Mr. Keynes on the Budget Problem', 17 July 1940, q. Peden, *Keynes, the Treasury and British Economic Policy*.
36. *CW*, xxii, 260, 264–5, 'A Supplementary Note on the Dimensions of the Budget Problem', 26 December 1940.
37. *Ibid.*, xxii, 326–7, L. Robbins to JMK, October/November 1940.
38. R. Stone, 'The Use and Development of National Income and Expenditure Estimates', in Chester (ed.), *Lessons of the British War Economy*, 85; see also Harrod, *Keynes*, 501.
39. JMK to N. Kaldor, 19 April 1941. The late Lord Kaldor showed me this letter from his personal papers.
40. As explained by Keynes in his 'The Theory of the "Gap"', 3 March 1941, T171/356. See also: H. Wilson Smith, 'The Size of the Gap', 28 February 1941; JMK to H. Wilson Smith, 28 March 1941.
41. Sayers, *Financial Policy*, 69.
42. See *CW*, xxii, 355–63.
43. *Ibid.*, 383–5.
44. *Ibid.*, 390, 16 January 1945.

45. *Ibid.*, 402–8; Sayers, *Financial Policy*, 210–18.
46. *CW*, xxii, 410–20.
47. KP: W/4, JMK to R. McKenna, 10 April 1941.
48. A. O. Bell (ed.), *Diary of Virginia Woolf*, v, 346.
49. Peden, *Keynes, the Treasury and British Economic Policy*, 40.
50. Sayers, *Financial Policy*, 73.
51. *CW*, xxii, 218, 'Notes on the Budget 1', 21 September 1940.

52. Littleboy, 'The Wider Significance of "How to Pay for the War" ', 88–95.
53. q. Sayers, *Financial Policy*, 91.
54. WLP: File 1315, R. C. Leffingwell to WL, 22 July 1942.
55. T172/1980. See Keynes Note on T. Balogh's letter to *The Times* on extension of rationing, 14 September 1942.
56. Cooley and Ohanian, 'Postwar British Economic Growth and the Legacy of Keynes', 439–72.

Chapter 4: Envoy Extraordinary

1. Halifax, Secret Diary, 17 February 1941.
2. Moser, *Twisting the Lion's Tail*, 127.
3. Halifax, Secret Diary, 25 June 1941.
4. Kimball, *Most Unsordid Act*, 33; Moser, *Twisting the Lion's Tail*, 124.
5. W Lippmann, *Herald Tribune*, 16 November 1939; KP: W/2, JMK to WL, 6 January 1940.
6. KP: L/40.
7. Blum, *Morgenthau Diaries*, ii, 171.
8. Kimball, *Most Unsordid Act*, 64–5. See also *ibid.*, 94.
9. *Ibid.*, 173.
10. Sayers, *Financial Policy*, p. 368.
11. T160/995/19422, Sir F. Phillips, 2 November 1940.
12. Kimball, *Most Unsordid Act*, 96.
13. T160/995/19422, Lord Lothian to PM, 28 November 1940.
14. *CW*, xxiii, 13–26.
15. T160/995/19422, Sir F. Phillips, 23 November 1940.
16. Feis, *1933*, 106–7.
17. Kimball, *Most Unsordid Act*, 5.
18. Feis, *1933*, 107.
19. Blum, *Morgenthau Diaries*, ii, 171.
20. Churchill, *The Second World War*, iii, 493–501.
21. T175/121, Sir F. Phillips to Sir R. Hopkins, 14 January 1941.
22. q. Kimball, *Juggler*, 14.
23. *Ibid.*, 9.
24. Sherwood, *White House Papers of Harry L. Hopkins*, 245.
25. *CW*, xxiii, 41–2.
26. *FRUS*, 1941, iii, 2, Churchill to Roosevelt, 2 January 1941.
27. *Ibid.*, 4, memo of conversation by Secretary of State, 11 January, 1941.
28. T175/122, JMK, 'The Course of Sir Frederick Phillips' Negotiations', 18 March 1941; see also Dormael, *Bretton Woods*, 13.

29. Blum, *Morganthau Diaries*, ii, 209.
30. Kimball, *Most Unsordid Act*, 104.
31. MD, vol. 404, 86.
32. Blum, *Morgenthau Diaries*, ii, 244–5.
33. *Ibid.*, 236.
34. *CW*, xxiii, 46–8, JMK to Nigel Roland.
35. *Ibid.*, 55, JMK to B. Cohen, 19 March 1941.
36. Kimball, 'Lend–Lease and the Open Door', 241.
37. *CW*, xxiii, 54–8.
38. *Ibid.*, 59, JMK to S. D. Waley, 22 March 1941.
39. *CW*, xxiii, 75.
40. *Ibid.*, 62–3, JMK to S. D. Waley and Sir R. Hopkins, 7 April 1941.
41. Dobson, *US Wartime Aid to Britain*, 93.
42. Pimlott (ed.), *Second World War Diary of Hugh Dalton*, 173, 258.
43. *CW*, xxiii. 61–2, JMK to Lord Catto and Sir H. Wilson, 2 April 1941.
44. MD, vol. 396, 266–9, J. Winant to H. Morgenthau, 9 May 1941.
45. Lucius Thompson's diary of 8–11 May 1941, in T247/113.
46. Roberts, *Holy Fox*, 277.
47. Halifax, Secret Diary, 7 March 1941.
48. Sherwood, *White House Papers of Harry L. Hopkins*, 246.
49. Howson and Moggridge (eds), *Wartime Diaries of Robbins and Meade*, 76.
50. Harrod, *Keynes*, 507; Sayers, *Financial Policy*, 379.
51. Harrod, *Keynes*, 557.
52. Harvey (ed.), *Diplomatic Diaries of Oliver Harvey*, ii, 32.
53. Leith-Ross, *Money Talks*, 316.
54. Reviewing Roy Harrod's biography in *The Times*, 31 January 1951.
55. Harrod, *Keynes*, 507–8.
56. MD, vol. 397, 221–4.
57. *CW*, xxiii, 87–8, JMK to Sir H. Wilson,

'The Course of my Negotiations', 19 May 1941.

58. T175/121, E. Playfair to S. D. Waley, 22 May 1941.
59. *CW*, xxiii, 74–7, JMK to H. Morgenthau, 16 May 1941.
60. T175/121, E. Playfair to S. D. Waley, 22 May 1941.
61. *Ibid.*, 16 May 1941.
62. *CW*, xxiii, 85, JMK, 'The Course of my Negotiations', 20 May 1941.
63. CMP: S. Courtauld to Christabel Aberconway, 9 May 1941.
64. T247/113, Lucius Thompson diary; T. J. Gifford to JMK, 19 May 1941.
65. MD, vol. 399, 407–11, vol. 400, 88, 220–3.
66. T247/113, JMK to Sir H. Wilson, 21 May 1941.
67. *CW*, xxiii, 98, JMK, 'The Course of my Negotiations: II', 25 May 1941.
68. T247/113, JMK to Lord Halifax, 24 May 1941; Lord Halifax to JMK, 26 May 1941.
69. KP: PP/80/9, JMK to P. A. S. Hadley, 10 September 1941.
70. JMK, 22 August 1941, q. Harrod, *Keynes*, 515.
71. Schlesinger, *Coming of the New Deal*, 511.
72. *CW*, xxiii, 105–6.
73. *Ibid.* 107, 154–5, JMK to Sir K. Wood, 2 June, 13 July 1941.
74. *Ibid.*, 108–12.
75. Halifax Diary, 28 May 1941.
76. *CW*, xxiii, 154.
77. Halifax Diary, 7 July 1941.
78. *CW*, xxiv, 212.
79. *CW*, xxvi, 102.
80. *CW*, xxiv, 195–6.
81. Skidelskky, *Keynes*, ii, 510.
82. *CW*, xxiii, 113.
83. Byrd L. Jones, 'The Role of Keynesians in Wartime Policy and Postwar Planning', 127–8.
84. For a summary of the discussions, see *CW*, xxiii, ch. 5.
85. See his letter to American economist Mordecai Ezekiel, 6 June 1941, in KP: W/8.
86. *CW*, xxiii, 122, JMK, 'The Course of my Negotiations: III'.
87. *Ibid.* 130. For the whole letter see *ibid.*, 130–3.
88. MD, vol. 404, 174.
89. *Ibid.*, vol. 410, 19 June 1941, 103f.
90. *Ibid.*, 106–11, 119–29.
91. *CW*, xxiii, 147–8, 149, JMK to H. Morgenthau, 2 July 1941. McCoy was old English slang for 'the real thing'; McCoy was also an official at the War Department.
92. Sayers, *Financial Policy*, 400–1.
93. T160/955/19422, Sir F. Phillips, 2 November 1941.
94. T247/67, JMK 1 January 1942.
95. KP: L/43, JMK to David Low, 25 April 1943, congratulating him on having spotted it.
96. *CW*, xxiii, 155–7, JMK to Sir K. Wood, 17 July 1941.
97. T175/121, E. Playfair to S. D. Waley, 16 May 1941.
98. *CW*, xxiii, 142, JMK to Sir K. Wood, 22 June 1941.
99. T175/121, E. Playfair to S. D. Waley, 16 May 1941.
100. Cairncross, *Years of Recovery*, 5.
101. Blum, *Morgenthau Diaries*, ii, 243.
102. Chace, *Acheson*, 73.
103. Acheson, *Present at the Creation*, 28–9.
104. *CW*, xxiii, 96–7.
105. For these discussions, which went on intermittently from 27 May to 9 July, see *CW*, xxvii, 20–31.
106. Blum, *Morgenthau Diaries*, ii, 243–4.
107. *CW*, xxiii, 121.
108. *Ibid.*, 125, 127–8.
109. T247/113, JMK to S. D. Waley, 18 June 1941; JMK to Harry Hopkins, 27 June 1941.
110. *CW*, xxiii, 138–40.
111. *Ibid.*, 125 and n.
112. T247/113, Sir K. Wood to JMK, 5 July 1941.
113. See Dobson, *US Wartime Aid to Britain*, 36–8; Moggridge, *Keynes: An Economist's Biography*, 660.
114. *CW*, xxiii, 144, editor's summary.
115. *Ibid.*, 145–6, JMK to Treasury, ? June 1941.
116. *FRUS*, 1941, iii, 21–2.
117. Kimball, 'Lend–Lease and the Open Door', 252–3.
118. *Ibid.* See also editor's summary, *CW*, xxiii, 143–4.
119. *CW*, xxvi, 245, JMK to R. Opie, 13 February 1942.
120. Dobson, *Us Wartime Aid to Britain*, 52.
121. Acheson, *Present at the Creation*, 29.
122. *CW*, xxiii, 162–5, JMK to Sir K. Wood, 15 July 1941.
123. T247/113, JMK to Sir K. Wood, 13 July 1941.
124. *CW*, xxiii, 173–5.
125. Harrod, *Keynes*, 512.

126. This account is conflated from Acheson, *Present at the Creation*, 30, and Acheson's 'Memorandum of Conversation', 28 July 1941, copy in FDR Library, PSF Box 16, File LL(3).
127. *CW*, xxiii, 177–8.

128. *Ibid.*, 151–2; Sayers, *Financial Policy*, 394–5.
129. Sayers, *Financial Policy*, 397.
130. Kolko, *Politics of War*, esp. ch. 12.
131. WLP: MS 326, Box 82/1217; KP: P/45, JMK to WL, 28 April 1942.

Chapter 5: Keynes in Wartime

1. *CW*, xxiii, 149, JMK to Sir H. Wilson, 2 July 1941.
2. LePan, *Bright Glass of Memory*, 62.
3. Clarke, *Anglo-American Economic Collaboration*, 71.
4. KP: PP/69, JMK to Sir E. H. Marsh, 11 December 1940.
5. KP: L/P, JMK to Sir F. Phillips, 14 January 1942.
6. Chester (ed.), *Lessons of the British War Economy*, 9.
7. RBP, File 198.
8. Harrod, *The Prof*, 88.
9. Chester (ed.), *Lessons of the British War Economy*, p. ix. See also *ibid.*, 31 for its remit.
10. KP: W/4, JMK to C. Clark, 23 January 1942.
11. Cairncross and Watts, *Economic Section*, 29.
12. *Ibid.*, 26–8.
13. *Ibid.* 53.
14. *CW*, xxv, 353, JMK to Sir W. Eady, 3 October 1943.
15. *The Times*, leading article, 22 September 1943, q. Sayers, *Financial Policy*, 45.
16. *CW*, xxii, 382, JMK to Florence Keynes, 28 March, 10 April 1943.
17. Isaiah Berlin, citing a story told him by Lionel Robbins, in Milo Keynes (ed.) *Lydia Lopokova*, 171–2.
18. So he was called by Lionel Robbins, *Autobiography*, 173.
19. *Ibid.*, 187.
20. *Ibid.*
21. Hopkins, *Tributes*, 29.
22. See Skidelsky, *Keynes*, ii, 358–61.
23. See Peden, 'Sir Richard Hopkins and the "Keynesian Revolution"', 285.
24. *CW*, xxv, 102.
25. KP: L/B, R. H. Brand to JMK, 18 May 1943.
26. Obituary, 13 August 1943, repr. in *CW*, x, 330.
27. Sir W. Eady to Florence Keynes, 3 June 1951.
28. Eady, 'Maynard Keynes at the Treasury', 903.
29. *DNB 1961–70*, 319.

30. Eady, 'Maynard Keynes at the Treasury'.
31. Moggridge, *Keynes: An Economist's Biography*, 663n.
32. Cairncross and Watts, *The Economic Section*, 54.
33. *Ibid.*, 53–4.
34. Robbins, *Autobiography*, 188.
35. *CW*, xxiii, 316–23.
36. Howson and Moggridge (eds), *Meade: The Cabinet Office Diary*, 26.
37. Moggridge, *Keynes: An Economist's Biography*, 663.
38. *John Maynard Keynes* (KCC), 26; Eady, 'Maynard Keynes at the Treasury'.
39. Eady, 'Maynard Keynes at the Treasury'.
40. Interview with the late Sir Frederick Harmer, 19 March 1987.
41. KP: W/1; see also T247/130.
42. T247/6, 'South American Correspondence'. For Playfair's letter see T175/121.
43. KP: L/K 147, JMK to RFK, 31 October 1941.
44. T247/4, JMK to S. D. Waley, 23 February 1942; to Lord Catto, N. E. Young, S. D. Waley, 3 March 1942.
45. T247/5, JMK memo, 26 April 1945.
46. See KP: PP/45 for correspondence with Ray Milburn about Madrid; KP: W/9 for correspondence with Stanley Jevons on Ethiopia.
47. E. A. G. Robinson, 'Keynes', *DNB 1941–50*, 456. See *ibid.*, 456–7 for a good account of Keynes's 'practical genius'.
48. Hubback, 'Sir Richard Clarke', 77.
49. LePan, *Bright Glass of Memory*, 62.
50. RBP: File 198, R. H. Brand to Barbara Wootton, 29 November 1946.
51. Skidelsky, *Keynes*, ii, 213, 509–10.
52. Kingsley Martin reviewing Harrod's biography in the *New Statesman*, 3 February 1951.
53. *Ibid.*
54. *Economist* review of Harrod's *Keynes*, 27 January 1951.

55. Phelps Brown, reviewing Harrod's *Keynes* in *Economica*, May 1951.
56. JMK to Florence Keynes, 23 February 1943.
57. RFKP: 13/57/479, JMK to RFK, 8 December 1943.
58. KP: L/42, JMK to Joan Robinson, 9 December 1942.
59. KP: L/43, JMK to E. Tillyard, 25 June 1943.
60. JTSP: 6.13, JMK to JTS, 15 February 1946.
61. This episode can be followed in KP: L/43, March/April 1943.
62. KP: PP/45, JMK to A. V. Hill, 18 February 1942.
63. *Ibid.*, Stephen Keynes to JMK, 10 January 1942.
64. *Ibid.*, Milo Keynes to JMK, 10 January 1942.
65. Jeremy Hutchinson to author, 28 January 1998.
66. KP: PP/45, Quentin Keynes to JMK, 16 April 1943; JMK to Quentin Keynes, 29 April 1943.
67. *Ibid.*, JMK to Milo Keynes, 21 July 1943.
68. *Ibid.*, JMK to David Hill, 3 February 1944.
69. This episode can be followed in KP: L/S.
70. KP: L/43, JMK to E. Tillyard, 25 June 1943.
71. KP: PP/79, G. Rylands to JMK, 3 December 1943.
72. *Ibid.*
73. Spalding, *Grant*, 375.
74. KP: PP/45, JMK to Frances Cornford, 30 March 1943.
75. KP: CO/1, JMK to Werner Stark, 18 April 1945.
76. KP: PP/45, JMK to G. B. Shaw, 4 May 1943. Leonard Woolf did it, but JMK still hankered after an appreciation of her economics.

77. Harrod, *Keynes*, 193–4.
78. See Spotts (ed.), *Letters of Leonard Woolf*, 348 and n.
79. KP: PP/45, JMK to Ivor Brown, 4 October 1942.
80. KP: L/42, JMK Reader's Report, 17 June 1942.
81. *Ibid.*, correspondence with J. H. Clapham May/September 1942.
82. KP: CO/1, 'Dr. W. Stark'.
83. KP: L/43, correspondence May/June 1943.
84. KP: CO/10, JMK to Joan Robinson, 20 August 1942.
85. 'The Book Collector', in Milo Keynes (ed.), *Essays on John Maynard Keynes*, 296.
86. KP: L/45, JMK to Cyril Connolly, 22 February 1945.
87. KP: GE/1/1, JMK to W. Hope-Jones, 25 August 1940.
88. KP: GE/1/2, JMK to Claude Elliott, 26 August 1942.
89. KP: GE/1/3, JMK to R. E. Marsden, 29 January 1943; JMK to C. H. K. Marten, 25 June 1943.
90. KP: GE/1/2, Claude Elliott to JMK, 11 August 1942; see also JMK to R. E. Marsden, 9 November 1942. KP: GE/1/3, JMK to R. E. Marsden, 12 March 1943.
91. KP: GE/1/4, J. Ridley to JMK, 8 March 1944; JMK to J. Ridley, (undated) March 1944.
92. KP: PP/45, JMK to William Temple, 3 December 1941.
93. *Ibid.*, correspondence, January/February 1945.
94. In *DNB 1951–60*, 202.
95. KP: GE/2, JMK to F. Cruso, 6, 24 February 1941.
96. KP: W/4, Sir G. Schuster to JMK 4 February 1943; JMK to Sir G. Schuster, 7 February 1943.

Chapter 6: Keynes's 'New Order'

1. KP: W/1, JMK to Dean Acheson, 17 October 1941.
2. *CW*, xxiii, 224–5, JMK (handwritten) minute, 30 December 1941.
3. See T175/123.
4. For an account of this see Dobson, *US Wartime Aid to Britain*, chs 3 and 4.
5. *CW*, xxv, 20.
6. This is the main thesis of Kindleberger, *World in Depression*; see esp. *ibid.*, 28, 291.

7. Skidelsky, *Keynes*, ii, 398.
8. Feis, *1933*, 139.
9. For two opposing views see Friedman and Schwartz, *Great Contraction*, and Temin, *Did Monetary Forces Cause the Great Depression?*
10. John Morton Blum, *Morgenthau Diaries*, i, 121.
11. Feis, *1933*, 125.
12. *Ibid.*, 283.
13. For an entertaining account of Roose-

velt's gold-buying spree, see Galbraith, *Money*, 209–12.

14. S. G. Waley, 1936, q. Drummond, *Floating Pound and the Sterling Area*, 205.

15. H. D. White Papers: Box 1, 4b, report on London trip, 13 June 1935.

16. *CW*, xxi, 360–9.

17. Blum, *Morgenthau Diaries*, i, 132–3; Rees, *Harry Dexter White*, 57.

18. Hull, *Memoirs*, i, 353.

19. Benjamin M. Rowland, in Rowland (ed.), *Balance of Power or Hegemony*, 203.

20. For a summary, see Horsefield, *International Monetary Fund*, i, 6–7.

21. Kimball, 'Lend–Lease and the Open Door', 231.

22. Hull, *Memoirs*, i, 530.

23. Feis, *1933*, 137.

24. Einzig, *Hitler's New Order in Europe*, 66.

25. A canonical statement of this retrospect can be found in Harry White's remarks to the American delegation at Bretton Woods, 1 July 1944: see MD, vol. 749, 16–17.

26. *CW*, iv, 139–40.

27. *CW*, ix, 219.

28. Skidelsky, *Keynes*, ii, 183–7.

29. *CW*, vi, 299.

30. *CW*, iv, 138.

31. *CW*, vi, 354–6.

32. *CW*, ix, 358; Skidelsky, *Keynes*, ii, 471–2, 481; Howson and Winch, *Economic Advisory Council*, 114–21.

33. *CW*, xxi, 273–7.

34. *Ibid.*, 239–40.

35. *CW*, xi, 501.

36. Schumpeter, *Ten Great Economists*, 274.

37. Dormael, *Bretton Woods*, 5–7; see also James, 'Post-War German Currency Plans', 205–18.

38. *CW*, xxv, 2.

39. JMK and E. Playfair, '¿Que Quiere Decir el Area?', November 1940; 'Proposals to Counter the German New Order', 1 December 1940, *ibid.*, 3–16. 'Professor' Keynes's memo can be found in PREM 4/100/5. Paul Addison surely goes too far in saying that the throwaway phrase 'social security' marks 'the beginning of the policies of social security for all' (Addison, *Road to 1945*, 168).

40. The phrase is Brendan Bracken's, quoted in Moggridge, *Keynes: An Economist's Biography*, 654.

41. T247/85, 'New Order File'.

42. *CW*, xxv, 8–9.

43. *Ibid.*, 16–19.

44. *Ibid.*, 9.

45. Eichengreen, 'Sterling and the Tariff', 32.

46. JMK, *The General Theory of Employment, Interest and Money*, *CW*, vii, 348–9. Hubert Henderson agreed: 'Of the various expedients which different Governments employed in the 1930s, none produced more unfortunate results than deliberate exchange depreciation. It was the least helpful to countries which tried it, and the most harmful to other countries': q. Dormael, *Bretton Woods*, 129.

47. T247/121, HDH memorandum, 3 September 1941.

48. *Ibid.*, 26 May 1941.

49. *Ibid.*, HDH, 'The Nineteen Thirties', 22 August 1941; 'The Balance of Payments Problem', 25 September 1941. The first paper was an early draft of the 'International Economic History of the Interwar Period', dated 3 December 1943, and published in Henderson, *The Interwar Years and Other Papers*.

50. T247/121, HDH to Sir R. Hopkins, 30 October 1941.

51. Harrod, *Keynes*, 526.

52. Penrose, *Economic Planning for Peace*, 16–17.

53. KP: L/K 135.

54. *CW*, xxv, 20, JMK to RFK, 21 August 1941.

55. OTFP2: OTF to R. Boothby, 28 January 1947; T. Boothby to OTF, 31 January 1947.

56. Hubert Henderson reviewing Harrod's *Keynes* in the *Spectator*, 26 January 1951.

57. KP: BE/1, W. Newbold to JMK, 1 October 1941.

58. FFP: F. Frankfurter to JMK, 19 September 1941; RFKP: 13/57/472, JMK to RFK, 9 September 1941.

59. q. Kynaston, *City of London*, iii, 483.

60. HCP: M. Norman to H. Clay, 19 June 1946.

61. *CW*, xxv, 67, D. H. Robertson to JMK, 27 November 1941.

62. *CW*, xxxvii, 22.

63. The first draft of the International Currency Union is reproduced in *CW*, xxv, 21–40. In my summary of Part I, I have rearranged the four sections in what, to me, seems a more logical order.

64. Moggridge, *Keynes: An Economist's Biography*, 674.

65. T247/116. JMK to H. Clay, 2 December

1941; KP: W/1, JMK to C. Guillebaud, 5 May 1942; see also *CW*, xxv, 28–9.

66. The progress of the Treasury 'sandwich' can be traced in T247/121.
67. *Ibid.* HDH, 'Post-War External Policy, Suggestion for a Reconciliation', 24 November 1941.
68. T247/122. Bank memo, 29 September 1941. This file contains the Bank of England's proposals and comments on the Keynes Plan.
69. *Ibid.*, Bank of England memo on Post-War Trade and Financial Policy, 17 October 1941; B. G. Catterns to Sir R. Hopkins, 4 November 1941; Bank memo, 4 November 1941. Keynes identified G. L. Bolton as the author of the last. Bank of England reactions can also be followed in BE: ADMIN 14/1–2.
70. T247/122, JMK, 'Bank of England Memorandum on Post-War Trade and Financial Policy', 22 October 1941.
71. *Ibid.*, HDH to JMK, 23 October 1941.
72. *Ibid.*, JMK, 'The Sterling Area', 9 November 1941; JMK to C. F. Cobbold, 26 November 1941.
73. *Ibid.*
74. T247/121, D. H. Robertson, 26 September 1941, 22 August 1941.
75. *Ibid.*, Note on Treasury memo, 12 October 1941.
76. *Ibid.*, undated.
77. *Ibid.*, 16 October 1941.
78. *Ibid.*, 'Post-War Currency', 21 September 1941.
79. *Ibid.*, Note on Treasury Memo, 13 November 1941.
80. BE: ADMIN 14/1, Sir R. Hopkins, 'Note on Post-War Monetary and Financial Policy'.
81. T247/121, 'Notes on Memorandum . . .', 17 November 1941.
82. *Ibid.*, HDH to Sir R. Hopkins, 22 October 1941.
83. Kynaston, *City of London*, iii, 497.
84. BE: ADMIN 14/1, H. A. Siepmann, 'Post-War Keynes Plan 1941', 12 September 1941.
85. *Ibid.*, L. P. Thompson-McCausland, 22 September 1941.
86. T247/122, L. P. Thompson-McCausland to JMK, 25 October 1941; JMK to L. P. Thompson-McCausland, 12 November 1941.
87. BE: ADMIN 14/1, G. L. F. Bolton, 'Keynes World Bank', 30 September 1941.

88. *Ibid.*, H. Clay, 'Keynes II and the Alternatives', 26 September 1941.
89. *Ibid.*, H. A. Siepmann, 'Results of Two Conversations with Keynes', 14 November 1941; G. L. F. Bolton's additions, 15 November 1941.
90. T247/16, 'Mr. Keynes's Proposal' 15 October 1941.
91. *Ibid.*, 24 December 1941.
92. RBP: File 198, R. H. Brand to JMK, 10 October 1941.
93. *CW*, xxvi, 247, JMK to L. Pasvolsky, 22 May 1942.
94. T247/116, J. E. Meade to JMK, 9 October 1941.
95. C.1 and C.2 of the 18 November draft, *CW*, xxv, 65. This was not in the first draft.
96. Penrose, *Economic Planning for Peace*, 15–16.
97. T247/121. Both letters written on 26 November 1941.
98. *CW*, xxv, 66.
99. BE: ADMIN 14/1, H. A. Siepmann to G. L. F. Bolton, 24 November 1941.
100. T247/121, 'Note of Meeting on 5 December to discuss Mr. Henderson's Memorandum'.
101. T247/122, Notes of first and second meetings with the Bank.
102. In T247/116.
103. These phrases are from a memorandum Harrod sent to Keynes on 4 April 1942 (T247/67), but he had been preaching this gospel throughout the autumn of 1941.
104. T247/121, RFH, 'Notes on Memorandum . . .', 17 November 1941; 'Note on Points Made in Discussion', 26 November 1941. See T272/63 for the development of Harrod's views.
105. T247/116.
106. T247/122, JMK to M. Norman, 19 December 1941.
107. BE: ADMIN 14/1, C. F. Cobbold to M. Norman, 29 December 1941.
108. *CW*, xxv, 69–94, Third draft of Proposals for an International Currency Union.
109. T241/116, D. H. Robertson to JMK, 22 December 1941; JMK to D. H. Robertson, 29 December 1941.
110. T247/116, Roy Harrod to Sir R. Hopkins, 18 December 1941.
111. *Ibid.*, Sir R. Hopkins to Roy Harrod, 24 December 1941.
112. KP: L/K/163.
113. Fourth draft of Keynes's Plan for an

International Currency Union, incorporated from para. 61 to para. 134 in the Treasury Memo on External Monetary and Economic Problems, *CW*, xxv, 108–39.

114. T247/116.
115. Pressnell, *External Economic Policy since the War*, i, 78.
116. T247/118. JMK to Sir R. Hopkins, 29 January 1942; Robbins Note, ? February 1942.
117. FO371/32450, C. Baring to N. Ronald, 6 February 1942, q. Dormael, *Bretton Woods*, 48.

118. Moggridge, *Keynes: An Economist's Biography*, 676.
119. T247/67, Harrod, 'Forthcoming Conversations with the United States', 15 April 1942; *CW*, xxv, 146–50, JMK to R. Harrod, 19 April 1942.
120. T247/67, Henderson, 'Notes on Post-War Problems', 7 April 1942; *CW*, xxv, 153–7, JMK to HDH, 9 May 1942.
121. B. Pimlott (ed.), *Second World War Diary of Hugh Dalton*, 406; *CW*, xxv, 140–3; Bullock, *Bevin*, ii, 204.
122. *CW*, xxv. 143, JMK to RFK, 11 May 1942.

Chapter 7: The Strange Case of Harry Dexter White

1. WLP: Box 82, File 656, WL to JMK, 18 April 1942.
2. T247/116, Roy Harrod to Sir R. Hopkins, 4 December 1941.
3. See *CW*, xxv, 24–5; see also Dobson, *US Wartime Aid to Britain*, 80–4.
4. *CW*, xxvii, 126.
5. *Ibid.* 111, JMK to Sir R. Hopkins, 15 April 1942.
6. *Ibid.*, 122–34.
7. *Ibid.*, 131.
8. *Ibid.*, 124.
9. See BE: ADMIN 14/2, L. P. Thompson-McCausland, 'Note on Buffer Stocks', 31 March 1942.
10. Cairncross and Watts, *Economic Section*, 67.
11. T247/110, JMK to Sir F. Phillips, 6 January 1943.
12. *CW*, xxvii, 166–8, JMK to Sir W. Eady, January 1943.
13. See Skidelsky, *Keynes*, ii, 476–8.
14. *CW*, xxvi, 253–72.
15. T247/2, JMK, 'Post-War Commercial Policy', 15 January 1943.
16. *Ibid.* Details of the discussions on the Commercial Union are in T247/2.
17. q. Dormael, *Bretton Woods*, p.40.
18. Oliver, *International Economic Cooperation and the World Bank*, 110–11.
19. Mikesell, 'Bretton Woods Debates', 5–6.
20. Rees, *Harry Dexter White*, 35.
21. *Ibid.*, 39, draft of a letter to Frank Taussig, undated.
22. *Ibid.*, 55–6.
23. *Ibid.*, 66.
24. *Ibid.*, 138.
25. Meade's Diary, 29 September 1943, in Howson and Moggridge (eds), *Wartime Diaries of Robbins and Meade*, 120.

26. Craig, 'Treasonable Doubt: The Harry Dexter White Case', 596–7.
27. Gardner, *Sterling–Dollar Diplomacy*, ch. 2.
28. Rees, *Harry Dexter White*, 53.
29. *Ibid.*, 100–2, 118, 143, 301–2.
30. See Keynes's comment in *CW*, xxv, 356.
31. The H. D. White Papers, Box 8, contains his drafts for the IMF and Reconstruction Bank.
32. Harrod, *Keynes*, 540.
33. For details, see Horsefield, *International Monetary Fund*, i, 21–5, iii, 41–82.
34. Dormael, *Bretton Woods*, 55.
35. As does Horsefield, *International Monetary Fund*, i, 28.
36. *CW*, xxv, 158–9. JMK to Sir R. Hopkins, 3 August 1942; JMK to Sir F. Phillips, 3 August 1942.
37. *Ibid.*, 160–7, JMK, 'Notes on the Memorandum ... transmitted by Sir F. Phillips'.
38. Moggridge, *Keynes: An Economist's Biography*, 688.
39. *CW*, xxv, 168–95. See *ibid.*, 173, 174, 183, 186, 187, 189, 191–2.
40. RFKP: L/K/203, JMK to RFK, 28 August 1942.
41. Horsefield, *International Monetary Fund*, i, 30.
42. FO371/31516, Sir F. Phillips to Treasury, 8 October 1942.
43. Penrose, *Economic Planning for Peace*, 48–9.
44. KP: L/K/237, JMK to RFK, 13 November 1942.
45. *CW*, xxv, 197, JMK to Sir F. Phillips, 16 December 1942.
46. T160/1281/18885/1, JMK to Sir W. Eady, 21 January 1942.
47. Dormael, *Bretton Woods*, 67–8.
48. *CW*, xxv, 210, JMK speech to meeting

of European Allies, London, 26 February 1943.

49. FO371/3530, JMK to N. Ronald, 25 February 1943.
50. *CW*, xxv, 238, JMK to Sir F. Phillips, 16 April 1943.
51. T160/1281/18885/1, JMK, 'The Berle Memorandum', 18 February 1943 – as the White Plan was then called.
52. *CW*, xxv, 215–26, JMK, 'A Comparative Analysis . . .', 1 March 1943.
53. Horsefield, *International Monetary Fund*, i, 45–6.
54. See Harrod, *Keynes*, 545–7; *CW*, xxv, 226–8.
55. *CW*, xxv, 230–2.
56. T160/1281/18885/3, JMK memo, 16 April 1943.
57. T247/67, Harrod, 'Foreign Investment, Industrialisation and the CU'; JMK to Roy Harrod, 15 September 1942.
58. *CW*, xxv, 268, JMK to Roy Harrod, 27 April 1943.

59. T160/18885/1, JMK to Lord Catto, Sir W. Eady, D. Proctor, 2 April 1943.
60. Dormael, *Bretton Woods*, 77.
61. T160/1281/18885/5, Lord Halifax to FO 13, June 1943.
62. q. Gardner, *Sterling-Dollar Diplomacy*, 78.
63. Lamont Papers: Folder 104–1, 1943–4, 'Bancor and Unitas', 3 June 1943.
64. q. Rowland (ed.), *Balance of Power or Hegemony*, 221.
65. 'Memoranda on Axis-Controlled Europe', no. 60, Review of the Foreign Press, Series A, 3 August 1943, Research Department Foreign Office. This copy is in BE 14/9.
66. *CW*, xxv, 258–9.
67. T160/1281/18885/5, JMK to D. H. Robinson, 2 June 1943.
68. Herbert H. Lehman Papers: JMK to H. H. Lehman, 16 April 1943.
69. *CW*, xxv, 269–80.

Chapter 8: Building a Better Britain

1 KP: PP/45, JMK to William Temple, 3 December 1941.
2 Partridge, *A Pacifist's War*, 140.
3. Harris, *Beveridge*, 386; Bullock, *Bevin*, ii, 226.
4. *CW*, xxvii, 249, JMK to Sir R. Hopkins, 13 October 1942.
5. *Ibid.*, 219, JMK to W. Beveridge, 25 June 1942.
6. *Ibid.*, 223, JMK to Sir R. Hopkins, 20 July 1942.
7. *Ibid.*, 237.
8. *Ibid.*, 230, 238–9.
9. *Ibid.*, 246–53, 255, JMK to Sir R. Hopkins, 13 October 1942; JMK to W. Beveridge, 14 October 1942.
10. Cairncross and Watts, *Economic Section*, 89; original of the Economic Section's memo, 'The Economic Aspects of the Proposed Reform of Social Security', dated 16 June 1942, can be found in HDHP: Box 3, Beveridge File.
11. HDHP: Box 3, Beveridge File, HDH to Sir Alexander Roger, 17 February 1943; to Sir R. Hopkins, 22 December 1942.
12. OTFP2: R. H. Brand to OTF, 8 December 1942.
13. Cairncross and Watts, *Economic Section*, 71.
14. *CW*, xxvii, 271, JMK to HDH and Sir R. Hopkins, 8 April 1942. For Henderson's paper see CAB87/55.

15. *CW*, xxvii, 314–15.
16. Pre-1914 figures are based on the records of trade unions that paid benefits to their members. The shortcomings of the data as a measure of unemployment in the labour force are well known. (See Feinstein, *National Income, Expenditure and Output of the United Kingdom*, 225.) What matters is how Keynes interpreted them. Even so, the percentages varied considerably across the cycle, from 2.0 per cent to 7.8 per cent (*ibid.*, 57). So the figure of 5 per cent is an average, not a minimum.
17. Lerner, *Economics of Employment*.
18. *CW*, xxvii, 280–1, 299, 301, JMK, 'National Income and Expenditure after the War', 28 May 1942; JMK to HDH, 3 June 1942.
19. Cairncross and Watts, *Economic Section*, 91–2.
20. *CW*, xxvii, 299, JMK to HDH.
21. *Ibid.* 381, JMK to W. Beveridge, 16 December 1944.
22. In Howson and Moggridge (ed.), *Collected Papers of James Meade*, iv, 63.
23. See Skidelsky, *Keynes*, ii, 265–8.
24. Skidelsky, 'Keynes and the State', 144–52.
25. In his essay 'The End of Laissez-Faire', *CW*, ix, 289.
26. In his paper 'The Public and Private

Concern', read to the Liberal Summer School, *CW*, xix, 696.

27. In the *General Theory*, *CW*, vii, 163–4.
28. *Ibid.*, 378.
29. *CW*, xxvii, 316, JMK to L. Robbins, 29 March 1943.
30. *Ibid.*, 225.
31. *Ibid.*, 227, JMK to Sir R. Hopkins and others, 15 May 1942; *ibid.*, 368, 'Post-War Employment Policy: Note by Lord Keynes on the Report of the Steering Committee', 14 February 1944; *ibid.*, 410–11, 'The Concept of a Capital Budget', 21 June 1945.
32. *Ibid.*, 352–3, JMK to Sir W. Eady, 10 June 1943; see also *ibid.*, 376–7, JMK to A. Barlow, 15 June 1944.
33. *Ibid.*, 226–8.
34. *Ibid.*, 319–20, JMK to James Meade, 25 April 1943.
35. *Ibid.*, 223–4.
36. KP: CO/2. Keynes attacked Lerner's paper 'Functional Finance and the Federal Debt', *Social Research*, February 1943, vol. 10, no. 1, in Washington in 1943. See JMK to Fritz Machlup, 24 October 1944; JMK to J. H. G. Pierson, 22 October 1943.
37. Wilson, *Churchill and the Prof*, 164–5.
38. For this shift see Tomlinson, *Employment Policy*.
39. Clark, 'Public Finance and Changes in the Value of Money', 371.
40. *CW*, xxvii, 206, 208.
41. *Ibid.*, 317, James Meade to JMK, 19 April 1943.
42. *Ibid.*, 310, JMK to James Meade, 25 August 1942.
43. *Ibid.*, 319–20, JMK to James Meade, 25 April 1943.
44. *Ibid.*, 322, 'The Long-Term Problem of Full Employment', 25 May 1943.
45. Henderson's paper is reproduced in Henderson, *The Inter-War Years and Other Papers*.
46. *CW*, xxvii, 321–4; see also *ibid.*, 350, JMK to Josiah Wedgwood, 7 July 1943.
47. 'Economic Possibilities for our Grandchildren' is published in *CW*, ix, 321–32. For a discussion, and critique, see Skidelsky, *Keynes*, ii, 236–8.
48. *CW*, ix, 384.
49. See Moggridge, *Keynes: An Economist's Biography*, 711.
50. *CW*, xxvii, 325–6.
51. *Ibid.*, 358.
52. Peden, 'Sir Richard Hopkins and the "Keynesian Revolution"', 289.
53. q. Booth, 'Simple Keynesianism and Whitehall'.
54. Beveridge's *Full Employment in a Free Society* was published in 1944.
55. *CW*, xxvii, 371–2, 'Note by Lord Keynes on the Report of the Steering Committee', 14 February 1944.
56. *Ibid.*, 366–7.
57. *Ibid.*, 336–42.
58. *Ibid.*, 354–7.
59. *Ibid.*, 369.
60. HDHP: Box 3, 'Brave New Worlds: Internal and External', 22 March 1944; 'The Employment Policy', 27 March 1944, 'Employment Policy and the Balance of Payments', 31 March 1944.
61. *CW*, xxvii, 373–4, JMK to Sir W. Eady, Sir R. Hopkins, 28 March 1944.
62. JMK to Austin Robinson, 5 June 1944, q. Moggridge, *Keynes: An Economist's Biography*, 709.
63. *CW*, xxvii, 385.
64. Hayek, *Road to Serfdom*, 90–1.
65. E.g. Barbara Wootton, *Freedom under Planning*, 30, 62, as q. Durbin, *New Jerusalems*, 269.
66. *CW*, xxvii, 385–8, JMK to F. A. Hayek, 28 June 1944.
67. KP: PP/84(1), R. A. Butler to JMK, 17 December 1941.
68. *The Times*, 26 February 1942.
69. See Mary Glasgow, 'The Concept of the Arts Council', in Milo Keynes (ed.), *Essays on Keynes*, 260–1, 262; also Glasgow, *Nineteen Hundreds*, 188.
70. Mary Glasgow, in Milo Keynes (ed.), *Essays on Keynes*, 267.
71. *CW*, xxviii, 341–9, 'Art and the State', reprinted from the *Listener*, 26 August 1936.
72. See Skidelsky, *Keynes*, ii, 384, 477–8.
73. See Clive Bell, *Old Friends*, 56–8.
74. *Listener*, 2 April 1942.
75. Kenneth Clark, *Other Half*, 27; Mary Glasgow in Milo Keynes (ed.), *Essays on Keynes*, 267.
76. Glasgow, *Nineteen Hundreds*, 192–3.
77. KP: PP/84(5), JMK to Michael Macowen, 5 June 1945.
78. A large file on 'Entertainments Tax' can be found in KP: PP/84(6).
79. Mary Glasgow in Milo Keynes (ed.), *Essays on Keynes* 266–7.
80. KP: PP/84 (5), JMK to Sir Alfred Barker, 23 January 1943.
81. *CW*, xxviii, 360, JMK, 'The Arts in Wartime', *The Times*, 11 May 1943.
82. *Ibid.*, 269.

83. KP: PP 84 (5), JMK to A. Dukes, 18 May 1943; for the antecedents to this row see also KP: PP/80(9).
84. KP: PP/84 (3) for these exchanges with R. A. Butler, February–April 1943.
85. *CW*, xxviii, 362–3. The Academicians' letter had appeared the previous day.
86. KP: PP/84 (5).
87. KP: PP/84(3), JMK to R. A. Butler, 6 April 1945.
88. *CW*, xxviii, 367–72, 'The Arts Council:

Its Policy and Hopes', published in the *Listener*, 12 July 1945.
89. KP: PP/84 (8).
90. Blunt, *Christie*, 228–33.
91. Kenneth Clark, *Other Half*, 131.
92. Mary Glasgow, in Milo Keynes (ed.), *Essays on Keynes*, 267.
93. Donaldson, *Royal Opera House in the Twentieth Century*, 45–8; Blunt, *Christie*, 235–7.
94. This account is based on the archives in the Royal Opera House.

Chapter 9: The Great Compromise

1. Penrose, *Economic Planning for Peace*, 120.
2. Howson and Moggridge (eds), *Wartime Diaries of Robbins and Meade*, 52.
3. Dormael, *Bretton Woods*, 87f.
4. *CW*, xxv, 292, D. H. Robertson, 'Notes', 3 June 1943.
5. *Ibid.*, 267, JMK to Roy Harrod, 27 April 1943; *ibid.*, 296, JMK to D. H. Robertson, 11 June 1943.
6. T247/5, JMK to T. E. Gregory, 11 June 1943.
7. T160/1281/18885/5, Lord Halifax to FO, 24 June 1943.
8. Howson and Moggridge (eds), *Wartime Diaries of Robbins and Meade*, 84.
9. Dormael, *Bretton Woods*, 90–1; see also *CW*, xxv, 317.
10. Moggridge, *Keynes: An Economist's Biography*, 723.
11. *CW*, xxv, 303, JMK to D. H. Robertson, 9 July 1943.
12. *Ibid.*, 318–19, 321, JMK to Sir W. Eady, 13 July 1943; JMK to J. Viner, 9 June 1943.
13. So Keynes told the Australian economist Herbert Coombs, who saw him in London that summer. See Turnell, 'A Clearing Union or a Stabilising Fund? Australian Economists and the Creation of the IMF', 7. Coombs was also promoting the Australian 'employment approach' – that members of the SF should commit themselves to full employment policies.
14. *CW*, xxv, 320–32, JMK to J. Viner, 9 June, 17 October 1943; J. Viner to JMK, 12 July 1943.
15. MD: vol. 654, 95, telegram from J. Winant, 5 August 1943; see also Dormael, *Bretton Woods*, 89–91.
16. Howson and Moggridge (eds), *Wartime Diaries of Robbins and Meade*, 76.

17. *CW*, xxv, 305–7, JMK to S. D. Waley, 22 June 1943; see also Moggridge, *Keynes: An Economist's Biography*, 724.
18. FO371/35336, R. Opie note of 23 August 1943.
19. Howson and Moggridge (eds), *Wartime Diaries of Robbins and Meade*, 97.
20. T160/1281/18885/6, JMK to E. Playfair, Sir W. Eady, 5 August 1943.
21. Howson and Moggridge (eds), *Wartime Diaries of Robbins and Meade*, 93.
22. *Ibid.*, 95–7.
23. *Ibid.*, 100.
24. *Ibid.*, 104, 109, 110.
25. T160/1281/18885/6, 'Note of Plenary Session', 21 September 1943.
26. Howson and Moggridge (eds), *Wartime Diaries of Robbins and Meade*, 105.
27. FO371/3536, R. Campbell to FO, 15 September 1943, contains JMK's report of the conversation. See also *CW*, xxv, 340.
28. Gardner, *Sterling–Dollar Diplomacy*, 112.
29. Howson and Moggridge (eds), *Wartime Diaries of Robbins and Meade*, 130.
30. Dormael, *Bretton Woods*, 101.
31. Interview with Edward Bernstein, 10 April 1989.
32. T160/1281/18885/6. fn. 89, T160/1281/1885/11. JMK to Treasury, 23 September 1943.
33. BE: ADMIN 14/9, L. P. Thompson-McCausland to C. F. Cobbold, 18 September 1943.
34. Howson and Moggridge (eds), *Wartime Diaries of Robbins and Meade*, 114; *CW*, xxv, 345–6.
35. *CW*, xxv, 334.
36. The phrase is from Pressnell, *External Economic Policy since the War*, 139.
37. Horsefield, *International Monetary Fund*, iii: *Documents*, 86.

38. Pimlott (ed.), *Second World War Diary of Hugh Dalton*, 631.

39. T160/1281/18885/6.

40. Pimlott (ed.), *Second World War Diary of Hugh Dalton*, 648; also T160/1281/18885/6, Telegrams 4174, 6356, 4274, 6702.

41. For Varvaressos's role, see Horsefield, *International Monetary Fund*, i, 58.

42. Howson and Moggridge (eds), *Wartime Diaries of Robbins and Meade*, 123.

43. *Ibid.* For Meade's comment on Thompson-McCausland, see *ibid.*, 121; for the Bank's instructions to him, *ibid.*, 150.

44. BE: ADMIN 14/9.

45. For Keynes's reasons, and plan, for monetising unitas, see *CW*, xxv, 321, 318–19, 341–4, 346–8; also L. P. Thompson-McCausland, 'Difference beween S. F. and Monetised Unitas . . .', 29 September 1943, in BE: ADMIN 14/9.

46. Howson and Moggridge (eds), *Wartime Diaries of Robbins and Meade*, 114; *CW*, xxv, 348, 349.

47. Mikesell, 'Bretton Woods Debates', 16.

48. *CW*, xxv, 379–87, 'Draft Statement'. See especially Clauses 2(ii), 6(ii), 13(iii), 4(ii).

49. Howson and Moggridge (eds), *Wartime Diaries of Robbins and Meade*, 118–19, 122, 124.

50. *CW*, xxv, 357, JMK to Sir W. Eady, 3 October 1943.

51. Howson and Moggridge (eds), *Wartime Diaries of Robbins and Meade*, 127.

52. MD: vol. 664, 30.

53. *CW*, xxv, 360–4, JMK to Sir W. Eady, 3 October 1943.

54. Howson and Moggridge (eds), *Wartime Diaries of Robbins and Meade*, 135.

55. *Ibid.*, 133; *CW*, xxv, 371.

56. MD, vol. 722, 17.

57. For the various documents resulting from the talks, see *CW*, xxv, 377–92. The comparisons are with the *CW*, xxv draft and the 10 July 1943 draft as reprinted in Horsefield, *International Monetary Fund*, iii, 83–96.

58. *CW*, xxv, 368, 369, JMK to Sir W. Eady, 8 October 1943.

59. Harrod, *Keynes*, 567–8.

60. *CW*, xxiii, 288, 312–13; information supplied by R. J. Sandilands.

61. *CW*, xxiii, 288, 312–13; Dobson, *US Wartime Aid to Britain*, ch. 5, esp. 139–40, 150; BE: ADMIN 14/9, Note by L. P. Thompson-McCausland of JMK lunch, at which were present Waley, Knollenberg, Charles Denby and Edward S. Acheson, reproduced in *CW*, xxiii, 286–290.

62. For JMK's comments, see *CW*, xxv, 354, 356, 363–4.

63. Harry White Papers: Washington Section, 1944 folder. Information supplied by James Boughton.

64. *CW*, xxiv, 1–18.

65. T160/1281/18885/7, JMK memo, 17 January 1944.

66. *CW*, xxv, 393–4; Gardner, *Sterling–Dollar Diplomacy*, 119–22.

67. Pimlott (ed.), *Second World War Diary of Hugh Dalton*, 670.

68. Dobson, *US Wartime Aid to Britain*, 173.

69. LePan, *Bright Glass of Memory*, 61.

70. MacDougall, *Don and Mandarin*, 40.

71. *CW*, xxv, 395–8, Sir W. Eady note, 9 January 1944.

72. HDHP: Box 3, HDH to JMK, 2 November 1943.

73. *Ibid.*, Box 5, Lord Catto, memo to Chancellor of the Exchequer on the International Monetary Fund, 16 February 1944.

74. *CW*, xxv, 408.

75. *Ibid.*, 399–408, JMK 'The Main Objects of the Plan'.

76. *Ibid.*, 409.

77. For the Bank memo and Dormael's comment, see Dormael, *Bretton Woods*, 132.

78. Pimlott (ed.), *Second World War Diary of Hugh Dalton*, 707–8.

79. *CW*, xxv, 410–13, JMK to Sir J. Anderson, 23 February 1944.

80. q. Kynaston, *City of London*, iii, 503, from a 'Note on Commercial Policy', BE: G 18/3, 20 March 1945.

81. Pimlott (ed.), *Second World War Diary of Hugh Dalton*, 710–12.

82. *CW*, xxv, 410–27, JMK, 'Note . . . on the US Proposals for a Bank of Reconstruction and Development', 7 March 1944.

83. JMK to L. G. Melville, 14 March 1944, q. Turnell, 'A Clearing Union or a Stabilising Fund?', 18.

84. *CW*, xxv, 427–9.

85. MacDougall, *Don and Mandarin*, 39.

86. For JMK's exchange with Beaverbrook 8–11 March, see *CW*, xxv, 415–18. For JMK's distinction between currency and commercial bilateralism, see his letter to Sir W. Eady, 29 March 1943, *Ibid.*, 430, and his correspondence with D. H. Robertson, *CW*, xxvi, 23–6.

87. Pimlott (ed.), *Second World War Diary of Hugh Dalton*, 735–6.
88. Dobson, *US Wartime Aid to Britain*, 173–4.
89. T160/1281/18885/1, JMK to Sir W. Eady, 9 May 1944.
90. T160/1281/18885/11, S. D. Waley to JMK, Sir W. Eady, 16 May 1944; JMK memo, 16 May 1944.
91. *CW*, xxvi, 3, JMK to F. Pethick-Lawrence, 16 May 1944.
92. As Balogh recalled in Thirlwall (ed.), *Keynes and International Monetary Relations*, 66.
93. LePan, *Bright Glass of Memory*, 101.
94. Letters to *The Times*, 10, 18 May 1943.
95. *CW*, xxvi, 29–30, JMK to L. Pasvolsky, 24 May 1944.
96. *Ibid.* 9–21.
97. Pasvolsky, q. Dormael, *Bretton Woods*, 160.
98. KP: PS/8, Alec Spearman to JMK (undated), but certainly referring to JMK's speech.

Chapter 10: The American Way of Business

1. *CW*, xxiv, 28–9, JMK to E. R. Stettinius, 18 April 1944.
2. See Moggridge, *Keynes: An Economist's Biography*, 657–60; *CW*, xxiii, ch. 8.
3. *CW*, xxiv, 26.
4. T247/28, JMK to S. D. Waley, Sir W. Eady, 30 May 1944; *CW*, xxvi, 41.
5. Pressnell, *External Economic Policy since the War*, 225.
6. *Ibid.*, 229.
7. *CW*, xxiv, 61.
8. *Ibid.*, 64.
9. Howson and Moggridge (eds), *Wartime Diaries of Robbins and Meade*, 156–7.
10. *CW*, xxvi, 59, JMK to Sir R. Hopkins, 25 June 1944.
11. Howson and Moggridge (eds), *Wartime Diaries of Robbins and Meade*, 158.
12. *Ibid.*, 158–9, Robbins Diary, 24 June 1944.
13. *CW*, xxvi, 48–54, JMK, 'The Bank for Reconstruction and Development', 9 June 1944.
14. *Ibid.*, 61, 64, JMK to Sir R. Hopkins, 25 June 1944; see also FO371/40948, 40589.
15. Howson and Moggridge (eds), *Wartime Diaries of Robbins and Meade*, 159.
16. *CW*, xxvi, 68, JMK to Sir R. Hopkins, 30 June 1944.
17. James, *International Monetary Cooperation since Bretton Woods*, 48.
18. *CW*, xxvi, 70, JMK to Sir R. Hopkins, 30 June 1944; Horsefield, *International Monetary Fund*, i, 85.
19. Howson and Moggridge (eds), *Wartime Diaries of Robbins and Meade*, 166.
20. *Ibid.*
21. *Ibid.*, 167.
22. MD, vol. 749, 210–11.
23. James, *International Monetary Cooperation since Bretton Woods*, 53.
24. Dormael, *Bretton Woods*, 179.
25. *CW*, xxvi, 86–7.
26. Dormael, *Bretton Woods*, 174, quoting Goldenweiser.
27. *CW*, xxvi, 109, JMK to Sir W. Hopkins, 22 July 1944.
28. EGP: BW Conference, Box 4.
29. Horsefield, *International Monetary Fund*, i, 95; Mikesell, 'The Bretton Woods Debates', 35–8.
30. q. Horsefield, *International Monetary Fund*, i, 97.
31. MD, vol. 754, 20–30.
32. Howson and Moggridge (eds), *Wartime Diaries of Robbins and Meade*, 176–7.
33. *Ibid.*, 176.
34. MD, vol. 753, 122–6.
35. *Ibid.*, 143–4; vol. 754, 4.
36. KP: W/1, JMK to Lord Catto, 22 July 1944; see also James, *International Monetary Cooperation since Bretton Woods*, 49 and n.49.
37. MD, vol. 756, 9.
38. *CW*, xxvi, 106, JMK to Sir J. Anderson, 21 July 1944.
39. *Ibid.*, 81, JMK to Lord Catto, 4 July 1944.
40. Eady in the *Listener*, 7 June 1951.
41. KP: W/1, JMK to Lord Catto, 22 July 1944.
42. A. W. Snelling, q. Pressnell, *External Economic Policy since the War*, 159.
43. Harrod, *Keynes*, 585.
44. Pressnell, *External Economic Policy since the War*, 189; *CW*, xxvi, 150–1; T247/50, JMK to Sir W. Eady, 1 March 1945.
45. EGP: Box 4.
46. From Malcolm MacDonald's *People and Places*, 1969, reproduced in Milo Keynes (ed.), *Lydia Lopokova*, 178–9.
47. *CW*, xxvi, 113, JMK to Lord Catto, 28 July 1944.
48. *CW*, xxiv, 97–107, JMK to Sir J. Anderson, 10 August 1944; Sayers, *British*

Financial Policy, 351–8; JMK to Florence Keynes, 7 August 1944.

49. Pressnell, *External Economic Policy since the War*, 216; Dobson, *US Wartime Aid to Britain*, 188–9.

50. Halifax Diary, 20 August 1944; *CW*, xxiii, ch. 8.

51. KP: L/44, JMK to A. P. Lerner, 27 September 1944.

52. Rees, *Harry Dexter White*, 251; see *ibid.*, 239–51 for the episode; also Penrose, *Economic Planning for Peace*, ch. 14.

53. KP: L/44, JMK to WL, 13 August 1944; MD, vol. 764, 90, H. D. White to H. Morgenthau, 20 August 1944.

54. Cairncross, *Price of War*, 27; *CW*, xxvi, 348–73.

55. Rees, *Harry Dexter White*, 241.

56. Blum, *Morgenthau Diary*, iii, 369; Dobson, *US Wartime Aid to Britain*, 194.

57. Woodward, British Foreign Policy, 476.

58. Dobson, *US Wartime Aid to Britain*, 195–6.

59. Churchill, *Second World War*, vi, 139; Penrose, *External Economic Policy since the War*, 255.

60. MD, vol. 773, 74.

61. *CW*, xxiv, 187, Frank Lee to F. E. Harmer, 6 December 1944.

62. *Ibid.*, 129, JMK to Sir J. Anderson, 1 October 1944.

63. *Ibid.*, 132, JMK to Sir J. Anderson, 4 October 1944.

64. *Ibid.*, 133–4; Halifax Diary, 2 November 1944; Penrose, *External Economic Policy since the War*, 255.

65. MacDougall Diary, 10 October 1944.

66. *CW*, xxiv, 186–7, Frank Lee to F. E. Harmer, 6 December 1944.

67. *Ibid.*, 214–15, JMK to Sir J. Anderson, 12 December 1944.

68. *Ibid.*, 151–2, JMK to Sir J. Anderson, 31 October 1944.

69. MacDougall Diary, 24 October 1944.

70. Isaiah Berlin, in Milo Keynes (ed.), *Lydia Lopokova*, 172–3. Berlin was stationed in Washington for most of the war.

71. *CW*, xxiv, 139, JMK to Sir J. Anderson, 21 October 1944.

72. q. Dobson, *US Wartime Aid to Britain*, 207.

73. For the Berlin story, see Milo Keynes (ed.), *Lydia Lopokova*, 173. A variant is given in a transcript of an interview with Michael Ignatieff, 5 June 1994.

74. In Milo Keynes (ed.), *Lydia Lopokova*, 184.

75. 23 October 1944. Letter in possession of Richard and Anne Keynes.

76. *CW*, xxiv, 166–8, JMK to H. Morgenthau, 16 November 1944.

77. *Ibid.*, 204, 217, 218, JMK to Sir J. Anderson, 12 December 1944.

78. Ben Pimlott (ed.), *Second World War Diary of Hugh Dalton*, 818.

79. *CW*, xxiv, 188, Frank Lee to F. E. Harmer, 6 December 1944.

80. Dobson, *US Wartime Aid to Britain*, 211. For Roosevelt's change of mind, see *ibid.*, 206–11.

81. *CW*, xxiv, 220–1, JMK to Sir J. Anderson, 12 December 1944.

Chapter 11: Temptation

1. For Meade's comments see Howson and Moggridge (eds), *Collected Papers of James Meade*, 46, 48, 61; also 'Lord Keynes's Notes', in *CW*, xxvii, 388–96.

2. Howson and Moggridge, (eds), *Collected Papers of James Meade*, 55.

3. *CW*, xxviii, 391–3, 398.

4. Sayers, 'Bank Rate in Keynes's Century', *Proceedings of the British Academy*, LXV (1979), 202, q. Howson, 'Cheap Money and Debt Management in Britain', 280.

5. Meade's description of Keynes in Howson and Moggridge (eds), *Collected Papers of James Meade*, 46.

6. KP: PP/45, JMK to Sir C. Gregg, 9 April 1945.

7. See T. P. McLaughlin, 'The Teaching of the Canonists on Usuary', *Mediaeval Studies*, 1, 1939.

8. KP: PP/45.

9. For the British draft see *FRUS*, 1945, vi, 56–60; For Keynes's views, see *ibid.*, 19–21, J. Winant to Cordell Hull, 8 February 1945; Currie Report on conversations with British officials, *ibid.*, 38.

10. Pressnell, *External Economic Policy since the War*, 237.

11. *CW*, xxiv, 249.

12. *FRUS*, 1945, vi, 28–9, 36–44.

13. *Ibid.* 10.

14. LePan, *Bright Glass of Memory*, 69.

15. *CW*, xxiv, 272.

16. The word 'bluff' occurs in the first version of Keynes's paper, but is left out

of redrafts. See 'Overseas Financial Arrangements . . .', para. 2, T247/49.

17. *CW*, xxiv, 276–9.
18. *Ibid.*, 281.
19. *Ibid.*, 289–90.
20. *Ibid.*, 292.
21. Clarke, *Anglo-American Economic Collaboration*, 55.
22. q. *ibid.* 56.
23. *CW*, xxiv, 262.
24. *Ibid.* 276.
25. Barnett, *Lost Victory*, 42–3.
26. *CW*, xxiv, 277.
27. T247/49, Sir W. Eady to JMK, 27 March 1945; cf. though JMK's comment to Brand on 3 May, that Eady was against an 'interim arrangement' with the US based on 'temporary borrowing', *CW*, xxv, 326.
28. *CW*, xxiv, 299–303, JMK to R. H. Brand, 6 April 1945.
29. T247/49, Lord Beaverbrook to JMK, 18 April 1945.
30. *CW*, xxiv, 330, JMK to Lord Beaverbrook, 27 April 1945.
31. T247/49, comments by E. Rowe-Dutton, 3 April 1945; S. D. Waley, 5 April, 12 April 1945; C. F. Cobbold, 13 July 1945. Notes of meeting of Overseas Finance Division, 18 April, with JMK in the chair. Present: Waley, Rowe-Dutton, G. S. Pinsent, Norman Young, H. E. Brooks, A. T. K. Grant, R. W. B. Clarke, E. Jones.
32. For Churchill's protest see his letter to Truman on 28 May 1945, *FRUS*, 1945, vi, 51. For Keynes's view see his letter to R. H. Brand, 11 July 1945, *CW*, xxiv, 373.
33. Moggridge, *Keynes: An Economist's Biography*, 790; Dobson, *US Wartime Aid to Britain*, 216–19.
34. *CW*, xxiv, 332, R. H. Brand to JMK, 14 May 1945.
35. Brand repeatedly emphasised this point: *ibid.*, 307–8, 332, 369.
36. *Ibid.*, 308, R. H. Brand to JMK, 5 April 1945.
37. *Ibid.*, 318, R. H. Brand to JMK, 25 April 1945.
38. *Ibid.*, 312, 340, JMK to R. H. Brand, 24 April, 30 May 1945.
39. *Ibid.*, 318, 321, 333.
40. Churchill, *Second World War*, vi, 498, 500–1.
41. *CW*, xxiv, 337–8.
42. T247/49, 'Towards a Balance of Payments', 11 May 1945; repr. in Clarke,

Anglo-American Economic Collaboration, 96–122.

43. Clarke, *Anglo-American Economic Collaboration*, 126–35.
44. T247/49, Sir W. Eady to JMK, 4 August 1945.
45. *CW*, xxiv, 366–7, JMK to Sir W. Eady, R. Clarke, 9 July 1945.
46. T247/49, R. H. Brand on 'Plan II', 20 July 1945.
47. *CW*, xxiv, 358–9, Editorial Note on Meeting in Keynes's room at the Treasury.
48. T247/49, S. D. Waley, 'Stage III'.
49. Clarke, *Anglo-American Economic Collaboration*, 6.
50. LePan, *Bright Glass of Memory*, 72.
51. *CW*, xxvi, 383, JMK to E. J. Passant, 30 December 1944.
52. *Ibid.*, 384–5, JMK to Sir J. Anderson, 26 February 1945.
53. *Ibid.*, 398, JMK to Sir J. Brand, 13 May 1945.
54. *Ibid.*, 400–1, JMK to Calvin Hoover, 6 December 1945.
55. LePan, *Bright Glass of Memory*, ch. 2. See particularly quotations at *ibid.*, 56, 91.
56. *FRUS*, 1945, vi, 54–6, Clayton to F. Vinson, 25 June 1945.
57. EGP: Box 4, 'Conversations and Reflections in Europe', Summer 1945.
58. *CW*, xxiv, 374, 376.
59. Pimlott, *Dalton*, 426.
60. *CW*, xxiv, 377–98, JMK, 'The Present Overseas Financial Position of the UK'.
61. *CW*, xxiv, 370, R. H. Brand to JMK, 23 June 1945.
62. Vinson Papers: Box 148, Harold Glasser to H. D. White, 8 August 1945.
63. *FRUS*, 1945, vi, 79–86, Memorandum of Conversation, 3 August 1945.
64. *Ibid.*, 90–2, 94–7, J. Winant to US Secretary of State, 11 and 16 August 1945.
65. *Ibid.*, 97–101, J. Winant to James F. Byrnes, 17 August 1945. A slightly different version is in the Vinson Papers, Box 148.
66. *FRUS*, 1945, vi, 103–5, W. Clayton to James F. Byrnes and Dean Acheson, 18 August 1945.
67. KP: L/45, JMK to Lord Halifax, 17 August 1945.
68. Bullen and Pelly (eds), *Documents on British Policy Overseas*, Series 1, iii (hereafter Bullen and Pelly) 44–9.

Chapter 12: Averting a Financial Dunkirk

1. *CW*, xxiv, 398–411, 'Our Overseas Financial Prospects', 13 August 1945.
2. Dalton, *High Tide and After*, 73–4.
3. Paul Bareau, Lecture II, 'The Loan Negotiations and Lend–Lease Settlement', 2.
4. KP: PP/45.
5. Bullen and Pelly, 72–7.
6. Pressnell, *External Economic Policy since the War*, 266.
7. Bullen and Pelly, 68, 72 n.2.
8. *Ibid.*, 73–4, n. 4; for American reactions, see *FRUS*, 1945, vi, 110.
9. Howson and Moggridge (eds), *Wartime Diaries of Robbins and Meade*, 223.
10. Pressnell, *External Economic Policy since the War*, 267–9.
11. T247/2, Minutes of Meeting of Ministers held at No 10, Downing Street on 31 August 1945.
12. Robbins, *Autobiography*, 205.
13. Lamont Papers: File 104–5, R. C. Leffingwell to C. Gifford, 31 August 1945.
14. Keynes's (undated) boat paper is reproduced in *CW*, xxiv, 427–51. See *ibid.*, 431–2 for revised figures.
15. Bullen and Pelly, 117, E. Hall-Patch to Sir A. Cadogan, 8 September 1945.
16. *CW*, xxiv, 425–6, JMK to Sir W. Eady and others, 4 September 1945; Bullen and Pelly, 125, enclosure to Eady and others, 10 September 1945.
17. *CW*, xxiv, 456–7, JMK to Sir W. Eady and others, 10 September 1945.
18. Howson and Moggridge (eds), *Collected Papers of James Meade*, iv, 132.
19. Bullen and Pelly, 128–32, and notes at 132–3.
20. Gardner, *Sterling–Dollar Diplomacy*, 194 and n.
21. So Moscow was informed on 29 October 1945. See Weinstein and Vassiliev, *Haunted Wood*, 168.
22. Bareau, Lecture II, 6.
23. In the *Washington Daily News*, 4 December 1945.
24. Bareau, Note of meeting of Joint Finance Committee, 19 September 1945.
25. *Ibid.*, Note of meeting of 20 September 1945.
26. Pressnell, *External Economic Policy since the War*, 279–81.
27. Bareau, Lecture II, 7.
28. Moggridge, *Keynes: An Economist's Biog-*

raphy, 803; Pressnell, *External Economic Policy since the War*, 273.
29. Pressnell, *External Economic Policy since the War*, 276.
30. Howson and Moggridge (eds), *Collected Papers of James Meade*, iv, 224.
31. Halifax Diary, 25 September 1945; Bullen and Pelly, 154, Lord Halifax to Ernest Bevin, 26 September 1945.
32. Bareau, Lecture II, 8.
33. *CW*, xxiv, 503–8, JMK, 'Terms of Assistance'; see also Bullen and Pelly, 155 n. 3; 158–9 n. 4.
34. *CW*, xxiv, 514, JMK to Hugh Dalton, 1 October 1945.
35. Bullen and Pelly, 169 n. 3.
36. Pimlott, *Dalton*, 430.
37. *CW*, xxiv, 521, 522, Sir W. Eady to JMK, 28 September 1945.
38. WLP: MS.326, Box 82, Folder 1217.
39. See comments in Halifax Diary, 26 September, 5, 9, 11 October 1945.
40. Bullen and Pelly, 196–9, Hugh Dalton to Lord Halifax, 8 October 1945.
41. *Ibid.*, 210–14, JMK to Hugh Dalton, 9 October 1945; *CW*, xxiv, 543.
42. Bullen and Pelly, 212, 214–15.
43. *CW*, xxiv, 542, JMK to Sir W. Eady, 12 October 1945.
44. Halifax Diary, 13 October 1945; Harmer Diary, 8 October 1945.
45. Bullen and Pelly, 219–22, Hugh Dalton to Lord Halifax, 13 October 1945.
46. Pressnell, *External Economic Policy since the War*, 285.
47. Bullen and Pelly, 223–4, Lord Halifax and JMK to Hugh Dalton, 16 October 1945.
48. *Ibid.*, 227–32, JMK to Hugh Dalton, 18 October 1945.
49. *CW*, xxiv, 543, JMK to Sir W. Eady, 12 October 1945.
50. Rees, *Harry Dexter White*, 348; Bernstein, 'Reflections on Bretton Woods'.
51. Rees, *Harry Dexter White*, 363–4; see also Gardner, *Sterling–Dollar Diplomacy*, 199–200.
52. *CW*, xxiv, 533–5, JMK, 'Dr. Harry White's Plan', 5 October 1945.
53. Pressnell, *External Economic Policy since the War*, 288–92.
54. Halifax Diary, 18 October 1945; Bullen and Pelly, 243–4, JMK to Hugh Dalton, 20 October 1945.
55. JMK's NABOB 191 to Hugh Dalton is reprinted in *CW*, xxiv, 557–63.

56. Harmer Diary, 8 October 1945; *CW*, xxiv, 541, JMK to Sir W. Eady, 12 October 1945.
57. Bullen and Pelly, 224, n. 5, JMK to Sir E. Bridges, 19 October 1945.
58. Robbins, *Autobiography*, 208–9.
59. Bullen and Pelly, 212, JMK to Hugh Dalton, 9 October 1945.
60. Harmer Diary, 27 October 1945.
61. Howson and Moggridge (eds), *Collected Papers of James Meade*, iv, 163.
62. Bullen and Pelly, 255–61, Hugh Dalton to British Mission, 27 October 1945.
63. Howson and Moggridge (eds), *Collected Papers of James Meade*, iv, 163–4.
64. Bullen and Pelly, 269–71, Lord Halifax and JMK to Hugh Dalton, 28 October 1945.
65. *Ibid.*, 243–4 n. 3.
66. Howson and Moggridge (eds), *Collected Papers of James Meade*, iv, 164.
67. *CW*, xxiv, 584, JMK to Sir W. Eady, 7 November 1945.
68. Bullen and Pelly, 259–60, Hugh Dalton to British Mission, 27 October 1945.
69. Pressnell, *External Economic Policy since the War*, 296.
70. Dalton, *High Tide and After*, 72, 77.
71. Bullen and Pelly, 289–92, Hugh Dalton to Lord Halifax and JMK, 6 November 1945; see also Howson and Moggridge (eds), *Collected Papers of James Meade*, iv, 165–6.
72. Bullen and Pelly, 302–4, 7 November 1945.
73. Bareau Note, 12 November 1945.
74. Bullen and Pelly, 320–1, E. Hall-Patch to J. E. Coulson, 15 November 1945.
75. Halifax Diary, 13, 14 November 1945.
76. *Ibid.*, 15 November 1945.
77. Bareau Note, 16 November 1945.
78. Bullen and Pelly, 335, British Mission to Hugh Dalton, 21 November 1945.
79. Bullen and Pelly, 323–44. This covers the set of NABOBS sent by the Mission between 18 and 21 November, as well as the American draft agreement.
80. *Ibid.*, 329.
81. *CW*, xxiv, 591.
82. *Ibid.*, 593–4.
83. RFKP: 13/57/518.
84. KP: PP/45, JMK to Janos Plesch, 6 January 1946.
85. Bullen and Pelly, 354–6, PM to Halifax, 24 November 1945; also *ibid.*, 358 n. 5.
86. *Ibid.*, 356–8, JMK to Hugh Dalton, 25 November 1945.
87. *Ibid.*, 359, British Mission to London, 25 November 1945.
88. *Ibid.*, 368–70, British Mission to London, 26 November 1945.
89. *Ibid.*, 371, Hugh Dalton to JMK, 26 November 1945.
90. *Ibid.*, 372–4, British Mission to Hugh Dalton, 27 November 1945.
91. *Ibid.*, 386–7, Hugh Dalton to Lord Halifax and JMK, 28 November 1945.
92. Richard Kahn, in Thirlwall (ed.), *Keynes and International Monetary Relations*, 57.
93. Bullen and Pelly, 375, n. 11, Sir W. Eady to JMK, JMK to Sir W. Eady, 27 November 1945.
94. *Ibid.* See the Eady note of 1 December 1945, at *ibid.*, 375, n.11.
95. *Ibid.*, 375–8 and n.12, JMK to Hugh Dalton, 27 November 1945.
96. *Ibid.* 389–94, 395–8, Annex to Cabinet Conclusions, 29 November 1945.
97. *Ibid.*, 405–6, British Mission to London, 30 November 1945.
98. *Ibid.*, 409, PM and Hugh Dalton to Lord Halifax, 30 November 1945.
99. Howson and Moggridge (eds), *Wartime Diaries of Robbins and Meade*, 241.
100. Bareau Note, 5 December 1945.
101. Howson and Moggridge (eds), *Wartime Diaries of Robbins and Meade*, 241.
102. Bullen and Pelly, 419–23; Telegram Nos 145, 146, 147 were sent from Washington on 3 December 1945; see also Bareau Note, 5 December 1945.
103. q. Pimlott, *Dalton*, 437–8.
104. Bullen and Pelly, 430, Sir E. Bridges to PM, 5 December 1945.
105. KP: L/45, Frank Lee to JMK, 26 December 1945.
106. q. Barnes and Nicolson, *Empire at Bay*, 1052.
107. Robbins, *Autobiography*, 210.
108. *CW*, xxiv, 605–24.
109. Howson and Moggridge (eds), *Collected Papers of James Meade*, iv, 166.
110. *CW*, xxiv, 625–8, JMK to Lord Halifax, 1 January 1946.
111. Jay, *Change and Fortune*, 137.
112. James, *International Monetary Cooperation*, 70–1.
113. Howson and Moggridge (eds), *Collected Papers of James Meade*, iv, 63.
114. Clarke, *Anglo-American Economic Collaboration*, 57.

Chapter 13: 'The Light is Gone'

1. Jay, *Change and Fortune*, 139.
2. JMK to Florence Keynes, 28 December 1945.
3. Howson and Moggridge (eds), *Collected Papers of James Meade*, iv, 196.
4. *CW*, xxvii, 444, 'The Balance of Payments of the United States'.
5. See Skidelsky, *Keynes*, ii, 522–3.
6. Johnson and Johnson, *Shadow of Keynes*, 132–4.
7. KP: PP/45, G. Rylands to JMK, 27 December 1945.
8. *Ibid.*, JMK to Molly McCarthy, 2 January 1946.
9. *Ibid.*, JMK to WL, 29 January 1946.
10. *CW*, xxvii, 463.
11. Howson and Moggridge (eds), *Collected Papers of James Meade*, iv, 216.
12. *CW*, xxvii, 467.
13. *CW*, xxvii, 465–81, 'Political and Military Expenditure Overseas', 11 February 1946.
14. *Ibid.*, 'Notes on Sterling Area Negotiations', 23 January 1946.
15. Howson and Moggridge, (eds), *Collected Papers of James Meade*, iv, 227; see also *CW*, xxvii, 454–6.
16. JTSP: 6–13, File 42–6, JMK to JTS, ? 1946.
17. Fonteyn, *Autobiography*, 97–8.
18. JMK to Florence Keynes, 23 February 1946.
19. Archives of the Royal Opera House: JMK to Ninette de Valois, 5 March 1946.
20. MD, Presidential Diary, vol. 8, 2 and 3 March 1946.
21. Dormael, *Bretton Woods*, 287, from H. D. White Papers, Box 7, Item 27c.
22. *CW*, xxvi, JMK to Treasury 7 March 1946, 211.
23. KP: L/46, JMK to Lord Halifax, 18 March 1946.
24. Bareau Note on 'Inaugural Meeting', 11 March 1946.
25. Keynes's speech is reproduced in *CW*, xxvi, 215–17.
26. Cited in Gardner, *Sterling–Dollar Diplomacy*, 266 n. 4.
27. Horsefield, *International Monetary Fund*, i, 134.
28. *CW*, xxvi, 218–19.
29. *Ibid.*, 225.
30. Dormael, *Bretton Woods*, 299.
31. *CW*, xxvi, 237.
32. Harrod, *Keynes*, 636.
33. KP: PP/45, JMK to Janos Plesch, 20 March 1946.
34. *Ibid.*
35. In Thirlwall (ed.), *Keynes and International Monetary Relations*, 27.
36. G. Bolton, 'Where the Critics Are as Wrong as Keynes Was', 1387.
37. *CW*, xxvi, 233–4.
38. 'Random Reflections from a Visit to the USA', *CW*, xxvi, 482–7.
39. RBP: Box 197, Sir W. Eady to R. H. Brand, 23 April 1946.
40. Howson and Moggridge (eds), *Collected Papers of James Meade*, iv, 251. Interview with J. E. Meade, 9 August 1980.
41. KP: PP/45, G. B. Shaw to JMK, 8 January 1946.
42. JMK's tribute is reproduced in *CW*, x, 375–81. It was published in June 1946 as *GBS at 90*, edited by S. Winsten.
43. HCP: H. Clay to M. Norman, 11 June 1946; M. Norman to H. Clay 19 June 1946.
44. KP: PP/45, JMK to A. V. Hill, 15 April 1946.
45. Texas University: Clive Bell to Mary Hutchinson, 23 April 1946. I am grateful to James Beechey for sending me a copy of this letter.
46. Harrod, *Keynes*, 641.
47. KP: PP/45, Florence Keynes, 'In Memoriam'.
48. Harrod, *Keynes*, 645; Clive Bell to Mary Hutchinson, 23 April 1946; Moggridge, *Keynes: An Economist's Biography*, 836. Keynes was sixty-two when he died, not sixty-three as Moggridge says.
49. V&A (NAL): Cockerell letters 86uu3. No. 27, G. L. Keynes to Sydney Cockerell, 28 April 1946. I am grateful to Fiona MacCarthy for sending me a copy of this letter.
50. Clarke, *Anglo-American Economic Collaboration*, 71.
51. Schumpeter, *Ten Great Economists*, 274.

Epilogue: Keynes's Legacy

1. Polly Hill and Richard Keynes (eds), *Lydia and Maynard*, published in 1989.
2. The account of Lydia which follows is based partly on the indispensable *Lydia Lopokova* edited by Milo Keynes; partly on Lydia Lopokova's correspondence in the Keynes Papers, especially LLK/5; partly on information supplied by members of the Keynes family and those who looked after her.
3. HDHP: Box 23B, D. H. Robertson to HDH, 3 April 1948.
4. Charleston Papers: Roy Harrod to Clive Bell, 17 April 1947; KP: PP/92, Roy Harrod to Geoffrey Keynes, 10 January 1949.
5. In the German journal *Deutsche Zeitschrift für europäisches Donken*, September 1951.
6. A. T. Peacock in the *Liberal News*, 23 February 1951.
7. For a succinct discussion, see A. Leijonhufvud, 'Keynes and the Classics', esp. 12–18.
8. Moses Abramovitz, 'Catching Up, Forging Ahead, and Falling Behind', 385.
9. *Ibid.* 395–6.
10. Hicks, *Crisis in Keynesian Economics*, 3.
11. WLP: File 1316, R. C. Leffingwell to WL, 12 July 1949.
12. Dormael, *Bretton Woods*, 307.
13. WLP: File 1316, R. C. Leffingwell to WL, 2 March 1960.
14. q. Timmins, *The Five Giants*, 265.
15. Stein, *Fiscal Revolution in America*, 227. For the whole discussion, see *ibid.*, 220–32.
16. Simon Keynes, 'Lydia at Tilton', September 1975, unpublished.

Dramatis Personae

This section should be read in conjunction with those at the end of the first and second volumes of this biography, pp. 421–31 and 685–708 respectively. *DNB* stands for the *Dictionary of National Biography*, KCC for King's College, Cambridge, LSE for the London School of Economics. Titles of people have been omitted where awarded after the years covered by this biography. The list of names is not intended to be exhaustive, either as regards coverage of people who appear in this book, or as regards the careers of those listed. Rather I have chosen those with whom Keynes was significantly involved, plus a sprinkling of the so-called statesmen, without whom the history of these years would have been very different. I have also briefly indicated the part they played in this story. For an exhaustive list of those who figured in JMK's life see Donald Moggridge, *Maynard Keynes: An Economist's Biography*, pp. 859–911.

ACHESON, DEAN (1893–1973), American lawyer. Assistant Secretary of State, 1941–5; Secretary of State, 1949–53. An Anglophile friend and admirer of JMK of outstanding ability, Acheson later played a key role in developing the 'Truman doctrine' of resistance to Soviet aggression.

AMERY, LEOPOLD (1873–1955), British politician and writer. Secretary of State for India, 1940–5, and a leading supporter of imperial preference in Churchill's government. It was said of him that 'had he been half a head taller and his speeches half an hour shorter' he might have been prime minister (*DNB*).

ANDERSON, SIR JOHN (1882–1958), civil servant. Lord President of the Council 1940–3; Chancellor of the Exchequer, 1943–5. Exceptionally, Anderson came into the Cabinet from the civil service. The greatest public servant of his age, he was also very pompous. He appreciated JMK, and was mainly guided by him in external finance, but the two men were not close.

ASHTON, FREDERICK (1904–88), choreographer. He found JMK rather terrifying, but adored Lydia.

ATTLEE, CLEMENT (1883–1967), Labour politician. Prime Minister, 1945–51. A laconic entry suits this laconic man.

AUDEN, WYSTAN (1907–73), British poet and playwright. JMK staged two plays he wrote with Isherwood (qv) – *The Ascent of F.6* (1937) and *On the Frontier* (1938) – at the Cambridge Arts Theatre. He thought that Auden's filthy, nail-bitten fingers explained something 'infantile' in his work.

BALDWIN, STANLEY, Earl Baldwin of Bewdley (1867–1947), British politician. Prime Minister, 1924–9, 1935–7. JMK referred to him as 'good King Baldwin' and approved of his foreign policy (or lack of it) in the mid-1930s.

BALOGH, THOMAS (1905–85), Hungarian-born British economist. Member of the Institute of Economics and Statistics, Oxford, 1940–5. Worked for 'Foxy' Falk (qv) in the City in the 1930s, then taken up by Hubert Henderson. The leading left-wing 'Schachtian', hostile to the Bretton Woods Agreement and American loan. In 1945 JMK called him a 'Jewish Nazi'.

BAREAU, PAUL (1901–2000), Belgian-born financial journalist. Attached to the Treasury, 1944–5.

BEAVERBROOK, LORD (Max Aitken) (1879–1964), Canadian-born British news-paper proprietor and politician. He was Minister of Aircraft Production from August 1940 to May 1941, helping win the Battle of Britain, and Lord Privy Seal, 1943–5. A strong imperialist, he opposed all JMK's international plans, but the two men had a friendly relationship which went back to the 1920s, when they had both opposed the restoration of the gold standard.

BELL family. The art critic CLIVE (1881–1954) and the painter VANESSA (1879–1961) were friends of JMK from pre-First World War Bloomsbury Group days. At Charleston, they were next-door neighbours of JMK in East Sussex. Their son QUENTIN (1910–97), later an art historian, was employed by JMK as a farm worker early in the war. His wages were £2 1s 0d per week.

BERLE, ADOLF (1895–1971), American lawyer, Assistant Secretary of State, 1938–44. An intellectual, lacking in common sense, married to an Anglophobic wife. JMK found him a 'queer attractive, unattractive figure in disequilibrium, with himself and the world'.

BERNSTEIN, EDWARD (1904–96), American economist. Assistant director of mon-etary research, US Treasury, 1941–6. He often infuriated JMK with his scholasti-cism, but got on famously with Dennis Robertson (qv).

BEVERIDGE, SIR WILLIAM (1879–1963), British administrator. Author of the Beveridge Report, and founder of the British welfare state. A man of powerful but exceedingly narrow intellect, he would have Sovietised the British economy had he been allowed to. His biographer writes that he believed that 'one could indefinitely expand the powers of the state without thereby modifying any of the basic structures of political, social, and family life' (José Harris in *DNB*). Only in a mature democracy could such a man be a benefactor rather than a menace.

BEVIN, ERNEST (1881–1951), British trade union leader. Minister of Labour, 1940–5; Foreign Secretary, 1945–51. JMK failed to win his support for his plan for deferred pay.

BOLTON, GEORGE (1900–82), British banker. Adviser to the Bank of England, 1941–8. Architect of Bank's preparations for foreign exchange control before the war, strongest advocate of their continuation after the war. Favoured Keynes's 'Starvation Corner' option in 1945.

BOOTHBY, ROBERT (1900–86), British Conservative MP, 1924–58. An early and leading parliamentary 'Keynesian', he was a 'Schachtian', mainly because of his intense hostility to the gold standard. The first edition of his autobiography *I Fight to Live* was misprinted *I Fight to Love*.

BRACKEN, BRENDAN (1901–58), British journalist and politician. Minister of Information, 1940–5; one of Churchill's intimates.

BRAND, ROBERT (1873–1963), British banker and public servant. Director of Lazard Bros, 1909–60, he was based in Washington after 1941 – as head of the British Food Mission, 1941–4; chairman of the British Supply Council, 1942; and Treasury representative, 1944–6. One of the first-class brains whom Britain threw into the financial struggle with the USA, Brand was dazzled but not overwhelmed by JMK's brilliance. Their friendship, which went back to the Paris Peace Conference of 1919, was durable, though not intimate. His *Times* obituary (24 August 1963) called him 'an outstanding example of a species which has dwindled in numbers over the years – the London private banker who is also economist, philosopher, and, within a certain range, a statesman'.

BRIDGES, SIR EDWARD (1892–1969), British civil servant. Secretary to the Cabinet, 1938–46; Permanent secretary, Treasury, 1945–56. Took over from JMK in the final week of the loan negotiations in 1945.

CANNY, SIR GERALD (1881–1954), British civil servant. Chairman of the Board of Inland Revenue, 1938–42. Canny aborted JMK's scheme for an income tax surcharge to pay for the war, but JMK's compromise with Canny on income tax credits made possible the 1941 budget.

CATTERNS, BASIL GAGE (1886–1969), British banker. Deputy governor of the Bank of England, 1936–45.

CATTO, LORD (Thomas) (1879–1959), British banker. Financial adviser to the Treasury, 1940–4; Governor of the Bank of England, 1944–9. 'Catto' to Keynes's 'Doggo' in the wartime Treasury. A working-class Scottish boy who made it to the top of the City 'through a combination of innate qualities and of grasping opportunities wherever they offered'. Very short. Some feeling, when he became Governor of the Bank, that he had 'gone native' at the Treasury.

CHAMBERLAIN, NEVILLE (1869–1940), British politician. Prime Minister, 1937–40. JMK shared his unwillingness to fight Hitler over Central Europe, but not his eagerness to reach an agreement with him.

CHERWELL, LORD (Frederick Alexander Lindemann) (1886–1957), British scientist. Known as the 'Prof.', he was head of the PM's Statistical Branch, and Paymaster-General, 1942–5. Apart from his support for weapons research, he specialised in criticising departmental statistics and providing Churchill with short digests of complicated matters, supplemented by coloured graphs and charts. 'His loyalty to Churchill was absolute, his influence on him profound' (*DNB*). Believed that the pastoralisation of Germany would solve Britain's export problem. Worked with JMK during Stage II negotiations in Washington in 1944.

CHRISTIE, JOHN (1882–1962), founder of Glyndebourne Opera, 1934. His cultural ambitions brought him into conflict with JMK in 1945.

CHURCHILL, WINSTON (1874–1965), British statesman. Prime Minister, 1940–5, 1951–5. Churchill's respect for JMK dated from the 1920s when JMK opposed the return to the gold standard, which Churchill came to regard as his greatest mistake. During the war, the two men met frequently at the Other Club.

CLARK, COLIN (1905–89), British economist and statistician. JMK thought him 'almost the only economic statistician I have ever met who seems to me quite first-class'. His pioneering work on national income statistics was the basis of Keynes's *How to Pay for the War*. His thesis of 25 per cent of national income as the safe upper limit of peacetime taxation won JMK's general agreement in 1945, and papers on JMK's desk after he died showed JMK was still thinking about it.

CLARK, KENNETH (1903–83), British arts administrator and connoisseur. Director of the National Gallery 1934–45, served on the Council of CEMA under JMK. Clark thought that JMK 'displayed his brilliance too unsparingly'.

CLARKE, RICHARD ('Otto') (1910–75), British civil servant. Served in various wartime ministries before being appointed assistant secretary, Treasury, 1945. Dazzled by JMK, but the most coherent Treasury critic of his loan negotiation strategy in 1945. Keynes's death left him the most formidable of the Treasury 'knights', partly because of his great speed in drafting.

CLAY, HENRY (1883–1954), British economist. Economic adviser to the governor of the Bank of England, 1933–44; Warden of Nuffield College, Oxford, 1944–9. 'He was a Gladstonian Liberal who, whilst recognizing that he was living in the twentieth century, felt that the liberty of the individual would be endangered by the continued growth of government economic activities' (*DNB*). Despite this, one of JMK's chief supporters at the Bank. Dalton called him 'Feet of Clay'.

CLAYTON, WILLIAM (1880–1966), American cotton merchant from Texas. Assistant Secretary of State, 1944–5; Under-Secretary of State for Economic Affairs, 1945–7. A self-made Southern businessman of liberal views, he represented his Secretary of State, James Byrnes, in the loan negotiations of 1945. 'Will Clayton was tall, strikingly handsome, beautifully attired, articulate, affable, assured and stubbornly his own man to the extent that he was not controlled by his always stubbornly liberal wife' (Galbraith). JMK found him too keen on 'business analogies'.

COBBOLD, CAMERON ('Kim') (1904–87), British banker. Executive director, Bank of England, 1938–45; deputy governor, 1945–9; governor, 1949–61. Chief Bank of England negotiator of the Tripartite Agreement of 1936. Protégé of Montagu Norman (qv).

COHEN, BENJAMIN (1894–1963), American lawyer. One of Frankfurter's protégés. Adviser to the US ambassador to London, 1941, when JMK discussed with him a loan, with Britain's North American securities put up as collateral.

COURTAULD, SAMUEL (1876–1947), British manufacturer, art connoisseur and patron, ballet lover. Old friend of Lydia, and one of those intellectual businessmen who appreciated JMK. JMK tried (unsuccessfully) to prevent the compulsory sale of his US subsidiary, Viscose, in 1940–1.

COX, OSCAR (1905–66), American lawyer. General counsel, Lend–Lease Administration, 1941–3; Foreign Economic Administration, 1943–5. In 1943 JMK called him 'the sole survivor of our old friends' in the Lend–Lease business, but warned that 'he often tells one, as though it was an accepted policy, his wishes rather than the unadorned facts'.

CRIPPS, SIR RICHARD STAFFORD (1889–1952), British Labour politician. Member of Churchill's wartime coalition, President of the Board of Trade, 1945–7; Chancellor of the Exchequer, 1947–50. Member of London's ministerial team handling the loan negotiations in 1945.

CROWLEY, LEO (??–1972), American businessman. Head of the Foreign Economic Administration, 1943–5. Of Irish descent, he was widely suspected by the British of manipulating Lend–Lease to Britain's disadvantage. JMK described his face as like 'the buttocks of a baboon', and BABOON was the code name for British telegrams to Washington during the loan negotiations of 1945.

CURRIE, LAUGHLIN (1902–93), Canadian-born American economist. Administrative assistant to the President, 1939–45; deputy administrator, Foreign Economic Administration, 1943–5. Currie agreed with the US Treasury policy of policing Lend–Lease to restrict Britain's gold and dollar reserves to $1bn. JMK thought him anti-British, especially on India. Probably was a Soviet agent, though there is still some reasonable doubt about this.

DALTON, HUGH (1887–1962), British economist and Labour politician. Minister of Economic Warfare 1940–2; President of the Board of Trade, 1942–5; Chancellor of the Exchequer, 1945–7. He supported JMK over Bretton Woods, and endorsed his department's free-trade outlook; but, as Chancellor, wobbled over the American Loan Agreement of 1945. There was some respect but little affection between the two men. Dalton was famous for his loud voice. Churchill once heard the familiar boom in an adjoining room. On being told that Dalton was talking to America, Churchill is reputed to have said: 'Why doesn't he use the telephone?'

DAVENPORT, NICHOLAS (1893–1979), British financial journalist. As City editor of the *Nation and Athenaeum*, 1923–30, of the *New Statesman and Nation* after 1930, and director of the National Mutual Life Assurance Company from 1931 to 1969, he worked with JMK for most of the inter-war years. He shared JMK's cheap-money outlook, but JMK opposed his plans to 'bolshevise' the British war economy in his book *Vested Interests or Common Pool* (1941).

DAVIES, CLEMENT (1884–1962), British politician. Liberal National and Liberal MP. 'At the beginning of the war in 1939 [he] became the chairman of an action committee in the House of Commons which sought the most effective prosecution of the war and which was supported by members of the three main parties in the House' (*DNB*).

DAWSON, GEOFFREY (1874–1944), British journalist. Editor of *The Times*, 1923–41. JMK disliked his line over Munich, but in November 1939 Dawson gave him the platform for the articles which were turned into the pamphlet *How to Pay for the War*.

DENT, EDWARD (1876–1967), British musicologist. Fellow of King's College, Cambridge, 1902–8, and Professor of Music, Cambridge, 1926–41. He hoped to do for opera what Ninette de Valois had done for ballet – develop a 'British' repertory, initially by getting operas sung in English. JMK brought him on to the Covent Garden Opera Trust in 1944.

DURBIN, EVAN (1906–48), British economist and Labour politician. In his efforts to persuade Labour to support *How to Pay for the War*, JMK (inexplicably) ignored Durbin and other Labour economists.

EADY, SIR WILFRID (1890–1962), British civil servant. Chairman of the Board of Customs and Excise, 1940–2; second secretary, Treasury, 1942–52, in charge of overseas finance. Admired JMK, but JMK was exasperated by his lack of technical acumen. Told him he lacked time and patience to teach him the rudiments of economics. Eady tried, without success, to resist JMK's complete dominance over overseas finance in the latter part of the war. Opposed JMK's strategy for the American loan negotiations, and came close to wrecking the negotiations themselves in November 1945.

ECCLES, MARINER (1890–1977), banker from Utah. Chairman, US Federal Reserve Board, 1936–48. JMK encountered his stentorian assurance and provincialism in the loan negotiations of 1945. He said of him: 'No wonder that man is a Mormon. No single woman could stand him.'

EDEN, ANTHONY (1897–1977), Conservative politician. Foreign Secretary, 1935–8, 1940–5. JMK supported his policy of 'heroic cunctation' in the 1930s, but was unallured by him in the war, and thought that Sir John Anderson (qv) should succeed Churchill as PM.

EINSTEIN, ALBERT (1879–1955), German-born physicist, Nobel prizewinner. His theory of relativity influenced JMK's conception of economics. JMK met him in Berlin in 1926, wrote about him in 1933, and saw him for the last time at Princeton in 1941, where Lydia described him in bed with a big toe sticking out.

EINZIG, PAUL (1897–1973), German-born financial journalist and prolific author on monetary questions. Political correspondent of the *Financial News*, 1939–45. His leak of the White Plan in the *Financial Times* precipitated the publication of both the Keynes and White Plans on 7 April 1943.

ELIOT, THOMAS STEARNS (1888–1965), American-born British poet. JMK and Eliot corresponded in 1945 on employment policy. JMK increasingly came to see his own economic theory as a secular application of Christianity.

ELMHIRST, DOROTHY (1887–1967) and LEONARD (1893–1974), an Anglo-American philanthropic team, co-founders of Dartington Hall in 1931. Their lives intersected with JMK's at three points: Dartington Hall was the home of the Ballets Jooss in the 1930s, JMK taught Michael Straight, Dorothy's son by her first marriage to Willard Straight, in the mid-1930s, and the Elmhirsts brought him news of US administration opinion in the autumn of 1939.

EPPS, SIR GEORGE (1885–1951), British actuary. Government actuary, 1936–44. With JMK considered the affordability of the Beveridge Report in 1942.

EVANS, IFOR (1897–1952), British economist and historian. Principal, University College of Wales, Aberystwyth, 1934–52. Served under JMK on CEMA.

FALK, OSWALD TOYNBEE ('Foxy') (1879–1972), British stockbroker and aesthete. Founder of the Tuesday Club, 1917, and long-standing friend and City associate of JMK, though their relationship cooled after 1931. Outstandingly clever and of philosophical bent he came to believe that Western civilisation was finished. One of the most perceptive judges of the mind and character of JMK he could have written an outstanding biography of him.

FERGUSSON, SIR DONALD (1891–1963), British civil servant. Permanent secretary, Ministry of Agriculture and Fisheries, he organised policy of reviving farming industry and increasing food production in the war. Attacked JMK's Buffer Stock Plan in 1942, opposed trade liberalisation schemes. JMK called his objections 'barmy'.

FLANDERS, ALLAN (1910–73), British industrial economist. Corresponded with JMK about *How to Pay for the War* when he was editing *Socialist Vanguard* in 1940.

FRANKFURTER, FELIX (1882–1965), American jurist and legal philosopher. US Supreme Court, 1939–62. He used his great manipulative skills in the service of the New Deal. Part of JMK's social and political circle in Washington.

FUNK, WALTHER (1890–1960), German Economics Minister, 1937–45. Author of the Funk Plan for the European 'New Order'. 'A notorious homosexual and habitual drunkard, the greasy-looking dwarfish Minister of Economics . . . proved after 1938 to carry little weight in the upper echelons of the [Nazi] Party' (Robert Wistrich).

GARVIN, JAMES LOUIS (1868–1947), British journalist. Editor of the *Observer*, 1908–42. Generally an admirer of JMK. Curiously, JMK never wrote for the *Observer*, despite its great influence at the time.

GLASGOW, MARY (1905–83), civil servant, arts administrator. Secretary-general of CEMA and the Arts Council, 1939–51. JMK wrote to her almost every day 1942–6, but always on business.

GRANT, DUNCAN JAMES CORROWER (1885–1978), British painter. JMK's oldest surviving friend and former lover. JMK continued to support his artistic enterprises during the war, including the wall painting of Berwick Church, and remembered him handsomely in his will.

GREGG, SIR CORNELIUS (d. 1959), British actuary. Chairman, Board of Inland Revenue, 1942–58. Fellow member with JMK of the National Debt Enquiry Committee, 1945. JMK told him that usury was the same as his liquidity preference theory of the rate of interest.

GUILLEBAUD, CLAUDE (1890–1971), British economist. Alfred Marshall's nephew and Fellow of St John's College, Cambridge, 1915–71. JMK got most of his information about Nazi Germany's economic system from Guillebaud.

GULICK, LUTHER (1892–1993), American economist. Special assistant, US Treasury, 1941–3. Gulick's proposal for an International Development Agency may have been a common influence on both the Keynes and the White Plans for post-war monetary institutions, leading, eventually, to the creation of the International Bank for Reconstruction and Development.

GUTT, CAMILLE (1884–1971), Belgian journalist and politician. First managing director of the IMF, 1946–51.

HALIFAX, LORD (Edward Wood) (1881–1959), British politician. Foreign Secretary, 1938–40; ambassador to the United States, 1940–6. Established a close relationship with JMK based on mutual respect which ripened into affection. Spent much time with JMK gossiping about Eton. Exercised a calming influence on JMK during the loan negotiations in 1945.

HALL-PATCH, EDMUND (1896–1975), civil servant. Assistant secretary, Treasury, 1935–44; assistant under-secretary of state, Foreign Office, 1944–6. Part of British team in the loan negotiations.

HARMER, FREDERIC (1908–95), businessman and Treasury official, he served as JMK's personal assistant during the Washington loan negotiations. His diary is an important source for JMK's moods during the negotiations.

HARROD, ROY (1900–78), British economist. PM's Statistical Branch 1940–2. Reshaped JMK's Clearing Union Plan in a more liberal direction. Failed to get the Treasury job which he coveted. JMK noticed his tendency to 'over-write'. His official biography of JMK was published in 1951.

HAWKINS, HARRY (1894–1983), American State Department official in charge of trade negotiations with the British. An enthusiastic executant of Cordell Hull's free-trade policies. Ran into the full barrage of JMK's evasive tactics.

HAWTREY, RALPH (1879–1975), British economist and Treasury official. From 1919 to 1945, as its director of financial enquiries, he was the Treasury's only trained economist. Occasionally the Treasury remembered he was still there. Wrote enormous memoranda on early drafts of JMK's ClearingUnion Plan.

HAYEK, FRIEDRICH (1899–1996), Austrian-born economist and philosopher of liberalism. During the war, JMK helped Hayek get a home in Cambridge, and sponsored his election to the British Academy. Hayek approved of his *How to Pay for the War*, Keynes approved of *The Road to Serfdom*, with reservations. The debate between the two on how much government intervention is compatible with a free society was never properly joined, because Keynes died. It would have been a battle of giants.

HENDERSON, SIR HUBERT (1890–1952), British economist and Treasury adviser, 1940–4. JMK's old sparring partner, their sparring went on during the war, when Henderson set out to torpedo 'utopian' schemes for post-war improvement. 'He carried realism to the point of contra-suggestibility, reacting critically to proposals rather than devising ways of making the best of what was to hand,' wrote Alec Cairncross. Isaiah Berlin called him a 'man of deep convictions, which he held with clarity and a kind of tranquil passion'.

HICKS, JOHN (1904–89), British economist and future Nobel prizewinner. Professor of Political Economy, Manchester University, 1938–46. Influenced JMK's *How to Pay for the War*.

HIGGINS, NORMAN (1898–1974), manager, managing director and Trustee of the Cambridge Arts Theatre, 1935–69.

HILL, ARCHIBALD VIVIEN (1886–1977), physiologist and Nobel prizewinner. Independent Conservative MP for Cambridge University, 1940–5. He married JMK's sister MARGARET (1885–1970). Their daughter Mary Eglantyne ('POLLY') (b. 1914) worked as a temporary civil servant during the war and, between September 1940 and May 1941 slept in the basement of 46 Gordon Square.

HITLER, ADOLF (1889–1945), German dictator. Chancellor, 1933–45. In the late 1930s JMK viewed him, much like A. J. P. Taylor later, as a rational opportunist. By 22 August 1939 he wrote that 'he seems to show in high degree what Scotland Yard says is particularly characteristic of all criminals, namely an inability to vary his methods'.

HOPKINS, HARRY (1890–1946), American politician and wheeler-dealer. From 1940 to 1945 special adviser to FDR.

HOPKINS, SIR RICHARD VALENTINE (1880–1955), British civil servant. Second secretary, Treasury, 1932–42; permanent secretary, 1942–5. Brought JMK into the Treasury in 1940. JMK had great respect and affection for 'Hoppy', who in turn was shifted by Keynes from his pre-war fiscal and monetary orthodoxies. Hopkins realised that JMK reinforced the Treasury's wartime position and kept him on a loose rein.

HUDSON, ROBERT (1886–1957), British politician. Minister of Agriculture and Fisheries 1940–5. Achieved an agricultural revolution in production and attitudes, decentralising powers and introducing guaranteed prices and markets. Opposed JMK's Buffer Stocks Plan and trade liberalisation.

HULL, CORDELL (1871–1955), US Secretary of State, 1933–44. His main war aim was to dismantle Britain's imperial preference system and in Article VII of the Lend–Lease Agreement found the instrument to do so. JMK regarded him not so much as wrong as monomaniacal in pursuit of this objective to the exclusion of any other.

ISHERWOOD, CHRISTOPHER (1904–86), writer. Visited Tilton with W. H. Auden (qv) in 1937 to discuss staging their play *On the Frontier* at the Cambridge Arts Theatre.

JAY, DOUGLAS (1907–96), British Labour politician and early Labour 'Keynesian'. JMK argued with him over *How to Pay for the War*.

JONES, JESSE (1874–1955), Texas businessman. Administrator, Federal Loan Agency, 1939–45; Secretary of Commerce, 1940–5. The 'Jesse Jones Loan' was one of JMK's achievements. 'I had been brought up', Jesse Jones once said, 'in the belief that the three most necessary things to a satisfactory life were family, religion, and money.' Arthur Schlesinger comments: 'Some might wonder whether this accurately stated the priority; but people learned not to fool with Jesse Jones.'

JONES, THOMAS (1870–1956), British administrator and prime ministerial wheeler-dealer. Secretary of the Pilgrim Trust, 1930–45.

JOOSS, KURT (1901–79), German-born dancer and choreographer. Exiled from Germany, he founded the Ballets Jooss, based on Dartington. JMK brought his ballet to Cambridge in December 1939. 'He was the 1st choreographer of international renown to attempt a synthesis of classical and modern dance...' (*The Concise Oxford Dictionary of Ballet*).

KAHN, RICHARD FERDINAND (1905–89), British economist and JMK's 'favourite pupil'. During the war he was a temporary civil servant, first at the Board of Trade, then as economic adviser to Oliver Lyttelton in the Middle East, then back in London at the Ministry of Supply, then the Ministry of Production. JMK failed to get him into the Treasury, and their close working relationship was suspended for most of the war. After the war, one of the two trustees of JMK's estate.

KALDOR, NICHOLAS (1908–86), Hungarian-born British economist. Lecturer and reader in economics, LSE, 1932–47, Kaldor spent the war years in Cambridge. JMK liked and respected him.

KALECKI, MICHAL (1899–1970), Polish economist. Suggested comprehensive rationing as an alternative to JMK's *How to Pay for the War*. Leffingwell (qv) described his scheme 'as a communist system to put everyone on the breadline. . . . It makes money worthless and gives us a government ration.'

KEYNES family. JMK's parents JOHN NEVILLE KEYNES (1852–1949) and FLOR-ENCE ADA KEYNES (1861–1958) both outlived him. His brother GEOFFREY KEYNES (1887–1982) was acting Air Vice-Marshal, and senior consulting surgeon, RAF, 1939–45. JMK took an avuncular interest in Geoffrey's four sons RICHARD (b. 1919), QUENTIN (b. 1921), MILO (b. 1924) and STEPHEN (b. 1927).

KINDERSLEY, SIR ROBERT (1871–1954), British banker. Partner in Lazards, and chairman of the National Savings Committee, 1920–46. Opposed JMK's compulsory saving plan.

LABORDÈRE, MARCEL (1869–1946), French financial journalist. JMK's favourite Frenchman. Their extensive correspondence, mainly on gold and money, starting in 1911, was broken off by the war, but resumed in 1945. Inexplicably, Don Moggridge does not mention him in his biography of JMK.

LASKI, HAROLD (1893–1950), British academic and Labour politician. Professor of Political Science, LSE, 1926–50. His garrulous presence in Labour's inner circle was an obstacle in the British loan negotiations in 1945. Attlee's putdown of Laski was classic: 'A period of silence on your part would be welcome,' he told him.

LAW, RICHARD (1905–80), British Conservative politician. Son of Andrew Bonar Law. Parliamentary under-secretary, Foreign Office, 1941–3; Minister of State, 1943–5; Minister of Education, 1945. The kind of liberal Conservative with whom JMK got on. Technically head of the British delegation at the Washington monetary and commercial talks September–October 1943. Published *Return from Utopia* (1950), an anti-planning polemic.

LAYTON, SIR WALTER (1884–1966), British economist and administrator. A Liberal Mandarin. One of the 'Old Dogs' who met with JMK at 46 Gordon Square in the autumn of 1939, later employed in the Ministries of Supply and Production.

LEE, FRANK (1903–71), British civil servant. Treasury delegation, Washington 1944–6.

LEFFINGWELL, RUSSELL (1870–1960), American lawyer and banker. Director of J. P. Morgan, 1940–59. Provided a running, but acute, critique of JMK's personality and policies from a conservative point of view from the Paris Peace Conference in 1919 onwards.

LEITH-ROSS, SIR FREDERICK ('Leithers') (1887–1968), British civil servant. Long-standing Treasury official, with anomalous status of chief economic adviser to the government, 1932–46. Director-general of the Ministry of Economic Warfare, 1939–42; chairman of the Inter-Allied Post-War Requirements Committee, 1941–3; deputy director-general, UNRRA, 1944–5. To JMK he typified Britain's 'Lady Bountiful' attitude – giving away money it did not have.

LEPAN, DOUGLAS (1914–98), Canadian author and diplomat. Joined Canadian High Commission in London, 1945, having fought in Italy as a volunteer gunner. His book *Bright Glass of Memory* (1979) contains a memorable chapter on JMK.

LERNER, ABBA (1903–82), Russian-born Canadian economist. Early convert to Keynesian economics, his 'functional finance' (1943) was a logical application of Keynesian ideas to public finance, shocking in its starkness. The first principle of 'functional finance' was that fiscal policy should be judged solely by its effect on the economy, not by its effect on the government's budget. This was not 'dressed up' enough to suit JMK.

LIESCHING, SIR PERCIVALE (1895–1973), British civil servant. Second secretary, Board of Trade, 1942–6. Led for Britain in trade negotiations with USA. 'A bit of a Tory no doubt, and a little solemn, solid and conventional. But good brains and a good Whitehall reputation . . .' (Dalton Diary).

LIPPMANN, WALTER (1889–1974), renowned American columnist. JMK got much of his information about US politics from Lippmann, and they frequently met in Washington and London.

LOTHIAN, MARQUESS OF (Philip Kerr) (1882–1940), British writer and politician. Extremely successful ambassador to Washington, 1939–40, despite his 'appeasing' past. He was converted to Christian Science by Nancy Astor. This held that all illnesses were mental, and all doctors quacks. He therefore refused to see a doctor for a treatable kidney complaint, and died.

MACDONALD, MALCOLM (1908–1981), British politician. UK high commissioner in Canada, 1941–6, where he was JMK's host on several missions. After the war, much involved in the winding up of the British Empire, which he did with tact and charm.

MACDOUGALL, DONALD (b. 1912), British economist. PM's Statistical Branch, 1940–5, where he supplied the coloured charts and graphs favoured by the PM. Accompanied Cherwell (qv) to Quebec and Washington, September–November 1944, where he kept a record of the Stage II negotiations.

MCKENNA, REGINALD (1863–1943), British Liberal politician and banker. JMK served under him as Chancellor of the Exchequer, 1915–16, and they kept in friendly touch till McKenna's death.

MACMILLAN, HAROLD (1894–1986), British politician and JMK's publisher. Published *How to Pay for the War* in 1940. Minister Resident at Allied HQ, North-West Africa, 1942–5; Prime Minister, 1956–63.

MACMILLAN, LORD (1873–1952), British lawyer and judge. Minister of Information, 1939–41, and first chairman of CEMA. JMK had served on the Committee on Finance and Industry, 1929–31, which Macmillan chaired.

MADGE, CHARLES (1912–96), British social scientist. Founded Mass Observation with Tom Harrisson, 1937. His studies of working-class saving habits and attitudes to compulsory saving were used by JMK in arguing for deferred pay in 1941.

MALKIN, SIR WILLIAM (1883–1945), British lawyer. Legal adviser, Foreign Office, 1929–45. Chaired the Malkin Committee on German reparations, 1943–4, on which JMK served.

MARCHANT, SIR STANLEY (1883–1949), British musician. Member of CEMA and the Arts Council, and Trustee of the Royal Opera House.

MARTEN, SIR HENRY (1872–1948), British schoolmaster. Taught JMK history at Eton. Contact re-established when JMK became a Fellow in 1940, Marten then being Vice-Provost. He succeeded Lord Quickswood (qv) as Provost in 1945.

MARTIN, KINGSLEY (1897–1969), British journalist. Edited *New Statesman*, 1931–60. Frequently clashed with JMK, who was chairman of the board, and who thought the *NS* was too muddled and left-wing (he often took these two terms to be synonymous).

MEADE, JAMES (1907–95), British economist and Nobel prizewinner. Served in the Economic Section of the War Cabinet, 1940–7. Worked part-time at the Board of Trade in the war. After JMK, the most fertile constructive mind in Whitehall, with key papers on employment policy and Commercial Union. JMK was often in vigorous dispute with Meade, who nevertheless regarded him as 'God'. Meade would rarely be diverted from the logic of an argument by questions of political practicability, and he had (to modern eyes) a ludicrous faith in the power of statistics to substitute for judgement.

MONICK, EMMANUEL (1893–1984), French public servant. Inspector-general of Finance, 1920–45; financial attaché in London, 1934–40; governor of the Bank of France, 1945–9. Prominent in the financial diplomacy of the 1930s, JMK saw him in London before the fall of France. One of the two Frenchmen he liked: the other was Marcel Labordère (qv).

MORGENTHAU, HENRY (1891–1967), American politician, intimate of FDR. Secretary of the Treasury, 1934–45. Morgenthau's support for Britain in the war coexisted with his determination to keep Britain dependent on the USA. His attitude started to change in 1944, but in FDR's last months he was in eclipse. He and JMK started off frostily in 1941, but in 1944 JMK won Morgenthau over at Bretton Woods. Morgenthau's weakness was a lack of understanding of finance. This meant he could be manipulated by Harry Dexter White (qv).

NEWBOLD, JOHN WALTON (1888–1943), Labour politician. Served with JMK on the Macmillan Committee on Finance and Industry, 1929–31. Affectionately appreciated JMK as (he hoped) a failed saviour of capitalism.

NORMAN, LORD (Montagu) (1871–1950), banker. Governor of the Bank of England, 1920–44. He and JMK had clashed bitterly over the gold standard in the 1920s, but there was a cautious rapprochement in the years covered by this volume. Norman's final assessment of JMK: 'A great economist, but a bad banker.' JMK's of Norman: 'Montagu Norman, always absolutely charming, always absolutely wrong.'

OPIE, REDVERS (1900–84), British economist, later naturalised American citizen. Counsellor and economic adviser, British Embassy, Washington, 1939–46. Married daughter of the American economist F. W. Taussig. Kept JMK informed of Washington gossip.

PASVOLSKY, LEO (1893–1953), American economist. Special assistant to US Secretary of State 1939–46.

PEACOCK, SIR EDWARD (1871–1962), Canadian-born British merchant banker. Director of Baring Bros, 1924–54; of the Bank of England, 1929–46. Involved with JMK in Jesse Jones Loan, 1941.

PETHICK-LAWRENCE, FREDERICK (1871–1961), Labour academic and politician. Fellow of Trinity College, Cambridge, 1897–1903. Old-fashioned Liberal, driven to left by social problems. Supported Bretton Woods. He and JMK in occasional touch throughout the war. But no real influence in Labour Party.

PHILLIPS, SIR FREDERICK (1884–1943), British civil servant. Entered Treasury 1908. Treasury representative in Washington, 1940–3, where he got on famously with Morgenthau (qv). Very dry, puffed away silently at his pipe, no imagination. JMK got on well with him.

PIGOU, ARTHUR CECIL (1877–1959), British economist. Fellow of KCC, 1902–59; Professor of Political Economy, Cambridge, 1908–43. Kept Economics Faculty at Cambridge going in first years of the war; complained to JMK about Joan Robinson.

PLAYFAIR, EDWARD (1909–99), British civil servant. Treasury, 1934–56. A lively source for JMK's Washington trip of 1941.

PLESCH, JANOS (1879–1950), Hungarian-born doctor. Started treating JMK in March 1939. A mixture of genius and charlatan. JMK credited him with having restored him to 'active life'.

PURVIS, ARTHUR (1890–1941), British businessman, who made his business career in Canada. From 1939 to 1941, as head of the Anglo-French (subsequently the British) Purchasing Board, and first chairman of the British Supply Council, he controlled British procurement of munitions and war-related goods in the USA. Is said to have influenced the size of the first Lend–Lease appropriation. Tragically killed in an aeroplane accident on 14 August 1941. To Morgenthau he was not only the 'ablest British representative in Washington, but one of the rarest persons I have ever known'.

QUICKSWOOD, LORD (Hugh Cecil) (1869–1956), British politician and High Churchman. He was the (increasingly eccentric) Provost of Eton (1936–44) during JMK's time as a Fellow. He resigned in 1944 with the classic words: 'I go to Bournemouth in lieu of Paradise.'

RASMINSKY, LOUIS (1908–98), Canadian economist. Chairman, Foreign Exchange Control Board, 1940–51. Encountered JMK not only on his visits to Ottawa but at Atlantic City, Bretton Woods and Savannah.

RATHBONE, ELEANOR (1872–1946), British social reformer. Independent MP, 1929–46. Helped persuade JMK to include family allowances in his *How to Pay for the War*.

RIDLEY, SIR JASPER (1887–1951), British banker. Served with JMK on Eton's Governing Body during the war.

ROBBINS, LIONEL (1898–1984), British economist. Director, Economic Section of the War Cabinet Offices, 1941–5. A staunch internationalist and economist–politician, he was JMK's most formidable ally in pushing through the Bretton Woods Agreement and in the loan negotiations. He supported JMK not only because he thought he was right, but because he felt guilty about his past opposition.

ROBERTSON, DENNIS HOLME (1890–1963), British economist. Temporary civil servant in the Treasury, 1939–44, when he left to become Pigou's successor as Professor of Political Economy at Cambridge. On the liberal side of the debates on the post-war economic order, partly because he had a greater belief in the price mechanism than did JMK. The most subtle mind in British economics in the first half of this century. His reconciliation with JMK was incomplete, as post-Bretton Woods arguments show.

ROBINSON, EDWARD AUSTIN (1897–1993), British economist. Economic Section of the War Cabinet Offices, 1939–42; Ministry of Production, 1942–5; assistant editor (1934) and joint editor (with JMK) of the *Economic Journal* (1944–6).

ROBINSON, JOAN (1903–83), British economist, wife of E. A Robinson. Lecturer in economics at Cambridge, 1937–49. JMK and she were close in the 1930s, but had little contact during the war.

RONALD, NIGEL (1894–1973), British diplomat. Foreign Office official most involved with JMK's economic and financial negotiations.

ROOSEVELT, FRANKLIN DELANO (1882–1945), President of the United States 1932–45. JMK saw him three times during the war. FDR duly made on him the impression he wanted to.

ROTHBARTH, ERWIN (1913–44), German-born statistician. JMK got him a job in the Institute of Statistical Research, Cambridge. He helped Keynes with *How to Pay for the War*. Killed in action 1944; JMK settled £200 a year on his widow.

ROWE-DUTTON, ERNEST (1891–1965), British civil servant. Assistant secretary, principal assistant secretary, Treasury, 1939–46.

RYLANDS, GEORGE ('Dadie'), (1902–99), British Shakespearian scholar, actor and producer. Fellow of KCC, 1927–99. An old Cambridge friend of JMK, he took over some of JMK's bursarial duties during the war, and succeeded him as chairman of the Arts Theatre Trust in 1946.

SALANT, WALTER (1911–99), American economist. Cambridge student of JMK in early 1930s; Office of Price Administration in Washington during the war. Clashed famously with JMK over inflation at meeting of economists in Washington in 1941.

SCHACHT, HJALMAR (1877–1970), German banker. President of the Reichsbank 1926–30, 1935–9; Minister of Economics, 1934–7. Creator of the 'Schachtian' system of bilateral barter for foreign trade.

SHACKLE, ROBERT JONES (1895–1950), British civil servant. Principal assistant secretary, Board of Trade 1942–7. Involved in Anglo-American trade negotiations.

SHAW, GEORGE BERNARD (1856–1950), Irish-born playwright. JMK hated his article 'Uncommon Sense about War', published in the *New Statesman* on 7 October 1939, but his gracious ninetieth birthday tribute to GBS in April 1946 was the last thing he wrote for publication. When GBS told him in 1939, 'The difference between us is that you are English and I am Irish,' he was not just referring to temperament.

SHEPPARD, JOHN TRESSIDER (1881–1968), British classicist, and one of JMK's oldest friends. A Cambridge character rather than scholar, he was Provost of KCC 1933–54.

SIEPMANN, HARRY ARTHUR (1889–1963), British civil servant. Ex-Treasury official, he was appointed special adviser at the Bank of England in 1926.

SIMON, LORD (SIR JOHN till 1940) (1873–1954), British Liberal politician. Chancellor of the Exchequer, 1937–40.

SRAFFA PIERO (1898–1983), Italian-born economist. Fellow of Trinity College, Cambridge, 1934–83. JMK helped him to track down papers in Ireland for his edition of Ricardo in 1944.

STALIN, JOSEF (1879–1953), Soviet dictator and war leader. General Secretary of the Communist Party of the USSR 1924–53.

STAMP, LORD (Sir Josiah till 1937) (1880–1941), economist and public servant. Led the Stamp Survey into war preparations, 1930–40. Killed by a bomb in 1941.

STIRLING, JOHN (1891–1965), British civil servant. Assistant secretary, Board of Trade, during the war. JMK 'stalled' his trade negotiations with Harry Hawkins on his mission to Washington in 1941.

STONE, RICHARD (1913–91), British economist and statistician. Central Statistical Office, 1940–5. JMK promoted and used his work on National Income Accounts.

THOMPSON-MCCAUSLAND, LUCIUS (1904–84), financial analyst and journalist. Studied economics at KCC. Bank of England staff, 1939–65. JMK's 'bag carrier' in Washington 1941.

THOMSON, LOGAN (d. 1980), farmer. JMK's farm manager, subsequently partner, Tilton Farm (from 1936) and Charleston Farm (from 1940).

TOWERS, GRAHAM (1897–1965), Canadian banker. Governor of the Bank of Canada, 1934–54. Keynes suggested him as governor of the Bank of England to succeed Montagu Norman in 1944. But Towers was not willing; and Norman found him 'too much JMK & $'.

Trouton, Rupert (1897–1965), economist and businessman. Studied economics at KCC, 1919–21. JMK invested in his Hector Whaling Company; Trouton alerted Keynes to the falsity of shipping statistics in 1941–2.

Truman, Harry (1884–1972), American politician. President of the United States, 1945–53. His importance in this narrative is that he cancelled Lend–Lease without warning on 19 August 1945.

Valois, Ninette de (b. 1898), British dancer, choreographer and founder of the Vic-Wells Ballet. JMK made possible the move of her ballet company to the Royal Opera House, Covent Garden in 1946. A friend, but not a close friend, of Lydia Keynes.

Viner, Jacob (1892–1970), American economist. Consultant, State Department, 1943–52. JMK corresponded with him about the IMF in 1943.

Vinson, Frederic ('Judge') (1890–1953), American lawyer from Kentucky. Secretary of the Treasury, 1945–6. JMK's two important passages of arms with him were at the Washington loan negotiations of 1945 and the Savannah Conference of 1946.

Waley, Sigismund David (1887–1962), British civil servant. Principal assistant secretary, under-secretary, Treasury, 1939–46, and head of the Overseas Finance division. Involved in the gestation of JMK's Clearing Union Plan and preparation for the American loan negotiations.

Wallace, Henry (1888–1965), American politician. FDR's Vice-President, 1941–5; Secretary of Commerce, 1945–6. On the left wing of the New Deal, and represented US agricultural interests. JMK tried to placate him with his Buffer Stock Plan.

Webster, David (1903–71), retailer. Worked closely with JMK in re-establishing Covent Garden, 1945–6, as the Royal Opera House's first general administrator.

White, Harry Dexter (1892–1948), American economist and public servant. Director of monetary research at the US Treasury, 1938–1945. Joint author with JMK of the Bretton Woods system. JMK's most important American relationship during the war, but there was more to Harry White than met the eye.

Williams, John Henry (1887–1980), American economist and banker. Author of the Williams 'key currency' plan, the New York bankers' alternative to the IMF and Bretton Woods system.

Wilson, Sir Horace (1882–1972), British civil servant. Permanent secretary, Treasury, 1939–42, when he was retired, having reached the minimum retiring age.

Winant, John Gilbert (1889–1947), American politician and public servant. US ambassador to London, 1941–6. Committed suicide. A strong Anglophile and friend of JMK.

WOLFIT, SIR DONALD (1902–68), actor–manager of the old school. JMK lectured him on his production of *'Tis Pity She's a Whore*, which the Arts Theatre was putting on, in April 1940.

WOOD, SIR KINGSLEY (1881–1943), British Conservative politician. Chancellor of the Exchequer, 1940–3. He introduced the first 'Keynesian' budget in 1941.

WOOLF, LEONARD (1880–1969) and VIRGINIA (1882–1941) were among JMK's oldest friends. They lived in Rodmell, a few miles away in East Sussex, and were regular Christmas visitors to Tilton. Virginia Woolf committed suicide in April 1941.

Index